D1192263

INTRODUCTION TO THE STUDY OF

PUBLIC ADMINISTRATION

THE MACMILLAN COMPANY
NEW YORK · BOSTON · CHICAGO
DALLAS · ATLANTA · SAN FRANCISCO

MACMILLAN AND CO., LIMITED
LONDON · BOMBAY · CALCUTTA
MADRAS · MELBOURNE

THE MACMILLAN COMPANY
OF CANADA, LIMITED
TORONTO

Introduction to the Study of Public Administration

by LEONARD D. WHITE, Ph.D.
Professor of Public Administration in the University of Chicago

REVISED EDITION

NEW YORK
THE MACMILLAN COMPANY

Printed in the United States of America
Revised Edition published April, 1939.
Defense and War Administration Supplement
published September, 1942.
Reprinted September, 1946.
Reprinted January, 1947.
Reprinted July, 1947.

FIRST EDITION COPYRIGHTED AND PUBLISHED, 1926,
BY THE MACMILLAN COMPANY

TO

MY FATHER AND MOTHER

PREFACE TO THE REVISED EDITION

The decade which has passed since the first edition of this book has shaken the economic and political foundations of the contemporary world. The effect of the repeated crises of these years upon public administration has been great, exactly how great we cannot yet be sure. As a nation we are, however, slowly accepting the fact that the loose-jointed, easy-going, somewhat irresponsible system of administration which we carried over from our rural, agricultural background is no longer adequate for present and future needs. The council-manager form of municipal government, the reconstruction of state governments and their administrative disciplining by federal authorities, and the pending reform of the federal structure itself are unmistakable signs of adaptation to new necessities.

These and other events of the last decade affecting the structure and operation of our system of administration are reflected in this second edition. The book has necessarily grown in volume. Its organization remains unchanged except by the addition of two new parts, one dealing with fiscal management, the other with forms of administrative action. The principal assumptions which underlay the first edition: that administration is a process which can best be treated as such without separate study of federal, state, or municipal administration; and that central management operations (such as personnel) can be dealt with apart from major substantive operations (such as police or health) also underlie this edition.

This volume is devoted to the American system of public administration. Despite occasional incidental references to the administrative organizations of other countries, this is not a study in comparative administration, a much larger task which remains to be undertaken.

The citations to literature are accordingly principally to American sources, although there are frequent references to the invaluable English publication, *Public Administration.* The quantity of writing, official and unofficial, about public administration in the United States is very considerable. I have tried to select that which would be most useful to the student, with emphasis upon the most recent output.

In preparing this revision I have been aided by the systematic works which in recent years have been written by friends and fellow workers in this field: W. F. Willoughby, John M. Pfiffner, Harvey Walker,

Marshall E. Dimock, Lewis Meriam, William E. Mosher and J. D. Kingsley, as well as by the publications of such bodies as the Commission of Inquiry on Public Service Personnel, the President's Committee on Administrative Management, and the National Resources Committee. Contrasting sharply with the situation a decade ago, the literature in the field is now abundant and is increasing rapidly.

Portions of the manuscript have been read by Professor John M. Gaus of the University of Wisconsin; Dr. Joseph P. Harris, research director of the Committee on Public Administration of the Social Science Research Council; Mr. Charles S. Ascher, secretary of the Committee on Public Administration; Dr. G. Lyle Belsley, director of the Civil Service Assembly of the United States and Canada; Mr. Carl H. Chatters, executive director of the Municipal Finance Officers' Association; Mr. Ismar Baruch, chief of the division of personnel classification of the United States Civil Service Commission, and Professors Floyd M. Reeves, Kenneth C. Sears, Marshall E. Dimock and Charles E. Merriam of the University of Chicago. My indebtedness to these generous critics is very great and it is a pleasure to acknowledge my appreciation while absolving them from any responsibility for the final outcome.

In the exacting task of collecting data and preparing the manuscript for publication I have been competently assisted by Karl Bosworth. Harmon J. Belinsky aided in checking data. The typing of the manuscript was handled with dispatch and precision by Diane Greeter Mulloy and her staff. Work on this edition was started with the assistance of my former secretary, Margaret E. Ringrose, of the United States Civil Service Commission, whose more recent aid in securing information is appreciated. My research secretary, Jean Schneider, has not only given me great assistance in collecting data, organizing material and criticizing the manuscript, but has also taken the principal responsibility for guiding the book through the press. I am indebted for this assistance to the Public Administration Fund of the University of Chicago.

L. D. W.

CHICAGO, ILLINOIS
February, 1939

PREFACE TO THE FIRST EDITION

Curiously enough, commentators on American political institutions have never produced a systematic analysis of our administrative system except from the point of view of the lawyer. Until the last few years even the textbooks have obstinately closed their eyes to this enormous terrain, studded with governmental problems of first magnitude and fascinating interest; and even today they dismiss the subject with a casual chapter. But certainly no one pretends that administration can still be put aside "as a practical detail which clerks could arrange after doctors had agreed upon principles."

The fact is that the last two decades have produced a voluminous literature dealing with the business side of government. The present volume represents an attempt to bring together the salient facts of American experience and observation and to deal with them analytically and critically. To accomplish this within the limits of a single volume is no easy task, implying as it does a constant danger of falling prey either to the Scylla of indiscriminate detail or the Charybdis of unsupported generalization. The total lack of any charted passage through these unexplored waters adds much to the hazards of the venture.

The book rests upon at least four assumptions. It assumes that administration is a single process, substantially uniform in its essential characteristics wherever observed, and therefore avoids the study of municipal administration, state administration, or federal administration as such. It assumes that the study of administration should start from the base of management rather than the foundation of law, and is therefore more absorbed in the affairs of the American Management Association than in the decisions of the courts. It assumes that administration is still primarily an art but attaches importance to the significant tendency to transform it into a science. It assumes that administration has become, and will continue to be the heart of the problem of modern government.

None of the technical phases of administration are developed. The student of public health administration, highway engineering, income tax collection, educational administration will consult the many admirable volumes dealing with these specialties. Running through all branches of administration, however, are certain common underlying problems: organization, personnel, control, finance, which it is the purpose of this book to explore. The particular audience to which it is directed is on the one hand the college and university student of political science, on the other hand the citizen who wishes to understand the basis of the executive phase of public affairs. The public official also may find that a systematic presentation in general terms will have the value of lending significance to his own task by disclosing it in a larger context.

The purpose has been to suggest problems rather than to present conclusions. If in spite of himself the author has occasionally slipped into dogmatism, he hopes that his readers will understand that he has his fingers crossed, and reserves the invaluable academic prerogative of leaving all questions open until all the evidence has been secured.

References have been supplied freely on account of the almost complete lack of guides to the existing literature, a gap only now partially closed by Miss Greer's admirable Bibliography of Public Administration.

If the book may provide a system of ordered relationships from which fruitful advances can be made by later writers it will have performed its chief function. If in addition it may stimulate research in a field which will abundantly repay attention, the labor of its preparation will be doubly repaid.

My colleagues, Professor Charles E. Merriam and Dr. Harold D. Lasswell, have given me invaluable systematic help in organizing the material of this volume. Professor Ernst Freund generously saved me from errors in chapter twenty, dealing with the administration and the courts. Mr. George C. Sikes, former secretary of the police pension board of Chicago, gave me the benefit of his informed judgment on the chapter dealing with retirement systems. All of these gentlemen, however, must be absolved from any responsibility for errors or misstatements of which the author may have been guilty.

L. D. W.

CHICAGO, ILLINOIS
August, 1926

TABLE OF CONTENTS

PART I

PUBLIC ADMINISTRATION: FORMS AND TRENDS

PART II

STRUCTURE AND ORGANIZATION

PART III

FISCAL MANAGEMENT

PART IV

PERSONNEL MANAGEMENT

PART V

FORMS OF ADMINISTRATIVE ACTION

PART VI

THE SYSTEM OF RESPONSIBILITY

LIST OF TABLES

PART 1

PUBLIC ADMINISTRATION: FORMS AND TRENDS

Chapter One

SCOPE AND NATURE OF PUBLIC ADMINISTRATION

SCATTERED about the country are thousands of buildings and offices in which public officials and employees are stationed in the performance of the daily work of government. In state capitals, county courthouses, city halls, post offices, customhouses, police stations, lighthouses, and in the great buildings which house the departments and commissions in Washington, over three million men and women are occupied in government service. What they do, by what means they are selected, and under what conditions they work are matters of prime importance to the success or failure of government. They and their work are to be examined in this book.

Clearly they do not comprise all of government, either in its strict official sense, or in the broader sense including the semiofficial agencies so intimately connected with government. Superior to officials are judges and legislators and members of constitutional conventions; beyond officialdom are the political parties and the pressure groups which in part fix the course which officials must follow. But officials and government employees are an essential and ever expanding portion of the whole of government, whose contribution to the public weal is of extraordinary importance. The study of their tasks is the study of public administration.

1. Scope and Nature of Public Administration

In its broadest sense public administration consists of all those operations having for their purpose the fulfillment or enforcement of public policy as declared by the competent authorities.[1] As such it is a special case of the larger category, administration, a process which is common

[1] John A. Fairlie, "Public Administration and Administrative Law," in C. G. Haines and M. E. Dimock, eds., *Essays on the Law and Practice of Governmental Administration* (1935), pp. 3-43; Woodrow Wilson, "The Study of Administration," 2 *Pol. Sci. Q.* 197-222 (1887); Marshall E. Dimock, "The Meaning and Scope of Public Administration," in John M. Gaus, L. D. White and M. E. Dimock, *The Frontiers of Public Administration* (1936); Marshall E. Dimock, "What is Public Administration?" 15 *Pub. Man.* 259-62 (1933); L. D. White, "Administration, Public," 1 *Encyclopaedia of the Social Sciences* 440-50 (1930); Ernst Freund, "Administrative Law," *ibid.*, pp. 452-55.

to all organized human effort and which is highly developed in modern corporate business, in the church, in the Red Cross, in education, and in international bodies, public and private.[1]

The quality and form of administrative systems vary widely. Administrative operations may be principally military in nature, as in warlike tribes; they may be chiefly concerned with the King's domain, as in seventeenth century Brandenburg; they may be largely limited to the maintenance of peace and order, as in rural America of the early nineteenth century; or they may be as vast in scope as those of a state in which production has become a public rather than a private function.

Over fifty years ago Woodrow Wilson described public administration in a brilliant essay.[2] "Public administration," he wrote, "is detailed and systematic execution of public law. Every particular application of general law is an act of administration. The assessment and raising of taxes, for instance, the hanging of a criminal, the transportation and delivery of the mails, the equipment and recruiting of the army and navy, *etc.*, are all obviously acts of administration. . . ." In its contemporary form public administration is also the prevention of soil erosion, the insurance of bank deposits, the control of agricultural production, the operation of unemployment offices, the maintenance of aircraft beacons, forecasting mineral output, research into the causes and cure of cancer, and planning long-time programs of government action.

To deal with public administration in the terms of this description would require analysis of the military as well as the judicial and civil arms of the government, and would lead into each of the many activities supported by the modern state—police, education, health, construction of public works, regulation of transportation, conservation, and many others.[3]

This treatise deals with only a part of the entire field. Despite its interest and importance, the military arm is excluded, except for certain instructive parallels in staff organization. The enforcement of civil policy by the armed forces is a relatively uncommon event, although in any state it is an ever present potentiality. In case of organized resistance to official authority, the first normal recourse is to the police, the sheriff or the United States marshal; their resources proving inadequate, the na-

[1] For some of its larger aspects the student may consult Luther Gulick and L. Urwick, eds., *Papers on the Science of Administration* (1937); and Henri Fayol, *Administration Industrielle et Générale* (1920), English edition *Industrial and General Administration* (1930); and Oliver Sheldon, *The Philosophy of Management* (1924).

[2] Wilson, *op. cit.*, p. 212.

[3] Studies by continental writers in the field of *droit administratif* follow this pattern; so also Lent D. Upson, *Practice of Municipal Administration* (1926), and in part Harvey Walker, *Public Administration in the United States* (1937).

tional guard of the state, or in extreme cases, the regular army may be called into play.

On the other hand the relation of the armed forces to the civil government is a problem which has always perplexed democratic governments and which bids fair to become again a leading issue of state organization. It is an aspect of public administration which deserves and will doubtless receive careful study.[1]

A common method of law enforcement which is also neglected in this study is judicial action. Although the American constitutional system recognizes the courts as a third and separate branch of the government, this constitutional structure need not obscure the fact that the primary function of the court is to enforce law. Judicial methods are specialized to a certain extent, but the major purpose of the court is the same as that of the administration: to enforce and to implement public policy as declared in law. During the first half century of our independence, the courts were among the principal administrative agencies.[2] Reliance upon the court for law enforcement, rather than upon a specialized branch of the executive, was projected into nineteenth century America from a long historic past in the colonies and in seventeenth and eighteenth century England. The rapid development of agencies in the executive branch designed to carry out public policy has diminished the one-time preponderance of the courts in administration, but in actual day-by-day procedure courts and officials operate in close conjunction and dependence, each on the other.

Due to the specialized nature of law enforcement by judicial decision, the judges as administrators will not be given systematic consideration in this volume. The court as an element in the system of responsibility of the administration will receive notice in the concluding chapter.

Operations peculiar to the special fields of administration also fall outside the scope of this volume—for example, the technique of determining liability to an income tax, of preventing soil erosion, or of identifying a suspected criminal. These are highly specialized procedures and are best dealt with by the specialists to whom they are of primary interest. They are, however, the primary substantive functions of administration and from one point of view it is artificial to describe public administration

[1] Consult Jean L. Jaurès, *L'Armée Nouvelle* (1910); abbreviated translation, *Democracy and Military Service* (1916); Sir Ian Hamilton, *The Soul and Body of an Army* (1921); Major General Frederick Maurice, *Governments and War* (1926); Lieutenant Colonel J. S. Omond, *Parliament and the Army, 1642–1904* (1933); Alfred Vagts, *History of Militarism* (1937); Lindsay Rogers, *Crisis Government* (1934), and "The War Machines Examined," 3 *Southern Review* 673-92 (1937–38).

[2] This point is dealt with in the next chapter.

apart from these major functions. It is feasible to analyze the problems of administration starting from the substantive activities toward which all official work is directed. By way of example, the problem of land use raises at once issues of public policy, public law, economics, technology, sociology, population, agronomy, and education as well as considerations of administration. Public administration always has such an immediate and varied context, and in the world of affairs the line between administration and that which is administered is often almost indistinguishable. For practical as well as technical reasons, however, it is necessary to stop short of describing all human problems and public policies in an effort to clear one path through the field of public administration.

Underlying the constant flow of such complex operations there are certain common procedures and problems characteristic of modern administration under any political system and in any field of government activity. They are concerned with the organization and structure of the administrative unit, large or small; with the provision and control of funds; with the recruitment and management of personnel; with certain typical methods of law enforcement; and with the system of responsibility – to the legislative body, to the courts, and in some degree to the electorate. These aspects of administration are broadly managerial in nature. They comprise the content of this volume.[1]

Without derogation therefore from the broad definition of the subject matter proposed above, this study will deal with that part of the field concerned with *the management of men and materials in the accomplishment of the purposes of the state.*[2]

This study, then, concentrates on the central core of the total complex of administration.[3] Since it is concerned with a process as process, it is neither necessary nor desirable to limit the analysis to either the na-

[1] The term, administration, is also used in a still more restricted sense to indicate the special function of planning, general direction, supervision, coordination and control within a department or agency. This is the function performed by the English "administrative" class. It is contrasted with the responsibility for carrying on established operations, and the performance of clerical and routine duties. The function of overhead management exists, of course, in the United States, although its exact nature is often debated. It is an essential part of the managerial aspect of public administration, and is discussed in chapters four and five.

[2] The principal bibliographies are these: Sarah Greer, *A Bibliography of Public Administration* (1926); same author, *A Bibliography of Public Administration* (1933), Part 1, "General Literature"; same author, *A Bibliography of Civil Service and Personnel Administration* (1935); Laurence F. Schmeckebier, *Government Publications and their Use* (1936); Laverne Burchfield, *Student's Guide to Materials in Political Science* (1935); and the current bibliographies in the *American Political Science Review.*

[3] Among the principal general works are the following: William F. Willoughby, *Principles of Public Administration* (1927); Leonard D. White, *Trends in Public Administration* (1933); John M. Pfiffner, *Public Administration* (1935); Harvey

tional, state or municipal governments. There is an essential unity in the process of administration that precludes a stratified treatment of the subject. To deal with it in terms of municipal administration, state administration, or national administration is to imply a logical distinction which in reality does not exist. The fundamental problems are the same.

The objective of public administration in the sense of management is the most efficient utilization of the resources at the disposal of officials and employees. In every direction good management seeks the elimination of waste, the conservation and effective use of materials and energy, and the protection of the welfare of the employees. In its broader context, the ends of administration are the ultimate ends of the state itself—the maintenance of peace and order, instruction of the young, equalization of opportunity, protection against disease and insecurity, adjustment and compromise of conflicting groups and interests, in short, the achievement so far as possible of the good life.[1]

The study of the content of public policy, on which all administration depends, is not necessary to the technical study of administrative procedures as such, although the success or failure of administration depends in part on the character of policy and the care with which it is formulated in legislation.

2. Public and Nonpublic Administration

Several generations of laissez faire policy and of theoretical emphasis upon sovereignty as the distinguishing mark of official action have accustomed us to draw a sharp and clear line between public and private undertakings. Thus the management of a grocery store is a private affair; the collection of taxes on the property of the owner is a branch of public administration.

While this distinction can still easily be made, it is significant that intermediate forms are developing which blur the line between that which is Caesar's and that which is not. The sharp differentiation began to get

---

Walker, *Public Administration in the United States* (1937); Marshall E. Dimock, *Modern Politics and Administration* (1937).

The principal works on state and municipal administration include John M. Mathews, *Principles of American State Administration* (1917); Arthur N. Holcombe, *State Government in the United States* (3rd ed. 1931); Frank G. Bates and Oliver P. Field, *State Government* (1928); W. Brooke Graves, *American State Government* (1936); Arthur W. Bromage, *State Government and Administration in the United States* (1936); Kirk H. Porter, *State Administration* (1938); Lent D. Upson, *Practice of Municipal Administration* (1926); William B. Munro, *Municipal Administration* (1934); Paul T. Stafford and W. S. Carpenter, *State and Local Government in the United States* (1936).

[1] Cf. John M. Gaus, L. D. White and M. E. Dimock, *The Frontiers of Public Administration* (1936), pp. 92-133.

out of focus when the courts introduced the doctrine of business affected with a public interest and thus opened the door for public supervision of some profit-making enterprises. It was affected also by the emergence of public ownership of many municipal utilities, and by the difficulty encountered by the courts in developing the law of municipal liability in "nongovernmental" matters.

Within recent years the line has perceptibly faded. The federal government has created a number of corporations, such as the Inland Waterways Corporation, the Federal Deposit Insurance Corporation, and others which are clearly more than mere private undertakings and which are nevertheless in a different legal position than an "ordinary" government department. These amphibians, however, are less puzzling than other intermediate agencies standing closer to the category of private enterprises. Is a credit union, the formation of which under federal law rests on the "necessary and proper" clause of the constitution, an instrumentality of the government? It has been so classified, but this would probably astonish the members of credit unions.

And what shall we say of the federal land banks, a majority of whose stock fluctuates from private to public and back again to private hands by the play of the investment market, but which remain constantly under the supervision of the Farm Credit Administration? Or, to push the case one step farther, how shall we classify a farmers' cooperative through which a farmer must proceed to negotiate a loan with a land bank? And what of the county farm bureau, recognized in some states as an official, in other states as a purely private body, but which in fact often controls the appointment and program of the county agent?

An allocation of these borderline cases to the category of public or private agencies is fortunately not necessary for present purposes. They are brought forward to suggest that the old categories of public and private undertakings are fraying at the edges, and that the student of public administration will in the future be concerned more closely than in the past with other than the normal forms in which public business has been conducted.[1]

3. Administration, Legislation, and Adjudication

The classical analysis of American government presupposes three

[1] For a statement of the similarities and differences between public and business administration, see the first edition of this book, pp. 17-21 (1926); J. D. Barnett, "Public Agencies and Private Agencies," 18 *Am. Pol. Sci. Rev.* 34-48 (1924); Sir Josiah C. Stamp, "The Contrast between the Administration of Business and Public Affairs," 1 *J. of Pub. Adm.* 158-71 (1923); John Lee, "The Parallels between Industrial Administration and Public Administration," 4 *Pub. Adm.* 216-22 (1926); Lane W. Lancaster, "Private Associations and Public Administration," 13 *Social Forces* 283-91 (1934).

branches each endowed with its own special type of activity. In its absolute form the theory was eloquently expressed by Samuel Adams in the Bill of Rights of the Massachusetts Constitution of 1780.

> In the government of this commonwealth, the legislative department shall never exercise the executive and judicial powers, or either of them: the executive shall never exercise the legislative and judicial powers, or either of them: the judicial shall never exercise the legislative and executive powers, or either of them: to the end it may be a government of laws and not of men.

Endless discussion, learned analysis, and opinions of the courts have failed to draw a recognized line between these three classes of powers, and recent decisions of the Supreme Court of the United States have again opened up questions once thought settled.[1]

What is the essential and peculiar nature of administrative operations, if any? Can they be differentiated from acts of legislation or of adjudication? Are they merely aspects of the "executive power," lacking elements of either law making or adjudication?

Most administrative action can be summed up by saying that it is the application of the law to individual cases on the basis of specific rules and regulations intended to guide and restrict the discretion of officials. Their work is normally subject to reasonably clear differentiation from policy making, which is the primary function of legislative bodies; and from adjudication, which is the primary function of the courts. Administration usually is no more than the application of public policy to the particular case, the characteristic function of the executive branch.

Some forms of administrative action, however, cannot be disposed of so simply. At times they are hardly to be distinguished from genuine legislation; at other times they seem almost identical with adjudication.[2] The essence of modern government is an obstinate intermingling of functions theoretically separate. The most we can say is that in each of the three constitutional branches there is a broad specialization and concentration of functions. The facts blur and obscure any sharp logical distinctions.[3]

[1] As to delegation of legislative power, *Schechter Poultry Corporation vs. U.S.*, 295 U.S. 495 (1935), and *Panama Refining Co. vs. Ryan*, 293 U.S. 388 (1935).

[2] See *infra*, chs. 33 and 34.

[3] A careful definition of terms is to be found from the pen of the editor of the *Illinois Law Review*, vol. 15, pp. 108-18 (1920–21). He writes in substance: Legislation is the declaration, independently of their application, of new rules of compulsory conduct, by an organ of the state, whose powers are specialized to exclude other functions except as incidental. Adjudication is the determination of a specific controversy, by the application of a rule of compulsory conduct, by an organ of the state, whose powers are specialized to exclude other functions except as incidental. The executive function is the factual and ultimate realization of a rule of compulsory conduct through an organ of the state, whose powers

With his usual insight, Herbert Croly noted this intermingling of powers in administrative agencies as early as 1914. After pointing out that the administrative commission exercises an authority which is in part executive, in part legislative, and in part judicial, Croly observes that the commission "is simply a means of consolidating the divided activities of government for certain practical social purposes." [1]

4. The Study of Public Administration

Formal recognition of the study of public administration as a phase of government distinct from the traditional "political" functions of the chief executive may be said to date from the brilliant essay by Woodrow Wilson in 1887.[2] Earlier writing by Charles Francis Adams and earlier studies in the field of educational administration had suggested rather than opened up this emerging field of activity. The faculty of political science of Columbia University began a series of systematic studies in 1896, all dealing with the process of state control over local administration; and Goodnow's works on administrative law, and on politics and administration, together with the writing of Fairlie and others went far to formulate the new discipline. Then came in quick succession the "muckrakers," the municipal reform movement, the bureaus of governmental research, and the increasing emphasis on "efficiency" and on technical operations—all aided by the steady pressure of the civil service reformers.

Out of these activities has grown a new, but a voluminous literature. The study of public administration developed steadily after the war, when the pressure of public debt forced discussion of administrative reorganization. The internal crisis caused by the depression of 1929 induced even greater concentration on public service problems, symbolized in the constructive reports of the Commission of Inquiry on Public Service Personnel and of the President's Committee on Administrative Management.

The gradual development of thought about public administration has

---

are specialized to exclude other functions except as incidental. Administrative power is a fourth term; its functions in pure theory must always be one of the three kinds of powers enumerated, but in practice may be and usually are a combination of two or more of these powers. Clear examples of this combination of powers are the Interstate Commerce Commission, the Federal Trade Commission, and the numerous state public utility commissions.

[1] Herbert D. Croly, *Progressive Democracy* (1914), ch. 17.

[2] Woodrow Wilson, *op. cit.*; see also National Institute of Public Affairs, *The Organization of Basic Courses in Public Administration* (1937); and a forthcoming study by Anna Haddow, *History of Political Science Teaching;* A. C. Stewart, "The Approach of British Universities to Public Administration," 11 *Pub. Adm.* 20-35 (1933).

served to differentiate more clearly its subject matter and center of interest from a number of neighboring fields. Before embarking on the long journey through a section of our field, it may therefore be useful to take bearings and observe the adjacent landmarks.[1]

a. Public administration and law. Law provides the immediate framework within which public administration operates. In the first place, statutory enactments define the tasks to be undertaken, establish the major administrative structure, provide the funds, and set forth general rules of procedure and methods of enforcing compliance. Obviously the form and content of the law may be an administrative asset or a liability. The law may lay down an objective beyond the competence of the service to achieve (enforcement of the eighteenth amendment); it may impose a sound or a faulty organization; it may grant or withhold effective sanctions. While, therefore, the law is not administration, it has a powerful influence upon administration.[2] Law is the formulation of policy; administration is its execution.

In the second place, law, both written and unwritten, provides the safeguards by which individuals may protect themselves against invasion of their rights by unauthorized official action.[3] In either case law acts as an external control over administration, or conversely administration must operate within the four corners of law. Legality therefore becomes a primary consideration of administrators, and legal advisers acquire an importance which far outweighs their strictly administrative contribution. In this respect business and public administration operate on a different basis, since the test of business success is profits rather than meticulous observance of the resolutions of the board of directors.

Public administration is embedded in law, and the student of the subject will often be with the statutes. Continental studies, indeed, are almost exclusively concerned with the legal framework of administration, rather than with either the process of management or the special techniques of given fields. American studies differentiate law and adminis-

[1] John M. Gaus, "The New Problem of Administration," 8 *Minn. Law Rev.* 217-31 (1923–24); same author, "The Present Status of the Study of Public Administration in the United States," 25 *Am. Pol. Sci. Rev.* 120-34 (1931); Phillips Bradley, "Administration: the Fourth Power in Modern Government," 27 *Social Studies* 320-27 (1936); R. C. Jarvis, "The Place of Public Administration in a Changing Society," 15 *Pub. Adm.* 406-18 (1937); Marshall E. Dimock, "The Study of Administration," 31 *Am. Pol. Sci. Rev.* 28-40 (1937); Sir Josiah C. Stamp, "The Administrator and a Planned Society," 16 *Pub. Adm.* 3-22 (1938).

[2] ". . . administration is more than the law—it is not less than the discretionary application of the rule of the law to every relevant instance which comes to the attention of the administrator." Gaus, White and Dimock, *op. cit.*, p. 14.

[3] Frank J. Goodnow, *The Principles of the Administrative Law of the United States* (1905); Leon Green, "From Law to Administration," 13 *Texas Law Rev.* 323-36 (1934–35).

tration, while recognizing their relationships. Administrative law, which is perhaps closest to public administration, has for its major purposes the legal organization of administrative power and the protection of public and private rights.[1] The objective of public administration is the effective conduct of the public business.

These two goals are different, if complementary. They are not always consistent, as Professor Ernst Freund indicated many years ago, pointing out that "increased administrative powers call for increased safeguards against their abuses, and as long as there is the possibility of official error, partiality or excess of zeal, the protection of private right is as important an object as the effectuation of some governmental policy."

b. Public administration and policy. In one of his early works, Goodnow differentiated politics, in the sense of policy, from administration.[2] A recent work by my colleague, Professor Marshall E. Dimock, renews this distinction, which is implicit in the definition of administration accepted for this volume.[3] From what has already been said, it appears that officials are concerned with the making of policy as well as its execution. One of the major trends of the last quarter century has been the growth of executive initiative in public policy. Mayors, governors and presidents are expected to have programs, and to seek their approval in law. Their programs, in turn, arise in part from the experience and wisdom of permanent officials.

Modern legislation is often compelled to forego detailed enactment of exact rules in favor of a general statement of policy to be made definite by subsequent executive orders, rules or regulations, or decisions in individual cases. In this way, officials participate immediately in the actual determination of policy, within the broad orientation fixed by law.[4] In many jurisdictions, especially in Washington, the advice of expert officials expressed at committee hearings often carries much weight. In general, however, the participation of permanent officials in major policy making is not overt, although it is substantial; in less than major policy, officials often play the leading part.

There is no reason to believe that administration is incompetent to

[1] The subject of administrative law is not included in this volume. The principal casebooks are Felix Frankfurter and J. F. Davison, eds., *Cases and Other Materials on Administrative Law* (1932); Robert A. Maurer, *Cases and Other Materials on Administrative Law* (1937); E. Blythe Stason, *The Law of Administrative Tribunals* (1937); Kenneth C. Sears, *Cases and Materials on Administrative Law* (1938). See also Frank J. Goodnow, *Comparative Administrative Law* (1893), and *The Principles of the Administrative Law of the United States* (1905); John M. Pfiffner, *Public Administration* (1935), chs. 18-21.

[2] Frank J. Goodnow, *Politics and Administration* (1900).

[3] Marshall E. Dimock, *Modern Politics and Administration* (1937).

[4] This aspect of administration is discussed at length in ch. 33.

make an important contribution to policy. In fact the impartiality, technical ability, and somewhat detached position of officials make them a useful counterweight to party and legislature in planning and in formulating policy. Administration may be the best equipped branch of government to make a genuinely public policy free from overwhelming favoritism to one particular pressure group.

c. Public administration and political parties. In a democratic government political parties are an essential agency for the formulation and expression of public opinion. Parties are the means by which 130,000,000 citizens influence the major direction in which government moves. Their importance in our national life is not diminishing, and in the light of antidemocratic movements in the post-war world, their influence in the United States ought to be preserved.[1]

In the American system, parties have always been closely associated with administration. By long tradition it is recognized that party leaders and party policy have a direct connection with the administrative service. The major purpose served by this connection is to ensure that public policy and its enforcement shall correspond to the will of the people as expressed at the polls. Thus party members in legislative bodies enact legislation; other party representatives serve as heads of departments and commissions. The official party organizations (national and state committees) take little direct part in the actual conduct of public affairs or their discussion, reserving their energies for the ever recurring campaigns.

In local administration, party workers often aid voters in their relations with officials, especially among the masses whose contacts with the city hall are rare and likely to be approached with apprehension. A peddler needs a license, a small merchant requires a permit, a youth needs bail, a housewife complains about the garbage collection—hundreds of such small but important things to be done or decisions to be made are facilitated for the citizen by the precinct worker, who knows the "right guy" in the city hall or the county courthouse. This task of mediation may be humble, but it is significant for the smooth working of the administrative machine.[2] In Washington it is performed by Congressmen.

The major problem of party contacts with administration is patronage. Party leaders and committees are expected to nominate to hundreds of thousands of small official appointments and employments in national, state and local governments. While enlightened politicians regret this duty, the party organization derives such vast power from its control

[1] Leonard D. White and T. V. Smith, *Politics and Public Service* (1939).

[2] See Charles E. Merriam and Harold F. Gosnell, *The American Party System* (rev. ed. 1929).

over patronage that it is seldom relinquished except under the compulsion of an overwhelming public opinion. To manage the huge number of patronage appointments in the national service subsequent to 1933, the Democratic National Committee organized an appointment bureau which for a time rivaled the United States Civil Service Commission.[1] All reports indicate that its work was efficiently performed, in the light of the end to be attained.

It is no exaggeration, therefore, to state that the conduct of public administration is influenced at every turn by the organized political party and by thousands of active politicians. The disastrous outcome of their activity in the administrative services has often been reported, obscuring the vast amount of public administration which quietly goes forward outside the range of partisan influences. Against the loss from partisan obstruction must be set the necessity of keeping administrative policy and law enforcement in fundamental harmony with the interests and the opinions of the mass of the people.

d. Pressure groups and public officials. Government in all its branches, especially the legislative and executive, is subject to a never ending complex of influences, only part of which are brought to bear through the party. These have recently been made the subject of a brilliant study by Herring, who for the first time has revealed the variety and intensity of these forces.[2] They are principally special interest groups, usually seeking some economic advantage. While their first attack may be on the legislative bodies, their second assault is on the citadel of administration. Such regulatory bodies as the Interstate Commerce Commission, the Federal Trade Commission, the Food and Drugs Administration, the Tariff Commission, and the Securities and Exchange Commission are especially exposed. Utility and railroad commissions in the states and inspection services in cities are subject to the same type of conflicting pressures. In the field of education, a different but no less ubiquitous set of pressures exists. They have been exposed in an illuminating volume by an historian, Professor Howard K. Beale.[3]

Realistic analysis of a police department's daily existence in any large city would disclose an amazing pattern of interrelated interests, sometimes seeking to purchase immunity from police surveillance, sometimes using the police force to compel a settlement of labor disputes, sometimes urging preferential treatment for individual policemen, but seldom pressing for an independent, vigorous and honest police department.

[1] The rise of the spoils system is noted in the following chapter, and treated in greater detail in ch. 18.

[2] E. Pendleton Herring, *Public Administration and the Public Interest* (1936)

[3] Howard K. Beale, *Are American Teachers Free?* (1936).

In short, wherever man's interests are, there his influence is at work to protect those interests. Officials cannot hope to escape this fact; the most they can do is to understand their environment and in Herring's phrase, to seek "the public interest" in their daily work and decisions. At another point will be found a discussion of the advisory committee, one of the means by which interest groups are brought into formal contact with officials, thus providing a complement if not a substitute for the informal contacts which have long been important.[1]

e. Public administration, technology and scientific management. The early history of the American administrative system discloses an organization whose principal equipment was quill pen and paper. The revolution in methods of business administration consequent upon the invention of modern office equipment and machinery has completely changed methods of conducting public business. The pen gave way to the typewriter, carbon copies to the multigraph and the multilith, hand counting to the punch card and the electric sorting machine, invented incidentally in the Bureau of the Census.

More fundamental is the change in the nature of administrative tasks introduced by invention and technological change in the life of the people, and by a wider application of our rapidly increasing scientific knowledge to everyday problems of community welfare. A century ago public health administration was limited to port inspection of incoming vessels at the largest ports only. Since the establishment of air line transport to Central and South America, the United States Public Health Service has been obliged to devise vacuum cleaner methods of safeguarding against the accidental importation of a single yellow fever mosquito in a Pan-American airship. The clipper ship has renewed the possibility of yellow fever epidemics under circumstances peculiarly difficult to control.

Comparison of the actual work performed and methods used by public officers in 1835 and 1935 shows startling changes in every direction. Then highways were dirt roads, built with shovels, picks, horses and human labor, on the basis of the "scientific" information of the town selectmen or the county commissioners. Schools were the province of the local "school-marm" and the town or county board of education, specializing in the three R's and plenty of applied discipline. Public sanitation was nobody's business; the country doctor treated the sick, and the undertaker disposed of those who failed to survive. The care of the poor and the feeble-minded, the custody of the criminal and the insane, were all entrusted to the "overseers" of the poor, with little or no thought

[1] See *infra*, ch. 7.

of classification, remediable treatment, scientific study or preventive action.

All the elaborate paraphernalia of technology, investigation, and scientific procedure were absent from the administrative technique of a hundred years ago. The whole technical equipment of present day administration rests upon science and invention, and the effectiveness of government action has been immeasurably increased as a result.[1]

The theory and practice of scientific management reflect these conditions. Formulated by Frederick W. Taylor at the close of the nineteenth century, scientific management was at first applied to problems of mechanical engineering. The basic philosophy of the existence of "the one best way," and of the responsibility of management to discover this method by scientific experimentation soon led, however, to an emphasis upon management as such and to an appreciation of the great waste in handling human beings in the production of goods.

Scientific management, in the sense of tested methods of work, is quite as broadly applicable to government as to industrial operations. Organized labor, however, has not been friendly to "stop watch" methods, and it can hardly be said that the scientific management movement as such has made great progress in government departments. It would be a mistake, however, to conclude that its influence has been negligible. The constant refinement of methods in government work, the invention and adoption of machine operations, the development of standards, all reflect in substantial measure the influence of the exponents of scientific management.[2]

The growth of science and technology and their application to the business side of government have already created a new environment in which old theories need to be readjusted. It is manifestly impossible in an age when public administration depends upon the slide rule, the clinical thermometer, the test tube, and higher mathematics, to continue on the Jacksonian notion that "the duties of all public officers are, or at least admit of being made, so plain and simple that men of intelligence may readily qualify themselves for their performance." The duties of public

[1] William F. Ogburn and S. C. Gilfillan, "The Influence of Invention and Discovery," in *Recent Social Trends* (1933), vol. 1, ch. 3; Read Bain, "Technology and State Government," 2 *Am. Sociology Rev.* 860-74 (1937).

[2] Scientific management as a method should not be confused with the so-called "science of administration." In the author's judgment, the process of administration in its present stage of development is more wisely described as an art rather than as a science. For the literature of scientific management consult Frank B. Copley, *Frederick W. Taylor, the Father of Scientific Management* (1923); *Bulletin of the Taylor Society;* The Society for the Advancement of Management, *Journal;* Morris L. Cooke, "Influence of Scientific Management upon Government–Federal, State and Muncipal," 9 *Bulletin of the Taylor Society* 31-38 (1924).

office are complicated, highly specialized, professional and immensely important. They can be adequately performed only by permanent officials, with suitable professional and technical training, acting under the direction of department heads of broad vision who are able by their personal leadership to mediate between the technician, the politician, and the public. The greater part of governmental work in this country is now carried on by employees and officials technically trained and well equipped for their task, a group exemplified by Julia Lathrop, first head of the Children's Bureau; Elwood Mead, for many years head of the Reclamation Service; George R. Putnam, former Commissioner of Lighthouses; and Dr. William Alanson White, late head of St. Elizabeths Hospital.

In an address before the Institute of Public Administration, Sir Stanley Baldwin once said: ". . . the application of the Act to the individual person is the task of the civil servant. He has to translate law into policy and apply power and pressure to the citizen throughout the multitudinous activities of the modern state. He has to fit the shoe to the foot with the minimum pinch and squeeze. Which, in more exalted language, means that administration is the essence of government and its quality a prime condition of civic comfort." [1]

Under circumstances differing in many respects from those surrounding the British civil service our public officials are engaged in the same task. The quality and nature of their work are better understood by a glimpse of the historical circumstances from which they have developed.

[1] 12 *Pub. Adm.* 7 (1934).

Chapter Two

TRENDS IN THE AMERICAN ADMINISTRATIVE SYSTEM

SYSTEMS of public administration, like all human organizations, are deeply affected by their origin and environment. To see our administrative institutions in the long perspective of a century and a half enables us to understand them better and to appreciate more vividly the contending forces which have combined to bring us where we are today.

These influences are in many cases still at work, and with others will continue to fashion the major aspects of our administrative organization and procedure. They are in part physical in nature (geographic, climatic), in part they flow from the economic and technological transformation of the country, and in part they comprise the underlying attitudes, preferences, beliefs, fears, and aspirations of the American people. They deserve a more extended treatment than space will here permit.[1]

1. The Foundations

The historical roots of the American administrative system are found in the English institutions of local government of the seventeenth and eighteenth centuries, in general the span of years from 1650 to 1750. Dutch, Swedish, and French origins (except in Louisiana) were quickly submerged by the predominant English pattern of government and administration. Institutions adapted to rural England were rapidly and normally reproduced in rural America.

Government was naturally on a minimum scale. Demand for governmental activities beyond the maintenance of internal peace and order (chiefly ensured by the courts and a night watch in the larger towns) was almost unknown. A "strong tradition of restraint upon and limitation of government" was projected well down into the nineteenth cen-

[1] For general background, see Charles E. Merriam, *A History of American Political Theories* (1903), and *American Political Ideas, 1865–1917* (1920); Vernon L. Parrington, *Main Currents in American Thought* (1927), especially vols. 2 and 3; Charles A. Beard and Mary R. Beard, *The Rise of American Civilization* (1927); President's Research Committee on Social Trends, *Recent Social Trends in the United States* (1933).

tury. The operations to be performed were of the simplest nature—maintenance of places of custody for the delinquent, aid to the indigent, safekeeping of such records as deeds, conveyances and similar documents at the county courthouse, inspection of certain products intended for export to determine standards of quality, the collection of the tax on real estate, and early spring work on the dirt roads—these cover the principal administrative activities, adapted to the simple needs of a rural civilization.

The administrative structure was equally simple. In the north it centered in the town meeting and town officers, in the south, in the county court and county officials. The difficulties of travel were such that contacts between the colonial or state capitals and either the towns or county seats were infrequent and unimportant. The great bulk of administrative work was done by the localities, not by the central state authorities.

Office holding was in the hands of an "upper class," set off both by social position and by economic advantages. Property qualifications for voting and for office holding were nearly universal, and while the governing class was perhaps more sharply defined in Virginia than in Massachusetts, it existed at most points. Jefferson, democrat that he was, unconsciously revealed the situation when in 1803 he wrote of a Massachusetts appointee, "His family is among the best on that shore."

Until well into the last half of the nineteenth century the principal means of law enforcement was trial by court and jury. Public authority was expressed in legislative rules and prohibitions, and in the decisions of judges. The law, whether written or customary, was normally called into action by the private citizen who, when injured by action of another, sought redress in the court. By awarding damages or by issuing judicial writ to compel or prohibit, the judge enforced the law in the particular instance. The jury played an important part in the whole law-enforcing process, thus bringing popular attitudes to bear on the degree to which a law was to be enforced.[1]

In the absence of actual appeal to a court, the law stood as a guide to action, with its potential penalties but without positive means to put them into effect. For years, few administrative officials existed whose duty it was either to observe the operation of the law, or to assist in making it effective, or to prevent its violation. With few exceptions, the law, the plaintiff and the court comprised the enforcement system, rather than a hierarchy of administrative officials.

Reliance on the judicial rather than the executive branch for law en-

[1] Roscoe Pound, *Criminal Justice in America* (1930).

forcement arose naturally from the fact that for two centuries the colonists on this continent were aggravated by imported royal governors who were often spoilsmen and usually out of sympathy with colonial interests. Hence there arose a strong anti-executive tradition in the American people which was introduced into the early state constitutions adopted from 1775 to 1800.

For generations the temper of the people, deeply affected by frontier conditions, favored a self-reliant, self-sufficient individual life. Doctrines of liberty and personal rights as against state interference were natural to the prevailing type of community and were emphasized first as resistance to Great Britain took form, and again as the population spread over the Alleghenies. In short, the administrative system was adapted to a simple type of civilization, a farming-fishing-trading community, a society of neighbors transacting affairs with persons whose reliability they were able to assess and whose responsibility could be enforced before the justice of the peace or the county court. They asked little from the state.

2. Basic Changes

The fundamental changes which have been responsible for transforming the simple administrative structure of 1800 into the complex organization of today are economic, scientific and technological in character or origin. They stem from the industrial revolution and the complex sequence of events consequent upon the application of steam to production, hastened by the course of invention and discovery. Here we find the major causes for the rise of the city, for the development of means of transportation, for the expansion of the corporation, for the swelling tides of immigration, and for the gradual rise of interest groups deeply concerned with government and administration.

As a direct result the immediate, personal relationships of early rural Americans, neighbors in small and self-contained communities, were obscured and supplanted by distant impersonal contacts of many types. It became necessary to transact business with men whose standing was not known through a lifetime of association; new and unaccustomed forms of business developed; individuals began to deal with corporations; the emerging city began to take over some of the activities which a colonial or a frontier citizen had managed for himself.

The growth of cities, and later of such metropolitan centers as New York, Boston, Chicago, San Francisco, is the most obvious symbol of the transformation of American life. The independent, self-sufficient, self-contained *rural* family expecting nothing from government apart from protection of person and property, has become predominantly an *urban* family dependent upon government and administration at every turn. The process of specialization has taken out of the urban home one function after another, requiring in most cases some administrative supervision to ensure that the interests of the family are properly conserved (disposal of refuse and sewage, inspection of milk supply, inspection of meat, weights and measures, etc.). The mere physical contiguity of hundreds of thousands of persons intensifies old problems and creates new ones, demanding public supervision.[1]

The rural family, too, has discovered that it is at the mercy of great forces which can be managed, if at all, only by government, often on a national scale. The improvement of farm methods is facilitated through the county agent, a salesman-educator-technician who represents at one and the same time county, state, and federal governments. The price and distribution of milk are fixed in some cases by state milk control boards. The production of basic crops is controlled, in cooperation with farmers, by the Agricultural Adjustment Administration. The conservation of the farmers' land is assisted by the Soil Conservation Service. Rural America, as well as industrial, has thus felt the impact of economic, scientific and technological change.

The direct, personal relationships of our forefathers, neighbors in small communities, have also been transformed by the rise of the business corporation. Until 1800 the corporation was practically unknown in the business life of the country; it was relatively unfamiliar for another quarter century. The industrial revolution favored this form of organization and after 1825 the number multiplied. Among the early corporations were banks, manufacturing enterprises, turnpike companies, railroads, insurance companies, later the municipal utilities.

The corporation profoundly altered the direct person-to-person relationship which had prevailed since the founding of the colonies. It was neither a neighbor, nor an individual whose standard of conduct could be assessed by those who had dealings with it. Its agents (especially those of the early insurance companies) were often irresponsible to the highest degree. And when injured citizens went to court they often found that the legal resources of the corporation by way of appeal and technicality were too great to be overcome, or that their suit for damages was useless owing to the complete bankruptcy of the corporation. Thus the whole structure of judicial protection of small property rights began to crumble.

Here the interests of individuals could not be safeguarded by the city,

[1] Arthur M. Schlesinger, *The Rise of the City, 1878–1898* (1933); Lewis Mumford, *The Culture of Cities* (1938); National Resources Committee, *Our Cities* (1937).

which was adding one service to another for its citizens. The authority of the state was required; and during the latter half of the last century state legislative and administrative supervision of corporations became steadily more specific and detailed, supplemented by subsequent regulation by the federal government.

As the course of modern industry developed, the relative equality of life in early America began to fade. Large fortunes accumulated, factory workers multiplied in number, and the line of separation between those who had much and those who had little became clearer and clearer. Political inequalities had been extinguished on the whole as these new economic extremes emerged; and now the government, responsive to the voting power of the masses, began to intervene to modify or to ameliorate the results of poverty and helplessness among the less fortunate. Factory inspection to eliminate hazards to life and limb, restriction of the hours of labor of women and children, minimum wages in special cases, heavy taxation of great fortunes through the inheritance and income taxes, all are examples of state intervention to protect those who are adversely affected by unregulated industrial competition, and to prevent the steady concentration of wealth in few hands. Here is one of the basic social changes which supports much modern administration.

Another important aspect of the changes underlying modern conditions of administration is the rise of organized groups each with a specific interest in some aspect of the public service, or utilized by the government as a means of making its administrative program more effective. The change is one away from a government dealing individually with its citizens as persons to a government dealing in large and significant measure with its citizens as members of a group. The importance of this alteration in relationship is very great.[1]

In Jefferson's administration various interests had, of course, to be attended by government—the New England shippers, the trans-Allegheny farmers, the southern tobacco growers. They were not yet organized interests; they spoke only as individuals; they maintained no representatives in Washington; they were not consulted as a group by the public authorities or associated with any administrative program. Much administration, and constantly more, is now transacted between officials and groups as groups; and organized interests are ubiquitous in the field of administration.

Illustrations could be multiplied. Of much contemporary significance is the new emphasis upon great interest groups as cooperating agencies

[1] E. Pendleton Herring, *Public Administration and the Public Interest* (1936); Harwood L. Childs, ed., *Pressure Groups and Propaganda*, 179 *Annals* (1935); Peter H. Odegard and E. Allen Helms, *American Politics* (1938), esp. chs. 7-11, 22.

in the administrative process. In several instances, the group affected has been deliberately organized, or an existing organization has been deliberately affiliated with government in order better to effectuate public policy. A dramatic instance is found in the work of the Agricultural Adjustment Administration.

After consultation with farming organizations, it was agreed to curtail production of certain basic farm commodities, such as wheat, cotton, corn and hogs. The problem of method immediately became of critical importance. No allocation could be worked out in Washington and imposed upon each individual farmer throughout the country. As an alternative, a voluntary but centrally guided method of procedure was devised, resting upon crop production associations in all the counties affected. These associations were open to all farmers, were locally organized on a democratic basis, were usually voluntary and not compulsory, and were directed by officers elected by the farmers concerned. The county agent was closely associated with the crop production association. The general plan of production control was debated and approved in these associations, which then became the agency for allocating to each cooperating farmer his share of the total production allocated to the county. Organized farmers thus became in substance a part of the administrative machinery of the national government.[1]

The basic importance of this change in the conditions under which American administrators operate is reflected in the interpretation given to it by John Dewey. What has happened, he argues, is the constant development of an interest which he calls public as each individual citizen finds that he is affected by the acts and decisions of other persons with whom he has no adequate channels of communication. Under these circumstances the provision of some organization through which the interests of these individuals can be brought into communication and coordination is essential to ensure that all interests are expressed and weighed in fixing upon a course of action. The system of administration is one of the means by which these disjointed publics are brought into effective contact each with the other.[2]

Accompanying these underlying changes there has been a considerable change in the climate of opinion with respect to government itself. The doctrine of the less government the better dominated the early

[1] Other striking illustrations may be drawn from the credit associations developed by Farm Credit Administration and Federal Home Loan Bank Board.

[2] John Dewey, *The Public and Its Problems* (1927); Mary P. Follett, *The New State* (1918). In the analysis underlying this chapter, I have been aided by an unpublished report prepared for the Social Science Research Council Committee on Public Administration by John M. Gaus, "A Study of Research in Public Administration" (1930).

years of our national life. It still persists in some quarters but has been fairly well submerged by popular willingness to turn to government and public officials for all kinds of aid. Labor and agriculture and business depend freely on government services, and find it useful to condemn only the expenditures caused by assistance to others than themselves. The great depression of 1929 magnified this change of attitude. In the desperation born of fear, bankers and brokers, industrialists and merchants, insurance companies and transportation lines went to the national government for aid and comfort. Aid was forthcoming, and the experience is not likely to be forgotten in future crises, however distasteful the recollection of need may be in conservative quarters. Among the great mass of citizens, the relief extended by government throughout a dark decade cannot fail to obscure the last vestiges of suspicion of government which as a people we inherited from pioneer days. We are now in danger of putting a heavier load on government than its present system of administration can support.

The industrial revolution and technological advances which appear to be responsible for the transformations of American life which have been outlined in the preceding paragraphs fortunately resulted also in an enlargement of the taxable wealth of the country sufficient to maintain the new activities. Administrative services cost money, and the revenue sources of Jackson's era would be wholly inadequate to meet present needs. The wealth of the country has increased by leaps and bounds and, until 1930, proved sufficient to care for all except war emergencies. To support the variety of administrative activities which are now thought necessary or desirable requires a proportion of the national income greater by far than that needed by the farming-fishing-trading communities of our forefathers.

3. Trends in Administrative Functions and Organization

It was inevitable that the transformation of the United States from a rural agricultural nation to one predominantly urban and industrial should have a profound effect upon its civil institutions. The modest local government idealized by Jefferson, limited in scope and managed by its citizens, was gradually submerged in large parts of the country by the complex, expensive, and powerful administrative machine of today. Rural administration is still important, but the principal administrative problems are found in the management of cities, of states, of regions and of the nation.[1]

[1] For problems of rural administration, consult such works as Lane W. Lancaster, *Government in Rural America* (1937); M. P. Catherwood, *Rural Government in New York*, Cornell University, Extension Bulletin 331, 1936; E. de S. Brunner and J. H. Kolb, *Rural Social Trends* (1933).

In a brief survey of a century's changes in the administrative structure of a nation as great as this, only some of the most significant aspects can be selected for attention. Other choices could well be made but there will perhaps be agreement that among the principal modifications are these: the great expansion of administrative functions, both regulatory and service, and in consequence the rise of organs of general management; the shift from law enforcement by judicial action alone to considerable law enforcement by administrative officials, entailing the growth of administrative discretion; the expansion of national administrative power and influence at the expense of the states, and of the states at the expense of the cities and counties; the early dispersion and eventual integration of internal administrative responsibility, involving a new concept of the office of chief executive; the gradual decline of patronage, accompanied by the increasing employment of specialists, professional men and scientists, and the rise of administrative planning.[1]

a. Expansion of administrative functions. It is unnecessary to emphasize the facts of administrative expansion. They are familiar signposts of the changing attitudes toward government which were noted in a previous paragraph. They are condemned, tolerated or praised by persons of different social philosophies, but the tide of expansion still flows strongly onward. It is possible that new administrative tasks will arise in the near future in health insurance and "socialized medicine," in the operation of railroads and various local utilities, and in the management of the radio; if not in these, it is reasonably certain that in other fields the expansionist pressure will result in more public administration rather than less.

In municipal government the forms of public undertaking are perhaps most varied. Their rise has been examined in studies of Detroit and Cincinnati.[2] Urban counties have felt the impact nearly as much, a conclusion demonstrated by a valuable study of Los Angeles County.[3] There is at least one corresponding study of the development of state activities.[4] For the federal government, the works of Professor Lloyd M.

[1] See Leonard D. White, *Trends in Public Administration* (1933) for a survey of some aspects of this subject since 1900.

[2] Lent D. Upson, *The Growth of a City Government* (1931); Cincinnati Municipal Reference Bureau, *Cincinnati (1802–1936): The March of City Government* (1937).

[3] Los Angeles County, Bureau of Efficiency, *Growth of County Functions* (mim. 1936).

[4] Elsey Hurt, *California State Government; an outline of its administrative organization from 1850 to 1936* (1937); H. Dewey Anderson, *Our California State Taxes* (1937), ch. 1.

Short and Dr. Carroll H. Wooddy give basic data.[1] The expansion of the educational and semi-educational activities of the schools reveals the same trend, the constant accretion of responsibilities discharged under public auspices.[2] It is rare for a function once undertaken by government to be abandoned by it.

The multiplication of functions has involved a corresponding increase in administrative agencies; and in consequence the recent development of organs of overhead management. These are still in a relatively primitive stage, but deserve notice as a probable harbinger of one line of important future evolution.

b. Rise of administrative agencies for law enforcement. In the previous section reference was made to the original dependence upon the courts for the enforcement of law, at the instance of private parties. As a result of the panic of 1837 came the invention of administrative agencies designed to enforce the law and conserve public interests not by prosecution but by supervision and prevention. The character of the change is illustrated by an early example drawn from the administrative history of Massachusetts.

The regulation of banks in the Bay State had gradually expanded since 1780. In essence the plan of bank regulation was, however, the same in 1830 as it was in 1780. The system comprised specific legislative requirements and prohibitions imposed upon the bank as a corporation, a schedule of penalties upon bank officials for violation thereof, and the customary right of an individual to sue the bank in the courts for damages. No official agency existed to inspect the bank or its transactions, except that the necessary initial capital was actually counted at the moment the charter of incorporation was granted.[3]

The growing demand for credit and bank facilities consequent upon the building of factories, canals and railroads led to the rapid increase in the number of banks, and to cutthroat competition between some of them. The panic of 1837 brought out a scandalous story of deception, misuse of funds, violation of law and betrayal of trust. It became obvious that mere legislative commands and prohibitions, enforced by suit on the part of injured individuals, were completely inadequate either as a restraint upon unsound banking practice or as a safeguard of the rights of depositors.

[1] Lloyd M. Short, *The Development of National Administrative Organization in the United States* (1923); Carroll H. Wooddy, *The Growth of the Federal Government, 1915–1932* (1934).

[2] Douglas E. Lawson, "The Development of Courses of Study in Ten Selected Large City School Systems" (ms. 1939), Ph.D. dissertation, Univ. of Chicago.

[3] Some enterprising bank speculators borrowed this capital for one day for the purpose of having it counted, repaying it on the next day.

In 1837 the General Court consequently established the State Bank Commission, the first administrative agency of its kind in the commonwealth, and one of the earliest in the country. The Commission was designed to see that the law was observed by the banks. To this end it had powers of visitation and inspection, power to require periodic statements, and in case of necessity power to require a bank to close its doors. The Commission thus became an instrument of the state to prevent the occurrence of unsound banking conditions, an alternative to judicial redress which experience had already demonstrated to be tardy and ineffective.

Implicit in this change was the recognition of a *public* interest requiring public protection through positive preventive action, in addition to the private interest for which judicial recourse had been thought adequate. The interest of the community in sound banking procedures, it was discovered, could not be left to the action of private creditors of a defunct bank. The recognition of a public interest, requiring public action, underlies not only the early bank commissions, but the insurance commissions, the railroad commissions, the utility commissions, and the whole movement in favor of official supervision of the economic order.

Implicit in the emergence of administrative regulatory and supervisory commissions was an expansion of discretionary power vested in administrative officers. Over the years the quantity of official discretion has enlarged, despite the reluctance of courts and some public opposition to administrative justice. In fact, however, both administrative rule making and administrative adjudication have served to amplify the discretion exercised by administrators. Subject to judicial review varying in extent from court to court and from time to time, it has become a characteristic feature of modern administrative procedure in many fields of governmental action.[1]

c. Shift in administrative balance of power. The center of gravity of the American administrative system at its inception was in the local governments; it has passed beyond the states and is now in the national capital. The march of power, constitutional, political, and administrative, to Washington has been one of the important governmental phenomena of the last fifty years. The results of the Civil War were decisive constitutionally; the arrival of "big business" was decisive politically and administratively. With the exception of the largest cities, there has been a notable centralization of authority within the states, as supervision and control of various sorts have been imposed on counties and

[1] The study of administrative discretion from the point of view of the administrator has never been undertaken. There is considerable literature on its legal aspects. Much work is needed in this area.

municipalities. The commerce power and conditional grants to the states have been the principal means of extending national authority at the expense of the states. New types of authority intermediate between the state and the nation, such as the Tennessee Valley Authority and the Port of New York Authority, suggest still further diminution of the administrative position of the commonwealth.[1]

d. Dispersion and integration of administrative responsibility. The expansion of governmental functions was reflected throughout the latter half of the nineteenth century in new administrative agencies. Distrust of the executive branch and preference for popular election of officials brought to pass the establishment of scores of small, independent, uncorrelated authorities, each designed to perform some specific activity. City governments had fallen into a chaotic state by 1900; state governments approached the complex and disorderly organization of cities a decade later.

The reform of municipal government, beginning with the commission plan and continuing with the council manager plan, brought order out of this chaos by consolidating these small units into relatively large and well-organized departments. This result was also effected by charter reform in many mayor-council cities. Within the states the trend toward integration commenced about 1915, and by 1935 had swept over the country. Much improvement resulted, but much remains yet to be done.

These and other parallel movements have transformed the character of city and state executives. In their original pattern they were designed as weak political leaders, the center of power remaining in legislative bodies. Since 1910, mayors and managers, school superintendents and governors have acquired much administrative authority. With some exceptions they are recognized now as the real heads of the administrative systems over which they long nominally presided. They retain also their political interests; and one of the unsettled problems of administration is to ascertain whether political leadership and administrative responsibility can be successfully discharged by one and the same person.[2]

e. Rise and decline of the spoils system. Rotation in office and selection of office holders for partisan reasons were the order of the day in the national government subsequent to 1829, in some states and cities from an even earlier date. Repeated efforts at reform were fruitless until 1883, when the merit system was adopted by Congress and by the state of New York. At present about two-thirds of all public employees are under a formal merit system or are protected by fixed standards. The

[1] For an extended discussion of this trend, see chs. 10-11.

[2] On this point see especially a monograph by Leslie M. Lipson, *The American Governor: From Figurehead to Leader* (1939).

struggle to extend the merit system still rages, with slow but certain gains.

While the original impulse for the merit system was reform of elections, its present support is principally the improvement of administration. The character of the civil service has been substantially changed since the merit system was introduced, not merely because a permanent staff was built up, but also because the traditional clerk has been supplemented by a new order of specialist personnel. These specialists include expanding numbers of the older professions, representatives of new branches of the professions and sciences, and a wide variety of technicians and experts often peculiar to the government service.

The old stereotype of the "government clerk" consequently no longer carries much meaning, although a large clerical force naturally remains. Their work is directed by a new breed of public official—men whose names are not found in the public press but who in their own circles are respected as leaders in their fields of endeavor. They are career men, the first generation of whom have already done their work, and whose tasks are now being picked up by an oncoming group of younger men.

f. Administrative planning. The great depression of 1929 accelerated national planning in all parts of the world, although planning in the field of government is far from new.[1] Modern administrative planning is illustrated by the town planning and zoning movement which developed rapidly into metropolitan and regional planning. In its early stages its objectives were partly esthetic, seeking to promote attractive and beautiful substitutes for the shabby surroundings of most cities. From the beginning, however, city planning had utilitarian purposes: effective transportation by land and water, good terminals, proper location of factories, zoning for restricted uses, and the like.[2]

A second type of planning was concerned with the conservation of natural resources. Its roots go far back into our national history as interest in forests, minerals, wild life, parks and other resources sprang into public consciousness.[3] Its modern evolution is traceable to the influence

[1] Charles E. Merriam, "Planning Agencies in America," 29 *Am. Pol. Sci. Rev.* 197-211 (1935); Katherine McNamara, *Bibliography of Planning, 1928–1935* (1936); Sir Henry N. Bunbury, "Governmental Planning Machinery," 16 *Pub. Adm.* 381-98 (1938). The principal journal is *Plan Age.*

[2] Thomas Adams, *Outline of Town and City Planning* (1935); Sir Gwilym Gibbon, *Problems of Town and Country Planning* (1937); Walter H. Blucher, "Planning and Zoning," in *Municipal Year Book,* 1936, 1937, 1938; William E. Cole and H. P. Crowe, *Recent Trends in Rural Planning* (1937).

[3] Charles R. Van Hise, *The Conservation of National Resources in the United States* (1910); revised edition, 1930, edited by Loomis Havemeyer, entitled *Conservation of Our Natural Resources;* basic data underlying planning activities are gathered in such volumes as President's Conference on Unemployment, *Recent Economic Changes in the United States* (1929); President's Research Committee on Social Trends, *Recent Social Trends in the United States* (1933).

of Theodore Roosevelt, who called the first Governors' Conference in 1908 to consider conservation and who gave a new impetus to the whole movement. The conservation of water, power, oil, gas, and soil suggested that the human resources of the nation were themselves proper objects of national planning. Hence arose the National Country Life Conference (1919) and the White House Conference on Child Health and Protection (1930), examples of a new orientation and a wider horizon.

A third type of administrative planning considers the national economic life as a whole, with special reference to the "strategic controls" through which economic activity can be guided into desired channels with a minimum of direct interference with the individual. This is essentially an attempt to create by central planning a better functioning of the economic and social order.[1] In the United States it has involved planning with reference to such strategic controls as public works, monetary and banking policy, investment policy, taxation, and agricultural production.[2]

The principal planning organ in the United States is the National Resources Committee, formerly the National Planning Board. It was first associated with Public Works Administration and was designed to advise and assist the Administrator through the preparation, development and maintenance of comprehensive plans related to the provision of public works in an emergency. Later it was separately organized as a committee of the Cabinet, comprising the Secretaries of Interior (chairman), War, Agriculture, Commerce, and Labor, the Works Progress Administrator and an advisory committee which took over the active direction of the organization.

The functions of the National Resources Committee as defined by Executive Order of June 30, 1934 are, "to prepare and present to the President a program and plan of procedure dealing with the physical, social, governmental and economic aspects of public policies for the development and use of land, water, and other national resources and such related subjects as may from time to time be referred to the Board by

[1] The complex problems of general economic and social planning may be pursued in the references already cited and in such articles as Lewis L. Lorwin, "Some Political Aspects of Economic Planning," 26 *Am. Pol. Sci. Rev.* 723-27 (1932); same author, "Social Aspects of the Planning State," 28 *Am. Pol. Sci. Rev.* 16-22 (1934); P. A. Sorokin, "Is Accurate Social Planning Possible?" 1 *Am. Sociology Rev.* 12-28 (1936).

[2] John M. Clark, *Economics of Planning Public Works* (1935); G. D. H. Cole, *Economic Planning* (1935); H. R. Burrows and J. K. Horsefield, *Economics of Planning* (1935); P. W. Martin, "The Present Status of Economic Planning," 33 *International Labour Rev.* 619-45 (1936); 35 *ibid.* 177-97 (1937).

the President." In the performance of these duties, the Committee has published an extraordinarily valuable series of basic reports.[1]

At the beginning of its work the National Resources Committee organized planning boards in the states. Within a period of two years most of the states had official planning boards or commissions, with appropriations which were often modest but which were supplemented by grants from the federal government. These appropriations have gradually expanded until by 1938 they amounted to about three quarters of a million dollars. The state planning bodies are encouraged to tackle their own problems, although there is naturally some coordination between their work and that of the National Resources Committee.

Another interesting type of planning agency is the Tennessee Valley Authority. The organic act authorized the President to make such general plans for the Tennessee basin as might be useful in guiding and controlling the orderly physical, economic and social development of this region.[2] Pivoted on the production of electric power and fertilizer, the Authority has in fact extended its influence into many phases of the economic and social life of the valley—schools, health, conservation, labor standards, adult education and others. There is already evidence that the T.V.A. is modifying the level of life in this and adjoining areas.[3]

Governmental planning of itself is preparatory, not executory. The plans are not self-enforcing, indeed they are not enforcible until they have been enacted into legislation or accepted by the public as good practice. Planning is a broad general guide to future objectives, not the immediate enforcement of a specific requirement. In fact the general mandate to the Tennessee Valley Authority for planning the economic improvement of the valley is being sought by force of example quite as frequently as by force of law. This world-wide attempt to discover more distant goals and the road to their realization suggests how broadly we must construe the nature of the administrative tasks of the future.[4]

[1] Their range and content may be noted from these sample titles: *Regional Factors in National Planning and Development* (1935); *Public Works Planning* (1936); *Regional Planning* (1936); *Technological Trends and National Policy* (1937); *Our Cities: Their Role in the National Economy* (1937); *The Problems of a Changing Population* (1938).

[2] 48 Stat. 58 (1933), sec. 22.

[3] Clarence L. Hodge, *The Tennessee Valley Authority* (1938); Howard W. Odum and H. E. Moore, *American Regionalism* (1938).

[4] Planners are organized in the American Society of Planning Officials, Chicago. See Arthur L. Shepard, "City Planning Personnel—A Critical Analysis," 27 *Nat. Mun. Rev.* 450-53 (1938).

4. Some General Qualities of the American Administrative System

As the result of well over a hundred years' uninterrupted development, an administrative structure has been evolved with characteristics peculiar to it. It is different from the Dutch, the Japanese, the Argentinean or the English civil service; it is peculiarly American.

In the first place, the prevailing American system like many others is based on the rule of law. Officials act on the basis of an authority created and limited by law; they are responsible to the courts for the observance of law; they must always act within the four corners of the statute and have no freedom to attack injustice wherever they see it. In the United States there is an emphasis on the right to be heard, an exaggeration of legal correctness, and in consequence an accentuation of the lawyer in administration which pushes the doctrine of the rule of law farther than in most other countries. An administrator must above all be on sound legal ground; he may exceed his budget but he cannot borrow from the courts.

Our system of administration is that of a democratic government. Real control is exercised by the elected representatives of the people; the voters themselves elect directly, indeed, something like 875,000 public officials, many purely administrative figures. There is a strong sense of localism, a sort of fireside democracy, which affects not only cities and states, but the field service of the national government. There is an intimate interlocking of political parties and administrative office, a special type of democratic influence upon the bureaucracy. There are no special classes within the civil service, such as the English administrative class. This is, in short, an example of administration by consent and by participation on a rare scale.

In its more extensive units, public administration has become an example of large-scale management, with many of the characteristic problems of large-scale organization in business. The Department of Agriculture in 1938 directed the efforts of over 80,000 men and women in all parts of the United States in a wide variety of activities; the Postmaster General manages a department employing over a quarter of a million; the mayor of New York heads an official organization of nearly 100,000 employees. The relations of the parts of a far-flung organization each to the other and to the central direction, the avoidance of "absentee" management by a relatively uninformed headquarters staff, the maintenance of adequate freedom and initiative on the periphery, the management of employees through the necessary means of an official hierarchy, these are among the common vexations of all large-scale structures, public and private.

The American civil service is managed generally by subject-matter specialists in preference to the men of "general competence." [1] Engineers, foresters, geologists, agronomists, social workers, accountants, journalists, economists in more recent years, these are the types who stand at the top of the operating departments, directly beneath the political heads. While the preference for the specialist-administrator is still strong, signs multiply that a different type may soon develop on a substantial scale. The early predominance of the engineer-city manager is weakening, especially in the larger cities, a change dramatized by the career of Clarence A. Dykstra, schólar, teacher, publicist, official, city manager, and since 1937, university president. Several important federal bureaus have definitely concluded that the subject-matter specialist cannot fully meet their administrative needs. Such specialists will doubtless continue to play a more important administrative part than in Great Britain, for example; but their monopoly in administration is being challenged.

Finally it may be pointed out that to an exceptional degree the American system of public administration is imbued with a strong sense of the doctrine of perfectibility. Standards have been, and in many instances still are low; but there is plenty of "divine discontent" with these deficiencies. There is a wholesome stirring of the waters among organizations of officials and among groups of employees, whose efforts toward better service and higher standards are very significant. They, in turn, are supported by a public sentiment for improvement which reflects a growing sense of the risks of failure on the administrative front. The expansion of administrative services to farmer and to city dweller alike is increasing the helpful contacts of government and governed. The masses of people are increasingly interested in administration as of practical, concrete concern to them instead of remotely antagonistic as in early years.

If, then, we seek to characterize the quality of the American public service, we may reflect on its attachment to the rule of law, its organization as an instrument of democratic self-government, the grand scale of its operations, its technical leadership by subject-matter specialists, and its strong internal capacity for improvement. These are not, naturally, universal traits; but even gross perversions of administrative integrity, unblushing partisanship, and occasional denial of the public interest do not destroy these essential qualities.

It is obvious that the system of administration found adequate for thirteen states fronting the Atlantic seaboard and backed by a wilderness is far different from the system which is now ministering to the needs of 130,000,000 people stretched solidly across the continent and harassed

[1] Léon Blum, *La Réforme Gouvernementale* (1936).

and perplexed by the civilization which they have created. An unbroken chain of events links the present to the past, and in the operation of the administrative machine of the twentieth century it is easy to discern the hand of the nineteenth, if not traces of the eighteenth. This history has not yet been told, nor the growth of opinion with reference to government and its administration. It will some day give insight into our administrative past and guides to our administrative future.

It seems clear that public policy will lay heavy loads upon the civil service of the next generation. The management of the economic estate of the country—lands, water, forests, minerals, power—is now under scrutiny from a long-range point of view; and long-range policies and administrative plans seem likely to result. Much more intricate and complex is the management in some measure of the whole economic system. Almost from the beginning of our national history we have attempted some direction, exemplified in tariff policy, internal improvements, and land policy. It is not likely that we shall now withdraw from the effort to guide a delicate but vast structure of production and distribution. The grave social consequences of indifference are balanced by those of clumsy intervention, but our past and present compel the effort at some degree of direction.

These are among the great ends which challenge government of the future, and which compel the radical and rapid improvement of the administrative organs through which policy works itself out. The stakes are beyond price, for if democratic policy and democratic administration fail, an autocratic alternative may await the opportunity to seize power.

PART II

STRUCTURE AND ORGANIZATION

Chapter Three

SOME GENERAL ASPECTS OF ORGANIZATION

WITH this chapter begins the study of the administrative system of the present, supplemented from time to time by further brief notes on the historical development of its special phases. The successive major divisions of this work will deal with structure and organization, with fiscal management, with personnel management, with some typical forms of action by which officials regulate the activities of citizens, and with the system of responsibility to which administration is subject. With an organization, funds, personnel, powers and responsibilities, government is ready to act in the execution of public policy.

A sound organization is intimately related to the effectiveness with which the personnel can work. Poor organization, i.e., one in which the parts are not well laid out, in which there is duplication of work, lack of clear responsibility, poor coordination, loose supervision, ineffective delegation, leads directly to loss of human effort, confusion of purpose, conflict of wills, and at times near paralysis of movement.[1] Good organization and smooth operation are inseparably connected. Even though competent personnel may make any organization work, there is no sense in requiring them to work with a poor one.

The point has been admirably put by Professor John M. Gaus, who writes: "Organization is the arrangement of personnel for facilitating the accomplishment of some agreed purpose through the allocation of functions and responsibilities. It is the relating of efforts and capacities of individuals and groups engaged upon a common task in such a way as to secure the desired objective with the least friction and the most satisfaction to those for whom the task is done and those engaged in the enterprise."[2]

The vital point is that structure is an arrangement of the working relationships of individuals, not merely an impersonal process of putting blocks together to make a building. As a system of arrangement of hu-

[1] An extraordinary example is found in the administrative history of N.R.A.; see Leverett S. Lyon and others, *The National Recovery Administration* (1935), chs. 4-10.

[2] Gaus, White and Dimock, *The Frontiers of Public Administration* (1936), pp. 66-67.

man beings, it is subject to such modifications, in particular cases, as given personality combinations may require. To what extent it is desirable to rearrange structure in preference to replacing personnel is a practical matter to be determined in the light of special cases. In the long run, the demands of sound organization require the fitting of personnel to it, rather than sacrificing normal organizational relationships to the needs or whims of individuals.

Before turning to the analysis and criticism of the prevailing structure of American public administration it is advantageous to consider the process of organization in its broader phases. Modern society contains an endless number and variety of associations. Among these organized groups exist governments and their administrative systems, possessing certain special characteristics, to be sure, but resembling in many ways the unofficial societies which flourish so abundantly.[1]

Experience and observation indicate that the technical problems of large-scale organization and management are much alike, whether the institution is official, as for example the Inland Waterways Corporation, or unofficial, as the Detroit and Cleveland Navigation Company. The intricate arrangements of government are not therefore without parallels in other forms of organization. They have significance as examples of what Urwick calls the "pure theory" of organization. Consequently it seems useful to explore the subject matter of organization as such, as a theoretical background for the special case of the structure of American public administration.[2]

"It is impossible for humanity to advance its knowledge of organization," writes Urwick, "unless the factor of structure is isolated from other considerations, however artificial such an isolation may appear."[3] While we yet lack a pure theory of structure, some parts are beginning to appear, and the nature and usefulness of such a theory are recognized. They may be illustrated by a simple analogy. In a shipyard we may observe piles of steel shapes, machines, lumber, implements, and tools. In themselves they are nothing; assembled on the basis of a plan of organization they become an ocean-going vessel, a structure of potential utility. But the assembly as such leads directly to no ultimate end; the ship has to be put in motion by providing a staff, operating mate-

[1] On industrial organization, see William B. Cornell, *Organization and Management in Industry and Business* (rev. ed. 1936); A. A. Farquhar, "Functional Organization," in H. S. Person, ed., *Scientific Management in American Industry* (1929); James O. McKinsey, *Organization Problems under Present Conditions*, Am. Man. Assoc., General Management Series 127 (1936).

[2] The reader who wishes to deal with concrete material before the general should reserve this chapter for later reading.

[3] L. Urwick, "The Function of Administration," in Luther Gulick and L. Urwick, eds., *Papers on the Science of Administration* (1937), p. 122.

rials, command, and a destination or plan of operations. It is the special task of organization to put the parts in their appropriate places and thus to create the potential utility of the structure as a whole.[1]

Hence we are led to the inquiry, what are the leading features of the formation and arrangement of the parts of a large-scale organization, public or private, which are conducive to the effective operation of the structure as a whole? Without exhausting this very large subject, we may consider five general aspects of the matter—the individual and his position, the unit cell of organization; the formation of administrative units; the hierarchical form of organization; the location and delegation of authority; and the coordination of the parts into an effective whole.

1. The Individual and His Position

The fundamental unit from which all organization is built is the position and its incumbent, the individual employee. Any composite structure is an aggregate of positions and incumbents, or conversely, the analysis of any organization into its divisions and subdivisions eventually leads to the irreducible unit, the position.

Classification technicians have been forced to define this unit, which is the principal object of their operations. From their lexicon we may take a formal definition in these terms: "A position is a specific civilian office, employment, or job, whether occupied or vacant, calling for the performance of certain duties and the carrying of certain responsibilities by one individual, either on a full-time or a part-time basis. . . ."[2]

The concept of a position is distinct from the concept of an employee. A position may be occupied or vacant. It is characterized by its duties and responsibilities, and as long as these criteria remain the same, the position remains the same although it may be occupied by different employees with different combinations of qualities at different times. A position often exists before it is occupied by anyone, and does not cease to exist with the death, resignation or removal of its incumbent. In government a position is usually created by administrative direction, in conformity with authority vested by law and by appropriation act.

As thus defined, the position is the universal building block of all organizations, official and unofficial. The army builds on the private, with

[1] The principal references to the subject matter of this chapter are: Henri Fayol, *Administration industrielle et générale* (1920); English edition, *Industrial and General Administration* (1930); James D. Mooney and Alan C. Reiley, *Onward Industry!* (1931); Luther Gulick and L. Urwick, *op. cit.; Investigation of Executive Agencies of the Government,* S. Rept. 1275, 75th Cong. 1st sess. (1937), ch. 1, "The Problem of Administrative Organization"; American University, *Groups and their Administration* (mim. 1938).

[2] U. S. Personnel Classification Board, *Closing Report of Wage and Personnel Survey* (1931), p. 131.

many specialized types of technical positions supplementing the positions of general command. A hospital is built on the nurse and physician, with many cooperating technical and subordinate positions. In a bank, a railroad company, a book club, a boy scout troop, a philanthropic foundation, in all human organizations, the position is the simple and universal unit of organization.

An employee or incumbent is an individual who occupies a position. The qualities desired of incumbents in positions rising in the hierarchy naturally vary widely. At the bottom of the ladder, physical strength or special skills may be principally needed. At the top, managerial skill and technical knowledge are essential.[1] These qualities correspond to the duties and responsibilities of the position.

Any organization, then, is an aggregate of positions and incumbents. Organizing skill brings about the effective relation of these positions and employees, each to the other, their combination into units of the first degree, and the relation of these units in larger and larger aggregates, eventually comprising the whole. In one direction sound organization leads into the function of classification; in another it leads into the formation of the parts of the whole.[2]

2. The Formation of Administrative Units

The aggregation of thousands of specific jobs into working units, and the combination of these into larger divisions reflect the double influence of specialization and combination. Specialization operates constantly to divide and subdivide work and to segregate workers, who are eventually combined into units and larger aggregates principally on the basis of the major purpose for which they exist.[3]

In government, the principal subdivisions of the whole administrative system are usually called departments or independent establishments (commissions, corporations, authorities, etc.). They are ordinarily organized on the basis of major substantive purpose, and are concerned "with the content matter" of their field. Thus for example we note a city police department, a county health unit, a state department of agriculture, and the United States Department of Commerce. Borrowing a figure of speech from army usage, such major substantive organizations are often called "line" departments.

Each large line department comprises a number of operating units

[1] For an interesting scale of qualities in the typical positions of an industrial hierarchy, see Henri Fayol, *Industrial and General Administration*, p. 11.

[2] Classification is considered in ch. 21.

[3] See especially Luther Gulick, "Notes on the Theory of Organization," in Gulick and Urwick, *op. cit.*, pp. 3-45; and *The Work Unit in Federal Administration*, Public Administration Service No. 56, 1937.

characterized by the singleness and unity of their task. They are the major units of administration, and are usually called bureaus. Thus the bureau of identification of a police department, the bureau of old-age pensions of a state welfare department, the Bureau of Mines of the Department of the Interior furnish examples. Their basis of organization is again purpose, but more specific, narrow, and unitary purpose than that which is usually found in the department.

The subdivisions of a bureau are designated by various terms, usually divisions. They are based on subject-matter specialties, specific projects, or special kinds of work. For example, the United States Office of Education had in 1936 divisions of higher education, American school systems, comparative education, special problems (a pseudonym for miscellaneous), statistics, and others. The Bureau of Internal Revenue was divided into the accounts and collections unit, the income tax unit, the miscellaneous tax unit, and the alcohol tax unit. The Bureau of Sanitary Engineering of the Illinois Department of Health was organized around these activities: public water supplies, stream pollution, mosquito and malaria control, sewerage, milk control, and laboratory service.[1]

In the not remote past, each major department or establishment was a self-contained unit. Each assumed full responsibility for all of its primary and secondary operations. The United States Department of Agriculture not only enforced interstate plant quarantines and conducted research, it also kept its own accounts, made its own disbursements, submitted its own budget to the House Appropriations Committee, purchased its own supplies, hired its own personnel, and rented its own quarters. Every department jealously guarded its own operating self-sufficiency and went its way without paying much attention to its neighbors.

Gradually, over a long period of years, the "major purpose" departments have been losing part of their responsibility for carrying on their auxiliary or secondary services. These services, responding to the pressure of specialization and presumed economies, have been separately organized partly outside, partly inside the line departments. The work specialized outside the departments is usually organized directly under the chief executive, but is sometimes attached to a central finance department. Thus we now find central purchasing offices, central personnel agencies, central disbursing offices and others, independent of any department, and corresponding subordinate offices inside the departments.[2]

No standard terminology has yet been accepted for this class of administrative agencies. Willoughby called them the institutional or house-

[1] The formation of field structure is not discussed at this point. See ch. 7.
[2] For further development, see ch. 7.

keeping services, terms which have merit but which have not been generally adopted. They are often erroneously called staff services, a confusion which should be avoided. Gaus suggests "auxiliary technical staff services," a useful suggestion. In order to propose a terminology which is not liable to confusion, I suggest and in this volume shall use the term, auxiliary services. This term is used in continental countries.

In large organizations, another type of specialization is developing, properly called the staff (alternatively general staff, administrative staff). Staff organization, first developed in the Prussian army, was introduced into American army organization by Secretary of War Elihu Root in 1903, and is slowly being segregated as a special organ in civil and large-scale business administration. A staff is an organ advisory to a responsible official, but without operating responsibilities. The function performed by the army staff is to plan, to advise, to assist the commanding officer, to supervise, but not to command.[1] The function of a civil staff is properly understood in the same terms, i.e., to study administrative problems, to plan, to advise, to observe, but not to act. A staff unit may be attached to a chief executive or to other principal administrators. The staff service of advice and counsel operates upward, downward and outward and across organizational lines. It is always advice, however, and never command.

The place of an industrial staff organ was described in these words by Fayol: "Whatever their ability and their capacity for work, the heads of great enterprises cannot fulfill alone all their obligations . . . they are thus forced to have recourse to a group of men who have the strength, competence, and time which the Head may lack. This group of men constitutes the Staff of the Management. It is a help, or reinforcement, a sort of extension of the manager's personality, to assist him in carrying out his duties. The Staff appears as a separate body only in large undertakings and its importance increases with the importance of the undertaking."[2]

The staff function and the function of the auxiliary services are therefore different and ought not to be confused. The auxiliary services are operating agencies, the staff is a thinking, planning and advisory agency. The auxiliary agencies are concerned with the maintenance of an exist-

[1] For development and illustration, see ch. 5.

[2] Henri Fayol, in Gulick and Urwick, *op. cit.*, p. 104. Compare J. D. Mooney in the same volume, p. 91, and pp. 95-96 in these words: "But if we take the broader view and consider *line* simply as the function of command, and *staff* as the service of information or counsel, we see at once that military organization can have no corner on these principles."

". . . Staff services, whether formally organized or not, are bound to grow up in every organization. Their formal organization, however, is demanded if we are to achieve the most efficient forms of concerted human effort."

ing organization, and are not concerned with major substantive policies; the staff is concerned with the revision of organization as new needs may dictate, and with the reformulation of major policies.[1]

This form of specialization, it must be emphasized, is still very incomplete, and is often entirely absent even in large governmental structures. This does not mean, of course, that no planning or thinking about administrative problems takes place. The line agencies are bound to plan their own work, and much planning and forecasting are carried forward by officials immediately responsible for operating decisions. Even when a staff agency has been set up, it acquires no monopoly of planning, for other agencies of government will continue to work out their own future programs and policies. A central staff agency is a useful specialization of the planning and coordinating function, but it is supplementary, not exclusive.

The formation of the parts of any large-scale organization, then, reflects the pressure of specialization and division of labor. Three principal types of administrative organs under the chief executive have emerged: the line agencies, the auxiliary services, and the staff. Within each, specialization breaks down the work into appropriate subdivisions, and eventually into specific positions. In actual practice, naturally, the allocation of functions does not always sharply recognize these logical categories; usually staff work is not clearly segregated; the work of the auxiliary services may only partly be placed in special organs; and auxiliary agencies may also perform genuine staff functions owing to lack of sharply exclusive differentiation of work.

While the usual basis of specialization for organizational ends will be by purpose, Gulick notes other types. Specialization by process brings about operating units which perform the same mechanical or other operation, as for example the familiar "stenographic pool"; specialization by clientele develops agencies which perform a wide variety of services for specified classes of persons, as for example, the mentally deranged under hospital care; specialization by area suggests administrative divisions responsible for diverse kinds of work in a given region.[2]

3. Hierarchy

The structure of an army provides the best recognized example of a hierarchy. All large-scale organizations tend to follow the same pattern, which in essence consists in the universal application of the superior-

[1] Cf. Gt. Britain, Machinery of Government Committee, *Report* (Cd 9230, 1918); Wilfred Spender, "A General Staff for the Civil Service," 112 *Nineteenth Century* 84-94 (1932).

[2] Gulick and Urwick, *op. cit.*, pp. 23-30.

subordinate relationship through a number of levels of responsibility reaching from the top to the bottom of the structure. This form of organization is called by Mooney and Reiley the "scalar process."[1] Every position in the organization finds its appropriate place in the hierarchy, designated by a distinctive title, the incumbent possessing authority to give orders to subordinates and bearing responsibility to receive and obey orders from superiors.

In view of the fact that the number of positions in any rank rapidly diminishes as the level of organization rises, the structure as a whole tends to appear as a pyramid, with a broad base rapidly diminishing to the apex, which is represented by the ultimate authority in charge of the organization. Governmental structure as a whole follows this pattern, with some modifications; and each organization unit (department, commission, bureau, etc.) repeats the same general formation.

The lines of responsibility and authority flow along the hierarchical structure. Through link after link, the chief executive is united with each individual worker, no matter how humble or routine his task. The whole organization is bound together as a work unit by the power of command, expressed in regulations, minutes, circulars, individual orders, and precedents.[2]

The degree of subordination may differ within certain limits, as well as the degree of the duty of obedience. In general it is less in civil than in military organizations; it varies with the nature and degree of official discretion; it is more precise in the lower ranks than in the higher; and it is sometimes vitiated by circumstances external to the hierarchy itself, as for instance the consciousness on the part of a subordinate of political irresponsibility. In general, however, the typical form of the hierarchy presupposes and requires the universal application of the rule of subordination and obedience.

From this point of view, indeed, we may consider any structure as an organization of centers of decision. While many questions flow upward to the head of the organization for decision, others are concluded at lower levels in the hierarchy. Analysis of any organization would reveal interesting allocations of the power of decision, together with appellate procedures both inside and outside the hierarchy.

The structure of public administration in the United States exhibits some well-established exceptions to the normal hierarchical form of organization. The principal exception concerns the independent regulatory commissions of the federal and state governments. They are not responsible to the chief executive, receive no instructions from him, and

[1] James D. Mooney and Alan C. Reiley, *Onward Industry!* (1931), ch. 4.
[2] Lt. Col. Émile Mayer, *La Psychologie du Commandement* (1924).

lo not submit their decisions to his review. They consequently operate)utside the hierarchy of offices which depends upon the president or governor.[1] Within each of these bodies, however, the rule of hierarchy)revails. Other historical exceptions are found in the cluster of inde-)endent constitutional offices established in most of the states, and in he traditional form of county government.

4. Location and Delegation of Authority

Administrative authority, like political authority, may be concen- rated or dispersed. In a constitutional state, constituent and legislative odies may distribute administrative power on the basis of two major ules. Much administrative authority may be vested by law or by con- titution in the local governing bodies of a governmental system, as for xample in the counties and cities within a state. In this case the adminis- rative system is decentralized. Conversely, much administrative power nay be vested in the hands of officials of the central government, with consequent diminution of the authority and discretion of officials in)wer governmental levels; the system is then called centralized. The rocess of transfer of administrative authority from a lower to a higher :vel of government is called centralization; the converse, decentralization.

Within any single level of government, as a city, a state, a county or ie nation, the administrative authority of a specific jurisdiction may so be concentrated or dispersed. An administrative system in which ithority is vested by law in the chief executive is an integrated system. ne in which authority is vested in a number of independent offices and ommissions may be described as a disintegrated system. The process of oncentrating administrative authority within one level of government, r within an operating unit is the process of integration.

In actual practice there are wide degrees of centralization and integra- on. Long-standing trends in the United States are gradually changing a ighly decentralized system into one less decentralized, and a highly dis- tegrated system into one which in some instances is highly integrated.

The establishment and maintenance of a smooth working organization e profoundly influenced by the location and delegation of authority. f cardinal importance is the rule of unity of command, a prescription ore generally observed in military and business than in civil adminis- ation. This rule emphasizes the desirability of a single source of final ithority in any organization, a reminder of the old saw, "No man can rve two masters." Failure to secure unity of command is followed by sorganization, irresponsibility, confusion and vacillation. It is elemen- ry to good organization.

[1] See ch. 8 for further discussion.

The location of authority, given unity of command, must be in the clearest terms. Lack of clarity at this point gives rise to uncertainty, conflict, and irresolution. Decisive allocation of authority is essential up and down the line; each official is entitled to know precisely what he is expected to do. Without such precision, responsibility can be enforced only with difficulty.

Power must be commensurate with responsibility. The official needs the legal and other means to accomplish that for which he has been made responsible. The end in view is to define responsibility so precisely that each official will be charged with definite duties, and will be vested with adequate power and authority, so that his success or failure will depend principally upon his own diligence and wisdom.

In public organizations, power and authority are commonly vested by law exclusively in the head of the department or independent establishment. Necessity compels the delegation and subdelegation of this power down through the various levels of the organization. At the end what is delegated is responsibility for the performance of a particular task by a single individual.

"Delegation means the conferring of a certain specified authority by a higher authority."[1] A few words are required on the procedure of delegation. Delegation of authority within an organ of public administration is revocable and subject to modification at the will of the delegating official. The delegation may be of several types. It may be delegation as to an *alter ego*, for example an authorization by the head of a department to a subordinate as *acting head*. It may be an *alter ego* delegation with respect to a specified subject matter, as in the customary delegation to an assistant head. Or, and more commonly, it is a specific delegation to perform the duties of a specific office, ranging from the bureau chief down to the messenger boy. Good administration requires that each delegation shall be as precise and specific as possible, an end greatly facilitated by the modern technique of classification.

5. Coordination of Parts

In any complex organism the parts have to work in coordination with each other in order to produce useful results. In a mechanical device the machine stalls if its parts do not gear together; in an organism the consequence of imperfect coordination is reduced efficiency. Coordination is the adjustment of the functions of the parts to each other, and of the movement and operation of parts in time so that each can make its maximum contribution to the product of the whole.

The coordination of the great number of parts of any large-scale o

[1] Mooney and Reiley, *op. cit.*, pp. 35-43.

ganization is so important that the industrialists, Mooney and Reiley, make it the center of their analysis. Viewing the machine in motion, effective coordination is an absolute essential to good administration.[1] This is a direct responsibility of overhead management. It is effected primarily by the orders, directions and commands of the chief executive, but long experience has demonstrated the need for supplementary means of coordination. Conferences of high executives under the chairmanship of the chief executive, and of their subordinates, interdepartmental committees, and specialized coordinating agencies such as the National Emergency Council are common devices. A staff is an effective coordinating organ, since its studies make it familiar with the consequences of poor coordination and it can suggest means of correction to the chief executive. Sound organization itself is conducive to easy coordination; as Mooney has suggested, there is a coordination of jobs which precedes the coordination of men.

The limits of coordination and supervision by one individual are suggested in the phrase, "span of control," a derivative of the psychological term, span of attention. This phrase refers to the obvious fact that there are limits to human capacity, and that when attention is spread too thinly over too many circumstances, unsatisfactory results occur. Graicunas has set forth the rapidly developing potential number of personal combinations which may prevail between one supervisor and an increasing number of subordinates.[2] Fortunately not all these potential combinations actually emerge, at least to the point where they require attention on the part of the supervisor.

The maximum number of subordinates who can be effectively supervised by one supervisor cannot be precisely determined by the application of a "law" of the span of control. The effective span of control varies with the type of work supervised (whether routine or discretionary), with the level of responsibility, with the personalities of the supervisor and subordinates, and with the necessary degree of supervision and direction. In general the structure of public administration has been such as to impose excessive tasks of direction and supervision upon the chief executive. A personnel and information service conducted with imagination may relieve the excessive task of the chief executive by

[1] Henry S. Dennison, *Organization Engineering* (1931), ch. 5; T. T. Craven and others, "Coordination in Public Administration," 17 *Bulletin of the Taylor Society* 1-86 (1932); I. G. Gibbon and Sydney Larkin, "Co-ordination," 10 *Pub. Adm.* 3-67 (1932); S. L. Post, "Coördination of National Administration," 29 *Am. Pol. Sci. Rev.* 269-74 (1935); Mary C. Trackett, "The Committee as an Instrument of Coördination in the New Deal," 31 *Am. Pol. Sci. Rev.* 301-10 (1937).

[2] V. A. Graicunas, "Relationship in Organization," *Bulletin of the International Management Institute*, March, 1933; reprinted in Gulick and Urwick, eds., *Papers on the Science of Administration*, pp. 183-87

bringing the whole personnel into awareness of the objectives and achievements of the department and thus create a sense of corporate sharing that not only simplifies but perhaps itself constitutes successful coordination.

These are not the only aspects of organization which might be described in general terms.[1] In due course of time, as associations of different types are analyzed and compared, and their likenesses and differences defined, a theory of organization will emerge. As yet we lack the analytical skill and the basic data to proceed far in this direction, valuable as have been recent contributions. The study of organization in other than military and naval units is still in its infancy, but long-time studies are on foot from which new insight will be forthcoming.

In the following chapters the general statements put forward here will be illustrated by the practice of the federal, state and local governments of the United States.

[1] For example, cf. the analysis of such concepts as magnitude, intensity, motion (in time), as aspects of organization.

Chapter Four

THE CHIEF EXECUTIVE AS GENERAL MANAGER

AMERICAN chief executives generally combine the three major functions of political leadership, administrative management, and ceremonial representation. The mixture varies widely from in-tance to instance, and in some cases one or the other ingredient may be lmost lacking, but there is wide similarity in a broad pattern which nites in the chief executive the duties of politician, administrator, and eremonial and legal representative. This study does some violence to he office by separating its administrative from its legal and political ac-ivities, since in practice each conditions the other.[1]

. Trends

The principal historical fact concerning the American chief executive s an administrator is that, until 1900, he had little to do with adminis-ration. In early years this situation arose in part from public preference or the legislative branch, a reaction against unpopular colonial gov-rnors; in part from the highly decentralized character of administration 1 the states; and in large part from the mere absence of much adminis-ration at any level of government, anywhere.

Mayors and governors and presidents, for a good century of our na-ional history, were chiefly interested in policy and politics. In some ases they still are. For years administration, in its numerous uncoordi-ated parts, was vaguely responsible to the people's representatives rather han to the chief executive. The early grant of "executive power" con-eyed military and political rather than administrative authority, and iere is no warrant in this grant alone for assuming that the founders itended or expected chief executives to become powerful administra-

[1] Study of the American executive in his manifold functions may be pursued in ie standard works on federal, state and local government, and in Grover Cleve-nd, *The Independence of the Executive* (1913); Russell M. Story, *The American Iunicipal Executive* (1918); Edward Stanwood, *A History of the Presidency* rev. ed. 1928); George W. Spicer, "From Political Chief to Administrative Chief," C. G. Haines and M. E. Dimock, eds., *Essays on the Law and Practice of Gov-rnmental Administration* (1935), pp. 94-124; Wilfred E. Binkley, *The Powers of e President* (1937); Lindsay Rogers, "The American Presidential System," 8 *Pol.* . 517-29 (1937); Leslie M. Lipson, *The American Governor: From Figurehead to eader* (1939).

tive figures. The inferior administrative position of the President of th United States was emphasized by the Tenure of Office Act of 186 (repealed 1887), denying the President's power to remove presidentia appointees except with the consent of the Senate; the secondary positior of governors, by the independent constitutional officers and by the in dependent charitable, correctional and other institutions; the administra tive weakness of mayors, by the multiplicity of administrative boards the membership of which was often beyond the mayor's sphere of influ ence. It was not, in short, until after much experience that the chie executive began to secure recognition as a principal administrator, or i other terms as the general manager of the public business. The transitio began in the cities with the reconstruction of the office of mayor.

Commencing with the ceremonial mayor of the English borough, th framers of city charters gradually evolved a powerful municipal office independent of the council, responsible directly to the electorate, an eventually vested with powers both of political leadership and of ad ministrative management. Mayor Josiah Quincy of Boston (1823–28 foreshadowed trends which came into their own subsequent to the Civi War. By 1870 council government "had been tried and found wanting. Between 1870 and 1900 "the mayor system, with comparatively fe exceptions, became the rule in those parts of the country where munici pal government was a problem of consequence."[1] While the temporar popularity of the commission plan obscured the rise of the mayor for decade (1905–1915), the later expansion of the council manager pla and of the "strong mayor" plan again emphasized the necessity for a re municipal executive.

Within the states, the governor began to secure recognition as a administrator about 1910, a transition symbolized by the new positio assigned to this office in 1917 by the Illinois Civil Administrative Cod With many variations in detail, the governor is now generally accepte as the central administrative official in the American commonwealth. H has not, however, ceased to be interested in politics and policy. Like th mayor, he still combines political leadership with administrative coord nation and direction.[2] Successful governors like Smith and Lehman c New York, Ritchie of Maryland, Lowden of Illinois and La Follette c Wisconsin illustrate the effective combination of administrative ar political leadership.

Until the passage of the Budget and Accounting Act of 1921, th President of the United States was principally a political leader, n

[1] Russell M. Story, *op. cit.*, p. 30.

[2] Consult the author's *Trends in Public Administration* (1933), ch. 14; and Les Lipson, *The American Governor* (1939).

merely because political leadership is inherent in this office but also because the President lacked almost every means of exerting administrative leadership. He still lacks many essential means, but despite these severe handicaps Woodrow Wilson, Herbert C. Hoover, and Franklin D. Roosevelt in turn expanded greatly the administrative influence of the office. The report of the President's Committee on Administrative Management indicates further essential steps to make the President an effective administrator.

The importance of this broad transition, which in the last thirty years (punctuated by emergency government) has built up one single predominant center of administrative responsibility in federal, state and local government, is very great. It marks a fundamental change from the uncoordinated, independent, administrative offices and agencies which de Tocqueville observed in his American travels in 1831. It establishes the possibility of unity of command, of effective coordination, of internal responsibility, and of administrative leadership. It does not, however, foreclose the possibility of spoils administration at the hands of shortsighted "statesmen."

Our historical inheritance, therefore, reveals a chief executive originally endowed with scanty administrative power but with ample opportunity for political and party leadership. Over a period of many years he has gained important administrative authority, but without any diminution of political interests except in such cases as the city manager and the superintendent of schools. At the apex of our administrative structure we therefore still find a political figure, closely related to a political organization. This type of general manager may be called the political, nonprofessional, independent administrator. It is the most frequent type, illustrated by hundreds of mayors, by governors and presidents.

During the last half century another type of general manager has been emerging who may be called the nonpolitical, professional, responsible type of administrator. The first notable example developed in the office of superintendent of schools.[1] This educational executive is appointed by the elective school board and is responsible to it. The selection is usually nonpartisan and often brings in a nonresident whose record elsewhere commands respect. Formal training, lifework, group organization, technical journals and conferences, and attitudes both of the school

[1] Thomas McD. Gilland, *The Origin and Development of the Powers and Duties of the City-School Superintendent* (1935); William C. Reavis, *Relations of School Principals to the Central Administrative Office in Large Cities* (1937); "Report of the Committee on Relation between Boards of Education and Superintendents of Schools," in National Education Association, Department of Superintendence, *Official Report,* 1932, pp. 282-86.

superintendent and the public emphasize the professional nature of his work.

A second example is found in the office of city manager.[1] The manager is elected by the city council, usually without term, and is responsible to the council. He has none of the duties of political leadership, which are the prerogative of the council and the mayor. Managers do not take an active part in municipal politics, and by the theory of their office are not expected to take any part. The university and other specialized training now available for preparation for this office and for improvement within it, the well-established International City Managers' Association, the managers' code of ethics, their many technical committees and their journal, *Public Management*, suggest the professional bearing of this group of public officials.

These two major types of general manager—the political, nonprofessional, independent type, and the nonpolitical, professional, responsible type—confront each other in conflict for supremacy. The issue is most sharply drawn in the cities, where mayor and manager represent the clash of different concepts of administrative organization. Mayors become mayors because they are able to command more votes than their rivals; managers are selected as a rule on the basis of their technical experience and competence. Mayors inevitably are local residents; managers need not be. The ambitions of mayors are usually political—to succeed themselves, to be elected later to the state legislature, to Congress, or to the office of governor. The ambitions of managers are usually to earn an appointment to a larger town on the basis of a good administrative record. The ambitions of mayors are achieved by an appeal to the electorate; those of managers by a record of administrative achievement. It was no accident that managers organized for mutual advice and the study of municipal problems a generation before the mayors.

While the manager type has steadily gained during the last twenty years, progress has not been rapid, and a few important reversions have occurred, among others Cleveland and Lima, Ohio; Binghamton, New York; and Fall River, Massachusetts. In the states, the political, nonprofessional type is unchallenged. In the face of the highly unsatisfactory administrative record of many of these elected executives, both city and state, how can the vitality of this form of administrative overhead be

[1] Space is lacking to discuss in detail the office of city manager. The development is important, and may be studied in the following references: Leonard D. White, *The City Manager* (1927); Louis Brownlow, "The City Manager in the United States," 9 *Pub. Adm.* 393-416 (1931); Charles P. Taft, *City Management: The Cincinnati Experiment* (1933); Clarence E. Ridley and Orin F. Nolting, *The City-Manager Profession* (1934); and a forthcoming volume by Donald Price, Harold Stone and Kathryn Stone on city manager cities. See also *Public Management*, and its predecessor, *City Manager Magazine*.

explained? On the other hand, why has the excellent administrative record of the managers failed to convince a substantial majority of all cities, large and small, and the states, of the superiority of this form of organization?

Some truth lies in the superficial observation of the power of resistance of the political organization. Nonpartisan administration spells the end of party patronage and the party machines will naturally fight to the last ditch to keep what they have.

Managers as a group have made their record on savings, on elimination of waste, on avoidance of extravagant building programs, on economy, rather than on a program of expansion, provision of new services, and spending. This attitude fitted in well with prevailing opinion from 1920 to 1932; but it lacks something of the public appeal which a more energetic and creative program possesses. Basically the "builder-booster" type has a glamor for Americans which is not wholly satisfied by the usually cautious and sometimes penny-wise manager.

There are other more fundamental considerations. The American people enjoy active, even spectacular political leadership, as well as good administration. The council manager plan has not produced the fire of political leadership which has emerged among the mayors—such men as Tom Johnson and Newton D. Baker of Cleveland, Daniel Hoan of Milwaukee, William H. Thompson of Chicago, Fiorello La Guardia of New York. Councils have been weak under all forms of city government, and the frequent subordination (in fact, not in theory) of the mayor in the council manager cities has either left the city without political leadership or has forced the manager to become civic leader as well as administrator, thus reverting in substance to the older type.

There is also a suspicion in some circles, including some groups of organized labor, that the council manager plan is undemocratic. This fear is unjustified, but it exists and buttresses the hostility of politicians who do not intend to lose their city patronage.

While, therefore, the battle between these two types of executive organization still proceeds and will doubtless carry forward into the next generation, the nonpolitical, professional type is making steady progress. It has substantially won the schools; it is strong in the cities; it has begun to secure a foothold in the counties; the states, however, remain indisputably in the command of the political, nonprofessional group of executives. The conflict between the two provides one of the major points of readjustment and growth in our administrative system.

2. Administrative Duties of Chief Executives

In either case, it is standard practice to vest the powers of chief executive in a single official, rather than in a plural body. The principal exceptions are found in instances where concentration of executive and administrative power is still denied, as in county government generally, and in the commission governed cities. A further interesting but relatively unimportant example is found in the New England towns, where the board of selectmen (usually three) acts as a collective executive. In cases such as the Port of New York Authority, the board acts in a legislative capacity; the director is the chief executive. The error of organization in the Tennessee Valley Authority was the failure of the board for several years to divest itself of administrative duties in favor of a general manager.

Whether he is a professional or a nonprofessional administrator, the chief executive as general manager performs much the same range of administrative functions. The context is different, the motivation is often quite different; but the technical operations are alike. What then are the principal managerial duties of mayors and managers, governors and presidents as the heads of their respective administrative organizations? Some administrative responsibilities are imposed by charter, constitution, or statute; others are defined in executive order; some are merely customary. With many variations in detail, they fall into the following main categories.[1]

a. To determine the main lines of administrative policy. Department heads and other principal officials necessarily come to the chief executive for consultation and advice about many matters, particularly those which are "hot" or important. Through such consultation and approval or disapproval the president, governor, mayor or manager guides and controls the work policy of the administration. Some chief executives expect much to be brought to them for approval, others prefer to delegate more widely, but in any event the major lines of work and policy will be fixed after approval by them. One aspect of this phase of central guidance is budget making.

Where legislative policy is expressed in general terms, administrative policy becomes the more important, transcending questions of internal management, finance, personnel or organization. It then deals with substantive issues of major importance.[2] In the federal government, all departmental proposals for legislation or comments on pending legislation

[1] See also Daniel Bloomfield, ed., *The Modern Executive* (1924); M. S. Culp, "Executive Power in Emergencies," 31 *Mich. Law Rev.* 1066-96 (1932–33); Erwin H. Schell, *The Technique of Executive Control* (4th ed. 1934); Herbert Emmerich, "Some Folklore of Executive Management," 20 *Pub. Man.* 264-67 (1938); Chester I. Barnard, *The Functions of the Executive* (1938).

[2] An impressive example of executive policy making may be studied in John D. Larkin, *The President's Control of the Tariff* (1936).

are cleared through the Bureau of the Budget, acting for the President.

b. To issue the necessary orders, directions, and commands. In any organization, the impulse to action derives from general or specific orders or directions. These may be oral or written. The great bulk of them are issued by the heads of the operating units and their subdivisions. Many must be issued by the chief executive in order to conform to statutory or even constitutional requirements. In the United States they usually take the form of executive orders, proclamations, or commissions, apart from the more informal letters, circulars, instructions, or oral directions which emanate from the White House and from departmental and other authorities. In municipal government, informal orders and directions are more common than formal executive instruments.

The quality and content of these executive acts are of primary importance in determining the quality and energy of administration. It is through them that the chief executive functions as an administrator; a weak executive will be revealed by the feeble leadership which he provides; a strong executive will make his influence effective to the far ends of his organization through the medium of his formal and informal orders, instructions and commands.

c. To coordinate the organization. The larger an organization the greater the number of points at which coordination is necessary. Most coordination can best be done at lower levels of responsibility than the chief executive, but some problems will force their way upward defying any solution other than one imposed by the chief executive himself. Such cases are usually the hardest ones. An effective administrator will find some means of coordination; if no adjustment is worked out the inner unity and smooth working of the parts are sacrificed. Unless a strong line is taken, feuds and discontents are likely to follow on conflicting claims and overlapping jurisdictions. At this point the chief executive is the court of last resort.

d. To authorize the details of organization. Legislation will usually establish the main operating units: departments, commissions, authorities, corporations and offices; the internal structure will often be left to executive discretion, in so far as it is not governed by the terms of appropriation acts. The initiative in determining the number and duties of the bureaus, divisions and units will be taken by the agency concerned, usually subject to approval by the chief executive in so far as the major subdivisions are concerned. In 1918, and again in 1932, Congress gave the President limited authority to modify structure by consolidating or transferring administrative units; this is an exceptional authority, and was refused in the defeat of the Reorganization Bill in 1938.

Incident to the formation of the internal structure is the allocation of work. As a rule, allocation of work follows from the statutes but in recent years there are increasingly numerous exceptions. The chief executive will be concerned only with major allocations, and usually only with marginal cases where alternative proposals by competing agencies require some final decision.[1]

The chief executive will authorize many temporary *ad hoc* committees or agencies to meet particular situations. These are important to iron out controversies, to adjust relationships, to formulate new policies or procedures, to meet emergencies of many sorts. In short, while the chief executive will find the major framework of his organization well set in the constitution or charter and in the statutes and ordinances, he will also find opportunity to modify, supplement and adjust in the interest of good administration. These adjustments will usually be made by his authority, or subject to his approval.

e. To control the management of finance. One of the principal marks of the contemporary chief executive is his responsibility for finance. It is his duty as a rule to develop a financial program, with respect both to revenue and expenditure, to prepare and submit a budget and, subsequent to the appropriation act, to supervise the course of expenditures. At any time this is a considerable power, but during fiscal emergencies it rises to great magnitude. While the legislative bodies retain ultimate control of the purse strings, the executive has seized fiscal initiative. In this field he who proposes usually disposes.

f. To appoint and remove personnel. The lower ranks will often be selected by competitive examination, beyond the sphere of influence of the chief executive; the higher personnel will be selected by or on the authority of the mayor or manager, the governor or the President, often with the advice and consent of the United States Senate, the state senate or the city council. Thus the chief executive nominates the heads of departments, the members of boards and commissions, and the responsible heads of authorities and government corporations; appointment is completed by confirmation by the upper branch of the legislative body. The President nominates to a wide range of positions, numbering in 1937 over sixteen thousand, including about 14,500 postmasters and excluding military and naval officers. In 1938 the selection of postmasters was transferred by law to the U. S. Civil Service Commission. Appointments by city managers are not usually subject to confirmation. The power to confirm is slowly losing ground in the state governments also.

In general the appointment of assistant heads of departments and bureau chiefs falls under two rules: they may be selected by the chief ex-

[1] For example in the federal government, the competition between P.W.A. and W.P.A. for use of emergency funds for construction.

ecutive; or they may be appointed by the head of the department concerned, with or without the informal approval of the chief executive. The appointment of bureau chiefs and lower ranks is best placed in the hands of the head of the department, not in the chief executive; and in most cases the selection can be made by recognized civil service procedures.

In national, state, and municipal governments, the power to nominate or appoint is one of the principal means by which the quality and tone of the administration are determined. Unfortunately at times chief executives find it necessary or useful to sacrifice their freedom of appointment in favor of support for legislation. The power of appointment then falls into the hands of unknown and irresponsible members of the legislature who bargain their votes for specified appointments. The public service almost invariably suffers. City managers are relatively free from the necessity of making this kind of a compromise.

In general the chief executive retains power to remove those officials whom he appoints or nominates. The power of removal of the chief executive may be summary, or he may be required to state cause, without, however, involving judicial control of his action. Removal of subordinate officials and employees is governed by special statutes in the civil service jurisdictions.[1] The power of removal is an important aspect of the authority of the executive over the administrative organization. It is often scandalously abused in jurisdictions which have no merit system whenever there is a change of administration.

The Myers case and the more recent Humphrey case bearing on the President's power of removal are so important as to require brief notice. In the former case the Supreme Court, in a majority opinion written by former President Taft, seemed to confirm the unlimited right of the President to remove all federal officials and to deny authority to Congress to restrict this power. Myers, the postmaster at Portland, Oregon, was removed by President Wilson on February 2, 1920, in disregard of the provision of law requiring the advice and consent of the Senate. The Supreme Court dismissed Myers' suit for pay for the remainder of his unexpired term, on the ground that the requirement of senatorial consent to the removal of a postmaster was unconstitutional. In the discussion of the case, the majority of the Court seemed prepared to extend its application to all federal officials, even those holding quasi judicial positions. This position was modified in the subsequent Humphrey case.[2]

[1] For further treatment, see ch. 25.

[2] *Myers vs. U.S.*, 272 U.S. 52 (1926); *Humphrey's Executor vs. U.S.*, 295 U.S. 602 (1935). These cases initiated reconsideration of the major issues of the administrative position of the President. Among other references, consult Howard L. McBain, "Consequences of the President's Unlimited Power of Removal." 41 *Pol. Sci.*

William E. Humphrey was appointed by President Hoover on December 10, 1931, to succeed himself as a member of the Federal Trade Commission for a term of seven years. On October 7, 1933, President Roosevelt removed him from office, without alleging or citing any of the causes for removal specified in the Trade Commission Act, to wit: inefficiency, neglect of duty, or malfeasance in office. Humphrey contested the power of the President to remove.

The Supreme Court sustained Humphrey's position. "We think it plain under the Constitution that illimitable power of removal is not possessed by the President in respect of officers of the character of those just named [i.e. Federal Trade Commission, Interstate Commerce Commission, and Court of Claims]. The authority of Congress, in creating quasi legislative or quasi judicial agencies, to require them to act in discharge of their duties independently of executive control cannot well be doubted; and that authority includes, as an appropriate incident, power to fix the period during which they shall continue, and to forbid their removal except for cause in the meantime." The present position is, therefore, that "an executive officer restricted to the performance of executive functions, . . . charged with no duty at all related to either the legislative or judicial power" may not be protected by act of Congress against the unrestricted power of the President to remove; but officials who share in the legislative or judicial power can be protected by legislation against the President's power to remove. The exact lines between these two classes remain to be drawn.[1]

g. *To supervise, facilitate and control administrative operations.* The chief executive is not himself an operating official, except in the smaller jurisdictions. It is his business to "see that the laws are executed," not himself to execute them. He is in command of the ship, but he does not

---

Q. 596-603 (1926); Edward S. Corwin, *The President's Removal Power under the Constitution* (1927); James Hart, *Tenure of Office under the Constitution* (1930), and "The President and Federal Administration," in C. G. Haines and M. E. Dimock, eds., *Essays on the Law and Practice of Governmental Administration* (1935), pp. 47-93; Albert Langeluttig, "The Bearing of Myers vs. United States upon the Independence of Federal Administrative Tribunals—a Criticism," 24 *Am. Pol. Sci. Rev.* 59-66 (1930); Charles E. Morganston, *The Appointing and Removal Power of the President of the United States,* S. Doc. 172, 70th Cong., 2d sess. (1929).

[1] Cf. a note in 51 *Harvard Law Rev.* 1246-51 (1937–38), "Morgan vs. United States: The President's Power of Removal"; for the power of the state governors, see Charles M. Kneier, "Some Legal Aspects of the Governor's Power to Remove Local Officials," 17 *Virginia Law Rev.* 355-68 (1930–31); John M. Dawley, "The Governor's Constitutional Powers of Appointment and Removal," 22 *Minn. Law Rev.* 451-78 (1937–38).

himself hold the steering wheel, run the engines, or give instructions to the galley. In any organization of substantial size, he must give up to others the actual performance of the work. He must delegate.[1]

This is a rule too often ignored. Energetic men in public office seem to delight in doing things themselves, or to feel uneasy lest they be poorly done by others. Hence the familiar sight of executives working at top speed all day, taking home fat brief cases of files, and spending Saturday afternoon and even Sunday at the office.

The law is often more at fault than the official, requiring that action be taken personally by the mayor, or governor, or president. When he was governor of New York, Alfred E. Smith described how we ruin our governors by heaping detail upon them.[2] In the Works Progress Administration allotments under the relief act of 1935, the President was required personally to allocate funds to projects, and actually sat in council with the officials of W.P.A. to secure the necessary information before authorizing specific allocations. Even worse, under the Economy Act of 1934, every retention of a civil employee beyond the retirement age required the specific approval of the President.[3]

Apart from such detail, it is the duty of the chief executive to keep informed of the course of administrative operations, to intervene where necessary to coordinate the work of related units, to settle jurisdictional disputes, to guide the policy and program of the whole organization, including the management of finance. If he does this, he will do enough; the operating details can best be left to others.

h. To investigate. The power to conduct informal inquiries is doubtless inherent in the chief executive's authority to see that the laws are enforced. This is, however, less effective than the formal power to investigate which has been conferred upon the governor of New York by the Moreland Act. The law provides that "The governor is authorized at any time, either in person or by one or more persons appointed by him for the purpose, to examine and investigate the management and affairs of any department, board, bureau or commission of the state." [4] New York governors have made effective use of this power from time to

[1] Cf. James Hart, "The President and Federal Administration," in Haines and Dimock, *op. cit.*, pp. 52-57, "The picture of the President as on his own initiative exercising a continuous and detailed direction of all phases of administration is thus a myth. He cannot do all the things which he may do." (p. 55).

[2] Alfred E. Smith, "How We Ruin Our Governors," 10 *Nat. Mun. Rev.* 277-80 (1921).

[3] For a time the President signed each individual case separately; eventually a journal was prepared including all cases arising each day, which the President validated *en masse* with a single signature.

[4] Cahill's Consolidated Laws of New York (1930), c. 18, sec. 8.

time, as for example the study of the Workmen's Compensation Bureau by Lindsay Rogers.[1]

i. To conduct public relations. The foregoing are internal aspects of overhead management; the chief executive also has responsibilities outside the organization itself. In the case of state and city executives, they, or their immediate representatives, manage some aspects of public relations. This means negotiating with legislators, interest groups and others, speaking on administrative and public questions, dealing with the press, consulting with groups of many kinds, in short representing the administration before the public.[2] The burden of this work is often very great. The chief executive also represents his jurisdiction in its negotiations with other jurisdictions. Thus the governor is the official who speaks for the state, the mayor for the city, in their relations with the national government, relations which year by year become more intimate and important.

3. Problems

These are important and far-reaching administrative powers. They reflect general acceptance of the proposition that administrative efficiency requires "the establishment of a responsible and effective chief executive as the center of energy, direction and administrative management." While this view is widely held, important reservations may be suggested.

Experience in some states leads to grave doubt whether an elected governor is likely to be either a responsible or an effective administrator. The administrative offices of Illinois were in the hands of an unblushing spoilsman for eight years, and in the hands of a weak governor for the next four years. Harvey Walker reports dissatisfaction with the elected governor-administrator in Ohio, and subsequent experience in this state more than confirms his reservations. Nor has a state with the long traditions of Massachusetts been able to avoid the election of governors who were ready to sacrifice administration to political exigencies. On the other hand, George W. Spicer explicitly records the excellent results secured in Virginia by the concentration of administrative responsibility in the governor of the Old Dominion.[3] A succession of able governors in New York also illustrates the proposition that good administration can be secured in some states under the direction of a politically

[1] New York Legislative Document 49, 1929.

[2] See ch. 30 for further development of the public relations field. For an exciting public relations episode, read L. P. Cookingham, "A Manager's Diary of a Power Strike," 19 *Pub. Man.* 291-95 (1937).

[3] Spicer, "From Political Chief to Administrative Chief," in Haines and Dimock, *op. cit.*, pp. 121-22.

elected chief executive. Any generalization is hazardous; we shall need to await a generation of experience.

It is probable, however, that the low standards which can be observed in some states which have concentrated administrative authority in the governor are due to the generally prevailing standards of government rather than to the concentration of power in itself. The possibility at least of securing a responsible administration is won by giving administrative authority to the governor; whether it will actually be achieved and at what level of competence depend on many factors beyond administration as such.

The second issue concerns the responsibility of the chief executive in his administrative role. Although the power of mayors and governors has been greatly increased, no means of control has been added to those which evolved around a formerly weak political office. In fact, once elected, mayors and governors are almost beyond effective control until the next election. While no serious issues have yet arisen, prudence suggests that additional means of balancing the administrative power of chief executives at all levels may be useful.[1]

A trenchant criticism of the prevailing assumptions favoring concentration of administrative authority in a politically elected chief executive has been written by Harvey Walker.[2] He advocates for the state substantially the same type of overhead organization as that of the council manager cities. He would restrict the role of the governor to that of political leader, and provide a qualified technical manager responsible to the state legislature, thus expecting to avoid both of the criticisms noted in the previous paragraphs.

Future trends may be in the direction of Professor Walker's proposals. Or they may be in the direction urged by William Y. Elliott and others toward a responsible executive on the model of English cabinet government.[3] On the other hand, they may be in the less spectacular direction of mitigating the dangers of political mismanagement of public administration by the extension and improvement of the merit system, and by gradually rising standards of popular choice of chief executives.

It is certain that the political, nonprofessional type of general manager of public business will be characteristic of a large area of the American system of public administration for a considerable period of time. In some way, the coordination of politics and administration is necessary in

[1] See ch. 36 for further discussion of this point.

[2] Harvey Walker, "Theory and Practice in State Administrative Organization," 19 *Nat. Mun. Rev.* 249-54 (1930), and in his *Public Administration in the United States* (1937), pp. 79-81. See also comments by Spicer, *op. cit.*, pp. 122-23.

[3] William Y. Elliott, *The Need for Constitutional Reform* (1935).

a democratic country, and under favorable circumstances such an executive may perform this function well. It is helpful to remember that a democracy requires responsible leadership, and that leaders must have means to ensure that their policy will not suffer in its administration. It is the special duty of political executives to supply administrative direction, driving power, and coordination of the legislative and executive branches of the government, and also to protect administration as an agency of the people from those who consider it only as an adjunct of a party.

Chapter Five

STAFF AND AUXILIARY AGENCIES

CHIEF executives, whether political and nonprofessional or professional and nonpolitical, are in command of administrative organizations which in many cases are of first magnitude. Like their military counterparts they need help in overhead management. To some extent this is forthcoming in recent years from staff agencies. The expansion of administrative work and the specialization of subsidiary functions have also resulted in another type of service designed primarily to assist the major operating departments, and in this book called the auxiliary agencies. Each form of specialization, staff and auxiliary agency, will be described in this chapter. Readers may be warned again, as in the third chapter, that the term staff is used in a more strict and limited sense than in much recent writing. Such agencies as central purchasing, personnel, accounting and printing offices are not included as staff agencies.

1. The Staff Agency

In any large-scale organization the head is forced to delegate the actual performance of many of his duties to others. This is especially true of executives in public administration upon whose time ceremonial, social, political and representative functions make heavy demands. The primary delegation is to the major substantive departments and agencies, in which the law directly vests much administrative authority and to which the chief executive may delegate more.[1] Practically all operating functions are thus taken off his shoulders.

The responsibilities of overhead management and general direction he cannot, however, avoid. He must be concerned with administrative policy, with the duty of command, with problems of organization, with finance and top personnel and public relations. Here again is a load too great for any one man to carry. He must have assistance in reaching the decisions which he cannot delegate to others.

In most American jurisdictions this help is casual and unsystematic.

[1] These are the so-called line agencies, responsible for a substantive activity of government.

In others it is forthcoming from an executive assistant or private secretary, although the latter may be primarily a political aid. In a few cases the necessary aid is assuming more formal status as a staff agency.

The generic function of a staff agency has already been stated.[1] It is the duty of a staff officer to study questions requiring a decision, to collect documents and information, to plan a course of action, and to advise his principal with reference thereto; and when the decision has been taken by the executive officer, to transmit and explain the orders and to observe and report upon the results. In theory he has no independent power or authority apart from his chief.

The basic assumptions of general staff work are implicit in the organic legislation enacted in 1903 under the impulse of Elihu Root's reforming genius.

> That the duties of the General Staff Corps shall be to prepare plans for the national defense and for the mobilization of the military forces in time of war; to investigate and report upon all questions affecting the efficiency of the Army and the state of preparation for military operations; to render professional aid and assistance to the Secretary of War and to general officers and other superior commanders, and to act as their agents in informing and coordinating the action of all the different officers who are subject under the terms of this act to the supervision of the Chief of Staff; and to perform such other military duties not otherwise assigned by law as may be from time to time prescribed by the President.[2]
>
> All officers detailed in said corps [General Staff Corps] shall be exclusively employed in the study of military problems, the preparation of plans for the national defense and the utilization of the armed forces in time of war, in investigating and reporting upon the efficiency and state of preparedness of such services for service in peace or war, or on appropriate general staff duties in connection with troops, . . . or on other duties not of an administrative nature. . . .[3]

This language describes an organism primarily devoted to thinking about military problems. It is an instrument for planning, for study and for observation, not an instrument of action.

In an organization of less than the first magnitude, such as a small city, or a thinly populated state, the character of the problems is such that the chief executive and the heads of the major departments may themselves work up the plans and make the observations necessary to guide their decisions and policy. The staff function may then be completely covered in the operating function.

In any large organization, however, the pressure of work and the complexity of problems are such that specialization is necessary. In actual

[1] See ch. 3; and John M. Gaus, "The General Administrative Staff," 3 *Plan Age* 10-14 (1937). Foreign analogies are suggested in the Haldane Report (Cd. 9230, 1918) and in the experience of the British cabinet secretariat.

[2] 32 Stat. 831 (1903).

[3] 39 Stat. 167 (1916).

fact the staff *function* is only partially segregated in specialized *agencies*, the degree of desirable specialization varying directly with the size of the organization and the character of its problems. In general it may be said that there has been too little special provision for staff work in the larger civil jurisdictions, especially in the national government.

The staff agency is outside the direct line of the administrative hierarchy. The paths of authority, of command, of subordination and responsibility do not pass through it. The staff agency stands somewhat apart, an adjunct to the office of the chief executive or of a major operating executive. Its special status invites misconception of its true function and value.

One danger is that the executive will assign to the staff operating functions which belong to departments. It is natural for him to say to a staff assistant in whom he has personal confidence, "Take charge of this situation until it is straightened out." A double responsibility, or at least a divided responsibility ensues and the position of the operating head is undermined. The appropriate staff activity in such a case is to study the situation, develop a remedy (preferably in cooperation with the department), report findings to the executive and leave him, in consultation with the department, to issue the necessary instructions. The National Resources Committee, in the early years of its work, and the Central Statistical Board were both forced to resist the invitation to assume operating duties.

There is also a tendency for a staff agency to become a control agency in its own right, acting in the light of what it knows or believes are executive policies. As programs develop new phases appear, or variations from the first formulation seem necessary, or changes in operation become essential. Should the staff agency issue the proper orders or directions within the agreed framework of policy, or should it bring the facts to the attention of the executive? The true staff function requires the latter course of action, but an active staff may be tempted to follow the line of direct intervention.

Hence arises another difficulty. The operating departments are likely to be jealous of their authority and to resist the investigation and recommendations of an "outside" body. The historical tradition of the departments is independence, and in the case of the "independent establishments" there is a well-founded body of doctrine in favor of autonomy. The departments can readily nullify the work of a staff agency by a policy of noncooperation or sabotage. In such cases the advantages of effective staff work are lost, but the justification for staff operations under favorable circumstances still exists. These and related difficulties of adjustment are illustrated in some measure by the official career of the first of the "brain-trusters," Mr. Raymond Moley. Mr. Thomas Corcoran, another staff man associated with another line agency (for convenience), has had greater success.

From the foregoing analysis it appears that the qualities of a successful staff officer are negotiating ability rather than highly developed capacity to command; the possession of a broad range of practical knowledge rather than specialized expertness in one field; patience and persistence rather than a tendency toward quick and fixed decisions; a willingness to remain in the background rather than a desire for personal prominence; loyalty toward the policies and views of superiors rather than insistence on one's own conclusions or recommendations. Such men can be found; and in the conduct of administration they are invaluable.

A delicate balance between the staff agency and the operating departments is required if the executive and the operating agencies are each to derive the advantages which are inherent in staff work. Under auspicious conditions the staff can aid the departments as well as the chief executive for whose assistance it is primarily designed. The larger the organization, the more conspicuously are needed specialized procedures for study, investigation, planning, coordination, conference and observation. Hence we may conclude that while duties of a staff nature were not specialized at all until recent years and are only imperfectly organized as yet, they are likely to become steadily more essential and more adequately appreciated in the public administration of the immediate future.

a. Staff agencies in the national government. Of all branches of public administration the national organization especially requires the aid which good staff work can bring. It is the largest, the most complex, the most resistant to change merely by reason of size and tradition. Only within recent years has the need for presidential administrative aides been recognized and partially met.

Curiously enough the usefulness of staff assistance was stated by John Vining of Delaware in the first session of Congress in language which deserves repetition today. Speaking of the chief executive on July 23, 1789, he said "that the President ought to be relieved from the inferior duties of his station, by officers assigned to attend to them under his inspection; he could then with a mind free and unembarrassed with the minutiae of business, attend to the operations of the whole machine. . . . The question he conceived to be reduced to this, whether a confidential officer would not be more useful than any other, and whether the duties could be distributed among the officers already instituted. For his part he conceived most of them foreign to either of those officers; and that they could not be performed with advantage any other way than by an officer appointed specially for the purpose. . . ."[1] In 1937, the President's Committee on Administrative Management went back to Vining, in their phrase, "*The President needs help.*"

In the civil administration of the national government much staff work is done, but not by a single agency. A number of units which are doing or might be expected to do work of this sort will be briefly reviewed in the following paragraphs.[2]

The American Cabinet, as such, has never developed as a staff agency. Apart from the subordinate position of its members vis-à-vis the President, their necessary preoccupation with political considerations, and their almost exclusive administrative concern with their own departments (whose interests they jealously defend against encroachment), the Cabinet lacks a secretariat. This is a fatal gap in its equipment as a collective organism.

The President's secretariat, also, has failed to develop into a staff agency concerned with such broad issues as fall to the army general staff. The White House personnel from 1930 to 1938 numbered about fifty; they have been principally concerned with the President's personal contacts and correspondence. Franklin D. Roosevelt's original secretariat consisted of his political adviser and two competent newspaper men; from 1935 to 1937 a former member of Congress was added to improve relations between the White House and the "Hill." While these secretaries are exceedingly helpful to the President, they are not recognized as having any organic connection with or relation to the departments and independent establishments. The duties assigned to James Roosevelt in 1937 as aide to the President more closely resembled staff functions.

The former Bureau of Efficiency (1913–33) made many studies of operating efficiency, principally designed to introduce better methods of business administration. In part, therefore, it resembled a staff agency, but it was never closely associated with the President, moving rather in the sphere of influence of the then senior senator from Utah, Mr. Reed Smoot. Its work was paralleled by the duties assigned to the Bureau of the Budget, and with the retirement of its senatorial backer it was abolished and its staff largely transferred to the Bureau of the Budget.

The Bureau of the Budget was intended to perform both auxiliary and staff functions. Despite its failure to study and investigate the operations of the various governmental agencies as authorized by law, it neverthe-

[1] *Annals of Congress*, vol. 1, pp. 667-68. This passage was called to my attention by Dr. Clifford J. Hynning.

[2] A more extensive account is contained in the author's article, "Historical Development of Administrative Agencies Auxiliary to the Chief Executive in the United States," 9 *Revue Internationale des Sciences Administratives* 7-20 (1936).

less ranks in 1938 as the principal existing staff agency in Washington as well as an operating auxiliary agency. The Bureau of the Budget advises the President with respect to expenditure and work programs (but not with respect to revenue); it studies legislation proposed by the departments, recommends approval or disapproval and transmits to the departments the President's decision; it reviews all proposed executive orders; it is called upon to advise with respect to problems of organization and method; it reviews all proposed new lines of activity arising in the operating agencies and recommends to the President the provision of funds, or the contrary. The director of the Bureau of the Budget has regularly been one of the principal advisers of the President on general administrative as well as fiscal problems. The chief failure of the Bureau as a staff agency consists in the fact that it has applied to itself the rule of parsimony which it enforced on others, and thus largely crippled its constructive usefulness. Fortunately its appropriation was materially increased for the fiscal year 1938–39.

The depression emergency, like the World War emergency, emphasized the need of effective coordination, liaison, and direction, especially in view of the rapid multiplication of unrelated New Deal agencies. The National Emergency Council, established in 1934 and comprising representatives of the departments and the most important recovery agencies, served for a brief time as an important coordinating agency. Its one-time director, Mr. Donald Richberg, was rashly hailed by the newspapers as an "Assistant President." This was an exaggeration, but it served to arouse jealousies on the part of officials who enjoyed the right of direct contact with the President and who feared lest they be forced to work through an intermediary.

The Central Statistical Board, created by executive order in 1933, was designed to coordinate the statistical work of the government and to provide for more effective utilization of statistical output. During 1933 and 1934 Winfield Riefler, the executive secretary of the Board, served in a strictly staff capacity for the President, presenting to and discussing with Mr. Roosevelt the trends of business and of recovery, week by week. The functions of the Board vis-à-vis the departments are strictly advisory. The Board does not itself produce statistics; it facilitates, suggests, assists, studies and criticizes. The technical staff is highly competent; the Board itself is drawn from the principal statistics-producing agencies. It is performing characteristic staff functions in a specific field.

The National Resources Committee, formerly the National Planning Board, is an agency primarily concerned with long-range planning and orientation. It has no administrative duties or responsibilities, and is not concerned with the improvement of day-by-day operations. It is interested in making explicit the basic knowledge necessary for the consideration of major policy. Its studies have been concerned with such data as land use, water conservation, mineral resources, the course and effect of invention, urbanism, technology, population and the history of planning. It is a staff agency.

This survey of federal agencies performing some staff functions indicates that a considerable number of such agencies exist, for the most part established subsequently to the World War. The trend has been unplanned, the function has not been clearly segregated, and existing staff agencies are not related effectively to each other, nor are they related effectively to the office of the President of the United States.[1] He lacks personal assistants to help him perform the administrative duty imposed upon him by the constitution to see that the laws are enforced. In the words of Franklin D. Roosevelt, the President cannot adequately handle his responsibilities; he is overworked; it is humanly impossible for him fully to carry out his constitutional duty as chief executive, because he is overwhelmed with minor details.

It was this situation which faced the President's Committee on Administrative Management in 1936. In order to facilitate the administrative work of the President, the Committee proposed to make three agencies of overhead management "part and parcel" of the executive office. These were the Bureau of the Budget, the Civil Service Administration, and the National Resources Committee. "Thus the President would have reporting to him directly the three managerial institutions whose work and activities would affect all of the administrative departments."

The Committee also recommended six executive assistants in addition to the present (1938) secretariat. The description of their status and duties indicates that they were intended to perform a strictly staff function. "These aides would have no power to make decisions or issue instructions in their own right. They would not be interposed between the President and the heads of his departments. They would not be assistant presidents in any sense. Their function would be, when any matter was

[1] The desirability of a more effective system of overhead management attracted the attention of the Institute for Government Research in 1929. In cooperation with a number of interested groups, a proposal was drafted under the leadership of W. F. Willoughby and presented to President Hoover for a Bureau of General Administration, including the Bureau of the Budget, the Civil Service Commission (somewhat reorganized), the General Supply Committee (since developed into the Procurement Division, Treasury Department), and the Bureau of Efficiency (abolished in 1933). Although this plan was not accepted by Hoover, it is an important step in the development of American thought about overhead management. See "Proposal for a Service of General Administration of the National Government of the United States," 7 *Public Personnel Studies* 166-79 (1929). The function to be performed by the proposed Bureau of General Administration was that of the auxiliary or institutional services, rather than the staff function as here defined.

presented to the President for action affecting any part of the administrative work of the Government, to assist him in obtaining quickly and without delay all pertinent information possessed by any of the executive departments so as to guide him in making his responsible decisions; and then when decisions have been made, to assist him in seeing to it that every administrative department and agency affected is promptly informed. Their effectiveness in assisting the President will, we think, be directly proportional to their ability to discharge their functions with restraint. They would remain in the background, issue no orders, make no decisions, emit no public statements. Men for these positions should be carefully chosen by the President from within and without the Government. They should be men in whom the President has personal confidence and whose character and attitude is such that they would not attempt to exercise power on their own account. They should be possessed of high competence, great physical vigor, and a passion for anonymity."[1]

Critics of this proposal asserted that it would increase to a dangerous degree the power of the President, and would unduly subordinate the departments and especially the independent establishments to presidential supervision.[2] The bill carrying these recommendations passed the Senate but was defeated in the House in 1938 by a narrow margin on the spurious issue of "dictatorship."[3]

b. Staff agencies in state and municipal governments. The expansion of governmental activities in cities and in states, and the gradual concentration of administrative authority in the hands of mayors, managers and governors have necessitated some specialization of staff work in these levels. Although many governors still work without adequate assistance for overhead management, in a number of states some provision for staff aid is available.

The first explicit and detailed recognition of the function of a staff agency in the states was drafted by the New York Bureau of Municipal Research in 1915.[4] This momentous report viewed the governor as a

[1] President's Committee on Administrative Management, *Report with Special Studies* (1937), p. 5. This report was printed in various forms; the citations in this volume are to the single volume *Report with Special Studies* which contains both the report and the supporting studies. Cf. William H. Taft, *The Need for the Organization of a Bureau of Central Administrative Control*, Sen. Doc. 1113, 62d Cong., 3d session, pp. 187-205 (1913).

[2] On the controversial issue of the independent regulatory commissions, see *infra*, ch. 8.

[3] Lindsay Rogers, "Reorganization: Post Mortem Notes," 53 *Pol. Sci. Q.* 161-72 (1938).

[4] N. Y. Bureau of Municipal Research, *The Constitution and Government of the State of New York: An Appraisal* (1915). See also Erwin H. Schell, *The Technique of Executive Control* (4th ed. 1934).

general manager and developed machinery for aiding him to operate as such. The proposed staff agencies included an executive office to receive reports, issue orders and handle the routine work of the chief executive; an executive cabinet made up of specialized vice governors as heads of functionally related administrative groups; and special agencies to which could be referred questions for study by experts. Although this proposal was defeated at the polls, it exerted a substantial influence upon later trends.

In general the fiscal officers in states and cities carry on most of the investigating, planning and coordinating work. In general also their strictly financial duties overshadow and sometimes hamper broader phases of overhead management. These offices, however, are frequently authorized, as in the language of the Illinois Civil Administrative Code, "To investigate duplication of work of departments and the efficiency of the organization and administration of departments, and to formulate plans for the better coordination of departments." [1]

The organization pattern for overhead management differs widely in the different states and it is not feasible to present the many varying details.[2] Specific staff functions are performed in most states through one or more permanently organized units, whether the governor's secretary, the budget officer, the comptroller, the commission on administration and finance, or other agency.[3] Since 1935 a new phase of long-range planning has evolved through the state planning boards, fostered by the National Resources Committee.[4]

Much of the staff work in states is done by the auxiliary agencies, the development of which since 1915 has been rapid. To them the governor has turned for assistance in planning, coordinating and often in controlling the system of which he is the head. Many studies and investigations have also been made by the line agencies.

In the cities, staff activities are relatively undeveloped. A recent unpublished study of New York City showed a considerable number of agencies engaged from time to time in the effort to work out plans for better administration and to study and comment upon the efficiency of current operations.[5] In the larger council manager towns, notably in

[1] Illinois Laws 1917, p. 2, sec. 36 (17).

[2] See L. D. White, *Trends in Public Administration*, ch. 14.

[3] Cf. a valuable study of staff and auxiliary agencies in Wisconsin by Walter R. Sharp, "The Chief Executive and Auxiliary Agencies in the State of Wisconsin," 9 *Revue Internationale des Sciences Administratives* 563-98 (1936).

[4] National Resources Committee, *The Future of State Planning* (1938).

[5] Lawrence H. Chamberlain, "Staff Aids to the Chief Executive in New York City," prepared under the auspices of the Institute of Public Administration (ms. 1936).

Cincinnati, the assistant to the manager is essentially a staff officer. In smaller cities the executive can seldom afford such advantages.

The absence of strong staff agencies in large cities is no criterion of the lack of need. This need has been supplied in many instances by the municipal research bureau, privately organized and supported, sometimes at war with the city fathers but often accepted by mayors and managers.[1] The record of the Cincinnati Bureau of Municipal Research indicates that to all intents and purposes it has been for ten years the principal staff agency of the city manager and the city government. Its studies on civil retirement allowances, on joint bond issues, on unemployment and industrial training, and on other subjects have all been influential in guiding the action of the city government. Other municipal bureaus have had the same fortunate relationships with the municipal authorities. In New York, Kansas City, Missouri, and other cities, however, the bureaus have sometimes been considered by city officials as enemies or as intruders.

c. Measurement as a staff tool. The measurement of operating results is a means of observation and control which is as useful to staff as to operating departments and which may consequently be briefly noticed at this point. The term measurement is taken to mean any technique which seeks objectively to appraise the results of a program of action or to compare the results of alternative programs.[2] Measurement of administrative activities and their products is the engineering approach to the ultimate test of success or failure. Difficult though the measurement of a complex organization is, the task of finding usable units has been under more or less constant consideration for many years. The conferences on the science of politics held by the American Political Science Association in 1923 and 1924 were devoted largely to the discovery of possible techniques of measurement, but the results were relatively meager.

In 1927 a large-scale research project was launched by the Association of Community Chests and Councils in cooperation with the University of Chicago to develop the statistical and record keeping bases for reporting, and eventually measuring, operating results in the field of social work. This undertaking was successfully concluded, and the new techniques were eventually taken over by the U. S. Department of Labor.[3] An equally extensive program was launched shortly afterward which led to the formulation of standard reporting and measuring de-

[1] See a forthcoming study by Norman N. Gill on the research bureau movement.

[2] Clarence E. Ridley and Herbert A. Simon, *Measuring Municipal Activities* (1938), p. iii.

[3] A. W. McMillen, *Measurement in Social Work* (1930).

vices in police administration.[1] Public works administration has also been studied on a large scale in the effort to develop usable measurement devices.[2] An extensive survey of contemporary measuring instruments was completed in 1938 by Clarence E. Ridley and Herbert A. Simon.[3]

These are merely illustrations of many efforts to apply a concrete unit of measurement to the complex phenomena of administration. They are frequently highly useful for administrative purposes but in most cases the facts are too difficult to capture to permit the precision of measurement which is characteristic of the natural sciences.

For administrative purposes, this degree of precision is unnecessary. In steadily greater measure executives are relying upon carefully organized statistical data and upon measurement devices to study, to plan and to control official programs. Measurement is a tool of operating and staff agencies alike which is making an important contribution to administrative improvement.

In one form or another, therefore, the exigencies of large-scale management are emphasizing and specializing the function of study, advice and assistance to principal executives. This staff function is designed to aid the chief executive and other responsible officials in the discharge of duties which cannot be delegated to others. It is the more essential, the larger the organization and the more complex the problems. The staff function is relatively a newcomer, and is still imperfectly understood. It is likely, however, to become more extensively developed as its usefulness is recognized and its relationships defined.

2. The Auxiliary Agencies

Until 1900, with few exceptions, every department or comparable administrative agency was a self-contained unit. Like the family in a primitive agricultural community, it carried on all the activities necessary for its maintenance. In addition to discharging its major responsibilities, each agency carried on all the essential "housekeeping" functions. It kept its own accounts on whatever system seemed satisfactory to it; it handled its own funds and kept its own earnings; it purchased necessary supplies and equipment when, where, and how it saw fit; it hired and fired employees; it made its own contracts, all of course within the four corners of the law and the appropriation acts.

As the volume of public business expanded, the process of specialization had its effect, and one by one the secondary operations which each

[1] International Association of Chiefs of Police, *Uniform Crime Reporting* (1929).
[2] Donald C. Stone, *Management of Municipal Public Works* (1938).
[3] *Op. cit.*

agency performed for itself began to split off as functions separately organized from any department, but serving all. Among the earliest thus to appear was the function of prescribing and operating the accounting system, for the chaos of accounts made auditing and other fiscal operations exceedingly difficult. Another such function was the recruitment of personnel, a specialization which was nourished in the early days less by considerations of administrative improvement than by demands for political reform. By the turn of the century, the purchase of supplies began to crystallize into a special "central" purchasing office, and along with it came central management of printing. The segregation of control over the preparation of estimates came into its own subsequent to 1910; and "centralized" paymaster operations somewhat later.

Thus over a considerable period the process of specialization has been pulling out of the omnicompetent administrative department or institution certain activities common to all or most line agencies, organizing each of them into a separate, single-purpose, specialized office. These are known as the auxiliary agencies whose function is to perform a common activity enabling the line agencies to maintain themselves as working organizations. The process is still in movement, and has developed to markedly different stages in different jurisdictions. Thus central accounting is almost universal; central purchasing is widespread, but by no means universal, while central recruiting is still the exception in the states and almost unknown in the counties. Potential auxiliary agencies which have not yet taken form in separate units include offices for in-service training, safety instruction and installation, and public reporting.

In any event complete separation of the auxiliary functions from the primary departments seldom if ever takes place. Thus, as will be noted later, much personnel administration remains within the departments despite the formation of civil service commissions. The same is true of purchasing, the provision of rented quarters and the like. The construction of public buildings for the use of major operating departments is usually entirely assigned to a special unit, but the plans are developed in consultation with the officials who are to occupy the structure. Specialization of these secondary activities therefore still leaves considerable responsibility with the line departments.

The specialized agencies which have thus been segregated from the departments have attracted much attention in the last quarter century. Their contribution to administrative improvement, especially that made by budget and purchasing offices, has certainly been substantial. They are, however, not the primary agencies of administration or government. They exist to serve and within limits to control the primary agencies; they do not perform services for or enforce regulations upon the public; they are subsidiary to the great departments which are the primary vehicles for the implementation of public policy.

In the actual organization of governments, clear-cut lines of demarcation are not always observed. The line departments are most likely to be clearly distinguished; but in them more or less staff work, unsegregated, may be tucked away. The auxiliary agencies are usually not difficult to identify, but confusion arises at times because they are incidentally employed by chief executives sometimes for staff, and sometimes for control purposes as well as for their own specific function. This does not destroy their essential nature. Staff agencies are usually more difficult to point to, partly because they are rare or nonexistent in smaller jurisdictions, partly because their special nature and function are only now emerging. Legislative bodies, moreover, in prescribing administrative forms, often vest two or more functions in the same agency, thus blurring the lines of distinction.

The broad purpose which underlies the development of the auxiliary agencies has been to secure economy. The debates and discussions attending their origin, especially the services for purchasing, budgeting and control of printing, speak eloquently of the financial savings which segregation of these activities would induce. While the actual demonstration of reduced cost is not always feasible, there is a consensus of informed opinion that substantial economies have generally been achieved, with reservations as to particular cases.

These economies result from the possibility of retaining experts to perform the functions in question, in lieu of their performance either by a specialist in another field or by that "jack-of-all-trades," the traditional chief clerk. They arise also from the gains due to increased scope of operations and reduced unit costs, as in large-scale purchasing. They flow, in part, from the possibility of reducing inventories by the provision of central stores. They are related to the closer supervision of these secondary operations and the more rapid introduction of the most recent methods. They are derived, finally, from the fact that chief executives have often given special attention to the enforcement of economy through the auxiliary agencies.

A further word may be useful on the dual function of service and control which the auxiliary agencies may be called upon to perform. Chronologically they were originally designed principally to facilitate, although the control function of the central personnel agency was always prominent. They are still primarily facilitating agencies, often exclusively such. The reorganization of state governments and corresponding trends in Washington have superimposed some functions of control, almost always as the recognized agent of the chief executive. The control is a control of operations, made by operating decisions, rather than one resulting from the typical staff advisory functions. An example is found in the discussion of central purchasing in the section immediately below.

The work of some of the auxiliary agencies is so important that it receives attention in later chapters, budget and personnel offices in particular.[1] It is unnecessary to describe the work of each of the remainder; their general nature and function will become sufficiently clear by dealing with central purchasing offices and central control of printing. With these data before us, we may then raise certain questions of general interest concerning the role of auxiliary agencies in the organization as a whole.

a. Central purchasing. In the words of the principal authority in this field, "The delegation, to one office, of the authority to buy the supplies, materials, and equipment needed by all the operating branches of an organization is known as centralized purchasing." [2] In large jurisdictions, the duties of a central purchasing office may include also the purchase of real estate, the rental of quarters, the provision of heat, light, telephone and telegraph, the provision of transportation, and similar activities.

The emergence of central purchasing on any substantial scale occurred subsequent to 1900.[3] While there has been a steady enlargement in the scope of work and an increase in the number of central purchasing agents, many of the smaller governments still allow their departments individually to purchase all, or most of their supplies and equipment.

In a survey conduced in 1926, Forbes noted 210 American cities with population exceeding 10,000 which had introduced central purchasing.[4]

[1] See chs. 14 and 18 respectively.

[2] Russell Forbes, *Governmental Purchasing* (1929), p. 1. Note that the term "centralized purchasing" has a different connotation from that given to the process of centralization as understood in this volume; see ch. 10.

[3] Model purchasing laws are found in Russell Forbes, *Purchasing Laws for State, County, and City Governments* (1931). See also Douglas M. Beck, *Central Purchasing* (1935), and several articles in *Public Administration:* H. S. Sadler, "The Case for the Supply Department," 9 *Pub. Adm.* 73-82 (1931); Sir Henry N. Bunbury, "Economy in Purchase and in Use," 10 *ibid.* 4-10 (1932); F. R. Cowell, "Central Purchasing," 10 *ibid.* 23-36; S. C. Bird, "Central Purchasing Schemes in Operation–Local Authorities," 14 *ibid.* 388-96 (1936). An older American work is Arthur G. Thomas, *Principles of Government Purchasing* (1919).

[4] Forbes, *Governmental Purchasing,* p. 51. Compare the data in Joel Gordon, *Purchasing Methods of New York State Municipalities* (1931), Publication No. 15 of the N. Y. State Conference of Mayors, p. 22, showing that of 68 New York cities, all but 24 had three or more officials authorized to make purchases. Experience in metropolitan Chicago is canvassed in Charlton F. Chute, "The Public Matériel Problem in the Chicago Metropolitan Region" (ms. 1935), Univ. of Chicago Library.

Most council manager cities adopted central purchasing along with the manager. By 1931, forty states had introduced some degree of central purchasing.[1] Five states also authorized their subdivisions to purchase through the state purchasing agency.

The development of purchasing methods in the federal government since the establishment of the General Supply Committee in 1910 shows a steady trend toward concentrating responsibility for purchasing.[2] The present situation was established by Executive Order 6166, June 10, 1933. This order created the Procurement Division in the Treasury Department, and transferred to it all powers of the General Supply Committee as well as supply functions of certain lesser agencies. The function "of determination of policies and methods of procurement, warehousing, and distribution" was vested in the new agency with wide discretion as to the extent to which it would exercise the full powers granted to it.[3] In principle, complete central purchasing in the federal government has existed since 1933, although the departments still purchase some items with the consent of the Procurement Division.[4]

The division of responsibility for purchasing between the department which uses and the agency which purchases is, in general terms, as follows. The department initiates the purchase (except for certain bulk commodities such as coal for which demand is well known), describes the articles desired and quantity needed, specifies time and place of delivery, and indicates any special aspects of the purchase in question. The requisition carrying this request and information is sent to the central purchasing officer, usually after being examined by the comptroller or fiscal officer to ensure that funds are available. The purchase is then made by the central purchasing officer, usually on the basis of open competitive bids. The authority to purchase is vested completely in him. Upon delivery, more or less elaborate inspection, sometimes including laboratory tests, is made to ensure the quality and quantity of materials supplied.

The principal problem of relationships in central purchasing arises over the question whether the purchasing officer may modify a requisi-

[1] L. D. White, *Trends in Public Administration* (1933), pp. 201-9.

[2] *Ibid.*, pp. 158-60.

[3] The Executive Order provides, "In respect of any kind of procurement, warehousing, or distribution for any agency the Procurement Division may, with the approval of the President, (a) undertake the performance . . . itself, or (b) permit such agency to perform such procurement, etc., or (c) entrust such performance to some other agency. . . ."

[4] For recommendations of the Byrd Committee to establish a General Supply Committee directly responsible to the chief executive, see *Investigation of Executive Agencies of the Government*, S. Rept. 1275, 75th Cong., 1st sess. (1937), pp. 231, 249.

tion, substituting a different grade or type of purchase or reducing the quantity, and whether he may refuse to buy if he thinks the purchase is unnecessary. Many battles have been fought over this issue, especially by such large users as highway departments.

Analysis of forty state purchasing acts in 1931 showed that in eighteen cases the power to modify a requisition had been specifically vested.[1] It is probable that in a number of other states the power to modify or refuse a requisition exists by implication in the power vested in finance departments.[2] In other cases the purchasing officer merely procures the requisitioned articles. Two types of purchasing officer therefore exist: one who may be called a purchasing clerk, the other who may be considered a comptroller of purchases.

An interesting and typical case of conflict of authority over purchase developed in Texas.[3] In 1924 the state highway department requisitioned two closed cars, specifying the manufacturer's name. The board of control (the purchasing office) declined to enter the order, considering the purchase of closed cars uneconomical. The attorney general ruled that the department could specify the type of equipment it needed, but without stipulating any brand or make; in the present case, the requisition for a closed car was sustained, but not the specified manufacturer.

A more serious case arose in 1928, when a difference of opinion developed over certain highway machinery, tractors, graders, rollers and trucks. In this case the department followed the earlier ruling and did not specify any particular make. After the bids were opened, however, the department made recommendations for preference among the bids received, which were defended on the ground of engineering advice, recommendations of highway superintendents, and lowest cost. The board of control rejected these recommendations and accepted bids for other equipment which was preferred on the ground of greater economy in operation. The attorney general upheld the right of the board to make the decision. The highway department thereupon withdrew the requisition.[4]

A practical complaint about central purchasing offices is delay. These complaints are often well founded. They suggest that there may be lim-

[1] White, *op. cit.*, pp 207-8.

[2] For example, in the Illinois Civil Administrative Code, Laws 1917, p. 2.

[3] Frank M. Stewart, "Purchasing of Highway Equipment in Texas," 24 *Am. Pol. Sci. Rev.* 409-15 (1930).

[4] These cases are of course exceptional; Stewart states that ninety-nine purchases out of every hundred are made by agreement between the department and the purchasing office. See the first edition of this book, pp. 146-47, for other cases. The story is told that the requisitioning officer of a state agricultural research station wrote his requisitions in Latin in order to avoid argument with the purchasing agent of the Agricultural College whose approval was necessary.

its beyond which the concentration of authority to purchase is a liability, not an asset. Emergency purchases and the purchase of highly specialized equipment are ordinarily left to the departments. Central purchasing offices like other agencies tend to extend their activities. While the authority to cover new types of materials under the aegis of the central purchasing office from time to time may properly be vested in the chief executive or in the central finance office, it is also desirable to provide for a periodic review of operating results in order to prevent overexpansion and congestion.

b. Central control of printing. Legislation in respect to public printing reaches back into the last century, when the chief concern was to eliminate favoritism by securing competition in bids and to guarantee proper fulfillment of contracts by taking the "spoils" out of printing. In the last twenty years there has been much legislation designed to impose administrative control upon printing, the purpose of which is primarily economy.[1]

Printing bills are large. The Government Printing Office in Washington does an annual business of $15,000,000, while Sparlin reports an estimated total state printing bill of $22,200,000 per biennium.[2] The separate management of printing by each department and agency resulted in highly unstandardized products, high costs, and at times excessive amounts.

In the federal government all printing must be done at the Government Printing Office. The new processes of reproduction have been seized upon by the departments and independent establishments to mimeograph, multilith, planotype and otherwise "print" material within their own offices. The inventory value of the equipment for such reproduction was $114,000 in 1920, and had risen to $650,000 in 1936. The departments and establishments were without doubt doing their "printing" more quickly and for small lots probably more cheaply than could have been done by the Government Printing Office. In 1937 this Office secured a ruling from the Comptroller General which if taken literally would practically confine the departments to "the reproduction of typewritten circular matter, making copies of official records and correspondence," and the like.

This incident is referred to because it illustrates the pull and tug of internal forces. We can only agree with the Brookings Institution that "complete centralization of the production of this material in the Gov-

[1] White, *op. cit.*, pp. 200-2.

[2] Estal E. Sparlin, *The Administration of Public Printing in the States* (1937), Appendix A.

ernment Printing Office or elsewhere does not offer a satisfactory solution."[1]

Within the states we find many detailed statutes prescribing printing procedure. The duties of central printing officers are twofold: some act merely in a ministerial capacity, while others exercise much authority as "comptrollers of printing." The tendency is in the latter direction, and considerable savings have been reported from some states.[2] As in the case of purchasing agents, the principal problem of organization has been to allocate final authority to print, or not to print. The issues are the same.

c. Observations on the auxiliary agencies. The almost uninterrupted trend of more than a quarter century in business and government alike toward specialized auxiliary agencies makes a strong prima facie case for them. At the same time, there are many complaints from the operating departments and some evidence to indicate that the process of tearing the departments apart in order to establish the auxiliary functions may go beyond the point where good administration results. One guiding rule is that the efficiency of the line departments is the primary consideration in organizational problems, since it is through them that the ends of government are attained. Moreover, the very large departments are able to derive most of the advantages of specialization entirely within their own framework.

While, therefore, experience indicates that it is useful to set up these secondary offices, it does not suggest that an absolute segregation of such activities is always advantageous. In most instances, only the test of actual operations will indicate where the line can best be drawn between advantageous specialization and the contrary. Enough central control is indicated, however, to prevent interdepartmental competition and to secure common procedures at key points.

The problem of controlling the discretion of the line departments by the decisions of the auxiliary agencies is a puzzling one, and no single or dogmatic answer can be given. At first thought it might appear that the major departments would be more competent to determine their needs, within the appropriation acts, than any other agency. On matters peculiar to the work on which they are primarily engaged, as sanitary engineering, the management of a library, or the maintenance of lighthouses, this conclusion is sound. Even here, however, some degree of fiscal supervision has developed.

The special knowledge and skill which auxiliary agencies can develop form in part the basis for accepting their decisions in their own fields

[1] S. Rept. 1275, 75th Cong., 1st sess., p. 240.

[2] Sparlin, *op. cit.*

of specialization. In part, however, they have acquired their position of control because they have been attached to the central office of the chief executive.

This is, indeed, one of the significant changes still in process. Before 1915 the auxiliary agency tended to be just another "independent" organization. The process of state and municipal reorganization had the effect of attaching each of them to the mayor or the governor. The fiscal officer especially tended to become a principal adviser of the chief executive. In strict conformity with this trend, the Committee on Administrative Management recommended closer connections between the personnel agency, the fiscal agency, the planning agency and the President, as well as expanded functions for the budget agency.

Some means of administrative control by chief executives must exist, and it is unlikely that the auxiliary agencies will wholly escape pressure to serve this end. In general it is true that the type of auxiliary agency which provides service only is slowly receding in favor of the type which combines some service functions with some control responsibilities.

With respect to cities, however, Upson writes, "There is no common practice . . . with respect to conflicting jurisdiction between the purchasing agent and the departments, but there is a tendency to overcome the difficulty by making the purchasing agent solely an ordering department. In other words, this official is under compulsion to fill the requisitions furnished to him by the departments, leaving to other branches of the government, primarily the auditor, the problem of determining whether a department is ordering supplies in unnecessary quantities and unsatisfactory qualities."[1] Upson deprecates this tendency, but something can be said in favor of separating the control functions and the service functions, which in many cases are combined in these auxiliary agencies. Here is a problem on which more data are needed.

The segregation of these secondary functions in the auxiliary agencies tends to complicate the organization, and to create additional points where friction may develop.[2] It follows consequently that attention to the coordination of the auxiliary agencies with the line agencies which they serve becomes a matter of importance. One means of securing

[1] Lent D. Upson, *Practice of Municipal Administration* (1926), p. 157.

[2] In a thoughtful essay, John Lee emphasizes the need for caution in extending the number and responsibilities of the auxiliary agencies, proceeding only as rapidly as "the sense of organization" already achieved permits. As a corrective for the dispersion which may attend upon the specialization of the auxiliary functions he urges wide understanding of the central purpose of the organization. See John Lee, "The Pros and Cons of Functionalization," reprinted in Luther Gulick and L. Urwick, eds., *Papers on the Science of Administration* (1937), p. 173.

smooth working is to establish the procedures of the auxiliary agencies by a joint committee representing all the interested parties; if the procedures are carefully thought out and adjusted to the needs of the user as well as of the purchaser, chronic friction will ordinarily be avoided. The function of a true staff agency is also invaluable in diminishing friction here and elsewhere; it can study conflict between user and purchaser as a disinterested party and work out a program for consideration of those concerned.

Increased efficiency and substantial economy may be expected from the formation of specialized auxiliary agencies for large-scale operations. In small organizations the benefits are proportionately likely to be less; and in large organizations it is chiefly in the mass operations that increased efficiency arises. While, therefore, the auxiliary agencies have ample justification under favorable circumstances, there is a point of marginal utility beyond which the unity and sense of full responsibility of the line department become the greater good. As yet, we can say only that experience in particular cases must indicate where the line should be drawn.

Chapter Six

THE DEPARTMENT

THE solid foundation of administration is within the departments. The chief executive is an essential center of responsibility and general management, but he does not himself enforce the laws or provide public services. The staff and auxiliary agencies are one step removed from the front line; they serve executives and line departments, not the mass of citizens. It is within the departments that the substantive work is done. Here it is that the arms of the executive branch reach abroad in the country to render services to some citizens and to restrain and direct others.

To the department, therefore, we now turn, observing its various external forms, its structure, the manner in which its ultimate authority is organized, and how it is managed from within. In the following chapter we shall examine the bureau, the principal unit of operation; observe the auxiliary agencies within the departmental framework; note the relations between field office and headquarters; summarize the system of internal control; and conclude with an analysis of the trend of reorganization of departments.

1. Types of Management Units

The chief executive has won a large measure of recognition as the general manager of public business; but in large organizations he cannot be concerned with the detail of actual day-by-day business. The endless flow of administrative operations is performed by officials and employees of high and low station organized into major units traditionally called departments. The national government started business in 1789 with three: state, war, and treasury. By 1880 the number had increased to eight, in 1938 it was ten, and others have been proposed from time to time, such as a department of education, of public works, and of public welfare. Corresponding increases in the number of departments, reflecting new governmental functions, are found in the states and the cities.

The department is not the only operating unit. In recent years new forms have developed. The independent board or commission[1] was familiar during the nineteenth century, especially in municipal affairs. The government corporation reappeared on the national scene with the Panama Railroad Company, later the war-time corporations, more recently the Inland Waterways Corporation and the emergency corporations related to the New Deal. The "authority" gives us at least a new terminology, although no well-defined status, for example the Alley Dwelling Authority. So also with the "administration"—the Public Works Administration, the Resettlement Administration and others. In Washington, there is a disposition to reserve the use of the term "office" to units which have advisory or research duties only, as the Office of Education. The time-honored term "committee" has been put to new uses in designating such organizations as the National Resources Committee. "Council" has also been pressed into use in such cases as the National Emergency Council (1934), and earlier the Council of National Defense; and "service" to designate the combined Immigration and Naturalization Service.

Beyond these specifically public agencies are such midway structures as the mixed enterprise, the code authority, the production control committees organized in counties at the instance of the Agricultural Adjustment Administration, the Federal Reserve Board and other organizations not possessing full status as public authorities, but performing what appear to be public functions. The forms and terminology of organization have therefore become diversified in recent years. Problems of internal structure remain much the same.[2]

This and the following chapter are concerned primarily with the department in the general sense of a major unit of organization dealing with a substantive field of administration. The states and the larger cities each normally possess from ten to twenty or more departments, representing a single zone of specialization: police and traffic, public health, education, services to agriculture, to labor, and to business, the collection of revenue, and others. They represent work generally recognized

[1] In this book the terms are used interchangeably.

[2] Studies of specific departments from the point of view of management and operation are numerous in the literature of the bureaus of research. Large-scale studies are less common, and there is room for an important contribution in an intimate view of the history, problems, traditions, and contributions of specific departments. An excellent study by William L. Wanlass, *The United States Department of Agriculture, a Study in Administration* (1920), will be supplemented by a forthcoming study of the same department by Professor John M. Gaus. The monograph series of Brookings Institution presents by far the most extensive account of the federal administrative agencies, but in formal rather than intimate terms. The history of each of the federal departments is given in Lloyd M. Short, *The Development of National Administrative Organization in the United States* (1923). A revealing account of the Department of Commerce is given in William C. Redfield, *With Congress and Cabinet* (1924).

as belonging to government, while newer or experimental activities are often assigned to commissions or temporary agencies. Their work is continuing, and generally expanding with population growth; over the years they generate well-defined departmental traditions.

The relative importance of the "old-line" departments as the principal agencies of administration has increased markedly during the last twenty-five years in states and cities; in the national government, their prestige was momentarily challenged by the New Deal "alphabetocracy." The five largest departments in Washington on June 30, 1938, were Post Office, 285,000; Agriculture, 102,000; War, 94,000; Navy, 68,000; Treasury, 67,000. Compare the five largest "establishments"—Veterans' Administration, 35,000; Works Progress Administration, 25,000; Home Owners' Loan Corporation, 13,000; Tennessee Valley Authority, 12,000; Social Security Board, 10,000.

Departments vary widely among themselves, although usually possessing the common quality of immediate relationship with the chief executive. They vary enormously in size; there are dwarfs and giants. At one extreme is the police department of any small town, comprising the chief and a few patrolmen, at the other the United States Post Office, with a personnel of over 280,000. This discussion is concerned only with the large organization.

Most departments have direct operating responsibilties. Thus the Post Office carries mail and the Department of Commerce takes the census. Some departments, however, are less operating than supervisory, directing and coordinating agencies; they have been called the "holding corporation" type. Farm Credit Administration is an excellent example. This organization is designed to extend credit to farmers; it supervises and operates through the intermediate credit banks, land banks, production credit corporations, and banks for cooperatives, assisted by the Federal Farm Mortgage Corporation. The overhead organization, F.C.A., has no dealings with farmers directly.

Some loosely organized departments, or those having relatively diverse functions, resemble the holding corporation type. Thus the Department of Interior comprises a heterogeneous group of bureaus and offices, ranging from the General Land Office through the Office of Indian Affairs, the Office of Education, the Alaska Railroad, the Division of Grazing, and the Petroleum Conservation Division. Here the "department" tends to become a collective name for a number of relatively autonomous operating units. The establishment of government corporations "within" a department (as in Agriculture, 1936, 1937) tends in the same direction. The traditions of some departments favor close control and direction by the head, in others tradition supports a relatively high degree of self-management. Naturally the smaller and more homogeneous the unit, the more compact its internal organization is likely to be.

Departments vary widely also in their degree of dispersion. The business of some departments is carried on almost entirely in their central offices; this is common in municipal and occasionally in state governments. In other cases, business is transacted almost entirely in field offices, and the degree of dispersion is great. This is the typical case in the national system. In a third instance, affairs are conducted partly in the field, partly in headquarters. Thus the United States Civil Service Commission transacts much of its business in its thirteen district offices, although most examinations are handled from Washington. In any case the district offices act under the instructions and supervision of the central office.[1]

2. Basis of Organization of Departments

The common basis of specialization on which government departments and other management units rest is function. The goal toward which the reorganization of departments during the last twenty years has been directed is to provide a small number of relatively large departments each possessing a single major function.[2]

Inspection of the number and duties of departments in any jurisdiction furnishes many examples of the unifunctional department. The Department of Justice of the United States government; the public health and public works departments in states; the police, fire and park departments in cities are typical examples. In many instances, however, departments are a hodgepodge of unrelated functions.

The concept of the unifunctional department, while simple on the surface, gives no automatic guide to the allocation of activities. Marginal cases in which two or even three departments appear to have valid claims are frequent. Should the care of the health of school children be assigned to the health department or to the schools? Should the development of child health on a national scale be assigned to the Public Health Service or to the Children's Bureau? Should the Forest Service be placed in the Department of Agriculture or in the Department of the Interior?

[1] The special problems of managing a widely dispersed organization offer a useful field of study.

[2] For a discussion of where authority to prescribe the form of organization should lie, see F. F. Blachly, "Who Should Organize State Administration?" 4 *Southwestern Political and Social Sci. Q.* 95-109 (1923–24); Peyton Hurt, "Who Should Reorganize the National Administration?" 26 *Am. Pol. Sci. Rev.* 1082-98 (1932); and the first edition of this volume, pp. 50-55.

When is a function of sufficient major importance to warrant organization as a department rather than as a bureau with other related functions in a broader unit? Decisions on such cases usually flow from other considerations than abstract principle: the pressure of interest groups; the capacity of those who possess to resist change; bureaucratic and political bargaining. The concept of function itself is not entirely precise, although it is a genuine guide.

The very fact that no department can be functionally self-sufficient and must inevitably have frontier problems with its neighbors is itself a further guide to the necessity for general staff and strong overhead management. The cooperation and coordination of these contiguous and overlapping organizations need to be facilitated.

Other bases of organization which may appear, usually in the subdivisions of a department, are by type of clientele, by geographical area, and by type of operation. Welfare departments deal with distinguishable types of individuals, the dependents, defectives and delinquents. The Veterans' Administration deals with all veteran problems. The Women's Bureau, the Children's Bureau, labor departments, deal with the interests of specific classes. They may also be considered as performing specific functions for these classes, such as rehabilitation, employment, or relief. The Department of State is partly organized internally on a geographical basis; the Division of Far Eastern Affairs handles all types of problems arising in this part of the globe, whether diplomatic, economic, legal, financial or commercial.

3. The Organization of Authority

In a large department, problems of internal organization are numerous and perplexing; in small units, many of them vanish and all are minimized. The large department spreads out these issues where they are conspicuous and often difficult, and accordingly the present discussion will take the "giant" organization as its object of interest.

The treatment falls into several sections: first the organization of the final authority in the department, involving brief notice of the role of the head; the debate between the advocates of a single head and those who prefer a plural body; the problem of interest representation within the authority where it is set up as a commission; finally, the forms of administrative management within a department, a matter of concern principally to the giant unit.

a. Administrative role of department head. In the federal departments and in some state and city departments, the office of head is as deeply concerned with policy as with administration. In most city and state units, however, policy is secondary to administration. The functions of a department head consequently vary in emphasis, but they will normally include duties in the field of law, policy, and administration.

In law the functions of the whole department are often vested exclusively or principally in the head. Thus the Illinois Civil Administrative Code provides that each department shall have a director "who shall . . . execute the powers and discharge the duties vested by law in his respective department." [1] Action taken is usually by or in the name of the head of the organization. Process is served upon the head, and his signature is necessary to validate in law all documents representing and declaring decisions of the department. From the point of view of the law, the head is the department.

The secretaries of the ten federal departments are important policy officials. In theory rather than practice, they are advisers to the President on general policy, internal and external, civil and military. In fact, they advise with the President principally on matters arising within or concerning their organization. Questions of the most intricate nature are constantly arising, and the secretary becomes the channel through which the organized views of the technical staff come to the attention of the chief executive. In state departments the same situation often prevails, on a somewhat less extensive scale.

Finally, the head is an administrator of the functions committed to his organization. Within it he duplicates the administrative functions of the chief executive: to plan, to command, to organize, to appoint and remove and in general to supervise and guide the work of the department. These are duties everywhere performed by department heads.

The question arises whether the head should be a layman or a technician, a man of general competence or a specialist. As in many administrative questions, there is no single answer. In the case of the federal departments and analogous state organizations, the functions of policy are so important that statesmen are needed rather than specialists. In technical state and city organizations, knowledge of the technique in question is important, if only to sustain the confidence of the staff in its head. Even here, however, specialist knowledge is not enough; the head needs breadth of view, ability to cooperate with other department heads, and capacity for leadership. For he is not merely to keep the wheels turning; he is critic, innovator, and buffer against the outside world.

The department head, moreover, has a symbolic role analogous to but different from that of the chief executive. He may represent or be especially related to an important interest group which thus secures cabinet representation in the national government or direct access to the gov-

[1] Illinois Laws 1917, p. 2, sec. 4.

ernor in the states. His representative position, either with respect to a special interest or to the public interest, may have important consequences. The use of his powers will be subject to pressures from many sides, suggesting the need for men of other than merely technical competence at these posts situated in the midst of the economic and social storms of contemporary society.[1]

In the national government it is accepted that the head of a department is primarily an outpost of the chief executive and a representative of a political party whose policies he is to pursue. Consequently he is appointed by the chief executive on the basis of political and personal acceptability, and for a limited term. While this doctrine generally prevails, it is not necessarily universally applicable. In a department whose operations are well established and are outside partisan controversy, the desirability of close political responsibility is slight. For example, there are no obvious administrative or governmental advantages in changing a postmaster general with every change in party control, and it is certainly anomalous to recognize him as the chief dispenser of patronage.

In the state and local governments the department heads are not always accepted as an outpost of the chief executive or his party. More commonly they are recognized as permanent technical officials. Where, however, controversial issues of policy prevail, or where patronage appointments are still to be made, rapidly changing department heads are the rule. The tradition of permanent department heads which prevails in Virginia (a one-party state) is worthy of emulation elsewhere.[2]

b. The administrator vs. the board. An old controversy concerning the relative merits of a single responsible administrator and a board or commission flared up again in the 1937–38 discussion over the proposal for a Civil Service Administrator in lieu of the United States Civil Service Commission. It will clarify the discussion if we start from the proposition that a conclusive case for the universal adoption of either form of structure cannot be sustained. It is more useful to inquire what ad-

[1] The broad question of expert and amateur in public administration is not dealt with in this volume. For literature see Ernest H. Hankin, *The Mental Limitations of the Expert* (1920); Harold J. Laski, "The Limitations of the Expert," 162 *Harpers Magazine* 101-10 (1930); Charles A. Beard, "Government by Technologists," 63 *New Republic* 115-20 (1930); E. B. Schulz, "An Unsolved Problem in City Government: Political Leadership and Expert Administration," 14 *Southwestern Social Sci. Q.* 120-32 (1933-34); Paul T. Stafford, "The New Amateur in Public Administration," 29 *Am. Pol. Sci. Rev.* 257-69 (1935); Ordway Tead, "Amateurs vs. Experts in Administration," 189 *Annals* 42-47 (1937).

[2] Unpublished data collected chiefly by Norman N. Gill for the Commission of Inquiry on Public Service Personnel (1934) reveal the greatest variation in the tenure and experience of department heads. In two cities, St. Paul and Milwaukee, Gill discovered career men serving as department heads in numerous instances; in others he found various degrees of instability.

vantages and disadvantages inhere in each type, and what administrative circumstances seem to call now for one, now for the other.

The "direct performance of work" in a field where major policy and objectives are generally accepted, where standards are well developed, and where the public interest is well defined and broadly recognized, normally calls for agencies managed by a single administrator, especially in those concerned with the vital interests of personal and community protection. Most government work falls in this class.

On the other hand the discovery and formulation of policy through specific decisions in particular cases or through inquiry and the promulgation of general rules and regulations, subject to the often vague phrases of the law; the exercise of wide discretionary or controlling powers affecting important private interests of person or property; the exercise of coercive power in controversial areas; the protection of administrative integrity against hostile outside pressure, these situations may call for action by a commission.[1] Even in these cases single-headed departments may operate satisfactorily, as for example the United States Department of Agriculture.

A few examples will illustrate the broad line of demarcation. The award of damages in compensation for industrial accidents, involving not merely a finding of fact but involving also a conflict of interest between owners and workers, calls for a determination by a board rather than the decision of one. The regulation of the activities of the stock exchange involves experimentation in a highly controversial field, making it desirable to organize the controlling agency as the Securities and Exchange Commission. The determination of banking policy in the Federal Reserve System affects such vast private interests that public confidence is greater in a group than it would be in an individual: hence the Federal Reserve Board. The balance of the conflicting interests of shippers, consumers, railroad investors, and competing cities in fixing rate structures is better achieved by the meeting of several minds than by the final decision of one. The evolution of an "unfair practice" policy in interstate business was, and remains, so experimental and controversial a subject that a "collegiate" form of organization is desirable.

Experience indicates that where a commission appears desirable, it is also advantageous for it to carry out its decisions through a single re-

[1] In particular cases where patronage and political pressure are strong, the commission may be effective as a protection against the spoilsmen; but when a spoils administration once acquires control of such a commission, it is the more difficult to drive it out. In general the remedy against "politics" is more likely found in the development of an effective merit system and in citizen support for a type of chief executive who will insist on good administration than in the somewhat dubious protection of a plural authority.

sponsible executive officer. This arrangement facilitates a clear segregation of the quasi legislative, quasi judicial, representative functions of the organization from its day-by-day operations. Substantially universal experience demonstrates the fatal weakness of the direction of day-by-day operations by a plural body. To "administer" in this sense of the term is the job of one, not of many.

Hence the growing number of commissions working through executive directors. Many health departments are organized on the New York model, including a health council for policy-forming purposes, which comprises a representative number of persons on a per diem basis, and a full-time executive officer who is responsible for the execution of policy. The 1937 Michigan State Civil Service Act draws a careful and well-conceived distinction between the duties of the commission and those of the state personnel director, recapitulating the division of work which long experience in this field has shown desirable.[1]

A striking example of the difficulty of management by a commission is afforded in the early history of the Tennessee Valley Authority. At the outset, this board divided the work of administration among the three members. The resultant confusion and friction finally induced the Authority to appoint Mr. John Blandford as "coordinator"; eventually after a long period of adjustment he became the responsible general manager of the Authority.[2]

A commission is sometimes chosen in order to segregate a particular function from the normal subordination of administrative agencies to the chief executive and to free it from some or all of the customary rules of operation, as for example the making of contracts, recruitment through the central personnel agency, or purchasing through the central purchasing office. The policy of "independence" is controversial and is considered in a subsequent chapter; here it is sufficient to note that the commission form makes easy contact with the chief executive more difficult, that the commission is at times deliberately preferred to break the direct supervision and control of the chief executive, and that the unity of the administrative system as a whole is somewhat impaired. Opinions differ as to the desirability of this breach of unity.

In general, the burden of proof is on the advocates of a board in preference to an administrator. Exigent demands for unity of purpose, for energy in execution, for well-defined responsibility, and for easy coordination press strongly in favor of one official rather than for a con-

[1] Act No. 346, sec. 6, 1937. Note also the shift in Wisconsin in 1937 from administrative commissions to single directors with advisory boards in charge of legislative policy.

[2] Cf. a forthcoming study by Herman Finer, *The Tennessee Valley Authority.*

joint authority. While commissions at times operate smoothly and energetically, too often they develop friction and conflict among their members. Differences spread inevitably into the subordinate staff, forming factions, one of the worst types of administrative plague. The commission is not an agency for effective management, and resort to it must be clearly indicated for the reasons already suggested–reasons which rest on the superior claims of healthy social adjustment and protection of socially important interests of individuals or groups.

c. Interest representation in the administrative structure. In view of the inevitable concern of special groups in the attitudes, program and decisions of administrative agencies operating in controversial fields, and in view of the desirability, if not necessity, of securing the consent and at times the active cooperation of these groups, the advisability of according them representation on the governing authority has been widely discussed. In some instances such representation is standard practice.

The case in point is not professional representation on professional boards, such as the appointment of medical experts on a board of health, or of engineers on an engineering licensing board. It is rather the representation of groups whose interests, usually economic, are affected by administrative action in a competitive or controversial situation. On the national scale, an example is found in the Federal Reserve Board membership, which must represent financial, agricultural, industrial and commercial interests, as well as the geographical divisions of the country. A study of interest representation in Oregon revealed on various boards the representatives of capital, labor, agriculture, wool growers, dairymen, the Oregon Taxpayers' League, seed dealers, and practical range stockmen.[1]

The advantages of such explicit representation are principally that the policy of the agency concerned will be worked out with full understanding of the preferences of those most directly affected, and of the probable effects of any given policy on each party; that consequently policy is likely to be more realistic; that the parties whose interests are affected are each educated to understand the point of view of the other, and of the public authority; that administrative policy so evolved is more easily enforced; that influences otherwise subterranean are brought into the open and given fair opportunity to be heard; and that this is a more democratic means of procedure than by the administrative fiat of a single official. Most of these advantages can be obtained also through advisory boards with a specific rather than a general function or purpose.

[1] James D. Barnett, "Representation of Interests in Administration," 12 *Nat. Mun. Rev.* 347-49 (1923). See especially a forthcoming study by Avery Leiserson, *Interest Representation in Administrative Commissions.*

The disadvantages flow from the possibility that the conflict of interest within a board organized to endow interest groups with voting power may be so fundamental that no agreement can be reached and in consequence administrative action is weakened or paralyzed. The balancing of two opposed groups with an impartial chairman (as in conciliation and arbitration boards) may lead to a series of majority-minority decisions, and to charges that one party or the other has captured the "impartial" member. On the other hand, in many cases the mediating common sense of the third member brings about a real meeting of minds. The process of reaching a decision may be retarded; but good administration consists certainly as much in doing the right thing as in doing something, however expeditiously and energetically.

In fields of social experimentation the representation of interests has special claims. Thus the code authorities under the National Recovery Administration were widely representative of the business groups affected, while the needs of labor and consumers were recognized in the formal organization of the Administration. Experience with the Consumers' Council of N.R.A. indicates that mere representation may be inadequate to secure effective results; power rests here as elsewhere with numbers and organization, and while the consumers are numerous they are not effectively organized as such.

Advisory boards furnish another means of enabling interest groups to be heard. They also link officials with citizens who have special knowledge or interest in a branch of government. In many instances such boards have enabled civic-minded individuals to render services of the greatest value to the community; their contributions have been especially marked in such fields as the social services, recreation, long-range planning and the like.

A double hazard has diminished their usefulness in some cases. On the one hand, the head of the department or agency may become so preoccupied in his daily work that he fails to call his advisory board, or to give it work to do, or to consider its recommendations; on the other hand, an advisory board with one or two active members may reach over into the field of operations and encroach on the responsibility of the department officials. Occasionally an executive with special confidence in an advisory board may try to pass his responsibilities to it, but this is less common than neglect.

A delicate balance is therefore needed in the relations between advisory boards and their principals. Board members should be free to advise, either on request or on their own initiative; they are entitled to see records and to be kept informed; their advice is worthy of consideration; they are entitled to know the reasons which may prompt an executive to follow a different line than that recommended to him. At the same time, the members of the board have no responsibility for decisions, for giving orders, for selecting personnel, for supervision of employees, or for purchases or fiscal operations. They are to advise, not to manage.

4. Administrative Management within the Department

In his trenchant discussion Arthur Macmahon points out that "so far as is possible, the tasks of supervision and coordination must be absorbed within departments, otherwise the problems that rise to the center become overwhelming in their detail." [1] To ensure this coordination, the federal departments have been slowly evolving during the last decade a managerial core above the level of the bureaus. A corresponding mechanism will doubtless eventually be found advantageous in large and dispersed organizations in state governments.

The objectives of overhead departmental management are threefold: to enable the department head to deal effectively with questions of policy, both in formulation and execution; to promote coordination both within the department and without; and to "liberate the energies of the operating units."

To attain these objectives, the *de facto* post of general manager has grown up, with many variations in detail, in the Treasury, Agriculture, Interior, Commerce, and Labor Departments, represented by such men as William H. McReynolds, W. A. Jump, Ebert K. Burlew, Malcolm Kerlin and Richardson Saunders. The office has not yet been recognized by name, or by a clear demarcation of status and duties.[2] Its original center of interest was the coordination of the auxiliary services and facilities, but "the group of virtual departmental managers have been drawn by sheer necessity into the broader and more difficult fields where facility meets formative policy." The emerging office resembles the post of permanent undersecretary, the normal apex of the department in other systems of administration than the American.[3]

Experience has already indicated that this office cannot be satisfactorily filled by nonpermanent incumbents. In some notorious cases, a secretary has been required for political reasons to accept as his immediate adviser a person who did not command his confidence, and the whole function of overhead management had to flow through devious and un-

[1] Arthur W. Macmahon, "Departmental Management," in President's Committee on Administrative Management, *Report with Special Studies* (1937), pp. 247-70. This brilliant study should be read in its entirety.

[2] Incumbents are often designated administrative assistants to the Secretary.

[3] A study of the legal offices of the departments and independent establishments is greatly needed in order to ascertain how far, if at all, they concern themselves with policy and administration as well as law.

official channels. The short service of assistant secretaries hampers functional assignments to them, and the unfamiliarity of incumbents with the business and traditions of the departments has clogged rather than opened the channels of communication between the head and the bureaus. These birds of passage, moreover, cannot expect to command the respect of the permanent technical services. It is impractical "to make impermanent assistant secretaries act as substantial links in the chain of directive and supervisory responsibility."

This criticism does not mean that a secretary of a department may not need policy advisers who come and go with him, and administrative assistants who act in a staff capacity outside the line of responsibility. The difference between the two groups is recognized in the English civil service as the distinction between the political and the permanent undersecretary. An analogous situation is recognized in Washington by the distinction between an assistant secretary and an administrative assistant to the secretary. The secretary of a federal department needs some policy men (for example M. L. Wilson in Agriculture), and some "old-timers" who know government procedures and how to get things done (for example E. K. Burlew in Interior).

With respect to both groups, the need is for men of general competence, who are also familiar with government organization and methods, rather than for specialists. The problem of general overhead management is a problem of balancing conflicting forces, of coordinating, of furnishing major guidance, of representing the department as a whole in its contacts with the outside world, official and private. These tasks require knowledge of the department's work, but do not require specialist knowledge or skill such as would be expected of a bureau or division chief. How to develop an adequate supply of such men of general competence, who know enough of the organization to work effectively, who are politically acceptable but not "politically minded," is an unsolved personnel problem.[1]

Intradepartmental coordination is a simple task in small organizations, but in large agencies with varied and changing programs it is a major problem. Here, as on the larger scale of interdepartmental coordination, the means include first of all a sound basic structure which keeps the essential points of potential friction at a minimum. Other essentials are clear assignment of duties, definite work orders and regulations, and conference at sufficiently frequent intervals to keep all units informed of the general program and of the part each plays in it. Intradepartmental committees to formulate procedures at junction points and to work over

[1] See the author's *Government Career Service* (1935) for one line of approach; and cf. Lewis Meriam's *Public Service and Special Training* (1936).

operating problems are helpful, but the need for many of them suggests a faulty underlying structure.

The reorganization of the United States Department of Agriculture in 1938 was designed to secure better internal coordination, especially in program planning. All major planning which formerly was scattered through the bureaus of the Department, with a heavy concentration in the Agricultural Adjustment Administration, was consolidated in the Bureau of Agricultural Economics. Earlier difficulties in coordinating field programs of different bureaus concerned with land use had led in 1937 to the establishment in the Secretary's Office of an Office of Land Use Coordination. By the 1938 changes, all marketing activities, which had been in four different sections, were brought under single direction. In probably no other administrative organization has the problem of intradepartmental coordination been more acute, both on account of the scale of operations, their diversity, their changing character, and their repercussions on local affairs throughout the country.

Chapter Seven

THE DEPARTMENT (*Continued*)

OUR study of the department up to this point has been concerned principally with overhead organization and management—the type of management units, the bases of major specialization, the organization of authority, and administrative management within the department. It remains to examine the formation and role of the bureau, the departmental auxiliary agencies, the field offices, the methods of internal control, and the movement for reorganization.

1. The Bureau

The internal structure of a large department is highly complex and differentiated. As the process of specialization advances with magnitude, the number of subdivisions increases, and important problems of direction and coordination arise. The management of the United States Department of Agriculture or the Treasury is a bigger job than the management of most state and city governments or private business enterprises. The Veterans' Administration and the Home Owners' Loan Corporation are larger organizations than are most state and city services.

The bureau is the principal internal unit of the department. Its head is responsible to and works under the direction of the head of the organization. The bureau is a homogeneous structure, built to perform one task or a series of closely related tasks. The Federal Bureau of Investigation, Department of Justice; the Bureau of Plant Industry in Agriculture; the Bureau of Labor Statistics; the Bureau of Internal Revenue; the Bureau of the Census; the fire prevention bureau of a city fire department—these typical designations suggest their unifunctional basis. The bureau is a highly stable unit; plans for "reorganization" move bureaus into new combinations with each other, but seldom tear them apart or abolish them. Within the bureau problems of general management, while not absent, tend to give way to technical problems. The bureau, in short, is the essential working unit of administration; the department is a coordinating device, keeping in effective contact related blocks of work and serving as the channel of communication with the chief executive and legislative bodies.

The primary basis of specialization within the department as within the system as a whole is therefore function. The breakdown within the bureau is usually governed by specific lines of work as designated in the statutes, or as fixed by administrative direction. Thus the United States Civil Service Commission in 1938 had among others an examining division, resting on the Civil Service Act of 1883, a retirement division administering the Retirement Act of 1920, and a classification division handling the Classification Act of 1923, as well as a research division and other divisions established by administrative direction.

Another basis of specialization within the bureaus is by the type of work or operation performed. Thus in the Bureau of the Census is the division of machine tabulation, probably the most extensive of its kind in the world; in the Office of the Fourth Assistant Postmaster General, the division of motor vehicle service. Still another example may be found in the National Bureau of Standards, the divisions of which are by scientific or technical specialty: the optics division, the electricity division, the metallurgy division and others.[1] The assignment of work to the various divisions of a bureau normally flows from the character of the work itself, but special circumstances, such as the quality of bureau chiefs, affect the distribution at times. An aggressive division chief who craves wide responsibility may extend his jurisdiction over near-by areas; a poor supervisor will in the long run tend to lose work rather than gain it.

2. The Auxiliary Services within the Departments

Each large department or agency segregates the auxiliary services along lines of specialization corresponding to the principal units serving the departments as a group. Thus within each of the departments of the national government is a budget or fiscal officer, whose duty it is to prepare the departmental estimates for the head of the department in much the same way that the Director of the Bureau of the Budget prepares the estimates for the President's budget. The budget officer is also sometimes responsible for keeping the departmental accounts, for preparing financial statements, and for watching the flow of expenditures within each bureau. He has close relations with the central fiscal office. Other auxiliary offices commonly found in the large departments in the

[1] It will be profitable to examine the bureau structure of any state system to discover the bases of specialization. Reports of state efficiency and economy commissions furnish much useful material on departmental organization, for example, National Institute of Public Administration, *State Administrative Consolidation in Maine* (1930); Indiana State Committee on Governmental Economy, *Report* (1935); Brookings Institution, *Report on a Survey of Organization and Administration of Oklahoma* (1935); *Report of the Connecticut Commission concerning the Reorganization of the State Departments* (1937).

national service are the personnel office, the purchasing and supplies office, the director of information (under a variety of titles), the office of legal counsel, library, accounts, and mail and files.

While the directors of these services are responsible to their department heads, they are also expected to work in harmony with the policies of the major auxiliary agencies serving the whole system. Thus bureau and departmental accounting officers must keep their accounts on the basis of the system fixed by the comptroller. General directions concerning the limits of annual budget estimates are addressed to the heads of departments, but it is the fiscal officers of the bureau and the department who have to prepare the estimates. They will plan within the maximums designated by central budget officers, but the internal pressure for funds is often irresistible. The duty of a departmental budget officer when the head of his department tries to secure bigger appropriations by subterfuge is differently construed—some "play ball" with the central budget agency by dropping hints which expose the true situation, others hew to the departmental line.

From time to time there has been discussion in favor of transferring responsibility for the departmental auxiliary agencies to the central auxiliary services. Thus in 1932 the U. S. Civil Service Commission proposed that the departmental personnel officers become officers of the Commission. Since the effect of this change would be to give the Commission the responsibility for handling the personnel work in each department and establishment, the Commission making the final decisions as to legality and propriety of all personnel movements, the departments resisted *en masse*. The proposal came to naught.

The precise relationship of the departmental auxiliary agencies to the corresponding central auxiliary bodies is one of the unsettled phases of organization. A distribution of authority in the personnel field is suggested in a later chapter,[1] and there has already been brief comment on the parallel problem in the purchasing field.[2] The expansion of departmental personnel work in Washington as a result of the Executive Order of June 24, 1938, will doubtless modify the balance between the U. S. Civil Service Commission and the line departments. My observation has brought me to the conclusion that good administration requires the strengthening of the departmental auxiliary services rather than their complete concentration in a central office. The task of the latter is guidance, the formulation of standards, stimulation, facilitation and to some extent supervision, rather than specific performance.

An interesting recent specialization within agencies operating in ex-

[1] Ch. 18.
[2] Ch. 5.

perimental fields is the planning division, as for example the division of program planning in the Agricultural Adjustment Administration; the division of statistical and historical research in the Bureau of Agricultural Economics and since 1938 the Bureau of Agricultural Economics itself, the central planning organ for the whole Department of Agriculture; the office of the economic adviser of the State Department; and, of longer standing, the War Department General Staff and the Army War College. These are of course staff rather than auxiliary agencies. Until the advent of the National Planning Board in 1933, later the National Resources Committee, no central long-range planning agency existed. Here again the most satisfactory balance suggests that the operating agencies plan their immediate programs in view of current administrative objectives and in the light of the findings of, but without responsibility to, the National Resources Committee.

3. Field Offices and Headquarters

Most state and national administrative offices require field offices, or field agents; in large cities there will be ward or district offices. In the cities distances are slight and communication is easy; but the national system is continental in scope. The Immigration and Naturalization Service operates almost exclusively through its field offices scattered all over the country; the headquarters office establishes policy and procedures, handles personnel and fiscal matters, inspects and supervises, but the actual work of admitting immigrants and of naturalizing them is done almost everywhere but in Washington.

This example is characteristic. Of 841,000 employees in the national service on June 30, 1937, 115,000 were in the District of Columbia and 726,000 were in the field. These proportions have been maintained for many years, and reflect the fact that the work of the national government, while supervised and directed from Washington, is actually carried on throughout the country. The major field offices of the national service tend to congregate in certain key cities—New York, Chicago, Atlanta, St. Louis, New Orleans, San Francisco and others.[1] This tendency is balanced by the pressure of Congressmen to locate federal offices in their districts.

Few studies have been made of the relations between headquarters and field staff.[2] While policies vary from case to case, in general the district offices operate on the basis of very detailed and explicit instructions, reducing the element of discretion in order to ensure consistency and uni-

[1] National Resources Committee, *Regional Factors in National Planning and Development* (1935).

[2] Consult W. F. Willoughby, *Principles of Public Administration* (1927), ch. 10.

formity of decisions. Appeal procedures are practically universal in order to allow the central office to review and correct errors. The central office usually maintains an inspectional service which visits the field offices at periodical intervals to advise local representatives, in addition to the accounting officers who move about in connection with their fiscal duties.[1]

Headquarters may hold a tight rein on field agents, permitting them little or no discretion, settling everything in the central office; in this case the system is technically known as a concentrated one. Or much discretion may be vested in local representatives, with power to give conclusive determinations in specified cases; then the system is referred to as deconcentrated. These terms are analogous to but not identical with the concept of centralization.[2] The top staff of the field offices will be assigned and transferred from Washington; the subordinate staff is usually permanently attached to the office. Postmasters, of course, are never transferred from one office to another, since until 1938 they were within the group of political appointments; at the time of appointment they are still required to be local residents. In general, there is relatively little transfer of personnel from field service to headquarters and vice versa, although conferences in Washington between the two groups are common.[3]

The connection between the central headquarters and the field office may be organized on either one of two lines. We may illustrate by a simplified version of the Social Security Board. When the Board was organizing its field service in 1935 it had the choice of establishing direct field contacts between each bureau with its field offices, or of setting up an intermediate regional office through which all the bureaus would communicate with their respective field agents. The distinction appears diagrammatically in charts A and B.

The Social Security Board chose the form of organization employing a regional office, twelve of which were established. It required considerable pressure, however, in the early days of the Board's work to prevent the operating bureaus from short-circuiting the regional offices in order to deal directly with their "own" field agents. Both forms of organization are in effect in different federal departments although the regional office type is exceptional. There is no clear evidence as yet of the superiority of one over the other. The point deserves further inquiry.

The local coordination of the field services of the national government

[1] May L. Dhonau, *Decentralisation in Government Departments* (1938).

[2] See *infra*, ch. 10.

[3] One phase of the connecting mechanism between headquarters and field offices has been reported by P. S. Wu, "Federal Inspectorate" (ms. 1929), Univ. of Chicago Library. For the related problems of adjustment of federal, state and local offices, see *infra*, chs. 10 and 11.

each with the other is a difficult problem. In principle it may be attacked through the coordination of headquarters offices, each sending the necessary instructions to its own agents, or it may be sought by local negotiation among the field offices. Both methods are useful, and neither can be fully successful without the other.[1]

Until 1921 apparently no serious effort had been made to link up the numerous field offices. The Federal Coordinating Service (1921–1933) was established by executive order to facilitate the disposal of war surplus materials held by federal agencies. Its work eventually extended to cover such matters as supervision of office space, use of motor vehicles, loan of equipment, purchase of supplies, and hospitalization of veterans.

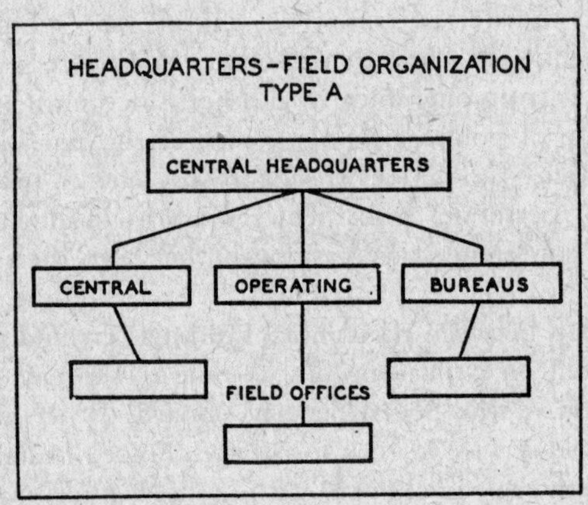

The Service, which was largely managed by army and navy officers on leave under the direction of the Chief Coordinator in the Bureau of the Budget, was almost entirely confined to the business or routine aspects of government. Conflicting policy was beyond its scope.

The Service operated in areas, ranging at different times from nine to twelve, with headquarters in the principal cities. It sponsored the Federal Business Associations, representing all the field offices in a given city and designed to secure coordination by cooperation rather than by direction from above.[2] In 1930 they numbered 293, but in 1936 they had diminished to 135, of which many are inactive. Since the termination of the Federal Coordinating Service in 1933 they have lacked support from Washington.

[1] The principal study on this point is by James W. Fesler, "Executive Management and the Federal Field Service," in President's Committee on Administrative Management, *Report with Special Studies* (1937), pp. 271-94.

[2] Leonard D. White, *Trends in Public Administration* (1933), pp. 154-61.

The depression emergency of 1929 led to the creation in 1933 of the National Emergency Council, which undertook to coordinate the new activities in the field. This venture was organized on a state-wide basis, in part because one of its functions was to serve as liaison agent between federal and state officials. Its various activities were not entirely compatible with each other, and in turn its work has diminished.

A third type of coordination in the field is illustrated by the Tennessee Valley Authority. Joint work in agriculture has been undertaken by the T.V.A., the Department of Agriculture, and the state agricultural colleges in the area. A forest council for the Tennessee Valley was formed, representing the United States Forest Service, the National Park Service,

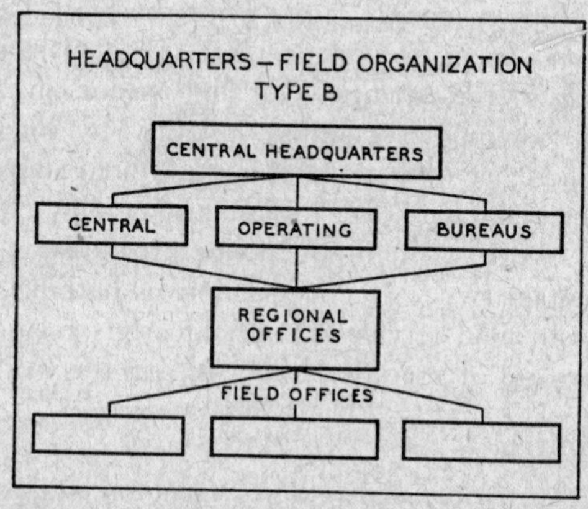

the forestry division of the Office of Indian Affairs, and each of the seven state forestry services in the valley. An advisory board on malaria control includes representatives of the T.V.A., the U. S. Public Health Service, the Department of Agriculture and the Rockefeller Foundation. Fesler reports that much of the accomplishment of the Authority in regional coordination has actually been based on negotiations in Washington and suggests that the experience demonstrates what can be done on a national scale for a region rather than what can be done by coordination through negotiations among field officials.

Permanent field officials who serve the respective departments, such as the district managers of the U. S. Civil Service Commission, necessarily develop close working relationships with other local officials. The Federal Business Associations have been helpful in extending personal acquaintance among federal officials working in the same city, but adequate coordination is lacking at some points. The necessity of coordinating federal and state work in new cooperative programs such as employment offices, social security payments, wage and hour determinations and others raises new and formidable issues.

There is little available evidence to permit a description of central-field relationships in state administration. So far as is known, the field agents of state offices work under closely written specifications designed to reduce the area of individual discretion in the application of law and rules. Distances are less and the problem of contact is consequently not so acute as in the national system. At this point further information is needed on a phase of organization which is universal.

Incidental notice may be given here to another element of administration which also has universal application, the means of communication. When John Adams represented his country abroad, he was forced to rely on packet ships to communicate with the State Department. His freedom of action was in proportion to the time span imposed by the uncertain crossing of the Atlantic. Our ambassadors in any part of the world may now communicate almost instantly by long-distance telephone with the Secretary of State. Within the United States the telegraph, telephone, and the Navy wireless are constantly used by civil officials. The change in police work wrought by police broadcasting and by squad cars able to maintain two-way conversations is nothing less than spectacular.[1] Obviously field service and headquarters relationships are far different in the world of 1930 than they were in the world of 1830.

4. Internal Control

The internal control of a large department or establishment, with a far-flung network of offices, is both important and difficult. The larger the organization and the more dispersed its parts, the greater is the problem of keeping it to the major line of departmental policy, of ensuring harmony and consistency of action, of maintaining satisfactory standards of efficiency, and of preventing the development of stresses and strains among the personnel. The customary means of control have already been suggested in part, but deserve recapitulation at this point. They must be directed to matters of policy as well as to operations and procedures.

a. Overhead management. The head of the department is the central control authority, acting through official orders, circulars, instructions and directions of various types, including the handling of funds and assignment of personnel. He is aided by his personal assistants and by assistant heads, if any. Upon the capacity of the head for reaching wise and timely decisions more than upon any other single element depends

[1] V. A. Leonard, *Police Communication Systems* (1938).

the quality and effectiveness of internal control, and the quality and tone of the organization as a whole.

b. Staff conference. Regular staff conferences are one of the most useful and most common means of internal control. Friction between operating units can sometimes be handled best by informal contacts; in other cases the influence of a group of operating heads on one of their number is beneficial. A common understanding of policy and program can be spread throughout the organization; changes in policy and organization can be discussed in their early stages; the lay and the professional groups within the organization educate each other.

c. Organization charts and work-flow charts. Within the last twenty years, efficiency experts have developed means of graphic representation of official relationships and of the flow of work which are useful devices both for clear allocation of work, for supervision and for control.[1]

d. Operating reports and fiscal control. Internal reports are principally of two sorts, fiscal and production. They are almost universal, and are constantly relied upon by the directing staff. Fiscal reports are presented at least monthly, sometimes more frequently. They are the chief means of checking rates of expenditure and activities beyond those authorized. They aid in keeping a balance between different phases of work. Unit costs may be a useful means of watching the efficiency of the organization. Production records are basic operating documents. They reflect the total work of the organization, the contribution of its parts and the output of individuals. They are effective instruments of control.

e. Supervision of correspondence. The life of the department and its subdivisions is reflected in its correspondence. Great care is therefore taken in well-managed organizations to review drafts of correspondence. Division chiefs in Washington read most, at times all, the dictated correspondence arising within their units; bureau chiefs read a great deal; the executive officer of a commission reads all letters involving complex issues, controversial cases, new policy, or important personages. Commissioners and heads of departments read mail which is "sent up" for their approval or consideration; the selection has to be made by the operating staff. Some overcautious executives sign "bushels" of mail.

f. Special investigations. In a large organization, special studies and investigations are in process much of the time. They are usually authorized and directed by the head of the organization. Secretary Ickes maintained a special unit for this purpose in the Interior Department and Public Works Administration. Recurrent field inspections and audit are

[1] Consult for this and related topics W. F. Willoughby, *Principles of Public Administration* (1927), ch. 13.

another type. Inquiries initiated by citizen complaint or by anonymous letters represent another type. The post office inspectorate is one of the best known units for intradepartmental investigation for control purposes.

g. *Morale-building activities.* The smooth working of an organization is greatly facilitated by positive as well as negative means of control. Whatever gives the members of a department a vital sense of participation facilitates internal control. Thus informational services intended to give the whole department some idea of its objectives and plans stimulate understanding and enthusiasm. Control through the type of leadership which creates the sense of power-with rather than power-over is as effective as the more formal devices suggested in these paragraphs.

5. Reorganization of Departments

The reorganization movement, originating about 1910, is a composite of several related trends, designed to secure greater efficiency and economy through closer administrative control of the spending agencies of government. It includes not only the consolidation of many small operating units into a few large ones, but also the extension of the authority of the governor and mayor or manager, the adoption of budget systems and methods of fiscal control,[1] the extension of the scope of the auxiliary agencies, and the application of better methods of coordination and central direction. This section looks at the reorganization movement principally from the point of view of the operating departments.

Before 1910 the American system of administration favored the direct subordination of administrative agencies to legislative and appropriating bodies, a situation which facilitated partisanship and patronage and which negated the possibility of effective managerial control. The gradual but steady increase in the number of separate units led to much confusion and overlapping of work, and to the cumulative irresponsibility of the operating agencies. The legislative body was inherently unfitted to act as the central directing agency, and the chief executive was both legally and practically unable to act as such.

The situation was aptly described in 1915 in the report of the Illinois Efficiency and Economy Committee. "The Committee finds that a condition of disorganization and confusion exists in the executive department of the State government which necessarily produces inefficiency and waste in the State services. . . . There is unnecessary duplication of positions and salaries. . . . The work that is undertaken is not well done. . . . The absence of definite correlation and cooperation between the

[1] See ch. 15 for discussion of this aspect.

nost closely related offices necessarily leads to loss and inefficient work. . . The present laws frequently give powers to several departments unler which each employ agents for purposes which could be more effiiently and economically performed by one agent at the same time." [1]

In municipal government the process of simplification and consolidaion was well under way when the Illinois report was written. The comnission plan broke through the resisting crust of accumulated tradition. Much antiquated machinery went on the scrap heap. While this form of nunicipal government was faulty in some respects, it did serve the esential purpose of re-establishing a fluid situation in municipal structure, nd paved the way for the council manager plan. Both drastically reuced the number of operating units, increased the size of the remainder, ied them closely to the chief executive, and set up more effective agenies of central coordination.

The proposed New York constitutional revision of 1915 set a new attern for the state departments, which was introduced in Illinois in 917. The Civil Administrative Code of this state became the inspiration nd model for state reorganization during the next twenty years despite vil days which overtook Illinois administration in 1921. Most states ave now adopted in greater or less degree the program of consolidation nd coordination of administrative agencies under the leadership of the overnor. Only a few, however, have terminated the traditionally indeendent constitutional offices—the secretary of state, treasurer, attorney eneral, superintendent of public instruction and others; these remain utside the main structure, for political rather than administrative easons.[2]

The effort to reorganize and consolidate the administrative agencies of the national government, commencing at the instance of President Taft and urged by Presidents Coolidge, Hoover and Roosevelt, still renains without major accomplishment.[3] The most recent statement of he problem was made in 1937 by the Committee on Administrative Management. "The Executive Branch of the Government of the United States," the Committee declared, "has thus grown up without plan or deign like the barns, shacks, silos, tool sheds, and garages of an old farm." The Committee recommended the consolidation, in varying degrees, of

[1] Illinois Efficiency and Economy Committee, *Report,* 1915, pp. 18 ff.

[2] The principal reference is A. E. Buck, *The Reorganization of State Governnents in the United States* (1938).

[3] The most recent report is that of the Brookings Institution for the Byrd Comnittee, *Investigation of Executive Agencies of the Government*, S. Rept. 1275, 75th Cong., 1st sess. (1937). See also W. F. Willoughby, *The Reorganization of the Administrative Branch of the National Government* (1923); L. F. Schmeckebier, *New Federal Organizations* (1934), and supplements in the *American Political Science Review.*

all the independent establishments with the ten existing departments an two new departments of public works and public welfare respectively

The course of departmental reorganization over two decades leave no doubt concerning the administrative soundness of the change from large number of small unrelated units directly dependent upon the leg islative body and exempt from executive supervision to a small numbe of important departments geared into the office of the chief executive. The wisdom of subordinating the independent regulatory commission to departmental supervision is hotly contested, and is discussed in th next chapter.

The independent position assigned to the "alphabetical" agencies i Washington during 1933 and 1934 is supported in principle by th Committee on Administrative Management as an emergency measure "New activities," say the Committee, ". . . should be given virtuall complete freedom, or extensive autonomy, within existing department In the nature of the case, new purposes cannot be carried out withou broad freedom to experiment. To tie a totally new activity either to th regular bureau pattern or to the regular controls may defeat its purpos entirely." [2] But when an activity has been organized, its major policie understood, and its work in the main placed upon a routine basis, i should be brought into the normal structure of organization and contro

At the end of twenty years' experience, several general observatior seem warranted. Reorganization is not a means of saving large sums o money; the principal method of reducing public expenditures is b eliminating government functions. Reorganization has greatly increase both the administrative and political authority and responsibility of th governor and mayor. It is or should be a continuing process, the prin cipal responsibility for which must rest in the executive branch. Stat reorganizations, without known exception, have frozen not only majo structure, but much detail in the terms of statute; easy adjustment made difficult, if not impossible.

In fact legislative bodies have shown a jealous concern to retain th authority to organize and reorganize the administrative system. Cor gress sought for a decade to handle this problem itself. It was finall apparent to everyone that affirmative action was impossible. Presider Hoover then invited Congress to allow him to transfer units from on department to another, authority which was finally granted with reluc tance, limited in point of time, subjected to Congressional veto, an

[1] The relative advantages of large and small departments are summarized b Arthur W. Macmahon, "Departmental Management," in President's Committee c Administrative Management, *Report with Special Studies* (1937), pp. 260-63.

[2] President's Committee on Administrative Management, *ibid.*, p. 37.

nally nullified by the refusal of a Democratic Congress to approve ransfers laid before it in the closing months of the Hoover administra-on. President Roosevelt made some adjustments under similar author-y granted to him during 1933 and 1934.

In the steady adjustment and readjustment of the parts of the machine sought not mere mechanical perfection, but an interrelation of parts which best facilitates the coordination of human beings. The personal actor may sometimes require a structural arrangement which mere ogic would condemn. Structure is designed to facilitate operation and o enhance results; it is not an end in itself.

"Government is a human institution. It is made up of men and women who work together in groups. . . . It is human throughout; it rests not nly on formal arrangement, skill, and numbers, but even more on atti-udes, enthusiasms, and loyalty. It is certainly not a machine, which can e taken apart, redesigned, and put together again on the basis of me-hanical laws. It is more akin to a living organism. The reorganization of he government is not a mechanical task. It is a human task and must be pproached as a problem of morale and personnel fully as much as a ask of logic and management." [1]

. Conclusion

Within the departments runs the life blood of administration. Their ivisions and subdivisions are the seat of the vital energy of the daily work of government. The impulse to action comes from beyond their oundaries, but the corrective and ameliorating and sustaining power of he state is situated within their frontiers. Man power is the source of heir energy, directed toward given ends and so organized and coordi-ated as to render the greatest return in human achievement for the re-ources employed. Organization and management are necessary to en-ble man power to assert itself effectively and it is in the end result that ound structure reveals and justifies itself.

Experience in organizing masses of men for action is most ancient in he armed forces, from which more can be learned than we yet know or civil purposes. But experience in organizing men for action in peace-ul undertakings is also ancient, and underlying the more formal con-iderations which comprise this and the preceding chapter are doubtless many social inheritances which we perceive only dimly, if at all. They acilitate mass action on an ever larger scale, but are themselves inade-quate for the scale of modern operations.

The comparative study of the structure and organization of all kinds f large-scale human institutions helps students of public administration

[1] *Ibid.*, p. 38.

to see more clearly the characteristic forms which facilitate as well a those which hamper and impede. The theory of structure of mass organization for administration is still to be written, but some of its aspect seem, none too clearly, to emerge in the light of common experience.

The formation and articulation of the parts of any organization ar necessarily objects of interest in the search for an effective instrumen of action. But in the last analysis, in a democratic society at least, th machine must correspond in broad outline to a pattern acceptable to th people. This may necessitate sacrifice of some measure of efficiency to sense of freedom or even to the prejudices of the governed. The searc for effective means of action is not paralyzed by this necessity; it i merely channeled.

It is probable that inquiry destined to reveal the secrets of organizatio will be fruitful not only in the higher ranges of large-scale structure but in the small subdivisions also. In final analysis, they must be stated i terms of the conditions of human association and leadership, for ultimately problems of structure are problems of human relationships.

Chapter Eight

THE INDEPENDENT REGULATORY COMMISSION

THE issue raised by recent discussion of the place of the independent regulatory commission in the federal government is much broader than this special case. In one form or another a similar roblem is found in state governments, where claims for autonomy have un squarely against the major reorganizing trend of the last twenty ears; and in city governments, where substantial traces of the administrative disintegration of the last century still persist.[1] The independent osition jealously guarded by school boards is another phase of the same uestion. The place of commissions, not "independent" but by their very rganization tending to find a place on the periphery of the central sysem, is still another angle of this many-sided problem of organization.[2]

To explore the many ramifications of the question of administrative ndependence as against the chief executive would take us too far afield.[3] 'wo principal instances which are particularly in the foreground of resent discussion will be dealt with in this and the following chapter: he independent regulatory commission and the government corpoation.

Until 1883 most work of the national government was performed hrough the departments and their subdivisions. While Congress often nposed specific duties and authority upon the department and bureau s such, and thus created the legal foundation for action independent of irection by the chief executive, in fact their administrative responsibily to the President was generally recognized. Years before the issue had een met and settled by President Jackson in removing a Secretary of he Treasury on the ground of difference of view on treasury policy. It now established in theory and practice alike that the work of the ten

[1] Data on the status of independent state regulatory commissions may be found C. O. Ruggles, *Aspects of the Organization, Functions, and Financing of State ublic Utility Commissions* (1937).

[2] On the general problem, see Robert M. Dawson, *The Principle of Official Indeendence* (1922).

[3] An important case in municipal administration is the zoning board of appeals; e Edward M. Bassett, *Zoning: the Laws, Administration, and Court Decisions uring the first Twenty Years* (1936), esp. ch. 6.

departments is subject, within the framework of the law, to the leadership and policy of the chief executive. Reorganization within the state since 1917 has emphasized a similar conclusion with relation to the governor and mayor.

In 1883 was established the United States Civil Service Commission an agency outside any of the departments but nevertheless directly subject to the authority and direction of the President. Four years late Congress created the Interstate Commerce Commission in a manne clearly indicative of its desire not to place the Commission under th immediate supervision of the President. The term of each member wa fixed at seven years, members retired in rotation, and the President power of removal was limited by the statute to inefficiency, neglect c duty or malfeasance in office. No member of the Commission has eve been removed.

From time to time other "independent" regulatory commissions hav been set up by Congress. The Federal Trade Commission in 1914 wa authorized to forbid "unfair practices" in interstate commerce; the Federal Power Commission, formed in 1920, was authorized to licens water power developments on navigable streams and to prepare futu policy; the Securities and Exchange Commission, established in 193 was designed to protect investors by enforcing the rule of publicit with respect to securities offered for sale; the Federal Communicatio Commission of 1934 took over the work of the former Radio Commi sion and the jurisdiction of the Interstate Commerce Commission ov telegraph and telephone companies; the National Labor Relations Boa became in 1935 "the first genuinely regulatory establishment" in th labor field, an agency empowered to prohibit unfair labor practices; th National Bituminous Coal Commission of 1935 was designed to contr competition by fixing minimum prices, but an adverse decision of th Supreme Court nullified this objective; finally the United States Mar time Commission of 1936 was vested with a modest authority over mar time shipping rates as well as the duty of operating the United Stat merchant fleet.

There were, therefore, in 1938 at least eight independent regulator commissions, of which two only had a substantial length of experien —the Interstate Commerce Commission and the Federal Trade Commi sion.[1] The present jurisdictions of five of them have been conferr since 1934.

In what sense of the term are these agencies "independent"? They a not independent of Congress, which created them, vested them wi

[1] Lindsay Rogers enumerates 14 such commissions in his article, "The Indepen ent Regulatory Commissions," 52 *Pol. Sci. Q.* 1-17 (1937).

ithority and from year to year supplies them with funds. Congress may erminate them, modify their powers, and expand or diminish their finanial resources at will. They are not independent of the courts, for the upreme Court upon petition of parties may review their decisions and ther confirm, modify or nullify them.

These commissions are not wholly independent of the President, since e nominates their members for confirmation by the Senate. The ower of the President to remove members has been definitely subjected) Congressional limitations by the decision of the Supreme Court in the lumphrey case.[1] The independent commissions are not subordinate to ıe White House as are the departments; and tradition combines with w to give them an actual position of substantial independence with espect to the President.

The marks of this independence are principally four. First, the term f office of members of the commission is longer than that of the Presient, and members retire only one at a time. The President cannot, ıerefore, control the membership upon his accession to authority.

Second, under the doctrine of the Humphrey case, Congress may preribe the causes for removal of members of the Federal Trade Commison, and presumably of similar regulatory bodies. The power of presiential removal for mere difference of opinion as to policy seems to have een destroyed at least so far as the Federal Trade Commission is conerned. No other authority to remove a commissioner exists, apart from e power of impeachment, or action by joint resolution of Congress.

Third, the decisions of the independent regulatory commissions are nal so far as the chief executive is concerned. Decisions are not submitd to the White House, they are not discussed with the White House, ey are not subject to review or to veto or to suspension by the Present. Immediately upon action by the commission they are complete ts of a competent authority in full force and vigor.

Finally, there have been no established channels of communication etween the President and the independent regulatory commissions. The ılf between the Interstate Commerce Commission and the President ıs been worn deep by usage of a half century. President Harding called ı the Commission one day, presumably to express his views on transortation policy. The incident has never been repeated. Upon the inauıration of a new President, the Interstate Commerce Commission does ot wait upon the chief executive to receive his policy, nor is there ther regular or intermittent exchange of views. Other independent

[1] *Humphrey's Executor vs. United States,* 295 U. S. 602 (1935); cf. James Hart, 'he Bearing of Myers v. United States upon the Independence of Federal Adminrative Tribunals," 23 *Am. Pol. Sci. Rev.* 657-72 (1929).

commissions tend toward the same general pattern of relationship, bu with significant modifications.

Their departures from the strict official aloofness of the Interstat Commerce Commission are in fact important clues to inner realities. Dur ing 1936 and 1937 the independent National Bituminous Coal Commis sion fell into such an internal conflict among its members, largely ove patronage, that they turned to the White House as the only means o restoring a semblance of capacity to act. The independent Federal Com munications Commission bogged down into such administrative confu sion that the President was forced to take advantage of a vacancy t appoint a personal representative to clear up the situation. The inde pendent Tennessee Valley Authority marched off in two directions a once, in the persons of the chairman and Mr. David Lilienthal. Eac fought out his position in the newspapers. Both parties appealed fo presidential guidance, but sufficient help was not forthcoming.[1]

The appointment of Mr. James Roosevelt as executive assistant to h father, the President, with the duty of acting as an intermediary betwee the commissions and the President, threw new light on the situatio Among the callers on the first day of the new regime were Mr. Josep P. Kennedy, then chairman of the independent Maritime Commissio and Mr. Clyde L. Seavey, chairman of the independent Federal Pow Commission. Mr. Kennedy remained for lunch; Mr. Seavey said, "I lai some troubles at his feet." In theory, however, an independent regul tory commission is one "wholly outside any regular executive depar ment" and "wholly free from control by the President." The Intersta Commerce Commission is the only genuinely pure example, althoug other regulatory bodies approach this status.[2]

The regulatory commissions have been endowed with "independence of the executive branch for reasons which command respect. Apart fro incidental circumstances they are principally two. In fields where publ policy is in an experimental and developmental stage it has been thoug essential to permit the gradual continuous definition of rules of condu by an expert agency protected so far as possible from the influence political or other external pressure. This is not merely partisan thirst f jobs, but much more the inevitable demand of interested groups f favorable consideration by the regulatory agency. Were the door n closed to political influence by virtue of the grant of independence,

[1] The unsuccessful efforts of some members of the Federal Tariff Commission assert an independent status in tariff policy determinations are also in point. S E. Pendleton Herring, *Public Administration and the Public Interest* (1936), ch.

[2] A thoughtful and sympathetic discussion of the independent position of t I.C.C. is found in I. L. Sharfman, *The Interstate Commerce Commission* (193 vol. 2, pp. 452-77.

has been feared, for example, that representatives of shippers, or railroads, or geographical sections of the country, "small business" or "big business" would call into play their Congressmen and Senators, if not the President himself to seek to control the decisions of the Interstate Commerce Commission. The tradition of independence has in fact enabled the Interstate Commerce Commission and some other federal regulatory agencies to withstand this kind of pressure.[1]

The second principal objective in setting up independent regulatory commissions was to separate the quasi judicial determinative powers of the commission from the executive branch. The quasi judicial determination, it was believed, should be subject to review only by a judicial body on the basis of legal, not political considerations. The process of reaching a decision in a reparations case before the Interstate Commerce Commission is in its nature such that a final review by an executive department could hardly be useful as a means of verifying facts or conclusions of law; and it might be objectionable as a means of modifying a decision on the basis of political pressures. To protect the integrity of quasi judicial determinations, therefore, the regulatory commission was placed outside of the sphere of influence of the executive branch.

Other incidental considerations, such as the apparent advantage in securing the services of experts,[2] the desirability of freedom in rule making, and the absence of any convenient department to receive a new activity, are of secondary importance or are related to the two principal reasons described in the preceding paragraphs.

While these reasons are of great weight, they have not been consistently applied. There are numerous examples of regulatory work involving interests of great importance, rule making and quasi judicial determinations which have been put within the departments and organized as operating bureaus. The enforcement of the Food and Drug Act (1906), the Meat Inspection Act (1907), the Plant Quarantine Act (1912), the Cotton Futures Act and the Warehouse Act (1916), and the Packers and Stockyards Act (1921) is assigned to the Department of Agriculture. The Packers and Stockyards Act indeed gives the Secretary of Agriculture a rate-making authority similar to that of the Interstate Commerce Commission.

The principal criticism leveled against the "independence" of the regulatory commissions is that they tend to diminish the constitutional power of the chief executive "to see that the laws are enforced," to destroy the unity of general direction of policy and of overhead man-

[1] Herring, *op. cit., passim.*

[2] E. P. Herring, "The Experts on Five Federal Commissions," 32 *Am. Pol. Sci. Rev.* 86-93 (1938).

agement, and to establish "areas of unaccountability." The essence of the matter is contained in the comment by Robert E. Cushman, "They occupy important fields of administration beyond the reach of Presidential direction and responsibility."

The dilemma thus precipitated is ably stated by Cushman in these words: "There is high respect, based on experience, for the independent commission as a device for federal regulation. . . . At the same time, the multiplication of these independent bodies tends inevitably toward a decentralized and chaotic administrative system." And at another point, "If the regulatory commissions . . . are wholly independent they are completely irresponsible for the doing of very important policy-determining and administrative work. . . . On the other hand, to rob the commissions of their independence is seriously to menace the impartial performance of their judicial and quasi judicial work."

From time to time an effort has been made to curtail the autonomous position of the regulatory agencies in relation to the President. The most recent suggestion is that made by the Committee on Administrative Management, supported by a careful analysis of the problem by Robert E. Cushman.[1]

In brief, the Committee proposed that each of the regulatory commissions be placed "within" a department. The present work of each commission would be broken down into two major branches. On the one hand the quasi judicial function, illustrated by the reparation cases of the Interstate Commerce Commission, would continue to be performed by the Commission as a "judicial section" and with the same complete independence of the department which now prevails. On the other hand, "all the work which is not essentially judicial in nature," for example to formulate rules, initiate action, investigate complaints, hold preliminary hearings, and prepare a formal record, as well as all "the purely administrative or sublegislative work," would be organized as an administrative section with the normal status of a bureau in the department concerned. In addition where the volume of business is large, and quick routine action is necessary, the administrative section itself would decide cases in the first instance and issue orders, which could be appealed to the judicial section on questions of law.[2]

[1] Robert E. Cushman, "The Problem of the Independent Regulatory Commissions," in President's Committee on Administrative Management, *Report with Special Studies* (1937), pp. 203-43.

[2] President's Committee on Administrative Management, *ibid.*, pp. 39-42. These proposals were subjected to adverse criticism in the report of Brookings Institution to the Senate Committee; see *Investigation of Executive Agencies of the Government*, S. Rept. 1275, 75th Cong., 1st sess. (1937), pp. 792-803. The Committee was supported by Lindsay Rogers, "The Independent Regulatory Commissions," 52 *Pol. Sci. Q.* 1-17 (1937).

The Committee on Administrative Management thus proposed to subordinate the administrative and "policy-determining work" of the regulatory commissions to the ultimate supervision of the President, through one of the major departments. This proposal rests on the undoubted fact that some, if not all, of the independent regulatory commissions deal with areas of public policy concerning which no President can be indifferent. It reflects the fact that a national program designed to secure a minimum degree of economic balance can hardly be executed unless the policy of the independent regulatory agencies be directed along lines in harmony with such a program. It recognizes that departments and bureaus responsible to the President are in fact dealing with some phases of the problems assigned to the independent commissions, and that confusion and conflict are certain to develop unless some form of policy coordination can be devised.

Objections to the proposed reforms often start from the proposition that the independent regulatory commission is "primarily an arm of Congress," that the great bulk of its duties are legislative in nature, and that Congress intended them to be so exercised that there might be "scrupulous regard for the rights of all concerned, some stability and continuity of policy, and freedom from political influence."[1] As an arm of Congress, and by an implied extension of the doctrine of separation of powers, it would follow that these commissions are completely external to the executive branch. But the independent commission is no more an arm of Congress than is any independent establishment or government corporation or department; all administrative organs are the agents of Congress, applying, interpreting and enforcing the laws which Congress assigned to them; and in all of them the rights of parties are to be conserved.

The real objection to the program of the Committee was stated a decade ago by Commissioner Joseph B. Eastman. "What purpose, then, would be served by bringing an independent commission within the jurisdiction of some executive department or cabinet officer? I can conceive of no purpose except to influence in some way the judgment of the commission or to bring it within the sway of some administration policy. But plainly, it seems to me, the cold neutrality of the commission, to use the expression of the Supreme Court, ought rather to be safeguarded jealously against precisely such extraneous influences. . . . As I see it, they [i.e., political considerations] have no place so far as the independent commissions are concerned."[2]

[1] Testimony of Joseph B. Eastman, in *Hearings before the Select Committee on Government Organization . . . on S. 2700*, 75th Cong., 1st sess. (1937), p. 179.

[2] Joseph B. Eastman, "The Place of the Independent Regulatory Commission," 12 *Constitutional Rev.* 95-102 (1928).

Commissioner Eastman wrote these lines in 1927, and while they have great weight today, the course of events since 1933 has put the policy problem of the independent commissions in a new framework. To understand the change, it is necessary to look more closely at the content of the phrase, policy making, as it is exemplified in the work of these commissions.

Much of the policy work of the Interstate Commerce Commission is of a technical nature requiring an exact knowledge of an exceedingly complex transportation system. Thus the determination of what is a "just and reasonable" classification, "present or future public convenience and necessity" with respect to extension or abandonment of lines, "safe and adequate facilities," or an "unduly preferential or prejudicial" regulation or practice, is a technical problem which ought to be settled in an atmosphere free from partisan or political considerations, even granting the important social implications of some of these decisions. An independent agency is a convenient, although not an exclusive means of obtaining an impartial judgment.

In other respects the policy work of the Interstate Commerce Commission transcends technical problems and is caught up in the broader aspects of the general social and economic programs of the government of the day. Here it is that the necessity for coordination of the policy of the Commission with that of the government becomes important; and it is at this level, rather than the level of technical determinations, that the proposal of the Committee on Administrative Management is directed. Thus, by way of example, in time of economic depression or recession railroad rate structures and by implication employee pay scales are important aspects of adjustment for recovery. The President must be interested in this area and may hope that the policy of the Interstate Commerce Commission will be reasonably consistent with his own broad program of economic rehabilitation. In case of conflict he has no administrative recourse. In 1935 the Resettlement Administration undertook to remove the population from sparsely watered regions of the west to other more promising agricultural sections. The rate structure on agricultural products from these areas can be so adjusted as to facilitate or to hamper this program. Again through the Reconstruction Finance Corporation Congress authorized loans to hard-pressed industrial and financial corporations during the depression. Policy with respect to loans to railroads quickly bumped against the policy of the Interstate Commerce Commission with respect to capital expenditures by railroad corporations. The impact of rate structure on such major problems as the balance of agriculture and industry, foreign commerce, and the retirement of marginal lands is unavoidable.

Another example. The effect of the policies of the Securities and Exchange Commission on market operations and price fluctuations may be very considerable. The sharp decline in the value of securities in 1937 was attributed in part by some observers to the margin requirements of the Commission; a change in these requirements (which incidentally followed a visit of the chairman of the Commission to the White House) apparently had a favorable effect upon the market. The President cannot fail to be concerned with policy decisions which may thus have an important influence upon general economic trends. In fact the policies of this "independent" Commission appear to have been developed and modified from time to time in the light of conversations with the President. It would, however, obviously be wholly unsatisfactory to expect the President to review or to guide the technical phases of policy involved in the regulation of stock exchange practices.

A final illustration may be taken from the Federal Power Commission. From 1920 to 1930 this authority was guided by an ex officio committee of members of the President's Cabinet. Congress had no well-defined power policy, nor had the members of the Cabinet or the White House; and the period was marked by fluctuations of policy and by ineffective administration. In 1930 the Commission was independently organized; after 1933 it received from Congress a more definite line of policy. The activities of the Power Commission were, however, complemented by the work of other units in the national government equally concerned with some aspects of power policy: the Department of the Interior and the Bureau of Reclamation; the Forest Service; the Tennessee Valley Authority; the Public Works Administration; the Water Resources Committee of the National Resources Committee, and others. It became impossible for the Power Commission to work in an administrative vacuum, blind to the policy and program of other units of the national government.

In each of the cases described in the preceding paragraphs, coordinating measures have been devised in one form or another. The office of Coordinator of Transportation (1934–37) was clearly an effort on the part of the President to link up the Interstate Commerce Commission with the central administration on the level of master planning. The informal visits of the chairman of the Securities and Exchange Commission to the White House reveal the inevitable administrative attraction of each to the other. The National Power Policy Committee, organized in 1934, brought the independent Federal Power Commission into contact with other power policy organs of the national government.

It is therefore not unreasonable to conclude that a degree of coordination is likely to arise so far as major policy problems are concerned.

Each of the independent regulatory commissions, with the exception of the Interstate Commerce Commission and perhaps the Federal Trade Commission, has found ways and means of clearance with the White House. But on other than major problems of policy, problems which are largely technical in nature, it is unnecessary to seek White House counsel, and in most cases it would be undesirable to do so.

In the light of this analysis, then, the case for placing the policy phases of the work of the independent regulatory commissions within the ambit of one of the major departments seems consistent with broad trends and defensible on the ground of securing unity in major governmental policy.

There is another phase of the matter, however, which raises a question of general importance. The Department of Commerce is an organization designed to give service and assistance to American industrialists and merchants; the Interstate Commerce Commission is intended to regulate, curb and prosecute common carriers who violate the law. The issue is whether it is wise to combine in one agency a service and a regulatory activity. There is danger that the sharp edge of regulation may be dulled within the house of a service organization; or vice versa that the usefulness of a service department may be diminished by hostility to its regulatory activities. There is no conclusive evidence to resolve doubts on this point.

Decisions on the allocation of functions to agencies do not always flow from pure reason, however. In the case in point, there would be understandable reluctance to place the Interstate Commerce Commission or the Federal Trade Commission within the Department of Commerce, simply because the Department does not command the public confidence which the Interstate Commerce Commission has won. The fear of political influence in railroad rate decisions, whether justified or not, would exist, and will delay any such coordination as the President's Committee recommended.

The proposal of the Committee respecting the separate organization of the quasi judicial functions involves other considerations. The Committee preserved the existing independence of the regulatory commission in so far as the judicial determination itself was involved, but proposed to place all the preliminary steps in the making of the record in the hands of the administrative section, responsible to the department rather than to the commission. One of the principal advantages of this separation would be to clear up a situation in which the same authority, i.e., the commission, appeared as the prosecuting officer and also as the judge, reaching a decision on the record prepared by its own officers.

The plan of "separation" would without doubt eliminate charges of unfairness arising from combining the offices of prosecutor and judge. The sequence of events by which appeals from Treasury decisions on tax liability were taken out of the Treasury and placed in the hands of the independent Board of Tax Appeals forms an analogous case, at least so far as the separation of prosecutor and judge is concerned. The commission, like any judge or court, would then become dependent on the case presented to it.

To reduce the authority of the commission to the final step of an adjudication on a record prepared by an organization not responsible to it would, however, alter substantially the existing status of the typical independent regulatory body. In such an event the course of adjudication would necessarily be subject in an important degree to the policy of the authority which initiates and prepares cases. While there is no reason to believe that the preparation of the case need be less technically competent, it is clear that the commission would lose to the department its present function of deciding what types of cases to prosecute and in consequence the pattern of administrative policy toward which to work.

Views on the desirability of such a change are diverse. They depend in part upon an understanding of the real nature of the action of a commission in reaching a decision in a case before it, and upon the status of the regulatory body. The commission may be conceived as an umpire, acting only upon appeal of private parties to it; or it may be considered as an active representative of a public interest, itself taking the initiative in investigations and prosecutions. It may be envisaged as a body formulating public policy or as an administrative court making decisions on controversies between private parties. The apparently quasi judicial work of the commissions is in fact often legislative in nature. The classic example is the issuance of a cease and desist order by the Federal Trade Commission, subsequent to an inquiry and a formal hearing before the Commission at which evidence is taken and the defendant has full opportunity to present his case. The action is a mixed one; the form of the proceeding resembles that of the courts in many, although not in all respects; the immediate conclusion of the proceeding may be an order directed to the defendant; the effect of the order is to define "an unfair practice in interstate trade" for the guidance of present and future business competitors; in short, an act legislative in nature and effect. This is the type of administrative action described by Commissioner Eastman in these words, "the duties which we perform are primarily quasi legislative. It is the procedure which is judicial." [1]

To the extent that such commission action is in fact policy making the proposal to coordinate the commission with the government of the

[1] Eastman, *op. cit.*

day may therefore rest on sound ground. The opposite view, that certain areas of policy can be more effectively developed in isolation from the central organization, is open to objection where major policy is concerned. The form of coordination is another problem.

In so far as the true judicial work of the commissions is concerned, as in the reparations procedure before the Interstate Commerce Commission involving the claims of contesting private parties, it is agreed that executive supervision is undesirable. There will be universal agreement also that the great mass of determinations by a commission should be free from review or control by the President. He should never intervene in a particular case. With or without any change in structure, however, it ought to be appropriate for a President at least to express to an independent regulatory commission his views concerning major orientation of commission policy in fields where wide discretion has been left by Congress.[1]

The main problem of the independent regulatory commissions is therefore the invention of some means by which the general tendency of such of their decisions and activities as affect substantially the major policy of the government of the day can be influenced by that government, while preserving impartiality and freedom from political influence in the area of technical aspects of policy making and in the area of quasi judicial determination of private rights. The ultimate form of organization which will conduce to this result has yet to be worked out.

The report of the President's Committee on Administrative Management rightly emphasized the danger inherent in the rapid multiplication of the independent regulatory commissions tending to establish a "headless fourth branch of government." There is need for stronger and more effective overhead management under presidential direction. The particular solution of the problem which the Committee proposed has not met general acceptance. In the eyes of its critics, it exaggerates the need for presidential direction, and underestimates the values of separate organization for a limited number of fields of governmental intervention.

It would be unfortunate nevertheless to establish new independent regulatory commissions except where the case is beyond doubt. No strong reason appears for an independent Maritime Commission, as now constituted. The trend toward the multiplication of the number of independent commissions appears to have been checked by the report of the Committee on Administrative Management, although the independent status of existing commissions has not been destroyed.

A degree of policy coordination can be secured by other means than by placing the independent regulatory commissions within a depart-

[1] Professor I. L. Sharfman, *op. cit.*, takes the opposite view.

ment. This end may be approached (a) through legislation suggested by the President from time to time restating the major line of policy to be pursued by a commission; (b) by the device of the interagency committee comparable to the National Power Policy Committee; (c) by the informal contacts and conferences which in fact obtain between the White House and most of the independent commissions and which might be facilitated by the work of executive assistants to the President; (d) by the renewal of such an office as the Coordinator of Transportation.

Changing circumstances throw administrative structures into new frameworks. An increasing emphasis upon a "planned" economic system would tend to undermine the separate position of the independent commissions since there cannot be many such plans. The relaxation of overhead influence upon production, wages, prices, distribution and a planned program of public works would, on the contrary, tend to remove the pressure for coordination of the independent commissions with the policy of the government of the day.

Likewise if Congress lays upon the independent commissions policy-forming tasks which are of a primary rather than a technical order, it is unlikely that the commissions can remain outside the presidential sphere of influence. For we must recognize that the Presidency is a policy-initiating office of major importance, in recent years overshadowing Congress in its own field. In so far as Congress fails to define in reasonably clear terms its major policy, in so far as Congress refers complex major issues to the independent commissions, it cultivates a tendency for the President of the United States to impose his views of policy upon the commissions in order to secure internal consistency of action in the executive branch of the government.

In short, on the level of technical determinations within an accepted major policy, and on the level of judicial proceedings, the independent regulatory commissions are entitled to preserve their independence of action vis-à-vis the White House. On the higher level of major programs of government, such independence is not likely to prevail.

Chapter Nine

GOVERNMENT CORPORATIONS

THE traditional unit of administration is the department with its bureaus and divisions. The head of a department, and through him all of its subdivisions, are directly subordinate to the chief executive and responsive to his policy. Another common type of administrative unit is the independent establishment, marked by substantial freedom from executive supervision. A third type, which has become important in recent years, is the government corporation. This form of organization may be as dependent on the chief executive as the department, or it may be more independent than the independent establishment. Its novelty and the wide diversity of opinion with respect to its usefulness warrant special treatment.[1]

1. Growth and Nature of Government Corporations

The Bank of North America, chartered by the Continental Congress in 1781, and the first United States Bank, chartered by Congress in 1791, were the earliest corporations in which the United States government held an interest.[2] Congress found rare occasion to use government corporations until the World War, but in 1904 acquired the Panama Railroad Company, a New York corporation. During the World War several corporations were established by Congress, including the War Finance Corporation, the Emergency Fleet Corporation, the United States Grain Corporation, the United States Housing Corporation, the United States Sugar Equalization Board, and the United States Spruce

[1] For consideration of the many legal problems concerning government corporations, see Stanley Reed and others, "Government-Controlled Corporations: a Symposium," 10 *Tulane Law Rev.* 79-101 (1935–36); Maurice S. Culp, "Creation of Government Corporations by the National Government," 33 *Mich. Law Rev.* 473-511 (1934–35); Robert H. Schnell, "Federally Owned Corporations and their Legal Problems," 14 *No. Car. Law Rev.* 238-73, 337-66 (1935–36); O. R. McGuire, "Some Problems arising from Government Corporations," 85 *Univ. of Penn. Law Rev.* 778-94 (1936–37); Lowe Watkins, "Federal Ownership of Corporations," 26 *Georgetown Law J.* 261-87, 637-65 (1937–38). An excellent survey is that by John A. McIntire, "Government Corporations as Administrative Agencies: an Approach," 4 *George Washington Law Rev.* 161-210 (1935–36).

[2] John T. Holdsworth and Davis R. Dewey, *The First and Second Banks of the United States*, S. Doc. 571, 61st Cong., 2d sess. (1910).

Production Corporation. Most of these were liquidated in the early postwar years. Their example was not, however, forgotten.

For two decades the extension of credit under national auspices has been effected by means of government owned and/or controlled banking corporations. Of these the earliest are the twelve federal land banks, authorized by the Federal Farm Loan Act of 1916. In 1923 Congress authorized twelve federal intermediate credit banks; eventually both groups came under the wing of the Farm Credit Administration (1933).

The management of the "heterogeneous assortment" of inland water craft acquired by the War Department in 1917–18 encountered such difficulties that Secretary Weeks sought to withdraw from this activity. The proponents of inland waterway development were sufficiently influential, however, to secure enactment of the act of June 3, 1924, creating the Inland Waterways Corporation and naming the Secretary of War as the incorporator and manager. This legislation embodied the somewhat ambiguous policy of preserving "in full vigor both rail and water transportation." Despite the fact that the Inland Waterways Corporation was established as a temporary, "pioneering" measure, intended to show private capital a lucrative opportunity for investment, no steps have yet been taken to terminate it.[1]

The depression commencing in 1929 again stimulated recourse to the government corporation as a form of organization thought to be well adapted to experimentation and rapidity of action. The curtain was raised in 1932 when the Reconstruction Finance Corporation appeared on the stage to perform a task analogous to that of the former War Finance Corporation. The stage suddenly became crowded in 1933 and 1934 as the program of the Roosevelt administration took shape. For the first time the place of the government corporation in the administrative structure became a problem of substantial proportions.

It is unnecessary to present here a complete list or description of existing government corporations, as variously defined.[2] They have been created for two major purposes. The principal use to which they were put during the depression was to facilitate the extension of credit to hard-pressed banking, insurance, transportation, manufacturing and other private corporations, and also to the states and their subdivisions. Here we meet such agencies as the Reconstruction Finance Corpora-

[1] See H. Rept. 375, 68th Cong., 1st sess. (1924); also for a full account, Marshall E. Dimock, *Developing America's Waterways* (1935).

[2] See John A. McIntire, *op. cit.*; John Thurston, "Government Proprietary Corporations," 21 *Virginia Law Rev.* 351-96, 465-503 (1934–35); C. Herman Pritchett, "Government Corporations in the United States," 19 *Southwestern Social Sci. Q.* 189-200 (1938–39), and "The Tennessee Valley Authority as a Government Corporation," 16 *Social Forces* 120-30 (1937–38).

tion, the Home Owners' Loan Corporation, the production credit corporations, the Commodity Credit Corporation, and in a somewhat different sense, the Federal Deposit Insurance Corporation.

The second principal use for which the government has resorted to incorporation is to carry on activities of a commercial or business nature.[1] The phrase includes, by way of specific example, operating a transportation system (Panama Railroad Company, Emergency Fleet Corporation, Inland Waterways Corporation); production and distribution, and/or regulation of prices (Federal Prison Industries, Inc., Cotton Stabilization Corporation); construction of public works (United States Housing Corporation, Public Works Emergency Housing Corporation); construction of dams and power plants (Tennessee Valley Authority); and extension of relief (Federal Subsistence Homesteads Corporation, Surplus Commodities Corporation, rural rehabilitation corporations).

At the close of 1936, it was reported that the number of government corporations (i.e., owned and controlled by the national government) was about 90.[2] At the close of the fiscal year 1935, the annual report of the Secretary of the Treasury indicated that the proprietary interest of the United States in corporations owned either completely or for the most part by it amounted to approximately $4,000,000,000. The total assets of these corporations were approximately $11,000,000,000.[3] In 1900 none of them existed.

Another view of the relative importance of the government corporation is secured by comparing the number of persons employed in the ten departments, in the independent establishments, and in the ten principal government corporations, as the term is used in this chapter. The number of persons employed on December 31, 1936, in the ten departments was 574,739; in the independent establishments 220,442; and in the government corporations 35,914. Of the latter number the Home Owners' Loan Corporation with 16,000 employees, the Tennessee Valley Authority with 13,000, the Reconstruction Finance Corporation with 3,000, and the Inland Waterways Corporation with 2,000 accounted for the great majority.

In the face of these figures critics of the trend toward government

[1] Cf. C. C. Abbott, "The Government Corporation as an Economic Institution," 15 *Harvard Business Rev.* 295-312 (1936–37). Special studies include forthcoming volumes by Herman Finer and C. Herman Pritchett on the Tennessee Valley Authority; John Thurston, *Government Proprietary Corporations in the English-Speaking Countries* (1937); Marshall E. Dimock, *Government-Operated Enterprises in the Panama Canal Zone* (1934), and *Developing America's Waterways* (1935).

[2] President's Committee on Administrative Management, *Report with Special Studies* (1937), p. 300.

[3] U. S. Secretary of the Treasury, *Annual Report*, 1935, p. 411.

corporations assert that the government has been transformed into "a tremendous super-holding company." In view of the continuing nature of the functions of many of the recent incorporations, it is unlikely that they will be liquidated with the rapidity of their World War predecessors; indeed, we apparently face a permanent modification of the administrative structure.

The unfortunate experience of the states with their holdings in defaulting corporations during the era of internal improvements before the Civil War resulted in widespread constitutional prohibitions forbidding the loan of the credit of the state, and there are still few examples of state owned or controlled corporations. The most spectacular instance is the Port of New York Authority, incorporated as the result of an interstate agreement between New York and New Jersey. This fruitful precedent has not been followed by other states in this or other fields. We may note, however, that in Michigan, Minnesota, and Idaho, the state universities are corporations. A public corporation was created in Wisconsin to build university buildings of a self-liquidating type in order to avoid constitutional prohibitions on loans for internal improvements. In a few states, also, government corporations have been established to administer relief.[1] The North Dakota State Mill and Elevator is operated through the corporate instrumentality of the North Dakota Mill and Elevator Association, but active management has regularly been in the hands of various state officials.[2] The state, subject to the limitations of its own constitution, has full authority to incorporate, but it has usually preferred the traditional forms of administrative agency.

Special cases among the cities, such as the Boston Elevated Railway, a private corporation managed by the city of Boston,[3] and the Cincinnati Southern Railway, built and owned but not operated by the city of Cincinnati, are exceptional.[4] Despite the frequency of public ownership and operation of municipal utilities, it is rare to find examples of the use of the corporation as an administrative device. It is probable, however, that municipal housing corporations will increase in number in the near future. In the further analysis of the government corporation we shall confine attention to the illustrations provided by the national government.

[1] Oliver P. Field, "Government Corporations: A Proposal," 48 *Harvard Law Rev.* 775-96, 778 (1934-35).

[2] Gilbert W. Cooke, "The North Dakota State Mill and Elevator," 46 *J. of Political Economy* 23-51 (1938).

[3] Margaret B. Bailey, "The Boston Elevated Railway" (ms. 1938), Univ. of Chicago Library.

[4] J. H. Hollander, *The Cincinnati Southern Railway: A Study in Municipal Activity*, Johns Hopkins University Studies in Historical and Political Science, vol. 12 (1894).

Analysis of these corporations reveals no simple or uniform type of corporate structure. They vary in the method of incorporation, in their relation to the central administrative structure, in the degree of operating independence, in the source of their capital funds, and in their internal organization. There is no generally accepted definition of the government corporation. Writing in 1926 when the number of such corporations was at a minimum, Van Dorn dealt with those corporations whose capital stock was owned wholly or largely by the government.[1]

The President's Committee on Administrative Management declined to define the term, although it distinguished between federal "business corporations" and federal "governmental corporations." The former class includes those which are chartered by the national government and in which private rights are represented by some degree of stock ownership and by board representation. On October 1, 1936, there were about 14,000 such corporations, including over 5,000 national banks, about 5,000 national farm loan associations, over 1,000 federal savings and loan associations, and 1,700 federal credit unions, each operating within a local community.[2] Others operate within a region, as the twelve Federal Reserve banks, the federal home loan banks and the business corporations associated with the Farm Credit Administration. Some of these are obviously agencies discharging a public function, but the credit unions resemble more closely an ordinary private corporation such as a building and loan association.

The "governmental corporation," in the sense of the Committee report, includes those owned and controlled by the national government, whether incorporated under federal or state charters. A majority of the stock is owned by the United States and no member of the board of directors is elected or appointed by private interests.

The principal basis of distinction among corporations from the point of view of their official characteristics is the degree to which the government owns and controls them. Using this as the criterion of definition, corporations fall into three reasonably distinct classes. First, there are corporations owned by the government either outright or in majority interest, and controlled by the government. These are appropriately known as government corporations. Second, there are corporations in which the government either has an investment or board representation or both, but in which control is vested in the hands of private parties.

[1] Harold A. Van Dorn, *Government Owned Corporations* (1926).

[2] President's Committee on Administrative Management, *Report with Special Studies* (1937), pp. 44-45, summarizing the special study by Herbert Emmerich, "Government Corporations and Independent Supervisory Agencies," pp. 299-308.

These are less than full-fledged government corporations and are conveniently termed "mixed enterprises." [1] Third, there are corporations established by private parties under authority of law, and subject to some degree of supervision by the government, but in which there is no element of government investment or board representation. This class of corporations comprises essentially private bodies beyond the proper meaning of the term, government corporation, although they may be utilized as a matter of convenience to cooperate in governmental activities.[2]

The present chapter is limited to the first class of government corporations in the narrow and strict sense of the term, illustrated by such agencies as the Reconstruction Finance Corporation, the Inland Waterways Corporation, and the Tennessee Valley Authority. The major issues with respect to them are: to what extent do they possess inherent advantage over the older form of administrative unit; in what way may they be geared into the major administrative structure? These problems are discussed in the succeeding sections.

2. The Government Corporation as an Administrative Device

The sudden popularity of the government corporation is due in part to the emergency nature of the period from 1930 to 1935, and to the unparalleled extent to which the national government came to the aid of its hard-pressed citizens. The permanent usefulness of the government corporation will depend upon its superiority as an administrative device in comparison with either the traditional departmental-bureau type of organization or any feasible modification of it. In order to appreciate some aspects of the relative value of the two types of organization, brief notice will be given to these points of comparison: (a) internal organization; (b) relations with legislative bodies; (c) relations with chief executives; (d) sources of revenue; (e) audit; (f) methods of personnel management; (g) freedom from political interference; (h) flexibility of policy and operations, and (i) legal status.

a. Internal organization. The prestige of the corporate form of organization in private affairs is so great that there is a natural tendency

[1] An English commentator defines a mixed undertaking to "include a joint undertaking carried on for mutual benefit and profit by a local authority and some private interest, such as a company carrying on business for profit." Sir William Hart, "Mixed Undertakings," 10 *Pub. Adm.* 138-56 (1932). See also Marshall E. Dimock, "Les Enterprises Mixtes," 20 *Nat. Mun. Rev.* 638-41 (1931).

[2] In the public law of the United States we must further distinguish the private corporation or activity "vested with a public interest" (*Munn vs. Illinois*, 94 U.S. 113 [1877]) which renders it liable to a special degree of governmental supervision. Any corporation, of course, is subject to the general law of corporations and to any peculiar provisions of its charter of incorporation.

to assume it is a superior type of organization, and its mere adoption by government in itself would tend to increase the efficiency of operations. The normal corporate structure is familiar, consisting essentially of a board of directors, a chairman having general executive duties, a general manager in whose hands is concentrated the complete responsibility for operations, and an independent auditor. The policy of the corporation is determined by the board of directors; administration is the duty of the general manager.

The structure of the government corporation sometimes conforms to this pattern, but not always. The Reconstruction Finance Corporation has a board of seven directors, the chairman of the Board performing the functions of the general executive officer. But the Inland Waterways Corporation is a corporation sole, the Secretary of War being the incorporator and vested with all the powers of the organization. Another type is the Tennessee Valley Authority, operating with a board of three directors and for several years with no executive officer. Each member of the board took a part of the work for his personal attention, a form of organization substantially the same as the discredited commission form of municipal government and weakened by the same fatal defects in the Tennessee Valley Authority.

The structure of many *nonincorporated* government organizations also conforms to the pattern of overhead organization found in the corporation. Thus the Michigan State Civil Service Commission has in effect a board of directors and a single executive officer; the former are responsible for policy and general supervision, the latter for current administration. This is the standard form of organization among civil service and other commissions whose main job is one of operations.

The first conclusion must be, then, that the government corporation does not always follow the traditional corporate form, and that nonincorporated agencies may and do sometimes follow this pattern of organization; in short that incorporation as such does not necessarily predicate whatever values there may be in overhead corporate structure, nor is it necessary to secure them.

Criticism of plural executives in organizations whose job is primarily operations leads to another observation. It is not certain that the overhead corporate structure as such has any advantage over the customary department-bureau structure in which definite responsibility is lodged in individual officers in a hierarchy.

Apart from the existence of the board of directors, the internal structure of the two types is likely to be substantially identical. In either case current operations are managed by a single executive; the various departments and their subdivisions follow the same general plan; the auxiliary agencies perform similar operations in the same organizational relationships.

The special relationship of the government corporation to other government agencies, rather than the internal form of organization, provides the principal points of superiority claimed for it. These range all the way from the contacts of the corporation with the legislative body and the chief executive to its freedom from detailed procedures which control the methods of the departments. They deserve careful examination.

b. Relations with the legislature. Over ten years ago Van Dorn wrote that although Congress was able by one means or another to direct the policies of the government corporations, "they nevertheless possess a greater amount of freedom from legislative interference than does the ordinary administrative agency." [1] This advantage arose from the fact that it required a positive legislative act to "interfere" with corporations; mere inaction, such as failure to appropriate, was not enough. Since 1936 this statement is only partially accurate, because the administrative expenses of some government corporations now require an annual appropriation. Another authority writes, "One of the greatest advantages of the public corporation is that it is removed . . . from constant interference from the legislature. . . ." [2] While it is true that some government corporations, notably the Panama Railroad Company, have not been the subject of frequent legislation or breaks in appropriation policy, the same observation could be made with respect to the Coast and Geodetic Survey, the Bureau of Lighthouses, the Naval Observatory, and other nonincorporated agencies.

The term "interference" used in these quotations implies more than is stated. No agency of government can be exempted from Congressional control, except to the extent that Congress may deem advisable from time to time. Any governmental agency, whether corporate or otherwise, especially one operating in a field where governmental policy is experimental or controversial, is and should be subject to the overriding authority of Congress. The smooth course of operations may be disturbed, but in a democracy this is a risk which cannot be avoided. In a field where governmental policy is broadly accepted, interference or undue control by Congress is unlikely in either corporation or department. The corporation, nevertheless, usually stands one step removed from legislative halls and is normally less likely to fall under legislative scrutiny so long as its affairs run smoothly.

c. Relations with chief executive. This aspect of the government cor-

[1] Van Dorn, *op. cit.*, p. 278.

[2] Marshall E. Dimock, "Principles Underlying Government-Owned Corporations," 13 *Pub. Adm.* 51-66 (1935).

poration is dealt with at some length in the subsequent section. Here it may suffice to state that the corporation as such may occupy almost any relation to the chief executive, differing in no degree from the department or independent establishment in this point.

d. Sources of revenue. "The principal advantages of a government-owned corporation over an ordinary government department are to be found in the ease and independence with which the undertaking's financial affairs and purchasing operations can be conducted. The ability to raise capital funds, the right to expand the business, the necessity of earning money before it can be spent, the assurance that income depends upon economic factors rather than upon the benevolence of the legislature, the right to borrow money on the corporation's credit, the freedom to build up reserves for the replacement of plant and the expansion of the business, the knowledge that accounts can be kept on a business basis and without periodic government audits, and the desire to run the business as efficiently as possible because the enterprise will be judged on its own financial showing—these are some of the respect in which the public corporation excels on the financial side in contras with the government department."[1]

This excerpt states succinctly a point at which the corporation ha undoubtedly greater freedom than the department. Recent trends in Washington give evidence of intent to curtail this freedom. Executive orders issued by President Roosevelt during 1935 required a number of government corporations to submit their estimates of expenditure for administrative purposes (i.e., operating expenses) to the Bureau of the Budget. Since 1936 Congress has required certain government corpora tions to obtain authorization for these expenditures from annual appro priations, a potent form of control.[2]

Fiscal independence, however, is not an exclusive attribute of the cor porate form. The departmental revolving fund is the substantial equiva lent of the capital fund of the government corporation. Capacity to borrow may be vested in a department or institution. Earnings may be retained by the operating agency if thought desirable by the legislature but for many years this practice has been deprecated. In practice, how ever, there can be no doubt that the government corporation enjoy privileges with respect to sources and management of funds which ar usually denied to the department. The existence of a considerable num

[1] Dimock, *ibid.*, p. 60. See also John McDiarmid, *Government Corporations an Federal Funds* (1938), and his "Government Corporations and Federal Funds," 3 *Am. Pol. Sci. Rev.* 1094-1107 (1937).

[2] Executive Orders 7126, 7150, 7174; First Deficiency Appropriation Act, 49 Sta 1597, 1647-48 (1936).

ber of separate corporate fiscal structures and policies may renew the difficulties which a quarter of a century ago started the campaign for fiscal consolidation.

e. Audit. The government corporation is frequently, but not invariably, released from the type of audit imposed upon the departments and independent establishments by the Comptroller General of the United States. Freedom from the delay and the meticulous decisions of the General Accounting Office is usually cited as one of the chief assets of the corporate form. The corporation's fiscal operations are audited, of course; but by its own auditor or by an outside firm of auditors. A midway position prevails with respect to the Tennessee Valley Authority, in accordance with which the detailed audit is performed by the Authority, while the Comptroller General retains the right to examine the audit and to report his findings and criticism to Congress.[1]

As a part of his audit, the Comptroller General interprets the statutes in relation to appropriations; this has at times been the source of controversy and eventual defeat of what the departments believe to have been the intent of Congress. The corporation relies upon the legal interpretations of its own law officers, which may be less restrictive than those of the Comptroller General. The regular departments and establishments have discovered a partial solution for the embarrassments of the audit in carefully prepared appropriation language (even drafted in collaboration with the Comptroller General), and in a cooperative rather than a belligerent attitude. At the same time, it must be agreed that in a situation requiring rapid adjustment of policy, where specific language in appropriations is hazardous, if not impossible, freedom from the restrictive rulings of the Comptroller General is desirable, and the corporate form is one way to secure such freedom. No government corporation objects to an audit of the commercial type.

f. Personnel. The government corporation is usually released from compliance with the customary methods of recruiting personnel and from provisions of law and rules governing status of employees. This position may be attained in greater or lesser degree in the regular form of organization. Those commentators who hail the corporation as a desirable form of organization in order to get free from the "red tape" of personnel regulations commit a double fault: they propose a course of action unnecessary for the end in view; and they misunderstand the real character of the personnel regulations, whose restrictive elements are frequently exaggerated. To the extent they are justified, they point

[1] For the controversy over the T.V.A. audit, see House Military Affairs Committee, *Tennessee Valley Authority Hearings*, 74th Cong., 1st sess. (1935), 2 vols.

to an improvement in the system beneficial to all government agencies, rather than to the necessity of evading the established personnel procedures by means of a government corporation.

g. Freedom from political influence. The government corporation is frequently associated with the myth that politicians will respectfully decline to seek its patronage. As a "business" organization it is supposed to be efficient and consequently proof against political pressure. This is a naïve view. While the corporation may, and in most instances has escaped the system of "political clearance" which engulfed many New Deal agencies, this fortunate result is not due to the corporate form of organization, but to the courage and stubbornness of the directors—for example, the Tennessee Valley Authority. The same personal qualities protected equally well the nonincorporated Rural Electrification Administration, and gradually restored order in the once malodorous Home Owners' Loan Corporation.

Professor Dimock states with reference to the Inland Waterways Corporation, "It is freely admitted by informed parties and by officials of the corporation that political appointments and removals have been made during the ten years that the Inland Waterways Corporation has been in existence." [1]

The unsavory patronage reputation of the Home Owners' Loan Corporation in its early years demonstrates that the corporate form is far from invulnerable. Mr. Vincent Dailey, the New York State manager of the corporation, is reported to have stated that the employees in New York were "taken from the ranks of the Democratic party." [2] Congressman Thomas Blanton of Texas said on the floor of the House of Representatives, "Every county appraiser in my nineteen counties was selected by me. Every county attorney in my nineteen counties was selected by me." [3]

On March 4, 1935, Mr. John Fahey, then Chairman of the Home Owners' Loan Corporation, to whom fell the task of cleaning the Augean stables, stated that the corporation had removed or required the resignation of 44 state, district and assistant state managers, that 236 attorneys had been discharged, and that 942 others had resigned or been discharged for political activities.[4] These figures mounted in later months.

The Panama Railroad Company has been relatively free from political patronage; so has the Forest Service, the Bureau of Reclamation, the

[1] M. E. Dimock, *Developing America's Waterways*, pp. 85-86.
[2] *New York Times*, Feb. 14, 1935.
[3] 79 *Congressional Record* 222 (Jan. 9, 1935).
[4] *New York Times*, March 5, 1935.

National Bureau of Standards, and most government bureaus and agencies. The government corporation lacks, in fact, one of the important means of protection against political influence—the formal requirements of the civil service act and rules. When these are absent, moreover, other forms of preference than political patronage may appear.

h. Flexibility of policy, organization and procedures. The corporate form of organization has definite advantages at this point, largely because its policy is not so closely defined by law, and because its internal organization is not so definitely fixed by the language of appropriations. Changes in organization are easier to effectuate, new procedures can be more readily introduced, and experimental methods can be tried and rejected or modified.

i. Legal status. The government corporation possesses a legal status different from that of a department or independent establishment. In general it may be said that the government corporation does not enjoy the status of an instrumentality of the sovereign power. It may sue and be sued; a corporation created by the national government may be taxed by the state in many instances; its liability is greater than in the case of a department. These qualities may be impressed by legislation upon a department or establishment, but usually they are not. The attributes of the nonincorporated Federal Housing Administration, however, are substantially equivalent to those of the government corporation.[1]

In the light of the foregoing comparison of the status and powers, actual and potential, of the department and the government corporation as alternative forms of organization, the advantages of the corporation seem in part genuine, in part adventitious and not always inherent in the corporation as such.

The President's Committee on Administrative Management described the government corporation as "a useful and efficient means" of executing the powers of the Federal government. "Its peculiar value," said the Committee, "lies in freedom of operation, flexibility, business efficiency, and opportunity for experimentation." These advantages are stated more

[1] "The President is authorized to create a Federal Housing Administration. . . . The Administrator may establish such agencies . . . and appoint such other officers and employees *as he may find necessary*, and may prescribe their authorities, duties, responsibilities, and tenure and fix their compensation, *without regard to the provisions of other laws*. . . . The Administrator . . . may make such expenditures . . . as are necessary to carry out the provisions of this title . . . *without regard to any other provisions of law governing the expenditure of public funds*. . . .

". . . the Reconstruction Finance Corporation shall make available to the Administrator such funds *as he may deem necessary*. . . . Provided, that the President, in his discretion, is authorized to provide such funds or any portion thereof by allotment to the Administrator from any funds that are available, or may hereafter be made available, to the President for emergency purposes." 48 Stat. 1245 (1934). Italics are author's. In addition the Administration retains its receipts.

explicitly as including financial self-sufficiency, including the right to borrow; freedom from annual appropriation, involving release from the supervision of the budget bureau; freedom from statutes and rules governing personnel, and such matters as purchase, travel, office space and property; ability to establish a separate system of accounts and to settle and adjust claims; possible participation of citizens in ownership; regional decentralization and local autonomy; subjection to suit by injured individuals, and to the operation of certain relevant state statutes; and the creation of an opportunity for the government to provide an economic service without entering directly into business itself.[1]

These are weighty considerations, in part representing inherent advantages of the corporation, in part reflecting dubious handicaps upon departments and bureaus, in part raising considerable question concerning their validity in government operations, whether under the corporate or any other form. Before reaching a final view of their value, another aspect of the problem of the government corporation involving its setting in the whole administrative system must be canvassed.

3. The Government Corporation and the Administrative Systen

The tendency toward dispersion and disintegration within the American administrative system has already been noted. From 1910 tc 1930 and beyond, a pronounced shift in the theory and practice of organization led toward a much more highly integrated type of adminis tration in cities, states, and nation. The lag in the national system wa noticeable, although repeated efforts were made to bring outlying ad ministrative agencies into closer relation with the main structure. Th sudden increase in number of the independent establishments and cor porations since 1932 has emphasized the potential difficulty arising fron a series of agencies performing a variety of functions, many related tc those performed elsewhere within the government, under condition which remove them to a greater or less degree from the coordinating in fluence of the chief executive. The problem was recognized by th President's Committee on Administrative Management, which con cluded that "some kind of semi-autonomous status in the regular de partments is desirable" for government corporations.

The major problem is the coordination and control of policy of th corporations to the end that the policy of the government as a whol shall be free from contradiction. The coordination of activities is als important, because the corporations and the departments and establish

[1] President's Committee on Administrative Management, *op. cit.*, pp. 43-44. Fo an adverse view see James M. Beck, *Our Wonderland of Bureaucracy* (1932 ch. 10.

nents occupy adjacent and at times overlapping areas with ample op-
portunity for duplication of effort. The question of subjecting the cor-
porations to the supervisory and controlling procedures of such agencies
as the Bureau of the Budget, the Civil Service Commission, and the
Procurement Division is less important in itself, since adequate budget-
ng, accounting, personnel management, and purchasing methods may
readily be developed by the corporation. This aspect of general coordi-
nation, however, plays into the others, and is entitled to weight in con-
clusions concerning the general status of the corporation as a govern-
nent agency. The essential problem is one of coordinating policy and
activities to ensure that the efforts of one agency are not nullified or
contradicted by those of another.

To secure coordination, the government corporation must have such
n organic relationship to the chief executive and the major administra-
ive agencies that its policy can be fixed in the light of knowledge con-
erning the programs of the President and his advisers. In case of di-
ergence of programs the controlling decision can then be made by the
President or his representative in the sense of a single policy. So long as
he administrative branch consisted exclusively of the departments and
heir subdivisions, roughly until 1910, this ultimate coordination was
nherent in the responsibility of the secretaries to the chief executive.
The independent establishments first disrupted this simple and effective
ype of organization. The government corporations are likely to make
ven greater gaps in the line of responsibility.

This suggests a survey of the typical relationships which exist be-
ween the government corporations and the central administrative struc-
ure. In some instances the connection is nearly as close and direct as
hat of the traditional bureau; in others, the relationship is remote and
neffective. The following examples illustrate the main types.

a. Inland Waterways Corporation. The organic act provides, "The
ecretary of War shall be deemed to be the incorporator. . . . The Sec-
etary of War shall govern and direct the corporation. . . ." The corpo-
ation is not technically a part of the War Department, but its relation to
he Secretary is certainly as intimate and direct in law as that of any of
he bureaus and agencies of his department. This type of corporate or-
anization is free from any objection of dispersion of authority.

b. Reconstruction Finance Corporation. The management of this gov-
rnment corporation is vested in a board of directors comprising the
ecretary of the Treasury (ex officio) and six others appointed by the
resident with the advice and consent of the Senate for a term of two
ears. The interlocking functions of the Treasury and the Reconstruc-
on Finance Corporation are recognized in the ex officio membership

of the Secretary, although in law the policy and decisions of the Reconstruction Finance Corporation may be independent of the Treasury. The position of the Secretary makes it certain at least that Treasury policy and Reconstruction Finance Corporation policy are settled with knowledge of each other's program.

c. Federal home loan banks. The Federal Home Loan Bank Board was established in June 1932. It comprises five members, appointed by the President with the advice and consent of the Senate for overlapping terms; the President appoints the chairman. The relations of this Board with the chief executive have been close throughout the Roosevelt administration. Although it is rated as an independent establishment, its policies have been cleared with the President. The Federal Home Loan Bank Board is authorized to establish federal home loan banks at such cities as may be designated. In this class of cases, Congress delegates the power to establish corporations to an administrative agency. They may be called corporations of the second degree, to distinguish them from those directly incorporated by Congress.

The management of each bank is vested in a board of twelve directors, of whom four are appointed by the Home Loan Bank Board in Washington. This Board, moreover, is authorized to supervise the banks and to "suspend or remove any director, officer, employee, or agent." They are, therefore, under close supervision, and their policy with respect to loans is not likely to vary to any important extent from the policy desired by the Home Loan Bank Board, which in turn clears through the White House.[1]

d. Tennessee Valley Authority. The organic act provides in this case ". . . there is hereby created a body corporate by the name of the Tennessee Valley Authority. . . . The Board of Directors first appointed shall be deemed the incorporators, and the incorporation shall be held to have been effected from the date of the first meeting of the Board." The Board consists of three members nominated by the President and confirmed by the Senate for terms of nine years, one retiring every third year. Removal is by concurrent resolution of the Senate and House of Representatives.[2] This type of relationship tends to remove the corporation from the organic structure of the administrative system. It is principally this type which bears the seeds of administrative disintegration.

[1] A parallel arrangement exists with the federal land banks and other credit institutions associated with the Farm Credit Administration.

[2] Removal of Chairman A. E. Morgan by the President is under judicial review at the time of writing.

The view that such corporations as the Tennessee Valley Authority have so distinct and separate a function that coordination of policy is irrelevant will hardly bear examination. To depend upon personal relations with the President is inadequate, especially as the number of separate corporations increases. The proposal to furnish the President with six executive assistants, while praiseworthy, does not place the independent government corporations in an organic relationship with the rest of the system. To place these corporations "within" one of the major departments of government, clearing on major policy with the secretary of the department while retaining a substantial degree of operating freedom, does create an organic relationship which ensures harmony of general program and responsiveness to the policy of the party in power. Essential coordination of policy is thus guaranteed by the type of relationship exemplified in the Inland Waterways Corporation.

Coordination of line activities between corporations and other agencies of administration presents no different problems than those encountered in coordinating the manifold agencies within the departments and among the independent establishments. The difficulties are aggravated by the very "separateness" of the corporation. Coordination by means of the auxiliary functions, especially budget supervision, the enforcement of the law of public employment applicable to the "old-line" agencies, and central purchasing, is deliberately resisted by the friends of the corporate device, since these procedures are alleged to result in over-rigidity.

The process of scattering administrative responsibility among corporations devoid of contact with the main structure has not yet produced serious consequences; it is a tendency which should be resisted. The Committee on Administrative Management, while recognizing the desirability of maintaining the separate identity of these agencies, asserted that their independence had already made the task of the President more burdensome. Continued resort to the corporation in preference to the older type of department will aggravate this fault. This emphasizes one's reservations concerning the general usefulness of the corporate device except to the extent that it can be properly coordinated with the rest of the administrative organization.

4. The Government Corporation: Conclusions

Experience with government corporations in the United States is still too limited to warrant more than tentative conclusions concerning their value and place in the administrative structure. They are the creatures of emergency, war and depression; and it is not clear what advantages and disadvantages they may reveal in the course of settled administration for handling long-range problems which involve the established branches within the main administrative structure.

In cases where it is desired to combine public and private ownership, the mixed corporation has great inherent advantage. These are usually cases involving proprietary interests, as, for example, the suburban or rural resettlement corporations instituted by Resettlement Administration. In many instances they represent cases in which the government is withdrawing from a field of activity in favor of private entrepreneurs, or is acquiring full control for itself. Such transitional situations are suitable for administration by the government corporation.

In some instances, the government desires to operate permanently a service of a commercial nature, i.e., one in which there is a producer-consumer, purchase-sale relationship, usually involving no government appropriation other than an initial capitalization. In the case of municipally owned utilities, these commercial services are usually administered without recourse to the corporate form of organization. The corporation has the advantage of separate unity which is likely to encourage esprit de corps and a sense of commercial enterprise. The government corporation is a convenient form of organization for such commercial undertakings. The same conclusion holds in respect to the extension of credit by government to private corporations or individuals, an emergency activity which probably will be liquidated as rapidly as possible.

The absence of the normal administrative controls is conducive to greater freedom of action by the government corporation, and in some types of situations this is desirable. These controls, however, developed over a long period of years as correctives of faults inherent in a government organization operating without controls. It is not yet proved that they should be permanently absent from the government corporation. Conversely, if they are harmful in relation to the government corporation, they are probably equally so in the case of the department, and should be modified or abandoned.

Too much emphasis has sometimes been given to the necessity of resorting to the government corporation to secure relief from the operating regulations which are in effect elsewhere. Freedom from the law of public employment means, to be sure, ability to hire employees without examination; but the corporation soon develops settled procedures of its own, if only as a matter of self-protection. Lack of competitive classified status conferred by examination means relative uncertainty of tenure for the employee, absence of transfer status to other "civil service" departments or agencies, usually scales of pay different from and often lower than those fixed by Congress, and loss of retirement rights.

Freedom from other procedures, and from some aspects of the public service law as well, is often conducive to operating flexibility, and many irritating instances of stupid control by the central auxiliary agencies may readily be cited. But freedom from the customary controls has not been found essential for such enterprises as managing a hospital—witness St. Elizabeths under the late Dr. White,[1] a model of its kind, or the hospital facilities of the Veterans' Administration; running a railroad—witness the Alaska Railroad, operated by the Department of the Interior; managing a municipal utility—for example the Los Angeles Power and Water Department; running a laundry—see the extensive laundry services of the Navy Department; operating a factory—the government arsenals; building dams and developing hydro-electric power—the Bureau of Reclamation and the Corps of Engineers; or "selling" materials or service—Rural Electrification Administration.

Despite these reservations government corporations and mixed enterprises may be destined to play a significant role in the changing world of the future. Much will depend upon the course of government intervention in the field of economic enterprise. The major drive of the last half century in favor of private undertakings subject to government regulation may persist with a gradually shifting weight of regulation. Or the results of this relationship between government and business may prove increasingly unsatisfactory, and direct government ownership and operation of commercial affairs at key points may develop. To the extent that government becomes an entrepreneur, the corporate form may be expected to find a useful function. The restrictions which surround most government operations certainly do not forecast official commercial or business success in a competitive world.

In the words of my colleague, Marshall E. Dimock, "The future success of the semi-public corporations would seem to depend in large part upon whether financial autonomy can be preserved and upon their being able to secure outstanding leadership and personnel. If these requirements can be satisfied, the borderline enterprises may constitute a permanent compromise between things public and things private, and they may be an instrumentality of outstanding social accomplishment." [2] In any event here is an aspect of public administration which will hold and deserve attention in the government of the future.

[1] *William Alanson White; the Autobiography of a Purpose* (1938).

[2] Marshall E. Dimock, "Public Corporations and Business Enterprise," 14 *Pub. Adm.* 417-28 (1936).

Chapter Ten

ADMINISTRATIVE RELATIONS BETWEEN THE STATE AND NATIONAL GOVERNMENTS

THE description and analysis of administrative organization to this point have disregarded the administrative consequences of the federal system of government. This is in accordance with the underlying assumption that the process of administration is essentially a single one, fundamentally the same in federal, state, municipal and rural government despite the variations caused by size. There are, however, important administrative relationships which arise just because the power to govern is distributed, constitutionally, between the states and the nation, and because long experience has demonstrated the necessity of coordinating these two independent governing authorities. In this and the following chapter, these relationships as they concern administration are the focus of attention.[1]

1. Administrative Centralization and Social Structure

In an earlier chapter the changing social structure of the United States was sketched in relation to the administrative process.[2] Certain aspects of these transformations need emphasis again in order to grasp the underlying significance of the broad trend toward administrative centralization in Washington which has steadily gone forward for decades, in recent years with almost headlong speed.

Basically the change in social structure which underlies centralizing trends is the transition from a local or village economy to a national and international economy. When Jefferson was President, production and exchange, banking and commercial operations, insurance and the making of contracts were characteristically carried on in a single community or within a narrowly confined area. It is unnecessary to review the stages by which our present complex national and international economy has been built up. Its symbols are the chain stores, the United States Steel Corporation, the American Federation of Labor, the Na

[1] The generalized form of relationship is analyzed in ch. 3, in the definition of centralization.

[2] See ch. 2.

tional City Bank, the Pan American Airways, and the Agricultural Adjustment Administration. It rests upon a profound change from a rural to an urban-industrial civilization.

Deeply involved in this primary alteration of our social structure is the shift from an economy characterized by dispersion of economic power to one characterized by concentration of power. Recent studies indicate that 200 great corporations dominate a large part of the industrial scene.[1] Concentration of private banking power in New York was modified by the Federal Reserve Act, but depression events have demonstrated anew the central place held by the United States Treasury and the Board of Governors of the Federal Reserve System. Agricultural interests have been stubborn in resisting concentration of farm leadership and farming operations, but with dramatic suddenness the Agricultural Adjustment Administration combined most of the scattered and hitherto ineffective agricultural groups behind a nation-wide program. How distant is national crop production control from the dispersed and self-sufficient farming community hailed by Jefferson as the bulwark of the republic!

In short we live in an era of concentrated economic power. From one great financial or industrial center may flow decisions which deeply affect the lives of hundreds or thousands, or which may spell prosperity or decline for whole communities. This is the situation analyzed by John Dewey in describing the growing helplessness of many "publics" in the face of the concentration of power which affects them but which they cannot influence. The need of interested groups to find a means of exerting pressure at centers of decision explains in large part the march of political power from the city hall and the county courthouse to the state capital, and thence to Washington.

The centralizing trend may be viewed from another salient, the transition from an economy of exploitation to an economy of conservation. For over 250 years the population of North America was engaged in the discovery and use of vast natural resources, present in an abundance far greater than contemporary needs could employ. This was an era in which laissez faire was the congenial climate of human activity. Little administration was required beyond that necessary to the orderly acquisition of title to the natural resources of the country: land, water, minerals, timber and power.

We now live definitely in an age of conservation. The new day is characterized by changes in land policy (notably soil conservation and rational land use), in forest policy, in water policy, and in the still rela-

[1] Adolf A. Berle, Jr., and G. C. Means, *The Modern Corporation and Private Property* (1932).

tively fruitless effort to conserve oil and gas. This is an era which necessitates unified, national governmental regulation to protect the public interest in exhaustible resources, now recognized to be none too ample for present and future needs. It is an age also in which problems require positive solution rather than mere negative prohibition.

The area of central administrative action is enlarged also by the gradual acceptance of the idea that in certain fields a national minimum standard is in the public interest, and by the invention and application of nation-wide procedures, largely administrative in nature, to secure such standards. In the field of education, this movement encountered strong opposition in favor of state autonomy, but in certain sectors, such as vocational education, national influence is widely felt. The point is illustrated by national action in the field of public employment offices where central influence is exercised by the U. S. Employment Service, and in the field of wages and hours in connection with the Wages and Hours Act of 1938.

In short, the social structure of America has been transformed from one in which problems requiring government action were both relatively few and severely limited in scope to one in which government intervention is required at more points and with a constantly expanding coverage. Inevitably the administrative structure has enlarged in response to these new needs, and in the light of their requirements has tended to depart from the county and municipality in order to become state-wide, regional or national in scope.

2. Constitutional Framework of Expanding Federal Administration

In a country with an unwritten constitution endowed with no superior status, such as Great Britain, the constitution forms no barrier to the progressive adaptation of administrative structure to changing needs. In the United States, the formal written division of governmental power between the nation and the states, enforced by the Supreme Court sometimes presents a formidable impediment to the ready adaptation of policy and administration to changing requirements. Over most of our national history, however, constitutional adaptation has favored an increasing degree of administrative centralization.

The constitutional basis of national administration may be amplified either by formal amendment or by judicial interpretation. By the eighteenth amendment, for example, the authority of the nation was temporarily expanded to deal with the manufacture, transportation and sale of intoxicating liquor. The weight of national expansion has rested however, on judicial construction. The commerce clause has been the chief means of expansion of national influence and control, covering in turn railroads, telegraph and telephone companies, pipe lines, packing houses, air commerce, and radio.

In a substantial line of decisions, the Supreme Court appeared to hold that the commerce power could properly be used "for the positive purposes of the national government," as well as for the immediate purpose of dealing with an aspect of interstate commerce.[1] Thus the court approved legislation prohibiting the interstate transportation of lottery tickets, in order to prevent "pollution" of the stream of interstate traffic; requiring the branding of oleomargarine, to prevent fraud; and requiring the inspection of meat and drugs intended for interstate shipment.

This line of cases was relied upon by Congress to support the prohibition of interstate transportation of products of child labor, but the Supreme Court by a five to four decision declared this legislation beyond the interstate commerce power.[2] This decision, supported later by a corresponding limitation on the taxing power in *Bailey vs. Drexel Furniture Company*, marked a recession of the tide of national expansion under the commerce clause.[3]

The constitutional issue was presented again in an acute form in the depression legislation of 1933 and 1934. The Railroad Retirement Act attempted to establish a pension plan for employees engaged in interstate commerce. Although the Supreme Court had been able to find constitutional authority for an injunction against strikers in a mine whose products entered interstate commerce, it denied Congressional power to impose a retirement act upon interstate carriers.[4] A second railroad pension law was subsequently enacted by Congress.

The National Industrial Recovery Act sought to favor economic recovery through action based on national control over the "indirect" aspects of interstate commerce. The underlying theory was that the depression hindered the free flow of interstate commerce, and that whatever national action was needed to remove these impediments was constitutionally permissible. In the Schechter case, the Supreme Court denied that Congress could legislate on such an ample scale.[5]

The Agricultural Adjustment Act of 1933 provided cash benefits to

[1] An incisive study of the decisions of the court is by Edward S. Corwin, *The Commerce Power versus States Rights* (1936).

[2] *Hammer vs. Dagenhart*, 247 U.S. 251 (1918).

[3] 259 U.S. 20 (1922).

[4] *Railroad Retirement Board vs. Alton R. Co.*, 295 U.S. 330 (1935).

[5] *Schechter Poultry Corp. vs. U.S.*, 295 U.S. 495 (1935).

farmers who cooperated in a program of crop reduction, the funds being derived from a processing tax. In the Hoosac Mills case, the Supreme Court again took a restrictive view of the power of Congress.[1]

In each of these cases elaborate administrative structures were struck down and the scope of direct federal administration was restrained and limited. But in 1936 the Supreme Court modified its view of permissible regulation under the interstate commerce clause in supporting the National Labor Relations Act (Wagner Act).[2] This decision and subsequent decisions of the Court apparently open up the possibility of a wide range of federal administration under the commerce power.[3]

While the constitutional framework has been thus modified, national authority and influence have been deeply affected by the ever widening use of conditional grants-in-aid by Congress to the states and their subdivisions. More detailed attention will be given this phase of the subject at a later point. Here it may be noted that under the decision of the Supreme Court in *Massachusetts vs. Mellon* federal grants-in-aid to states have been judicially accepted.[4] Their extent is therefore an issue of administrative convenience and advantage. Congress may purchase a degree of administrative coordination within the states by appropriate grants which it might never be able to secure either by constitutional amendment or by legislative enactment.

The constitutional barriers have also been weakened by the doctrine of *Missouri vs. Holland*, authorizing Congress to enact supporting legislation under the treaty power which it could not enact under its enumerated powers.[5] The administrative activities of the United States game wardens in the Bureau of Biological Survey rest in part upon this constitutional basis.

This brief summary of the changing constitutional framework of administration indicates some of the limitations attending the general trend toward administrative centralization, as well as the means by which some constitutional obstructions have been surmounted. The process of administrative centralization, however, flows around and over formal constitutional structures. The pressure of events forces the states and the national government together at a thousand points, and out of these contacts develop cooperative arrangements, contractual agreements, interchange of personnel, loan of facilities, exchange of data, joint ap

[1] *U.S. vs. Butler*, 297 U.S. 1 (1936).

[2] *National Labor Relations Board vs. Jones and Laughlin*, 301 U.S. 1 (1937), and associated cases.

[3] Cf. the decisions upholding the Social Security Act: *Steward Machine Co. v. Davis*, 301 U.S. 548 (1937); *Helvering vs. Davis*, 301 U.S. 619 (1937).

[4] 262 U.S. 447 (1923).

[5] 252 U.S. 416 (1920).

pointments, and other operating devices in most of which the superior administrative resources of the national government tend toward national leadership.

The depression exaggerated a growing public expectation that in most major administrative areas leadership would be forthcoming from Washington. This is still balanced by a lively sense of state autonomy and local pride, but the power of resistance of state officials is diminished by public demands in each state for effective solution of pressing problems. The heat of public opinion is melting the dividing lines of "sovereign" jurisdictions in favor of national action on national problems.

With these brief observations we may now turn to consider selected examples of the redistribution of administrative responsibility between the national government and the states.

3. Trends toward National Administration

Three fields of public administration common to the state and national governments reflect the tendency to centralize authority in Washington: highways, education, and social security. Important aspects of federal-state relations in finance, crime control, forest preservation, planning, airport development and other fields can be studied elsewhere.[1]

a. Highway construction. In his monograph on the Bureau of Public Roads, W. S. Holt points out that the relation of the national government to highway construction has passed through an almost complete cycle.[2] During the early period of internal improvements, the federal government participated directly; later it withdrew in favor of the states, which in turn left the work to counties or their subdivisions. The reversal of this long trend was marked in 1891 when New Jersey granted state aid for county highways; the new tendency, largely induced by

[1] The monograph literature dealing with administrative aspects of federal-state relations includes Walter Thompson, *Federal Centralization* (1923); *Federal Versus State Jurisdiction in American Life*, 129 *Annals* (1927), *passim;* L. D. White, *Trends in Public Administration* (1933); V. O. Key, Jr., *The Administration of Federal Grants to States* (1937); Henry J. Bittermann, *State and Federal Grants-in-Aid* (1938); Jane Perry Clark, *The Rise of a New Federalism* (1938). Articles of special importance include Arthur N. Holcombe, "The States as Agents of the Nation," 1 *Southwestern Political Sci. Q.* 307-27 (1920–21); Walter F. Dodd, "The Growth of National Power," 32 *Yale Law J.* 452-59 (1922–23); James D. Barnett, "Cooperation between the Federal and State Governments," 17 *Nat. Mun. Rev.* 283-91 (1928); Roscoe Pound, "Cooperation in Enforcement of Law," 17 *Am. Bar Assoc. J.* 9-14, 63-64 (1931); Henry W. Toll, "Is Federal Centralization the only Practicable Alternative?" 8 *Rocky Mountain Law Rev.* 9-14 (1935–36); Jane P. Clark, "Joint Activity between Federal and State Officials," 51 *Pol. Sci. Q.* 230-69 (1936); Edward S. Corwin, "National-State Cooperation–its Present Possibilities," 46 *Yale Law J.* 599-623 (1936–37); John Dickinson, "States and the Nation," 42 *Commercial Law J.* 5-11 (1937).

[2] W. Stull Holt, *The Bureau of Public Roads* (1923), pp. 2 ff.

the advent of the automobile and the demand for expensive hard roads was accelerated by the first national highway grants in 1916.

The interest of the national government in highways commenced in 1893 with an appropriation to establish the Office of Road Inquiry, later the Office of Public Roads. An excerpt from the language of the formal letter of instructions to the first agent in charge suggests the narrow scope of national functions at that time.

> . . . it is not the province of this department to seek to control or influence said action [in building highways] except in so far as advice and wise suggestions shall contribute toward it. . . . The department is to furnish information, not to direct and formulate any system of organization, however efficient or desirable it may be. Any such effort on its part would soon make it subject to hostile criticism.[1]

From 1893 to 1912 the Office of Public Roads was devoted to experimentation, advice to state and county highway agents, the construction of demonstration roads, and the dissemination of information. In 1912 it was authorized to construct post roads. In 1916 the first major highway act went on the books, setting up a system of grants to the states for highway construction. The national government soon acquired a position of leadership in this field, which has progressively become more widely accepted.

The states are now the basic units for major highway construction. They receive a substantial proportion of their highway funds from Washington, and the Bureau of Public Roads sets the standards, approves the projects, audits the accounts, inspects the completed work, and exercises some administrative supervision over state highway departments.

The shift in responsibility is symbolized in two passages taken from the Highway Act of 1916 and of 1921, respectively, which should be compared with the excerpt from the letter of instructions of 1893 quoted above. In 1916 the National Highway Act required each cooperating state to maintain a "state highway department," which was construed as "any department of another name, or commission, or official or officials, of a State empowered, under its laws, to exercise the functions ordinarily exercised by a State highway department. . . ."[2] Five years later the same term was defined in the 1921 Highway Act to include "any State department, commission, board, or official *having adequate powers and suitably equipped and organized to discharge to the satisfaction of the Secretary of Agriculture the duties herein re-*

[1] Quoted in *ibid.*, p. 7.

[2] 39 Stat. 355 (1916), sec. 2. In 1916 six states had no highway department, and nine others were not eligible for recognition by the Bureau of Public Roads. In 1917 each state had a recognized highway department.

quired."[1] Obviously the center of gravity had shifted considerably in the passage of years since 1893.

Relative expenditures on highways were thrown out of balance in 1933 and the later years of the depression as a result of the huge emergency expenditures for public works and the resulting grants and loans to the states. From the fiscal point of view, the national government has emerged in the crisis as the senior partner in the firm.

It is no exaggeration to state that in the twenty years since the first federal highway act a national highway system has been established at the direction of Congress by the Bureau of Public Roads, and that the standards of construction and maintenance by the states and their subdivisions have been greatly improved as a direct result of national intervention through the grant-in-aid device. It is impossible to conceive that the transportation needs of the present could be met without the coordination, guidance and supervision furnished by the national administration and the support of national funds.

b. Education. Responsibility for public education was originally reserved *in toto* to the states, and organized school groups have been jealous of any federal influence. Since the first Morrill Act (1862) granting federal aid to state colleges of agriculture, the amount of federal grants for educational purposes has steadily increased. In 1914 the federal government appropriated to support direct instruction in agriculture and home economics through the county agent; in 1917 further aid was forthcoming for vocational education including training in trades, industry and agriculture;[2] in 1920 aid was provided for vocational rehabilitation. In 1935 the Social Security Act put on a permanent basis federal grants for educational assistance to certain underprivileged or handicapped groups. Other federal aid to education was derived from Works Progress Administration and the National Youth Administration.

Meanwhile proposals for large conditional grants to the states for general educational purposes were blocked by fear of "regimentation" of education from Washington. In 1938 the President's Advisory Committee on Education recommended general and unrestricted federal grants for elementary and secondary education rising over a period of years from forty to one hundred forty million dollars annually, as well as further grants for teacher preparation, school buildings, state departments of education, adult education and library service.

These proposals, now pending (1938), represent an effort to extend federal aid without national dictation of (although not without influ-

[1] 42 Stat. 212 (1921), sec. 2; italics are author's.

[2] The Advisory Committee on Education, *Report of the Committee* (1938), pp. 5 *et seq.*

ence upon) state educational policy. The proposed means of federal influence are four: joint approval of plans; effective state systems of reports to the federal government; federal audit of funds; and reserved authority to suspend payments during any period in which the state fails to maintain an adequate administrative agency or fails to make reports with reasonable promptness. If this program is accepted by Congress, it will be of great interest to observe to what extent the mere weight of finance upon policy can be avoided.

c. Social Security Act. In no field has so rapid a readjustment of the responsibility of the national, state and local governments taken place as in the relief of dependents. Throughout our history until 1932 the care of dependents was a principal responsibility of the local community, supplemented for certain special types of cases by state aid or care in state institutions. Traditionally also the care of the unfortunate has been largely a private rather than a public undertaking. From 1932 to 1935 this ancient edifice was turned upside down, as private charity, local public resources, and state aid in turn collapsed. The national government was forced to intervene. It not only took the burden of emergency relief, it organized a national system of social security which marks an historic break with traditional forms of public action in this field.

With respect to emergency relief, the national government first entered the field in 1932 with an appropriation authorizing loans to the states amounting to $300,000,000. These came in the nick of time to save the situation in several large industrial states. In 1933 the Federal Emergency Relief Administration (F.E.R.A.) and the Public Works Administration (P.W.A.) came on the scene, together with the Civil Works Administration (C.W.A.) which carried about 4,000,000 unemployed through the winter months of 1933–34. In 1935 the national government turned back to the states full responsibility for the relief and care of unemployables, and retained the responsibility for finding work for the employable through the medium of Works Progress Administration (W.P.A.). These are only the major efforts. In addition the national government maintained the Civilian Conservation Corps (C.C.C.) with a "normal" enrollment of 300,000 young men; the Federal Surplus Commodities Corporation; the Commodity Credit Corporation; and the Resettlement Administration; it also increased expenditures in many of the regular departments and establishments.

All this impressive array was not designed to accelerate the flow of power to Washington; it merely reflected the collapse of the states and their subdivisions. Implicit in the almost universal recognition of the national government as the only agency competent to deal with the internal crisis, was a subtle loss of status by the states. This was evidenced in the never ending procession of the officials of states and cities who went to Washington to ask for funds, and who in their desperation forgot the "sovereign power" and reserved rights proclaimed in their constitutions. The return of prosperity may result in the complete withdrawal of the national government from the field of direct relief, but the psychological loss of prestige by the states will not soon be restored.

The enactment of the Social Security Act involved a change in legal relationships which illustrates and confirms the shift of power in this area. By this legislation a permanent nation-wide program of aiding the dependent aged, the unemployed, dependent children and handicapped persons is established. The administration is divided in most cases between the central and the state governments, the former providing a share of the funds, the latter organizing and maintaining the necessary services. The authority of the national government is exercised through the conditional grants-in-aid.

The general pattern is shown in the provision for old-age assistance. Legislation specifies under seven headings the essential characteristics of state plans, including the requirement that the state shall "provide such methods of administration (other than those relating to selection, tenure of office, and compensation of personnel) *as are found by the Board to be necessary* for the efficient operation of the plan" [i.e., the state plan]. It is the duty of the Social Security Board to approve any state plan which corresponds to these requirements, but the Board is also authorized to refuse payments in case of failure to comply. The central government may thus exert considerable influence.

As a rule this influence is effective principally at the time when plans are submitted for approval by the Social Security Board. The Social Security Board, however, maintains close contacts with the cooperating states in an advisory and supervisory capacity, and has exerted constant influence in the development of state programs and state administration. In three cases within the first three years of the life of the Board, however, it has demonstrated its capacity to take drastic action to enforce compliance with the law by withholding funds.

On July 30, 1937, the Social Security Board suspended grants to Illinois for old-age assistance. The state had failed to establish adequate accounting records, to make reasonably prompt decisions on eligibility, to give hearings to rejected applicants, and to give adequate instructions to county officials. There was evidence furthermore of "chiseling" on the part of some officials high in the state government, who took care of their relatives irrespective of need. All these matters had been called to the attention of state officials, but no improvement was made. The Governor of Illinois called the suspension of funds "tyrannical," and reminded the Board that his was "still a sovereign state." Despite this bold language, the state director of old-age assistance was discharged, other changes were made, and eventually the payments were restored.

The Oklahoma case was even more flagrant, involving maladministration in grants for old-age assistance, aid to the blind, and aid to dependent children. The causes of this unsatisfactory situation were repeatedly called to the attention of the state commission but without avail. On March 2, 1938, grants were suspended. The state records showed "many payments over long periods of time" to dead persons, to persons under the statutory minimum of sixty-five and to persons not in need. Illegal payments mounted into several millions. Here, too, the state reluctantly but gradually came to terms.

Equally disturbing were the facts which led to the suspension of payments to Ohio on September 30, 1938. The Social Security Board found "a lack of effective administrative direction and control of the agency. . . . repeated interference with orderly procedure by the governor, . . . executive responsibility diffused . . . wholesale violation of the Ohio civil service laws and rules . . . serious and excessive delays . . . discrimination in the handling of complaints" and other administrative failures all reflected in exceptions by federal auditors to state payments amounting to $1,900,000. The retirement of the Governor of Ohio in 1938 cleared the way for administrative reform.

d. Use of federal taxing power. Another potentially powerful means of influencing state action from Washington is found in the use of the taxing power. The federal estate tax imposed upon all specified inheritances authorizes a credit or rebate to the amount of eighty per cent of any estate or inheritance tax paid to a state or territory or the District of Columbia. The effect of this credit was to induce the states to enact an inheritance tax, in order to secure this revenue which otherwise would all flow to the federal government.[1]

A comparable use of the taxing power to hasten the adoption of state unemployment compensation laws is found in the Social Security Act. Every employer as defined in the act is now required to pay an excise tax of three per cent of his total pay roll to the Unemployment Trust Fund. The taxpayer is allowed a federal credit of ninety per cent of the amount which he pays into a state unemployment fund, provided the state law meets the approval of the Social Security Board. Among the conditions specified as a prerequisite for approval are that the state funds shall be turned over to the U. S. Treasury; and that unemployment compensation shall not be denied an individual for refusing to accept new work if the position offered is vacant on account of a strike, if the

[1] U.S. Code (1934 ed.), Title 26, sec. 413 (b).

wages, hours or other conditions of work are less favorable than those generally prevailing, or if a condition of employment is joining a company union or refraining from joining a bona fide labor organization. Employees in any state are ineligible to participate in unemployment benefits except under a state law; employers are in any event subject to the federal tax; the combined interest of both groups is, therefore, to secure state legislation. The potential influence of this means of stimulating and directing state action is great.

4. Federal-State Cooperation

Highways, education and social security are among the principal directions in which national power is expanding in formal relationships with the states.[1] These are, however, only the slightest indications of the vast number of administrative relations between Washington and the forty-eight commonwealths. Miss Clark rightly says, "Wherever federal and state interests meet, there informal cooperation is found—in varying and changing quantity, but always present in some degree."[2] Nor is this a recent phenomenon. In 1922 there were 553 separate cooperative research projects involving an expenditure of over $42,000,000.[3]

The field of police administration is reserved to the states and their subdivisions, apart from special police problems chiefly concerned with coinage and with interstate or foreign commerce.[4] There are inevitably close contacts between the federal Secret Service, the Federal Bureau of Identification, and the Bureau of Narcotics on the one hand, and city police officers on the other.[5] In the control of narcotics, the federal offi-

[1] Other centralizing fields are dealt with in such references, among many, as these: Simeon E. Leland, "The Coordination of Federal, State and Local Fiscal Systems," 6 *Municipal Finance* 35-46 (1933); Milton Conover, "National, State, and Local Cooperation in Food and Drug Control," 22 *Am. Pol. Sci. Rev.* 910-28 (1928); James A. Tobey, *Federal and State Control of Milk Prices* (1937); Francis D. Burke, "Federal-State Employment Services," 18 *Southwestern Social Sci. Q.* 210-14 (1937–38); Justin Miller "Crime Control as an Interstate Problem," 22 *Wash. Univ. Law Q.* 382-90 (1936–37); J. Carroll Cone, "The Dividing Line between Federal and State Promotion of Aeronautics," 4 *J. of Air Law* 473-78 (1933); Martin L. Lindahl, "Cooperation between the Interstate Commerce Commission and the State Commissions in Railroad Regulation," 33 *Mich. Law Rev.* 338-97 (1934–35); Paul G. Kauper, "Utilization of State Commissioners in the Administration of the Federal Motor Carrier Act," 34 *Mich. Law Rev.* 37-84 (1935–36).

[2] Jane P. Clark, *The Rise of a New Federalism* (1938), p. 10; and "Federal-State Cooperation in Labor Legislation," 27 *Am. Labor Legislation Rev.* 167-72 (1937).

[3] E. W. Allen, *Co-operation with the Federal Government in Scientific Work*, National Research Council, Bulletin 26, 1922.

[4] See 1 *Law and Contemporary Problems* 399-508 (1933–34), *Extending Federal Powers over Crime.*

[5] Arthur C. Millspaugh, *Crime Control by the National Government* (1937).

cers concentrate on smuggling and interstate traffic, while city police fight street peddling and opium resorts; but the lines cannot be sharply drawn.

The Interstate Commerce Commission and state utility commissions are concerned with many problems involving at the same time both state and federal jurisdictions. Over a long period of time, informal joint hearings have been held, and in 1922 an agreement between the I.C.C. and the state commissions was adopted. This type of cooperation was extended in the Motor Carrier Act of 1935. In matters affecting carriers operating in more than three states, the Commission may establish a joint board, representing each state. This joint board is given the same powers of inquiry as a member or examiner of the Commission; its recommended orders are dealt with in the same manner as the proposals of an examiner. The Commission is further authorized to avail itself of the cooperation, services, records, and facilities of state authorities.

In the emerging field of planning there is a large-scale demonstration of cooperative work. The National Planning Board (now National Resources Committee) was established in 1933 and shortly thereafter urged the states to organize independent state planning agencies. By 1937 there were forty-five such state agencies. The National Resources Committee furnishes some technical assistance and consultants to help the states, and suggests certain basic lines of inquiry, but each state board works on its own responsibility. Initiative and leadership, but not control, come from Washington.

Other cooperative arrangements, somewhat more formal, are worked out in written agreements between federal and state officials. Most federal departments "are honeycombed" with cooperative agreements on a great variety of subjects. Miss Clark reports more than four hundred such in the Bureau of Agricultural Economics of the United States Department of Agriculture alone.[1]

Quite apart from such arrangements, but in most cases supporting them, there is a subtle form of transfer of influence from the states to Washington. It is reflected in a growing sense of federal leadership in common fields of administration flowing from the greater prestige of the national government, from the more extensive scope of its operations and the more substantial financial support, from a generally higher standard of technical competence, and as a rule from a greater freedom from partisan interference than is characteristic of most state and local governments. These circumstances count for much in the "invisible transfer" of power.

[1] Jane P. Clark, *The Rise of a New Federalism* (1938), p. 47. On this topic I have followed Miss Clark, especially the third chapter of her book.

5. A Note on Grants-in-Aid

In both the present and following chapters reference is made to grants-in-aid as one of the means by which readjustment of administrative influence is taking place. This note is designed to deal in summary fashion with its essential features and to refer the reader to the principal literature.

A grant-in-aid is a sum of money assigned by a superior to an inferior governmental authority.[1] The grant may be outright or it may be conditional, typically the latter. The general purpose of a grant-in-aid is to improve the quality or quantity of governmental service in backward areas by transferring public funds from the more wealthy to the less wealthy regions through the medium of the central treasury.

Grants-in-aid for schools were originated in New York in 1795 and have been traditional in American public finance for about a century.[2] Continuing federal grants to the states commenced in 1862 with the passage of the first Morrill Act making grants to the state agricultural colleges. In both state and national systems, grants-in-aid have steadily expanded in number and in volume; growth has been especially rapid since the depression.

The techniques of the national conditional grant-in-aid include (1) formal acceptance of national grants by the state, usually through legislation; (2) local initiative in preparing plans and establishing organization; (3) central approval of plans by a national administrative agency, but not requiring assent of the President; (4) joint provision of funds, usually but not always on the basis of equality; (5) execution of the project by state or local authorities, directly or on contract; (6) separate central and local inspection and audit; (7) eventual payment of obligated sums to the state upon satisfactory completion of the project, usually with partial payments in advance.

The central government retains sanctions to ensure effective state participation. Federal authorities may refuse to approve suggested plans, and in some cases may decline to cooperate because the state has faulty administrative organization or procedures. They may decline to make payments if the conditions of agreement are not observed, and in case of a continuing grant, may suspend further payments. Normally the state has no recourse beyond the federal department, as to the President or to Congress, but Senators and Congressmen are brought into action by laggard states in time of crisis. Study of Canadian grants-in-aid

[1] Herman Finer, "Grants-in-Aid," 7 *Encyclopaedia of the Social Sciences* 152-55 (1932).

[2] Henry J. Bittermann, *State and Federal Grants-in-Aid* (1938), pp. 60 ff.

demonstrates that good results are endangered when decisions are made by the political rather than the administrative authorities.[1]

6. The Interstate Compact as an Alternative to Federal Power

Some commentators expect the state to yield the battle to the national government, remaining as geographical areas and administrative subdivisions of the nation where suitable. Certainly the tide is floating the states in this direction although the destination is still remote; but the tide may conceivably turn under the influence of future events; or the states may exert themselves to swim against the current.

It can hardly be expected that the states will retain or strengthen their position unless they are administratively and fiscally competent. Senator Henry Toll, a staunch friend of the states, is correct in declaring, "Any claim of States' rights must now be justified by a demonstration of States' competence."[2] As if bent on suicide, many states obstinately refuse to put their houses in order. But aside from this consideration, the states may be able to stem the tide by affirmative, cooperative action on their part, undertaking in concert certain tasks which one could not do alone, and which otherwise would be undertaken by the central government. The principal means by which the states can proceed is by interstate compact, authorized in 1789 by the federal constitution.

A compact between Virginia and Kentucky concerning rights in lands severed from Virginia and also jurisdiction over the Ohio River was ratified by the first Congress on December 18, 1789. Boundary line compacts occurred from time to time in the period before the Civil War, as well as later. Determination of criminal jurisdiction on public waters lying between states became a frequent source of interstate compacts commencing in 1905. No significant use of the compact power for broad purposes of public policy occurred until 1911, when Congress gave general *prior* consent to agreements between states for the conservation of

[1] The principal literature includes Sidney Webb, *Grants in Aid: a Criticism and a Proposal* (2d ed. 1920); Austin F. MacDonald, *Federal Aid* (1928); Paul H. Douglas, "The Development of a System of Federal Grants-in-Aid," 35 *Pol. Sci. Q.* 255-71; 522-44 (1920); Fletcher H. Swift, *Federal and State Policies in Public School Finance in the United States* (1931); V. O. Key, Jr., *The Administration of Federal Grants to States* (1937); Henry J. Bittermann, *State and Federal Grants-in-Aid* (1938); Jane Perry Clark, *The Rise of a New Federalism: Federal-State Cooperation in the United States* (1938); Luella Gettys, *The Administration of Canadian Conditional Grants* (1938); James A. Maxwell, *Federal Subsidies to the Provincial Governments of Canada* (1937).

[2] Henry W. Toll, "Is Federal Centralization the Only Practicable Alternative?" 8 *Rocky Mountain Law Rev.* 10 (1935-36).

forests and water supply. No state has taken advantage of this consent.[1]

Harbor and transportation problems in and around New York offered a new field of joint action leading to compacts between New York and New Jersey in 1919 for the construction of a tunnel under the Hudson River, and two years later for the creation of the Port of New York Authority.

These agreements led to the rediscovery of the "compact clause" by the National Conference of Commissioners on Uniform State Laws. A distinguished committee of the Conference, headed by Dean John H. Wigmore, concluded that "the most feasible and promising remedy" for the extraordinary inconvenience due to independence of state laws and consequent "disharmony of action or inaction" lay in the use of interstate compacts. Despite reservations by Mr. Freund, the committee endorsed the usefulness of state compacts even with foreign powers, and hopefully observed, "By the method of State Compacts, the progressive commercial States will have it in their power to go onwards independently, without waiting for the cooperation of other slow and tardy States. . . ."[2]

In the light of further experience and of present problems does the interstate compact today appear as an effective means of solving problems which are superstate in scope or nature?[3] The evidence indicates that compacts and agreements are adequate to deal with definitely localized interstate problems which have only an incidental national interest. The disposition of water resources in an interstate watershed, the unification of an interstate port development, the prevention of water contamination in a specified area, the extension of criminal jurisdiction over

[1] Lists of interstate compacts are available in 9 *State Government* 118-21 (1936), and in a report by the General Committee on Compacts and Agreements between States of the National Conference of Commissioners on Uniform State Laws, entitled *Compacts and Agreements between States* (1937).

[2] Report of the Committee on Inter-state Compacts, in *Handbook of the National Conference of Commissioners on Uniform State Laws* (1921), pp. 297 ff.

[3] The principal secondary literature of general interest on interstate compacts includes: Felix Frankfurter and James M. Landis, "The Compact Clause of the Constitution—a Study in Interstate Adjustments," 34 *Yale Law J.* 685-758 (1924-25); Emerson D. Fite, *Government by Cooperation* (1932); W. Brooke Graves, *Uniform State Action: a Possible Substitute for Centralization* (1934); C. Herman Pritchett, "Regional Authorities through Interstate Compacts," 14 *Social Forces* 200-10 (1935-36); Jane Perry Clark, "Interstate Compacts and Social Legislation," 50 *Pol. Sci. Q.* 502-24 (1935), 51 *ibid.* 36-60 (1936); National Resources Committee, *Regional Factors in National Planning and Development* (1935), chs. 6-7; Edwin M. Duerbeck, "Economic Control by Interstate Compact," 15 *Social Forces* 104-11 (1936-37); Marshall E. Dimock and George C. S. Benson, *Can Interstate Compacts Succeed?* (1937); Joseph J. Spengler, "The Economic Limitations to Certain Uses of Interstate Compacts," 31 *Am. Pol. Sci. Rev.* 41-51 (1937).

waters lying between states, the construction of an interstate utility such as a tunnel or bridge have all been successfully handled by interstate compact. These types of problems, it is important to observe, are usually localized, do not involve competitive interests of states or their citizens, usually require little or no continuing administration, can be settled once and for all by a single agreement, and do not involve any important national interest. In this type of problem the compact is a useful means of interstate cooperation.

For national problems, the interstate compact has doubtful value. It cannot operate as a substitute for the established national organs of government: Congress, the President and the national administration. It is quite inadequate to deal with complex large-scale problems requiring constant readjustment of policy or method. To rely upon cooperative state action by compact or agreement to solve the agricultural problem, to coordinate the revenue systems of state and nation or of the several states, to fix standards for intrastate productive and industrial enterprise, or to eliminate child labor is to postpone effective action indefinitely.

There is a third class of cases neither specifically local nor national, involving the interests of a group of states but not directly concerning all. The conservation of oil involves twelve or fifteen states in the first instance. The conservation of forests involves a larger number, but not the states lying in the "treeless plains" east of the Rocky Mountains. A uniform minimum wage is primarily an issue in the more highly industrialized states, although a potential issue anywhere. Within very recent years the interstate compact has been applied to some of these problems, but so recently that final judgment as to its effectiveness must be withheld. Three recent instances will be examined: the "Concord compact" on minimum wage; the effort to form a compact to support minimum wages after the fall of the National Recovery Administration; and the oil compact.

Subsequent to several preliminary conferences a compact looking toward a uniform minimum wage for women and children was signed at Concord, New Hampshire, May 29, 1934, by representatives of seven states—Maine, New Hampshire, Massachusetts, Connecticut, Rhode Island, New York and Pennsylvania. The essential substantive provision of the compact recites that, "No employer shall pay a woman, or a minor child under twenty-one years of age, an unfair oppressive wage."[1]

[1] 50 Stat. 633 (1937). See Ethel M. Johnson, "Interstate Compacts on Labour Legislation in the United States," 33 *International Labour Rev.* 790-815 (1936); and Abraham C. Weinfeld, *Labor Treaties and Labor Compacts* (1937).

These are general phrases, and their approval alone does not approach a solution of the evil of low wages for a relatively defenseless class of workers. By August, 1938, this agreement had been ratified by only three of the negotiating states, Massachusetts, New Hampshire and Rhode Island. The problem of industrial competition from the southern states, not parties to the compact, remains untouched.

The compact has interest, however, from the point of view of the enforcement of its provisions. Each state agrees (Title II, sec. 6) to enact the necessary legislation to maintain the minimum standards described in the preceding paragraph, and also to enforce and supervise their operation through the state's "appropriate administrative agencies" (Title II, sec. 7). Each commonwealth also establishes an unpaid commission, the chairmen of which collectively comprise an interstate commission, to which the United States may appoint a member.

The agreement provides no interstate sanction other than publicity, but the publicity requirements are of interest. Any question arising out of the compact, or state laws in pursuance thereof, "shall be brought before the interstate commission for consideration"; the commission shall make an investigation and publish its findings and recommendations. The self-interest of each compacting state is relied upon to disclose any substantial departure from the spirit of the agreement.

The difficulties of material progress in dealing with problems involving interstate economic competition through the interstate compact were revealed at a conference at Spring Lake, New Jersey (1935), subsequent to the adverse decision of the Supreme Court in the National Recovery Administration case. It was believed by some that an interstate compact might restore a basis for minimum wages. But the Governor of New Jersey, while welcoming the delegates, said, "I caution you against precipitate action in negotiating compacts. Once done, they are irrevocable, and we should not rush wildly into these compacts."

Employers and their associations were also on hand. The secretary of the Manufacturers' Association of New Jersey criticized the compacts as too complex in structure, and as calling for a "regimentation distasteful to American labor and to American employers." The president of the Employers' Association of North Jersey was quoted as saying, "The result of making laws uniform in the several states . . . would therefore be in many cases to take away an advantage which permits a New Jersey industry to meet competition and to transfer that advantage to a competitor in another state." [1]

The history of the effort to conserve oil and gas resources is much too

[1] *New York Times,* June 29, 1935.

long to include here.[1] It illustrates most clearly the unwillingness of the states to permit interference in the production of oil by either the national government or by an interstate agency. Some of the oil states have sought to conserve their own resources by various devices, including production quotas. Others have declined, and the discovery and exploitation of new fields have not only demoralized the market, but have placed the conserving states at a marked disadvantage. An effort to correlate state production with estimates of market demands prepared by the United States Bureau of Mines met with only partial success, especially when the Bureau of Mines sought to alter the balance between states or fields.

Section 9c of the National Industrial Recovery Act sought to protect the conservation states by outlawing interstate transportation of "hot oil," i.e., oil produced in excess of quotas as fixed by the several states. In the Panama Refining Company case, the Supreme Court invalidated this legislation.[2]

The major oil producing states then sought an adjustment through an interstate compact, executed in Dallas, Texas, February 16, 1935. This compact fell far short of effective management of oil production. Its stated purpose in fact was to conserve oil and gas, not to adjust production to market needs. The compact specifically asserted, furthermore, that its purpose was not to limit the production of oil or gas for the purpose of stabilizing or fixing its price, creating monopoly or promoting "regimentation." The several methods for conservation enumerated in the compact are doubtless useful to the extent they are enforced; but even if well enforced, they leave the major problem of oil production untouched. This problem is the control of production to approximate demand, and the allocation of production to different competing fields.

There is nothing in the compact to require any producing state to fix a quota, or to force or allow others to enforce a quota; total production is left to the discretion of each state, with no provision for adjusting it to market conditions; the power of Congress to control imports of oil is not related to the power of the states to fix production quotas each for its own producers; the production of one state is not brought into relation with the production of other states. No authority outside the state is created, nor is there even the modest sanction of publicity found in the Concord minimum wage compact. The compact was renewed in

[1] See Northcutt Ely, *Oil Conservation through Interstate Agreement* (1933), published by the Government Printing Office for the Federal Oil Conservation Board; Samuel B. Pettengill, *Hot Oil: the Problem of Petroleum* (1936); Myron W. Watkins, *Oil: Stabilization or Conservation?* (1937).

[2] *Panama Refining Co. vs. Ryan*, 293 U.S. 388 (1935).

1937. On October 1, 1936, it had been ratified by six of eighteen oil producing states, covering about two-thirds of total production.

Study of the minimum wage compact and the oil compact leads to the conclusion that this type of problem is not likely to be solved by this method. Although the interests of a part of the states only are directly involved, these are national problems; and in one way or another they call for a national solution, administered and executed by the national administration.[1]

In short, while the compact is a useful device to secure agreement on a localized, noncompetitive problem, its difficulties in other fields are great. These are not primarily the amount of time consumed in negotiation, nor the reserved right of withdrawal by the states, nor the inflexibility of the compact, nor the possible failure of Congress to ratify. The major weakness is the practical impossibility of securing an agreement among all the interested parties as the number of states increases, and as agreement is sought on controversial matters, especially those involving the competitive standing of states in the national market. No means exists to compel any state to agree to a compact against its real or supposed interests, and in one case only has Congress ratified a compact against the opposition of an interested party (Colorado River Compact). No means has yet been found to enforce the terms of a compact against a member state. Intervention of the Supreme Court of the United States may be possible in some instances, but the method of enforcing its judgment against a state is not obvious.[2]

The general conclusion is, therefore, that the interstate compact is not an effective barrier against the trend toward national centralization, and cannot be relied upon to stay the course of events by which leadership and administrative authority in national problems are moving to Washington.

7. Interstate Cooperation

The interstate compact is not the only means by which the states may coordinate their activities. The National Conference of Commissioners on Uniform State Laws, organized in 1899, has been instrumental in facilitating uniform state legislation in the field of private law. Its work has been useful but progress has been slow.

There are a considerable number of organizations of state officials, to

[1] Cf. the conflict between federal and state governments over water power development in New England, 1937–39.

[2] See *Virginia vs. West Virginia*, 246 U.S. 565 (1918); Thomas Reed Powell, 'Coercing a State to Pay a Judgment: Virginia v. West Virginia," 17 *Mich. Law Rev.* 1-32 (1918–19).

which further reference is made in a later chapter, which facilitate the exchange of technical information and experience.[1] They are professional in character, and although extremely helpful to their members are not a means of resisting centralizing trends directly.

The Council of State Governments (Cosgo) is the most impressive organization which has yet developed to assist in maintaining a fair balance between national and state governments. This federation of principal state officials and of legislators developed on the foundation of the American Legislators' Association, the creation of Senator Henry W. Toll of Colorado. In 1938 the Council included this Association, the National Association of Secretaries of State, the National Association of Attorney-Generals, and the Governors' Conference, each served by the Central Secretariat of the Council.

The Council works in large part through interstate commissions, representing some or all of the states as the case may require and officially authorized by the state governments. In 1938 there were interstate commissions on conflicting taxation, on crime, on social security, on the Delaware River basin, and on the Ohio basin. A general assembly is held each year, usually in Washington.[2]

The period from 1925 to 1935 was a decade of slow and at times discouraging progress in organization. The final result was a triumph of organizing skill which for the first time in our history gave the states a mechanism for cooperative action. The weight which Cosgo will carry in future federal-state relations cannot yet be ascertained, but it is likely to be substantial.

8. Future Trends

He would be a hasty prophet who would predict the end of the forty-eight commonwealth governments, or even their eclipse by the central sun. While they have lost something to the federal government, they have gained much, partly from their subdivisions but more from taking on new activities. The states still have a range of work more ample than that of the nation, and in some ways closer to the mass of people. They are also powerful political units as well as constitutional and administrative organs, and from this point of view are primary while the nation is derivative. The tides of national power must run for long before the states will be submerged as mere administrative subdivisions of the whole.

Writing in 1933 I said, "The general conditions of social and public

[1] See ch. 27.

[2] See Council of State Governments, *The Book of the States*, an annual publication commencing in 1937; W. Brooke Graves, *Uniform State Action* (1934).

ife at the present time suggest that further progress toward centraliza-ion is probable."[1] In 1938 there seems to be no reason to modify this pinion. It is likely, however, that the actual transfer of administrative ubject matter from the states to the nation will be relatively uncommon. t is more probable that cooperative joint activity will develop on an ven larger scale. In cooperative fields, however, leadership will probably ettle in the hands of the national government, while operations will fall o the states and their subdivisions.

In the light of present and probable future trends, the technique of co-peration between officials responsible to different "sovereign" powers ecomes of primary importance. The interaction of federal and state fficials is one of the emerging major problems of structure, inherent in ll federal governments. It may be desirable eventually to transfer all oint operations to state officials acting under federal supervision and irection; or it may be found that a double set of officials in a given area an be geared together without too much lost motion. In any event this oordination on the scale of a continent is a major undertaking.

[1] L. D. White, *Trends in Public Administration* (1933), p. 48.

Chapter Eleven

STATE AND NATIONAL ADMINISTRATIVE RELATIONS WITH LOCAL OFFICIALS

READJUSTMENT of power is taking place within the states, as well as between the states and the nation. Here also administrative responsibility flows upward into wider areas and into jurisdictions with greater financial resources. The net result is in part a transference of subject matter from the local authorities to the state, in part the extension of state supervision over activities, the performance of which is still left to the locality. This readjustment has been in process for well over fifty years, but so great was the dispersion of power that even today the internal state systems of administration are relatively decentralized in comparison with the institutions of other countries.

While these movements have been long in process, a new aspect of centralizing drifts appeared as a consequence of the depression of 1929 and the sudden and unforeseen extension of direct administrative relationships between municipal governments and rural populations on the one hand and the national government on the other. Brief notice of this significant trend precedes more extensive discussion of administrative relations between the states and their subdivisions.

1. Administrative Relations between the National and Local Governments

Constitutionally speaking, the national government is not aware of the existence of municipalities. Political connections, however, have long been close and administrative relations are rapidly developing. Writing in 1925 William Anderson noted a number of instances in which national activities affected municipal administration and predicted that "the future holds in store even closer contacts between the national and municipal authorities." He suggested that the national government "should make itself one of the principal agencies for providing municipal information, for educating local officials, and for promoting the improvement of local governmental processes." [1]

In 1931 Paul V. Betters published a systematic survey of federal serv

[1] William Anderson, *American City Government* (1925).

ices to municipal governments.[1] "The wide range of activities of the national government which touch intimately on current problems of municipal administration," said Mr. Betters, "may surprise many." He found that federal agencies developed standards not only in weights and measures, but in traffic and safety, in zoning and building, in highway construction, and in milk sanitation; they carried on studies not only in vital statistics and population estimates, but in financial statistics, employment figures, and crime rates; upon request they made specific surveys and reports in education, in public health, and in national resources and land use; they undertook cooperative enterprises in food and drug administration, in municipal water control and in other fields; they maintained informational services in a wide range of activities; recently they entered the field of training of municipal employees.[2]

The financial pressure of the depression induced a more direct and effective relationship between Washington and the city halls than had ever been contemplated. Municipal revenues, dependent largely upon real estate taxes, diminished rapidly at the very moment when heavy relief expenditures were forced upon the city treasury. Curtailment of normal operating expenditures proved completely inadequate to meet the crisis; the legal authority to incur debt had been exhausted in some instances and the market for municipal loans was practically nonexistent. This financial crisis precipitated national action. The relief load was shifted to national credit through loans and grants to the states for cities, and in some cases directly to the cities; the Public Works Administration entered into direct negotiation with cities for construction of municipal works; the Housing Division of P.W.A., the Resettlement Administration, and other emergency agencies dealt directly with city authorities. City revenue collections were improved by loans to householders through the Home Owners' Loan Corporation and the whole community structure was strengthened by work opportunities created

[1] Paul V. Betters, *Federal Services to Municipal Governments* (1931).

[2] On federal-city relations consult Harvey Walker, *Federal Limitations upon Municipal Ordinance Making Power* (1929); Paul V. Betters, "Washington and the Cities: 1934," 23 *Nat. Mun. Rev.* 415-19, 423 (1934); same author, with others, *Recent Federal-City Relations* (1936); same author, "The Federal Government and the Cities," 199 *Annals* 190-98 (1938); Earl D. Mallery, "Federal-City Relations in 1937," *Municipal Year Book*, 1938, pp. 197-209; C. C. Ludwig, "Cities and the National Government under the New Deal," 29 *Am. Pol. Sci. Rev.* 640-48 (1935); Harold W. Dodds, "Federal Aid for the City," 25 *Yale Rev.* 96-112 (1935-36); Roland R. Renne, "Probable Effects of Federal Land Purchase on Local Government," 25 *Nat. Mun. Rev.* 401-6, 411 (1936); Wylie Kilpatrick, "Federal Assistance to Municipal Recovery," 26 *Nat. Mun. Rev.* 337-44, 351 (1937); same author, "Federal Regulation of Local Debit," *ibid.*, 283-90, 298; E. H. Foley, Jr., "Recent Developments in Federal-Municipal Relationships," 86 *Univ. of Penn. Law Rev.* 485-516 (1937-38).

by one or more of the national agencies active in the fight against the depression. It is no exaggeration to state that the spending and lending programs of the national government saved many cities from financial disintegration and from social disorder.

The fiscal affairs of some local authorities were so involved, however, that they could not be saved. In order to facilitate an orderly procedure to safeguard the interests of holders of municipal securities so far as possible in the light of practical bankruptcy, Congress enacted the Sumner-Wilcox bill allowing cities to make an adjustment of their outstanding obligations through the mediation of the United States District Court This legislation facilitated the composition and adjustment of municipal debts in "desperate" cases until it was declared unconstitutional by the Supreme Court.[1] In revised form, it was re-enacted by Congress in 1937

The extent to which actual control over municipal affairs was lodged in Washington as a result of these emergency measures is not easy to define. The federal government did not attempt to weaken the control of the state over its political subdivisions, and no change in the legal status of the city was imposed. In some cases city officials dealt with state authorities as intermediaries with Washington; in other cases the relations were direct.

Cities accepting Public Works Administration grants and loans had to agree to a schedule of wages, hours and conditions of employment prescribed by the federal authorities, to allow federal inspection and a federal audit. The P.W.A. reserved the right to disallow payments for technical and engineering plans which seemed excessive. These limitations did not apply of course to other than joint federal projects, and were in each case voluntarily accepted by the municipality.[2] The depression contacts between cities and the national government were broad and in their extent spectacular; but the states were not dispossessed of their traditional constitutional position as guardians of municipal government The change has been a change in climate rather than a change in topography.

Future lines of development are not clear, but it seems likely that the research and advisory services of the national government to cities are destined to increase in importance.[3] So far as the cities enter into debtor-creditor relations with Washington, an element of fiscal supervision may appear, although this is not likely to develop toward a highly centralize

[1] *Ashton vs. Cameron County Water Improvement District*, 298 U.S. 513 (1936

[2] National Resources Committee, *Public Works Planning* (1936), Part 3, "Division of Costs and Responsibility."

[3] National Resources Committee, *Our Cities: Their Role in the National Economy* (1937).

system such as the French. Movement has been rapid since 1933, and a federal bureau of municipal relations is much more within the realm of the practical than it was before the events of the depression. Here is an aspect of central tendencies which in the case of the great urban centers may be of special significance, for they have as little to derive from the state capitals as they have much to gain from Washington.

Before leaving the relations of the national to the local groups, it is important to note parallel changes in direct federal contacts with the rural population.[1] Until the advent of the Agricultural Adjustment Administration, they had been almost nonexistent, although indirectly the federal government had been active in aiding education and research in agriculture, and in financing the county agent movement.[2]

The dramatic and absorbing story of agricultural production control by means of voluntary cooperation of farmers with the A.A.A. deserves more space than can be given to a brief survey of this novel administrative relationship.[3] In broad perspective, during the years 1933 to 1938 a national administrative organization for planning crop production, for ascertaining farmer approval of programs, for adjusting production to established quotas, and for securing payments to cooperating farmers on proof of compliance with contracts was established and put into operation with respect to four staple crops: wheat, cotton, corn-hogs and tobacco.

This huge administrative machine, largely ignoring the states as intermediate agencies, was composed of two basic elements, the Agricultural Adjustment Administration in Washington which fixed total quantities, and thousands of county production control associations (in 1935, 4,600) comprising (in 1934) over 3,000,000 cooperating farmers. Each county production control association included all cooperating farmers who signed a contract with the A.A.A. It was managed by a board of directors made up of the chairmen or representatives of the township or community production control committees within the county. These chairmen in turn were elected by the farmers themselves.

Each county production control association maintained a number of committees, the most important of which was the allotment committee, responsible for checking and adjusting individual farmer's allotments. In each community were local committee members, charged with such du-

[1] Lane W. Lancaster, *Government in Rural America* (1937), ch. 14.

[2] See a forthcoming study by Gladys Baker, *The County Agent.*

[3] Edwin G. Nourse, J. S. Davis, and J. D. Black, *Three Years of the Agricultural Adjustment Administration* (1937); Carlton Ball, *Federal, State and Local Relations in Agriculture* (1938).

ties as securing contracts, appraising yield, certifying production records, and making investigations with reference to contracts. For the corn-hog program alone, there were 2,182 county corn-hog control associations and about 55,000 community committeemen.

The national government thus became the most satisfactory, if not the only means of enabling farmers to cooperate in the management of production. Farmers signed contracts directly with the authorities in Washington; they received cash payments for contract compliance directly from the United States Treasury; they planned, organized, planted and reaped in a coordinated program devised in Washington on the basis of information prepared by farmers themselves. No one, except the Supreme Court, stopped to inquire about the sovereign state.

Congress has no delegated constitutional authority to order a referendum on any phase of public policy. Voting is a matter controlled almost exclusively by the states and is jealously guarded by them. But the Agricultural Adjustment Administration found it possible to conduct a *de facto* referendum among farmers to ascertain whether they wished to continue the 1934 production control program in 1935. Over 4,000,000 farmers, whether under contract or not during 1934, participated in a mass referendum and by a large majority approved the extension of the agricultural adjustment plan. This is probably the first time that citizens of the United States ever expressed even an informal opinion by ballot under national guidance, and is perhaps the most spectacular demonstration of the short-circuiting of the states. No recourse was had to the official county or state election officials; the referendum was conducted by the farmers at the request of the national government and under its general supervision.

The influence of this new type of contact between the rural communities and the farming population with Washington in facilitating the growth of national administration is certain to be substantial.[1]

[1] An interesting example of the quiet way in which federal bureaus may influence local activities is found in the inspection of county jails by the U. S. Bureau of Prisons. Legislation in 1930 authorized the Bureau to use approved county jails for the custody of federal prisoners, the rates to take into consideration the character of quarters furnished and to encourage "reasonably decent, sanitary, and healthful quarters and subsistence. . . ." The federal government of course has no right to dictate to local officials how to operate their county jails, but it can refuse to use jails which it does not approve. There are states where intolerable conditions exist, and the rating of county jails revealed a very low general level of suitability. Refusal to use a county jail, or payment of less than the maximum per diem, or removal of federal prisoners has already effected a marked improvement. The attitude of county officials is revealed in excerpts from this letter of a county jailer, "If you see fit to return federal prisoners to this jail I assure you that I will use my utmost endeavor in caring for them in a manner that will meet your approval. . . ." See Nina Kinsella, "County Jails and the Federal Government," 24 *J. of the American Institute of Criminal Law and Criminology* 428-39 (1933-34).

2. Centralizing Trends within the States

The same tendency toward an upward flow of administrative leadership and supervision which stirs eloquent appeals to "state rights" is at work within the forty-eight commonwealths, transferring authority from the counties and the cities to the state capitals. Despite the fact that the tide has been running toward the state capitals for many years, the state administrative systems are still relatively decentralized in nature.[1]

This is due in part to the extreme decentralization which prevailed in the early years of our national history, in part to a strong sense of local responsibility, in part to a conflict of interest between urban and rural populations in the same state, in part to the power of resistance of the local political organizations which are in command of the local scene. It is also a reflection of the fact that a large part of the area of the United States is still sparsely settled, is rural and agricultural in nature, and neither requires the administrative services nor the elaborate administrative organization which an urban population demands.

The states in which the trend toward administrative centralization has been most definite fall into two groups: on the one hand, the more highly industrialized and urbanized, such as New York, Massachusetts, and New Jersey; on the other hand, certain states in which centralization has been forced by the breakdown of local finance, such as North Carolina. Study of trends in a few state-local functions will make more clear the character of the movement and its present boundaries.[2]

a. Finance. The sources of local revenue have usually been fixed by

[1] The early history of centralization within the states is covered in an able series of dissertations at Columbia University: William C. Webster, *Recent Centralizing Tendencies in State Educational Administration*, Columbia University Studies in History, Economics and Public Law, vol. 8, no. 2 (1897); Milo R. Maltbie, *English Local Government of To-day, a Study of the Relations of Central and Local Government, ibid.*, vol. 9, no. 1 (1897); Robert H. Whitten, *Public Administration in Massachusetts, the Relation of Central to Local Activity, ibid.*, vol. 8, no. 4 (1898); John A. Fairlie, *The Centralization of Administration in New York State, ibid.*, vol. 9, no. 3 (1898); Clement M. L. Sites, *Centralized Administration of Liquor Laws in the American Commonwealths, ibid.*, vol. 10, no. 3 (1899); Samuel P. Orth, *The Centralization of Administration in Ohio, ibid.*, vol. 16, no. 3 (1903); William A. Rawles, *Centralizing Tendencies in the Administration of Indiana, ibid.*, vol. 17, no. 1 (1903); Harold M. Bowman, *The Administration of Iowa, a Study in Centralization, ibid.*, vol. 18, no. 1 (1903).

[2] The principal general references on this subject include: John R. Commons, "State Supervision for Cities," 5 *Annals* 865-81 (1894-95); Schuyler C. Wallace, *State Administrative Supervision over Cities in the United States* (1928); Leonard D. White, *Trends in Public Administration* (1933); Lane W. Lancaster, *Government in Rural America* (1937); Henry J. Bittermann, *State and Federal Grants-in-Aid* (1938).

the state from the beginning. The fiscal officers in counties and citie have also been specified by law, including the familiar assessor, collecto and treasurer, and later budget and accounting officers. Within this ad ministrative framework, the local authorities were originally left com pletely free to work out their own financial salvation. The amounts t be raised by taxation or by the issuance of bonds were subject to n supervision; the allocation of funds among services was entirely a loc responsibility; and fiscal methods with respect to collection, accountin and ensuring the security of funds and the solvency of the communit were left strictly to the county boards and the city fathers. The stat even turned over to its subdivisions responsibility for collecting its ow revenue.

Over a long period and to a widely varying extent the state has sinc intervened in the revenue systems of its subdivisions. To correct gro undervaluations by competing assessors, state boards of equalization an review were established. To limit the fiscal burdens placed on son communities by irresponsible local authorities or to lighten the weight real estate taxes, tax limits and debt limits were fixed by legislation, occ sionally by constitutional amendment. Fiscal methods were made un form and much more effective by state law.

The assessment of certain types of property such as railroads and uti ities was taken away from the local governments by the states. Th state developed new sources of revenue—the inheritance tax, the incon tax, the sales tax and others—which were generally directly administere by it without reliance upon local agencies. The state is developing stat administered locally-shared taxes in which initiative lies at the state cap tal rather than in local offices.[1] In most states, central supervision w made more effective by the creation of state tax commissions, sometim with authority to prescribe rules for the conduct of county, and to lesser extent, city fiscal officers. Active tax commissions have assum leadership in training and guiding local assessing officials as well as supervising their work.

With respect to expenditures within debt and tax limits, local autho ties are still largely masters in their own houses. State tax limitatior however, have had a very restrictive effect upon local programs in r cent years. State law in many instances imposes various procedural r quirements, especially budget methods and accounting systems, and t requirement of fiscal reports to state authorities is gradually extendin State supervision of revenue is substantially greater than of expenditur

[1] Ruth G. Hutchinson, *State-Administered Locally-Shared Taxes* (1931).

ut in both cases the original pattern of local autonomy has been con-iderably modified.[1]

b. Highways. Early highway construction was either a town or county ndertaking, or a private enterprise by a turnpike corporation charging olls. Until the era of hard roads, highway building and maintenance re-nained a job for local contractors and country folk who "worked out" heir taxes on road improvement. The use of the automobile has caused great change in responsibility for highway finance, design, construc-ion and maintenance. The initiative in research in highway design was aken by the United States Bureau of Public Roads from its inception, lthough considerable research was carried on by some state highway epartments. The financing of expensive macadam or concrete roads ould not be carried by the local communities. It was first shared by he states, which floated large bond issues, later by the United States hrough the grant-in-aid and more recently by direct construction as a elief measure. Most of the hard road construction of the country has een done under state or federal supervision.

In North Carolina all highway maintenance and construction, and in Virginia most of such work, have been transferred from the county to he state, a shift induced by the financial weakness of the county but acilitated by a recognition of the superior technical capacity of the ate. This degree of state assumption of local administration is still ex-eptional.

c. Police. The management and direction of police forces remain pri-narily a municipal or a county function. The inadequacy of a host of ndependent and often jealous local constabularies is well recognized. Certain recent developments point to a greater degree of central super-ision and coordination. Over fifteen states supplement the local police ith either a state police or a highway patrol. Teletype systems connect nany metropolitan police departments with their satellites, and radio is oordinating neighboring police forces. The International Association f Chiefs of Police is now (1938) working on a regional radio network.[2]

Twenty states had established bureaus of criminal identification by

[1] There is a voluminous literature on state supervision of local finance. Consult nong other references, Royal S. Van de Woestyne, *State Control of Local Finance Massachusetts* (1935); Harley L. Lutz, "State Supervision of Local Finance," 43 *of Political Economy* 289-305 (1935); Frank G. Bates, "State Control of Local nance in Indiana," in C. G. Haines and M. E. Dimock, eds., *Essays on the Law d Practice of Governmental Administration* (1935); the exceptionally valuable re-orts of the New York State Commission for the Revision of the Tax Laws since 30; Robert K. Carr, *State Control of Local Finance in Oklahoma* (1937).

[2] V. A. Leonard, *Police Communication Systems* (1938); August Vollmer and lfred E. Parker, *Crime and the State Police* (1935).

1933, often with power to require reports of offenses known to the police and arrests. A voluntary national reporting system of offenses known to the police, initiated by the International Association of Chiefs of Police, is now maintained by the Federal Bureau of Investigation of the Department of Justice. In a few cases state authorities may remove local peace officers, but this power is seldom used.[1]

These references indicate that there is a modest tendency toward state influence upon local police departments. It remains slight. Police departments are notoriously self-contained and particularistic, due in part to exclusively local recruitment and to a rigid policy of internal promotion from the lowest ranks to the chief, due also in some cases to close connections between the local political organization and the police force, and to a reluctance on the part of a liberty-loving population to allow themselves to be policed by an organization not subject directly to local sentiment.

d. Education. Local control of education in the United States contrasts with central control of education in such countries as France or Germany. "The influence of the frontier on the organization of American schools is further reflected in the fact that these schools have long been and are today largely controlled by local authorities. Most of the countries of Europe have central ministries of education endowed with large powers of control over schools and universities. In the United States the federal government exercises no direct control over schools. Even the states, which are politically responsible for the schools within their boundaries . . . leave the administration of education largely to representatives of local communities and to private enterprise." [2]

At many points, however, the influence of the state in education is expanding. One significant aspect is the establishment and enforcement of teaching standards by means of certification. The number of state systems of certification increased steadily during the last quarter century so that by 1936 county certification had almost disappeared. Thus a uniform standard for all localities is fixed by the state.

Standards for secondary schools are also determined by the state through the process of accrediting which in 1932 had been established in forty-two states. These standards usually relate to such matters as organization, curriculum, library, building and equipment. When coupled with a system of grants-in-aid, which is common but apparently

[1] See the author's *Trends in Public Administration* (1933), pp. 125-28.

[2] President's Research Committee on Social Trends, *Recent Social Trends in the United States* (1933), vol. 1, p. 326; George D. Strayer, Jr., *Centralizing Tendencies in the Administration of Public Education* (1934); John H. McNeely, *Authority of State Executive Agencies over Higher Education*, U. S. Office of Education, Bulletin 15, 1936.

not increasing rapidly in scope, the state is able to go far in determining the nature and effectiveness of local education. It is of interest to note that the number of state inspectors of rural schools shows a marked increase.

The curriculum in the secondary schools is primarily determined by the local school board. The state may require certain subjects to be taught, and in fact the number of prescribed subjects tends to increase. We may conclude that while the trend toward administrative centralization is at work in the field of education, it has not yet substantially modified the pattern of a highly decentralized, locally controlled system. Private accrediting bodies such as the North Central Association of Colleges and Secondary Schools have replaced or supplemented state action in educational standards.

e. Relief. The catastrophic depression starting in 1929 has completely changed the administrative organization for relief and philanthropy within the states. Reference has already been made to the intervention of the national government, commencing in 1932 after the breakdown of private philanthropy and of local public assistance. Within the states a state-wide organization to handle the emergency problem was extemporized almost overnight. It is still too early to ascertain what type of permanent public authority for welfare purposes is likely to emerge, but state systems resting upon and coordinating county and city units are already developing.[1] Under the provisions of the Social Security Act the states must assume responsibility for the supervision of the administration of old-age assistance and other forms of public assistance receiving federal aid unless the state administers the act directly. Unemployment compensation is uniformly state administered. This is also true of the management of public employment offices, which until a few years ago were generally regarded as a local responsibility where they existed.

Local responsibility in such an intimate phase of government work is nevertheless exceedingly important. The prevention of waste and the elimination of unworthy recipients of public relief are, in the long run, greatly accelerated by a local organization responsive to local sentiment. On the other hand, the influence of a local political machine may in some cases overweigh this consideration. Politics in relief is especially intolerable; and is likely eventually to induce its own corrective. While, therefore, it is quite uncertain what type of welfare and relief organization will become the accepted pattern, it appears certain first, that private philanthropy will not be able again to carry the major share of the load; second, that welfare activities have become a permanent and important branch of public administration; and third, that a substantial

[1] Marietta Stevenson, *Public Welfare Administration* (1938).

amount of state and national influence on local standards is likely to b combined with immediate county and city responsibility.

Well before the depression the states had generally taken over certai welfare and charitable institutions which were in the early days man aged by the county, such as hospitals for the insane and feeble-minde and schools for the defectives. County jails still remain in the hands o the locally elected sheriff, despite wide criticism of the lax and inade quate standards which characterize them as a group.

f. Trends in other fields of administration. Although the state is vi tally interested in the purity of elections, it has sought to ensure hones management of the polls by elaborate legislation rather than by admin istrative supervision. A leading authority in this field, Dr. Joseph P Harris, stated in 1929, "Election machinery has remained almost com pletely decentralized despite the movement of the last half century to ward centralization. There is practically no state administrative contr over elections. The supervision of the precinct officers is left to th county or city officers, and quite commonly the precinct boards are law unto themselves." [1]

In the field of public health administration, on the other hand, the in fluence of the state is steadily expanding. This development involve state action in the collection of vital statistics, supervision of waterwork and sewerage systems, inspection of local hospitals, control of venere diseases and the extension of rural health units. The Shepard-Towne Act, authorizing grants for child and maternity welfare, accelerated th establishment of state units for child hygiene, now found in each of th states.[2] The grants of the Social Security Board strengthened the state county connection.

In the matter of public personnel management, the states are with few exceptions entirely decentralized. The methods of selection of ap pointed local officials and employees, their standards of qualificatio their status and tenure, their compensation, their removal and retir ment, are strictly matters of local concern alone.[3] This is one of th major handicaps to a career service in local government. Exceptions a found to the general rule in Massachusetts, New York, New Jersey an Ohio, where in varying degrees the state civil service commissions infl ence the standards of county and/or city service commissions. In co nection with some grants-in-aid, the federal government can influen local standards; for example, the United States Employment Service ca fix standards for the state employment agencies cooperating with it. B

[1] Joseph P. Harris, *Registration of Voters in the United States* (1929), pp. 113-1

[2] White, *op. cit.*, ch. 7.

[3] George C. S. Benson, *The Administration of the Civil Service in Massachuset with Special Reference to State Control of City Service* (1935).

he Social Security Board is specifically prohibited by law from con-
erning itself with tenure, compensation and method of selection of co-
perating state services.

Other examples may be drawn from any field of administrative activ-
ty.[1] The trend toward some degree of central supervision, guidance or
ontrol will be evident in many of them, although the degree and the
peed of movement will vary greatly from state to state and from sub-
ect to subject. A broad perspective of the whole area of administration
eveals without doubt that power, political and administrative, is march-
ng from the city halls and the county courthouses to the state capitals,
nd from the state capitals to Washington.

3. Municipal Home Rule as a Barrier to Centralization

The law of municipal corporations assigns cities no protection against
he overruling authority of the state legislature. Abuse of power by po-
itically controlled assemblies, coupled with a growing reluctance of
rban populations to be governed by a legislative body dominated by
ural areas, induced the home rule movement. By constitutional amend-
nent the unrestricted authority of the legislature over cities has been
urtailed in order to vest in the municipality final authority over "mat-
ers of local concern."

Home rule for cities began in 1875 in Missouri, and for specified
lasses of municipalities has been adopted in fifteen states, although the
ecessary supplementary legislation has not (1938) been enacted in
ennsylvania. There have been no adoptions of this system in any state
ince 1924. Home rule for counties was initiated in California in 1911,
nd was adopted by Maryland in 1915. In other states local power to
elect the form of city government by adopting one of several optional
orms established by state law has given some degree of home rule.

Home rule is therefore geographically restricted. What degree of self-
dministration is conferred under home rule powers? In general, the
ourts have construed local authority very strictly, finding many mat-
ers which cities sought to regulate under their constitutional powers to
e not subjects of local concern, but subjects in which the state has an
nterest and which consequently have not been transferred to the
unicipality.

A leading study of municipal home rule reaches conclusions which

[1] For example, Leonard D. White, *An Evaluation of the System of Central inancial Control of Research in State Governments*, National Research Council ulletin, vol. 9, no. 49 (1924); American Library Association, *The State Library gency* (2d ed. 1937); Paul V. Betters, ed., *State Centralization in North Carolina* 932); Paul W. Wager, "Effects of North Carolina's Centralization," 26 *Nat. un. Rev.* 572-77 (1937).

suggest that centralizing trends are not likely to be seriously retarded by local privileges. "The nub of the home rule problem," says Professor McGoldrick, "is the assignment of functions to state and municipal authorities respectively." [1] He continues, "The number of matters, which can be assigned completely and excusively to local discretion will ultimately prove few indeed. . . . If the courts are forced to deny all state control in order to permit local control of specific problems, it may be expected that more and more matters will be declared state concerns."

Any division of governmental power is not likely to endure through changing circumstances. The tendency is almost invariably in the sense of recognizing state-wide interest in matters once of local concern. Traffic regulation provides an apt illustration. We may recall also that the evil which home rule was intended to cure was political interference in local affairs. Home rule was not invented to prevent the type of administrative supervision which has developed in the last quarter century. Nor has it operated to balk administrative relationships, especially in view of the restricted meaning of "municipal affairs."

A desirable administrative balance between cities and states is gradually emerging in fact as both state and city governments rise to higher levels of competence and integrity. An able and honest municipal official has nothing to fear from competent and well-meaning officials of the state; indeed he may have much to gain from them, or much to give them. The rise of official organizations in many functional areas, such as health, education, welfare, public works and fire prevention, is gradually sidetracking an older sense of hostility between city and state; and on the other hand the existence of a strong league of municipalities in a state is a strong deterrent to hostile legislation.

The formal division of power sought in the home rule system, then has not proved a barrier to the extension of the administrative influence of the state over its municipalities. The stagnation of the home rule plan and the strict interpretation of its provisions give little indication that in the future it will be more effective as a countervailing force than in the past. It is more likely that a new network of administrative relationships will make home rule more and more an anachronism in our administrative system.

4. Technique of Centralization

With no powerful countermovement yet induced by the trend toward political and administrative centralization, and in light of the un-

[1] Joseph D. McGoldrick, *Law and Practice of Municipal Home Rule, 1916–1930* (1933), p. 317; see also Howard L. McBain, *The Law and the Practice of Municipal Home Rule* (1916).

derlying social and economic trends, it seems probable that the tendency toward the state capitals and Washington will continue. Before undertaking a broad evaluation of the movement from the point of view of good administration, we may pause to survey briefly the methods by which central influence and authority are brought to bear upon lower jurisdictions.

Not all methods which have been used elsewhere are in effect in the United States. Thus we have no field representative of the federal or state government corresponding to the French prefect, nor is there administrative power to compel specific performance of a mandatory duty by a local authority. We have no system of penalties which can be imposed by higher administration for failure of local bodies to perform their duties, apart from withdrawal of grants.

In the United States many devices have been employed, either in the state-nation or in the state-local relationship. The forms of centralization are too varied to permit complete enumeration, but in the following classification some of the more common methods are exhibited.[1] They range from those which prescribe the least to those which impose the greatest degree of central control.

a. Advice and information. The central authority may content itself by maintaining research and informational services, available to other administrative agencies. John Stuart Mill conceived this to be the primary duty of the central authority. The case is admirably illustrated by the scientific, research and informational services of the Department of Agriculture. The United States Bureau of Public Roads and the Office of Education furnish other instances of far-flung advisory and research services primarily maintained for the advantage of the states and their subdivisions. Within the states analogous services are often maintained by the health departments for the use of local health officers. States generally have been relatively inactive in this field, however, but state leagues of municipalities have developed admirable informational services in lieu of state assistance.

b. Cooperative administration. In this case formal or informal work relations are established by which two separate jurisdictions cooperate on a basis of equality, neither party having superior right of direction or control. Precise illustrations, not connected with grants-in-aid or other supervisory influence, are not common. Cooperation between state and national game wardens is, however, a good case. Considerable cooperative research also falls in this category. The grain inspection work of the U. S. Department of Agriculture is carried out in part by state grain

[1] Cf. a more detailed analysis in a forthcoming study by Spencer D. Parratt and Finla G. Crawford.

inspectors who are licensed by the United States after qualifying ex aminations. National and state planning programs are linked together b cooperative means.

c. Periodic reports. Local authorities may be left free to perform thei respective duties, but are required to report to the central governmen The form of the report is usually prescribed by the central body in th interest of uniformity. The most extensive and important reports ar those of a fiscal nature. A substantial majority of the states require on or more types of periodic reports in this class.[1] Closely related is th power to prescribe and install the accounting system, from which fisc reports are derived; this is now frequent within the states, and in th case of federal grants, is imposed upon each jurisdiction receiving fed eral money. The authority of the central body to audit local accoun may also be noticed here; it is not yet standard practice, although qui frequent.[2]

d. Inspection and advice. As a transitional stage, central officials ar sometimes authorized to inspect and advise, but without authority compel compliance with their recommendations. They report to th central authorities, which may induce further legislation. A widesprea instance of this type of centralization is the inspection of schools b visiting teachers. Inspection of sanitary installations, such as seweraş systems, is another example. This type of supervision is often associate with the grant-in-aid, although not necessarily. An important ne agency of administration is the federal inspectorate, using the term the sense of federal representatives who contact and inspect cooperati work within the states.[3] The numbers and activities of federal inspecto have increased rapidly in recent years.

e. Central review. Most administrative operations by local authoriti are final; in some instances they are regularly reviewed by a state a ministrative body before they become binding. An excellent illustrati is furnished by the act of assessment. Boards of equalization and mo recently tax commissions are directed to review the original assessmer in order to equalize any variation in general standards which inte county competition for tax relief may have brought to pass. In sor cases, individual taxpayers may appeal to the state tax commission, variation of the type of central control designated as review. The stu and analysis of city applications for grants and loans from the Pub Works Administration is a closer example.

f. Grant-in-aid. The conditional grant of money by a higher to

[1] L. D. White, *Trends in Public Administration* (1933), pp. 51-54.

[2] *Ibid.*, pp. 63-65.

[3] See P. S. Wu, "The Federal Inspectorate" (ms. 1930), Univ. of Chicago Libra

lower authority is a powerful means of administrative control, especially since it serves to expand the influence of the national government beyond the scope of the specifically enumerated powers. On the other hand state grants to its subdivisions are less likely to be accompanied by conditions or by administrative supervision and enforcement of the conditions. Thus state departments of education have not exercised much influence on city school systems despite the grants which they have administered. The means of control lies in the power of the granting authority to decline to allow a grant in the first instance, to impose conditions, or to withdraw a grant for failure to observe the conditions. To all intents and purposes, the action of central officials in such cases is final. Of all methods of expanding central influence and power over lesser agencies, this is one of the most effective, for the demands of the local taxpayer to benefit by his share of the grant (to support which he is paying taxes) are compelling.[1]

g. Fixing of standards. As a result of the operation of central supervision through the means already enumerated, there is a definite tendency to work toward common standards in scattered and unrelated administrative units. These standards may have reference to administrative methods, to the amount and character of expenditures, to qualifications for appointment, and to other aspects of official work. The drive for higher standards is widespread in many fields, and it cannot be doubted that, in general, central influence has been steadily in favor of better local administration. Noteworthy results have already been achieved in education, health, and finance. On the other hand, there are always progressive communities which are well in advance of any standards which the state or national authorities could suggest as desirable minima.

h. Requirement of prior permission. In a growing number of cases, plans developed by the locality or the state must be presented to the state or to the national authorities respectively for approval. This requirement is often associated with a grant of money, but not always. Thus approval of plans for county and city hospitals by a state board of health is now frequent.[2] Approval of highway construction by the state is also common.[3] Under the Federal Employment Service Act, a state is entitled to a grant only if "the Director finds that a state has complied with the requirements [of the Act] and if plans have been submitted and approved. . . ."[4]

The Social Security Act affords several typical illustrations. Provision

[1] See references in ch. 10; and also Tipton R. Snavely, D. C. Hyde and A. B. Biscoe, *State Grants-in-Aid in Virginia* (1933).

[2] White, *op. cit.*, p. 99.

[3] *Ibid.*, p. 113.

[4] 48 Stat. 113 (1933).

is made for payments for old-age assistance (sec. 3) for "approved" plans submitted by states; the elements of a plan which is eligible for approval by the Social Security Board are stated in the statute, leaving to the Board discretion as to compliance. Other sections provide for payments in aid of needy dependent children (sec. 401 ff.) on the basis of an "approved plan," on the same general model.

Approval of fiscal plans finds an extraordinary illustration in New Mexico. An act of 1921 authorized the state tax commission to approve in whole or in part or to amend the budget estimates of each and every county.[1] In Iowa the state director of the budget upon the request of five taxpayers must examine proposals for local improvements, "and if the director shall find that the plans and specifications and form of contract are suitable for the improvement proposed and that *it is best for the interests of the municipality* . . . the director shall approve the same." [2] These are exceptional cases.

i. Appointment and removal of officers. In general it may be stated that the appointment and removal of personnel are not common means of central supervision over localities.[3] Hundreds of thousands of local officials are elected, and in all cases the community has retained nearly complete control of its official family. State officials are beyond the legal control of the national agencies.

Some exceptions exist, of which the following are illustrations. Since 1918 candidates for county assessor in Kentucky are required to possess a certificate from the state tax commission before their names are allowed on the ballot. This certificate is given on the basis of a written examination. In a few states the governor or some state official may remove local assessors after a hearing.[4] Illinois and Ohio require local health officers to be appointed from lists prepared by the state board of health after competitive examination.[5] State appointment and removal of rural local health officers are provided in some states. Employees of health districts in Ohio are appointed from state civil service lists if no eligibles are available from the registers of local commissions.[6] In 1913 the Wisconsin state commission of highways was authorized to examine applicants for county superintendent. In a small number of states local peace officers

[1] New Mexico Laws 1921, c. 188.

[2] Italics are author's.

[3] See Charles M. Kneier, "Some Legal Aspects of the Governor's Power to Remove Local Officers," 17 *Virginia Law Rev.* 355-68 (1930-31); M. H. Satterfield, "State Appointment and Removal of Local Law Enforcement Officers," 12 *Southwestern Social Sci. Q.* 277-95 (1931-32).

[4] White, *op. cit.*, pp. 62-63.

[5] *Ibid.*, p. 95.

[6] *Ibid.*, p. 101.

may be removed by state officials. In general, these powers are scattered and their use is infrequent.[1] The most spectacular instance on record is the resignation of Mayor Walker of New York in 1932 in the face of charges being heard by Governor Franklin D. Roosevelt.

j. Issuance of orders. Central authority may be vested with the right to issue general regulations binding upon the locality, or orders applicable to a single authority. Both types are widely enforced in the field of public health. Here the initiative passes from the local to the central agencies. Performance is enforced usually through the courts. This type of control is rare in the federal-state relationship.

k. Partial or total assumption of activity. The logical end of this series is reached when responsibility is transferred outright from the city or county to the state. Railroad regulation was subject to county boards until 1869, when Massachusetts established the first railroad commission; much power over even intrastate rail transportation has now shifted to the Interstate Commerce Commission. The assessment of utilities spreading from one end of a state to the other was once a duty of county assessors; it is now the task of the state tax commission.

The principal method by which central authority in administration has been amplified is not, however, the outright transfer of power. Supervision and review, setting standards and maintaining them by conditional grants are the historic means by which the state is gradually assuming responsibility for the kind and quality of local administration, and by which, in certain fields, the national government is exerting an influence upon and within the states. These devices permit a gradual adjustment between urban and rural communities and the state, and between the state and nation, without raising too sharply the political issues of state rights and local autonomy. Without disturbing the constitutional structure they facilitate such administrative adjustments as seem desirable from time to time in the light of changing problems and changing circumstances.

5. Values and Limitations of Administrative Centralization

A readjustment of an administrative system which has proceeded in a single direction over a period of three-quarters of a century and which is still in full flood is obviously more than a superficial trend. It is reasonable to conclude that it represents a major response of an administrative system originally designed for a rural agricultural economy to a type of organization better adapted to an urban industrial economy.

In seeking to reach a broad evaluation of this readjustment, therefore, we may start with the blunt assertion that the services and responsibili-

[1] *Ibid.*, p. 127.

ties which Americans desire from their government cannot be secured by reliance upon 3,000 counties and many thousands of uncorrelated towns and cities. Operating independently, they are incompetent to sustain the load of modern administrative requirements.

This conclusion, however, does not imply that counties, towns and cities are not prepared to carry a substantial share of the responsibility for contemporary administration. They are now discharging many important functions, and in many instances are doing work of high quality. They must necessarily carry a very substantial portion of the burden, for no degree of centralization which is either possible or desirable in a country as vast as the United States could transfer administrative responsibility for the bulk of public work to Washington.

Realization of the interlocking character of many governmental problems, of the interlocking interests which are affected by action at any one point, and of the impossibility of reaching either wise or effective solutions unless all factors are taken into consideration tends toward vesting responsibility in higher governmental units with a broader geographical base. The national implications of public action are forcing one problem after another into the arena of national administration—economic security for city and country, relief, public works, credit facilities, truth in advertising, elimination of child labor, transportation by motor vehicle—the list is long. Within the states, the desire to equalize opportunity for all citizens in education, in care for the handicapped, in protection of health, in access to markets, promotes state intervention in areas of administration once left to the local communities. These are desirable objectives.

With recognized exceptions, the highest standards of administration are generally associated with the national government. Its standards are certainly subject to improvement, but in comparison with those characteristic of many states, most counties and some cities, they are definitely superior, in some instances by a wide margin. The extension of national influence in state administration generally results, therefore, in raising the level of the commonwealths. The influence of the United States Bureau of Public Roads in highway construction, of the Department of Agriculture in state experiment stations, of the Public Health Service in state and municipal health departments, of the United States Employment Service in state employment offices has meant better administration.

In general it appears that officials of the national administration as a class are likely to be more competent than state or local officials as a group. State administration under favorable circumstances usually commands abler officials than the counties, although in some of the less progressive states no sharp distinction can be drawn. The larger and better managed cities usually are extremely well served by their official staffs, and the level of competence compares favorably with the states and at times with the national government. This superiority of national administration, to which many individual exceptions must be made, is due in part to the greater responsibilities involved, in part to the wider opportunity for specialization, in part to the greater prestige of the national system which attracts well-qualified officials and employees, and in part to its methods of recruitment and personnel management. National centralization tends, therefore, on the whole to put power in more competent hands.

More clearly with each decade it becomes certain that national problems can only be dealt with effectively through national instruments. Given the multiplication of public issues which present superstate problems, we can be sure of the expansion of the federal administration despite the difficulties of effective large-scale management which arise. These can be solved more easily than the hazards of trying to handle national issues through local authorities can be overcome.

The states as instruments of progress are definitely losing ground. Their leadership, with rare exceptions, is mediocre; their administrative organization, again with occasional exceptions, is inadequate. The inspiring example of such a state as Wisconsin has had almost no effect throughout the whole Mississippi Valley. The failure of the state to become a strong instrument of government is one of the leading reasons for the transfer of influence to Washington.

It seems possible indeed that the future structure of the American administrative system will rest primarily upon the national government and the cities, at least so far as the urban population (now approaching sixty per cent) is concerned. Ten years ago Charles E. Merriam wrote, "Those interested in preserving the balance of powers between the national and local governments might find the urban community a more effective counterweight . . . than the feebly struggling states. . . . A city would not be obliged to climb far to go beyond a state. Already there are seventeen cities of a population of over 500,000; nine states with less population than that. And if economic resources and cultural prestige are added to numbers, the contrast is more striking."

Certainly the record of administrative improvement in cities during the last twenty-five years is exceedingly impressive. In many states, municipal administration is far superior to state administration, just as progressive work in school management is found in city schools rather than in the state departments of education. The technical municipal services even in towns ridden by a low order of politicians are often surprisingly good. In cities which have the benefit of wholesome municipal government, cities like Milwaukee, Cincinnati, Berkeley, Richmond, Springfield (Massachusetts), they are entitled to recognition as equal to the quality of any administrative work at any level of government in the United States.

The weakness of the states may result eventually in the development of important administrative regions which will serve as the coordinating centers for planning administrative enterprises locally undertaken, and also as the connecting links between cities and the national authorities. The states would doubtless continue, but with further loss of position. This line of evolution is suggested by the Tennessee Valley Authority. The vitality of the state in many parts of the country, however, is such that effective regionalism is not likely to be an early achievement, and it is possible that the states can improve their administrative capacity to the point where they will play a larger part in the future system of administration in this country.

One of the important assets of a democracy is an active, energetic local government, meeting local needs and giving an immediate opportunity to citizens to participate in their own public affairs. While in some instances state or even national uniformity is desirable, in many cases variety and local adaptation are the essence of good administration. Both aspects of our common life deserve respect.

The gains to citizenship from an active system of local government are sometimes more obvious than the gains to efficient administration. In the last analysis, the former are entitled to great weight in a democracy. Nor is it certain that an undisturbed trend toward centralization may not eventually create an administrative organization so huge and so complex that it becomes much less efficient than a simpler structure. We have too little evidence to know at what point increase of size spells decrease of efficiency, but that such a point exists is probable.

Centralization in administration is, after all, a process which grows out of the social environment of the age, in response to the necessity for dealing with specific, concrete situations. Each generation makes its contribution for or against the growth of the national system as its problems and attitudes dictate.

The limits of useful centralization are defined by the prevailing technique of large-scale management and the prevailing social environment. In America we are living in a complex social organization which is constantly building itself upward and outward, creating larger social and administrative units which tend to replace in whole or in part the smaller units of earlier decades.

The social profile shows centralization progressing at various rates of speed and reaching a "saturation point" at different stages. No specific demarcation of the useful limits of centralization can be suggested which has any promise of stability. One may suggest as tests or standards the effective attainment of prevailing social ideals and objectives; the preservation of community and personal sense of initiative and responsibility; and the preservation of adequate democratic control.

Chapter Twelve

ADMINISTRATIVE AREAS

THE subject matter of administrative organization and structure has another aspect, the construction and arrangement of the geographical areas within which administrative functions are carried on. In a mythical city state, geographical subdivisions for administrative purposes might be unnecessary; the area limits of each administrative agency would reach to every corner of the state. In actual government much, if not most, public administration is organized on the basis of an area less extensive than that of the whole state, or the whole city.

The geographical basis of public administration has not been widely studied, apart from the important work of William Anderson.[1] In principle, however, there can be no doubt that areas may be well or poorly adapted to the work in hand, and that the relation of one area to another may be important in securing a smooth-working machine. The observations on administrative areas in this chapter are designed less to present any accepted conclusions than to call attention to a neglected cluster of problems.

The question of areas is related to the issue of centralization. The transfer of a public function from the county to the state is a shift from a small to a larger area, with all that is implied by way of increased population, greater financial resources, and more ample legal powers. The extension of supervisory influence of a central over a local government with respect to functions performed by it reflects also a readjustment of areal resources in terms of man power and money power. While the problems of administrative areas are not all involved in this special aspect, this is an important phase which may be observed in passing.

1. Types of Administrative Areas

Every public official and employee is related to an administrative area. He possesses not only a jurisdiction in the legal sense, but also in the

[1] William Anderson, *The Units of Government in the United States,* Public Administration Service No. 42, 1934; Phillips Bradley, "Administrative Areas," 1 *Encyclopaedia of the Social Sciences* 450-52 (1930); note also the works of Charles B. Fawcett, *Frontiers: A Study in Political Geography* (1918); *Provinces of England* (1919); *A Political Geography of the British Empire* (1933).

geographical sense. The area may be as large as the continental United States, or as small as a New England township or a city precinct. The geographical limits of the United States are divided and subdivided into hundreds of thousands of governmental and administrative areas whose present boundaries often reflect an historical inheritance rather than a rational adjustment of area to function, or area to area. In some metropolitan districts areas are piled up one on the other, overlapping each other in utmost confusion. In such a state as Virginia, on the contrary, the areas of government possess relative simplicity and orderliness.

Areas employed for administrative purposes fall into two major categories. They are, respectively, the area for a unit of government and the purely administrative district. The accepted definition of a unit of government is that devised by William Anderson.[1]

1. The unit has its own separate continuing governmental organization, either a board or a council, or in some cases even a single elective or appointive officer.
2. This governing body has the power year after year to provide some governmental service, or some quasi governmental service like a public utility, on its own responsibility, and subject to its own control.
3. This governing body is independent of other local governments, and is not a mere board handling some function of government on behalf of, or as a department of, another local corporation.
4. The area covered by a unit of local government may or may not coincide with the area of some other local government. If the areas coincide the test is whether the corporate existence is separate for the two or more units occupying the same area. There can be separate public corporations in the same area, of course, if they are organized for different purposes.
5. Among the important powers for any unit of local government, the power to raise revenue by taxation, or by special assessment, or by fixing rates for service rendered must be considered one of the most important. When other tests fail, this test may decide the case.

Areas laid out for purposes of general government are widely employed also as administrative districts. They may, however, be subdivided, combined, or entirely ignored for administrative purposes.

The second type of unit is the administrative district, formed without necessary reference to existing boundary lines of governmental units, having no "governmental" organization, no independent existence, and no power to raise revenue in its own right and by its own action. It is important to differentiate these two types of administrative areas. The considerations affecting their formation, their degree of permanence, their flexibility in the face of changing conditions, and their ease of coordination with other areas vary in substantial measure.

The number of units of government in the United States, 1930–1933,

[1] Anderson, *op. cit.*, p. 2.

is estimated by Anderson as 175,418. Their distribution is shown in the following table.[1]

TABLE I

Number of Units of Government in the United States, 1930–1933

Jurisdiction	Number
The nation	1
The states	48
Counties and parishes (Louisiana)	3,053
Incorporated places (cities, villages, D.C.)	16,366
Towns and townships (in 23 states)	20,262
School districts	127,108
Other units	8,580
Total	175,418

The number of local governments in the Chicago metropolitan region in 1933 reached the disgraceful total of 1,642. Their distribution is shown in the following table.[2]

TABLE II

Local Governments in the Metropolitan Region of Chicago[a]

	Number in the Whole Region	Number in Regional Section of Illinois	Number in Cook County	Number in Chicago
Cities	204	175	89	1
Counties	15	9	1	1
Townships	165	124	30	—
School districts	978	901	195	1
Park districts	70	70	56	22
Forest preserve districts	4	4	1	1
Sanitary districts	11	11	4	1
Drainage districts	190	188	40	—
Mosquito abatement districts	4	4	2	—
Health districts	1	1	1	—
Total	1,642	1,487	419	27

[a] In this study, a government was defined as an agency which independently exercises the power of initiating tax levies and assuming indebtedness and has legally constituted officials responsible for certain governmental services within a definite area.

[1] Adapted from Anderson's Table I, *op. cit.*, p. 1.

[2] Charles E. Merriam, Spencer D. Parratt and Albert Lepawsky, *The Government of the Metropolitan Region of Chicago* (1933), p. 9; cf. Simeon E. Leland, "Waste through Multiplicity of Governmental Units," 22 *Bulletin of the National Tax Association* 162-68 (1937); Milton Chernik and Samuel C. May, "Local Government in the San Francisco Bay Region," 199 *Annals* 99-105 (1938).

The number of purely administrative districts which underlie these units of government is entirely unknown, but it is certainly great. The territorial area of the United States is divided for national administration into 106 different series of districts, typically twelve districts in each series.[1] The states are subdivided for most administrative purposes: highway construction, health, police, inspection, forest protection, game and fish protection and many others. It is a reasonable assumption that each of the forty-eight states is divided into at least ten series of districts with a minimum of five districts in each series. The rural county uses principally the regular units of local government for administrative purposes, but the urban county and the city possess a large number of administrative subdivisions. In all, the purely administrative districts will number many thousands.

The establishment of boundary lines for these governmental and administrative units is governed by many considerations, legal, historical, geographical, prudential, political, and financial.[2] The main pattern of local government subdivisions is fixed for a large part of the United States by the familiar six-mile-square township lines; the county and city lines are affected somewhat by the concentration of population, but lag far behind the movement of the people. In broken country, geography suggests many boundaries, but in the open prairie or the flat coastal plain geographical considerations have little consequence.

Boundaries of the governmental units which also serve as administrative subdivisions are exceedingly difficult to readjust. Vested political interests are usually disturbed; community sentiment is often aroused; conflict between village and farm, between city and suburb, is sometimes involved. Recent efforts to organize metropolitan districts reveal the rigidity of boundaries in urban centers and when the metropolitan city cuts across state lines, the difficulty of adjustment is greatly enhanced.

The fact is that the governmental-administrative units often acquire a definite sense of community. They have emotional values which can be whipped into action for defense against consolidation with a large neighbor to which little sense of attachment exists, and against which is directed a sense of fear, hostility and conflict of interest. Americans share with other peoples a sense of attachment to locality, a loyalty which has

[1] These are mapped in National Resources Committee, *Regional Factors in National Planning and Development* (1935), pp. 203-23; for an account of a new administrative area, the soil conservation district, see Albert Lepawsky, "The Farmer Practices Public Administration," 27 *Nat. Mun. Rev.* 485-89 (1938).

[2] This topic is ably discussed in a series of articles by Sir Josiah C. Stamp and others in 3 *J. of Pub. Adm.* 300-97 (1925); see also John A. Fairlie, "Administrative Regions in Great Britain," 31 *Am. Pol. Sci. Rev.* 937-41 (1937).

civic values but which complicates the easy adjustment of boundaries to changed conditions.

The purely administrative district, on the other hand, is relatively fluid. Rarely, indeed, are the boundaries of the administrative district known outside official circles. Citizens send their income tax returns to a collector of internal revenue, but they do not know, and are indifferent to the geographical limits of his jurisdiction. Highway patrols safeguard the main thoroughfares, but the motoring public realize they have passed from one district to another only when they see a patrol headquarters. The boundaries of administrative districts are fixed to suit administrative convenience, and as a rule are readily altered in the light of changing circumstances. When, however, complex installations are involved, as in the communication system of a city fire department, even administrative districts acquire a degree of fixity. Apart from such exceptions, the administrative district has a flexibility and an anonymity quite different from that of the unit of government.

2. Trends in Area Reorganization

The settlement of the country throughout the last century and the concentration of population in cities rapidly increased the number of units of government and of administrative districts. Since 1890 the number of units of government has continued to increase, but less rapidly. The expansion in governmental functions and activities has been especially marked since 1910, and has required the very rapid multiplication of the purely administrative districts. Since 1920 there has been much discussion of the need for reducing the number and simplifying the structure of units of government, and a modest trend in this direction can be observed.

Recent movements are summarized by Anderson.[1] "With the turn of the tide toward industry and away from agriculture in recent decades, there has come the abandonment of many farms and even some villages, and the flow of population back into urban centers. While dispersion of population was once the rule, a reconcentration of it in large centers has recently become the order of the day. In very few places in the hinterland are new units of local government now needed. Many can be and are being abandoned. While there will probably be many new cities and villages incorporated in the future, particularly in the larger metropolitan areas, a definite decline in the units of rural local government may be expected. The statistics may not show these changes very quickly. Many units, without actually dissolving, will probably first merely be-

[1] Anderson, *op. cit.*, p. 13.

come inactive. Even when their main functions as well as much of their population have been sucked away, they may remain a long time as shells of what they once were. Centralization of power and functions, together with concentration of pooulation, must ultimately have its effect."

In the rural part of the United States, the elimination of small school districts is the principal trend in area reconstruction. There still remain over 125,000 school districts, nearly three times as many units of government as are required for the conduct of all other public activities, federal, state and local. The reconstruction of rural county lines meets with stubborn opposition. They are relatively immobile, although the plight of many small, sparsely populated rural counties is desperate. The principal sources of resistance are the county political organizations and certain vested interests profiting by status quo.[1] The principal gains have been in the combination of counties for joint support of common activities, thus forming an administrative district larger than the county without destroying it as the traditional governmental unit.

The process of annexation of outlying suburbs to the central city went on rapidly during the latter part of the nineteenth and the early part of the twentieth centuries. This trend has slowed down to a marked degree, so greatly indeed as to suggest that the city of the future may become an aggregate of contiguous but more or less independent areas.[2]

Despite some change, thererore, the areas of local government exhibit a substantial degree of stability and permanence. The boundary lines of the states are beyond the range of adjustment. Administrative problems, however, exhibit no respect whatever for these established governmental boundaries. The necessity for adjustment and innovation is widely felt; in the superstate, subnational area we already find significant changes in the formation of regions and in the discussion of regionalism.

3. Regionalism

Two converging movements are laying the foundations for administrative and perhaps governmental areas larger than the state, but smaller

[1] In discussing a plan for area reconstruction in the state of Washington, Menefee observes, "Any such comprehensive plan as that proposed in this study would undoubtedly be opposed by office-holders under the present county system, by leaders of political parties, by editors of newspapers carrying official advertising, and by merchants located in the county seats." Selden C. Menefee, *A Plan for Regional Administrative Districts in the State of Washington*, Univ. of Washington Publications in the Social Sciences, vol. 8, no. 2 (1935), p. 77.

[2] Winston W. Crouch, "Extraterritorial Powers of Cities as Factors in California Metropolitan Government," 31 *Am. Pol. Sci. Rev.* 286-91 (1937).

than the nation.[1] On the one hand, the states through the medium of interstate compacts are forming new areas including two or more states or parts of states for specific administrative purposes. The New York harbor area has been organized as an administrative unit by the Port of New York Authority. The tide waters in the neighborhood of New York City have been formed into an administrative area for water purification. Not every interstate agreement, however, produces a new administrative area.

On the other hand, the national government has created the Tennessee Valley Authority with an area covering the states and counties in the Tennessee Valley. Proposals are pending to establish regional authorities for other parts of the continental area of the United States. The Tennessee Valley Authority is a unit of government, not merely an administrative district. It is responsible to the Congress, but it must cooperate in many ways with the states.

From still another point of view, the administrative subdivisions of many of the national departments and agencies represent regional areas. These are formed on the basis of many considerations relevant to the special problem of the agency concerned. They are not uniform, but they tend to cluster around a small number of "natural" regional centers.

With the constitutional and political effects of regionalism we are not primarily concerned. As an administrative device, the regional area has many advantages. From the point of view of the national government, the region facilitates a deconcentration of authority which is conducive to useful specialization of effort, to more expeditious action, to easier coordination of national, state and local authorities, and to the comprehensive planning and treatment of the problems peculiar to a single watershed or other functional area. From the point of view of the state governments, the interstate region established by the national govern-

[1] The extensive literature on regionalism is represented by the following items: New York State Bureau of Housing and Regional Planning reports; Charles E. Merriam, "Metropolitan Regions," 20 *Univ. of Chicago Magazine* 364-70 (1928); C. E. Merriam, S. D. Parratt and A. Lepawsky, *The Government of the Metropolitan Region of Chicago* (1933); Paul Studenski, *The Government of Metropolitan Areas in the United States* (1930); Amry Vandenbosch, "Regions versus States," 21 *Kentucky Law J.* 432-42 (1932–33); C. Herman Pritchett, "Regional Authorities Through Interstate Compacts," 14 *Social Forces* 200-10 (1935–36); National Resources Committee, *Regional Factors in National Planning and Development* (1935), and *Regional Planning*, Parts 1-7 (1936–37); James W. Fesler, "Federal Administrative Regions" (ms. 1935), Harvard Univ.; same author, "Federal Administrative Regions," 30 *Am. Pol. Sci. Rev.* 257-68 (1936); Meredith F. Burrill, *A Socio-Economic Atlas of Oklahoma* (1936); Howard W. Odum, *Southern Regions of the United States* (1936); George H. Hansen, *A Regional Redistricting Plan for the State of Utah* (1937); Donald Davidson, *The Attack on Leviathan: Regionalism and Nationalism in the United States* (1938); Howard W. Odum and H. E. Moore, *American Regionalism* (1938).

ment probably facilitates local contacts and coordination; the region created by state compact is both a useful means of cooperative action and also a partial protection against the further loss of power to Washington. From the point of view of effective governmental action concerning problems which are superstate but less than national in scope, such as the use of water derived from Boulder Dam, the region is almost a necessity. While, therefore, the region as a *political* unit (i.e., as a superstate) is not yet in the present view of things, the region as a governmental unit (Tennessee Valley Authority, Port of New York Authority) and as an administrative district is well established and is apparently destined to become of greater use and significance.

4. Relation of Area to Area

In general, each administrative agency has organized its districts to suit its own convenience and necessities, without much attention to the districts of other agencies. Major geographical features, such as the Ohio River, the Mississippi River, and the Rocky Mountains, often direct different agencies toward some common boundaries. A study of the districts developed by the federal agencies shows little correlation one with another, and little tendency to use the same blocks of states as units. Thus "even such a traditional unit as New England is dismembered more frequently than not."

At the other end of the scale, inspection of the myriad of administrative districts in a metropolitan area reveals the same disregard for coordination of areas as such. Even police and fire districts, which bear an organic relation to each other, are planned independently. For some purposes, research rather than administrative in character, the census tract is becoming the common unit cell area in the larger cities.

The multiplicity of overlapping units of government in some metropolitan areas is traceable to the tax and debt limitations imposed upon local governments by state constitutions. Thus in Cook County (Chicago) the tax and debt limitations are such that a single area of local government, such as a consolidated city-county, would be fiscally incompetent to maintain existing services. The establishment of separate tax and debt incurring authorities in areas coincident with the city or county, such as the Park District, the Library District, the Forest Preserve District, and the Sanitary District was necessitated in order to avoid the constitutional limitations on fiscal capacity of local governments. The inhabitants of Cook County thus live under several layers of local authorities, at times with identical boundaries.

Obviously, not every area can bear a reasoned relation to all other districts in a given geographical and governmental unity. Administrative areas must be constructed primarily with an eye to the function which they serve. Many of these functions are interrelated and some are interdependent. These relationships are usually recognized, formally or informally, in day-by-day operations, but they have been overlooked in constructing administrative districts. The coordination of districts by joint use of the same district, by building larger units from smaller, by consolidating the number of separate boundary lines, and by relating administrative districts to units of government would tend toward simplicity, the convenience of citizens, and better coordination of different phases of administration itself. The consolidation of local units of government tends in the same direction.

Many of the advantages of coordination of administrative areas may be secured by establishing a common center of administration for areas which overlap each other. In large cities, for example, district police stations and fire stations are seldom put in the same or neighboring buildings. District health and welfare services are likely to operate from independent stations despite the related character of their work and clientele. Distances within cities are relatively small, but psychic distances overlook the standard units of length. The state and federal administrative distances are greater and the usefulness of common centers of administration is correspondingly enhanced.[1]

5. Criteria of Evaluation

What marks a suitable area of administration? Separate answers to this question are required for areas which are units of government, and for those which are purely administrative districts.[2]

a. The unit of government viewed as an administrative area. These units include the city, the incorporated village, school district, town or township, the county and the state, all basic governmental agencies of the United States characterized by the power to maintain a local responsible governing body, to raise revenue, and to provide services.

Small local areas of government may be deliberately subsidized by state governments by means of grants-in-aid. In the absence of such subsidies one of the principal criteria of the adequacy of areas is that they should be sufficiently extensive to permit the raising of enough revenue

[1] James W. Fesler, "Standardization of Federal Administrative Regions," 15 *Social Forces* 12-21 (1936–37).

[2] Much thought and attention have been given to the delineation of areas for school purposes. See among other citations Howard A. Dawson, *Satisfactory Local School Units: Functions and Principles of Formation, Organization, and Administration* (1934); Alonzo O. Briscoe, *The Size of the Local Unit for Administration and Supervision of Public Schools* (1935); Francis G. Cornell, *A Measure of Taxpaying Ability of Local School Administrative Units* (1936).

to support the services required by law or desired by citizens. The revenue-producing capacities of areas of local government and of the states vary enormously; but the services which cities, counties, and school districts are required or expected to provide are respectively about the same in a given state. Concentration of population and wealth makes the tax burden for these services relatively slight in some local units, crushingly heavy in others. The fiscal incapacity of rural school districts and rural towns in such areas as northern Maine or the Adirondack region in New York, the Blue Ridge region in the southeastern states and other sections spells the doom of the historic pattern of local government in these parts.[1] The small rural county in some parts of the country is equally impotent to serve by itself as an effective area of administration in the face of the costs of what are now accepted as essential services.

These fiscally dependent areas have been carried along in increasing measure by state subsidies, and in some measure the state grant-in-aid will remain a helpful instrument of equalization of resources. The test of fiscal capacity is, however, a genuine criterion of the adequacy of an area of local government.

A corollary of this criterion is population. There appears to be no ascertainable maximum limit to the population of effective units of local government. Skill in administrative organization and operation has developed to the point where five, seven, ten million people can live in a single metropolitan area in reasonable security and comfort, enjoying the amenities of modern civilization. The minimum number of persons requisite for the simple services of a rural area cannot be dogmatically stated, but it is clear that a minimum exists. Menefee's study in the state of Washington indicated a desirable population of 30,000 or more in the principal subdivisions of the state in order to be able to furnish adequate services at a minimum per capita cost.[2] Necessary health service cannot be provided separately and independently for each hamlet, or for each rural township, not merely for lack of revenue but also for lack of clientele.

The township and county were originally delimited so that any resident could reach the county seat and return to his home within a day's journey. With earlier methods of transportation, this meant that the county seat could not be much more than twenty miles from its perimeter. Modern means of transportation and communication have so "collapsed" space that on the basis of the same criterion of convenience, a county might now readily stretch fifty or sixty miles from its central

[1] O. J. Scoville, "Liquidating Town Government in Decadent Rural Areas of Maine," 13 *J. of Land and Public Utility Economics* 285-91 (1937).
[2] Menefee, *op. cit.*, p. 68.

point. With suitable district offices in the various population centers, the convenience of citizens in 1935 would be as effectively served in a county 100 miles square as in 1835 in a county of one-fourth this size.[1]

From quite a different point of view, the area of government and of administration should correspond to the geographical scope of the subject matter administered. It is this consideration especially which has forced the transfer of many functions of government from the county to the state, and in some cases from the state to the region or to the national government. Thus the regulation of railways in their infancy was at times confided to the county. The state eventually was forced to replace the county, and the national character of the problem eventually compelled its treatment on national lines, as a single geographical entity. The jurisdiction of the governing body and administrative officials must approximate the extent of the subject matter under public supervision.

These, then, are the principal criteria for the evaluation of a unit of local government as an administrative area: fiscal adequacy, sufficiency of population, accessibility to the seat of government, and coincidence of area with the subject matter of administration. From another point of view it is advantageous to organize local areas around trading centers, thus combining the area of government with an economic area. In turn this union will often reflect natural geographic features, which in some cases practically dictate jurisdictional, economic, and social boundaries

b. The administrative district. Here we consider the area established by administrative fiat for the convenience of officials and citizens, th area within which an official works on his daily assignment. The princi pal criterion by which to judge this type of area is convenience, both o officials and of citizens.

In terms of official convenience, the area will include a sufficient mini mum to provide enough business to warrant the employment of a full time staff not less than the size which experience indicates is necessary to avoid excessive unit costs. If the area provides institutional service, i will be large enough to maintain the institution as an efficient, well rounded unit.

From the point of view of the public, the principal consideration o convenience is accessibility. The citizen who needs to confer with a pub lic official or who wishes to transact business with a public authority wants to find an office in the vicinity. The limits of accessibility are se by appropriation acts. In general, public offices are found where the pub lic business has to be transacted. Customs districts, judicial districts health districts, police districts are organized to meet public needs. Th

[1] Carlton C. Sims, "County Government in Tennessee" (ms. 1932), Univ. o Chicago.

United States Civil Service Commission, to take a particular case, maintains thirteen districts, each with a district office, organized principally to meet the convenience of departmental field offices requisitioning employees. It also has about 3,600 examining districts, organized to meet the convenience of those who desire to take examinations.

The concentration of state business is normally at the state capital. Where large interests are found elsewhere, state administration will follow. Thus the public business of New York state is conducted for upstate New York at Albany, but for New York City in the state offices maintained on Manhattan Island. In Illinois some of the principal state offices are in Chicago, rather than Springfield. In California, state offices are required in San Francisco and Los Angeles on a scale comparable to those in Sacramento.

Public and official convenience therefore governs the formation of the administrative districts and the location of the field offices. While these districts may also acquire a degree of permanence, they are not so firmly entrenched as the areas of local government. The never ending stream of population is constantly stranding some units of local government along the shore and sweeping others into midcurrent, where they may have to carry a burden too heavy for them to support. Like awkward rafts they drift along or stick fast while the stream courses by. Fortunately new and better structures designed merely for administrative purposes can be built quickly by administrative action.

PART III

FISCAL MANAGEMENT

Chapter Thirteen

ORGANIZATION FOR FISCAL MANAGEMENT

AT THIS point problems of organization and relationships give way to a second major aspect of public administration, fiscal management. Reverting to a figure of speech used in an earlier chapter, ve may say that the many parts of the administrative vessel have been ssembled and put in place so that a seaworthy craft now lies in the haror. To put it to work funds and a crew are essential. In succession the rincipal aspects of getting, using, and accounting for funds, and of hirng the crew are brought forward for analysis and observation.

1. Definition and Scope of Fiscal Management

Fiscal management includes those operations designed to make funds vailable to officials and to ensure their lawful and efficient use. In a mall city and in rural government generally fiscal management is relaively simple; in great cities fiscal management is usually the most perlexing phase of local government; and in the heavily populated states nd the federal government the organization, procedures and problems re extremely complex.

Fiscal management includes as its principal subdivisions budget making, followed by the formal act of appropriation; executive supervision f expenditures (budget execution); the control of the accounting and eporting system; treasury management and revenue collection; and udit. To perform these functions an extensive organization is required, ie study of which is the main purpose of this chapter.[1]

The analysis of fiscal organization and procedures incidentally throws ght on other aspects of administration. An appropriation act involves nportant executive-legislative relationships, and has direct and practical ffect upon public planning. Modern devices for extending the influence f the chief executive over administrative spending illustrate the new osition of mayors, governors and the president as true heads of the hole official family. The complex and difficult set of relationships beveen the central finance office and the operating departments is somehat paralleled by the corresponding relation of the civil service com-

[1] State supervision over local finance has already been noted in ch. 11.

mission with the same departments. The organization of the fiscal offices, partly in one or more central units, partly as departmental finance offices not directly responsible to the central finance agency, presents an important general issue. Finally, the procedures by which fiscal officers collect the revenue from willing or reluctant citizens illustrate in many ways the modes of law enforcement which are dealt with in a later division of this work. While, therefore, these chapters will be primarily concerned with the arrangements by which officials get funds and use them, the broader implications of the subject matter will not disappear from view.

Finance and administration are in fact inseparable. Every administrative act has its financial implications, either creating a charge on the treasury or making a contribution to it. Nothing can be done without the expenditure of money, at the very minimum for the payment of the salary or wage of the official or employee who acts. Available financial resources set a maximum limit on administrative activity as a whole and on each of its separate parts. The management of finance is therefore one of the first and one of the inescapable responsibilities of administrators.

In their broader implications financial operations may affect or may be deliberately designed to consummate some general aspect of public policy. The tariff has been a means of effectuating policy quite as much as a source of revenue. The taxation of sulphur matches by the federal government is merely a convenient means of driving them from use. Chain store taxes are less revenue measures than means to protect the small proprietor. The control of production through taxation of surpluses was sought in the Bituminous Coal Act of 1937. The social security tax for unemployment compensation was designed to bring effective pressure on the states to establish state compensation plans.[1] Expenditures may also be designed to effectuate both an immediate specific purpose and more general end, as for example the "pump-priming" outlays of the federal government since 1933. The use of public expenditures to secure social reform is exemplified in the Walsh-Healy Act which set up minimum conditions of labor to be observed by bidders on public contracts.

These are aspects of fiscal management which lie outside the scope of this volume, although their social significance is of primary importance. They concern great questions of public policy more than matters of administration; or as phases of administration they involve substantive problems which are excluded from consideration here.

[1] Harvey W. Peck, "The Use of the Taxing Power for Non-Fiscal Purposes," 183 *Annals* 57-62 (1936); E. P. Herring, "The Politics of Fiscal Policy," 47 *Yale Law Rev.* 724-45 (1937-38).

It follows that most of the field of public finance falls outside this ook.[1] Of its three main divisions, public expenditures, revenue, and nancial administration, we are concerned only with the latter. In the llowing chapters, therefore, nothing will be said about the various urces of public revenue, their distribution among different areas of overnment, their incidence, and their economic and social effects. We all not examine the many and rapidly changing types of public ex-enditures reflecting changing attitudes toward the role of government our social structure. Nor shall we consider fiscal policy in the sense f the relative merits of a balanced budget, a favorable balance of trade, long-term capital expenditure plan, the elimination of social injustice y taxation or their opposites.

Instead, the point of view underlying this study of fiscal management that of the operating official or chief executive who is responsible for e execution and enforcement of legislation and who needs funds to em-loy the necessary personnel, to purchase equipment, and to incur other roper expenditures. His first task is, therefore, to secure funds, his sec-nd task is to use the funds in the performance of his prescribed tasks; he ust also maintain accounts to show the flow of funds and to indicate e results of their expenditure; finally, he must submit his records for independent audit to determine the legality and propriety of his action every particular. The most important aspects of fiscal management as part of public administration concern the relationships involved in this ries of operations, not in the amount of revenue and expenditure in eneral or in particular. It is with these relationships, consequently, at we shall deal rather than with figures and trend lines.

To carry on these activities a considerable organization is required, art of which lies within the major operating departments, part of which outside, consisting of budget officers, directors of finance, comptrol-rs, accountants and auditors. The evolution of these offices throws con-derable light on their present character.

Trends in Fiscal Organization

Within the constitutional system of the United States, the executive ranch is unable to levy or collect revenue or spend money without leg-lative authorization. This basic requirement is part of our historic in-eritance from Great Britain, where the principle of legislative suprem-cy in finance had become established beyond challenge—after centuries f conflict—by the time of the American revolution. It was written into

[1] This field is covered in such works as Clyde L. King, *Public Finance* (1935); arley L. Lutz, *Public Finance* (3d ed. 1936); George F. Shirras, *Science of Public nance* (3d ed. 1936), 2 vols.; and Jens P. Jensen, *Government Finance* (1937).

the national constitution and the constitutions of the states, and is uni versally recognized as one of the fundamentals of a constitutional de mocracy, although the form and nature of the authorization vary fro case to case.

At the outset, in harmony with accepted political theory, the majo responsibility for most of the basic operations in finance rested with th legislature or its recognized agents. Congress and the state legislatur authorized all revenues, usually for one year only; the state legislatu frequently elected the state treasurer who was custodian of funds, an for years the Secretary of the Treasury was recognized as responsib to Congress in a peculiar degree; expenditures were authorized by legi lative appropriations made directly to each spending agency, and th auditor was usually elected by the legislative body or the voters. Th governor and the President were generally excluded from close conta with money matters.

For a hundred years the fiscal machinery of the country gradually ex panded, but without modification of the general ideas upon which it wa originally based. The legislature remained the center of gravity of th whole system, but its parts eventually multiplied to such an extent th many of them seemed to move in orbits of their own, independent the central sun. The legislative task of considering appropriations w frequently divided among several committees and subcommittees; sep rate committees handled revenues and expenditures. This dispersion responsibility made impossible any general view directed toward fina cial planning. Likewise it made easy pork-barrel and other wasteful ap propriations.

The dispersion of legislative responsibility for fiscal affairs was para leled by the disintegration of the administrative and fiscal establishmen The independent position of the traditional fiscal officers—assessors, co lectors, treasurers, comptrollers and auditors—defeated their proper c ordination. Bookkeeping methods, accounting and office procedur were devised to suit the convenience of the individual office, and gene ally without respect to the needs of other fiscal offices. The statuto independence of fiscal officers did not always result in the anticipat balance of one against the other. While old fiscal offices remained, ma new and independent fiscal agencies were created. This was especial true on the state level where such new agencies as tax commissions, de commissions, investment commissions and special revenue collecti agencies emerged, frequently with little or no coordination among the selves or with the older offices.

Larger sums were constantly passing into the hands of more agenci in the shape of earnings, which for years were allowed to be retain y the departments for their own use, supplementing regular appropria-ions. These earnings tended to escape adequate accounting, and compli-ated the financial structure. The long list of fee officers added to fiscal onfusion.

Although there are exceptions to this generalized description, the net esult was an extraordinary dispersion of responsibility for fiscal admin-tration in the numerous offices concerned with public finance and a orresponding confusion of responsibility for fiscal policy in an incom-etent and badly organized legislative body.

The history of the last quarter century has been steadily in the direc-on of consolidation on all fronts.[1] Legislative procedure has been im-roved and executive integration has gone far toward creating an or-erly and responsible financial system. The number of independent dministrative agencies has been greatly reduced, minimizing the num-er of separate requests for appropriations; coordination of fiscal policy as been improved by establishing finance departments and budget agen-ies; executive control has been extended over administrative agencies id expenditures; earnings of departments are covered into the treasury id the fee officers are on their way to extinction, however desperate ie fighting. Leadership in financial matters has been definitely trans-rred to fiscal officers, sometimes but not always subject to the chief ecutive, and year by year it is becoming more effective.

The new pattern of consolidated fiscal agency is well illustrated by ie Department of Finance in Illinois. The director of the department appointed by and is directly responsible to the governor. The princi-l fiscal officers are the director, assistant director, administrative audi-r, superintendent of the budget, superintendent of departmental reports, atistician, state purchasing agent, superintendent of printing and the x commissioners. The Director of Finance is the secretary and execu-ve officer of the Tax Commission, but so far as the assessment of prop-ty for taxation is concerned the Commission operates independently the Department of Finance. The organization chart of this office in-cates the internal relationships.

Inevitably the rate of progress in different jurisdictions has varied eatly, and the present position is quite uneven as we pass from one ite to another, or one city to a second. In general, the fiscal procedures the national government never became so involved as in some of the ites and municipalities, although they were in grave need of reform

See L. D. White, *Trends in Public Administration* (1933), chs. 5 and 14; Wil-m Anderson, *Local Government and Finance in Minnesota* (1935); Carl H. atters, "Local Government Finance in the United States of America," 2 *Local overnment Administration* 4-12 (1936).

when Congress finally enacted the Budget and Accounting Act of 1921 The large industrial states of the east and middle west along with California took the lead in reorganization of fiscal machinery, although in recent years improvements are noted in all parts of the country. Seriou weaknesses in the fiscal situation of some states and many units of loca government became apparent in the recent depression, but these wer due rather to failure of revenue than to unsatisfactory fiscal procedure or dishonest officials.

ILLINOIS DEPARTMENT OF FINANCE

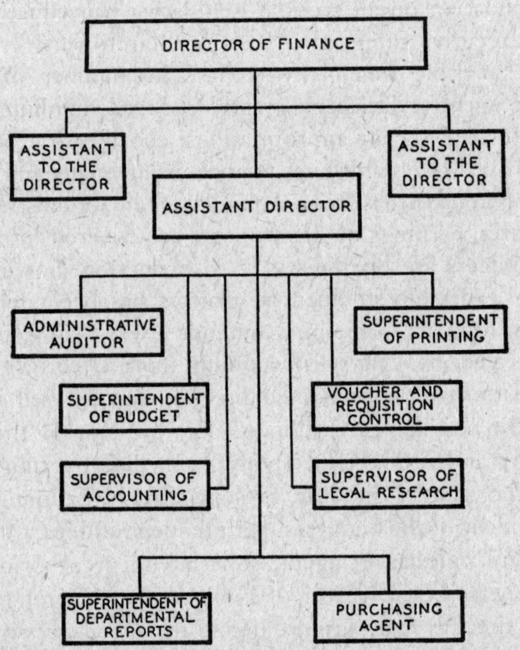

The broad reasons for this transition are four: loss of confidence i legislative bodies as agencies for fiscal management; realization of th desirability for fixing responsibility for the management of fiscal affair rapidly rising governmental expenditures and debts which emphasize the necessity for fiscal reform; and the studies of research bureaus, whic made apparent the waste due to disorganized fiscal management ar which offered promising, reasonable alternatives.

3. Present Organization for Fiscal Management

While all sorts of patterns of organization, good and bad, can b viewed in actual operation, the result of the last forty years' discussi f fiscal management has been to outline a standard form to which actual iscal structures tend to conform.[1] Present-day fiscal offices fall into hree separate groups: (a) the central finance departments, illustrated y the Illinois Department of Finance; (b) the principal fiscal officials n the operating departments; (c) the auditors. A brief survey of each f these groups will be followed by a statement of the division of work mong them.

The central finance offices other than those collecting the revenue in- lude principally the treasury and the finance department, which often mbraces the budget office, the central accounting staff, and the execu- ive comptroller; in large jurisdictions the office of comptroller may be eparately organized. The treasury is the old historical finance office, the hief responsibility of which is to receive, to have custody of and to pay ut public funds. In the states and cities, it is usually an independent of- ice; the Office of the Treasurer of the United States is a part of the reasury Department. There is a slow trend to terminate the independ- nt status of the office.

Budget officers were a later invention. The movement for better budg- ting began in the cities with the municipal reform group, and was well nder way by 1900. In the states, budget agencies were initiated in 1911 y California and Wisconsin; by 1926 every one of the forty-eight states ad a formal state budget of one type or another, and most of the states ad executive budget agencies.[2]

In a few jurisdictions the office of comptroller, an executive authority mpowered to review and control proposed expenditures on behalf of ne chief executive, has been separately organized and differentiated rom the auditor, the agent of the legislative branch.[3] Massachusetts fur- ishes an excellent example.

In this state the Comptroller's Bureau is a subdivision of the Commis- on on Administration and Finance, and the comptroller is appointed or a term of four years by the governor and council. The comptroller xamines all accounts and demands against the commonwealth and cer-

[1] Space limitations prohibit the description of fiscal organizations in any single risdiction, but at least one specific case study should be undertaken by students. he most recent exposition of the fiscal system of the federal government is in the port prepared by the Brookings Institution, *Investigation of Executive Agencies the Government*, S. Rept. 1275, 75th Cong., 1st sess. (1937), ch. 3. Various re- orts by state reorganization committees describe state fiscal systems. A generalized escription of the fiscal systems of the American states may be found in J. Wilner ndelson, *Budgetary Methods in National and State Governments*, Special Report the N. Y. State Tax Commission No. 14, 1938. See also standard works on merican state and local government.

[2] White, *Trends in Public Administration*, p. 189.

[3] See *infra*, ch. 17, for further discussion of these offices.

tifies the amounts due and allowed on each account or demand. He designs and installs the accounting system and keeps general books of account, examines all state printing, and keeps all original bills and vouchers which are examined in the settlement of claims. The comptroller, in short, is the central executive officer for the review and control of expenditures as they occur from day to day.[1]

The state auditor is an auditor and nothing more. He is forbidden to keep any books or records except records of audit. Even in the procedures of audit, he must comply with regulations made by the governor and council.[2]

These three offices then are the principal central agencies for fiscal management: the treasury, the budget office, and the comptroller. They are slowly tending toward a union of forces although a long way yet from a "Ministry of Finance."

Within the operating departments responsibility for managing financial matters tends to settle into a common pattern. Authority to incur specific expenditures within the terms of the appropriation act is normally vested in the head of the agency; in the case of a commission it is sometimes vested in the president or chairman, sometimes in the board as a whole. This authority is evidenced by the countersignature of the head on pay rolls, requisitions and other financial documents. In very large or dispersed agencies the authority to incur expenditures may be devolved on bureau or office heads.

The operating head of an organization of any size usually does not himself act as the fiscal officer. Consequently a fiscal office inside the department is established to carry on all the preparatory steps in reaching fiscal decisions, to record fiscal transactions, and to have custody of fiscal documents. This office is one of first-rate importance in large departments, admirably illustrated by the Office of Budget and Finance of the Department of Agriculture.

Another primary fiscal office is that of the auditor. This, too, is an historic office reaching back to the foundations of our government. The auditor is the agent of the legislature; it is his duty to ensure that all expenditures authorized by administrative officials are legal and regular in every respect.

Apart from the legislative act of appropriation, the various operations by which money is made available for public purposes, is expended, and is accounted for are distributed among the foregoing fiscal agencies: the central controlling bodies, the spending agencies, and the auditor. Their smooth coordination is one of the major problems of fiscal management.

[1] Massachusetts General Laws, 1932, vol. 1, pp. 132, 135.

[2] *Ibid.*, pp. 154-55.

'heir interrelationships are never ending and necessarily involve situa-ons where differences of opinion are certain and sometimes profound.

The general distribution of authority is normally this. The line or perating departments are responsible for the preparation of estimates, ut the budget office reviews and may modify them. The line depart-ents initiate expenditures, but their validation may require the ap-roval of the comptroller. The line departments prepare and validate the nancial documents showing expenditures, which are the basis of the ntral accounts maintained by the specialized fiscal offices and of the idits performed by the auditor. Some line departments keep their own ooks of account; others do not. As an incident of operations, they may ollect fees and other miscellaneous revenue.

The central fiscal agencies are essentially organs of control superim-osed on the spending departments. Experience indicates that the inter-ts of the taxpayer cannot be safely left to the unregulated discretion the line agencies. Consequently the fiscal agencies review the depart-ental estimates, watch the flow of expenditures, retain the custody of nds, and audit the results.[1]

Personnel in Fiscal Administration

The delicate and important position held by the directors of the cen-l fiscal agencies lends special emphasis to the quality of mind of the cupants of the key posts: finance directors, budget officers, treasurers, mptrollers, and auditors. They hold positions of great power, and ex-rience indicates that it is not always easy to strike a happy balance be-een their responsibilities and those of the major departments.

The controlling consideration lies in the proposition that administra-e agencies exist to perform a public function authorized and financed a representative body on behalf of the citizens. Primacy of purpose s with the line agencies, not with the fiscal offices. Government does t exist for the keeping of books and accounts, for reviewing expendi-es and fiscal programs, or even for executing an audit. Government d its administrative organs exist to serve and to achieve great human jectives in terms of the health, education, safety and convenience of mass of the population.

It is also true that these ends are to be sought within the law and sub-t to the limitations imposed by law and appropriation acts, for the en-cement of which fiscal agencies and auditors were created. In the rginal area where differences of opinion arise concerning what is law-

For the court review of expenditure decisions, see Harvey C. Mansfield, lministrative Finality and Federal Expenditures," 47 *Yale Law Rev.* 603-21 37-38).

ful the emphasis may be on the judgment of the line, or the auxiliar agencies of administration. It is the view of this book that the opinio of the operating heads acting under their responsibility to the chief exec utive is entitled to primary consideration where differences of opinio on expenditure programs can reasonably be entertained, subject c course to the examination of the auditor.

Fiscal agencies and operating agencies are constantly thrown togethe and in some instances the former necessarily have the final decisio Hence arises the special necessity for a superior personnel in the fisc offices. It is easy for fiscal officers to think in terms of money only an necessarily difficult for them to weigh and appreciate the thousand di ferent services and values which lie behind the expenditure of mone It is also inevitable and indeed proper that fiscal officers should be prin cipally concerned with a balanced budget and with the avoidance unauthorized expenditures. From this point of view it is easy to fall int an attitude of not spending, rather than an attitude of spending. Fisc officers in fact usually correspond to the stereotype of the mythical Sco

Central fiscal agencies are in part designed to counterbalance tl spending proclivities of the operating departments, and no one shou complain if they perform this function. The critical problem is wheth in selecting certain subjects of expenditure for approval and others f disapproval or for diminution, they are aware of the social as well as th financial implications of their decisions.

Since this issue is discussed in the next chapter, it is enough to state here in order to suggest that finance officers need to be statesmen as w as accountants, bankers, or economizers. While the function they are perform is essential, it is not yet clear that the manner of its performan is adequately adjusted to the ends for which government exists. Wh are our fiscal governors, from what social origins they spring, with wh philosophy they are endowed, with what breadth of outlook they ma their decisions are matters of which we know little, but of which wholesome scheme of fiscal control must take full measure.

Chapter Fourteen

BUDGETARY PROCEDURES AND PROBLEMS

AMONG the astonishing features of our administrative history is the fact that until about 1910 there were no executive budgets in nation, states or cities. Every spending agency went directly to ts appropriating body and it was no responsibility of the chief executive to influence or control the amount asked or granted except in the inal act of a veto. The possibilities of extravagance, waste and favoritism nder such a disorganized regime were endless. No country except one lessed with a rapidly expanding economy could have tolerated the lack f financial order and care which was almost universal until three decdes ago.[1]

The essence of the great change which has been introduced in fiscal nethods since 1910 (in the national government since 1920) is the grant o the chief executive of authority to control both the budget estimates nd to some extent the use of the funds subsequently appropriated by he legislative body.[2] Coordination, supervision and control of finance re gradually replacing the unregulated and chaotic freedom of the arious administrative agencies to deal directly with appropriations comnittees.

The immediate result has been a marked improvement in the care vith which estimates are prepared for legislative consideration. In 1923 he chairman of the House Appropriations Committee said, "I have ever seen estimates of appropriation so free from obvious padding, so arefully squared to actual needs, or so void of proposed extravagant exansion of government activities as these." In 1924 the chairman of the enate Appropriations Committee said, "Now an estimate means somehing." The same results followed the introduction of state and city udget systems.

[1] For a theoretical discussion of budgeting on different lines than those adopted y this chapter see J. Wilner Sundelson, "Budgetary Principles," 50 *Pol. Sci. Q.* 36-63 (1935). Budget procedures and problems in education are discussed in Oscar W. Irvin, *State Budget Control of State Institutions of Higher Learning* 1929).

[2] For an example see Finla G. Crawford, "The Executive Budget Decision in New York," 24 *Am. Pol. Sci. Rev.* 403-8 (1930).

A secondary consequence has been to amplify the administrative authority of the chief executive. Inevitably he who controls finance is in command so far as expediency and policy may dictate. The fiscal aspects of administrative reorganization form one of the principal bases on which the new leadership in administration rests.

A third effect has been to reduce the influence of members of appropriations committees on administrative problems, but by no means to eliminate their contacts with officials. Before the reform of fiscal procedures leading members of appropriations committees, who are usually legislative old-timers, were frequently the real power behind the administrative scenes. Their power was used for political as well as official ends. Such legislators still have and are bound to have great influence in administrative circles, but their freedom to influence officials is somewhat diminished.[1]

Budget practices in actual operation vary widely from place to place and from time to time under the influence of personalities and special conditions. In the following paragraphs a generalized account of the main stages in budget making is presented, briefly discussing a few of the more significant issues.[2]

1. Preparation of Estimates

The first step in budget making is the preparation of estimates by each administrative agency. At this initial point one of the basic changes in

[1] In the Independent Office Appropriation Act of 1937–38, the salary of the Executive Director of the Social Security Board was reduced $500 at the instance of a powerful senator who had been crossed in a patronage appointment by the director.

[2] Excellent general discussions of fiscal management are available in W. F. Willoughby, *Principles of Public Administration* (1927), chs. 28-43; John M. Pfiffner, *Public Administration* (1935), chs. 13-17; Harvey Walker, *Public Administration in the United States* (1937), chs. 5-10. Industrial budgeting is discussed in John H. Williams, *The Flexible Budget* (1934).

Among the many books and monographs dealing with budgets, the following will be found useful: U.S. Commission on Economy and Efficiency, *The Need for a National Budget*, H. Doc. 854, 62d Cong., 2d sess. (1912); René Stourm, *Le Budget* (1889), English edition, *The Budget* (1917); Luther H. Gulick, *The Evolution of the Budget in Massachusetts* (1920); F. A. Cleveland and A. E. Buck, *The Budget and Responsible Government* (1920); Charles G. Dawes, *The First Year of the Budget of the United States* (1923); R. E. Taylor, *Municipal Budget Making* (1926); W. F. Willoughby, *The National Budget System* (1927); National Municipal League, "A Model Municipal Budget Law," 17 *Nat. Mun. Rev.* 437-45 (1928); A. E. Buck, *Public Budgeting* (1929); same author, *Budgeting for Small Cities* (1931); same author, *The Budget in Governments of Today* (1934); Roscoe C. Martin, *Budget Manual for Texas Cities* (1934); J. Wilner Sundelson, *Budgetary Methods in National and State Governments* (1938). The most recent description and analysis of federal budget procedure is found in *Investigation of the Executive Agencies of the Government*, S. Rept. 1275, 75th Cong., 1st sess. (1937), ch. 3.

fiscal procedure has developed. Traditionally each operating unit was solely responsible for the amount and nature of its requests for the succeeding fiscal period. Naturally it prepared its estimates in the light of its own needs without much attention to the existence of similar or overlapping activities in other agencies and necessarily without regard to the total requests since they were not known until a clerk had finally assembled them. This uncoordinated and uncontrolled procedure lent itself to a sort of competitive bidding in padded estimates. It was customary to overestimate in order to balance reductions certain to be made by legislative committees. Honest estimates were rare, because no conscientious administrator dared run the risk of heavy cuts from an honest figure. Appropriations committees and applicants for funds consequently played a game of poker; either might hold the higher cards. A consistent, balanced financial program was unknown, the proper relation of expenditures to revenue was relegated to the background, and deficits were as common as mosquitoes in New Jersey.

Budget estimates are still prepared in the first instance by the departments and other agencies receiving appropriations. They are prepared, however, on the basis of instructions which grow out of the general financial program developed and announced by the chief executive. This program is based on the revenue which existing laws are expected to produce with any increases or decreases which the chief executive may think wise or necessary, reflecting the particular emphasis which he desires to give to public activities. Thus in a period of depression it may be the policy of the president, the governor or mayor to fix the estimates at the figure of the preceding year, or to impose a flat percentage decrease over the previous appropriation, or to allow no promotions nor increments of pay.[1] Executive policy, however, does not affect the estimates of the legislative branch, which are usually prepared by the clerks of the houses, or those of the judiciary, or those of the independent state constitutional officers or institutions such as the state auditor, treasurer, or the state university.

Within these limits fixed by executive policy, the budget officials of the various departments and agencies set to work, having before them the record of expenditures of the present and previous years, any general instructions concerning financial policy which may be given by the

[1] In some states, general financial policy may be worked out through an administrative board, or through a board representing the executive and legislative branches. The influence of the governor tends to dominate these boards, although the independent auditor or comptroller is often a figure to be reckoned with. Political affiliations may make any combination possible, sometimes to the detriment of executive leadership. See author's *Trends in Public Administration* (1933) pp. 188-91.

head of the department, and the informally expressed hopes of the bureau chiefs and division heads. At this stage the departmental budget officer will work out a schedule of promotions and advances for members of the organization, a task which is usually shared with (or even controlled by) the departmental personnel office. In a large organization, weeks will be devoted to the task of setting up estimates for consideration by the head of the department or agency, involving repeated conferences between operating officials and departmental budget experts.

In a large department such as the United States Treasury or Department of Agriculture, the first consideration of the estimates involves something of the same tug of war that reaches its full strength at later stages. The departmental budget officer is inclined to hold expenditures down, while the operating units tend to push them up. A delicate balancing of claims ensues. Most bureaus have legitimate requests, the total of which far exceeds any reasonable hope of departmental approval; each bureau must therefore reach its own conclusions as to which items to put forward at any given point of time. One division competes against sister divisions, the balance being struck eventually by the head of the department with the advice of his budget officer, often after protracted figuring and more conferences. Here, too, pressure from interested groups may be felt. Ample funds mean more activity; shrinking appropriations mean less activity; and both ends may be desired by different parties, for different reasons.

There is an interesting "professional" influence at work tending to hold down the departmental estimates. This is the desire on the part of the departmental budget officer to submit estimates which will be regarded as professionally competent by the budget experts in the central fiscal agency. Excessive, unwarranted, "out-of-line," padded, or ill-considered estimates will not be regarded as professionally competent, and the departmental budget officer does not wish to be placed in the position of trying to defend them before his peers in the budget bureau.

The form of the estimates is sometimes fixed by law, more frequently by the chief executive or the budget officer. It varies from case to case, but will usually include summary statements of total requests compared with previous appropriations; detailed and itemized requests by each operating unit; requests for each major object (personnel, material, services, etc.); and anticipated revenue from departmental earnings, if any. It is uncommon for the estimates to be presented in terms of work units to be performed, although this would often be the most significant presentation. For example, when Mr. Frank Bane was Commissioner of Public Welfare in Virginia, he presented a budget showing the number of inmates of the various institutions, the quantity of food required and other corresponding data, and then invited the state budget director to estimate the cost.

The estimates will also include more or less elaborate explanations intended to convince the budget director and the chief executive of the essential reasonableness of the proposals. The arguments are largely relative in nature, explaining new work requirements imposed by statute or by growth of activities, arrearages and delays in operation under previous appropriations, and recommendations for new undertakings. These documents are known in federal parlance as the "justification sheets."

On or about the appointed day, final approval is given to the estimates by the head of the organization. Bureau chiefs secretly congratulate themselves that no worse fate has befallen their hopes. The estimates are transmitted to the bureau of the budget or finance director with the prayers and aspirations of all concerned.

2. Review of Estimates

In the days of unreformed fiscal procedure, the multifarious operating units presented their estimates directly to the appropriations committee where they were assembled for the first time by a clerk. Standard practice now introduces a preliminary review and adjustment of all estimates of the executive branch either directly by the chief executive, as in small jurisdictions, or by his agent, the budget bureau or the finance director. Thus the United States Budget and Accounting Act of 1921 provides that the Bureau of the Budget "shall have authority to assemble, correlate, revise, reduce, or increase the estimates," and corresponding language is found in state and city finance acts.

After preliminary study by the budget examiners formal hearings are usually held between the budget agency and the departments at which the latter are given opportunity to explain and defend their estimates, now under fire. Most departments complain that the budget examiners are "hard-boiled" and deplore their lack of insight into the real problems of the operating agencies. Something can be said both in criticism and defense of the budgeteers. The general impression left upon the author as a result of three years' official contact with the United States Bureau of the Budget was that its staff worked under too great pressure to function as intelligently and effectively as might be desired, and in individual cases the examiner seemed to be influenced too much by a desire to conform to the "hard-boiled" stereotype which presumably commanded respect in his group.

However this may be, the United States Bureau of the Budget cuts hundreds of millions from the departmental estimates. The amount of reductions in the "normal" predepression years is shown in the following table,[1] which may be compared with Table IV on page 220. These are not merely reductions of "padded" estimates, but are cuts in programs which departments can usually defend with justice.

TABLE III

Reductions Effected by the Bureau of the Budget in Original Estimates, 1924–1930

Budget for Year Ending June 30	Reductions (000 omitted)	Percentage of Budget
1924	$307,404	10.0
1925	318,208	10.5
1926	324,324	10.5
1927	150,286	4.8
1928	112,735	3.5
1929	189,881	5.4
1930	280,778	7.6

The budget officials themselves must in the last analysis take the initial responsibility for allowing or disallowing estimates. In considering the estimates for 1938–39, the United States Bureau of the Budget sought advice on certain types of proposed expenditures from the National Resources Committee. This precedent suggests that other sources of advice might also be used to advantage by budget examiners, such as civil service commission experts on personnel proposals and the purchasing experts on large procurement estimates. Such coordination is rare apart from informal and unsystematic personal contacts.

The necessity for some central coordination and balancing of expenditure programs is now admitted on all sides, however great the resistance to budget making was twenty-five years ago. The power to refuse to recommend expenditures proposed by the various departments is an essential phase of this central review of the estimates; a mere compilation and summary is not enough. This power is a drastic one, and is usually exercised under the immediate direction of and responsibility to the chief executive himself. Great though the power is, it is inescapable if expenditures and revenues are to balance and if a coordinated program is to be undertaken.

The crucial issue is, on what grounds and on what evidence do budget officials approve, eliminate or reduce proposals for expenditure? Budget officers do not disclose specific reasons for rejecting or reducing an estimate. In Washington a phrase is current to the effect that a proposed expenditure is not in harmony with the President's financial policy, a

[1] Taken from the author's *Trends in Public Administration*. p. 152.

formula which precludes discussion except with the President. The real reasons are various, and are sometimes remote from fiscal considerations.

The most obvious reason for reducing estimates is to bring the total within the maximum fixed by the chief executive. Budget procedure is intended among other things to keep expenditures in check, and implicit in reformed fiscal procedure is the authority of the president, governor, manager or mayor to determine the maximum amount which he will recommend to the appropriating body. Estimates inevitably exceed this maximum and the budget officer, representing the chief executive, must reduce them in varying degrees to meet the total. At this point, by a process which has never been described by the participants, the relative merit of competing claims for funds on the part of different departments is weighed and determined.

Budget officials may of course have specific instructions from the chief executive. They may believe that a proposed expenditure can be postponed without loss to the public interest. They may find that a proposed undertaking overlaps work in another agency. They may be satisfied that a department or agency consistently overestimates its requirements, or handles its funds carelessly; or they may believe that the estimates are too high for the purpose intended. In fact, the views of the spending agencies and the budget bureau are often at variance on this point.

Finally, the budget officials may believe that a proposed expenditure is plainly unnecessary, or is obviously unwise; that is, a difference of opinion concerning substantive policy may exist. Thus a publicly supported municipal hospital may propose an appropriation for an improved X-ray apparatus. The budget officer asserts that the present apparatus is adequate, and declines to recommend the estimate. The superintendent of a state institution for the insane requests an appropriation for instruction in occupational therapy. "The budget" doubts the value of such instruction. The civil service commission requests funds to expand its classification staff. The budget bureau declines to admit the necessity for such expansion.

Case studies which would indicate precisely who makes such decisions as these, for what reasons, and under the influence of what predispositions would be extremely significant, however difficult to secure. Here the claims of the armed forces of the nation clash against the claims of the civilian branch; the interests of farmers compete against those of business and of labor; special interests seek to support or to weaken administration by increasing or reducing appropriations. It is well understood that any effort by budgeteers to reduce certain estimates will stir up a storm of opposition from outside interests, and that not even the chief executive could safely cut at these points. These conflicting force are felt more openly at the later stage of legislative consideration, bu are not unknown here.

Unexplored issues of sound public policy abound in this *terra incog nita*. Whose judgment is more likely to reflect the public interest in sucl cases? Who is more fully informed concerning actual need for funds? Are officials trained in fiscal operations more likely to reach socially de sirable conclusions than professionally trained civil servants? Obviousl if some balance between competing claims must be reached within th executive branch, it can only be attained under the authority of th chief executive himself, who in most cases must act through agents. Hov should these agents be prepared for such a difficult and delicate task fraught with social consequences often of considerable importance?

One thing is clear: few budget agencies have had the resources to en-able them to make reasoned decisions. They have envisaged their func-tion in very limited terms—chiefly to curb the "sinful art" of expendi-ture. Spending may at times be more important than saving, but thi doctrine would be heresy in a budget office. The United States Burea of the Budget has seriously curtailed its usefulness and missed its large opportunities by applying to itself the rule of parsimony which it en-forced against others. If executive control of estimates is necessary, an in my judgment it is, then that control should at least be based on th widest possible knowledge of what each department or agency is doin and on some understanding of the social importance of its function. Th mere judgment of an accountant or an efficiency expert is not enough.

Implicit in these paragraphs is the assumption that budget official exert influence upon departmental policy. Most budget experts assert that they have no policy except that which they receive from their prin-cipal. They are doubtless sincere in their opinion that they are neutral before great public issues, but acquaintance with them quickly dispels any such illusion from the minds of their friends. They are doubtless sincere also in asserting that they have no views on the usefulness of spending money here rather than there; but their daily decisions betray them.[1] This is not a criticism of budget experts, but a notice to those who may have to deal with them.

3. Approval and Submission of Budget

The revised estimates are eventually given formal approval by the

[1] A tragic example was the reported decision of a budget examiner in the U. S. Bureau of the Budget denying estimates to relieve an appalling overcrowding in the public hospital of the District of Columbia because in his judgment the care of the indigent sick should be assumed by private charity.

chief executive (or in a few states and cities by a budget commission) and are submitted to the legislative body. Major controversies between budget officials and spending agencies will have been finally determined by the chief executive himself. Here lies a delicate piece of strategy: when to appeal over the head of the budget director. Department heads weigh carefully all "angles" before they take this final desperate step to unhorse budget bureau decisions. It is folly to appeal on other than major issues, and not always wise to appeal for review of them. The final decision may be negative, in which case the only result is to incur the ill will of the budget experts before whom the next year's estimates must be brought. The decision may be favorable, but it may be bought at the price of strained relations with the budget office. As a rule the cost is thought too great and however reluctantly, the departments accept the decisions of the budget experts. While the possibility of appeal is always present, it is infrequently taken. This is a fact of considerable significance in weighing the internal balance of fiscal power.

The completed budget will usually include a transmitting message conveying executive recommendations, summary statements, detailed exhibits of proposed expenditures compared item by item with the latest appropriation and with actual expenditures of the last year or two years. There will be explanations of any increase and proposals for revenue adequate to meet the anticipated expenditure. The budget is, in short, a complete and detailed financial plan and work program, so arranged as to facilitate comparison with the current fiscal plan and program. It enables the appropriating authority to act on the basis of a definite program carefully considered by the executive branch and specifically recommended by the chief executive.

4. Consideration and Enactment of Appropriation Act

The department head who needs funds to carry out his official duties now must transfer his attention to the legislative body. In most American jurisdictions, the legislature still retains full authority to modify, increase, diminish or abandon the budget estimates submitted by the chief executive. In fact, however, a carefully prepared and comprehensive plan cannot easily be ignored and appropriations tend to follow closely executive recommendations. The comparative record of the President's budget and Congressional appropriations in pre-emergency years is convincing evidence.[1]

[1] In 1933 the Appropriations Committee of the House reported the Independent Office Bill carrying a total of $535,568,883. This was $5,053 more than recommended by the Bureau of the Budget.

TABLE IV

Variation between Congressional Appropriations and Presidential Budgets

Year	Amount of Decrease (000 omitted)	Per Cent of Total Budget
1925	$10,599	.35
1926	10,653	.34
1927	4,945	.35
1928	5,350	.16
1929	6,555	.18
1930	4,613[a]	.11

[a] Increase.

In a few states there are constitutional limitations upon legislative power to modify the governor's financial recommendations. Of these Maryland is perhaps the most restrictive. A constitutional amendment drafted under the leadership of Dr. Frank J. Goodnow and approved in 1916 severely reduces the legislature's authority. The governor's estimates for the executive branch cannot be increased, but may be reduced by the Maryland assembly; the estimates for the courts (prepared by the judges) cannot be reduced, but may be increased; and estimates for the legislative branch may be either increased or reduced. No item of appropriation other than those in the governor's budget may be initiated by either house until the budget has been enacted into law. Additional subsequent appropriations must carry specific revenue provisions, and are subject to the veto power of the governor.[1]

In Congress, however, and in most state legislatures and city councils, representatives may modify executive proposals at will. How far may department officials go in urging the appropriations committee to restore and approve their original estimates? Before reformed budget procedure, each department had *carte blanche* to make its case on its own terms. Although it is difficult to change this long-established tradition, the federal departments formally recognize their duty to accept the President's estimates and to forget their original plans.

In fact, however, it is difficult to prevent aggressive officials from conveying their real views to the appropriations committees. Three years after the introduction of the federal budget procedure, President Coolidge found it necessary to warn the higher bureaucracy in these terms:

> I regret that there are still some officials who apparently feel that the estimates transmitted to the Bureau of the Budget are the estimates which they are authorized to advocate before Committees of the Congress. Let me say here that under

[1] Constitution of Maryland, Art. III, Sec. 52 (1916).

the Budget and Accounting Act the only lawful estimates are those which the chief executive transmits to the Congress. It is these estimates that call for your loyal support. . . . I herewith serve notice again as chief executive that I propose to protect the integrity of my budget.[1]

It has not been necessary to repeat this warning in recent years, but there is a certain amount of informal contact between some officials and individual members of appropriations committees. Nothing can prevent a member of these committees from interrogating an official during hearings on the estimates in such a way as to make it easy for the official to reveal his real views. Nor is there any means at the disposal of the chief executive to bar from budget hearings the representatives of groups who stand to gain by increased appropriations. These unofficial persons may of course secure ammunition *sub rosa* from the bureaus. There is no implication in this that the departments regularly or frequently sabotage the adverse decisions of budget directors; but for a realistic understanding of fiscal and group pressures one cannot overlook the likelihood that ends may be thus attained by indirection. Since the President does not possess the item veto, he has no effective ultimate protection of the integrity of his budget against the will of Congress.

In some of the states a different rule prevails. The budget as transmitted to the legislature may contain both the original and the revised estimates. The departmental officials then retain their freedom to argue their case *de novo* before the appropriations committee, although with the handicap of adverse executive recommendations. If their eloquence prevails, the governor still has the item veto in many states, which is usually the final word despite the possibility of a legislative vote to override the veto. In general, the views of the governor and his budget officer are likely to be accepted by the state administrative agencies, for an open break with the governor is dangerous.

A letter from a former state official suggests one reaction of the spending departments to modern budgetary controls. Some years ago he wrote, "With regard to budget making, my experience has been entirely satisfactory, largely due, I believe, to the fact that I have had personal acquaintance with the chairmen of the appropriations committee in House and Senate, and have been in position to insist on fair consideration for our needs, or to go over the head of the budget officer to his embarrassment. . . . The point is that the budget official is sub-

[1] Cf. 42 Stat. 21; sec. 206 of the Budget and Accounting Act, 1921: "No estimate or request for an appropriation and no request for an increase in an item of any such estimate or request, and no recommendation as to how the revenue needs of the government should be met, shall be submitted to Congress or any committee thereof by any officer or employee of any department or establishment, unless at the request of either House of Congress."

ject to arbitrary orders of the governor and in many if not most cases the subordinate head of a division has no recourse and is supposed to lie down and roll over after filing his formal request."

In the cities practice varies. The physical concentration of municipal offices, the closer contact of officials and city councils, the interest of the local newspapers, the smaller scale of operations (excepting the metropolitan areas) and the consequent personal interest on the part of the councilmen, all tend to blur the sharper lines of distinction which buttress executive authority in the fiscal affairs of the states and nation. City managers, however, as a rule secure recognition of their responsibility for controlling estimates; and powerful mayors like Anton J. Cermak of Chicago have no difficulty in maintaining their dominant control of financial operations. Much depends on party unity between mayor and council, or between governor and legislature.

The Senate and House appropriations committees and ways and means committees are among the most important, the most diligent, and the most ably manned of all legislative committees. Leaders of both parties are found here, and members with the longest experience. Clerks of appropriations committees often serve for many years and build up unrivaled stores of information as bases for their shrewd judgments. Budgets are consequently given attention under relatively favorable circumstances. It must be added, however, that legislative bodies have never equipped themselves with a staff of examiners who could make independent inquiries for the information of the committee members. They receive an immense amount of information and misinformation; but they take few positive steps to make first-hand, on-the-spot inquiries to ascertain actual conditions. Such a staff would be of substantial aid.[1]

The appropriations committee of the U. S. House of Representatives is divided into subcommittees, each of which considers the budget of specified departments and independent establishments. Departmental representatives are given a hearing and are subjected to close and sometimes hostile questioning. Further information is often requested to support the estimates. The contact between administration and the legislature in the appropriations committee is one of the most vital, and will richly repay systematic study.

The record of legislators with respect to appropriations has not been reassuring. Members tend to take a local view of state or national finance, and in the old days formed many indefensible combinations to push through funds for special or local interests. The congressional

[1] For example, observe the work done by the Los Angeles City Bureau of Budget and Efficiency, the Chicago Finance Committee staff, and the New York Board of Estimate staff.

"pork-barrel" was only the most conspicuous of many other barrels. Even today the records of Congressmen who make loud demands for retrenchment and who then vote for the soldiers' bonus or free seeds for farmers illustrate how readily pressure groups with voting power may affect financial considerations.

Legislative consideration and approval of revenue and expenditure programs are nevertheless essential aspects of a democratic constitutional state. The representatives of the voters are entitled to determine for what purposes and in what amounts taxpayers' money shall be spent. Criticism of the methods of legislative action is not intended to question the propriety and desirability of legislative control of fiscal policy. A legislature can perform its work best, however, in general rather than in specific terms.

Subsequent to final action by the appropriating body, appropriation acts are presented to the President, to the governors of every state but North Carolina, and to most mayors for their approval or disapproval. The governors of many states possess the item veto, which greatly increases their power to influence legislative action. Informal notice that the governor will veto an item if enacted by the legislature is often sufficient to modify action as desired by the chief executive. Obviously, too, this authority increases the dependence of the departments and institutions upon the governor. It is rare and in many states practically unknown for the governor's veto to be overridden by subsequent vote in the legislature.

Where, however, the governor or mayor can veto only the entire bill, the balance of power rests with the legislature, whose action is in most cases final. The President has no item veto, and his authority is substantially weakened in consequence.

5. The Form of the Appropriation Act

The form of the appropriation act is especially important from the point of view of the line departments.[1] An appropriation may be made in general terms, in a lump sum; or it may be made in specific terms, highly itemized or segregated. In actual practice all sorts of variations are found, not only from one jurisdiction to another, but from time to time in a single jurisdiction, or even in different places in the same appropriation act.

From the point of view of legislative control of administrative operations, the itemized appropriation act is obviously more effective. If it so desires, the legislature may indicate not only for what specific pur-

[1] The issues are ably discussed by Frank J. Goodnow, "The Limit of Budgetary Control," 9 *Proceedings of the American Political Science Association* 68-77 (1912).

poses money will be spent, but how many persons shall be employed, what salary shall be paid each one, and other particulars. The agitation for better budget methods which commenced about 1905 laid great emphasis upon itemized *estimates*, from which it was inferred that itemized *appropriations* were equally desirable. This mistaken conclusion led to some extraordinarily minute appropriation acts, and eventually caused such administrative difficulties as to compel a revision in the direction of less specific headings.

The purpose underlying this excessive itemization was sound enough. It was intended to keep spending officers within the bounds of public policy, to prevent deficits, to ensure care in the use of funds, to prevent misuse of funds and to facilitate the audit. The means chosen was inappropriate. It assumed that a legislative body was competent to prescribe, always months and sometimes over a year in advance, how money should be spent in detail for each and every state activity. Such prevision is impossible on the part of anyone and especially on the part of a numerous assembly, many of whose members are always new to their task. Detailed prescriptions of this sort have the effect of placing the administrative services in a legislative strait-jacket, which is certainly not in the interest of effective and intelligent administration.

The trend of financial development eventually provided another solution to the problem which preserved the proper discretionary power of the administration. Itemized estimates are still required in the preparation and drafting of the budget; but the appropriations tend to become general in nature—"lump sum" in the current phrase. Standard appropriation headings in Massachusetts furnish an excellent illustration. The appropriation act of 1937 carried 758 items, numbered serially.[1] The customary form is shown in the following excerpt:

DIVISION OF CIVIL SERVICE

411	For the salaries of the commissioner and associate commissioners, sums not exceeding nine thousand dollars..	$ 9,000
412	For other personal services of the division, a sum not exceeding one hundred fifty-one thousand dollars....	151,000
413	For other services and for printing the annual report, and for office supplies and equipment necessary for the administration of the civil service law, a sum not exceeding twenty-nine thousand dollars.............	29,000
	TOTAL.................	$189,000

In such lump sum appropriations, how is effective control maintained? Is this procedure not identical with the discredited uncontrolled appro-

[1] Massachusetts Acts and Resolves 1937, c. 234.

priation practice of the nineteenth century? The answer is in the negative. Modern control devices ensure orderly and equitable use of funds.

The largest single item of expenditure is for personal service. Duties classification, enforced by an agency within the executive branch but separate from the departments, ensures that salaries will be properly adjusted to the kind of work involved and prevents favoritism, lack of standardization, and competitive interdepartmental bidding. In Massachusetts, but not in most jurisdictions, specific authority must be secured by the departments from the Commission on Administration and Finance to fill any vacancy or to create a new position.[1]

The second largest item of expense is for material. Well-organized central purchasing agencies, working on published specifications and requiring bids on the open market, ensure that this part of the public funds will be properly used. With respect to these and other items of expense, the rapidly developing techniques of executive supervision furnish a means of close inspection and planned use of money made available in lump sums.[2] In short, the establishment of integrated administrative operation and central control services permits a legislative body to appropriate safely in large and unrestricted sums. All this is buttressed by the customary "gentleman's understanding" that the detailed estimates presented in the budget are the guide to the general allowances authorized by the appropriation act.

These assumptions largely broke down in the emergency relief act of the 74th Congress. This extraordinary statute and later relief acts authorized expenditures in terms of a blank check of unexampled proportions. The act reads:

> That in order to provide relief, work relief and to increase employment by providing useful projects, there is hereby appropriated . . . to be used in the discretion and under the direction of the President . . . the sum of $4,000,000,000 . . .; not exceeding $500,000,000 in the aggregate of any savings or unexpended balances in the funds of the Reconstruction Finance Corporation; and not exceeding $380,-000,000 [of other unexpended balances]. . . . Provided, that except as to such part of the appropriation made herein as the President may deem necessary for continuing relief as authorized . . . this appropriation shall be available for the following classes of projects, and the amounts to be used for each class shall not, except as hereinafter provided, exceed the amounts stated, namely: (a) Highways, roads, streets and grade crossing elimination, $800,000,000; (b) rural rehabilitation and relief in stricken agricultural areas, and water conservation, trans-mountain water diversion and irrigation and reclamation, $500,000,000; (c) rural electrification, $100,-000,000; (d) housing, $450,000,000; (e) assistance for educational, professional and clerical persons, $300,000,000; (f) Civilian Conservation Corps, $600,000,000; (g) loans or grants [for state and local projects], $900,000,000; (h) sanitation, preven-

[1] See ch. 21 for an explanation of classification procedures.
[2] See ch. 4 and ch. 15 for a description of these devices.

tion of soil erosion, prevention of stream pollution, sea-coast erosion, reforestation, forestation, flood control, rivers and harbors and miscellaneous projects, $350,-000,000; *Provided further*. That not to exceed 20 percentum of the amount herein appropriated may be used by the President to increase any one or more of the foregoing limitations. . . .[1]

No schedules of projects supported these huge sums and no plan was laid before Congress. Moreover, although the established contract procedure was imposed, the usual safeguards of appointment through the Civil Service Commission and payment of employees on the basis of the Classification Act were set aside. Congress, in short, authorized expenditures greatly exceeding the total appropriation of an ordinary fiscal year without knowledge of the particular purposes to which the funds would be put and without many of the controls which normally govern lump sum appropriations. Naturally these emergency procedures are no precedent for normal operations. Indeed at the very moment the relief agencies were receiving these huge sums the estimates of the established agencies were being pruned by the Bureau of the Budget with its accustomed severity.

The form of the appropriation act has great influence upon the nature of the subsequent audit. A highly itemized appropriation act enables and indeed requires a meticulous supervision on the part of the auditor, who must be satisfied that the intent of the legislative body has been observed in each particular. Each additional item sets up requirements which the auditor must enforce. An item for a junior file clerk at $1200 per annum can be used only for this purpose and not for a typist, however greatly changing needs of the service may require the latter rather than the former employee.

A lump sum appropriation avoids this narrow type of audit. Proper control still prevails, however, for the general laws with respect to employment of personnel, purchase of supplies, making of contracts, custody of funds and the like govern all financial transactions.

The grave handicap to good administration which is inherent in the itemized appropriation lies in the severe limitation or even destruction of administrative discretion in the best use of funds for the purposes authorized by law. The effect of itemized appropriations is to determine operating problems *a priori* by an agency outside the administration and inherently unfitted for the task. The effect of the safeguarded type of general appropriation is to restore discretion where it can be effectively used. Administrative authority in a word is being returned to the administration. But, as never before, it is a responsible administration.

[1] 49 Stat. 115 (1935).

6. Summary

The principal underlying tendency in budget making which is revealed in the analysis of past and present methods is the growth in influence and authority of the chief executive. Hardly a generation ago mayors, governors and even the President himself were destitute of fiscal power except in the political act of a veto. This gap in the authority of the chief executive is a formidable evidence of the weak administrative position which theory and practice ascribed to him. Now he may dictate the maximum estimates of most spending agencies.

From the point of view of the operating departments and agencies, the adoption of executive budgets in the last thirty years has transformed their means of access to public funds. They are still not insulated from the legislature, but their contacts are canalized and governed by executive direction. They must defend their proposals twice, once before the budget officials and again before the appropriations committee. Their hardest battles for funds are fought with budget bureaus, not with legislators. Their opportunity to profit by personal and political vantage points in the quest for funds is greatly diminished.

From the point of view of members of the appropriating bodies, the preliminary review and balance by the executive branch is an unmixed gain. The range and variety of appropriations have grown far beyond the ken of all except the most experienced representatives. The tentative selection of items and the achievement of a balance between revenue and expenditure give the legislators "something to work on," and protect them in some measure against importunate demands for bigger grants.

Careful estimating has without doubt diminished the total amount of public expenditures, although no statistical proof of this conclusion can be offered. With expanding activities expenditures have soared despite budget control, but they would have soared still higher without the restraint imposed by budget officials.

Future lines of development may reasonably include larger staffs for budget bureaus, with men trained in other fields than accounting; closer liaison with other staff and auxiliary agencies, such as personnel, purchasing and planning; small technical staffs for legislative committees dealing with revenues and expenditures; and in the federal government, further consideration of the desirability of granting the President the item veto which is possessed by many state and municipal executives.[1]

[1] Cf. the specific recommendations for the U. S. Bureau of the Budget made by the President's Committee on Administrative Management, *Report with Special Studies* (1937), pp. 16-20.

Whether the direction into which public expenditures have been diverted by budget experts is wiser than that which might have been taken without their guidance cannot be ascertained. While it is true that in the last analysis fiscal policy is determined by the chief executive and by the legislative bodies, their judgment is affected by the recommendations they receive in a tightly balanced fiscal program worked out by anonymous experts in a subordinate administrative agency. The net result of whatever degree of influence may be exerted is conjectural, but is in the direction of saving, not of spending.

Chapter Fifteen

EXECUTIVE SUPERVISION OF EXPENDITURES

1. Growth and Character of Expenditure Control

Until about twenty years ago, the final authorization for public expenditures was the appropriation act, the various sections of which were construed as commands to administrative agencies to pursue various subjects of public interest to the full extent of appropriated monies. Each office had unchallenged control of the funds granted by the appropriation act. Governors and presidents were vested with no direct power or right to question the use of funds by administrative officers, even beyond those appropriated. The chief executive had influence wherever he could remove subordinates, but in the states this carried him not far beyond the doors of the executive mansion; nor were mayors more powerful until after 1900.

Compliance with the terms of the appropriation act was the immediate duty of its beneficiaries, whose decisions were checked eventually by the auditor. In practice, however, the auditor was not able to prevent deficits or to question the use of funds which, although legal, was extravagant. No authority existed to curtail expenditures in case of unforeseen emergency. The result was a long record of deficits in federal, state and local finance which were regularly covered by deficiency appropriations.

An early object of fiscal reform was to secure more careful and better balanced estimates of expenditure and revenue. At first it was hoped that deficiencies would thus disappear. Experience, however, soon scuttled this aspiration and in the general increase of executive power there developed new devices intended to impose greater restriction on the spending agencies throughout the fiscal year. City managers, mayors, governors, and to a certain extent the President were authorized in diverse ways to "execute the budget." In the cities an early example is found in the finance sections of the Cleveland charter of 1913; in the states the first major step was taken in Illinois in 1917; in Washington certain phases of control developed from the Budget and Accounting Act of 1921, although "anti-deficiency" legislation dates from 1906.

The extent to which this new type of executive supervision of expenditures had proceeded in the states, to 1932, is indicated in detail in the author's *Trends in Public Administration*.[1] In one form or another it has affected most states, but the degree of control varies greatly from one to another. Similar procedures have been emerging in the cities, usually in the office of the comptroller, mayor or manager. The trend of the last twenty years has been in the direction of amplifying these procedures and the depression years sharply accelerated the movement. Standard practice now includes one or more devices intended to permit executive surveillance or control over the expenditure of funds already duly authorized by the legislature.

This type of executive authorization marks the abandonment of the long-established doctrine that an appropriation is not merely an authorization but an order to spend the sums appropriated. An appropriation has gradually become an authority effective only so far as may be necessary, and subject to the specific or general authorization of the chief executive. This change reflects the new position of the chief executive both with respect to the legislature and to administrative bodies. Within limits it places the head of an administrative agency in a position of fiscal dependence upon the chief executive, and inevitably gives the latter considerable influence over the policy and activities of the former.

The process of executive supervision of expenditures, often called budget execution, is from one point of view chiefly negative in character. Each operating unit has its own definite plans based on its estimates, confirmed in the appropriation act, and reflecting as a rule a continuing administrative load. The chief executive is not likely to add to existing work programs and in the nature of things cannot change them much. His action, where other than merely confirmatory, is likely to be negative in the sense of reducing operations, or requiring postponements, or facilitating coordination with other activities pursued elsewhere in the organization. The principal interest of the chief executive in financial supervision is to avoid deficits and to ensure economy. His usual point of view is restrictive. Executive supervision of administrative use of funds, in short, is control.

In some instances, the machinery of control has been used for political purposes, either in factional warfare or in recurrent battles between the parties. These perversions may be expected where electors are unable to distinguish between honest men and demagogues, or where they have only the unsatisfactory privilege of choosing the lesser of political evils. Occasionally the administrative system as a whole has suffered

[1] L. D. White, *Trends in Public Administration* (1933), pp. 191-95.

because means exist by which a chief executive can control the course of expenditures. The remedy is not to forego means of internal supervision, but rather to improve the quality of the supervisors. In some communities this may be a long and discouraging task, but it is the way of good administration.

Since 1910 there has been no reversal of the tide of expanding central control of expenditures. The broad results have been generally commended by students of government and public finance and no body of opinion exists which favors a return to the era of departmental "rugged individualism" which was universal in the days of William McKinley. Careful analytical studies of the operating results of overhead executive management of expenditures have not yet been made and, until they appear, satisfactory evaluations cannot be undertaken. At some points the amount of control may be excessive and unnecessary in the interests of good administration, if not positively harmful. In any event, here is one of the major innovations of the last thirty years.

All forms of fiscal management, including budget making, depend upon the fiscal information secured from the accounting system. The special forms of executive supervision of expenditures which are the subject matter of this chapter are especially dependent upon accurate and current accounts. It is therefore in point to turn briefly to the topic of public accounting as a preface to the forms of control which are discussed in later paragraphs.

2. Public Accounts and Accounting Control

A common phrase in the state reorganization statutes vests power in the director of finance "to supervise accounts and expenditure" and "to keep controlling accounts." To understand the amount and kind of fiscal control which flows from such phraseology it is necessary to describe briefly the essential character of public accounting.

"Accounting is the science of producing promptly and presenting clearly the facts relating to financial condition and operations that are required as a basis of management." [1] The primary functions of a system of accounts are to make a financial record, to protect those handling funds, to reveal the financial condition of the organization in all its branches or purposes at any time, to facilitate necessary adjustments in rate of expenditure, to give information to those in responsible posi-

[1] Francis Oakey, *Principles of Government Accounting and Reporting* (1921), p. 1. The federal accounting system of 1937 is described in *Investigation of Executive Agencies of the Government*, S. Rept. 1275, 75th Cong., 1st sess. (1937), pp. 143-57. Present practice is set forth in the reports of the Municipal Finance Officers' Association, *Standard Practice in Municipal Accounting and Financial Procedure* (1937), and *County Finance and Accounting Standards* (1937).

tion on the basis of which plans for future financial and operating programs can rest, and to aid in the making of an audit.[1]

Authority to devise, install and operate the accounting system is generally an administrative responsibility although in some jurisdictions it is vested in the independent auditor. A 1938 study disclosed that forty-three states had a central accounting office; in seventeen of these states accounting was set up in the office of the comptroller, while seventeen others still gave accounting to the auditor. Various arrangements prevail in other states.[2] For many years accounting procedures were customarily left to the discretion and wisdom of the respective departments, each of which set up a system supposedly adapted to its needs. Naturally the greatest diversity resulted. As a part of the general movement toward integration of the administrative system, central supervision over the form and maintenance of accounts tended to be placed first in the auditor's office, and later in the finance department or comptroller's office. In 1921, authority to prescribe the accounting system was transferred from the United States Treasury to the General Accounting Office but in 1938 it was agreed that this was an error.

From the point of view of the department head or the chief executive, early and accurate accounting reports are necessary in order to direct the course of work and future expenditures. They also provide the essential record to demonstrate the appropriate and legal use of funds, making certain that each subdivision of an organization is actually using money for the purposes for which it was appropriated. The accounts and supporting financial documents provide the evidence on the basis of which each spending officer justifies his expenditures, either to the finance director or to the auditor.

While the accounting system is thus essential as a means of preventing the wrongful use of funds, it also underlies all other types of executive control of fiscal operations. It is the basis on which executives act to prevent deficits, as well as the documentary foundation for questioning the care and wisdom with which funds have been used.

In the business world the information currently disclosed by the accounting system is one of the main sources on which business policy is predicated. In the field of government, accounts could hardly be use

[1] Among the works on public accounting the following will be found especiall useful to students of public administration: Richard Brown, ed., *History of Accounting and Accountants* (1905); A. E. Buck, *Municipal Finance* (1926), chs. 5-6 A. C. Littleton, *Accounting Evolution to 1900* (1933); Lloyd Morey, *Introductio to Government Accounting* (2d ed. 1936); National Committee on Municipal Accounting, *Bibliography of Municipal and State Accounting* (1937). A useful volume on business accounting is Monard V. Hayes, *Accounting for Executive Control* (1929).

[2] National Association of State Auditors, Comptrollers and Treasurers, *Tabula Analysis of State Fiscal Offices* (1938), p. 49.

for planning or controlling purposes until a reorganized administrative system established an effective seat of responsibility. In well-managed public jurisdictions, the monthly, quarterly and annual accounting reports are now relied upon, as in business, for guidance as to executive policy and program. This use of accounts has naturally been emphasized during the depression when revenues were shrinking and deficits rising n every direction. One of the principal emerging values of an accountng system is consequently the aid it furnishes in supervising, planning and adjusting work programs in the light of rapidly changing economic conditions. The center of gravity of the accounting system has thus een forced out of the department or auditing office into the supervisory gencies attached to the office of the chief executive.

Since the accounting system is the means by which the necessary data re made available for making and reviewing estimates, it is important o key the accounting system to the budget, or vice versa, and to organze the accounts so that they will produce the desired information for udgetary purposes. This adjustment has been made in progressive jurisictions.

Before taking summary leave of government accounting, a brief note needed with reference to cost accounting. In its essentials, cost acounting is the determination of inclusive costs per unit, usually of production or of service; for example, the unit cost of an army rifle manuactured at a government arsenal, or the unit cost of maintenance of a atient per day in a state hospital. Cost accounting procedures were deeloped in construction, manufacturing, and transportation, and have een widely taken over in the field of government services and operaons. The accounting officer of the United States Civil Service Commison, for example, calculates the unit cost of holding examinations of ifferent types. Unit costs in public construction, such as highways, ublic buildings and sewer systems are commonly obtained.

The chief uses of the unit cost as an element of expenditure control e twofold. Costs may be compared in a single institution or single opation over successive periods of time; and the comparative costs of nilar operations in different agencies or in different jurisdictions may approximated. Variations in operating conditions from place to place well as from time to time naturally have to be taken into consideraon, but with proper discretion the unit cost may be an effective means executive control of expenditures and operations.

Types of Expenditure Control

Despite endless diversity in the law and practice of fiscal management the nation, the states, and their subdivisions, it is possible to segregate ur principal types of expenditure control. All but one of them occur subsequent to the appropriation act; all operate within the terms of the appropriation; and all normally depend upon the will of the chief executive, directly or indirectly. These four types are: control of future policy affecting expenditures; control to prevent improper use of funds; control to prevent deficits; and finally control to review the wisdom and reasonableness of proposed expenditures. The four categories are not entirely separable, but they afford convenient heads for classifying a variety of fiscal devices.[1]

a. Control of future policy. Sound budget procedure is itself an important means of reviewing future policy, as reflected in the estimates. In addition, the President of the United States has a second positive means of controlling future policy which was forecast by the Budget and Accounting Act of 1921 and developed by various subsequent executive orders. The first indication of this type of policy control came in December 1921 in an executive order requiring all recommendations for new legislation which would create a charge on the public treasury to be submitted to the President through the Bureau of the Budget before presentation to Congress. During the administration of Franklin D. Roosevelt, this procedure was renewed and strengthened by requiring all departmental correspondence with Congress concerning legislation to clear with the Bureau of the Budget. Control of department policy and expression of opinion was thus effectively secured. In the states there is greater latitude for departments although major legislation is usually discussed with the governor. In the cities plans for ordinances or by-laws are normally cleared with the mayor or manager, since the number of proposals is relatively few and contacts are easy to make. The forms and degree of policy control involving expenditures are more explicit and specific in the national government than elsewhere.

b. Control to prevent misappropriation of funds. The principal internal fiscal controls to ensure the proper use of funds include the administrative audit, approval of contracts, control of purchasing and printing, supervision of personnel expenditures, and approval of transfers from one appropriation item to another. Each of these forms of supervision will be noted in the following paragraphs.

Administrative audit. The supervision of expenditures by a comptroller, an administrative official in the executive branch, is gradually emerg-

[1] References to the subject matter of this chapter are scanty. The principal items are J. W. Sundelson, *Budgetary Methods in National and State Governments*, New York State Tax Commission Special Report No. 14, 1938; A. E. Buck, "Financial Control and Accountability," in President's Committee on Administrative Management, *Report with Special Studies* (1937), pp. 135-68; L. D. White, *Trends in Public Administration* (1933); Denzel C. Cline, *Executive Control over State Expenditures in New Jersey* (1934).

ing as overhead management is strengthened. In essence this form of control requires approval by an administrative officer of all vouchers and claims before they are forwarded from the spending unit to the treasurer for payment. The independent audit may also take place at this point. Review by the comptroller is designed principally to ensure that the expenditure is in accordance with executive policy, that it is legal, that the supporting documents are in proper shape, and that funds are available in the appropriate account. In substance, the operation resembles the subsequent independent audit.[1]

Approval of contracts. The comptroller or the director of finance may also have authority to approve or disapprove contracts involving certain types or amounts of expenditure. The legal form of the contract may also be reviewed by the attorney general. In the federal government contracts are reviewed and approved by the Comptroller General.

Purchase of supplies and control of printing. The purchase of supplies by a central purchasing office facilitates central control of a large block of expenditures. The central purchasing agency, for example, not only purchases upon requisition, but in some cases may substitute its judgment for that of the requisitioning agency as to quality or quantity or price, or may even decline to purchase.[2] Similarly, the printing office may not merely secure the bids for a job, but may edit the manuscript, and decline to authorize publication if it thinks wise.[3] The essential elements were written into an early California statute of 1895 (c. 188), providing that the Superintendent of State Printing "shall have discretionary authority to revise, reduce, or decline to execute any order, or part of any order, which in his judgment is unnecessary or unwarranted by law, and which will tend to unnecessarily consume the appropriation for support of the State Printing Office."

Personnel control. A similar control of personnel costs arises from the classification plan maintained and policed by a central personnel agency. Standard rates of pay for carefully defined kinds of work are set either by legislation or by administrative action; the central personnel office classifies each position and thereby assigns it to its proper scale of pay. The department can pay neither more nor less than this scale.

In Massachusetts, the Commission on Administration and Finance must approve the filling of each vacancy and the creation of each new position. This authority is rare among the states. In Washington, the economy legislation of 1933 required the President to give his personal approval to the

[1] See ch. 17 for discussion of this form of administrative control and the audit.

[2] In 1931 the purchasing agents of sixteen states had statutory authority to modify purchase requisitions; see the author's *Trends in Public Administration*, pp. 207-8.

[3] White, *ibid.*, pp. 200 ff.

filling of every vacancy. The preliminary stages of this huge task were assumed by the Bureau of the Budget, leaving the President only the duty of signing a daily journal of recommendations. These procedures were devised, not in the interest of a personnel program, but in the interest of a financial program.

Transfers and emergency funds. Finally we may note that transfers of funds from one appropriation head to another now usually require the approval of an executive agency outside the department and not infrequently the consent of the mayor, manager or governor. The department cannot on its own responsibility transfer its funds to meet its emerging needs. Contingency and emergency funds allowed a department are usually subject only to its own later allocation. Such funds however, in Illinois and elsewhere are disappearing as central contingency funds handled by governors or administrative boards take their place. The result again is to expand central control of current expenditures.

Over a long period of years, therefore, but especially within the last two decades, methods have been devised to prevent the misuse of funds through a number of provisions involving central fiscal control by a finance officer acting usually under the chief executive. These include the checking of expenditures, the review of contracts, centralized purchasing, central review of printing, control of pay scales, and supervision of transfers and contingency funds.

c. Control to prevent deficits. During the nineteenth century the occurrence of deficits in all levels of government was common. They were covered by subsequent deficiency appropriations. Reaction against recurring deficits has led to several countermeasures, some of which are drastic in their bearing. Congress first sought to cure the disease by the "anti-deficiency" act of 1906, but in the absence of effective means of enforcement there was no relief.[1]

The extension of the general power of control and direction in the hands of governors, mayors and managers since 1910 has had a beneficial effect upon deficits, providing a means of suppression which prior to 1910 was rare. Experience indicated, however, that this authority in and of itself was insufficient; it needed special techniques to support it. These were found in the apportionment procedure which was formally introduced by Congress in 1906, but which became effective in Washington only subsequent to the formation of the Bureau of the Budget. By executive order the apportionments were put on a monthly basis in 1933, and the consent of the Bureau of the Budget was required for an

[1] A. E. Buck, "Financial Control and Accountability," in President's Committee on Administrative Management, *Report with Special Studies* (1937), pp. 155-. Violation of the act was punishable by summary removal, a fine of not less than $100 or imprisonment for not less than one month. These penalties were never invoked, despite many violations; 34 Stat. 49 (1906).

variation. The apportionment plan (sometimes called allotments) was a common feature also of the reorganized state systems of administration initiated in 1917 by Illinois. It has been widely introduced in cities and is now standard, although not universal practice.

The procedure is simple. The total annual appropriation is divided by the agency concerned into twelve parts which need not be uniform but which correspond to the expected rate of expenditure. These apportionments, which require careful advance planning of the year's work, are then submitted to the mayor, manager, governor, or finance director, usually for approval but sometimes merely for record. In either case the chief executive may question and take means to correct any indefensible proposals, and of course can ensure himself that no deficit is in sight. The course of expenditures or commitments is carefully observed month by month, or quarter by quarter. If expenditures above the allotment for any month are incurred, a reduction can be imposed during succeeding months. In this way steady pressure to avoid deficits is facilitated.[1]

A variation of this procedure is the general reserve devised by the United States Bureau of the Budget in 1921. General Dawes, then Director of the Bureau, required each department and independent establishment to set up a general reserve of estimated savings under each appropriation. This reserve was reported to the Bureau of the Budget and was allowed to be spent only on the personal authority of the secretary or head of the establishment. The Bureau of the Budget could exert only a persuasive influence to protect these funds, but when supported by the President it was effective. The following table shows the amounts covered into the Treasury from these reserves in the predepression years.[2]

TABLE V

General Reserve Covered into the Treasury

Year	Amount (000 omitted)
1922	$116,690
1923	81,875
1924	25,575
1925	24,564
1926	45,707
1927	37,586
1928	60,751
1929	17,395

[1] This and other aspects of the subject are dealt with in an unpublished ms. by r. W. H. Edwards, "The Position of the Governor in Recent Administrative Reganizations in the States" (1937), Ohio State University Library.

[2] White, *op. cit.*, p. 154.

The depression emergency accelerated executive control over rates of expenditure. As early as 1923 Utah authorized the governor to withhold appropriations temporarily if the condition of the treasury warranted such action.[1] In 1932 Alabama sought to cut expenditures to match shrinking revenues by allowing the governor drastic powers of curtailment within the appropriation. All appropriations were declared to be "maximum, conditional and proportionate." The governor was directed to restrict allotments to prevent an overdraft or deficit "by prorating without discriminating against any department [or] institution . . . the available revenues . . ." [2]

A more highly developed but analogous plan was introduced in West Virginia in 1933. If revenues prove inadequate, the governor is directed to reduce expenditures in multiples of five per cent in accordance with five classes of organization units.[3] These are (1) fiscal agencies; (2) law enforcement agencies; (3) state institutions; (4) other departments and services; (5) transfers from the general fund. In case the governor finds that pro rata reductions will seriously impair the most essential agencies of government, the law directs differential reductions. These begin with five per cent on class five; next ten per cent on class five and five per cent on class four; then fifteen per cent on class five, ten per cent on class four, and five per cent on class three, with an outside limit of twenty-five per cent reduction on class five.[4] Other examples are reported by Sundelson.[5]

d. Control to ensure wisdom and reasonableness of expenditure. This form of executive control of expenditures reaches well beyond efforts to ensure legality and regularity or to avoid unwelcome deficits. In principle it extends to a review of the sound judgment of the spending officers in particular cases, and at times has actually been used for such purposes, although more commonly it resembles the administrative audit.

The classic formal statement of this authority is found in provisions of the Illinois Civil Administrative Code of 1917 conferring power upon the Department of Finance in these terms: [6]

> To examine and approve, or disapprove, vouchers, bills and claims of the several departments, and such as are by law made subject to the approval of the Governor.

[1] Utah Laws 1923, c. 108, sec. 6.

[2] Alabama General Acts, extra sess. 1932, Act No. 37.

[3] West Virginia Acts 1933, 1st Extraordinary Sess., c. 56.

[4] A valuable discussion is found in S. E. Dadisman, "Budget Control and Separation of Powers," 40 *West Virginia Law Q.* 166-74 (1933-34).

[5] J. W. Sundelson, *Budgetary Methods in National and State Governments*, N. Y. State Tax Commission, Special Report No. 14, 1938, chs. 45-47.

[6] Illinois Laws 1917, p. 3, sec. 36, subsections 9 and 11.

> . . . and no voucher, bill or claim of any department shall be allowed without its approval and certificate. . . .
>
> In settling the accounts of the several departments, to inquire into and make an inspection of articles and materials furnished or work and labor performed, for the purpose of ascertaining that the prices, quality and amount of such articles or labor are fair, just and reasonable, and that all the requirements, express and implied, pertaining thereto have been complied with, and to reject and disallow any excess; . . .

Similar language was subsequently introduced in the administrative codes of a number of states.

The Illinois Department of Finance, acting on behalf of the governor, has used this authority freely from time to time. Thus a requisition for fifty cases of grapefruit, then out of season, was canceled because it appeared they were intended for the doctors and nurses, not for the patients in a public hospital. Proposed expenditures for certain pedagogical magazines for a normal school were refused because they were deemed unnecessary. In Texas a similar system resulted in a feud between the Department of Highways and the Board of Control over the type of truck to be used by the highway engineers.[1] In Massachusetts a former president of the State Agricultural College resigned on account of "interference" by the Commission on Administration and Finance.

In states where such a review prevails, there has been considerable resistance on the part of the administrative agencies. An innovation of this sort naturally involved potentially a serious lessening of their authority. They were quite unaccustomed to such "outside meddling," although they recognized the long-established jurisdiction of the auditor. In principle, moreover, no obvious boundaries to this type of supervision could be drawn.

No cause is assigned in the Illinois Civil Administrative Code on the basis of which vouchers may be disallowed, but the words "fair, just, and reasonable," have been construed to vest in the finance department the power to review questions of expediency as well as questions of law arising from the expenditures of other departments and institutions. During Governor Lowden's administration a controversy arose on this issue and was referred to the governor's advisers for opinion. It was said that unless the director of a department could depend upon appropriations regularly made by the legislature and approved by the governor, his executive and administrative efficiency would be greatly impaired. It was alleged further that when the finance department undertakes to criticize individual decisions of a division or institution, without know-

[1] See Frank M. Stewart, "Purchasing of Highway Equipment in Texas," 24 *Am. Pol. Sci. Rev.* 409-15 (1930).

ing or being in a position to know the reason for the decision, it transcends its authority.

The opinion given to the governor supported a broad interpretation of the powers of the director of finance. The Code was intended, the opinion held, to embody the ideas of supervision of expenditures, review of current business transactions, critical inspection of vouchers and documents, and the determination of the legality and justness of claims against public funds. "As a matter of power, therefore, considered in the abstract, it is my judgment that the director of finance can question the expediency or propriety of any expenditure. But power is not always coupled with right. It is to be presumed that in the exercise of this vast power the director will be guided by prudence, moderation, zea for successful, efficient and harmonious administration, as well as by a consideration of the express powers vested in other departments." [1]

No first-hand study of the actual balance of power between the spending agencies in the Illinois state government and the finance director has ever been made. Under Governor Lowden (1917–1921) supervision was close and at times meticulous. Governor Small (1921–1929 was less interested in sound administration than in the political success of himself and his Chicago associates. Governor Emmerson (1929–1933 was relatively weak and made little use of the Department of Financ for the purposes for which it was devised.

Governor Horner (1933–1940) entered office committed to a policy of fiscal retrenchment and economy in the achievement of which h made good use of the Department of Finance. He did much to restor the power and prestige of the department to the position it enjoye under Lowden. Numerous advances were made in the techniques an procedures within the department but little was accomplished in ex tending the control of the department over the elective offices. It is sti restricted in its operation largely to the "Code" offices. The departmen moreover, has become more concerned, with the passage of time, wit the administration of taxes than with the control of finances or the exe cution of the budget. There is some belief, too, that certain adminis trative positions in the department have been more closely connecte with party patronage throughout the government than appears desi able. This condition crept into the department with Governor Smal

Controversies in other states involving the powers of finance directo were taken to the courts, and on the whole the courts have been rath hostile to this type of expenditure control. In Ohio a case arose on tl following statement of facts.[2] Junk, a contractor, presented to the D

[1] Unpublished opinion prepared by W. E. Woodward (1918).

[2] *State ex rel. Junk vs. Herrick*, 107 Ohio St. 611, 140 N.E. 314 (1923).

partment of Highways and Public Works a contract in good legal form for the construction of certain state highways. The director of the department forwarded the contract to the director of finance for his approval. The director of finance refused to sign the contract on the ground that he did not regard it as an appropriate or desirable contract for the state to enter into. Junk therefore asked for a writ of mandamus to compel the director of highways and public works to sign the contract, alleging that the contract did not require approval by the finance department.

The Supreme Court of Ohio sustained this view. In announcing its decision the court adopted a tone distinctly hostile to the Department of Finance. "The inquiry is . . . to what extent, if at all, the finance department is authorized to control the policy of the highway department in the matter of state aid in the construction of highways throughout the state. . . . We shall not attempt in this proceeding to define the duties and limitations of the director of finance in his relations to the directors of the other departments, but we do find it necessary and do not hesitate to say that his duties do not reach even in the remotest degree to a control of the policies of the department of highways and public works."

A similar view was expressed by the Supreme Court of Indiana.[1] In its decision the Court declared, "There is absolutely nothing in any of the legislation relating to this subject which tends in the slightest degree to authorize the department [of inspection and supervision of public offices] to control the discretion of any public officer, administrative board, or other governmental agency whatever."

In 1925 the Ohio Supreme Court denied the power of the governor himself under the Civil Administrative Code to control the discretion of the director of highways and public works. The case turned on the constitutional position of this official, but again the tone of the Supreme Court was unfriendly to executive authority.[2]

A Michigan case reaches an analogous conclusion, on the basis of the constitutional status of the state Agricultural College.[3] The legislature of the state of Michigan established a state administrative board and authorized it to exercise general supervisory control over funds appropriated by the state legislature. Acting under this authority the administrative board undertook to direct some phases of the work of the Michigan Agricultural College. The college authorities took the view that inasmuch as the institution was established by the constitution, it was

[1] *State ex rel. Licking Township vs. Clamme et al.*, 134 N.E. 676 (1922).
[2] *State vs. Baker; State vs. Donahey*, 112 Ohio St. 356 (1925).
[3] *State Board of Agriculture vs. Auditor General*, 226 Michigan 417 (1924).

impossible for the legislature to impose a financial control of this sort upon them. The Supreme Court by divided decision sustained this view. In the course of its decision the Court said: "Clearly, in saying that the legislature can attach to an appropriation any condition which it may deem expedient and wise, the court had in mind only such a condition as the legislature had power to make. It did not mean that a condition could be imposed that would be an invasion of the constitutional rights and powers of the governing board of the college. It did not mean to say that in order to avail itself of the money appropriated, the state board of agriculture must turn over to the legislature management and control of the college, or of any of its activities."

An Idaho case takes much the same view.[1] The Supreme Court declared, ". . . the board of regents [of the University of Idaho] is a constitutional corporation with granted powers and while functioning within the scope of its authority is not subject to the control or supervision of any other branch, board or department of the state government. . . ."

The general tenor of these decisions is unfriendly to this type of fisca control. The courts commonly find that such a degree of control goe to the heart of departmental policy and assert that the discretion of th department in the use of funds appropriated to it cannot be diminishe by the intervention of a finance department. Such decisions could doubt less be modified by subsequent legislation for all except the independen state constitutional offices.

In fact, however, these decisions of state supreme courts coincide wit actual operating tendencies. Unless supported by energetic and coura geous, even ruthless governors, finance departments lack the mora authority to impose their decisions on resisting departments. Such gov ernors have been conspicuously absent in most states, and this type o fiscal supervision has run down like a clock which needs winding. S far as can be ascertained the depression emergency was met, not b reviving detailed forms of control, but by resort to measures which dea with lump sums rather than with specific expenditures, or with ne sources of revenue.

4. An Evaluation of Executive Supervision of Expenditures

In 1910 most administrative agencies and institutions were fiscally ir dependent of the chief executive. They prepared their own estimate submitted them directly to the appropriations committee, ultimatel received a direct appropriation, and spent the money without any supe vision other than that provided by the auditor. The administrative hea

[1] *State vs. State Board of Education and Regents of the University of Idaho al.*, 33 Idaho 415 (1921).

might or might not have been appointed by the chief executive in the first instance; in either case the latter did not interfere with the former in the ordinary course of affairs.

Now by contrast many administrative agencies find their estimates reviewed and often reduced by a budget officer, and usually the appropriations committee does not see the department's own figures. After the appropriation, the financial officer intervenes between the spending agencies and the money, requiring apportionments or allotments on the basis of a considered plan of expenditure and sometimes reserving the right to examine each and every expenditure to be sure both of its legality and of its administrative expediency. Funds for personnel, which usually range from sixty to seventy per cent of total appropriations, are often controlled by the classification system imposed from without; funds for supplies and materials, from fifteen to twenty-five per cent of total expenditures, are often controlled by an independent central purchasing agency; and contracts usually require the approval of the central legal officer and finance officer. Since 1910 a considerable number of fiscal restraints have thus been laid upon the free discretion of spending authorities.

The spirit of the new system is revealed by its exponents. Writing in *Texas Municipalities*, City Manager John N. Edy stated, "I consider it the obligation of the executive to enforce budget provisions and to keep expenditures within appropriations and within receipts."[1] A. E. Buck implies the same point of view in asking the question (with reference to the United States system), "Does it not appear . . . that the bureau chiefs still have their own way to a very large extent in the expenditures of the appropriations granted by Congress?"[2] The view expressed by City Manager Edy is widely accepted. The new management definitely recognizes the manager, mayor, governor or president as the effective head of the administration. This does not mean, of course, that the chief executive undertakes to make all manner of operating decisions in all the varied aspects of government activities.

The question remains how far it is necessary or desirable for the chief executive to take responsibility for executing the terms of an appropriation act rather than the departments. The problem deserves more extended treatment than can be given here, as it is central to the proper internal balance of the administrative system.

In so far as the independent governmental authorities are concerned, whether in the state or national governments, the conclusion must be

[1] John N. Edy, "Modern Budgetary Practice and Budgetary Control," 21 *Texas Municipalities* 193, 197 (1934).

[2] A. E. Buck, *Public Budgeting* (1929), p. 467.

that in principle central fiscal control by the chief executive and his subordinates is incompatible with full autonomy. The degree of subordination which results from central purchasing and salary standardization is however relatively slight and is standard practice in the national system. Apportionments are required by the U. S. Bureau of the Budget from the independent establishments.

An analogous case is municipal control of the fiscal affairs of school districts. The historic pattern has separated school finance from city finance, although various exceptions exist. Opinions differ as to the wisest organization of these two intimately related fiscal systems. Schoolmen usually stand firmly for independence; students of public finance and public administration for some type of coordination, with exceptions in each group. The depression emphasized the usefulness of some sort of relationship, not necessarily one of school subordination.[1]

Setting aside these special cases and considering henceforth the central hierarchy, we may observe that the extension of executive authority in the execution of the budget raises in principle the constitutional issue of separation of powers. To date, executive modifications of legislative fiscal enactments have not been seriously challenged, and presumably fall within the recognized power of the executive branch to "deal with the details." In any event the legislative mandate clearly controls where it is unequivocally expressed. Fiscal control by the executive runs only so far as the legislative body directs or permits.

Within the area of executive discretion, to what extent is it in the interests of good administration to support central rather than dispersed authority? So far as the control of future policy is concerned, the chief executive is entitled to review the recommendations of the departments and agencies for new legislation and to make sure at least that the legislative body is informed of his own views on departmental plans. Since future program is reflected in budgetary estimates, it follows that central review and coordination of estimates before presentation to the appropriating authority are also well justified. Executive control to prevent or at least to regulate the incurring of deficits is in the interest of good administration. Hence the apportionment system and central approval of any deviations from approved plans stand on firm ground.

The functions of an executive comptroller are well established in business and seem to have equal justification in government. It is not an improper interference with departmental prerogative to scrutinize the flow of vouchers reflecting expenditures to ensure that they are legally made, are regular in form, and are within executive apportionments and legislative appropriations. This type of fiscal control within the execu-

[1] Nelson B. Henry and Jerome G. Kerwin, *Schools and City Government* (1938

tive branch is not widespread, although universal in the parallel legislative audit.

The independent administrative examination of vouchers as provided by the Illinois Civil Code is not designed to prevent deficits; it gives the fiscal officer opportunity to question the judgment of the bureau chief, and, if he deems it necessary, to substitute his judgment on particular expenditures for that of the bureau chief. Whose judgment is to be preferred?

While this issue is not entirely one sided, much can be said for leaving the bureau chief wide discretion. He and his subordinates are technically competent in their field; the fiscal officer is not. The bureau chief is familiar with the details of operating conditions and with actual problems arising from day to day; the fiscal officer is not. The bureau chief knows the personnel of the bureau and their reactions more intimately than an outside fiscal agency. Decisions can be reached more quickly if he can act on his own authority. More important, he is responsible for results. If experience demonstrates that he is not technically competent or is weak in administration, the remedy is to secure a bureau chief who is competent and who can get results.

On the other hand, some considerations suggest the need of supervision of expenditures from outside the operating unit. New policy may be initiated on a small scale within an existing appropriation which may involve ultimate expenditure beyond any reasonable limits. Bureau chiefs cannot be left free to mortgage the future in this respect without supervision. This safeguard can be adequately supplied, however, through proper budget procedure and allotments. Two or more bureaus may engage in related and overlapping work; they cannot readily adjust their programs and expenditures without guidance. Bureau chiefs, who are usually technicians, sometimes are not good business administrators. Hence the desirability of central purchasing, rentals and construction. Or programs endorsed by the technicians may bid fair to stir up hostile public reactions which are properly of concern to chief executives. These instances point to some type of supervision. They do not demonstrate the need for the Illinois type of voucher inspection. Control of estimates, supervision of apportionments, and central management of the specialized auxiliary activities such as purchase, personnel, and rentals are adequate.

At the same time, it is feasible to allow fiscal agents to question the wisdom and expediency of proposed expenditures, if the ultimate decision is made by the department, rather than by the finance official. If the latter feels that the case is important enough, he may call it to the attention of the chief executive, who makes a conclusive decision. The finance official need not fear that his observations will pass unheeded, for his authority over succeeding estimates and his influence with appropriations committees are more than sufficient to entitle him to respectful hearing, even though his status as a principal representative of the chief executive be ignored. In the long run the lesser power over individual department expenditures might prove to be the greater influence.

The substantive decisions taken in the course of day-by-day administration of the line departments can be taken most intelligently and wisely by their responsible officials. This is generally recognized by fiscal officers in principle, if not always in practice. The remedy for weak or bad administration is not to transfer power to fiscal officers, but to secure competent administrators. In short, it is largely by means of better personnel, rather than highly concentrated fiscal procedure that effective administration is likely to be attained.

It seems clear that there are limits to the usefulness of fiscal supervision and control. Such supervision has overstepped the limits of its usefulness when it interferes substantially with the freedom of departments to carry out the programs imposed upon them by law. It has overstepped its usefulness when it takes the initiative in preparing department plans instead of surveying those submitted by the proper officials. It goes too far in attempting to substitute its judgment on technical questions for the judgment of the department. It operates to the detriment of sound administration when it impairs the sense of responsibility within the department for its work.

The real value of fiscal control lies, first, in compelling reconsideration of and conference about doubtful items of expenditures. It enables the department to see clearly all the implications of a proposed line of conduct and brings to it the informed business judgment of an office in touch with all departments of government. The usefulness of fiscal control consists, second, in furnishing an opportunity for the evaluation of different branches of administration in terms of their relative importance and in framing a financial program which gives precedence to the more pressing projects.

Chapter Sixteen

TREASURY MANAGEMENT

A TREASURY may be compared to a reservoir into which the stream of revenue flows and out of which it takes its course in the form of expenditures. It is the duty of the treasurer to record the inflow and to account for the outgo, without in any way assuming responsibility for determining the amount of intake or the conditions and magnitude of discharge, except to prevent any unauthorized person from dipping his bucket into the pool.

This figure of speech is, however, a gross oversimplification, except in the case of very small jurisdictions. Nevertheless much of the work of a treasurer's office is ministerial and routine; the decisions concerning fiscal policy and administration are made elsewhere, and the principal role of the treasurer remains that of a custodian. His chief qualifications are therefore managerial ability and knowledge of bookkeeping and accounting, and his chief need is protection against political pressure to subordinate his accounts to permit political use of public funds.

The Treasury Department of the United States government presents a unique case—so special and so complex that it will not be dealt with in this discussion. Among many other fiscal and nonfiscal agencies the department includes the Treasurer of the United States. His office is principally custodial, and is overshadowed by other branches of the Treasury concerned with revenue, accounts, debt administration, currency, foreign loans and collections, and general fiscal and monetary policy. The scale of operations of the United States Treasury, the problems involved in currency and banking control, the management of an enormous reserve of gold and silver bullion raise questions less of fiscal management than of public policy, the study of which would take us far afield. The typical cases of treasury management are to be found in the states and their subdivisions.[1]

1. Problems of Treasury Management

The administrative problems involved in treasury management at such

[1] Data concerning the offices of state auditor, treasurer and comptroller are found in the National Association of State Auditors, Comptrollers and Treasurers, *Tabular Analysis of State Fiscal Offices* (1938).

levels are, among others, these: the custody and safekeeping of funds, the investment of surplus funds and the disposition of interest, the disbursement of funds, and the maintenance of adequate cash reserves.[1]

In every respect the scale of operations of treasury management has been transformed since 1900. The great expansion of public functions during the last two generations has necessitated a new scale of fiscal administration. Total expenditures of New York State in 1850 amounted to $2,011,000; by 1900 they had risen only to $22,900,000.[2] In 1930 the expenditures from the general fund were over $259,000,000. Total revenue receipts of all state governments amounted to a little over 450 million dollars in 1915; by 1932 they had swollen to over 2,200 million. The character of the revenue was changing rapidly also as emergency taxes such as the sales tax were added to the sources of income, and as federal grants to the states increased. Revenue receipts of counties expanded from 370 million in 1912 to 1,300 million in 1932; city, town, village and borough treasurers received 1,090 millions in 1912, and 3,370 millions in 1932.

In the face of these heavy responsibilities, the office of treasurer in state, county and city has remained substantially unchanged except for the addition of more clerks and bookkeepers. Its history reveals it to have been one of the weakest and least satisfactory of the major public offices. Traditionally the treasurer has been an elective official, which implies that the incumbent is one active in politics, usually in debt to a political machine, and probably politically ambitious. The extraordinary power which control of public funds involves has made the office politically important in the first degree.

The authority of the treasurer is usually established by the state constitution for states and counties, and by the city charter for municipalities. The result has been to make the treasurer almost completely irresponsible. Thus Governor Caulfield of Missouri sought to remove the state treasurer in 1930 upon discovering an alleged misfeasance in depositing state funds for personal advantage. Upon quo warranto proceedings the Missouri Supreme Court held that the governor had no power to remove this constitutional officer, and that impeachment was the only remedy. Impeachment proceedings were taken but a vote of two-thirds to convict could not be obtained and the defendant thus not only escaped punishment but retained his office.[3]

[1] Brief studies of treasury management are found in A. E. Buck, *Municipal Finance* (1926), ch. 10; Lent D. Upson, *Practice of Municipal Administration* (1926), ch. 7; Harvey Walker, *Public Administration in the United States* (1937), ch. 10.

[2] Cited in Frank G. Bates and Oliver P. Field, *State Government* (1928), p. 220

[3] Martin L. Faust, "Irregularities in Custody of State Funds in Missouri," 20 *Nat. Mun. Rev.* 74-77 (1931).

The leading authority in this field, Professor Martin L. Faust, summarized his inquiries in these terms: "From the general surveys and special studies it is at once apparent that an almost chronic condition of misfeasance, corruption and mismanagement exists in connection with the handling of state funds. . . . The more important forms of graft and treasury misfeasance are outright embezzlement of the treasury funds, refusing to turn over interest earned by the public deposits, placing large deposits of state moneys in banks controlled and run by politicians, extending credit on liberal terms directly or indirectly to the official able to influence the selection of the depository, withholding state moneys from the treasury, and using them for private purposes."[1] It is impossible not to accept his verdict that as long as the state treasurer is an elective officer, the office will be in politics and political considerations will be a decisive factor in the distribution of public deposits.

While the general standards of rectitude prevailing in the community will broadly govern the ethics of public office, and while a mere change in organization form is no guarantee of high moral standards, it may nevertheless be urged that the existing form of organization of the treasurer's office exposes it most completely to the hazards of mismanagement. The office could be taken out of the front line political trenches, and it could be made administratively responsible. Such action has been taken, for example, in Virginia. In 1928, the independent elective constitutional office was abandoned, and the treasurer is now appointed by the governor and assembly for a four-year term. In New York State the office of treasurer has been abolished; its functions are performed by the comptroller.

Extension of the merit system to the employees of the state and local treasurers would accelerate the rejuvenation of this ancient, important, but somewhat discredited office. Considering that there are 47 state treasurers, over 3,000 county treasurers, over 16,000 city and village treasurers, and over 127,000 treasurers of school districts, almost all elected and politically committed, we may imagine the extent and difficulty of reform at this point. The public stake in the proper performance of their work is enormous, for these officials have custody of over four billion dollars of public funds belonging to the states and their subdivisions.[2]

2. The Custody of Public Funds

We thus come face to face with one of the chief problems of treasury management in the states, counties and cities, the safekeeping of public funds. Throughout much of our early history, funds were actually held in the vaults and strong boxes of the treasurers, much as in the

[1] Martin L. Faust, *The Custody of State Funds* (1925), p. 62.

[2] Federal Deposit Insurance Corporation, *Annual Report*, 1934, p. 196.

day of William the Conqueror, except that the rule of seven keys was no longer observed. The alternative procedure of placing the funds in banks was looked upon with suspicion which, in view of the "wildcat" banking of early times, was not wholly unjustified.

Until the formation of the Federal Reserve System, Congress required federal officials charged with the custody of federal funds to hold them in such official places of safekeeping as the vaults of the customhouses, the mints, and the central treasury in Washington. This, the independent treasury system, has now been discarded in favor of deposit in the banks of the Federal Reserve System, except that the huge stock of gold bullion is held in a specially constructed "strong-box" in Kentucky, and much silver at West Point.

Within the states and their subdivisions, also, the idea of actual physical possession of the cash by the treasurer has been abandoned in favor of the bank depository method. The security of public deposits still remains an unsolved problem, especially in the midst of such an economic and financial disaster as that commencing in 1929. It is estimated that at least $450,000,000 of public funds were impounded in banks during 1933.[1]

This extraordinary banking crash merely accentuated the problem and laid bare the issues more clearly.[2] Who shall determine the banks where public funds shall be deposited? On the basis of what considerations shall the choice be made? What security shall be exacted to ensure the safety of the funds on deposit? The answers to these questions reveal the principal sources of protection which bitter experience is gradually developing. While all variations of practice can still be observed, the preferred practice is stated in the following paragraphs.

Who shall choose the banks in which public funds may be deposited? The free discretion of the treasurer is giving way to the action of a board, or the decision of the governing authority. In the states, depository boards comprising the governor, the auditor, the attorney general and other officials are common; in only twelve cases in 1925 was the treasurer able to select depositories on his own responsibility. In the counties Porter reports that the solution normally has been to authorize the county governing board to indicate the banks in which county

[1] Martin L. Faust, *The Custody of State Funds* (1925), *passim;* and, by the same author, *The Security of Public Deposits,* Public Administration Service No. 51, 1936. This section relies heavily upon these two valuable studies.

[2] Losses through failure of depositories had not been great until recent years, although not uncommon. A survey covering 47 states showed that from 1912 to 1917 the aggregate losses amounted to only $26,000. In 1923 about $2,275,000 was tied up in defunct banks, recovery of most of which was expected. Faust, *The Custody of State Funds,* p. 24, and Appendix 2.

'unds may be deposited.[1] In cities, various arrangements exist, but the ıncontrolled discretion of the treasurer is becoming less common.

What considerations govern the selection of depositories? The law ɔf most jurisdictions still leaves the basis of selection to the judgment of he proper authority, occasionally specifying a minimum paid-up capi- al as a condition of eligibility, and in rare instances requiring a distribu- ion of depositories in different counties. A requirement gradually spread- ng among the states and localities is competitive bidding on interest ɔffered; in recent years the banks have not been active bidders, and a ıigh bid may indicate lack of security.

What security shall be exacted to ensure the safety of funds on de- ɔosit? Over the years, all sorts of devices have been tried and most found wanting in time of emergency. An early plan gave preferred creditor status to public deposits in a defaulting bank. Apart from the ɔossibility that assets might be lacking to pay even the public deposi- ors, this plan is open to criticism as imposing an undue and undesirable ıardship on private creditors.

In the New England states and in New Jersey, principal reliance was placed until the 1929 depression upon bank supervision, or upon per- sonal liability. The high character of banking institutions in this region gave adequate protection until the bank crisis of 1933 when some losses ɔccurred. Personal liability of the treasurer is wholly unsatisfactory.

For a time it seemed that surety bonds might provide a satisfactory means of safeguarding public funds on deposit, and the surety system is still widely used. But, faced with losses of over $33,000,000 from 1928 to 1933, the surety companies have come to regard depository bonds as a "highly undesirable" class of business. During the banking difficulties of recent years, sureties themselves proved unreliable in some cases, costs became prohibitive, and recovery too often involved liti- gation.

The most common method of handling the problem of security is to require the pledge of collateral security. Faust regards this plan as the most satisfactory of those which have been tried, although he recog- nizes that the necessary competence in the evaluation of collateral is most likely to be found in large rather than small jurisdictions.

Three states, Iowa, Wisconsin and Indiana, have systems of state in- surance for public deposits. Both Iowa and Wisconsin insurance funds have been "in the red," although their situation seems to be improving with aid from the Reconstruction Finance Corporation. The Indiana plan is of post-depression origin. In general it appears unlikely that a

[1] Kirk Porter, *State Administration* (1937), p. 107.

plan of deposit insurance limited to one state is sufficiently stable to provide adequate protection.

On the other hand, the insurance of deposits on a nation-wide scale, as by the Federal Deposit Insurance Corporation, holds much greater promise. Local governments, like other depositors, are taking advantage of the existing protection up to $5,000. Faust recommends that the system of federal insurance be extended to cover public deposits in full, the cost to be assessed against the deposits. From the point of view of administrative convenience as well as of the safety of deposits, this plan appears superior to any that have yet been tried, especially if coupled with strict safeguards against placing large sums in small or weak banks.

The unsatisfactory character of the American banking system has magnified the difficulties of this phase of treasury management, and a complete solution will probably have to await the improvement of the bank structure. At the same time, the weakness of treasury administration in states and local governments must bear a large share of the responsibility for repeated loss of public funds on deposit. This phase of treasury management, while well handled in many communities, has broken down in many others.

3. Interest on Public Funds

A commentary on the extraordinary methods of handling public money is found in the practice, almost universal until about 1900, of allowing treasurers to retain for personal use the interest on deposits of public funds. The theory underlying this practice was that the treasurer was responsible only for the safety of the funds committed to him, that the funds were not required nor expected to earn interest, and that any such interest was merely a personal "windfall" of the treasurer. Actually the interest earnings, often very large sums, were widely recognized as the due of the party in power or of the faction to which the treasurer belonged.

By 1920 this remarkable doctrine had been generally replaced by the recognition that interest earned on public funds was as truly the property of the government as the funds themselves. In 1925 Faust reported that Alabama was the only state not receiving interest on its bank balances. No data are available with reference to contemporary practice in counties and cities, but the covering of interest into the treasury is now the common practice.

Repeated scandals in private appropriation of interest on public funds have been aired in the courts. One of the most sensational involved Governor Small of Illinois, who with four other former state treasurers was sued in 1921 for withholding approximately $2,500,000 of interest on treasury deposits. Small had placed state deposits in an obscure private bank, on which two per cent interest was paid to the state. The bank, controlled by the interest ring, then purchased notes of certain large Chicago packing houses on which seven per cent was earned, thus profiting the principals by five per cent. In a civil suit, Small was found guilty and ordered to make restitution of over $400,000 of interest wrongfully withheld from the treasury.[1]

The investment of funds, as distinguished from their deposit in banks, is usually managed by an investment board or commission, comprising ex officio three or more of the principal state or local officials. Investment is required principally for trust funds and for sinking funds. The steady preference for serial bonds is gradually eliminating sinking funds and is thus reducing the magnitude of the investment problem. Safety in investments has usually been sought by limiting the choice to those securities in which insurance companies may legally invest. There is a definite tendency, not yet widespread, to require the state to handle the investment of local funds.

This colorful aspect of treasury management, characterized in the past by bold and unscrupulous appropriation of interest earnings for personal and party benefit, has already passed into the more staid and less reprehensible period of accurate accounting and public control. The huge interest takings of the past will not recur, unless by outright fraud and peculation.

4. Maintenance of Cash Reserves

A technical problem of treasury management to which only passing notice can be given concerns the maintenance of an adequate daily cash reserve. Treasury income and outgo are not even or steady streams; both fluctuate widely as tax payments become due, and as heavy cash requirements for construction, debt retirement or other purposes are met. Underlying these peaks is the normal and relatively steady flow of current operating expenses. The treasurer has to maintain cash reserves to meet all current demands, a program requiring some planning and foresight. To tide over low points, relief may be sought in tax anticipation warrants or in short-term borrowing; to take care of operating surpluses, investment in short-term securities may be made. During the depression cash balances completely disappeared in some jurisdictions, leading to municipal bankruptcy, "foreclosure," payless pay days, and

[1] See Faust, *The Custody of State Funds*, for details of this and other cases; C. S. Hexton, "The Liability of Public Officers in Illinois for Funds in their Custody," 1 *John Marshall Law Q.* 213-19 (1936-37).

other expedients. This aspect of treasury management has been peculiarly difficult since 1929.

5. Disbursement of Funds

One would hardly look to the disbursement of funds by public treasurers for the dramatic, but many exciting episodes are tucked away in this unlikely corner. The payment by check of nearly 2,000,000 Civil Works Administration workers on November 15, 1933, for their first two weeks' work is one of the truly extraordinary administrative feats of this generation. With less than six weeks' notice of the whole undertaking, and with only two weeks' notice of the names of persons entitled to payment, it was necessary to write checks in Washington for distribution in every community in the United States. At the direction of the President the Government Printing Office stopped all work to print millions of blank checks; an emergency staff for night and day shifts was extemporized, and the checks went out on time.

The duties of the state and local treasurers in the disbursements of funds are ministerial. They receive warrants from the comptroller or auditor to pay certain sums to certain individuals, and on this authority draw the proper check for payment. In relatively few cases are payments made in cash except for day labor and sometimes for employees paid on a weekly rate. The use of checks is standard practice. The volume of checks in large jurisdictions is tremendous, and to relieve the countersigning officers a machine has been devised which enables an individual to sign several checks at one time.

In city governments the advance of funds to departmental officers for disbursement is rare. In the state governments the advance of funds to officers and institutions located at a distance from the capital is relatively common. In a diminishing number of cases, fees collected locally are retained for payment of bills due. In general, only the state universities retain an important degree of fiscal autonomy in the state governments; there are only rare examples, apart from some municipal universities, in the cities. The government corporations of the United States, however, act as their own disbursing agents. With such infrequent exceptions, however, the function of federal disbursement was consolidated in 1933 in the chief disbursing officer of the Treasury.[1]

The task of disbursement is principally one requiring accuracy and care. It reflects completely the characteristic treasury features of bookkeeping, accounting, and proper authorization. It reveals the treasurer's office as one principally devoted to the maintenance of financial records and indicates how completely it should be removed from the influence

[1] Executive Order 6166, June 10, 1933.

of political considerations. It is a technical office, for the filling of which popular election is not a desirable form of selection.

The credit operations of government grow steadily more impressive. The principal issues are economic rather than administrative in nature, and may best be approached from another point of view than administration. For the same reason the special functions of the United States Treasury Department concerning coinage, currency, international movement of specie or debt payments, and management of the public debt are not dealt with, important though they are to the national welfare.

In short, in the states, counties and cities, treasury management is principally concerned with the receipt of funds, their custody and safekeeping, their investment and disbursement. These functions are important but secondary to such aspects of fiscal management as budget making, current control of expenditures and audit. They require for their successful performance honesty and competence in bookkeeping and accounting, together with some knowledge of investment procedures. They do not involve wide discretion, except in the case of investments. The office of treasurer has been one of the weakest links in the reformed fiscal procedures of the last quarter century. Repeated violation of trust and consequent loss of public funds have been traced to the political obligations of treasurers, and to their independence of any control save impeachment. The office should be deflated by destroying its privileged constitutional position and then related to other fiscal offices and made responsible to the chief executive.

Chapter Seventeen

AUDIT

THE final stage in fiscal management is the audit. The long sequence of fiscal events including the initial preparation of estimates, submission of the budget, appropriation by the legislative body, apportionments to the spending agencies, setting up accounts, making obligations, and eventual payment of money to vendors, contractors and employees terminates with a review of these steps to ascertain that they have been legally and regularly taken.

1. Nature of Audit and the "Administrative Audit"

The audit is a function undertaken on behalf of the appropriating body, and is therefore a legislative, not an executive task. It is part of the external control over administration maintained by the representative body, not a part of the internal responsibility of officials to the chief executive. In principle it is unrelated to and independent of any means of fiscal control which executives may require to facilitate the overhead management and direction of work for which they are responsible.[1]

Much confusion exists between the functions of audit and of fiscal control by executives, of which the "administrative audit" or, better, the administrative examination of accounts is a part. Audit is much the older form of review, since it runs back through state and federal governments into the colonial period and beyond. Executive control of expenditures including the administrative audit is a modern phenomenon, reaching back not much more than thirty years and in many instances

[1] The principal monographs and studies on government auditing include, Willard E. Hotchkiss, *The Judicial Work of the Comptroller of the Treasury* (1911); Albert G. Langeluttig, *The Department of Justice of the United States* (1927), ch. 13; Darrell H. Smith, *The General Accounting Office* (1927); W. F. Willoughby, *The Legal Status and Functions of the General Accounting Office of the National Government* (1927); George C. S. Benson, *Financial Control and Integration* (1934); Harvey C. Mansfield, "The General Accounting Office," in President's Committee on Administrative Management, *Report with Special Studies* (1937), pp. 169-202; *Investigation of Executive Agencies of the Government*, S. Rept. 1275, 75th Cong., 1st sess. (1937), ch. 3; Daniel T. Selko, *The Administration of Federal Finances* (1937); National Association of State Auditors, Comptrollers and Treasurers, *Tabular Analysis of State Fiscal Offices* (1938).

even less. It is a phase of the new position of the chief executive which was rare in states and cities before the reorganization movement.[1]

The difficulty of clear distinction is increased because the exact function of a true audit is understood differently by the authorities. In this discussion the following definition is accepted as the point of departure.

> Auditing is a systematic examination of the books and records of a business or other organization, in order to ascertain or verify, and to report upon, the facts regarding its financial operations and the results thereof.[2]

The task of auditing is not entirely the same in government as in business. A commercial auditor is consulted principally to verify the records of corporate officers. He is not usually responsible for ascertaining whether they followed instructions or acted without proper authorization. The validity of payments made is not contingent upon the findings of the auditor nor does he participate in the final settlement and payment of sums owed to or by the corporation. He verifies the records by comparing books of account with cash, property, bills and other evidences to see that all entries are properly made and that they indicate correctly the results of operations as reflected in profit and loss.

Governmental auditing in the United States is usually more than a mere verification.[3] It is also a determination whether amounts paid or claimed were legally and regularly subject to disbursement. In this case the validation of the audit is the ultimate authorization to pay; failing validation the payment either cannot be legally made or, if already disbursed, recovery may be sought from the disbursing officer or the payee.[4] This is the nature of the auditing system of the federal government and most states; in other states and a large number of cities, audit is a verification only.

Neither type of audit replaces the operations involved in administrative control of expenditure, although the procedures are similar in part. The basic objectives of an audit are to see that funds have been

[1] See *supra*, ch. 7.

[2] Robert H. Montgomery, *Auditing, Theory and Practice* (5th ed. 1934), p. 3.

[3] See the comment by the Brookings staff on this point in *Investigation of Executive Agencies of the Government*, S. Rept. 1275, 75th Cong., 1st sess. (1937), pp. 157-58.

[4] This dual nature of auditing is reflected in the *Corpus Juris* definition: ". . . sometimes it [i.e., the audit] is restricted in meaning to a check-up of the correctness of the account or claim and excludes any element of discretion on the part of the auditor; . . . at other times, it may embrace not only an examination of accounts and a comparison of charges with vouchers, but also an allowance or rejection of charges . . . involving an exercise of discretion by the auditing officer or board. . . ." 7 *Corpus Juris Secundum* 1274-75.

used only for the purposes and in accordance with the conditions established by law, to check the accuracy of accounts and inventories, to ensure against embezzlement or loss of funds, and to report findings to the proper agency: the administrative agency in case of unauthorized expenditures, the prosecuting officers in case of wrongdoing, the legislative body in case of inefficiency or unsatisfactory operation of the fiscal system. The purpose of administrative control of expenditures is to ensure regularity and accuracy as well as care and good business judgment in the use of funds, and more broadly to enable the chief executive to bring his influence to bear upon work programs and administrative policy as reflected in expenditures. The end of an audit is to ensure regularity and legality; of administrative control, to avoid deficits, to supervise current expenditures, and to ensure that all fiscal programs are in conformity with the master plan of the government of the day. These objectives overlap in part, but not entirely.

Historically, an audit took place subsequent to expenditure. In its simplest form, it was a scrutiny of books and supporting documents (pay rolls, vouchers, etc.) at the close of a fiscal year. The full year's operations were then available for study and criticism, surpluses or deficits were disclosed, and the net result of fiscal operations could be ascertained and reported to the appropriating body. The deterrent effect upon misuse of funds lay in the danger of ultimate discovery, not in prohibition at the moment. In its more highly developed form, audit became a continuous operation, the flow of financial transactions through the auditor's office being uninterrupted throughout the fiscal year. It still remained, however, subsequent to the event. More recently the pre-audit was invented, by which pay rolls, bills and claims pass through the auditor's hands before payment. An audit is still usually, although not necessarily, an operation conducted after payments have been fully authorized and actually made, while administrative control occurs prior to and as a part of the decision to authorize an expenditure.

It results that in principle two separate and distinct officers are responsible, one for audit and one for administrative control. The former is an arm of the legislative branch and is properly called an auditor, the latter is a branch of the executive and is properly called a comptroller.[1] In practice, however, these terms are often confused, partly because the auditing function is performed by an official described in the constitution or laws as a comptroller, partly because the function of adminis-

[1] Practically all states have created the office of auditor, but less than one half that of comptroller. In 1938, state auditors' staffs ranged from 2 to 648, typically from 10 to 50; the comptrollers' staffs ranged from 25 to 75. *Tabular Analysis of State Fiscal Offices*, p. 7.

trative control is exercised in part, or in whole by the nominal auditor.[1]

The necessity of an audit is questioned by no student of government. The usefulness of some form of executive control of current expenditures is also widely acknowledged. There is a growing sentiment that the duplication of effort between the comptroller, acting for the executive, and the auditor, acting for the legislative branch, should be curtailed, but the need for duality of control is not in dispute.

The principal issue concerns the form and effect of the audit, an issue which has been placed in the front rank of current problems by the proposals of the President's Committee on Administrative Management to modify the character of the functions performed by the Comptroller General of the United States. Since the controversy over this proposal throws light on the nature and role of the audit, it will be helpful to examine the powers of the Comptroller General as a case study and to consider the proposals of the Committee to curtail them.[2]

[1] Benson correctly identifies these two forms of financial control: "The first, which for convenience sake we may call internal control, is what is usually thought of as the 'Comptroller's' or 'Financial executive's' job in American business. It is primarily the duty of the comptroller to pass on all expenditures of the business or administration, i.e., to approve vouchers or issue warrants for payment and thus exercise a continuous check on the financial conduct of affairs. Particularly in government administration this power goes hand in hand with the power of preparing the budget. The second which we call external control is necessary only when some party outside of the actual administration, stockholder or taxpayer or legislature, has a definite interest in conduct of affairs. It is known in American and English business as auditing and usually means a periodical (sometimes continuous) check on validity of accounts and payments by someone who is definitely outside of the administration, after payment has been made." George C. S. Benson, *Financial Control and Integration* (1934), p. 1.

[2] Excepting the *Tabular Analysis of State Fiscal Offices*, noted above, there is no comprehensive study of auditing in state and local government, apart from occasional studies of the system of one state, or of one city or group of cities. Great variety of practice prevails, since the auditing laws are far from comparable and practice does not always conform to law. Massachusetts and Virginia are among the states which have differentiated between audit and the administrative examination of accounts. In the council manager cities, the city manager is often himself the actual controller of daily expenditures, although he bears no such title. In the larger council manager cities, the manager will appoint a finance director who watches expenditures and enforces managerial and council policy. In many cities of all types, however, auditing, budget making, bookkeeping and accounting, expenditure control, paymaster operations, debt management and other phases of fiscal operations are confused and mingled in the single office of city comptroller. For a forward-looking proposal see Lent D. Upson, "A Municipal Auditor-General," 26 *Nat. Mun. Rev.* 428-31 (1937). Study of auditing in the state governments may begin with Harvey Walker, *Public Administration in the United States* (1937), pp. 254-60 and references cited on p. 262. Much city auditing is done by private auditing firms or by state leagues of municipalities. See William A. Lafferty, Jr., *The Auditing of Municipal Accounts in New York State*, New York State Conference of Mayors, Publication No. 28, 1933, pp. 52-57; National Committee on Municipal Accounting, *Municipal Audit Procedure* (1938).

2. The Growth and Character of Functions Performed by the General Accounting Office

Prior to the establishment of the General Accounting Office in 1921 the audit of federal expenditures had been performed in the Treasury Department by six auditors, acting under interpretations and findings of the Comptroller of the Treasury. The Budget and Accounting Act of 1921 established an independent auditing office representing the legislative branch of the government. This change accords with the theory of governmental auditing, and was emphasized by the fifteen-year term of the Comptroller General with removal only for specific causes by a joint resolution of Congress after notice and hearing. The independent character of the office was duly asserted by its first incumbent, Comptroller General John R. McCarl.[1]

The powers vested in this office are numerous and weighty. They include by specific enumeration authority to settle and adjust all claims and demands by the government or against it; to prescribe the form and procedure for accounting; to investigate all matters relating to the receipt, disbursement and application of public funds; and to report to Congress every expenditure or contract made in violation of law. They include by implication or construction authority to interpret all statutes affecting the receipt, expenditure or use of public funds, to approve contracts, and to have the custody of original documents necessary to support the validity of payments. Mere enumeration of these powers reveals the central position which the General Accounting Office has come to occupy; their steady expansion for fifteen years eventually precipitated a strong reaction. In the following paragraphs each of the principal activities of the General Accounting Office will be noted.

a. Audit. "All claims and demands whatever by the government of the United States or against it, and all accounts whatever, in which the government of the United States is concerned, either as debtor or creditor, shall be settled and adjusted in the General Accounting Office." This is the fundamental authority of the Comptroller General. It involves the examination of financial transactions to ascertain their accuracy, regularity, and legality and the availability of credits in the appropriation affected. In the performance of this task, covering expenditures of billions of dollars a year and requiring examination of millions of accounts and

[1] W. F. Willoughby, *The Legal Status and Functions of the General Accounting Office of the National Government* (1927); Albert Langeluttig, "Legal Status of the Comptroller General of the United States," 23 *Ill. Law Rev.* 556-90 (1928–29); President's Committee on Administrative Management, *Report with Special Studies* (1937), pp. 21-25, and pp. 169-202, containing the study by Harvey C. Mansfield, "The General Accounting Office"; *Investigation of Executive Agencies of the Government*, S. Rept. 1275, 75th Cong., 1st sess. (1937), pp. 134-74.

documents, the services of over 5,000 employees were required in 1937, and still the work was seriously in arrears.

The General Accounting Office has never accepted the practice of test audit which prevails in the corresponding British Office of the Auditor and Comptroller General. A test audit is one which scrutinizes a part, rather than all of the financial transactions and is satisfied if the portion selected for examination reveals no irregularities. The test audit is based upon confidence in and acceptance of the administrative examination of accounts and expenditures which is made before bills are certified for payment. In the federal government, "administrative audits prior to the approval of vouchers are conducted for the most part with great care in order to determine that all payments are properly authorized and that no appropriation or limitation thereof, is exceeded."[1] This review of expenditures is not recognized, however, by the Comptroller General as permitting any relaxation of his audit, item by item.

The audit, as already noted, may either precede or follow the payment of a voucher by a disbursing officer. The Comptroller General has sought to impose a system of preaudit and by agreement with a number of agencies operates on this basis. Other agencies have declined to accept a preaudit and the Navy Department reverted to a postaudit after trying the preaudit for five years. The so-called "administrative audit" always precedes certification for payment.

It is the duty of the auditor to see that all legal requirements for expenditure have been observed, and this duty often leads far afield from the primary issues. The law, for example, requires competitive bidding on most contracts; before a valid claim can be established, proof of compliance must be affirmatively established. Most agencies of the national government are subject to the Classification Act of 1923; the auditor must be satisfied that the position has been allocated to a class and that the incumbent is receiving compensation in accordance with the allocation. Appointment of experts by the departments is sometimes allowed without competitive examination; but the Comptroller General requires proof that the position and the incumbent are in fact "expert." The United States Civil Service Commission cooperates with the General Accounting Office in this connection.

The jurisdiction of the Comptroller General of the United States has, however, its limits. The broad nature of these limits may be indicated by two or three examples. Reverting for the moment to classification procedures, it is not a duty of the Comptroller General to inquire whether the classification made by the Civil Service Commission is the

[1] *Investigation of Executive Agencies of the Government*, S. Rept. 1275, 75th Cong., 1st sess. (1937), p. 159.

correct one, or that which he would have made in the first instance. The final responsibility for classification rests with the Commission, including most positions in the General Accounting Office itself. If it appears that a classification has been established in due and proper course, the General Accounting Office is bound thereby.

A similar situation exists in the income tax unit of the Bureau of Internal Revenue. Determination of tax liability is the responsibility of Treasury officials, and it is beyond the competence of the General Accounting Office to reopen individual returns. A dissatisfied taxpayer may appeal to the Board of Tax Appeals, or eventually to the courts, but not to the Comptroller General. A corresponding rule prevails in customs classification and the imposition of duties. Were the contrary rule to prevail, the General Accounting Office would in principle be obliged to review all the decisions of all the departments and independent establishments on all aspects of the substantive law involving financial transactions which they respectively administer. The duty of an auditor is to audit, not to administer.

This basic limitation, however, is easier to state than to apply in the multifarious circumstances of government operations, and there is a common tendency for auditing offices to extend their authority into definitely administrative matters. This tendency is facilitated by the laws which often erroneously impose administrative functions upon auditors, and by the view which auditors sometimes take that they are the judges of their own jurisdiction. It is consequently easy for auditors to expand their activities into the field of operations and to assume decisions which belong to others.

In case the General Accounting Office disallows a payment, the sum disallowed is charged against the account of the disbursing officer. His first recourse is to attempt to convince the General Accounting Office that it has made an error, and much correspondence is always on foot between the auditors and the disbursing officers. If the General Accounting Office remains unsatisfied, and the payment has been made, the disbursing officer, or the Attorney General, may try to collect from the person to whom the payment was erroneously made. If this proves impossible, the charge rests upon the disbursing officer and his bondsman. The final source of relief is an act of Congress discharging the disbursing officer from liability. Since most disputed sums are due to honest difference of opinion and not fraud nor embezzlement, such relief is normally forthcoming if no other adjustment is possible.

b. Advance decisions. This procedure leads directly to another activity of the Comptroller General. Administrative and disbursing officers naturally prefer to avoid doubtful payments. In order to protect themselves, they have been authorized since 1894 to request "advance opinions" which determine whether a proposed payment is legal and proper or the contrary. The number of such advance opinions is steadily increasing, fostered by the meticulous audit which has been developed by the General Accounting Office. In 1914–15 the number was about 250; in 1936–37 the number ran into the thousands.

This procedure is a reasonable one up to the point where administrative officers seek to validate every new line of action by preliminary appeal to the Comptroller General. The tendency is inevitably in this direction for every new or unusual expenditure; the end result may be to make the General Accounting Office the supreme administrative authority rather than a legislative auditing office.

c. Interpretation of statutes. The advance opinion is related to another important phase of the work of the General Accounting Office, the interpretation of statutes affecting expenditures. A long-standing controversy between the Attorney General and the auditing officials turns on their respective responsibilities for legal interpretation of statutes. Before 1921 the Comptroller of the Treasury recognized the authority of interpretations given in the Opinions of the Attorney General. Subsequent to the establishment of the office of Comptroller General, the Attorney General declined to interpret statutes directly governing expenditures, but continued under the terms of the law to render opinions on other statutes. The Comptroller General refused to submit any disputed questions to the Attorney General or to modify his decisions in conformity with the Opinions of the Attorney General. He reserved and exercised the right to make conclusive determinations wherever the course of expenditures was affected directly or indirectly. The resulting conflict, which has led "to a great deal of uncertainty, delay, and expense, and at times reaches almost to the point of administrative paralysis," may be examined in three illustrative cases.

The first conflict of jurisdiction arose in 1922.[1] The Comptroller General issued regulations to the War Department requiring transportation accounts to be certified to the General Accounting Office for direct payment, omitting the prevailing administrative examination and certification for payment by the War Department disbursing officers. The War Department denied the right of the Comptroller General to issue the regulations, and the Attorney General sustained this view in a formal opinion. The War Department consequently declined to comply with the regulations, which, however, were not withdrawn and which were followed by certain other departments. Langeluttig

[1] See Willoughby, *op. cit.*, pp. 50-61.

makes this comment. "Certain things should be noted regarding this opinion. The first is that the Attorney General expressly disclaims any authority on his part to review or revise a settlement of a claim by the Comptroller General, but he does assert the right to construe the law for the purpose of determining the scope of the powers of the Comptroller General. The second is that the Comptroller General has ignored this decision by continuing in force the regulations and has succeeded in having them observed at least in part. The Comptroller General has thus taken the position that it is proper for him to construe his own powers as well as to act finally upon the settlement of accounts." [1]

A case involving transportation accounts in the Navy arose in 1935. In 1920 Congress authorized payment of traveling expenses of the wives and dependent children of naval officers when the officer was ordered "to make a permanent change of station." The Navy Department sought to authorize payment of traveling expenses in the case of a naval officer ordered home for retirement. The General Accounting Office disallowed the claim in a series of cases, and a number of officers including one Bullard, sued in the Court of Claims. Their contention was upheld. The General Accounting Office declined to follow the ruling in the Bullard case, alleging that previous cases had not been properly presented to the Court of Claims by the Attorney General The Navy Department, following the opinion of the Attorney Genera and of the Court of Claims, advised the Comptroller General that i had instructed its disbursing officers to continue to make payment o traveling expenses for dependents of naval officers in these circum stances.

Comptroller General McCarl thereupon addressed a lengthy lette to the Secretary of the Navy stating the facts in the case, discussin the status of the General Accounting Office, and concluding wit these sharp words:

> . . . in view of your announced conclusion to ignore the decisions of this offic with respect to the legal availability of existing appropriations for such paymen and to require such payments by accountable officers under your military contro you are advised that there is ended the effort this office has made to assist you Department in its seeming difficulties . . . and that hereafter . . . appropriations wi not be available for payment of traveling expenses of dependents of officers of th Navy to their homes when such officers are ordered home to await orders fo retirement.[2]

[1] Albert G. Langeluttig, *The Department of Justice of the United States* (1927 p. 165.

[2] The letter is printed *in extenso* in House *Hearings*, Navy Department Appro priation Bill for 1936, pp. 841-46. The case of the Navy Department is stated at p 848-51.

'our days later, President Roosevelt announced that he and his Cabinet ad decided to back the Secretary of the Navy. Members of the Senate nd House, however, expressed their determination to support the Comptroller General, and for a moment it appeared likely that heavy ighting was the order of the day. In due course of time, however, almer counsels prevailed and it was decided to seek an amendment of he law governing travel allowances. Meanwhile the Comptroller Genral prevailed.

A third case arose from the Employees' Compensation Commission. n the exercise of its discretion, this Commission held that occupational iseases were included in the term "personal injuries." The Attorney General confirmed this opinion. The Comptroller General ruled in a ontrary sense. The Commission followed the opinion of the Attorney General, and subsequently Congress gave it conclusive power to inerpret the compensation act.[1]

In general, it may be stated that the vast majority of decisions, interretations and rulings made by the Comptroller General are conclusive nd final in fact. Most cases of conflict between the Attorney General nd the Comptroller General can be solved only by action of Congress. ome, involving withholding of salary, have reached the courts, and each of such cases noted by Langeluttig (to 1927) the courts susined the view of the Attorney General. In 1918 the Supreme Court ntimated broadly that the federal auditors should follow the legal pinions of the Attorney General.[2] The Court, after referring to the pinion of the Attorney General in the case, said, ". . . this ruling ould have put the subject at rest . . . we are of the opinion that it obvious on the face of the statement of case that the Auditor had o power to refuse to carry out the law and that any doubt which e might have had should have been subordinated, first to the ruling f the Attorney General and, second, beyond all possible question to e judgments of the courts below." The Comptroller General, hower, still declines to accept this view of his relations to the Attorney General, and the feeling between the two offices is at times far from iendly.

d. Comptroller General determinations and judicial decisions. This rings us to the view of the Comptroller General concerning the govning force of court decisions. The present situation may be briefly ated. The Comptroller General will yield only to an opinion of the

[1] 43 Stat. 389 (1924).

[2] *Smith vs. Jackson*, 246 U.S. 388 (1918); see also O. R. McGuire, "The Opinns of the Attorney General and the General Accounting Office," 15 *Georgetown w J.* 115-26 (1926–27).

Supreme Court of the United States. Opinions of other federal courts, including the Court of Claims, are recognized as "persuasive" and as entitled to "great weight," but not as conclusive.

The position of the Comptroller General is put in these terms. The accounting officers are not a part of the federal judicial system, and the rule governing judges that decisions of higher courts are binding on all inferior courts is therefore not applicable. If, moreover, the General Accounting Office should follow the decisions of the Court of Claims, the rights of the United States might be sacrificed if upon appeal the Supreme Court should reverse a Court of Claims decision, the claim meanwhile having been settled. So far as the lower federal courts are concerned, the General Accounting Office points out that there is no necessary consistency among them and consequently no one line of decisions to guide accounting officers.[1] The Comptroller General consequently recognizes the controlling force of decisions only of the Supreme Court itself.

e. Control of accounting forms. Other aspects of the authority of the Comptroller General are less spectacular in their consequences. The power to prescribe the forms, systems and procedure for accounting was transferred from the Treasury to the General Accounting Office in 1921. This authority has been implemented by gradual improvements in the federal accounting system and by partial installations.

The reason for giving the auditor authority to prescribe the accounting systems for the administrative agencies is to ensure that the form of accounts will furnish the type of information needed for auditing purposes. This consideration overlooks the fact that the principal use of accounts is to furnish information for operating officials and that consequently the form of accounts should be such as to produce the information needed by them. There is general although not complete agreement that the power to prescribe and supervise the accounting systems should consequently be vested in the executive branch, not in the auditing service. There is also dissatisfaction among accounting experts over the failure of the General Accounting Office to bring the federal system up to date by introducing the most modern methods.

At one time the Comptroller General sought to take charge of paymaster operations, which were then carried on by each department and agency. This program was blocked, and in 1933 the function of disbursement was concentrated in the Treasury.

f. Deposit of original documents. As a part of auditing routine, the

[1] O. R. McGuire, "The Accounting Officers of the United States and Judicial Precedents," 19 *Ill. Law Rev.* 523–32 (1924–25). McGuire served for many years as counsel to Comptroller General McCarl.

Comptroller General requires the deposit in his office of all original documents supporting expenditures. Carbon copies or photostatic reproductions are not accepted. Considerable inconvenience is said to arise in the administrative offices as a result. The Federal Power Commission refused to turn over the original copies of all franchises granted under the Federal Power Act of 1920 and Resettlement Administration declined to submit the documents proving title to the land they were purchasing. Other instances of refusal exist but a huge volume of documents is constantly pouring into the General Accounting Office, great enough, it is said, to fill the National Archives building in ten years if they were deposited there instead of in warehouses. Mansfield asserts that, "Probably no other single factor weighs so heavily among the reasons why Government-owned corporations object strenuously to being brought within the jurisdiction of the General Accounting Office. . . ."[1]

g. Power to investigate. Finally the Comptroller General is authorized and directed to investigate matters concerning public funds, to report expenditures or contracts in violation of law, and to make such special inquiries as may be directed. There have been a number of valuable special investigations of agencies or institutions.

This summary view of the authority of the Comptroller General reveals that his is an office of great power. He is wholly independent of the President, and in practice is substantially independent of the courts.[2] In theory he is responsible to Congress, but even this connection is hardly one of substance. The work of the Comptroller General has not been subjected to periodic review by Congress or by a congressional committee; his decisions are not brought to the attention of Congress except in case of serious controversy; Congressmen have no effective means of knowing what balance is maintained between audit and administrative discretion nor of assuring themselves that these relationships are satisfactory; nor has Congress had leadership from the Comptroller General in major aspects of fiscal administration. Instead of reporting to Congress expenditures in violation of law, the Comptroller General has imposed his interpretation of legality upon the departments. Mansfield therefore concludes, "Thus the main feature of the act has broken down completely. Administrative action by the Comptroller General has been substituted for reports to Congress."[3]

[1] President's Committee on Administrative Management, *Report with Special Studies* (1937), p. 183.

[2] Harvey C. Mansfield, "Judicial Review of the Comptroller General," 20 *Cornell Law Q.* 459-79 (1934-35).

[3] Harvey C. Mansfield, "The General Accounting Office," in President's Committee on Administrative Management, *op. cit.*, p. 191.

The mounting tide of complaints against a form of current financia control which tended to become a "judicial rather than an executiv process" came to a focus in the studies of the President's Committe on Administrative Management in 1937.[1] Their recommendations, whic

[1] "A large number of arbitrary and technical decisions by the General Account ing Office is another conspicuous result of the present system of fiscal contro This is not a matter of isolated instances but of the wholesale hampering of almos every agency whose accounts are settled by the Comptroller General. A few exan ples serve to illustrate.

"The Comptroller General objects to delegation to an assistant of authorit vested in the head of a department. Thus, in spite of an act of Congress permittin the Secretary of the Interior to delegate to his executive assistant power to sig 'such official papers and documents as the Secretary may direct,' the Comptroll General refused to allow credit for travel expenses for Interior Department em ployees changing official duty stations on orders so signed. Such delegations mus be limited to pro forma matters or routine work. Travel authorizations in the opir ion of the Comptroller General, are matters of discretion requiring personal actio by the Secretary (15 Comp. Gen. 171 [1935]).

"Similarly the Comptroller General held that since the Securities Exchange Ac authorized the Commission to appoint and fix the compensation of its officers an employees, there was no authority to delegate any part of the appointing power t a director of employment research, and consequently no authority to pay the sa aries of employees appointed through him (15 Comp. Gen. 226 [1935]).

"In connection with Government contracts the Comptroller General attemp to review specifications and to determine whether or not they meet administrativ needs and are at the same time not unduly restrictive. This has led him far into field in which from every point of view he is ill-equipped to act. . . .

"A very recent decision (16 Comp. Gen. 23 [1936]) holds that mileage in lieu c actual expenses for travel on official business in a personally owned automobi cannot be paid to an employee who used a car registered in his wife's name, eve though under the law of the State where the travel was performed the property c husband and wife is common.

"By another recent technical ruling, credit was refused for travel expenses of a Internal Revenue agent sent at the express direction of the Secretary of the Trea ury to investigate the murder of a narcotic agent. Despite the obvious interest c the administrative officers in the matter, and its interest to the next agent assigne to that position, the Comptroller General held:

> The investigation of the murder of a narcotic agent has no connection with the assessment and collection of the internal revenue itself, . . . the investigation of the murder of a Government agent is a matter primarily for the State authorities, unless committed under such conditions as to constitute a Federal crime; . . . in which case the proper bureau of the Department of Justice would be charged . . . (16 Comp. Gen. 32 [1936]).

"Suspensions of 1 cent are occasionally made (see 16 Comp. Gen. 25, 26 [1936] although the cost of handling these items must far outweigh the recoveries. Sim larly, the Comptroller General has required fourth-class postmasters to insta meters, at a charge of $1.50 a month, to measure accurately the electric power co sumed for lighting in little post offices where the average monthly charge for cu rent consumed was $1.

"A more important instance was the Comptroller General's refusal to allow th Public Works Administration to dedicate part of the site acquired for the Tec wood low-cost housing project in Atlanta to the local government for use as publ streets and parks. This decision was made on the ground that there was no autho were accepted by the Senate in 1938 but defeated by the House of Representatives on final roll call, were intended substantially to deflate what had come to be the most powerful fiscal agency in the United States, if not in the world.

3. Proposals of the President's Committee on Administrative Management

The recommendations of the Committee were based on the premise that the authority of the Comptroller General was excessive and had been used to the detriment of effective administration. Their proposals, modeled on the office of Comptroller and Auditor General of Great Britain, strip the U. S. Comptroller General of power to settle and adjust claims and to disallow expenditures, leaving him authority to examine all financial transactions and to report questionable items to Congress.[1] These drastic alterations may best be presented in the language of the Committee.[2]

1. For the purpose of providing the Chief Executive with the essential vehicles for current financial management and administrative control, the authority to prescribe and supervise accounting systems, forms, and procedures in the Federal establishments should be transferred to and vested in the Secretary of the Treasury. . . .

2. For the purpose of fixing responsibility for the fiscal management of the Government establishment on the Chief Executive in conformity with the constitutional principle that the President 'shall take Care that the Laws be faithfully executed,' claims and demands by the Government of the United States or against it and accounts in which the Government of the United States is concerned, either as debtor or as creditor, should be settled and adjusted in the Treasury Department.

3. To avoid conflict and dispute between the Secretary of the Treasury and the departments as to the jurisdiction of the Secretary to settle public accounts, which conflicts and disputes have so marred the relationship between the Comptroller General and the departments in the past, and to make it impossible for the Secretary of the Treasury to usurp any of the powers vested in the heads of departments by the Congress, the Attorney General should be authorized to render opinions on such questions of jurisdiction (but not on the merits of the case) upon the request of the head of the department or upon the request of the Secretary of the

---

y to give away property of the United States, although all that in fact was being given away was the future cost of maintenance of the streets and parks.

"Instances of this sort could be multiplied indefinitely. In practical effect many of them amount either to denials of substantial justice to individual employees, or they insist on procedures that fly in the face of common sense. Whatever their individual significance, taken together they are a serious indictment of detailed outside control." Harvey C. Mansfield, *ibid.*, pp. 193-94.

[1] John McDiarmid, "Reorganization of the General Accounting Office," 31 *Am. Pol. Sci. Rev.* 508-16 (1937); George P. Auld and M. L. Seidman, "Government Reorganization and the Independent Audit," 65 *J. of Accountancy* 224-31 (1938).

[2] President's Committee on Administrative Management, *op. cit.*, pp. 24-25.

Treasury, and the opinion of the Attorney General on such questions of jurisdiction should be final and binding.

4. In order to conform to the limitations in the functions remaining within the jurisdiction of the Comptroller General, the titles of the Comptroller General and the Assistant Comptroller General should be changed to Auditor General and Assistant Auditor General, respectively, and the name of the General Accounting Office should be changed to the General Auditing Office.

5. The Auditor General should be authorized and required to assign representatives of his office to such stations in the District of Columbia and the field as will enable them currently to audit the accounts of the accountable officers, and they should be required to certify forthwith such exceptions as may be taken to the transactions involved (*a*) to the officer whose account is involved; (*b*) to the Auditor General; and (*c*) to the Secretary of the Treasury. . . .

6. In the event of the failure of the Secretary of the Treasury and the Auditor General to reach an agreement with respect to any exception reported by representatives of the Auditor General concerning any expenditure, it should be the duty of the Auditor General to report such exception to the Congress through such committees or joint committees as the Congress may choose to designate.

The final settlement of claims would thus pass from the Comptroller General to the Treasury, a branch of the executive department. Payment would proceed on Treasury certification, and the only recourse of the Auditor General would be to report to Congress. The auditors however, would examine all transactions before settlement by the Treasury (i.e., a preaudit), and would have an opportunity to question any item and to seek to convince the Treasury officials that payment should be suspended or denied. The final disposition would remain with the Treasury.[1]

In the light of the previous analysis of the powers of the Comptroller General, the following further changes were proposed. The interpretation of statutes would become a duty of the Attorney General, not of the Auditor General. Advance decisions by the Comptroller General would presumably disappear. The custody and control of original documents would remain with the departments and establishments. The accounting system would be organized and directed by the Treasury. In short, the central management of finance would be specifically veste

[1] Cf. the statement by George C. S. Benson, "One conclusion of logic which backed by experience is that while the independent auditor may and should mak as thorough an audit as possible, any attempt of his to interfere with the actu conduct of administration will, by violating the sole responsibility of the head administration, lead to considerable friction. . . . If he checks balances, reconcil bank statements and investigates supporting vouchers, he is an auditor. But if h allows or disallows accounts or prescribes book-keeping forms or passes on con tracts, he becomes an administrator and may make trouble for the responsible ad ministrators. Nevertheless an auditor can be of great value to the administration, his authority includes the power to make remarks on the efficiency and econom of business, yet does not extend to mandatory powers." *Financial Control and Integration* (1934), p. 4.

n the Treasury Department and the sole function of an audit without ›ower of disallowance would be reserved to the Auditor General.

Proposals as drastic as these naturally did not command universal acceptance. Systematic criticism came from Brookings Institution, al-though this group concurred in principle with some of the Committee recommendations.[1] Thus there was agreement to transfer accounting o the Treasury Department, although the Brookings experts suggested a joint committee representing the Bureau of the Budget and the Audi-or General to establish the forms and procedures.

The basic disagreement turned on the final settlement of claims, which Brookings steadfastly declared should remain with the Auditor General, and on the power of the Auditor General to make suspensions and disallowances. The issue may be put in these terms: does the pub-ic interest require vesting in an auditor power to prevent the making of a payment which he believes is illegal or irregular, but which the iscal agents of the executive branch approve as legal and regular? The difference of view reflects in part a difference of definition of an udit.

The President's Committee started from the concept of an auditor s one who verifies after the event, without authority to prohibit a challenged payment; the Brookings Institution started from the concept of an auditor as one who inherently and necessarily, as an agent of Congress, must be vested with power to prevent payment of an obli-ation questioned by it.[2] The power to prohibit, in the view of the President's Committee, was appropriate to an office within the executive branch, but not to one external to it.

[1] The whole subject was exhaustively discussed in the *Hearings before the Joint ommittee on Government Organization*, Feb., March and April, 1937; in the *earings before the* [*Senate*] *Select Committee on Government Organization on . 2700*, August, 1937; and in the *Hearings before a* [*Senate*] *Select Committee to ivestigate Executive Agencies of the Government on S. Res. 217*, 74th Cong., ıne, July and August, 1937.

[2] A close comparison of the following definitions suggests how easy it is to fore-ose argument by skillful statement of the premise.

"An audit is an examination and verification of the accounts after transactions e completed in order to discover and report to the legislative body any unauthor-ed, illegal or irregular expenditures, any financial practices that are unsound, and hether the administration has faithfully discharged its responsibility." President's ommittee on Administrative Management, *op. cit.*, p. 21.

"*Audit.* [An] independent examination made by the General Accounting Office its representatives of the accounts of accountable officers for legality, regularity, ıd accuracy. Audit is an inseparable part of the settlement of an account and ould be distinguished from *administrative examination.*" D. T. Selko, *The Ad-inistration of Federal Finances*, p. 68. Cf. W. F. Willoughby's analysis, from hich Selko has departed, in *The Legal Status and Functions of the General Ac-›unting Office*, pp. 29-30.

More fundamentally the difference of opinion turns on the relativ weight to be given on the one hand to safeguards to ensure the legalit of expenditures and on the other to means of facilitating adminis trative operations. The Committee on Administrative Management wa concerned with more effective overhead management; the Brooking Institution was concerned with preventing scandals in the dispositio of public funds. Both ends are legitimate and both deserve consid eration.

The present author favors the recommendations of the President' Committee on Administrative Management. There is ample evidence t support their claims that speed, decision, vigor and common sense i the conduct of national affairs have been subordinated to technica rulings on doubtful questions; and to demonstrate that it has becom increasingly difficult and at times impossible for the government t manage its business with dispatch, with efficiency, and with economi sagacity.

The safeguards proposed by the Committee against the illegal or th irregular expenditure of public money are adequate in the federal sys tem. The audit would be improved, both by its proposed decentraliza tion and by its immediate review of pending expenditures. There no conflict concerning the propriety of a preaudit. The examination vouchers, bills and claims by Treasury accountants can be fully truste to correct any irregularities; the Opinions of the Attorney General o the meaning of statutes and appropriation acts can be trusted to pro tect the interests of the United States as well as the Opinions of th Comptroller General; and no department or Treasury accountant woul care to be brought before a congressional committee on a report b the Auditor General that an irregular expenditure had been allowe unless an honest and reasonable difference of opinion existed. In an case the work of the government should not be interrupted by th veto of an office in no way responsible to the executive branch and onl imperfectly responsible to Congress.

These conclusions do not suggest in any way that an effective aud is unnecessary, or that auditing can be properly performed within th executive branch. The real problem is to balance an effective aud with effective administration. The end of administration is not to secu an auditor's clearance for money spent; great social purposes are be achieved as quickly, completely and intelligently as possible. The ends must, of course, be sought within the law, but the general term of laws and of appropriation acts leave and are intended to leave muc discretion to officials. The Comptroller General has tended to arroga to himself the discretion which is left in the law; and he is not qual ed to exercise this discretion or intended by Congress to do so. There as been "an invasion of administrative responsibility" which is not dvantageous to the public interest. The weight of legality, meticulously onstrued, has overbalanced the weight of administrative discretion nd judgment.

These pages are written while the ultimate fate of the proposals to odify the character of the General Accounting Office is still in abeyice. In some form or other it is desirable to restore a better balance etween the responsibility for making expenditures and the duty of diting them.

PART IV

PERSONNEL MANAGEMENT

Chapter Eighteen

RISE OF PUBLIC PERSONNEL MANAGEMENT

MANY elements combine to make good administration: leadership, organization, finance, morale, methods and procedures, but greater than any of these is man power. To find and to hold capable men and women and to help create and maintain working conditions under which they can do their best are the great tasks of personnel management.

Not all personnel work is done by the central civil service commission, as we shall see in the course of this chapter; the line departments are necessarily bound to carry a considerable part. At one point or another, however, effective personnel management will be concerned with questions of recruitment, examination and certification; position-classification, pay policy, assignment of duties and job supervision; training, especially in-service training, and promotion; service records, discipline and removal; safety and welfare programs, accident compensation and retirement on pension; professional and union organization within the public service; morale, prestige and the means of creating a career service. Behind these issues, often technical in nature, lie broad problems of the adjustment of a permanent bureaucracy to political parties, to overhead management, and to the conditions of democratic government. Most of these questions will receive notice in the chapters which follow.

This and the succeeding chapter are devoted to the general framework of the American system of public personnel administration, following which the more specific, technical procedures are passed in review. "Hiring and firing" public employees and officials has had a long and checkered history. We start, therefore, with a sketch of the historical development of methods and purposes of appointment. This phase of the inquiry brings us face to face with the most perplexing long-range problem of public service relationships, the adjustment of the respective interests of the political party and of a nonpartisan, permanent civil service. Finally we turn in this chapter to consider the distribution of contemporary personnel activities between the central personnel agency and the departmental personnel offices and the form of organization which each normally takes. In the following chapter we inquire more closely into the characteristics of the present-day public service and the prospects of extending the ideal of a career service.

1. Rise and Decline of the Spoils System

The most conspicuous feature of the history of personnel in American public administration has been the rise, persistence and gradual decline of the spoils system.[1] Before parties were organized on a national scale, the country was launched on a merit system by George Washington, but party warfare quickly denied the possibility of keeping the public service outside the sphere of influence of party forces.

The issue was first clearly drawn in 1801 when the Jeffersonian Democrats replaced the Federalists. Jefferson invented the doctrine of "due participation" of each party in public service appointments, a doctrine which he originally conceived in terms of substantial equality but which with the decline of the Federalists was reduced practically to terms of proportionate voting power. His early dilemma and his solution are revealed in this quotation from his writings.

> If a due participation of office is a matter of right, how are vacancies to be obtained? Those by death are few: by resignation, none. Can any other mode than that of removal be proposed? This is a painful office; but it is made my duty, and I meet it as such. I proceed in the operation with deliberation and inquiry, that it may injure the best men least, and effect the purposes of justice and public utility with the least private distress; that it may be thrown, as much as possible, on delinquency, on oppression, on intolerance, on ante-revolutionary adherence to our enemies. It would have been to me a circumstance of great relief, had I found a moderate participation of office in the hands of the majority. I would gladly have left to time and accident to raise them to their just share. But their total exclusion calls for prompter corrections. I shall correct the procedure; but that done, return with joy to that state of things, when the only questions concerning a candidate shall be, is he honest? Is he capable? Is he faithful to the Constitution? [2]

By 1803 a proper balance had been reached and further removals were not made. The long succession of Democratic presidents from

[1] The principal works in this field include Carl R. Fish, *The Civil Service and the Patronage* (1904); Howard L. McBain, *DeWitt Clinton and the Origin of the Spoils System in New York* (1907); William D. Foulke, *Fighting the Spoilsmen* (1919); Samuel P. Orth, *The Boss and the Machine* (1919); Charles E. Merriam and Harold F. Gosnell, *The American Party System* (rev. ed. 1929), chs. 4-7; Frank M. Stewart, *The National Civil Service Reform League* (1929); the publications of the National Civil Service Reform League, including the magazine *Good Government.*

[2] Jefferson, *Writings* (Washington ed.), vol. 4, pp. 402-5, quoted in Fish, *op. cit.,* pp. 35-36.

1801 to 1829 and the final disappearance of the Federalists shelved the problem of national party patronage for a generation. It was destined, however, to reappear.

Within the states, however, the spoils system was not slow in establishing itself.[1] Pennsylvania, New York, and Massachusetts became centers for sharp battles between factions in which one of the most powerful weapons was control of the appointing power. That the lessons thus learned in state politics would eventually be applied on a national scale was almost inevitable. Political leaders in the states were unwilling, in short, to accept Jefferson's tolerant doctrine of due participation. They developed and in 1829 Jackson accepted the doctrine of party monopoly.

On the national scene the first step in this evolution was taken in 1820 by the passage of the Tenure of Office Act, as a result of which the term of certain specified federal officials was limited to four years. The Tenure of Office Act was extended from time to time to other classes of officials, although it was not used for patronage until the advent of Jackson. It is still a barrier to the extension of the merit system over a century after its origin. The inauguration of Jackson in 1829 gave early signs of the impending change in the character of the federal service. "The trimly dressed gentlemen of the old regime with their high stocks and good breeding were jostled by hack politicians from New York and country editors and farmers from the West."[2] An office-seeking friend of Amos Kendall said, "I am ashamed of myself, for I feel as if every man I meet knew what I came for." "Don't distress yourself," replied Kendall, "for every man you meet is on the same business."

The wholesale removal of Adams' men and the appointment of friends of Jackson was not merely an episode in political reprisals. Jackson was undoubtedly concerned about the apparent growth of an "un-American" bureaucracy which in his opinion challenged the equalitarian basis of American democracy.[3] Without doubt he interpreted accurately the opinions and attitudes of great masses of citizens in the formal justification of the theory of rotation in office which he presented to Congress in his first annual message in December, 1829. His philosophy is so congenial to the American democrat and has exercised such influence that it deserves quotation.

[1] See Howard L. McBain, *op. cit.;* and Carl J. Friedrich, "The Rise and Decline of the Spoils Tradition," 189 *Annals* 10-16 (1937), pointing out colonial origins of state and national patronage.

[2] Fish, *op. cit.*, p. 109.

[3] Marquis James, *Andrew Jackson* (1938), ch. 28.

There are, perhaps, few men who can for any great length of time enjoy office and power without being more or less under the influence of feelings unfavorable to the faithful discharge of their public duties. Their integrity may be proof against improper considerations immediately addressed to themselves, but they are apt to acquire a habit of looking with indifference upon the public interests and of tolerating conduct from which an unpracticed man would revolt. Office is considered as a species of property, and government rather as a means of promoting individual interests than as an instrument created solely for the service of the people. Corruption in some and in others a perversion of correct feelings and principles divert government from its legitimate ends, and make it an engine for the support of the few at the expense of the many. The duties of all public officers are, or at least admit of being made, so plain and simple that men of intelligence may readily qualify themselves for their performance; and I can not but believe that more is lost by the long continuance of men in office than is generally to be gained by their experience. I submit, therefore, to your consideration whether the efficiency of the government would not be promoted, and official industry and integrity better secured, by a general extension of the law which limits appointments to four years.

In a country where offices are created solely for the benefit of the people no one man has any more intrinsic right to official station than another. Offices were not established to give support to particular men at the public expense. No individual wrong is, therefore, done by removal, since neither appointment to nor continuance in office is matter of right. The incumbent became an officer with a view to public benefits, and when these require his removal they are not to be sacrificed to private interests. It is the people, and they alone, who have the right to complain when a bad officer is substituted for a good one. He who is removed has the same means of obtaining a living that are enjoyed by the millions who never held office. The proposed limitation would destroy the idea of property now so generally connected with official station, and although individual distress may be sometimes produced, it would, by promoting that rotation which constitutes a leading principle in the republican creed, give healthful action to the system.[1]

The immediate results of the wholesale removals and appointments which Jackson made were those which might have been expected. The efficiency of the administration rapidly declined. The standard of integrity which had on the whole been well maintained until 1829 began to suffer. Notable instances of peculation occurred during Jackson's own administration. Of these perhaps the most remarkable was the case of Swartwout, Jackson's collector of the port of New York, who fled to Spain in 1837 with something over $1,250,000. The land offices were very loosely conducted. Fish reports the case of the receiver of public money at Columbus who had speculated with government funds. The inspector who examined the case wrote to the Secretary of the Interior, "The man seems really penitent; and I am inclined to think,

[1] James D. Richardson, ed., *A Compilation of the Messages and Papers of the Presidents* (1908), vol. 2, pp. 448-49.

in common with his friends, that he is honest, and has been led away from his duty by the example of his predecessor, and a certain looseness in the code of morality which here does not move in so limited a circle as it does with us at home. . . . He has, moreover, pledged his word that, if retained, he will strictly obey the law. . . ."[1]

It would have been supposed from the repeated declarations of the Whig leaders that with the election of Harrison in 1840 the country would have been restored to the traditional practices of the Massachusetts and Virginia statesmen. But the pressure upon the leaders of the Whig party, which now came into power for the first time, was too great to be withstood and the record of the Harrison-Tyler administration is not substantially different from that of Jackson. There followed during the next twenty years a constant alternation of parties which fixed the spoils system upon the country so thoroughly that it has not yet been wholly shaken off.

Although the Jacksonian concept of democracy is still dominant, the exigencies of the public service are more and more making inroads upon the theory that any man of intelligence may readily qualify himself to hold any office. The urgent necessity of technical competence in the administrative service is compelling the gradual extension of the ideas of merit and capacity.

As early as 1853 Congress prescribed that no clerk should be appointed until he had been examined and found qualified by a board of three examiners selected by the head of the department. The enforcement of this law gradually weakened and eventually the law was abandoned.[2]

Congress made no further comprehensive attempt to deal with the selection of personnel until 1871. In that year the President was authorized "to prescribe such regulations for the admission of persons into the civil service of the United States as may best promote the efficiency thereof, and ascertain the fitness of each candidate in respect to age, health, character, knowledge, and ability for the branch of the service into which he seeks to enter, and for this purpose he may employ suitable persons to conduct such inquiries and may prescribe their duties and establish regulations for the conduct of persons who may receive appointments in the Civil Service."[3] An eminent Civil Service Commission was appointed by President Grant on the basis of this legislation but the Commission was forced to abandon its work in 1873 owing to

[1] Fish, *op. cit.*, p. 138.

[2] See Lewis Mayers, *The Federal Service* (1922), pp. 41-42.

[3] 16 Stat. 514 (1871); U.S. Code (1934 ed.), Title 5, sec. 631.

lack of appropriation and absence of support from Congress. The law still remains, however, an integral and important part of the statutes regulating personnel in the federal government.

Agitation for the merit system was incessant. The National Civil Service Reform League was organized in 1879 and the issue of reform took on national scope. It is interesting to note that the principal concern of the great band of original civil service reformers was not greater administrative efficiency but purified elections and a more wholesome democracy. The moral fervor of reform is unmistakably presented in the words of George William Curtis: "Partisan prostitution of the public service is radical treachery to popular government because it makes private interest and not the public welfare the motive of political action. . . . It is one of the chief evils of the spoils system that reckless abuse of patronage, the most lavish and acknowledged corruption, have made party despotism so absolute that the conscience and intelligence of the country are largely enslaved by unprincipled ignorance and insolent cunning."

The assassination of President Garfield in 1881 by a disappointed office seeker finally crystallized public sentiment and forced a reluctant Congress to approve the Pendleton Act, the basis of the civil service regulations in force and effect today. This legislation initiated the doctrine of party neutrality, the counterpoise of the Jacksonian doctrine of party monopoly.

The Pendleton Act extended the merit system only to about 14,000 positions, chiefly in the post office and the customhouses. The President, however, was authorized to extend the new plan by executive order, and the great expansion of the federal classified service is due chiefly to the successive orders of each president from Grover Cleveland to the present day. Congress extended the merit system to the Foreign Service, the former prohibition unit (after disastrous experience with patronage), and to other agencies, including the Social Security Board. But the chief executive is chiefly responsible for the growth of the merit system from an original nucleus of 14,000 to an army of 532,000 positions in 1937.[1]

Renewed agitation in favor of the merit system in the national service broke out in 1934 in view of the action of Congress in excepting most of the 200,000 employees in the "New Deal" agencies from the provisions of the merit system.

In principle, appointments to New Deal agencies not under civil

[1] The detailed steps in the growth of the classified executive civil service are set forth in a publication of the U. S. Civil Service Commission entitled *The Classified Executive Civil Service of the United States Government* (1933).

service were made by the proper appointing authority; in practice applicants were usually required to secure "clearance" through the headquarters office of the Democratic National Committee. "Clearance" meant a certificate of political endorsement, either that of a Congressman, a state or local committee, or an active member of the party. At times it was evaded, at other times it became a formality; but in general endorsement was the essential "open sesame" to this huge block of 200,000 posts.[1] In all this there is nothing new in principle, for a record of active partisanship was equally valuable under Republican administrations; however, the country had seen nothing on this scale nor, according to some, had the rule of political endorsement ever been applied with such rigor.

To perform its functions of certifying the Democratic allegiance of seekers for office, the Democratic National Committee organized itself efficiently. A huge central file was established, dockets were prepared, and political information sought concerning the applicants. In many of the major organs of government the Committee appointed a representative whose duties included the constant search for vacancies or new positions, liaison between the administrative organization and the Committee, and the maintenance of good relations between one and the other despite obvious points of friction. Thus in effect a new personnel agency was established, unofficial in nature to be sure, but none the less real in its own sphere of influence.

In the midst of these exceptional additions to federal patronage rose the slow but steady tide of merit. By executive order the Farm Credit Administration and other smaller agencies came under the merit system; by act of Congress the Central Statistical Board, the Bureau of Motor Carriers, the Social Security Board and other agencies were included in the merit system.

Government corporations are usually not subject to the requirements of the Civil Service Act of 1883; they may or may not be subject to the Classification Act of 1923. Their personnel record has on the whole been good, and in some cases, such as the Tennessee Valley Authority, it has been excellent. In the long run it will be found desirable to place most classes of government corporation employees under the formal merit system.

In 1938 the President proposed the reorganization bill which would have authorized him to extend the merit system "upward, outward and downward" to include all but policy-determining posts. Although the virtual extinction of federal patronage was deferred by the defeat of

[1] The official description of this procedure is by James A. Farley, "Passing Out the Patronage," 126 *American Magazine* 20-22 (August, 1938).

this bill, the President pushed rapidly forward in the same direction by his Executive Order of June 24, 1938, extending the merit system to about 100,000 unprotected positions. Congress, after a bitter struggle, enacted legislation in 1938 placing about 14,000 first, second and third class postmasters under full civil service status.

On a broad view, therefore, progress in establishing and expanding the merit system over a half century has been sustained, and while large numbers of positions still are left to be brought under the merit system, the fact remains that over 600,000 employees of the national government have merit status—the largest single group of permanent civil service employees in the world.

The merit system has grown more slowly in the states. New York enacted the first state merit law in 1883, Massachusetts followed in 1884. From 1884 to 1937 only eight other states adopted merit system legislation—New Jersey, Maryland, Ohio, Illinois, Wisconsin, Colorado, California, and Kansas. In the latter state the law has long been ineffective for lack of appropriations, and in more than one state, administration falls far short of reasonable expectation.[1]

In 1937 popular demand for a better public service resulted in the enactment of merit legislation in five states: Arkansas, Tennessee, Michigan, Maine, and Connecticut.[2] These laws may be credited largely to the favorable sentiment created by the National Civil Service Reform League, the National League of Women Voters, and the Junior Chamber of Commerce. National action is supported by the same groups and by the organized federal employees.

In other states a customary merit system prevails over a considerable part of the service. New Hampshire and Vermont in the east, and Virginia in the south are cases in point. In most states the technical and professional services are likely to be free from gross political raids. The public social services are rapidly being placed on a merit basis throughout the country. But even with these allowances, we are driven to the conclusion that the states have been slow in adopting the merit system, either formally or informally.[3]

There are still too many states like Missouri. A change of party control occurred there in 1932; at the end of the two-year term of the new incumbents, such triumphs as the following had been achieved. In the

[1] V. O. Key, "Methods of Evasion of Civil Service Law," 15 *Southwestern Social Sci. Q.* 337-47 (1934-35).

[2] An earlier merit system in Connecticut was abolished in 1921.

[3] An exceptionally able article revealing the strength and weakness of state personnel systems is by Dr. Ellen C. Potter, "Personnel in the Public Service from the Administrator's Point of View," 24 *Nat. Mun. Rev.* 517-21, 534 (1935); cf. Katherine A. Frederic, "Public Personnel Trends in the States," 189 *Annals* 173-79 (1937).

office of State Auditor, there were 55 new employees, one holdover; in the office of Secretary of State, 147 new faces, one old-timer; but the Treasurer, Attorney General, the Department of Labor Inspection, the Adjutant General, the Building and Loan Bureau and other agencies had made a really clean sweep—no former employees were left.[1] The inevitable result is that the states are losing in the race with the national government for dominant administrative authority.

In the cities there has been much progress, both formal and informal, in favor of the merit system. The drive for municipal civil service commissions largely spent itself by 1910, leaving 439 municipal commissions in existence in 1937, chiefly in the eastern and north central states and the west coast states.[2] Southern cities and states alike have been slow in adopting the merit system, but by 1936 the new interest in reform had reached these parts. Since 1910 the improvement of municipal personnel practice has come about chiefly through the general lifting of standards of city government, especially in the council manager cities. With hardly an exception these 450 communities have excellent records in handling local personnel problems, although very many have no civil service commission.

In the great metropolitan areas, standards of performance are not infrequently low. Commissioners are sometimes politicians first, and officials second; a Chicago commissioner is reported to have said, "Sure, I believe in civil service, but I think the Democrats should get the jobs." The record in New York (excepting the brilliant progress under Mayor La Guardia), Buffalo, Philadelphia, Pittsburgh, Cleveland, Chicago, Minneapolis, Seattle, Los Angeles, cities all of which have had civil service commissions for years, is far from satisfactory and in some cases represents nothing less than the collapse of the merit system. Here are being fought out the most difficult battles between spoils and merit with the patronage system well entrenched and in command of almost impregnable defenses.[3]

So far as the counties are concerned, the patronage system still maintains almost complete sway. Among the few notable exceptions are Los Angeles County, which has had an exceptional record for many years under the guidance of chief examiners Doty, Stevens, and Amsden; Hamilton County (Cincinnati, Ohio); and a few of the counties

[1] Data compiled under the direction of Dr. Martin L. Faust from the official manuals of the State of Missouri.

[2] Civil Service Assembly of the United States and Canada, *Civil Service Agencies in the United States: A 1937 Census* (1938), p. 7.

[3] For a defense of patronage see W. R. Davies, "Why I Believe in the Patronage System," 19 *Nat. Mun. Rev.* 18-21 (1930); and William Turn, "In Defense of Patronage," 189 *Annals* 22-28 (1937).

of New Jersey and Massachusetts. Cook County (Chicago) has an adequate merit law which is too largely ignored in practice; by contrast there is an admirable extra-legal merit system for the county social services, conducted with the aid of an unofficial citizens' committee. By and large the counties remain the chief stronghold of patronage and of discreditable political rings, which are endowed, however, with extraordinary vitality and capacity for self-protection.

A general view of the total situation is, however, encouraging. The Commission of Inquiry on Public Service Personnel reported a large proportion of all levels of the public service as protected either by the merit system or by formal standards of selection. The following table summarizes their finding: [1]

TABLE VI

NUMBER AND PER CENT OF PUBLIC EMPLOYEES UNDER THE MERIT SYSTEM OR CHOSEN BY FIXED STANDARDS, 1932; AND PAY ROLLS

JURISDICTION	TOTAL NUMBER OF EMPLOYEES	EMPLOYEES UNDER CIVIL SERVICE		PAY ROLL (in Millions)
		Number	Per Cent	
Federal	583,196	467,161	80.0	$1,171.2
State	252,000[a]	96,750	38.4	338.7
Municipal	591,500[a]	350,000	59.2	895.5
County, township and district	302,000[a]	45,000	14.4	450.8
Public education	1,189,000	1,189,000[b]	100.00	1,664.7
TOTAL	2,917,696	2,147,911	73.6	4,520.9

[a] Estimated.
[b] Chosen by fixed standards.

As we survey the present situation, it is clear that there are two powerful systems of "personnel administration," each irreconcilable with the other, in control of different sectors of the public service. In some jurisdictions one has eliminated the other, victory resting at times on a precarious basis; in other jurisdictions and especially in the great cities the battle sways back and forth from year to year, with ultimate triumph not yet assured to either system; in still others the issue is dormant by reason of the complete command of patronage or merit as the case may be.

This battle has been raging for more than fifty years. Great gains

[1] Table adapted from report of the Commission of Inquiry on Public Service Personnel, *Better Government Personnel* (1935), p. 90 and p. 92, omitting military personnel in federal government.

have been made by the merit system in these years, greater than is usually realized. The basic conditions of government are such that the eventual triumph of the merit system seems inevitable. The ever increasing technological aspects of governmental operations; the greatly intensified social responsibility of government, making the risk of administrative failure equivalent to the risk of social catastrophe; the emerging professional point of view in many branches of administration; and the expansion of civil service unions intent on protecting their own interests by the steady application of the merit system, these and other circumstances forecast the certain destruction of patronage in due course of time.

2. Reconciliation of Party and Bureaucracy

The record of the last fifty years of reform leaves no doubt of the reluctance of the party organization to yield its power over patronage.[1] The party has stubbornly resisted every advance of the merit system and has undermined the administration of the merit system wherever possible in order to retain a hold on appointments. Political favoritism is still the principal handicap to good administration despite the gains of the last six decades.

The historic opponents of party patronage have been the organized reformers, but the civil service itself is gradually finding its voice in resisting the pressure of politicians. Professional groups in the public service recognized their enemy many years ago; more recently the organized rank and file civil service unions have added the weight of their influence in favor of the merit system and against patronage. From this point of view, therefore, there is a definite and increasingly conscious conflict of interest between public service employees and the party organization.[2]

The issue is the termination of patronage. A rough calculation indicates that in 1937 there were potentially about 300,000 patronage positions in the federal service, about 125,000 in the states, 225,000 in the cities, and 250,000 in the counties and rural subdivisions, a total of 900,000 positions carrying an annual pay roll of at least $1,200,000,000. The stakes are impressive, although by no means all of these positions outside the merit system are actually used for party purposes. Consider-

[1] This problem is discussed from the point of view of the party in Charles E. Merriam and Harold F. Gosnell, *The American Party System* (3rd ed. forthcoming); and in D. W. Brogan, *Government of the People* (1933); see also *Annals*, vol. 189 (1937), and Lane W. Lancaster, "Political Parties and City Government," 199 *Annals* 199-205 (1938).

[2] This problem is discussed in L. D. White and T. V. Smith, *Politics and Public Service* (1939); see also *Annals*, vol. 189 (1937), *passim*.

able reductions would be needed to identify the real amount of patronage actually possessed.

The attitude of the party toward patronage is not merely an example of original sin. For generations the party has depended in considerable measure upon patronage as a means of paying for the work which is required in campaigns. A political party has legitimate uses for money. It must pay, like any other consumer, for telephone and telegraph, for rent, for traveling expenses, and for other supplies and services. It must have funds or their equivalent to pay its creditors.

Considerable cash and much "unpaid" work are available to party organizations as a result of the power to appoint to civil positions. The political machine of the city of Chicago, for example, normally controls from 3,000 to 5,000 political appointments; this is enough to support one active worker in each precinct with a comfortable margin left over for headquarters. Employees not under the merit system, moreover, are easy targets for political contributions, and a pay roll tax for party purposes ranging from three to five per cent is common. Despite laws to the contrary, party leaders are often tempted to collect from the competitive civil service employees; thus in 1935 it was necessary for the U. S. Civil Service Commission to order the removal of the Collector of Internal Revenue in Philadelphia for collecting from the wrong parties.

A tax of even one per cent on an unprotected pay roll of $1,200,000,000 amounts to $12,000,000, a sum which is greatly exceeded by the value of the political work performed by those who hold patronage positions or who aspire to them. From the party point of view, the loss of revenue on a scale such as this might seem almost equivalent to destruction.[1]

Realization of this dilemma, which apparently suggests we must choose either party with patronage, or government without party, prompted an English commentator on American affairs to write these words: "The spoils system met a need of democratic government as old as Periclean Athens. It provided party funds. The exploitation of the public service was not a good method, but are its substitutes much better? . . . No democracy has solved, to any reasonable man's satisfaction, the problem of the cost of political organization. The American system which regarded office as a prize to be fought for, and to be enjoyed, was at least candid and the reformers never did, one may

[1] Miss Overacker's analysis of 1936 campaign contributions in sums of $1,000 or more revealed that officeholders contributed almost as much as manufacturers (the heaviest contributors); Louise Overacker, "Campaign Funds in the Presidential Election of 1936," 31 *Am. Pol. Sci. Rev.* 473-98 (1937).

say never dared, to attempt to answer the question, who shall pay the costs of political war." [1]

Political parties are an essential characteristic of a self-governing people, and to preserve the party as an effective organ of opinion is an important object of public policy. The practical issue is, where can parties obtain the necessary funds to enable them to organize public opinion on the issues of the day? Contributions might come from large corporations and individuals of great wealth; from organized economic groups and interests, such as labor, capital, agriculture; or from public treasuries on a per capita party membership basis. No one of these is free from serious objection.

These are not, however, the only alternatives to the currency of patronage. The La Follettes, father and sons, have maintained an effective state-wide party in Wisconsin for a generation with almost no patronage. They depend upon the voluntary effort of those who believe deeply in the political program for which these leaders stand. Mayor Daniel W. Hoan has been reelected chief executive of Milwaukee without a break since 1916, the candidate of the Socialist party which has neither local nor state patronage. It is financed by small voluntary contributions and by unpaid work. The City Charter Committee has regularly defeated the Republican Party in Cincinnati since 1926, without the aid of patronage. Hundreds of small cities throughout America, the lesser Middletowns, carry on their party campaigns without patronage.

On the national scale, parties now have more patronage than they need, and much more than serves the public interest. In fact, a healthy party system in a democracy needs little support from patronage. Professor Charles E. Merriam has put the matter most cogently. "As party principles and policies rise, the spoils system sinks. The party system and party spirit do not need spoils. On the contrary, they are incompatible; and the stronger is the one, the weaker is the other." [2]

Certain it is that from the sole point of view of good administration, party patronage is the proverbial old man of the sea. The case for a nonpartisan civil service rests squarely upon the public interest in the impartial, competent, technical management of public affairs. The public interest means the safety, protection, convenience, comfort and advantage of citizens and groups of citizens, under the law.

A civil service organized without respect to the shifting needs of party or faction can pursue these ends without diversion. A civil service buffeted here and there at the dictation of the party in momentary

[1] Brogan, *op. cit.*, p. 194.

[2] Merriam and Gosnell, *The American Party System* (rev. ed. 1929), p. 133.

control must sacrifice the interests of all citizens to the demands of some.

This does not mean that the political party has no function to perform with respect to the public service. The party is or might be a beneficial regulator of the bureaucracy. That bureaucracy is not congenial to American devotion to liberty and equality is clear from various quotations gathered by President Harold W. Dodds.[1] Thus Senator Borah: "that meddlesome, irritating, confusing, undermining, destructive thing called bureaucracy"; or former President Hoover: "There are three implacable spirits in bureaucracy—self-perpetuation, expansion, and demand for more power"; or Alfred E. Smith: "The next thing I view as dangerous to our national liberty is government by bureaucracy. . . . We don't want any autocrats. We wouldn't even take a good one."[2]

Party politicians, who provide the ultimate overhead management of administration, who guide its course and provide its funds, who mediate between citizens and officials, perform an indispensable function in keeping the expert on tap, not on top. It is sometimes hard for a policeman to remember that he was made for the public and not the public for him. The opportunity of humble citizens to talk with their precinct captain or their alderman, and of other citizens to talk with Congressmen and Senators and the secretaries of the great departments of state is a means of curbing officiousness through the mediation of politicians which no one would wish to diminish.

With due emphasis upon these allowances, the readjustment of party and civil service will demand more sacrifices of the party in the future than of officialdom. Our needs as a nation require less politics in the administrative departments and more technical competence; less clearance by political committees and more by civil service commissions; less discontinuity and more stability in management.

3. Organization for Personnel Management

Until 1883 each federal department and agency managed its own personnel matters on its own responsibility, subject to the embryonic law of public employment.[3] The Pendleton Act introduced the concept

[1] Harold W. Dodds, "Bureaucracy and Representative Government," 189 *Annals* 165-72 (1937). See also P. C. Lyel, "Some Psychological Factors in Public Administration," 8 *Pub. Adm.* 131-47 (1930); L. Urwick, "Bureaucracy and Democracy," 14 *ibid.* 134-42 (1936).

[2] See especially the illuminating article by Arnold Brecht, "Bureaucratic Sabotage," 189 *Annals* 48-57 (1937); E. P. Herring, "The Future of Patronage," 14 *Virginia Quarterly Rev.* 44-56 (1938).

[3] On this topic, see especially William E. Mosher and J. D. Kingsley, *Public Personnel Administration* (1936), chs. 1-6. The law of public employment is treated in a work by Oliver P. Field, *Civil Service Law* (1939).

hat some aspects of personnel management could best be handled by central agency. The principal original authority thus taken away from he departments was the examination and certification of eligibles. rom time to time in the course of the last fifty years other personnel ctivities have been pulled out of the departments and vested in the entral personnel agency.

While the degree of such specialization varies from case to case, t is now standard practice to place responsibility in the central agency or examination and certification; position-classification; service rec- ords; promotional examinations wherever in force; central record keep- ng; and often but not always the management of the retirement sys- em. The departments have thus been required to give to the personnel ffice a considerable range of activity.

They keep for themselves, however, many important responsibilities. They usually retain freedom to choose one of three names certified or appointment; they prescribe the duties of each employee and assign im to his particular task; they supervise and direct his work; they levelop in-service training; they impose whatever disciplinary measures nay be required, sometimes with an appeal to the central agency for eview of discharge; they make out the service ratings in the first in- tance; they develop programs of employee safety and welfare. In hort, in the more intimate and morale-building aspects of personnel nanagement, the department still retains its full authority.[1]

This division of personnel management requires a dual organization. On the one hand is the central personnel agency, commonly the civil ervice commission; on the other are the department personnel offices, ong undeveloped but now coming into their own. In the federal gov- rnment, the most effective departmental personnel work has been arried on by the Department of Agriculture. Its Office of Personnel vas reorganized and expanded in 1938. The revised organization is hown in the following chart.

The Department of Labor followed the lone example of Agriculture n 1936, but a number of New Deal agencies such as Farm Credit Administration, Resettlement Administration, and Home Owners' Loan Corporation had already embarked upon progressive personnel pro- grams. The Executive Order of June 24, 1938, forecast the rapid in- tallation of personnel directors in all the large national departments nd establishments.

The Personnel Department of the Tennessee Valley Authority is vell organized and ably staffed. Its principal units are the employment

[1] A. J. Altmeyer, "The Scope of Departmental Personnel Activities," 189 *Annals* 88-91 (1937).

division, the classification division, the personnel relations division, the training division, and the field offices at the construction sites.

In few cities or states are there separate departmental personnel offices. Several such exist in New York City, especially in the Department of Welfare, the Department of Hospitals and the Department of

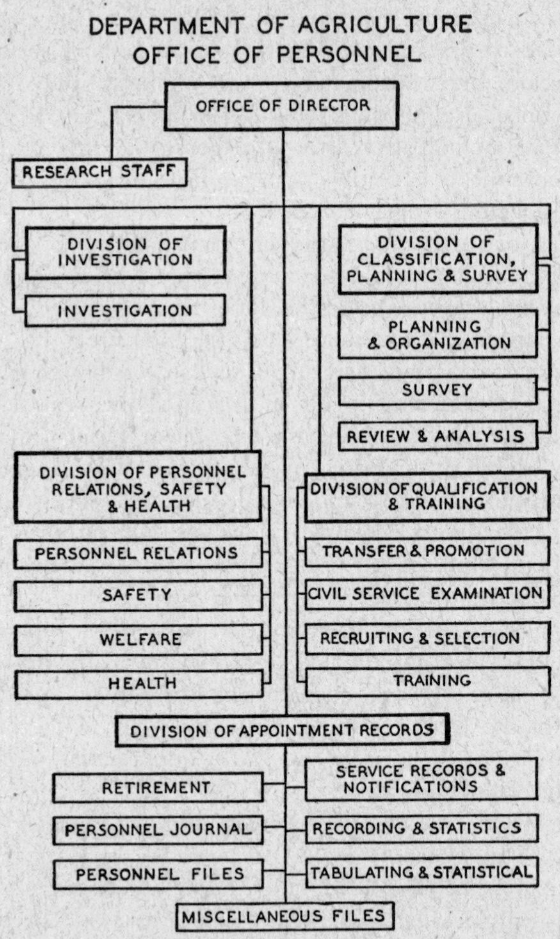

Sanitation. In Wisconsin there are part-time personnel men in a few of the major departments. As a rule, departmental personnel work has been developed chiefly in the federal government.

The organizational form of the central personnel agency was originally and still is predominantly the commission, usually a body of three persons with overlapping terms. This form of organization was imposed for reasons of reform, not of administration. It was believed essential to have a commission so constituted that the minority party representative could prevent the majority from "stealing the works." Experience as a member of two commissions satisfies the writer that the usefulness of this form of organization is exaggerated. As a member of the Chicago Civil Service Commission the minority member found himself powerless to prevent what seemed to him unjustifiable practices; as a member of the United States Civil Service Commission, he found his services as a watchdog were wholly unnecessary, since his colleagues were as sincere defenders of the merit system as he.

The commission form is preferred by some on the ground that in the making of the rules, which govern policy, and in the hearing of disciplinary cases on appeal, the concurrent judgment of three is better than the sole determination of one. This view has merit, especially where public or employee confidence would be strengthened.

In the case of the United States Civil Service Commission, this point of view is less relevant, since the rules are made by the President and their technical preparation is done by the staff of the Commission and checked by the Bureau of the Budget and the Attorney General. The United States Civil Service Commission, moreover, does not act as an appellate body except when an employee comes forward with offer of proof that his discharge was due to religious or political reasons—an exceedingly rare event.

The ineptness of commissions as administrative agencies performing day-by-day routine operations has already been discussed.[1] Their common weaknesses have been well illustrated by civil service bodies. As a result, modifications of the traditional structure are growing more and more common. An early example was developed in Massachusetts in 1919.[2] A civil service commission comprising a commissioner and two associate commissioners retained authority as a body to make rules and regulations and to decide appeals. The commissioner became the executive and administrative head of the organization and with the exceptions just noted was given all the functions of the former commission. In 1931 this example was followed in substance by Wisconsin, and in 1937 by Michigan and other states.

In a few city manager towns, the charter provides for a director of personnel immediately responsible to the city manager, in lieu of the traditional commission. Managers generally prefer this newer form of organization. The Tennessee Valley Authority organized its personnel work under a director in preference to a commission. The drive for a

[1] See ch. 6.

[2] Massachusetts Laws 1919, c. 350, sec. 66.

single personnel director and the elimination of the historical commission were given new impetus by the proposals of President Hoover in 1932 [1] and of President Roosevelt in 1937 to install a civil service administrator in place of the United States Civil Service Commission.[2]

The President's Committee on Administrative Management adopted the idea of an administrator chiefly because they conceived the national personnel agency as one of the three major administrative aids of the President, the others being the Bureau of the Budget and, for long-time problems, the National Resources Committee. A body which must act collectively, which must caucus before it knows its official mind, cannot be an effective agency to advise the President on the daily problems of administration; and if the personnel office is to discharge this function, it must be put in the hands of one responsible official.

The Committee also reached the same conclusion on the ground that central personnel management in Washington would be more energetically and effectively pursued by one administrator than by three commissioners. The Senate accepted this proposal, but it was eventually defeated in the House of Representatives.

Opponents of the plan for an administrator urged that a commission is necessary in order to withstand the pressure from Congressmen and others for special favors. That this pressure exists I can testify, but it is probably no more severe than that experienced regularly by the Director of the Bureau of the Budget. The issue is rather whether qualified men can be found who can stand the strain.

The loss of minority party representation, the fear of the uncontrolled whims of a single official, the absence of a woman on the personnel agency and the impossibility of securing regional or religious representation were also urged as objections to the plan for an administrator. In the author's opinion, they carry less weight than the reasons which suggest the replacement of the Civil Service Commission in the federal service by an administrator.

Where, however, independent rule making and appellate authority are vested in the personnel agency and where it is clear that public and employee confidence in the competence, impartiality and integrity of a single administrator would not be forthcoming, some form of plural organization is preferable. The Massachusetts type is well adapted to combining representative capacity with administrative energy. The trend is toward this form of organization or to the administrator.

The emerging form of organization for personnel management par-

[1] H. Doc. 254, 72d Cong., 1st sess. (1932).

[2] President's Committee on Administrative Management, *Report with Special Studies* (1937), pp. 7-12; 55-133.

allels that already established in the budget field: a structure composed in part of a central, in part of departmental offices. The same problems of coordination arise, especially, in this instance, the problem of uniting effectively in the central authority the police and service aspects of civil service administration.

To harmonize different views and secure effective leadership, President Hoover established the Council of Personnel Administration in 1931. The chairman of the Council, on which representatives of the various departments and independent establishments had representatives, was the president of the Civil Service Commission. In 1938, President Roosevelt terminated this ex officio chairmanship, and confined membership to the personnel officers of the federal agencies. No corresponding organization is known in any state or city.

In view of the wide ground which this chapter has covered, we may pull its threads together in this closing paragraph. Here as elsewhere the hand of the past lies heavily on the present; the dead weight of patronage and spoils, illegitimate offspring of devotion to democracy and equality, still burdens the upward struggling, technical, nonpartisan and permanent services which such a civilization as ours now seems to require. The form and temper of the new public service are, however, plain: it is basically neutral, impartial, skilled and impersonal. Its very qualities make it a stranger to the party politician whose world is personal, human, partisan, and colored by all the disparate ambitions of a competing society. Until 1883 party dominance of public employment was complete; since then it has been in slow but steady retreat. In its wake it leaves a more or less extensive and formal system of personnel administration shared by the departments and a central personnel agency, whose traditional form of organization as a commission is beginning to give way to intermediate forms apparently tending toward a single civil service administrator. This trend reflects the emerging belief that personnel management and fiscal management are two of the principal agencies of overhead management, the task of the chief executive.

Chapter Nineteen

GOVERNMENT CAREER SERVICE

IN DECEMBER, 1933, the Social Science Research Council appointed a Commission of Inquiry on Public Service Personnel. The report of this distinguished unofficial body gave popular currency to the idea of government career service, which also had acquired a sudden but not wholly artificial popularity as a result of the closing of doors in the business world subsequent to the depression of 1929.

In the words of the Commission, "we . . . recommend that the day-to-day administrative work of government be definitely made a career service. By this we mean that steps shall be taken to make public employment a worth-while life work, with entrance to the service open and attractive to young men and women of capacity and character, and with opportunity of advancement through service and growth to posts of distinction and honor."[1] This admirable definition implies a clear distinction between a career service and mere life work. The adoption of the merit system ensured life work, but only laid the necessary foundations for a career service.

Within the protecting walls of the merit system, however, a career service has already made substantial progress. The work of the great departments and commissions in the federal government is carried on by career men and women, civil servants of such eminence as W. H. McReynolds in the Treasury, W. W. Stockberger in Agriculture,

[1] *Better Government Personnel* (1935), p. 3. The members of this Commission were L. D. Coffman, President of the University of Minnesota; Louis Brownlow Director of Public Administration Clearing House; Ralph Budd, President of the Chicago, Burlington and Quincy Railroad; Arthur L. Day, Vice President of the Corning Glass Works, and Charles E. Merriam, Professor of Political Science University of Chicago. Dr. Luther Gulick, Director of the Institute of Public Administration and Eaton Professor of Municipal Science and Administration at Columbia University, was director of research. Other volumes published by the Committee include the *Minutes of Evidence* (1935), and supporting volumes by Sarah Greer, *A Bibliography of Civil Service and Personnel Administration* (1935); Leonard D. White, C. H. Bland, W. R. Sharp, and F. M. Marx, *Civil Service Abroad Great Britain, Canada, France, Germany* (1935); Harvey Walker, *Training Employees in Great Britain* (1935); Carl J. Friedrich, W. C. Beyer, S. D. Spero, J. F. Miller, and George A. Graham, *Problems of the American Public Service* (1935) and Lucius Wilmerding, Jr., *Government by Merit: an Analysis of the Problem of Government Personnel* (1935).

Malcolm Kerlin in Commerce, L. J. Briggs in the National Bureau of Standards, Katherine F. Lenroot in the Children's Bureau, Ismar Baruch in the Civil Service Commission, George R. Putnam,[1] recently retired from the Bureau of Lighthouses, the late Elwood Mead of the Bureau of Reclamation and the late Dr. William A. White of St. Elizabeths Hospital.[2] The state services of Massachusetts, New York, New Jersey, Wisconsin, California and other states would reveal a corresponding group of career men and women, especially in the scientific, medical, engineering and welfare fields. In the cities the managers are the principal type of career men, flanked by able technical careerists in public health, recreation, public welfare and other less developed career fields.

The United States is, therefore, not without its brilliant public service career men, fully able to hold their own with the career men of other countries. The significance of the report of the Commission of Inquiry lies not in the discovery of a new type of public service organization, but rather in demanding that career opportunities be widened, that handicaps to a career service be eliminated, and that backward areas be brought within hailing distance of progressive outposts. The development of thought about the public service during post-war years turned chiefly on technical matters of test technique, classification, efficiency rating and statistical analysis. The Commission of Inquiry raised more fundamental questions concerning the kind of a public service we are building or wish to build and fixed attention on a long-range ideal. The report coincided in point of time with a growing realization that the tasks of contemporary government are such that we can rely on nothing short of a public service commanding the best brains of our generation—not only as a temporary "brain-trust" but as an integral part of the administrative system.

In the course of the pages of this chapter we shall discuss first, some of the features of the American public service which affect deeply the actual achievement of a career service of this order; second, the foundations of a career service consonant with American traditions; and finally, the problem of a career service in general administration.[3]

[1] Mr. Putnam has given an illuminating account of his life in the public service in his autobiography, *Sentinels of the Coast* (1937).

[2] Among the indispensable books in public administration is Dr. White's autobiography, entitled *William Alanson White: The Autobiography of a Purpose* (1938). Other valuable biographies or autobiographies illustrating public service careers are William C. Redfield, *With Congress and Cabinet* (1924); Allan Nevins, *Henry White; Thirty Years of American Diplomacy* (1930); Herbert Croly, *Willard Straight* (1925); Charles E. A. Winslow, *The Life of Hermann M. Biggs, M.D., D.Sc., LL.D., Physician and Statesman of the Public Health* (1929); David Fairchild, *The World was my Garden* (1938).

[3] Although the point will not be dealt with here, the opportunities for careers in quasi public bodies such as bureaus of governmental research and organizations of officials deserve treatment. They are steadily increasing.

1. The Quality of the American Public Service

Skeptics, pointing to the patronage which still flourishes in all level of government and to the formidable handicaps to a challenging caree in government, are wont to conclude that in competition with business, government will continue to draw into its ranks only the secon or the third best. That government must compete with business in th labor market for scientists, engineers, technicians, and executives a well as skilled mechanics and routine workers is certain.

Government is only one of many competitors in the open labo market, and it is subject to the same conditions and limitations as an other large employer of labor, except in time of war for military service Government tenders certain terms and conditions of employment; s do manufacturers, bankers, railroads, retail traders and other employers Workers by hand or by brain tend to seek employment where the pay hours and other conditions of service are on the whole most attractive If the conditions of government work are distinctly less satisfactor than those obtaining in private employment, the standard of skill an competence attracted to the public service will be lowered.

In some respects, such as the opportunity to make a fortune, govern ment cannot compete at all with private employment. In other re spects, such as security, prestige, and identification with socially signifi cant work, government can compete on equal or better terms. In layin the foundations for a career service, it is elementary that governmen should make the most of those qualities of the public service whic count in securing and keeping a highly qualified personnel.[1]

It is, therefore, relevant to examine the public service from the poin of view of security, opportunity, mobility, and routine for the broa purpose of laying bare some of the important conditions which in fluence government career service.

a. Security. Among the tribal deities of America, the goddess Secu rity has been traditionally entitled to little respect. Exploiting a ne country which offered dazzling prizes to the self-reliant and the ad venturous, Americans worshiped courage and initiative and chanc not security. But even in the golden days of rugged individualism, silent mass of humble citizens cast anxious eyes toward the futur when advancing years would first diminish and then destroy the earning power.

In the second quarter of the twentieth century the old gods a tumbling from their thrones, and the anxieties of the mass of perso are becoming the concern of most. The rapid growth of old-age pensio

[1] Cf. the thoughtful article by Arnold Brecht, "Civil Service," 3 *Social Researc* 202-21 (1936).

plans, the recent approval of unemployment reserves or unemployment nsurance, the spread of insurance and compensation against the hazards of industrial accident and disease, most striking of all, the recognition of a national responsibility for personal security evidenced in the fornation of the Social Security Board, all these are tokens of new emphasis upon security.

Where the merit system is in force, public employment affords a legree of security greater than that normally prevailing in the indusrial world. Since 1929 the search for security has doubtless been one of the main reasons which has prompted millions to take civil service examinations. And while before 1929 the public service lost caste because t was peopled with many who were motivated by the desire for ecurity, since the hard experiences of the depression the public service tands to gain, not lose prestige by reason of this quality.

The degree of security inherent in public employment is, however, often exaggerated. In politically controlled governments and agencies, ecurity is nonexistent except where one party controls over many ears, and factional fights always endanger whatever stability coninued party success may promise. The most complete guarantees of tatus under the merit system give no protection against lay-off in case of reduction of force or termination of an activity. The unfortunate xperience of the foreign commercial agents of the Department of Commerce who, in 1933, were given twenty-four hours to start for heir home shores is only one of the most indefensible illustrations of ruthless program of liquidating an activity against which no claims of civil service status are potent. The lay-off of thousands of employees n Washington in 1933, and in state, institutional and municipal servces from 1930 to 1934 is a more normal case of the same procedure. and salary and wage levels may be modified downward by legislative r executive action in case of need.

Nor are civil service employees protected by law against discharge or proper cause, contrary to a widespread opinion. In the federal ervice discharge is practically in the free discretion of the head of the epartment or establishment; in the states and cities a somewhat greater egree of protection is sometimes encountered, but in any case there re adequate provisions to discharge for incompetence, insubordinaon, neglect of duty, drunkenness or dishonesty, provided the responble official has the courage to proceed.

Severe limitations to the actual security of merit system employees ierefore do exist; and anyone familiar with the psychology of public nployees during 1930–1935 understands how real the sense of inseirity has been. At the same time, if we compare the *relative* degree of security in public employment with the conditions prevailing in private enterprise, we are bound to conclude that the public service is the more stable of the two.

b. Opportunity. There is a widespread illusion that there is little opportunity in the public service, that civil service employees "get in a rut," and that there is no escape from devastating monotony. On the basis of personal observation at close range for a number of years, the writer does not share this opinion. There is excellent opportunity in the public service for those who are adapted to the conditions of work in a large organization and who have the ability to do difficult work. In government or industry, persons with second-rate ability are not likely to hold first-rate jobs. The opportunity of an able person to rise to a first-rate job in government is probably as good as in private employment. The same sifting process goes on in government offices under the merit system that is found elsewhere; officials are constantly on the lookout for promising understudies; unusually competent younger employees move ahead about as rapidly as they are ready for more responsible work.

Opportunity is of course a relative term, and it is idle to expect the same kind of success in public office as some achieve in the competitive world. The maximum financial success for merit system employees in the federal service is rarely in excess of $6,500 a year, a figure which is roughly comparable to top-flight merit positions in the larger states and cities. Public service opportunity is intelligible chiefly in terms of making a direct personal contribution to the great ends of democratic government. My observation satisfies me that highly competent men will choose a government career on the basis of these rewards. Their principal concern must always be that full use will be made of their ability, for as soon as they are occupied on work which does not command all their powers, they become dissatisfied.

For this reason it is necessary to organize a career service so far as possible to build up effective opportunity for personal development. Not everyone has the qualities which warrant promotion to the highest administrative and technical positions, but those who have superior ability must be given a suitable outlet for their energy if the public service is to retain them. It was this philosophy which underlay the writer's proposal for a career group in higher administration paralleling an established career service in scientific, technical and professional aspects of government work.[1]

The changing quality of the public service is gradually expanding career opportunities, especially as the proportion of scientific and pro

[1] L. D. White, *Government Career Service* (1935).

fessional positions increases. In 1896 there were 4,089 positions involving professional, scientific or technical subject matter, or 2.3 per cent of the total number of 178,717 civilian positions. On January 31, 1937, an analysis of 234,254 positions among the then total of over 800,000 showed 29,795 or 12.72 per cent in the professional and scientific service and 35,132 or 15 per cent in the subprofessional service, a combined percentage of 27.72. In these professional and subprofessional classes, the largest occupational group was engineering and drafting, 25.56 per cent; then in order, law, 18.22 per cent; economics, statistics, political and social sciences, 14.17 per cent; the medical sciences, 10.35 per cent; the physical sciences, 8.59 per cent; the agricultural and biological sciences, 7.34 per cent; and library science, 7.99 per cent.[1]

c. Mobility. We must recognize, however, that it has not been so easy to move around in the public service as would be desirable. Opportunity to advance by changing employers is gradually increasing; and as states and nation grow more closely together in cooperative activities, freedom of movement will expand. By the phrase, mobility, we mean the degree of movement of personnel from one position to another. It is a broader term than the expression "turnover," which has been more widely used in industrial than in public employment. In public office the degree of mobility is governed by the law and regulations, by practice and tradition.

In its various phases mobility includes reassignment within the same organization and class or grade; advancement in salary scale and promotion to a higher class; transfer from one official agency to another with or without change in duties and responsibility; change of employment by moving from one jurisdiction to another; change from official to private employment and vice versa. Although the calculation of rate of turnover has been standardized, no index of mobility has yet been devised. No inherent difficulty (apart from the absence of the basic statistics in some cases) in the development of such an index is apparent; and it would be a very useful tool in the better understanding of the practical operation of the personnel system.

In general the mobility of public service personnel is probably low in comparison with the mobility of industrial groups. Any general statement, however, is subject to many important exceptions since the freedom of movement in government work is highly variable from case to case. Reassignments vary in frequency with the size of the organization and character of work. In such groups as the Foreign Service, the Forest Service, and the United States Public Health Service, reassignment is a

[1] Data compiled by Ismar Baruch, chief of the personnel classification division, U. S. Civil Service Commission.

deliberate policy. Transfer and promotion opportunities vary both with the size of the unit and with its general trend toward expansion or contraction, as well as with the special terms of the law in particular cases. Transfer to a different department or agency is limited by diversity of function, but where similarity of function prevails (as in staff and auxiliary operations) this type of movement is more common. Opportunity to move to another governmental authority (as from city to city or city to state) is severely limited in all but the established professions. Change from unofficial to official employment is common, since practica experience is usually required prior to appointment; but the contrary movement is less frequent.

A number of circumstances hamper freedom of movement in public employment. Local pride emphasizes the sentiment that "home town boys are as good as any." There is also a widespread belief that an official or employee needs to be familiar with local conditions and personalities. Sectional prejudice still plays some part in closing the door to the outsider. To the extent that political preference controls appointments, residence within the state for state appointments, or within the city for municipal positions is almost universally required. The gradual accrual of pension benefits is a powerful incentive to remain in the same jurisdiction. Finally the effects of a depression are to increase the sentiment for local appointments.

Movement from state and local positions to national positions is much greater than the reverse, and has been particularly marked since about 1933. Interchange between states is less common than between the state and Washington, and probably less than between the cities. Interchange between city service and state service is slight. Movement from political office into administrative positions is probably greater than the opposit trend. In general the recognition of a professional point of view favor easy exchange of personnel in every direction; per contra, the influenc of patronage eliminates the interchange of personnel.

The mobility of public officials and employees is gradually increasing Barriers are slowly dropping in section after section and with respec to group after group. While many sectors of the public service sti remain tightly frozen, in others a thaw has set in. Consideration of number of cases will illustrate the prevailing diversity.

Superintendents of schools. Here there is wide public acceptance o complete freedom of movement and relative freedom from politic considerations. Superintendents in the larger cities are quite as likely t come from "abroad" as from the locality. Other career openings in th field of educational administration include the positions of president and deans of state normal schools and state universities, in which loc residence requirements have been forgotten. *City Managers.* Local sentiment varies considerably but in general there is wide opportunity to move from city to city. Occasionally municipalities even refuse to consider a local man; in many the outsider has a free field, and nation-wide competition is common. Some managers have served with success in four, five, or six cities. *Municipal health officers.* In the middle-size cities, outside appointments are common. Professional qualifications are well established, and considerable freedom of movement exists in fact. *Finance officers,* state and municipal. State or local residence is usually required of this group and the chance to move from one jurisdiction to another is limited. These appointments are usually personal, requiring the confidence of the chief executive. Auditors and comptrollers, on the other hand, are frequently elected; and in this case local residence is universally demanded. *Police chiefs.* With rare exceptions, the police chiefs are local appointees, usually having grown up in their own department. *Clerical and supervisory staff.* Here the rule of local residence is almost universal. Higher appointments are made from within the office in state, county and city governments, or are made politically from local residents. *Social service group.* Under pressure of emergency conditions, an unusual degree of mobility has prevailed in recent years. Considerable prejudice against the outsider exists, however, emphasized by the delicate nature of the social worker's task. *Personnel experts.* Local residence is frequently waived in this group and there have been several recent nation-wide competitions for important personnel posts.

To the extent that they prevail, artificial handicaps to free movement tend to deter the most energetic and promising young people from choosing the public service as a career; they bottle up real talent in watertight compartments; they foster a provincial satisfaction with mediocrity; they short-circuit the stimulating effect of new experience and broader horizons; they sometimes drive the most competent persons out of public into private employment. They hamper the growth of a professional point of view.

To what extent the interchange of personnel between government and business should be facilitated is a moot point. A better understanding between government and business may well arise from interchange of this sort, and a few years' training of a future industrialist in a government office may have considerable value to industry and eventually to government itself. In my *Government Career Service,* I pointed out a well-known risk in these words, "There is no defense for a cynical practice by which able young men spend a few years in the public service becoming familiar with the laws and regulations with the more or less open expectation of capitalizing their knowledge by deserting the public service to enter private employment where they turn their training against the government." [1]

On the other hand, much can be said for an "interneship" for certain classes of officials in the business organizations with which they are in contact. Commissioner Joseph B. Eastman once observed that the staff of the Interstate Commerce Commission ought to know as much about the railroads as the rail executives themselves. A friendly interchange on special assignment both ways has possibilities.

d. Routine, monotony, repetitive operations. While there is a large amount of routine operations in government work as in any large organization, the public service does not suffer in comparison with other types of employment on this point. Industrial fabrication tends toward the repetitive operations of the assembly line more completely than do the ordinary tasks of government.[2] The opportunity to exercise judgment in official work is in fact widespread, although naturally in varying degrees.

In the higher administrative and the various levels of supervisory positions, discretion and judgment in handling staff and in reaching decisions on substantive matters are inherent. In the scientific field, the same type of reasoning from data toward a demonstrable conclusion exists in government as in private employment. In the professional classes engineering, medicine, and especially law, routine is at a minimum. Most operations which are usually classified as repetitive fall in the clerical force. Even here there is considerable room for the exercise of good judgment, and many clerical operations require an accurate knowledge of laws, rules, and judicial decisions.

Many types of work peculiar to government require unusual discretion and judgment, for example, the customs patrol inspector, immigration inspector, income tax collector, food and drug inspector, utility examiner, personnel officer, assessor, policeman, and scores of similar illustrations. Mere routine, repetitive operations are less common than is usually supposed.

2. Foundations of a Career Service

These considerations bring us directly to the foundations on which an American career service must rest.[3] Permanence of tenure during good behavior and satisfactory work is an obvious *sine qua non.* A career service is incompatible with appointment and tenure on the basis o

[1] White, *op. cit.*, p. 71.

[2] Elton Mayo, *The Human Problems of an Industrial Civilization* (1933).

[3] See especially Lewis Meriam, *Public Personnel Problems from the Standpoint the Operating Office* (1938), ch. 13; and Katherine A. Frederic, *Trained Personn for Public Service* (1935).

›mporary partisan supremacy. Nor is a career service compatible with ıe rule of local residence, for the ablest men are not willing to tie them- ːlves to a life work in a single city or county (with exceptions) or even ı a single state. Quite apart from popular prejudices against outsiders, owever, the invention of practical means to open up transfers from one ırisdiction to another, involving classification status, pension accruals ıd other matters, is surrounded by serious technical difficulties. These vo handicaps to careers, the rule of politics and the rule of local resi- ence, are still serious obstacles to state and local career possibilities, though they are substantially avoided in the federal service.

Government career service in the United States must start with full ːcognition of the underlying American devotion to the doctrine of]ual opportunity for all citizens. The special privileges which are ɔssessed by the English administrative class do not fit the American ːene. Nor can a career service in other than the scientific and profes- onal group rest on any specific educational preparation. There is wide- read conviction that careers in government must be careers open in :inciple to any who can qualify for them, irrespective of formal edu- tional achievements.[1]

The need for actually qualified career men and women is not, how- 'er, in dispute; our equalitarianism is directed against "artificial" bar- ːrs rather than good standards, although it sometimes defeats the too pid raising of standards. Career service stands on the recognition of ility and assumes that superior ability and attainments will be the basis r original selection and for eventual promotion to more responsible sts. Anything short of this is fatal to a career service, for the morale a career group cannot withstand personal or political favoritism.

Career service would be facilitated by the closer coordination of civil rvice examinations with the educational system. On any impartial view is extraordinary that these examinations have gone their way with so tle regard to selecting, year after year, the brightest secondary school d college or university graduates for public service careers. The ex- ıinations of the federal Civil Service Commission for junior professional d scientific positions and for junior civil service examiner are geared, newhat inadequately, to college graduation, but these are relatively ːe exceptions. A career service places less emphasis on specific prepa- ːion, more on general education and mental alertness; less emphasis on

That university men and women are finding their place in government work is strated by Lewis Meriam's comment on the technical services: "Ph.D.'s and Phi a Kappa keys are more common in the national service than anywhere else ex- t on a university faculty," *Public Service and Special Training* (1936), pp. 15- and again, "As I have watched the ever changing stream, the university men n to me to be steadily gaining ground," *ibid.*, pp. 18-19.

practical experience, more on capacity to learn on the job and to pro gress. These considerations suggest the closer correlation of public edu cation and public service.

Government career service, as indicated above, implies also opportunit for personal growth and for the full exercise of one's best ability. In th early years this is facilitated by various forms of in-service training, i later years by promotion to more difficult and exacting duties. Stagna tion in promotion leads usually to resignations or to stagnation of ambi tion and activity.

A final characteristic of a career service in the United States is th open road from the junior to the top positions. This has been achieve in the organization of many departments and agencies, but is defeate in others. The principal obstacle is the reservation of high positions fo political appointment. There are usually no internal barriers until th political level is reached, but this level is reached too soon.

What are the principal obstacles to broader recognition of career serv ice in the American government? Most of them have been indicated i the previous paragraphs, but they may be summarized here.[1] In the stat and local governments and to some extent in the field service of th national government local residence restrictions are the chief obstacl In many cases temporary political tenure of all positions or politic control of the higher positions ruins career service prospects. Low sa ary levels in some jurisdictions are a handicap although not an absolu bar. The presumed absence of promising opportunity for personal grow is a deterrent in some cases. The low prestige of the public service h been a special handicap in some instances, though not in others.[2]

These are serious but not insurmountable obstacles. They have be banished in many instances and the trend is generally in favor of the elimination. Even a brief sketch of some career possibilities indicat that there is already reason for some gratification with the progre which has been made.

In the national government the best known career group is the Fo eign Service of the State Department, organized since 1924 on the ba of the Rogers Act.[3] While all foreign service problems have not y been solved, there is general agreement that the quality of the consul and diplomatic service recruits has been notably improved and th stable conditions of service have created a better esprit de corps. L

[1] These and other obstacles are discussed in a committee report issued by International City Managers' Association, *A Career Service in Local Governm* (1937).

[2] See the author's *The Prestige Value of Public Employment in Chicago* (19 and *Further Contributions to the Prestige Value of Public Employment* (1932).

[3] Tracy H. Lay, *The Foreign Service of the United States* (1925).

well known but well established as career services are certain types of scientific work in the national government, such as the Forest Service, the meat inspection service, the National Park Service, the United States Public Health Service and the engineering service of the United States Bureau of Public Roads.[1] The national legal service is only partially organized on a career basis, since many such appointments are made on the basis of political affiliation. Personnel work is steadily emerging as a career field.

Within the state governments the principal illustrations of genuine career services are found in the expanding field of public welfare, the field of education and the scientific and professional services, of which public health and highway construction and maintenance are perhaps the leading examples.[2] The broad field of public welfare and the public social services connected with the Social Security Board and the state employment services seem likely to provide new and important career opportunities.

Within the cities, career opportunities exist in some instances, and are rapidly forming in others.[3] In the field of public education, a career service has long been firmly established, both in teaching and in educational administration. A less extensive but also well-established career opportunity is available in public library administration. The city manager profession illustrates a situation in which careers are being worked out in many individual instances. A few managers have exceeded twenty years of continuous employment in one or more cities. Public health administrators are already in the career class. Career openings for social workers are multiplying rapidly in recent years, despite considerable criticism of other than local appointments.

3. Careers in General Administration

General administration is understood to mean those duties concerned with the formation of policy, with the coordination and improvement of government machinery and with the general management and con-

[1] See Isador Lubin, "Government Employment as a Professional Career in Economics," 27 *Am. Econ. Rev.* Supplement 216-24 (1937); W. W. Stockberger, "The Need for Career Administrators," 189 *Annals* 91-96 (1937); L. D. White, "Careers in Government," 101 *Scribner's Magazine* 58-61 (March, 1937); William E. Mosher, "A Critique of Federal Personnel Policies as Applied to the Professional Social Science Positions," 27 *Am. Econ. Rev.* Supplement 199-209 (1937).

[2] Marietta Stevenson, *Public Welfare Administration* (1938); Ward W. Keesecker, *Selection, Qualification and Tenure of Principal State School Officers*, U. S. Office of Education, Circular No. 166, 1936.

[3] Gerald W. Shaw, "Tenure of Chief Municipal Officials in the United States," 17 *Pub. Man.* 227-31 (1935); Norman N. Gill, "Career Personnel in Six Large Cities," *ibid.* 260-63; Luther Gulick, "Toward a Municipal Career Service," *ibid.* 331-33.

trol of the departments of the public service. It is an essential element of any system of administration, and increases in importance with the size of the organization. Perhaps the first formal recognition of this group was given by the New York City Civil Service Commission in a resolution of July 1, 1938, creating the positions of Junior Administrative Assistant ($3,000–4,000); Administrative Assistant ($4,000–5,000); Senior Administrative Assistant ($5,000–6,000); and Administrator ($6,000 and over).

The performance of the duties of this class of employment calls for "a trained mental equipment of a high order. . . . In some spheres what is most wanted is judgment, *savoir-faire*, insight, and fair-mindedness; in others an intellectual equipment capable of the mastery of complex and abstruse problems in, for instance, taxation or other economic subjects, in others, imagination and constructive ability." [1]

In municipal government the office of city manager is clearly one devoted to general management. In public education the office of superintendent of schools is concerned with general management. The superintendents or general managers of public institutions in city and state fall in the same category. The general manager of the Tennessee Valley Authority is another clear example.

In the national government, a considerable number of positions concerned with general administration exist, but they have never been specifically identified nor are they recognized as belonging to a special class of employment. No special procedures for recruiting junior administrators and no special preparation or training prevail.[2] The positions include such posts as undersecretary and assistant secretary, the five general managers of departments observed by Macmahon, administrative assistants, bureau chiefs and assistant bureau chiefs in some cases, and the heads of many federal institutions such as the Beltville Agricultural Experiment Station, Alcatraz, and St. Elizabeths Hospital.[3]

[1] Quoted from English sources in White, Bland, Sharp and Marx, *Civil Service Abroad* (1935), p. 20. Career groups in general administration have long since been developed in older civil services such as the English, French, German, Dutch and Scandinavian. They rest upon (1) an extensive educational preparation, either in legal subjects principally (Germany, Austria) or in literary and philosophical subjects (France, Belgium) or in the humanities or sciences (England); (2) direct recruitment into a category to which higher administrative duties are chiefly assigned; (3) early assumption of responsibility; (4) promotion strictly on the basis of merit to such important posts as a permanent undersecretaryship.

[2] Emerging exceptions to this generalization exist in Home Owners' Loan Corporation and the Department of Agriculture.

[3] Arthur W. Macmahon, "Selection and Tenure of Bureau Chiefs in the National Administration of the United States," 20 *Am. Pol. Sci. Rev.* 548-82, 770-811 (1926); E. P. Herring, *Federal Commissioners: a Study of their Careers and Qualifications* (1936).

The essential characteristics of these and similar posts, in Luther Gulick's formulation, are seven, the first letters of which form the word, Posdcorb: planning, organizing, staffing, directing, coordinating, reporting, and budgeting.[1] In his lectures, *Public Service and Special Training*, Lewis Meriam accepts these categories as common to practically all administrative positions, but argues that an essential element is omitted, knowledge of subject matter. "You have to plan something, you have to organize something, you have to direct something," writes this practical observer of the federal scene. "Intimate knowledge of the subject matter with which an administrative agency is primarily concerned is indispensable to the effective, intelligent administration of that agency." [2] "Public administration is an instrument with two blades, like a pair of scissors. One blade may be a knowledge of the fields covered by Posdcorb, the other blade is knowledge of the subject matter in which these techniques are applied. Both blades must be good to make an effective tool." [3]

This point of view leads Meriam to deny the existence of "such a thing as a general administrator or an administrator per se," since each case of general administration is specially conditioned by its peculiar subject matter.

Dr. Meriam is correct in pointing out that an administrator necessarily deals with a special field and in emphasizing that knowledge of the subject matter of the field is useful. In the opinion of the present writer the requisite degree of subject-matter knowledge is much less than that required of the subject-matter specialists who serve in every department and is not necessarily precedent to actual experience in administration. Knowledge of special subject-matter content does not, moreover, replace skill in general administration, nor does it submerge the qualities which distinguish the general administrator and make it possible for him to serve with equal distinction in successive subject-matter fields.

This position can be illustrated by specific examples. Mr. William H. McReynolds entered the national service in the post office, later was employed in the Bureau of Efficiency, then was transferred to the staff of the Personnel Classification Board, of which he became eventually the director. In 1933 he became executive officer of Farm Credit Administration and in 1934 administrative assistant to the Secretary of the Treasury, in reality the general manager of this huge department. To an exceptional degree he possesses that combination of qualities which shine administratively in any department and which is basically independent

[1] Luther Gulick, "Notes on the Theory of Organization," in Gulick and L. Urwick, eds., *Papers on the Science of Management* (1937), p. 13.
[2] Lewis Meriam, *Public Service and Special Training* (1936), p. 2.
[3] *Ibid.*, p. 26.

of subject-matter knowledge. Such men quickly sense the "feel" of new administrative situations. Such figures as Governor William I. Myers of Farm Credit Administration, Louis Brownlow and Herbert Emmerich of Public Administration Clearing House, each with a rich and varied administrative experience, Robert Moses,[1] Director of Parks of New York State, James V. Bennett, Director of Prisons, United States Department of Justice, illustrate the same type of administrative skill.

Assuming that there is a special function which may be called general administration, is it desirable to set up a special administrative service as a recognized career with its own original entrance gate and its own special pathway to upper administrative positions? In *Government Career Service*, the author proposed a special service organized as a career open on equal terms both to present civil service employees, without reference to educational achievements, and to eligibles selected by open competitive examination at the college level. The proposal recognized a degree and form of preparation carefully planned to maximize their eventual contribution to overhead direction.[2]

In 1920 the advisers of the Congressional Joint Commission on Reclassification opposed a special corps in administration and upon reviewing the situation again in 1936, Lewis Meriam, who served with this Commission, repeated his former conviction. He feared that a special form of selection and preparation for higher administration would stir up jealousies and lower morale; he believed that the professional and scientific services should be administered only by professional and scientific men; he stressed the subject-matter content of administration rather than its function of coordination, initiation, and general management and control.[3]

With Meriam's conviction that administrative positions in other than the distinctly scientific and professional services should be left open both to men with university education and to those who work up in the ranks on a foundation of less formal education the writer has always agreed. The principal difference is whether men and women can wisely be assigned at an early date to a special class of employment comprising the duties of general management, for the purpose of securing special training and experience in this field and for the more certain elimination

[1] Among many references to the career of Robert Moses, see Beverly Smith, "Bigger than Politics," 118 *American Magazine* 55, 104 (Oct., 1934); H. C. Herring, "Robert Moses and His Parks," 176 *Harper's Magazine* 26-37 (Dec., 1937); an unsigned article in 17 *Fortune* 70 (June, 1938) entitled, "Robert (or I'll resign) Moses."

[2] L. D. White, *Government Career Service* (1935); see also by the same author an article in 10 *Fortune* 76-77, 150-61 (Nov., 1934) entitled "Toward a New U. S. Civil Service."

[3] Meriam, *Public Service and Special Training*, ch. 1.

of those who show little aptitude for it, all without discrimination against men with scientific or any other form of training; or whether alternatively the relatively unorganized existing methods emphasizing knowledge of subject matter and depending upon trial and error for ascertaining administrative skill fit better the temper of the federal service. My observation in Washington leads me to believe that special selection, special training, special experience and careful elimination will produce a better group of overhead administrators than those developed by present methods. This opinion reflects less emphasis upon subject-matter content, more upon skill in leadership, representation, coordination, and negotiation.

In one form or another, the provision of careers in general administration is one of the major needs of the present day. The technical, scientific and professional services are far ahead of the administrative services. The new forms of public service require to an unparalleled degree competent general administration, because so many and such vital public interests are affected. Modern public administration presents an immense task of keeping masses of people in sympathy with government policy. For this task special qualities of personality and special types of experience are needed; they are not the qualities which distinguish the scientist as such, although scientists may also have the qualities which make good administrators.

From among such scientists in part and from among men and women who have the mixture of personal qualities conducive to success in management a group of general administrators has already emerged and will continue to maintain itself. The method is less important than the end; but here as elsewhere well-devised special methods would seem to promise better results than those procedures which, like Topsy, "just growed."

It would be misleading to close this discussion without emphasizing the fact that despite lack of formal organization public service careers are and for a generation have been possible. Public education is a huge career service counting over a million members; most of the half million (by 1939, perhaps 650,000) federal employees under the merit system are potentially careerists and not merely "lifers"; in the public welfare, public health, public recreation, library, and engineering services of many states and cities significant career opportunities are well established; public personnel work is definitely in the career stage; the state-federal public employment service is emerging into the same brighter prospect; the establishment of unemployment insurance and the prospective establishment of public health insurance and assistance point to new career opportunities. Nor are these careers confined to college and university graduates; many able men and women entering the service from secondary schools are making their way to the top on the basis of merit.

There is, therefore, no occasion for the friends of government career service to become defeatist; there certainly are obstacles to overcome, but there are major achievements in the past and ample prospects in the attainable future.

Chapter Twenty

RECRUITMENT, EXAMINATION, AND CERTIFICATION

WITH this introduction to the broad background and general objectives of personnel administration, we may now turn to its more technical phases. The oldest and still one of the most important branches of the work of civil service commissions is to supply qualified men and women for all the varied kinds of positions which the civil service requires. This difficult and, in increasing measure, scientific task is discussed in the present chapter, to be followed in turn by summary presentation of the technical operations of position-classification, salary standardization, training, promotion, service records, discipline, and retirement systems. We shall then turn again to more general problems involved in the trend toward professionalization and civil service unions, and in the morale and prestige of the public service.[1]

1. Recruitment

The terms, recruitment and examination, are often used interchangeably. In this book, the word recruitment is limited to the specific steps taken to attract suitable candidates to apply for examinations. Examination will be understood to mean the formal process of testing as a means of determining either mere qualification or rank order of merit and the establishment of an eligible register. Certification is the process of sending to an appointing officer the names of those who are eligible for appointment. Chronologically, therefore, the sequence is recruitment, examination, certification.

The traditional approach of American civil service commissions toward recruitment is one of relative passivity.[2] Recruitment has often been considered simply a matter of the publication and distribution of unattractive announcements, often necessarily written in rather forbidding "official English." A different plan of recruitment has been evolved

[1] On all these questions, the reader may profitably supplement his reading by reference to William E. Mosher and J. Donald Kingsley, *Public Personnel Administration* (1936), and Lewis Meriam, *Public Personnel Problems from the Standpoint of the Operating Office* (1938).

[2] Lucius Wilmerding, Jr., *Government by Merit* (1935), chs. 5-7.

in progressive jurisdictions which accept a responsibility for arousing the interest of specially qualified persons. It is not enough, in this view, merely to sort out by examination those who come forward voluntarily; there is a positive duty of finding peculiarly well-qualified persons and of inducing them to take the examinations.

The theory and practice of passively accepting what turns up are open to criticism in any case, but are particularly indefensible in recruiting for specialized middle-and-upper-bracket positions. A special duty to make an active search for exceptionally well-qualified applicants clearly rests both upon the central examining agency and upon the operating departments. The latter, in fact, are more likely to be active in hunting out competent individuals than the former, partly because they know their specialized field, partly because they are the ones who will feel the consequences of an unsatisfactory appointment. Civil service commissions have failed to push selective recruitment partly because their funds have seldom permitted much work at this point, partly because they fear criticism on charges of favoritism.

The process of recruitment illustrates admirably the tug and pull of the opposing forces of equalitarianism and humanitarianism on the one hand against the claims of special competence on the other. Our national predilection for equality and for a humane social order leads in the direction of giving everyone a chance at the civil service examinations.[1] The desirability of special competence and of conserving commission funds suggests barriers in the form of examination prerequisites which will keep out those who are unlikely to succeed. Very difficult problems, aggravated by the depression, thus arise concerning such prerequisites as age, education and experience.

It is obviously advantageous to the government to recruit its employees at an early age, and thus to capitalize the special skill which they acquire throughout a lifetime in the public service. It is also obviously advantageous to avoid recruiting men and women in middle life or beyond who have failed to maintain themselves in private employment, and who, as one of them once put it, "seek peace" in the security of a government job. A career service, moreover, is best worked out by recruiting young men and women and by training them in the service for higher positions. For these and other reasons, the civil service examinations of many other countries impose low age limitations, sixteen, eighteen, twenty-four, or for professional work thirty, the ages being related to school diplomas.

Widely divergent age limits exist in the United States, but in general

[1] It is for this reason that only a very few civil service commissions require an examination fee.

he emphasis upon "giving everyone a chance" pushes the limits to the point where they fail to serve their most useful purpose. In the national government, the normal age limit for other than scientific and professional positions is fifty-three, a year fixed in the light of the retirement act. For scientific and professional positions, the limits are thirty-five, forty, forty-five and fifty-three for the junior and higher grades respectively. These limits are subject to constant criticism by some members of Congress, and in 1937 the Senate passed a bill (which was killed in the House) to abolish all age limits whatever. A similar measure was enacted in 1938 by New York for the New York City service, subject to the minimum age of eighteen fixed by the child labor law and the maximum of eighty fixed by the retirement law. The force behind these proposals is pure humanitarianism, overriding the lesser consideration of administrative efficiency.

Considerations of equality of opportunity govern the drive against educational prerequisites. So far as the recognized sciences and professions are concerned, there is agreement that appropriate education may be required; the same rule holds for occupations wherever an official license is required as a prerequisite to practice. In most other fields the requirement of some formal education encounters strong opposition on the ground that every American citizen is entitled to an equal chance to take the examination.[1] This position cannot fail to appeal to all who sense the strong emotional attachment to equal opportunity which prevails in this country, although the result is to admit many who cannot pass the examinations, thus wasting public funds, arousing false hopes and creating painful disappointment. The invention of general intelligence and other short answer tests has diminished the potential waste of energy by providing an examination which can be quickly and inexpensively scored.

The same conflict rages over the experience prerequisites, which are difficult in any case to adjust precisely to the needs of a particular type of employment. Economy in the use of examination funds suggests strict experience specifications for specialist jobs; a sense of equality and a commonly expressed desire to find employment for the unemployed suggest the contrary. The experience and the educational prerequisites,

[1] In 1935 Massachusetts prohibited any educational requirement as a condition of taking a civil service examination except in respect to professional and other positions for which the law imposes such requirements (Mass. Acts and Resolves 1935, c. 228). The same measure was enacted in Ohio in 1938 (Baldwin's Ohio Code, sec. 486-9a). An Ohio act of 1937 provided that appointments to the state relief commission should be made without discrimination "by reason of their having or not having attended any college or other educational activity where social science is taught"; Baldwin's Ohio Code Service, June, 1938, Temporary Legislation, p. 23, sec. 9.

indeed, are in conflict between themselves. Pfiffner is right in pointing out that "The American recruiting system is stacked heavily against the promising youngster and in favor of the mediocre mature person. This is due to the fact that entry to tests requires specific periods of experience in work similar to the position for which the test is given." [1]

Somewhat different considerations support the preference given to veterans in different degrees by practically all public recruiting bodies. Here a sense of national gratitude for past service in the military forces sustains exemptions from the customary prerequisites. In the eyes of Congress and state legislatures whatever lessening of administrative efficiency may result is outweighed by the discharge of a debt to veterans. It is a nice point to judge where the interests of the public service and of veterans can most justly be balanced.[2]

The various concrete means of recruitment need not detain us, since they are of principal concern to the specialist. The normal method is the printed announcement posted in various public places, especially post offices, supplemented by newspaper advertisements. Announcements are regularly sent to technical schools, colleges and universities Special clienteles are cultivated through trade journals and specially prepared mailing lists. The civil service has generally neglected to follow the lead of the army, navy, and marine corps in using posters. Some agencies, especially in time of rapid expansion, use the radio.

Recruitment, in short, revolves around the problem of attracting the best, not the most, although both selective and general programs are justified. The task is one both for the civil service commission and for the operating departments. It calls for special skill and in any large commission deserves separate organization. Recruitment involves more than mere announcement and passive acceptance; to meet the requirements of our present public service, it must be active, searching, selective, persistent and continuous.[3]

2. Examination

The origin of the written examination as a means of selecting man's rulers is lost in the ancient history of China.[4] Modern examinations for

[1] John M. Pfiffner, *Public Administration* (1935), p. 173.

[2] The subject of veterans' preference is not discussed in this book. An excellent treatment is that by John F. Miller, "Veteran Preference in the Public Service," in Carl J. Friedrich and others, *Problems of the American Public Service* (1935).

[3] The principal references on this topic are William Brownrigg and Louis J Kroeger, *Toward Effective Recruiting*, Civil Service Assembly Pamphlet No. 7 1937; and a forthcoming study by Russell Barthell, *Government Recruiting*, in preparation under the joint direction of the University of Chicago and the Civil Service Assembly of the United States and Canada.

[4] P. C. Hsieh, *The Government of China* (1925)

what we now call the civil service arose in Brandenburg where they were recognized by 1730 and formally established in the General Code of 1794. The United States borrowed the practice of civil service examinations from Great Britain where they had been in effect since the 1820's for the Customs and Excise Department. A general scheme of pass examinations set up in London in 1855 gave way in 1870 to the rule of open competition.

In 1883 the examination system was adopted by both the federal government and the state of New York, and has subsequently spread throughout the United States. Unfortunately no history of American civil service examinations has yet been written.[1] In broad outline we know that early civil service examiners tended to lay considerable emphasis on arithmetic, spelling, geography, the use of English, and similar subjects. Later there was a change of emphasis to "duties" tests made up of material which in content had to do with the work to be performed. Commencing with the World War, examiners turned in increasing measure to tests of fundamental traits, aptitudes and skills in place of or in addition to subject-matter knowledge.

Resort to examinations in 1883 was dictated by the need of finding some substitute for the unrestrained and much abused choice of public employees by politicians on the basis of political allegiance. Examinations can still be justified on the basis of this consideration, certainly until politicians can give a satisfactory demonstration of their capacity and will to pick competent men for the varied work of government. The principal justification for modern testing, however, is not only that it is impartial and impersonal, but that it actually results in the elimination of the unqualified and places the qualified in reasonably accurate order of merit. While no one asserts that the results of formal examination are infallible and while candid examiners are free to admit the mar-

[1] The present discussion of the field of testing is less than an introduction. A more extensive treatment is found in William E. Mosher and J. D. Kingsley, *Public Personnel Administration* (1936), chs. 2 and 3. Among the many works dealing with the subject the student may use profitably Lewis M. Terman and Maud A. Merrill, *Measuring Intelligence* (1937); Rudolf Pintner, *Intelligence Testing, Methods and Results* (rev. ed. 1931); Morris S. Viteles, *Industrial Psychology* (1932), and *The Science of Work* (1934); Henry E. Garrett and M. R. Schneck, *Psychological Tests, Methods and Results* (1933); Raymond B. Cattell, *Guide to Mental Testing* (1936); Walter V. Bingham, *Aptitudes and Aptitude Testing* (1937); Frank N. Freeman, *Mental Tests* (2d ed. 1938). Further literature is noted in the following bibliographies: Grace E. Manson, "Bibliography on Psychological Tests," 4 *J. of Personnel Research* 301-28 (1925–26); Gertrude Hildreth, *A Bibliography of Mental Tests and Rating Scales* (1933); Earl B. South, *An Index of Periodical Literature on Testing . . . 1921–1936* (1937); and the guides to tests prepared by Oscar K. Buros, *Educational, Psychological and Personality Tests of 1936* (1937), and earlier years.

gin of error in their results, nevertheless the relative order of merit reached by carefully prepared tests does correspond to the real capacity of applicants. Examinations are constantly becoming more nearly accurate predictions of performance on the job.[1]

The short answer type of examination permits the testing of the test itself. A good test is one which is a dependable guide to vocational success or failure. A standardized test is one whose dependability has been ascertained. Dependability in turn is measured by the validity and the reliability of the test. The term validity is used to indicate the degree to which the test measures the ability it is designed to measure. If there is little relationship between the scores made by persons on a test designed to measure ability to do a certain task and their known ability to do the task, the test has little validity. Per contra, if the relationship is high, the test has high validity. The reliability of a test is the extent to which it consistently measures what it measures, that is, the extent to which persons would be ranked in the same relative order by their scores on alternate forms of the test or on successive experiences with the test.[2]

Not only may the test as a whole be tested, but the selective value of each item may be ascertained.[3] New tests whose selective value can be forecast may then be constructed from items whose selectivity is known. Short answer examinations are carefully balanced with a proper distribution of easy and difficult items.

Many civil service laws require examinations to be "practical," and fear of public reaction to apparently irrelevant psychological tests keeps civil service examiners close to what elected representatives recognize as practical. In a recent study of New York City practice, the conclusion was reached that despite a noticeable trend toward educational content, "the primary characteristic of the written test in New York City is its adherence to the 'practical' tradition of American civil service recruitment," the outcome both of law and of long acceptance of the premise that experience is preferable to education.[4] In fact, it is possible to prepare examinations testing mental qualities (as distinguished from knowledge or achievement) in terms of subject matter which practical men

[1] I. L. Kandel, *Examinations and Their Substitutes in the United States* (1936).

[2] L. J. O'Rourke, "Office Employment Tests," in W. J. Donald, ed., *Handbook of Business Administration* (1931), p. 792.

[3] Norman J. Powell, "Item Evaluation in a Civil Service Examination," 21 *J. of Applied Psychology* 494-503 (1937); Charles M. Davidson, "Evaluation of Clerical Tests," 16 *Personnel J.* 57-64, 95-98 (1937–38); Dorothy M. Andrew, "An Analysis of the Minnesota Vocational Test for Clerical Workers," 21 *J. of Applied Psychology* 18-47, 139-71 (1937).

[4] Wallace S. Sayre and Milton Mandell, *Education and the Civil Service in New York City*, U. S. Office of Education (1938), p. 25.

accept as practical. An example is the police test developed by Dr. L. J. O'Rourke, director of the research division of the United States Civil Service Commission.

The effort to be practical has had some unfortunate results. It overemphasizes experience as against capacity to learn. It has helped to block the coordination of schools and civil service examinations. It has tended to produce tests closely identified with narrow "pigeonhole" jobs. It has hindered the development of examinations related to the selection of men for careers rather than jobs. It has delayed the acceptance of tests of aptitude and personality in favor of tests of knowledge and specialized skill. On the other hand, many jobs require practical skill or knowledge for which a specific test is well adapted.

In the course of twenty years' experimentation with testing devices, a large number and variety of examinations have been invented, from which civil service examiners select those which seem best adapted to their special ends. For the purposes of this volume it is unnecessary to enter upon a detailed study of test procedures. A general view of American examinations, which Herman Finer once declared to be one of our chief contributions to the world's stock of civil service ideas, is the most that can be done.

At the outset we may say that on account of lack of time and resources few, if any, public examining agencies are able to use the most refined procedures which are available. Civil service examinations usually involve large numbers, and time is always pressing. For example, the United States Civil Service Commission examined about 250,000 persons annually in the years before the depression; since 1933 this figure has mounted to more than 750,000. The New York City Commission examined 98,000 in 1937, and active state commissions such as New York or California have their hundreds of thousands. Examinations on a scale such as this must be affected by administrative as well as by technical examining considerations. The pressure of numbers has driven commissions to use the short answer form to the exclusion of the essay type, which has specific values of its own; to avoid the more refined types of aptitude and personality tests; and to use the oral test only where the number of candidates is strictly limited. In consequence there has been a certain overemphasis upon the so-called general intelligence test.

The classification of tests employed by Mosher and Kingsley is adopted for the following summary. The major categories are tests of capacity or aptitude, tests of achievement, and physical tests. In form the test may be written, oral, or a demonstration of skill. In administration, the test may be assembled or nonassembled, i.e., examinations in which the candidates are or are not brought together in one or more examination rooms.

The general intelligence test was devised in 1905 by Binet and Simon in an effort to segregate subnormal children in the schools of Paris. It was introduced generally in the United States by the Goddard translation of 1908 and became standardized in American usage by the Stanford revision of 1916, developed by Terman.[1] The use of mental tests for other than schoolroom purposes was launched by the army alpha test, devised in 1917 and applied to over 1,700,000 men. It was used principally to identify potential officer material among draft recruits and to segregate the lowest range of mentality for other than combatant duty.[2] Widespread interest in this form of "measurement of mind" led to the development of numerous other forms of general intelligence tests, among which are the Terman Group Tests of Mental Ability, the Otis Group Intelligence Scale and the Pressey Senior Classification and Verification Series. In one form or another this type of test has been widely used by civil service commissions, although often supplemented by other sifting devices. The general intelligence test is frequently used to exclude those who make less than a given score; those who pass are then given other tests for knowledge, aptitudes or skills. Since it can be scored rapidly and inexpensively, it is a useful device administratively.

Its selective value is generally accepted for a wide variety of positions requiring mental alertness, capacity to learn, and ability to comprehend. It is commonly used in one form or another in police examinations. The Detroit police department requires a score of at least 100 on the army alpha test; Berkeley, California, sets the high standard of 135. It is a part of many tests given by the United States Civil Service Commission: for example, in the stenographer-typist examination its value has been well established. On the other hand, it has less relevance to selection for jobs in the skilled and semiskilled trades where trade knowledge and special skills are predominant. Morris S. Viteles discounts general intelligence testing in determining vocational fitness, although accepting its value in shutting out the low-grade feeble-minded and in suggesting superior ability for executive posts.[3]

Recent work by L. L. Thurstone and others opens up new possibilities of mental testing in civil service employment. Thurstone developed methods for identifying unit traits, and has now succeeded in isolating

[1] Lewis M. Terman and Maud A. Merrill, *Measuring Intelligence; A Guide to the Administration of the New Revised Stanford-Binet Tests of Intelligence* (1937).

[2] C. S. Yoakum and R. M. Yerkes, *Army Mental Tests* (1920).

[3] Morris S. Viteles, *Industrial Psychology* (1932), p. 133.

a number, among which the factor of general intelligence has yet failed to appear.[1] Seven unit traits clearly identified include S, spacial and visual imagery; P, perception; N, number ability; V, verbal relations; W, word fluency; M, memory; I, induction; two others not so clearly identified are R, reasoning ability, and D, deduction. The process of identifying unit traits has not yet run its course, and it is consequently too early to form an opinion concerning their applicability to civil service examinations. It is possible that examining procedures may be substantially modified.

Another form of capacity or aptitude test is the social intelligence test. This quality is defined as the ability to adjust to new situations involving relations with people and to adopt a course of action which is effective in the sense that it leads others to do consistently and voluntarily the thing it is desired they should do.[2] The value of this characteristic to all civil servants who are in contact with the public, especially policemen, is obvious. So far as is known, however, civil service examiners rarely examine for this quality.

Mechanical intelligence, on the other hand, is more frequently given recognition in civil service examinations. Among the accepted tests in this field are the Stenquist Assembly Test and the Minnesota Mechanical Ability Test. This form of test is useful in the skilled and semiskilled trades and in positions involving skill in the use of clerical machines.

Aptitude tests and the related vocational interest tests are not widely used by civil service commissions, a reflection of the fact that commissions have been chiefly concerned in discovering whether an individual is now prepared to do a given job, rather than to discover his aptitude for a general type of work. The duties of railway postal clerks require memorizing difficult distribution schemes; a test for memory is therefore an obvious part of the examination given applicants for this position. Mosher and Kingsley report that the Detroit Commission has used the Porteus Maze Test in selecting playground directors; the test is designed to measure the individual's planning capacity, prudence and mental alertness. Capacity for accurate observation is a desirable trait in police work, and a number of tests have been devised to measure this characteristic. One form consists of a picture presenting evidence of the commission of a crime from which candidates report the significant

[1] L. L. Thurstone, *Primary Mental Abilities* (1938), and *The Vectors of Mind* (1935).

[2] See an unsigned article, "Partially Standardized Tests of Social Intelligence," 8 *Public Personnel Studies* 73-79 (1930). The George Washington University Series Social Intelligence Test is the principal example. See also F. A. Moss, "Preliminary Report of a Study of Social Intelligence and Executive Ability," 9 *Public Personnel Studies* 2-9 (1931).

facts. The wide variety of aptitude tests which are commonly used in vocational counseling is less frequently encountered in civil service examinations.

Successful public employees are distinguished not merely by adequate general and special abilities, but also by character and personality. Civil service examiners, however, seldom use personality and emotional tests, depending rather upon the probationary period to weed out the emotionally unstable or unfit. Adequate studies to indicate at what point individuals should be barred from examination or employment on account of emotional or personality unfitness have not been made, although it is certain that personality traits count very heavily in maintaining a smooth working organization. Measures of introversion-extraversion, such as the Laird Personal Inventory, C-3; of confidence and sociability, such as the Bernreuter-Flanagan personality inventory; of ascendance-submission, such as the Allport A-S Test; and a variety of other personality tests or inventories have been developed.[1] Their wider use in civil service examinations will probably await much larger appropriations for examiners or much smaller classes of applicants.

From this brief sketch of capacity and aptitude tests we turn to tests of achievement. The traditional academic examination is an achievement test, revealing the amount of knowledge acquired in a given field. Tests of knowledge are the most common form of civil service examinations; they may be, of course, either free answer or short answer. The unwritten nonassembled test involving an evaluation of experience and education is another form of achievement test. The various trade tests are achievement tests. Demonstration tests, such as skill in driving a truck, operating a comptometer or taking dictation, also fall in this category. In general civil service examiners rely on the achievement test, again a reflection of the practical character of American tests. For many types of work they are satisfactory.

Character is tested by inquiry and investigation rather than by formal examinations, although tests for deceit have been invented. The United States Civil Service Commission makes an exceedingly careful character investigation for all law-enforcing positions and positions involving special trust. Only individuals who give every indication of trustworthiness are placed on the eligible lists. The results are sometimes extraordinary. In 1926 the former prohibition unit, to which appointments had been made politically, came under civil service regulations and all incumbents were required to meet the character investigation. Over 2,000 were re-

[1] See Oscar K. Buros, *Educational, Psychological and Personality Tests of 1933/34* (1935); and similar title for 1936.

fused further employment. Generally speaking, the civil service is a moral elite in this and in other countries.

Physical examinations fall in two general groups: the first, which in principle is universal, is designed to ensure freedom from contagious disease or from any condition which would make the applicant a poor risk from the point of view of the retirement fund; the second is designed to ensure the possession of essential physical qualities, such as adequate sight or hearing or the minimum strength requirements for manual labor. Physical examinations are rigid for policeman and fireman, border patrol inspector, coast guard and similar positions, but much less rigorous for the sedentary occupations.

In form, examinations may be written, oral, or demonstration. Most tests are written, either the free answer essay type or the short answer form. The latter includes true-false questions, completions, correspondences, proverbs, word relations and the meaning of words or paragraphs, or questions which can be answered by supplying a date or figure. Difficult and complex case problems may be so presented also as to permit an answer in the form of a specific choice of alternatives. The short answer form is favored by civil service examiners because the answer is objective and certain, scoring is easy and inexpensive, the range is wide, the material is open to standardization and lends itself to a variety of purposes. The weakness of the short answer form is that it gives no evidence of capacity to use English, of originality of mind or quality of knowledge, of ability to prepare analyses of complex material, and similar qualities which may be touched in a free answer test. For some positions these qualities are all-important.

The oral test is the *bête noire* of civil service examiners. It is frequently used in examinations for higher-bracket positions and for those which deal intimately with the public. The object is to assess the personality of the candidates and to eliminate such as seem clearly disqualified by reason of unsatisfactory personal qualities. Personality is not revealed on the written examination and if it is to be dealt with at all, it must be on the basis of an oral interview.

While the object is defensible, great difficulties attend the use of oral tests.[1] The judgments of the examining board are necessarily subjective and have been shown by experiment to be subject to a wide margin of variation. The test situation is somewhat artificial and it is not certain that all candidates do themselves an equal degree of justice. Where, due to large numbers, several examining boards are required on the same test, the possibility of unreliable results rapidly increases. Moreover in case of appeal there is no written or other record to put

[1] The New York Courts adopted a critical view of oral examinations in 1936.

in evidence, and no defense for the usual complaints of prejudice or bias which are brought forward by those rejected. Despite these difficulties, the use of oral tests is increasing rather than diminishing. In some instances a dictaphone record is made of the oral interview in order to reproduce the evidence if the conclusions of the board are challenged. With an examining board which commands public confidence and with precautions to ensure recognition by the examiners of the sources of error, the oral test may add useful data to the information available on the written test. At best, however, it can hardly be expected to do more than to eliminate the clearly unfit or to identify the unusually superior applicants. The interview which usually takes place between the appointing officer and the individuals certified for consideration is another form of the oral test, and one which gives rise to practically no criticism. It is an adequate barrier against the employment of the personality misfits so far as any oral interview may serve to this end, although appointing officers may rightly expect to be spared the task of interviewing the obviously unfit.

So far as they reach, American tests have become progressively more selective; indeed they are much more highly developed than the examining procedures of most foreign countries. They are by no means infallible although they are now rarely poisoned by fraud. Examiners do not yet examine for such important qualities as executive ability capacity to work with others, courage, decisiveness, foresight, ability to handle details, initiative, industry, and emotional balance or self-control. Perhaps these qualities can better be appraised by observation during the probationary period, or be allowed to play their part in the eventual future promotion or lack of promotion.

These brief comments on an extensive and technical subject suggest that modern test construction is a task for an expert. A quarter century ago a school teacher was considered exceptionally well qualified. Today a specific and technical training and considerable experience are essential for proper construction of an examination. This training includes a wide knowledge of the characteristics and requirements of positions. It also requires the technical knowledge of item construction which has been built up in most advanced examining agencies. In such agencies a small number of experts have been at work, for the most part during less than fifteen years. Their contribution has already been substantial and is likely to increase with cumulative force.

Future lines of progress in the testing field are twofold: scientific and administrative. From the scientific point of view, new and better tests will be devised. From the administrative point of view there will be closer coordination between the examinations of different jurisdictions thus avoiding the indefensible waste of repeating the same test at spasmodic intervals for federal, state and city jurisdictions respectively.

3. Certification

The process of recruitment and examination comes to its logical end in the certification of names of eligibles for the consideration of the appointing officer and his selection of an eligible. In most jurisdictions the first three names on the register are certified, and the appointing officer may select any one of these. The rule of three is criticized by some because it opens the door to selection on a party basis. Within limits this is possible and in politically ridden organizations may occur. My observation is that in the federal service it is rare, and that the potential harm is overbalanced by the desirability (in the national government the constitutional necessity) of allowing the appointing officer a minimum of discretion. There are other, and legitimate, criteria of selection for civil service appointment than mere ability to pass examinations, although party affiliation is not one.

In actual practice the process of certification is a high art, since the rule of three is undercut by other requirements. A disabled veteran must be certified first, in some jurisdictions, irrespective of his earned grade; persons on a reinstatement list may have prior claims to those on an original register; a man or a woman may be specified by the appointing officer; two or more registers may compete for use on a given certification; an appointing officer may desire the eligible holding seventh place, and consequently awaits the appointment of those in preferred position. The effective use of registers is made or marred by the wisdom and good sense of those who make up the certificates for consideration for appointment. Often a delicate line has to be drawn between the desires of the operating departments and the requirements of the rule of open competition. While the latter must prevail, it is the duty of the civil service commission to meet so far as possible the needs and preferences of the line agencies, in whose interest the entire procedure is initiated.

Chapter Twenty-one

POSITION-CLASSIFICATION

PRESENT-DAY personnel management rests on two major foundations, tests of fitness and position-classification. Without derogation from other important aspects of personnel work, these are the two essentials. Without each of them the personnel system of any large organization lacks the basis on which most other branches of personnel management depend.[1]

Government requires, as we have already observed, hundreds of thousands of workers, representing almost every vocation, occupation and profession. To deal with every position individually would be chaos; it is necessary to group positions into classes in order to settle readily and wisely prerequisites for employment, questions of pay lines of promotion, requirements for transfer and other day-by-day matters. Hypothetically positions might be grouped on the basis of any one of many criteria, as, for example, the rate of pay, the unit in which the position is located, the necessary education and training, the type and amount of experience required to perform the work, the specific appropriation from which incumbents are paid, or the specific employment law to which they are subject. Experience demonstrates that efficient performance of most personnel operations is facilitated by grouping positions on the basis of their duties and responsibilities.

A well-known classification system is that found in a police force in which the customary ranks rise from the patrolman through the sergeant, lieutenant, captain and police chief. This is primarily a classification by responsibilities rather than by duties; supplementing it are specialized positions in separate duties classifications, such as radio engineer, fingerprint expert, photographer, and garage mechanic. A simple system such as this is inadequate for the complex array of positions found in the civil service as a whole, but the essentials are illustrated in this example. In general terms the objective of a duties classification is to lay the foundation for equitable treatment of public employees.

[1] In preparing this brief summary of a complex subject, I have been greatly aided by the published and unpublished work of Ismar Baruch, chief of the personnel classification division of the United States Civil Service Commission, and one of the principal experts in this field.

by the accurate definition, orderly arrangement, and fair evaluation of positions in the public service.

1. Historical Development of Classification Plans

Although the general ideas underlying position-classification are old, its technique is of relatively recent development. The equity and the administrative logic of using duties and responsibilities as a basis for position-classification were recognized by federal employees and by committees of the United States Congress a century ago,[1] and frequently thereafter; but the actual procedures for developing, installing, and administering a position-classification plan, as we now recognize them, were not devised until 1911. In that year, the first genuine duties classification was installed in Chicago.[2] The experiment aroused widespread interest and even during the World War other cities began to follow. The major impetus to the movement came as a result of the report of the Congressional Joint Commission on Reclassification of Salaries (1920), which, with the classification report for Canada prepared by Arthur Young and Company, gave a reasoned explanation of the theory and practice of the new movement.[3]

In the post-war period, duties classification spread steadily. The federal classification act was put on the books in 1923, largely at the instance of the National Federation of Federal Employees; the postal service was reclassified in 1925; and in 1928 a general survey looking toward the extension of the federal system to the field service was authorized. The depression has delayed legislation authorizing the installation. A survey in 1932 showed that eleven states, a considerable number of the larger cities and a few urban counties had formally adopted a classification system.[4] It is practically impossible to make an exact enumeration, since every jurisdiction necessarily has some record of its positions which it may call a "classification." This may consist solely of a list of occupational titles which are only remotely related to duties and responsibilities, or it may be

[1] See, for example, the following: S. Doc. 71, vol. 1, 25th Cong., 2d sess. (Jan. 3, 1838); S. Doc. 239, vol. 3 (Feb. 26, 1838); S. Res., March 5, 1838. A comprehensive history of federal classification and pay policy is forthcoming by Ismar Baruch.

[2] In view of the low estate to which the Chicago Civil Service Commission later fell, it is of interest to note that in 1914 the Philadelphia Civil Service Commission sent a representative to report on the work of the Chicago Commission. He reported in part, "The activity and advancement of civil service systems in the United States have probably reached the highest point yet attained in the city of Chicago. . . . The Chicago system is entirely built up upon a modern engineering system of efficiency and economy."

[3] Arthur Young and Co., *Report of Transmission to Accompany the Classification of the Civil Service of Canada* (1919); *Report of the Congressional Joint Commission on Reclassification of Salaries*, H. Doc. 686, 66th Cong., 2d sess. (1920).

[4] L. D. White, *Trends in Public Administration* (1933), pp. 255-58.

a system once well planned but allowed to go to wrack and ruin, or it ma be a good duties classification well maintained.

The full influence of the position-classification plan is hardly con veyed by the list of actual adoptions. Among public personnel expert a position-classification plan is universally accepted as the proper an necessary basis on which to erect a sound personnel program. Th technique of position-classification is a rapidly developing art and th influence of classification philosophy is steadily increasing. At th present time there is no American alternative to the major proposition of position-classification on the basis of duties and responsibilitie although there are differences of opinion on specific procedures. Th English classification plan, while similar in fundamentals, varies widel in its application, tending toward a much broader class description tha is favored in this country. In short, among the many devices intro duced in personnel management during the last quarter century, th duties classification ranks as one of the most important and influential.

A position-classification plan in very small towns is reduced to suc a narrow scale that it hardly needs formalization. In towns from 25,00 to 200,000 a formal system is desirable, but major difficulties of admir istration are encountered both in the original development and install tion and in the current maintenance. Outside consultants are usuall relied upon to make the original installation. When these experts hav left town all the pressures for exceptions, for leaving classificatio alone despite change in duties, for preferential treatment for this that class come to bear upon the often very weak defenses provided b the local personnel agency. Before many years the classification pla has not infrequently become only a pale reflection of the actual fact

The most plausible solution of this common small-town problem to rely on a periodic audit by an outside agency. In many states th service can be had from the state league of municipalities. Or alte natively the cities can contract with the state league, with larger neig bors, or with private consultants to carry on current classification wor In some way these cities need help to maintain their classification pla in good order.

There has been some difference of opinion as to whether classificati work should be undertaken by the personnel agency or the centr finance office. A three-man board, representing the former Unit States Bureau of Efficiency, the Bureau of the Budget, and the Ci Service Commission, known as the Personnel Classification Board, in tiated the federal classification plan.[1] The work was transferred to t Civil Service Commission in 1932. In the writer's opinion, the analy

[1] Paul V. Betters, *The Personnel Classification Board* (1931).

of duties and responsibilities and the classification of positions can be handled best by the personnel agency; there are financial implications in the results of classification but they should not be put in a dominating position. The psychology of budget examiners is to avoid expenditures, a point of view which is important but which ought not to govern allocations of positions. The determination of salary scales stands on a different footing, however; it is primarily a fiscal problem.

2. Construction of a Classification Plan

The process of classifying a position involves two major operations: first the construction of the classification plan, and second the allocation of the position to its proper pigeonhole or "class," designated in the plan by a class title.[1]

The construction of a classification plan grows out of and is intimately related to the actual positions which are found in a jurisdiction. In its final form a classification plan consists of a number of classes adequate to enable a place to be found for each existing position, arranged in orderly fashion with respect to each other, and supplemented

[1] There is no systematic study of position-classification. The principal single authoritative presentation is contained in the *Closing Report of Wage and Personnel Survey* (1931) of the U. S. Personnel Classification Board. An excellent general presentation of the whole subject is *Classification and Compensation Plans, Their Development, Adoption, and Administration*, Civil Service Assembly Technical Bulletin 1, 1928.

The Civil Service Assembly also mimeographed the *Report of the Technical Committee on Rules for the Installation and Administration of Classification and Compensation Plans* (1930). A series of papers, chiefly by E. O. Griffenhagen and Fred Telford, in volumes 2 and 3 of *Public Personnel Studies* (1924–25), contain much valuable data.

Recent illustrative classification studies of particular jurisdictions include, among others, Harvey Walker and Fred Telford, *Proposed Classification and Compensation Plan for the Public Service of the State of Ohio* (1931); J. L. Jacobs and Co., *Classification and Compensation Plans of the Personal Service in the Executive Departments of Philadelphia* (1930); U. S. Personnel Classification Board, *Preliminary Class Specifications of Positions in the Field Service* (1931); New York State, *Report of the Joint Legislative Committee on Classification of Positions in the Civil Service* (1932); Commonwealth of Pennsylvania, *Classification and Compensation System of Personnel Service* and supplement (1933); Farm Credit Administration, *Preliminary Class Specifications for Positions in Field Organizations* (1935); Griffenhagen and associates, *Report on Classification and Compensation of Positions in the Service of the Commonwealth of Virginia,* and supplement, *Definitions of Classes of Positions* (1937); Home Owners' Loan Corporation, *Class Specifications for Positions in State and Other Field Offices* (mim. 1938).

General functional classification studies are illustrated by: Bureau of Public Personnel Administration, *Proposed Classification and Compensation Plans for Library Positions* (1927); Federal Board for Vocational Education, *Fire Fighting, an Analysis of the Fireman's Job,* Bulletin 155, 1931; California State Department of Education, *Job Analysis of Police Service*, Bulletin 4, 1933; American Public Welfare Association, *A Public Welfare Job Study* (1938).

by a set of rules and regulations for their administration, interpretation and amendment. The structure of the plan becomes more specific as we examine the fundamental concepts on which it is based. These appear in the ideas of position, class, class specification, service and grade.

The fundamental unit in the classification plan is the position.[1] A *position* is a specific civilian office, employment or job, whether occupied or vacant, calling for the performance of certain duties and the carrying of certain responsibilities by one individual, either on a full-time or a part-time basis. The concept of position is distinct from the concept of employee. A position may be occupied or vacant. It is characterized by its duties and responsibilities and as long as these criteria remain the same, the position remains the same regardless of the fact that it may be occupied by different employees at different times. A position often exists before it is occupied by anyone and it does not necessarily cease to exist with the death, resignation or removal of its incumbent.

These basic units are combined into classes through analysis of their relevant characteristics. A *class* or *class of positions* comprises all positions which are sufficiently similar in respect to their duties and responsibilities so that (a) the same requirements as to education, experience, knowledge and ability may be demanded of incumbents, (b) the same test of fitness may be used to choose qualified employees, and (c) the same schedule of compensation is made to apply with equity under the same or substantially the same employment conditions.

Each class is identified by an explicit statement written in a standardized form and including the essential facts which mark it off from every other class. This statement, called a *class specification* or class description, is defined as a formal statement of the duties and responsibilities of the positions in one class, illustrated by examples of work performed and of the qualification requirements of the positions in the class.[2] It

[1] The following analysis and definitions are borrowed from the standard treatment of classification procedures, *Closing Report of Wage and Personnel Survey* (1931), prepared by the U. S. Personnel Classification Board.

[2] An illustrative class specification, from E. O. Griffenhagen and associates, supplement to *Report on Classification and Compensation of Positions in . . . Virginia* (1937), pp. 315-16, follows:

Senior Factory Inspector Executive

CHARACTERISTIC DUTIES

Under administrative direction, to assist in the formulation of administrative policies pertaining to inspection of industrial plants and other establishments coming within the scope of the State laws and regulations pertaining to labor conditions onsists of four or sometimes five parts: (1) the title of the class; (2) he statement of duties and responsibilities; (3) examples of work perormed or typical tasks; (4) the statement of minimum qualifications; 5) in some systems a statement of lines of promotion and scales of pay.[1]

The term *service* as used in the national government means the broadst division of related classes of positions. It refers to a general aggreation of classes of positions grouped on some broad basis selected to id in the process of classification and of fixing compensation. Positions ow under the Classification Act of 1923 are grouped into five services: he professional and scientific service; the subprofessional service; the lerical, administrative and fiscal service; the custodial service; and the lerical-mechanical service. In other jurisdictions a service may be less nclusive and there may be more of them.

Grade. In the federal classification plan each service is divided into rades ranging from the simplest work in that service to the most diffiult and responsible. The term "grade" means a subdivision of a service, ncluding one or more classes of positions for which comparable basic ualifications and compensation are prescribed, the distinction between rades being based upon differences in the importance, difficulty, reponsibility, and value of the work. To each grade (junior, senior, prinipal and others), it is customary to attach a definite salary range. Like

---

afety of employment, and safety in places of public assembly; to supervise the ork of inspectors; and to do related work as required.

Examples.—Planning, laying out, and directing the work of inspectors; conferring nd advising with superiors and others relative to the administration of the laws nd regulations; seeing to the compilation of statistical data; supervising inquiries nto the practices of private employment agencies and the conditions of employent of women and children; assigning work to and supervising inspectors; reiewing reports of inspectors; conducting special investigations; making periodic nspections in assigned territories; securing evidence, instituting proceedings, and ssisting in prosecutions; conciliating labor disputes; compiling and submitting reorts as required.

QUALIFICATIONS

Minimum Essential.—High school education, preferably completion of a special echnical course in industrial safety, and seven years of industrial plant experience, f which one year shall have been in safety work, or any equivalent combination of ducation and experience; familiarity with modern industrial machinery, processes, nd safety methods, and with the laws and regulations pertaining to industrial safety nd employment of labor; ability to lay out work for others and secure their coperation; ability to secure cooperation of employers and employes and to avoid nnecessary antagonisms; initiative; resourcefulness; good observation; firmness; nd good judgment.

[1] The most elaborate and extensive set of job specifications which has probably ver been prepared is that now in process under the direction of the division of andards and research of the United States Employment Service. These are for se in the first instance by public employment offices. The *Job Descriptions for the 'onstruction Industry* (1936), for example, fill five volumes.

a contour on a topographic map that passes through all points of th same elevation, a grade level marks off within a service all classes o positions of equal importance, difficulty, and responsibility.

The service identification mark in the federal classification plan i by letter: P for professional, CAF for clerical, administrative and fisca and so on. The grades within each service are identified by numbe commencing at the lowest grade with number one, and are designate briefly as P-2, CAF-9, SP-5, etc. Classes are identified not only by th appropriate grade symbol, but also by appropriate titles as well: fo example, *junior* statistician, P-1; *assistant* attorney, P-2; *senior* accoun ant, CAF-10; *principal* bacteriologist, P-6; *principal* aeronautical eng neer, P-6; and so on.[1]

The structure of the classification system, then, is built on the positio and class as the fundamental units; classes involving naturally associate lines of work are grouped into services; different degrees of respons bility are indicated by grades and titles, or in some systems by titl alone. The class is the essential unit.

[1] Using the federal professional and scientific service as an example, we find th following statutory language describing the relative difficulty of work (U.S. Coc [1934 ed.] Title 5, sec. 673):

P-1. "simple and elementary work."

P-2. "work requiring . . . previous experience, and, to a limited extent, th exercise of independent judgment."

P-3. "responsible work requiring extended professional, scientific, or technic training and considerable previous experience."

P-4. "difficult and responsible work requiring considerable . . . training an experience, and the exercise of independent judgment."

P-5. "important specialized work requiring extended . . . training and exper ence, the exercise of independent judgment, and the assumption of r sponsibility for results, or for the administration of a small scientific technical organization."

P-6. "duties . . . to act as assistant head of a major professional or scientif organization, or to act as administrative head of a major subdivision such an organization, or to act as head of a small professional or scie tific organization, or to serve as a consulting specialist, or independent to plan, organize, and conduct investigations in original research or deve opment work in a professional, scientific, or technical field."

P-7. "duties . . . to act as assistant head of one of the largest and most impo tant professional or scientific bureaus, or to act as the scientific and a ministrative head of a major professional or scientific bureau, or to act professional consultant to a department head or a commission or boa dealing with professional, scientific, or technical problems, or to perfor professional or scientific work of equal importance, difficulty and respo sibility."

P-8. "duties . . . to act as the administrative head of one of the largest an most important professional or scientific bureaus, or to perform profe sional or scientific work of equal importance, difficulty and responsibility

Similar definitions were established for the grades in the other services.

The formal enactment of a classification system is usually the duty ›f the legislature. Congress, in the Classification Act of 1923, fixed the nain structure of services and grades, leaving the establishment and lefinition of specific classes to the former Personnel Classification Board, 1ow to the Civil Service Commission. To cover the federal service ›ver 1,500 classes have been found necessary, the population of which nay vary from one to thousands.

Reflection upon the nature of a classification plan reveals that it is elated to the major structural plan of the administrative system. The ;ross structure of an administrative organization normally includes de- artments, bureaus, divisions, and sections or units. If the idea of struc- ure is pushed into the section or unit, the system of classes immediately ppears. The classes of employment are the subdivisions of the small- st unit in the gross structure. They may be illustrated in a particular ection or unit by only one individual or by many individuals. In any ase, the internal relationships defined by the statement of duties and esponsibilities carry the structure of the administrative system to its ›gical conclusion. The classification is the internal structure of the mallest operating unit.

The position-classification plan as a whole is the skeleton on which ıe personnel requirements of the service are built. It is derived from logical analysis of the various types of work and degrees of responsi- ility which are found within public employment. It reduces what may e an exceedingly complicated mass of positions to an orderly relation- ıip and by emphasis upon duties and responsibility aids greatly in ıtelligent consideration of operating problems. It is essential to the evelopment of a career service, because it sets out the successive steps y which a beginner may advance to responsible positions.

The exact description of jobs has sometimes been misunderstood as handicap to the career service idea. This is an error; the difficulty es not in close classification but in too narrow recruiting, inadequate ı-service training and above all in severe limitations on transfer. These andicaps are not essentially related to a system of closely defined classes r grades.

Allocation of Positions to Classes

The construction of a classification system, apart from the pay struc- ıre which is associated with but is a separate entity from the classifi- ıtion plan, involves many intricate and sometimes controversial issues. he real battles start, however, when the allocation of positions to the etwork of classes begins. The assignment of a position to a class deter- ines the scale of pay of the incumbent, and endless pocketbook nerves are likely to be set on edge, either in apprehension or in realization. The allocation also fixes the normal lines of promotion, placing the position in one of the major services. Since the prestige value of a professional service is higher than that of a subprofessional or clerical, there is pressure by marginal groups to secure a professional allocation. Individuals struggle for the best terms they can get, and one class compares its status with the allocation of others. Nor are these isolated episodes occurring once and then forever past; they carry on year after year, with new problems arising as rapidly as old ones are settled.

Other interests are also involved. The taxpaying public is concerned to hold allocation and pay within the strict limits of law; so far as its influence is effective it is deflationary, while that of the employees is naturally inflationary. Bureau chiefs often use their influence for better allocations, since this means they are more certain of satisfying and keeping their better (or favored) employees. Responsible officials are inclined to be impatient of the restrictions of classification and pay scales when they desperately need (or think they need) a certain individua who is already being paid in private employment more than Congres or state legislatures have determined shall be paid for this kind of work in government.

In the midst of these conflicting pressures stands the body author ized to make and enforce the allocation, normally the civil service com mission. Its line of action may be loosely or tightly drawn by a classi fication statute or ordinance, or by the classification plan itself a approved by the chief executive of the jurisdiction. But no law ca or should be drafted so precisely and in so much detail as to exclud the necessity for informed judgment in allocating positions; and n set of class specifications is regarded as a rigid administrative instru ment, unsusceptible of revision upon a proper showing. The law is th outer limit, within which an informed discretion acting on successiv cases gradually sets finer discriminations which, acting as precedent and reflected in revisions of the class specifications, gradually reduc discretion to a minimum.

The process of allocation in a settled system thus becomes one c comparison and of relativity. Ambitious employees search the horizo for favorable omens in the form of comparisons supporting their hope while classification examiners make as objective studies as they ca to discover and record all the precedents, analogies, and differentiatin factors.

A close study of the elaborate techniques of fact-finding, analysi and comparison which have been developed would take us too f afield. The primary task is to ascertain the exact duties and respons bilities of the position; this is sometimes simple, but often requires study over days or weeks. It is necessary to observe at first hand not only what is done but also how it is done, to what extent the work is checked or reviewed, what is the relationship between the duties of the position and the functions of the office in which it is located, and where the position is located in the network of authority and flow of work. Honest differences of opinion develop over the mere facts of luties and responsibilities. One of my vivid recollections as a member of the United States Civil Service Commission is a formal hearing at which a member of an important regulatory commission read a brief ending to show that the classification examiners had misunderstood he duties of a group of positions—a brief which despite its clarity and orce was eventually found itself to rest upon a misapprehension.

In the process of getting at the facts the employee himself and his upervisors naturally have full opportunity to state their case. They o not always agree, and the inquiry not infrequently teaches division nd bureau chiefs much about their own organization. Incidentally, conusion in the distribution of authority, overlapping duties, and other ources of poor administration are almost certain to appear in the process of getting at the facts on which an allocation rests. This is one of e subsidiary but important advantages of a classification plan.

In reaching a conclusion concerning the proper allocation of a posion, a classification investigator and analyst is guided solely by these onsiderations: (a) the field of work, subject matter or activity of a osition; (b) the kind and degree of supervision or authority flowing om higher positions in the organization; (c) the kind and degree of pervision or authority, if any, flowing from the position to subordite positions; (d) responsibilities other than supervisory, if any; (e) e difficulty and complexity of the work; and, to the limited extent at they may not be involved in the foregoing factors, (f) the qualiation prerequisites that are or should be established for employment that position.[1] The analyst has no recommendatory or other author- to modify the assignment of work, or to require changes in internal ganization, or to demote or promote or transfer any employee. He ust take the positions as they are and allocate them as they stand. uite apart from the process of allocation he may informally advise e head of the unit on improvements in organization or assignments work, but this is purely a by-product.

Following this approach, the personnel classification division of the U. S. Civil vice Commission has prepared, out of experience with actual cases, a compresive manual for use in training new classification investigators and analysts in federal service, *The Analysis and Evaluation of the Duties and Responsibilities Positions for Purposes of Classification* (mim. 1934).

The facts once ascertained, the analysis proceeds until the closes available correspondence is discovered in the set of class specification or in the record of other correctly allocated positions. In most in stances, the facts point directly to a given class in a given service There are always marginal cases, however, and it usually is these whic cause the greatest difficulty. In the federal service, a dissatisfied em ployee or administrative officer is entitled to refer a case to the Boar of Appeals and Review, a body of three experienced members of th Civil Service Commission staff who study the case *de novo*. If thei decision is also adverse, he may, and in some cases does secure a hear ing before the Commission as a body. This is a more elaborate pro cedure than obtains in smaller jurisdictions. The decision of the Com mission is final; Congress might make a specific exception for the positio in question but this occurs only in the rarest cases for the highe positions.

In the ordinary course of position-classification a number of con mon operating problems are encountered which throw light upon th inner nature of classification work. The public service is necessaril a constantly changing organism, and a system of allocations which correct at one time will almost certainly be incorrect a year or tw hence. To meet these changes individual cases are constantly brough to the classification examiners when duties have been added or in creased in difficulty or responsibility. When the job has gone dow however, it is not so likely to be reported, notwithstanding the requir ments of law or rule. The only satisfactory remedy is a periodic aud in which all positions are resurveyed.[1] This procedure was initiate about ten years ago in the federal service and has proved so useful the departments that more requests for a general audit are made b them than can readily be handled.

A common fallacy in position-classification is that the allocation a position should take into account the capabilities, qualifications an efficiency of the incumbent. Each employee, it is argued, "stamps h own imprint on his position and consequently positions are seldom t same when occupied by different incumbents." In placement and ser ice rating it is legitimate and even necessary to classify the employ as such, but the pay scale, which is related directly to the classificati plan, has to be based on what the individual employee actually do not what he is qualified to do.[2] Differences of efficiency on a giv

[1] Ismar Baruch, *The Administration of a Classification Plan Through Perio Audits*, Civil Service Assembly Pamphlet No. 5, 1936.

[2] Ismar Baruch, *Facts and Fallacies about Position-Classification*, Civil Serv Assembly Pamphlet No. 10, 1937.

ob are recognized by the different points on the pay scale established or the position, and by early selection of the more efficient for pronotion to the next higher class or grade.

Any fixed or statutory system of pay scales in which the applicaility of a given pay scale depends on the allocation of the position nder the classification plan will have the occasional effect of preventing he public service from employing individuals who are well qualified, erhaps peculiarly qualified for a particular office or employment. This esults from the fact that such individuals may be earning a larger alary in private employment than the government can offer. Heavy ressure is sometimes brought to bear upon the classification agency to uthorize a higher classification (and consequently better pay) which vould attract the desired individual. These "special cases," which are sually in the highest brackets, are often especially difficult; no question f politics or favoritism is involved and there is no doubt that the indiidual is really exceptionally qualified. A change in allocation to a higher lass or grade than that which was originally determined (if correct) vould, however, be a plain violation of the standards fixed by legistive or other authority and is beyond the power of the classification gency. The problem is primarily one of pay levels and not positionassification.

Allocation to a specific grade or class increases in difficulty with the umber of grades or classes and the consequent diminution of their spective spans. Within the allocating authority of the civil service ommission there are fifteen grades in the federal clerical-administrave-fiscal service, a number which is more defensible as a means of curing flexibility of administration than as a means of sharply differenating levels of responsibility. In any event marginal cases will occur, d a large number of grades or classes results in greater homogeneity ithin each of them.

The correct classification of positions is clearly a difficult and hazdous task. To perform it well requires classification investigators and alysts who are both technically proficient and endowed with more an an average degree of social intelligence, since their opportunity create enmity as well as disappointment is almost without bounds. hey must be so eminently fair that even disappointed employees and ministrative officers will recognize their fairness; they must possess e impartiality and objectivity of the judge while collecting the evince and examining the witnesses. They must acquire a knowledge the organization and functions of the department in which a classifiion is made comparable with that possessed by most of those employed in the department, as well as a much greater knowledge abou corresponding or analogous organizations or functions elsewhere. They must have exceptional capacity to get at the facts, to weigh their rela tive importance, and to reason from them. They must have a govern ment-wide, not an insular viewpoint. Their first loyalty is to th position-classification plan and to the civil service commission, bu they must also recognize a responsibility to aid the departments to th utmost, within the terms of the law or position-classification plan. Thei recommendations are likely to be conclusive, but they must guar against the illusion of omnipotence. They require plenty of courag because their conclusions are likely to be attacked from high quarter but while they must be steadfast they cannot be stubborn. They mus in addition have technical competence: trained ability to write specifi cations, wide and specific knowledge of occupations, and a thoroug knowledge of the general principles and objectives of position-classifi cation.

These are difficult specifications but they are approximated by class fication technicians in all the stronger jurisdictions. Unless the front line trenches are manned by first-class troops, the battle to maintain a equitable and consistent classification system is soon lost; and in to many instances this outcome may be discerned.

4. Uses of a Classification Plan

Position-classification on the basis of duties and responsibilities w originally devised in order to secure a closer approximation of the ru of "equal pay for equal work." Favoritism of the rankest sort had cre in under cover of fancy position titles, and even where outright pre erence was missing there was only the vaguest correspondence betwe work and pay. The inevitable result was resentment or discourageme on the part of some and intrigue on the part of others, with grou morale shattered in consequence.[1] Pressure over many years had usual resulted in substantial total overpayments. A sound classification pla currently maintained has demonstrated its capacity substantially to elin inate this serious fault.

[1] The situation had become so serious in the federal service by 1920 that the Co gressional Joint Commission made the following finding: "The Commission fin that there is serious discontent, accompanied by an excessive turnover and lo among the best trained and most efficient employees; that the morale of the pe sonnel has been impaired; that the national service has become unattractive to a sirable type of technical employee; and that the government has put itself in t position of wasting funds on the one hand and doing serious injustice to individu on the other. . . ." H. Doc. 686, 66th Cong., 2d sess. (1920), p. 54.

Other phases of personnel work are also aided by a good classification plan. The minimum qualifications developed in class specifications provide the foundation on which examination prerequisites are based and suggest the subject matter of the examination. The examination prerequisites are usually more closely drawn than the minimum qualifications. Before the modern duties classification, civil service examiners were often puzzled to know for what to test, since all kinds of employment were in fact concealed under such general titles as clerk or file clerk. With all like positions sorted into one homogeneous class, it is possible to prepare an intelligent examination, but not otherwise.

A classification plan is also essential as the basis for an orderly system of promotions and transfers. Without it, the duties performed under one title may have little or no relation to the duties performed under a similar or corresponding title carrying a lower or higher salary. The ack of arrangement or the disarrangement of positions in relation to luties and responsibilities would prevent the intelligent development of promotional avenues. Proper outlets for promotion would be frequently obscured by misleading titles in higher posts. Eligibility for promotion to a higher position would rest less on qualifications arising rom knowledge of duties, more on the somewhat fortuitous correpondence of often meaningless titles.

The operation of a service record (or efficiency rating) plan is likewise facilitated by a good classification plan. All the employees in a iven class can be judged on their performance on a single or homoeneous type of work, rather than on many different and even unrelated inds of work.

Budget estimates for personnel become intelligible only through the ise of the meaningful titles and symbols involved in a duties classifiation. Budget examiners can form no reasonable estimate of the actual ersonnel needs of a department when the work of its employees is isguised by fictitious titles. When, on the other hand, positions are orted out into homogeneous classes, it is much more feasible to judge hether the estimates are well founded or are inflated.

A position-classification plan also tends to eliminate the evil of specific alary legislation for individual employees or minority groups. Salary evels are enacted by the appropriating body, not individual salaries. s a result the personal lobbying for salary increases which disgraced ome city halls has greatly diminished and in many places has praccally disappeared. Most city councilmen, state legislators and Conressmen welcome relief from this type of personal pressure, but a few still try to manipulate the classification system to secure favors for their friends.[1]

These are the principal uses to which the duties classification is put. Taken together they comprise assets of first-rate importance. Position-classification on the basis of duties and responsibilities has introduced order into a chaotic situation. It has improved the conditions of work and the morale of the public service. It is supported by most organized civil service groups as the principal safeguard against favoritism and the principal source of fair and equitable treatment. It advances the interests of the employees, the management, the legislative body and the taxpayers. While differences of opinion often exist concerning the correctness of an individual allocation, there are almost no differences of opinion concerning the usefulness, indeed the necessity of a well-planned, currently maintained classification plan.

[1] Before 1910 the finance committee of the Chicago City Council recommended for individual employees, instead of positions. Kingsbury states that the committee was occupied for weeks and sometimes months, while the corridors would be filled with employees waiting for a personal hearing. By 1915 lobbying for personal increases was practically eliminated (although it later reappeared) and the budget carrying standard rates of pay for standard positions, was passed "without change and practically without debate." Joseph B. Kingsbury, "The Merit System in Chicago from 1895 to 1923," a series of articles in *Public Personnel Studies,* vols. 3 and 4 (1925–1926).

Chapter Twenty-two

COMPENSATION

THE amounts annually paid in salaries and wages to public employees and officials in the United States are staggering. A reasonable estimate places the figure at approximately $4,000,000,000. In times of prosperity these huge sums arouse little attention, but in times of depression they are an easy mark for controversy and attack. Exaggerated claims are put forward about possible savings on behalf of the hard-pressed taxpayer, and a latent conflict of interest flares into open assault and spirited defense.

The general considerations governing pay in the public service consequently become of great importance. Unwise pay policy probably can cause more havoc in the morale of a public service than any other influence. However, until very recent years the adjustment of wages and salaries was on anything but a sound or systematic basis, and was characterized by gross inequalities which led to the invention and installation of the classification technique described in the previous chapter.

1. Development of Pay Policy

The history of public pay policy in the federal service was sketched in 1920 in studies preparatory to the Classification Act of 1923. The general situation was summarized in this statement.

> The only conclusion that can be drawn from these varied rates of increase is that the Government raises salaries only when it is forced to do so in order to keep its employees, and then only so far as to withstand outside competition. When there is no such competition, . . . salaries tend to remain stationary, or are advanced slowly and uncertainly to an extent which is wholly insufficient to meet the increase in the cost of living. This policy of drift is the more easily followed because Government employees have never shown any inclination to a strike, have only recently organized themselves into a union, and have made it one of the basic principles of that union that they shall neither themselves strike nor be called upon to support any strike against the Government.[1]

[1] Mary Conyngton, "The Government's Wage Policy During the Last Quarter Century," 10 *Monthly Labor Rev.* 1325-41 (1920). See also the confirming data in New York Senate Committee on Civil Service, *Report in Relation to the Standardization of the Public Employments of the State*, S. Rept. 40 (1916); *Report*

For many years in the federal service prior to 1923, basic salaries were fixed either by specific enactment of individual salaries in the so-called "statutory roll," or by administrative discretion within the terms of a lump sum appropriation. In the one case there was no administrative discretion; in the other there was no legislative control. During the war the competition between appointing officers who could offer the salary necessary to secure an acceptance and those whose hands were tied by salary amounts stated in specific appropriations led to a demoralizing competitive bidding for employees. This in turn induced legislative restrictions on transfers so rigid as to result in grave injustice and serious handicaps to good administration. For the same kind of work highly variable rates of pay were actually in force, a reflection of the absence of any central control over the relationship between salaries and duties.

The deadlock between a Congress unwilling to yield control over scales of pay and a service which was being ruined by lack of proper administrative discretion in adjusting pay was broken in 1923 by the device of position-classification. Control and discretion were balanced each against the other in proportions which experience is proving to be basically sound.

Conditions equally unsatisfactory were practically universal throughout the states and cities.[1] In some cases control over compensation was part of the political domination of public offices; in others, unsavory combinations were made between leaders of organized employee groups and members of city councils. In the old days, aldermen and county commissioners and legislators in state and nation played a complicated game of personal favors and punishments with the pay checks of friends and enemies. This practice, ruinous to the morale of any group, still flourishes in a few jurisdictions and lingers to a small degree in more. Prior to 1910 the broad generalization holds that no reasoned plan or program existed to handle the various phases of the compensation problem. Methods were slovenly, unsystematic and wasteful even

of the Congressional Joint Commission on Reclassification of Salaries, H. Doc. 686, 66th Cong., 2d sess. (1920); U. S. Personnel Classification Board, *Report of Wage and Personnel Survey*, H. Doc. 602, 70th Cong., 2d sess. (1929), and *Closing Report of Wage and Personnel Survey* (1931).

[1] Of New York it has been said, "In the history of the state government there has never been—and there is not at the present time—an exact or logical basis for fixing salary rates or titles of positions. Standards of compensation as a basis for making salary appropriations are unknown. Civil service employments are from the viewpoint of salary standards and related working conditions in a chaotic state. . . In a large number of cases, salaries are fixed by accident, expediency, or political preference. Increases in salary have been irregular, uncertain, and too often without regard to the relative merit of employees."

where they were not shady. They fulfilled none of the requirements of good administration and served neither the interests of the employees, of the government, or of the taxpayer. They lent themselves to sharp practice, collusion, and gross discrimination.

2. Major Objectives

These historical notes suggest the main purposes which a compensation plan should seek. They include (a) an equitable relationship between the salaries and wages of public employees and those of corresponding classes of private employment; (b) an equitable relationship between the salaries of individuals performing the same kind of work; (c) a fair relationship between the salaries of individuals doing different kinds of work; (d) reasonable promptness in adjusting salaries to changing price levels; (e) reasonable opportunity for presentation of claims and grievances and of different points of view.[1] In the following discussion it will be assumed that a sound classification plan has been developed and installed. The pay structure is intimately related to the classification plan, but is an independent entity.[2]

a. Public and private pay levels. A consideration of the relation between public and private pay levels requires attention to at least three occupational groups: the organized crafts, public employments having substantial counterparts in industry, and employments peculiar to the public service. The organized crafts usually receive the same hourly wage scale in the public service as prevails in private employment in the locality. Laws or rules frequently provide for payment of the "prevailing wage," and public pay scales follow private pay levels. As a result the craftsman employed by government usually benefits by a substantial margin when reckoned either in relative annual earnings or otherwise. He has the advantage of regular employment, less hazard of lay-off, no strikes, assured vacation and sick leave, and in many instances a retirement allowance. Accident compensation is usually the same as in private industry.

A second large group comprises employees found in both public and private enterprise, such as typists, stenographers, clerks, bookkeepers, accountants, draftsmen, nurses, operators of business machines, and the like. The general rule in this group is that public levels of compensation tend to follow those already established in the competitive labor market. Most pay structures worked out in connection with position-classi-

[1] An excellent discussion of pay policy is found in Herman Feldman, *A Personnel Program for the Federal Civil Service*, H. Doc. 773, 71st Cong., 3d sess. (1931).

[2] Theoretical consideration of the various bases upon which salary and wage levels rest, or may rest, is available in such volumes as Paul H. Douglas, *The Theory of Wages* (1934); E. M. Burns, *Wages and the State* (1926).

fications are based on elaborate surveys of industrial pay levels. The theoretical reasons for attempting to secure a reasonable correspondence in this respect are obvious. A scale of pay in public employment higher than that in corresponding private circles is likely to lead to complaints from taxpayers as well as from private concerns competing in the same labor market. A scale of pay below the industrial level means failure to attract and to keep a desirable type of employee in the public service. The mass of positions in this group are found outside government and in consequence the general level of industrial compensation has a strong influence on the level in the public service for the same kinds of employment.

But certain qualifications and exceptions require notice. The scales of pay in the public service are very much less flexible than those in competitive undertakings. A pay structure once set by legislative enactment stands unmoved by ordinary oscillations. Changes occur, but with nothing like the rapidity or extent which characterize private scales of pay, especially during a period of rapidly rising costs of living or the disturbed years of an economic depression. In time of falling industrial pay scales, the public service benefits; but when industry raises its bids for workers, government is not able to compete by rapid upward adjustments of its own salaries.

A second qualification: in the federal service, pay levels below $2,000 per annum tend to be somewhat higher than for corresponding types of work outside; but in the higher levels the public scales are progressively less than those in the industrial world. A recent proposal to increase from $9,000 to $15,000 the maximum under the Classification Act of 1923 failed to receive serious consideration by Congressmen, whose salaries are $10,000 per annum. Some federal agencies have been handicapped seriously by the relatively low salaries in higher brackets, especially by failure to recruit or hold unusually competent executives, lawyers, economists and scientists. The same general situation prevails in state and municipal government. In the latter, the modest margin between the pay envelopes of organized workers and the pay checks of their administrative or professional supervisors is often painfully apparent.

The third group of occupations to be considered in this problem includes employments peculiar to the public service—postal clerks and carriers, street cleaners, police and firemen, customs inspectors, penitentiary guards, and others. No direct comparison with industry is possible. Analogy supplies a general guide, comparing these with other types of employment requiring similar education and experience and involving corresponding degrees of responsibility. In the municipal field, the most common comparisons are those made with other cities. Thus the Chicago rates of pay for policemen are definitely influenced by the New York scales.

From the point of view of the public service it is desirable that scales of pay compare favorably with salary rates elsewhere. Real compensation, however, is not measured merely by the number of dollars and cents per hour or month. The public service, especially where the merit system prevails, possesses the important assets of relative security of tenure, generous sick and annual leave provisions, old-age pension (now paralleled, but not equaled by the provisions of the Social Security Act for large groups of nonpublic employees) and hours of work which for many years were shorter than those of private corporations and which are likely to be always as short as those imposed by government upon industry. While the public service may capitalize these and other advantages, they may be offset to some extent by uncompensated overtime and other disadvantages.

Broad social considerations make it desirable that the government accept the role of the "model employer." This is an application of the "yardstick" doctrine which is making its way as a means of setting standards for social amelioration. It is also good business, for pay levels which workers recognize as favorable and which taxpayers accept as reasonable are one of the most important bases of efficient service and high morale. Candor compels one to add that the doctrine of the "model employer" has been effectively accepted in few jurisdictions, the Tennessee Valley Authority and the Panama Canal Zone being conspicuous illustrations of good practice.

The pay levels in the various grades and services of the federal government are shown at the end of this chapter.

b. Pay relation between individuals performing the same type of work. This compensation problem is solved by a duties classification plan, properly administered. Placing all positions similar in duties, in responsibilities, and in difficulty of work in the same class almost automatically realizes the doctrine of equal pay for equal work, omitting for the moment individual differences in productivity. Borderline cases will always be present, where differences of opinion as to proper classification and pay may arise. In general, however, the claim is well founded that in the departmental service in Washington, in the postal service, and in well-administered classifications in the states and cities, a fair relationship has been worked out between persons performing the same kind of work. This achievement represents a notable advance beyond the chaotic situation prevailing in 1910.

c. Pay relations between different kinds of work. Acceptance by government of the "prevailing rate" sidesteps one of the most difficul compensation problems, that of determining the relative value of on kind of employment as compared with another. Should a court stenographer, for instance, receive more or less than a junior engineer or janitor? There is no compelling answer to such a question and no accepted method of reaching a conclusion. The labor market reaches conclusion on the balance of many complex forces and circumstances The relative standards thus developed may be criticized, especially a points where a decent minimum is not sustained, but there is no genera alternative for government short of an arbitrary standard set in th light of principles which are certain to be challenged. There is a desirable tendency in government to set a minimum wage, however, independent of the labor market.

d. Adjustment of salaries and wages to changes in the cost of living Abrupt changes in the general level of the cost of living quickly throw established pay structures out of gear. Two such crises have develope in recent years—one during the World War, the other during the depression. In the former case, federal employees at the lower pay level were given a horizontal increase, popularly called a "bonus," over an above the regular pay which with some exceptions eventually amounte to $240. The bonus was a crude and unsatisfactory device which exaggerated some of the inequalities already serious enough. In 1923 th bonus was absorbed in the new scales of pay. These scales were raise in 1928, and again slightly in 1930.

During the depression the cost of living was substantially reduced To meet the crisis caused by shrinkage in revenue and increased expenditure, wages and salaries of public employees and officials wer reduced in most jurisdictions. In the federal service a fifteen per cen cut was introduced upon all wage and salary payments, which wa gradually reduced to ten and five per cent before its termination in 1935

The most careful method of adjustment of salaries to cost of livin has been worked out in St. Paul. Originating in 1920 and dropped fo five months during the depression on account of the resistance of city employees whose salaries were being adversely affected, this plan provides for a semi-annual adjustment of salaries and wages to correspon to the index of the cost of living. As prices rise, wages follow; as price drop, wages decline.[1]

It is desirable that scales of pay in the public service be reasonably

[1] J. B. Probst, "The St. Paul Plan of Adjusting Salaries to Cost of Living," 1 *Pub. Man.* 163-66 (1933). For an analogous plan effective in the British Civil Service from 1920 to 1933, see the author's *Whitley Councils in the British Civil Servic* (1933), pp. 165-72.

stable, from which it follows that they must be fixed neither at a mere subsistence level nor at a level far above that established by the better private employers. They should stand at a point where some fluctuation in the scales of the competitive labor market, up or down, will not throw official scales too obviously out of line. If employees are expected to carry the margin of loss in purchasing power when cost-of-living levels rise, the government may properly be expected to carry the load of unusually favorable scales of pay when the cost of living and competitive wages fall. In either case, if the maladjustment continues over a period of time or is severe, changes in pay structure, up or down, may be expected to follow.

e. Collective bargaining on pay issues. In Great Britain elaborate arrangements have been developed since 1920 to permit employees or their representatives and employee organizations to confer with departmental officials on pay questions. These arrangements include (1) opportunity for the staff to discuss changes in the scale of pay or increments; (2) opportunity to require arbitration on compensation issues before the Industrial Court; (3) proposal of individuals or groups deserving of promotion; (4) appeal from selections for promotion actually proposed.

Obviously British civil servants have privileges not common in this country. Here employees are heard informally or formally on matters touching their interest, especially when they are organized. In point of fact, changes in scales of pay favorable to the federal employees are usually initiated and pushed through Congress by their representatives, and similar activity is common where municipal or state unions exist. Likewise reductions in pay are resisted by concerted action.

The pay problem in the United States is not one, however, which the employees *as a group* ordinarily deal with in individual cases. Administrative officials grant or withhold pay changes to their subordinates without outside intervention except in cases of apparently flagrant injustice. Nor is there any tribunal of appeal other than the appropriating body and the public except where the correctness of a classification is challenged.

The process of collective bargaining which is the normal method of fixing scales of pay for many types of industrial employment is consequently extremely attenuated in the public service. Some declare with their eyes on the sovereign power of the state and the formal appropriating procedure that it does not exist. This view overlooks the realities of the situation, for the weight of organized employees does count in the decision. Negotiations take place between mayors and finance committees on the one hand and organized city employees on the other in which conflicting forces reach an adjustment. A mayor in a precarious political situation may be hard pressed by the municipal unions in the negotiations. The major organizations of federal employees maintain effective lobbies in Washington highly skilled in negotiation to extract the last bit of favorable consideration for their proposals.

The employee relationship policy of the Tennessee Valley Authority accepts the principle of collective bargaining (sec. 3) as a means of determining the prevailing rate of wages for laborers and mechanics. The rates are established annually on the basis of a thoroughgoing study by the Personnel Department and direct discussions with the representatives of organized labor. The contacts between management and employees have been cordial and the results of this form of collective bargaining, in the shape of good morale and absence of friction, are impressive.[1]

Normally the process of collective bargaining in the public service does not proceed to the ultimate test of a strike. In numerous instances in Chicago and elsewhere, however, particular groups of employees have quit their jobs to demonstrate their power, and in one exceptional case in Chicago they were tacitly supported by the mayor and some members of the council. As a rule, however, collective bargaining in the public service is a process *sui generis*. But in the recognized crafts, government accepts the results of private collective bargaining, fixing standard rates of pay for skilled and unskilled labor.[2]

3. Other Aspects of Pay Policy

In conclusion brief notice may be taken of certain more technical aspects of compensation structure and policy. Good practice now provides, in lieu of a single flat rate, compensation schedules or pay ranges. These comprise a minimum, a series of increments, and a maximum the number of increments being commonly five. Advances by increments are usually authorized by administrative direction within the limits of current appropriations. These increments make it possible to differentiate between good and passable work in a given group. In the national service, the award of increments is related to the efficiency ratings. As a rule entrance to a grade or class is required at the minimum salary and usually there are provisions governing the rate of advancement within the pay range.

[1] Floyd W. Reeves, "Personnel Administration in the Tennessee Valley Authority," 2 *Southern Economic J.* 61-74 (April, 1936). The employee relationship policy is reprinted in full in this article; it is also separately printed by the T.V.A.

[2] See ch. 28 for further discussion of employee organization and activities.

Whether or not increments should be granted automatically year by year for satisfactory service remains an open question. A considerable proportion of the national service enjoys automatic increments, including the Post Office; inspectors in the Immigration and Naturalization Service; certain groups in the Bureau of Customs; the Foreign Service; the commissioned officers in the Coast and Geodetic Survey, the Coast Guard; the Public Health Service; and the District of Columbia policemen, firemen, and school teachers. They are standard practice in the army, navy, and marine corps. All automatic increments, however, were suspended by act of Congress during the depression. Teachers in city schools frequently enjoy automatic increments, as well as police and fire forces. The clerical services on the other hand seldom enjoy this privilege.

From the point of view of the employees automatic increments are naturally preferred. From the point of view of the public they are also desirable, provided supervisory officers have courage enough to withhold them for unsatisfactory service. The danger is that mediocre work will be accepted and increments allowed so long as an employee is retained, thus destroying an important incentive to efficient work. In any event the employee rises only to the top point of a given scale, and does not automatically proceed onward to a higher scale. Needless to say it is unfortunate for part of a service to secure automatic advances while others equally deserving are denied increases either by lack of a system, or by failure to appropriate, or by administrative action.

One aspect of an automatic increment system is that within a few years most members of a given group, if relatively stable, may be paid at the maximum of the range for that class. To avoid this outcome under the Classification Act of 1923, where the increments are largely discretionary, Congress established a requirement of law known as the "average provision," which provides that "the average of the salaries of the total number of persons under any grade in any bureau, office, or other appropriation unit shall not at any time exceed the average of the compensation rates specified for the grade. . . ." In a largely populated grade in a given bureau this provision is administratively feasible. In a small group it operates to cause the greatest administrative difficulties. When a grade becomes "locked," by reason of having reached this average, new employees coming in at the minimum can receive no increments, nor can older employees with excellent efficiency ratings receive an increase in pay until the blockade is broken by the death, resignation, or transfer of one or more employees from the group. So serious were the inequities caused by the "average provision" clause that in 1931 the Personnel Classification Board recommended its repeal, but Congress has not yet (1938) taken action.

Despite some discussion of the desirability of geographic differentials in compensation scales, the national government disregards differences in regional cost of living. The Personnel Classification Board reached the conclusion in 1931 that "The injustice, uncertainty, controversy, and administrative difficulty which would be caused in an attempt to carry out such a system broadly would more than offset its benefits to the government or to the employees as a whole." [1] Experience with differential scales of pay under the Public Works Administration tends to confirm this conclusion, although the U. S. Wages and Hours Act

United States Classification Pay Scale

Act of March 4, 1923, as amended

Service and Grade[a]		Compensation Range							Service and Grade	
P	CAF	A	B	C	D	E	F	G	CU	SP
		600	600	660	720	780	840	840	1	
		1020	1080	1140	1200	1260	1320	1380		1
		1080	1140	1200	1260	1320	1380	1380	2	
		1200	1260	1320	1380	1440	1500	1500	3	
	1	1260	1320	1380	1440	1500	1560	1620		2
		1320	1380	1440	1500	1560	1620	1680	4	
	2	1440	1500	1560	1620	1680	1740	1800		3
		1500	1560	1620	1680	1740	1800	1860	5	
	3	1620	1680	1740	1800	1860	1920	1980		4
		1680	1740	1800	1860	1920	1980	2040	6	
	4	1800	1860	1920	1980	2040	2100	2160		5
		1860	1920	1980	2040	2100	2200	2300	7	
1	5	2000	2100	2200	2300	2400	2500	2600	8	6
	6	2300	2400	2500	2600	2700	2800	2900	9	7
2	7	2600	2700	2800	2900	3000	3100	3200	10	8
	8	2900	3000	3100	3200	3300	3400	3500		
3	9	3200	3300	3400	3500	3600	3700	3800		
	10	3500	3600	3700	3800	3900	4000	4100		
4	11		3800	4000	4200	4400	4600			
5	12		4600	4800	5000	5200	5400			
6	13		5600	5800	6000	6200	6400			
7	14			6500	7000	7500				
8	15			8000	8500	9000				
9	16			In excess of 9000						

[a] Symbols as follows: P, Professional; CAF, Clerical, Administrative and Fiscal; CU, Custodial; SP, Sub-Professional.

[1] U. S. Personnel Classification Board, *Closing Report of Wage and Personnel Survey* (1931), p. 298.

of 1938 recognized regional wage differentials in private industry. A few exceptions to the standard rates exist in the federal service. Thus employees of the Panama Canal in the Canal Zone have a differential of twenty-five per cent of their basic salary. But postal employees have uniform rates in all parts of the country, a precedent which stands against the recognition of geographic differentials in other parts of the service.[1]

If, however, we examine the compensation levels collectively in state and municipal governments, we observe definite broad geographic differentials, corresponding in general to the wage and salary level of the community and region. Thus public service scales are lower in the south than in the north. Careful study would doubtless demonstrate also that rural scales are substantially lower than urban levels in the same section, and that rates of pay for organized groups are relatively higher than for the unorganized.

[1] Geographic differentials are common in other countries. In Great Britain, the provincial rates are less than those in greater London. In Switzerland a number of differentials are recognized, including one for employees in places over 3,000 meters above sea level.

Chapter Twenty-three

EDUCATION AND TRAINING FOR THE PUBLIC SERVICE

1. Trends

The history of education and training for the public service in the United States falls into three periods. Of these the first, during which training was almost entirely confined to the military, naval, and educational services, terminated in 1906 with the foundation of the New York Bureau of Municipal Research and its training school; the second ended with the World War, which interrupted a healthy growth of interest in public service training along many lines; finally, commencing about 1920–1922 a renewed drive toward old goals has swept forward with increasing strength and ever broader achievements. In 1938 training opportunities in federal, state, and municipal governments were widespread, were multiplying rapidly on all fronts and were steadily building up higher standards of performance.

The underlying conditions and the training developments in each of these three periods may profitably be examined more closely. From early years when the doctrine of rotation in office became a fixed national policy to the opening of the twentieth century, the public services were characterized almost without exception by the dominance of laissez faire philosophy. Hence they were restricted in scope and were predominantly clerical and record-keeping in character. Furthermore the various departments and offices were strongly political, definitely nonprofessional, and from time to time were swept bare by the change of party control.

As a direct result, training for civil employment was scattered and inconsequential, with the exception of the teachers in the public school system. Two conspicuous training institutions were connected with the armed forces, West Point and Annapolis. In 1883 Massachusetts Institute of Technology commenced specific training for public health services, but no degrees were granted until much later. In short, training for the public service, prior to 1906, was practically limited to the educational field, where a professional status developed at an early date and where permanent tenure was making strides both in law and in practice. In the great bulk of the service, there was no training; indeed the basic prerequisites for a training program were wanting.[1]

This unfortunate state of affairs did not pass unchallenged. The municipal reformers and the civil service reformers never tired of denouncing the unsatisfactory character of the public service. Since 1883 there has been a steady extension of permanent tenure for civil employees under federal, state and municipal civil service laws and ordinances; permanent public employees have replaced the shifting groups of political henchmen. Gradually, too, the idea took root that the rule of merit as tested by examination should be applied to promotions as well as to entrance. With increasing momentum, professional interests began to loom up in the civil service; engineers and lawyers found working beside them medical men, laboratory technicians, statisticians, and economists. This reflected the passing of laissez faire and marked the accelerating expansion of public functions with emphasis upon regulatory activities. Technical operations (as in conservation, valuation of public utilities, factory inspection and industrial safety) supplemented the old record-keeping operations. With the turn of the century the muckraking period solidified a public demand for higher standards of character and competence.

Out of this changing order developed for the first time an effective interest in training for civil employment. The founding of the New York Bureau of Municipal Research in 1906 symbolized a new order. One of its earliest interests was training for city service; the election of John Purroy Mitchel as Mayor of New York in 1912 opened the door to placement of trained persons on a scale which attracted nationwide attention. Other cities, including the new council manager towns, took note, and from 1910 to 1917 there was intense interest in the municipal service and in training for a professional career therein, especially among young college men whose idealism was challenged by these new perspectives.

At the University of Wisconsin President Van Hise built a strong bridge between the university and the state service. Faculty members secured important appointments in the state administration and state officials lectured in university halls, while among the students arose an unexampled interest in public affairs. Paul Reinsch, John R. Commons, Richard Ely and Charles McCarthy illustrate the distinguished group which united the state university and the state and national governments. During these years, progressive Wisconsin and reformed New

[1] A brief sketch of the history of public service training is found in O. Glenn Stahl, *Training Career Public Servants for the City of New York* (mim. 1936), Ph.D. thesis, New York University.

York pioneered new ideals of public service training and official careers.

New ideas and enthusiasm were obviously bubbling in the years subsequent to the foundation of the New York Bureau of Municipal Research. Absorption in the gigantic events of the war, its aftermath of "normalcy" in government and business, the reaction against Wilsonian liberalism and reform all took heavy toll. For five years (1917–1922) special training for the American administrative system marked time.

While the span of years in the third period of development runs from about 1922 to the present, the tone was given not by the boom years prior to 1929 but by the subsequent depression years. The stage was set in 1931 by the University of Minnesota Conference on Training for the National Service. Recent training developments have been influenced by fierce competition for employment, public or private, stressing again the value of special preparation; by a new emphasis in government operations which may be broadly characterized as social service in nature (relief, employment, public works, social security); by the relative prominence of public as contrasted with private undertaking; by the greatly enlarged consequences of success or failure which now attach to government operations as compared with the day when they were record-keeping in character; and consequently by wider recognition of the necessity for high-grade and well-prepared personnel.

The general drift of opinion at the present time with reference to training for the public service may be summarized in these terms. There is a growing acceptance of the need for training at various stages. There is a much clearer recognition of the difference between preentry education for the public service (in the French phrase, *préparation*) and in-service or post-entry training (*formation*). There is a gradual recognition of the relation between examination procedures and training programs. Among the colleges and universities there is marked expansion of "training" for the public service, due in part to the closing of normal channels of employment during the depression.

Within the last twenty years a number of university programs have been well established, partly for students contemplating public service, partly for officials.[1] Among them may be mentioned:

a. The School of Citizenship and Public Affairs at Syracuse University, 1924. Syracuse now trains men for city manager posts and positions in other fields of administration in a two-year course.

[1] For the voluminous literature, some of it ephemeral, see Dorothy C. Culver *Training for Public Service: A Bibliography* (mim. 1937).

b. The training program of Cincinnati University, 1927. This is characterized by a connection with a strong engineering school and by alternate study-work periods. Courses are offered for engineers, nontechnical students, and public welfare students, with interneship arrangements in the city government.

c. Princeton University School of Public and International Affairs, 1930, devoted to the training of men who expect to enter public life or public administration or engage in international business and affairs, or enter journalism or law.

d. The University of California which, since 1920, has sent a considerable number of men from its department of political science into the state and municipal service, and which gives advanced training to men in the public service.

e. The courses in public administration at the University of Southern California, Los Angeles, which cater especially to men and women in the city and county services of Los Angeles and environs by extensive short courses and summer courses. The first short course was held in 1928.

f. The University of Minnesota, which in the last decade has held many short courses for municipal and county officials, and which instituted in 1936 a new training program including interneships and in-service fellowships.

g. American University, which initiated an in-service training program for federal employees in Washington in 1935 with early emphasis upon personnel and finance administration.

h. The Institute of Public Affairs, a Washington, D. C., nonprofit-making organization which (since 1936) has administered a joint graduate study-interneship program for about forty fellows selected on a national basis.

i. Harvard University's Littauer Graduate School of Public Administration, founded in 1936 and devoted principally to aiding men already established in city, state or federal administration.

These are only some examples of an impressive contemporary movement. They omit the contribution of many other universities, such as Columbia, Chicago, Stanford, Virginia, and others which offer broad, general education in the social sciences to undergraduate and graduate students, many of whom find their way directly or indirectly into public service employment.[1]

The acceptance of a program of education for the public service and of training within it marks the abandonment of some old ideas and the adoption of new ones. The historical belief that the duties of public office are simple and may be readily understood by any man of good intelligence is long out of date; one wonders what the harassed staff of the Social Security Board or the Agricultural Adjustment Administration might say on this point! Training programs imply permanent service; that is, a bureaucracy but an intelligent one. It is an obvious waste of public money to train mere "birds of passage." Training sug-

[1] For a full display, see Charles S. Ascher, "Educational Preparation for Public Administration," in *Municipal Year Book*, 1938, pp. 354-64; see also O. Glenn Stahl, "Public Service Training in Universities," 31 *Am. Pol. Sci. Rev.* 870-78 (1937).

gests a career service and implies the existence of future prospects which make special effort on the part of employees rational. These ideas are by no means universally accepted, but a survey of recent trends indicates that they are winning more and more support.[1] The future, one may surmise, belongs to them, rather than to the doctrines of an earlier era.

2. Education for the Public Service

Analysis of public service training requires a differentiation between education for the public service prior to appointment, and training within the service subsequent to appointment. This distinction rests on a substantial difference in circumstances and objectives. Pre-entry "training" is intended to enable an aspirant to pass an examination or otherwise to show fitness for appointment, or more broadly to develop the knowledge and qualities of mind which will make for subsequent success. There is no certainty of selection for a civil service post and the object is properly, therefore, to prepare the would-be civil servant on sufficiently broad lines (without overlooking examination requirements) so that his efforts will not be wasted if he is unsuccessful in entering public work. The principal instruments of preparation are the public school system and the colleges and universities. They are unable, for reasons which will appear shortly, to offer specific courses for specific jobs in a given office; and their responsibility for education is universally conceived in terms which make educators unwilling to narrow their offerings to such a vocational purpose. "Cram schools" of varying degrees of merit coach for specific examinations.

By contrast, in-service training is directed toward individuals who are actually at work. Such training is a recognizable investment in long-time service. The employee is performing a particular function which in the public interest should be well performed; and he is eligible for promotion to other positions where competence and special knowledge are equally desirable. The specific object in view is performance. Training to improve performance may be special or general, but the immediate objective is definable in terms of present or future responsibility. The instrument of training is not the public school system primarily

[1] On this general topic see Lewis Meriam, *Public Service and Special Training* (1936), and William E. Mosher and J. D. Kingsley, *Public Personnel Administration* (1936), ch. 13. A comparison of training in business and in public administration is available in the study by George A. Graham, "Personnel Practices in Business and Governmental Organizations," in C. J. Friedrich and others, *Problems of the American Public Service* (1935); see also the work of William C. Beyer, "Municipal Civil Service in the United States," in Friedrich and others, *op. cit.*

but the service itself. For these reasons, it is desirable to make a distinction between pre-entry *education* and post-entry *training*.[1]

The general issue concerning pre-entry education is whether this preparation shall be specifically designed for the needs of government or on the contrary more general and cultural in nature. A single and dogmatic answer is not feasible, but there is one obvious consideration which precludes any simple program of public service preparation. There is no single "public service." There are on the contrary a bewildering variety of services, almost matching the range of occupations which are "private" in common acceptation.

At the same time there are certain professional fields which government dominates and in which consequently professional or vocational training is *ipso facto* training for government service. One of the earliest of these fields to develop was forestry, and the curriculum of forestry schools is closely articulated with government requirements. Another such field is veterinary science which is dominated by the official meat inspection services. The most recent to emerge is public welfare. The professional schools of social work now turn a large najority of their graduates into the public social services and the curiculum is appropriately built in the light of the needs of the public serv-ce. At the nonprofessional level, fire fighting and sanitary inspection re almost entirely governmental.

For a few types of positions specific educational preparation is not ieeded. Some examinations given by civil service commissions are of he general intelligence type, which do not require specialized educa-ion. These examinations are gradually increasing in number, and the chools are under less compulsion than a decade ago to attempt the mpossible feat of "educating" for specific vocational outlets. Thus the nterests of the public service and of the school system are coalescing n favor of broad general education for a few groups of positions, lthough in the sciences and professions education will necessarily be pecialized. This tendency deserves more conscious attention and sup-ort than it has received.

Both general and specialized education for the civil service appear,

[1] Public service training has been the subject of a series of conferences, reported nd unreported, since 1931. The principal conference reports are, in order, *Univer-ty Training for the National Service* (Univ. of Minnesota, 1932); Morris B. ambie, ed., *Training for the Public Service*, Public Administration Service No. 49, 935; Committee report of the International City Managers' Association, *Training or Municipal Administration* (1936); *The Training of Public Servants*, Interna-onal Institute of the Administrative Sciences and the International Union of Local uthorities, Publication No. 3, 1937; American Municipal Association in coopera-on with the International City Managers' Association and the Civil Service As-mbly, *Toward Competent Government* (mim. 1936).

therefore, to have a place. Their respective contributions become more clear from consideration of several specific cases: the role of the professional schools; the nonprofessional graduate schools in the universities; the liberal arts college; and the secondary schools.[1]

a. The professional and technical schools. The professional schools—law, medicine, engineering, education, in an older group; forestry, social service and business among a newer group—offer instruction in well-recognized fields some of which are primarily private in nature, others of which are primarily public. Law and business represent the former, education and social service the latter. In the latter group, professional schools educate with the public service definitely in mind and the curriculum is organized to this end. In the former case, the curriculum has been slow in recognizing that an increasing proportion of graduates enter public service. Only within the last few years have the faculties of engineering schools and law schools begun to offer courses for the man who looks to official appointment. In medicine, on the contrary, the field of public health has been well recognized since about 1910.

So far as adequate training for the public service in the professional schools is concerned, the chief need is to supplement the definitely technical training with some information concerning special phases of technique which apply to public work (such as quarantine, methods of public contracting, or administrative law) and also with some insight into the conditions under which public work is conducted. The latter information is perhaps the special contribution of public administration.

b. The graduate schools. For a great number of positions in the public service—clerical, supervisory, custodial, manipulative, specialist, and labor—the university can make very little contribution. In the case of two important but numerically small groups, the scientific and the professional, university education is either essential or highly advantageous. It is clear, however, that the universities cannot expect to place large numbers in the public service. Compared with the annual university output, the public service intake is negligible.

In the scientific departments, the graduate schools offer adequate training in basic knowledge and practical techniques. Students majoring in biology, geology, mathematics, or chemistry are well equipped to pass the appropriate examinations. If the student definitely looks forward to government work, supplementary study in political science and public administration is useful.

Among the social sciences and the humanities the problem is more difficult. The need of government for historians, sociologists, philol-

[1] See especially Wallace S. Sayre and Milton Mandell, *Education and the Civil Service in New York City*, U. S. Office of Education (1938).

ɔgists, and classicists as such is extremely limited. The demand for tatisticians, economists and students of public administration is somewhat greater and is expanding. But appointing officers do not expect or desire junior statisticians to know the special problems of the paricular statistical field into which they may be plunged. If mastery of he tool has been acquired, the appointing officer is content. Some speialization in economics is frequently preferred, as in agricultural ecoıomics, labor economics, or the economics of transportation. These pecialist fields, however, are normal features of graduate instruction in nany departments of economics.

The general conclusion concerning graduate school preparation for he public service (apart from some of the professional schools) is, herefore, that on the whole a fundamental education in a field of knowledge with some work in public administration is preferable to specialiation for a government position.[1]

c. The liberal arts college. Preparation for government positions requiring a college degree does not call for any substantial modification of normal college course. If the collegian is interested in the natural or biological sciences or in such tool subjects as statistics and accounting, he can usually obtain enough instruction in connection with his major work to compete in the examinations for the junior grade.

If he is interested in the social sciences, his lot is more difficult. Until 1934, civil service commissions almost completely neglected this imporant source of public service recruits. In 1934 the United States Civil Service Commission offered an examination adapted to this group of tudents under the title, "Junior Civil Service Examiner." The results were very satisfactory; over 7,900 college graduates competed, and over 3,600 were successful in passing a difficult general intelligencegeneral information test. A considerable number (about 1,200 in the irst two years) have been appointed to a wide variety of nonspecialized unior positions in many departments or agencies.

Such an examination provides an important source of unusually prom-

[1] Cf. a recent manuscript report from the University of Minnesota (Morris B. Lambie). "While both public and private services include in general the same occupations and professions, there are certain phases of the training program in each professional and vocational school which call for special emphasis where the candidates intend to enter public service. The basic training will be the same . . . but the point of view may be somewhat different. . . . Those who enter the public service will be better qualified if they are led to an understanding of the nature and significance of the duties which they are to perform for the public; to an appreciation of the responsibilities which they will have, and the environment in which they will work; to a clearer view of the relationships which exist among government agencies and units; and to a knowledge of the financial and legal foundations upon which public offices are established."

ising young men and women. It is in harmony with the almost universa conviction of college authorities that their duty is to educate the whol man, not to "train" him vocationally. As state and municipal commis sions open up the same type of examination, much good will result fron every point of view. A second type of examination for students ir political science, economics and sociology was offered for the first tim in 1936 under the title, "Social Science Analyst." It, too, attracted large number of well-qualified candidates.

The potential value of such examinations is indicated by the respons of college and university graduates to the State Department examina tion for the Foreign Service subsequent to the passage of the Roger Act in 1924. Hundreds of exceptional undergraduates prepare them selves for this examination, academic in nature, with special emphasi on the social sciences and law. The Foreign Service at once was enable to draw on the best product of the universities and colleges for th junior positions.

d. The secondary schools. So far as most positions are concerned, ap pointments in the public service require no education beyond the second ary schools. These schools have no specific program of education fo work in public offices. They do not need to develop any. The greates assets which the secondary schools can give to the young person who seek work in public office or elsewhere are ability to use the English lan guage effectively, both in speech and in writing, ability to handle simpl mathematical computations, broad familiarity with the common field of knowledge and so far as possible capacity for independent though The general intelligence test adapted to high school graduates used b the United States Civil Service Commission and other commissions i the open door through which secondary school graduates who hav followed such a course may enter the public service. The George-Dee Act of 1936, however, may stimulate more specialized secondary schoc preparation for certain public service vocations.

Effective correlation of the educational system and public service en trance requirements has never been established in this country. This i due partly to the diversity of educational standards, controlled by forty eight "sovereign" states, partly to the undisciplined scheme of entranc age limits which almost universally prevails, and partly to the slov growth of an examination system which, as yet, covers only a part o the public service. The net result is to throw a heavier burden on sub sequent in-service training.

From time to time a proposal is brought forward to establish a civ service West Point as the principal training center for future civil serv ants. Superficially the idea is attractive. Too close an analogy canno

›e drawn, however, between officer preparation for the army at the Ailitary Academy and training for the higher posts in the civil service. Vest Point trains for an officer class, sharply distinguished from the ank and file who advance to the officer grades only in exceptional cases. The civil service has no such officer class; on the contrary there is a vell-established tradition in favor of free and open opportunity for the owest grades to seek promotion to the highest. Most responsible non-›olitical positions are filled in fact by promotion, with no bar from the ›ottom to the top. Furthermore, the civil service is not a single profes-ion or vocation for which a homogeneous curriculum could be con-tructed, such as is found in West Point. If the students are selected ›rior to attaining status, as at West Point and Annapolis, there is no ;uarantee that they will be eligible for appointment upon graduation, ınless to unclassified or exempt positions. In short, those who are famil-ar with the federal service doubt the value of a specialized civil service raining academy, especially at the pre-entry stage.

. Internes and Apprentices

Realization of the value of learning by doing has kept alive the idea f interneship and apprenticeship in public service training since 1906, lthough such opportunities are still painfully few. In strict parlance an nterneship is an opportunity to observe and to participate without regu-ar or permanent status, an apprenticeship is an opportunity to learn by loing under close direction with a permanent status and the expectation f passing from the apprenticeship into regular employment. The terms re often used interchangeably, and in the following discussion no effort vill be made to distinguish between them.

The concept of an apprenticeship in connection with public service raining was inaugurated by the New York Bureau of Municipal Re-earch. The object in view was to give the student a practical and real-stic view of administrative operations and problems by exposing him o the sight, sound, touch, taste and smell of the thing itself. After some ormal preparation, therefore, the student was required either (a) to ›repare a report on some actual situation or problem, or (b) to serve as junior assistant to some municipal official. Experience demonstrated he exceptional value of this first-hand contact. A few months spent rappling with real problems encountered by real officials and vexed by eal obstacles proved to be worth a year in the library or lecture hall.

Other institutions have adopted the apprenticeship program.[1] Syra-use University and the University of California especially have applied

[1] Tennessee Valley Authority, *Training Program for Interns in Public Adminis-ation . . .* (mim. 1937).

it widely and with good results. An important variation has been worked out at Cincinnati University (similar to the work-study program of Antioch College) by which selected students study governmental problems at the university for one month and then work in the city hall for a month. Two students work and study in alternation so that the city job is continuously filled.

In 1934 the National Institute of Public Affairs initiated an interneship program in Washington. The objects were twofold—partly to give a realistic turn to a college education in political science, partly to interest men and women in and prepare them for public employment. In addition to lectures by prominent officials, each interne is assigned, by previous arrangement, to some office where he can observe the wheels go round at close range. With rare exceptions, most internes report very favorably on their experience.[1] In 1935 Colgate University established a Washington center for a small group of undergraduates, who combine regular course lectures by an ambulatory faculty member with close contacts with Congress, the courts, and the administrative offices. The city managers have long approved the idea of an interneship in principle, but have been handicapped in putting principle into practice on account of local objections to "outsiders." [2] In 1936 Los Angeles County initiated an important program of apprenticeships, which in 1938 opened places for eight college graduates from southern California institutions.

The interneship idea, while attractive, has certain potential defects. An undue concentration of internes in Washington, or in any state capital or city hall, would quickly cause a revulsion among busy officials. The training and experience acquired during an interneship may never be capitalized in the public service, especially where the rule of open competitive examinations prevails. If attention is to be given by public officials to training young persons, it would seem more useful to train those who have already acquired a probationary appointment. A group of internes may also stir up critical comment from established employees who fear loss of future prospects. On the other hand a well-planned program in the hands of sympathetic public officials has great promise and it is to be hoped that such opportunities will expand rapidly in future years.

4. In-Service Training

Scattered examples of training of present staff may be found here and there over a long period of years, but systematic in-service training is

[1] Henry Reining, Jr., "Problems of Training for the Public Service," 16 *Pub Adm.* 294-302 (1938).

[2] A study by the International City Managers' Association in 1934 indicated that most cities had no interneships, 16 *Pub. Man.* 167-71 (1934).

:hiefly a product of the post-war period. There are two major objec-ives: one the better performance of present work, the other preparation or a higher position. Both the government and the employee have an nterest in each but in different proportions. The interest of the govern-nent is sufficient to warrant some allowance of official time and some inancial support. At present, however, in-service training is usually lone at the expense of the employee, on the ground without doubt that ɪe has already been found competent by examination to do his assigned ob. It is clearly not the responsibility of the government to provide for ›ublic employees at public expense general educational facilities of a ultural nature other than those which are available to all citizens. It s equally clear, however, that training which improves present perform-nce or which is designed to prepare employees for future tasks is a roper object of public expense.

In the light of the objectives of in-service training, the instruction is ractical and specific in most cases, although a substantial margin of eneral but relevant study may be found in more highly developed lans. A variety of schemes have already been established. The simplest an arrangement by which the new employee is turned over to an ex-erienced one for instruction and guidance. At its best this plan corre-ponds to the tutorial system which is used for the higher British civil ervants.[1] This ideal is seldom reached, and in practice this kind of training" is of very limited value. It is the most common.

Another plan, adapted to training a batch of recruits entering at the me time, offers an introductory series of lectures and inspection trips r the purpose of acquiring a bird's-eye view of the whole organiza-on. This is usually very helpful although it may convey only a super-cial impression.

One of the most valuable methods for training junior professional and ecialist employees is a "circular" training course by means of frequent assignments to different divisions of the organization. Here the initiate arns by doing, which is perhaps the best single training method. An-her well-recognized scheme, effectively used by the Farm Credit dministration, consists of full-time attendance at a brief course of in-ruction. Here the student masters the details of organization, studies e law and regulations, and becomes acquainted with personnel and ethods of operation [2]

[1] Harvey Walker, *Training Public Employees in Great Britain* (1935), pp. 8-22. e also Louis J. Kroeger, *Training for Public Personnel Administration in Califor-ı* (mim. 1936); Rowland A. Egger, H. I. Baumes and R. Uhl, *Training for Pub-Service in Virginia* (mim. 1937); Earl Brooks, *In-Service Training of Federal nployees* (1938).

[2] New methods of training are forecast in John E. Devine, *Films as an Aid in aining Public Employees* (1937).

These illustrations are concerned with training of the raw recruit In-service training is just as much concerned with a continuing pro- gram for established personnel.[1] Without question the most elaborat and most successful in-service training institution is the Graduate Schoo of the Department of Agriculture. The object of this school is to pro- mote the efficiency of the department by means of formal and extensiv training facilities. The work is given out of office hours, is supporte entirely by the students, and although resting on somewhat vague statu tory authority until the Executive Order of 1938 is in effect only semi official in nature. The school is, however, supervised and encouraged b the department. Registration is open to any qualified student and nearl all government departments and many universities and colleges are rep resented among the students. The curriculum is based principally upo an impressive group of scientific and economic courses, of which th following are illustrative: History of American Agriculture; History c Economic Thought; International Trade; Statistics, elementary and ac vanced; Organic Chemistry; Plant Ecology; Plant Diseases; Anim Parasitology, and the like. Another group includes the modern lar guages, emphasizing the use of scientific terms. Finally mention may b made of a group of courses in personnel administration initiated in 193 and continued in cooperation with American University. It is no acc dent that this first impressive example of in-service training develope in a department devoted largely to scientific investigation, a field whe the progress of science is so rapid that "refresher" courses are almo essential. The high standards of instruction and the breadth of trainin afforded by the Graduate School mark it as one of the foremost trai ing institutions of its kind in the world.

From time to time officials are detailed to make special studies, eith here or abroad, or to attend professional conferences and convention Such experiences form one type of in-service training. They should cultivated so far as possible and expanded to include definite traini assignments on leave with pay. The suggestion of an official sabbatic leave has also been made, and among the county agents, for exampl has actually been introduced in a few cases.

Among the most interesting recent developments are training pr grams at the University of Minnesota (1936) and at Harvard Universi (1937) which are analogous to the sabbatical leave idea. Substantial fe lowships for men in active service are available in limited numbers both institutions, on the basis of which it is possible for young gover ment executives to take a year for further study and to return to th

[1] Gordon R. Clapp, *Supervisory Training in the Tennessee Valley Author* (1936).

egular positions at its conclusion. Such opportunities lend dignity and restige to the public service.

In the field of in-service training in local government, exceptionally ood work has been done for municipal employees through the semi-fficial leagues of municipalities, notably in Minnesota, Kansas, Virginia, nd New York. The program of the New York Conference of Mayors the most extensive. It began in 1928 with the establishment of training hools for police and firemen on a state-wide regional basis. In 1930 aining for four other groups was arranged—financial officers, civil serv-e commissioners, building inspectors, and welfare officials. The success f these schools was so marked that in 1931 the Conference received a rant for the purpose of developing training schools for municipal offi-ials and making studies of municipal problems. A Bureau of Training nd Research was established and training programs for twenty groups f officials worked out. In 1935 this work was placed on strong founda-ons by the incorporation of the Municipal Training Institute under the ipervision of the Regents of the State of New York.

The expansion of the training schools under municipal league auspices shown in the following table:[1]

TABLE VII

NUMBER OF AND ATTENDANCE AT MUNICIPAL TRAINING SCHOOLS

YEAR	NUMBER OF SCHOOLS	ATTENDANCE
1928	2	302
1929	29	4,523
1930	48	5,625
1931	54	6,808
1932	75	7,415
1933	67	6,315
1934	80	8,855
1935	113	13,674
1936	98	11,660
Total	566	65,177

The municipalities take full responsibility for providing facilities and ithorizing attendance. Although fees are required and attendance is oluntary, there are definite indications that the future belongs to those embers of the lower grades who take advantage of these training cilities. The New York Director of Research summarizes recent hievements in these words:

[1] Table adapted from data in a report prepared by the American Municipal As-ciation in cooperation with the International City Managers' Association and the vil Service Assembly, *Toward Competent Government* (mim. 1936), appendix 4.

These schools have reduced the costly apprenticeship period of public official decreased municipal administrative expenses and are lessening public dissatisfactio with city and village administrators. Further, schools have raised the standard c municipal service, lengthened the tenure of office, reduced personnel turnover, ir creased the efficiency of officials and employees and convinced the public that mu nicipal service is not just a political job but a technical and highly specialized work

Federal aid to public service training was initiated by the George Deen Act of 1936 (49 Stat. 1488), authorizing appropriations supple mentary to the Smith-Hughes Act of 1917 for training in "public an other service occupations." [2] This has been construed so that instructio under public bodies other than boards of education, for example, league of municipalities, is permissible, and such leagues, led by Ne York and Michigan, are taking advantage of this new source of suppor for training. Many "public service occupations" overlap similar work i private employment, such as water supply and purification or electri and gas plant operations; many are peculiar to public jurisdiction, suc as fire fighting, police protection, building inspection, health inspectio factory inspection and the like.[3]

Developments in Michigan indicate early lines of in-service trainin under the George-Deen Act. The Michigan Municipal League and th State Board for Vocational Education joined in appointing the sam director of public service training. Four lines were initially selected fc intensive work: fire, police, assessment and electric utility plant oper tion; the expansion of courses in Wayne University (Detroit) in suc subjects as assessment, elections, report writing, public speaking an transportation was facilitated; and a number of three-day explorator conferences with executives in public works, personnel, weights an measures and finance were arranged. In principle, the George-Deen Ac represents an important development in public service training. Expanc ing federal functions make it appear probable that national leadershi in various sectors of public service training is likely, although the ce ter of gravity will remain in the states.

Apart from these official or semiofficial enterprises the most notab example of in-service education and training at the level of local go ernment is that sponsored by the School of Public Affairs at the Un versity of Southern California. During the academic year courses a

[1] N. Y. State Conference of Mayors and other Municipal Officials, *Municip Training Schools in New York State*, Publication No. 31, 1934, p. 13.

[2] Note also the work of the Division of Labor Standards; see U. S. Departme of Labor, Division of Labor Standards, *Report of Proceedings of a Training Cour for State Factory Inspectors*, Bulletin 6, 1936.

[3] Jerry R. Hawke, *Training for the Public-Service Occupations*, U. S. Office Education, Vocational Educational Bulletin 192, 1938.

;iven in the County Hall of Records and in the City Hall. Every summer one-week institute is arranged which in 1938 was attended by over ,000 city, county and state employees in the southern California region. 'uture trends are likely to reproduce such regional centers in other arts of the country.

From a practical point of view, in-service training programs necesarily deal principally with the more numerous lower-grade jobs. Vocaional training in the industrial field is primarily intended to give emloyees an opportunity to become more efficient on the jobs which they ave, or to equip them for jobs which are within their reach. Training ıe lower grades has, however, an important incidental result. It forces ıe higher grades to "keep on their toes" in order not to be put to ıame before their subordinates. This may be noticed in local police orces; and in the long run, a properly trained rank and file will produce roperly trained supervisory officers.

State and county governments as a group are still lagging behind the xample provided by the cities and the national government. Despite ıis, as the whole scene is surveyed in perspective it is clear that a renaisınce in governmental standards is upon us. In increasing measure the leal of settled, stable administration based on superior competence is ıking hold of the American people. The extension of college and uniersity preparation for the public service is not only helpful, it is symolic of the new status which public service is acquiring. But of equal gnificance is the desire of public employees and officials themselves to nprove their work by following courses and programs of post-entry aining. Here lies the possibility of indefinite improvement of the public ırvice and the continued enhancement of its standing in the community.

Chapter Twenty-four

PROMOTION AND SERVICE RECORDS

1. Promotions

The management of promotions is partly a technical question, but i is also deeply affected by common-sense judgment and fairness. A badl planned promotion system harms an organization not merely by push ing ahead unqualified persons but also by undermining the morale c the whole group. The hope for timely promotion is so normal and s widespread that the influence of a good promotion system is all-per vasive. It is one of the means of holding in government service the bes qualified men and women who enter the lower grades and is thus a important phase of a career service. Conversely the lack of promotio may become one of the surest means of driving them out of the publi service. In any large-scale organization it cannot be left to chance or t the casual attention of the persons most concerned in particular case for the larger the organization the greater the likelihood that promisin employees may be shunted off into dead-ends. In an expanding admini trative system, such as has on the whole characterized all levels of th American government, new positions are frequently created and pro motion is accelerated so far as the merit system prevails; but in a stat or contracting system, promotion prospects are greatly reduced.[1]

The principal object of a promotion system is to secure the best po sible incumbents for the higher positions, while maintaining the mora of the whole organization. The main interest to be served is the publ interest, not the personal interest of members of the official group co cerned. The public interest is best secured when reasonable opportuniti

[1] In these pages promotion means an appointment from a given position to a po tion of higher grade, involving a change of duties to a more difficult type of wo and greater responsibility, accompanied by change of title and usually an increa of pay. The terms "advancement" and "administrative promotion" refer to an a vance in pay by a prescribed increment within the scale of pay appropriate to given position. They do not involve change of duties, responsibility or title. A assignment is merely a change of task within the same class, grade and scale of p and implies no change of status. A transfer is a change of assignment from one e ploying agency within a given jurisdiction to another in the same jurisdiction, n necessarily involving any change of pay, duties or responsibility. A promotion s tem is the aggregate of laws, rules and practices which govern the making of p motions in any governmental agency.

or promotion exist for all qualified employees, when really superior :ivil servants are enabled to move as rapidly up the promotion ladder as heir merits deserve and as vacancies occur, and when selection for romotion is made on the sole basis of merit. For the merit system ought o apply as specifically in making promotions as in original recruitment.[1]

In discussing promotion problems different figures of speech are ometimes employed, such as promotion ladder, or promotion pyramid. The figure of a pyramid permits graphic representation of the dimen- ions of the promotion problem—the vertical ascent, and also the hori- ontal base and proportionate dimensions at any stage along the vertical. The character of these dimensions governs actual promotion possi- ilities.

Inspection of any organization reveals the fact that the number of upervisory and directing positions is small in comparison with the num- er of junior or rank-and-file positions. The figures in the following able indicate how rapidly the promotion pyramid narrows toward the pex.

TABLE VIII

Proportion of Higher to Lower Positions

Grade	United States Public Health Service[a]	Boston Police[b]	Detroit Hospital Service[c]	New York City Fire Department[d]
V	1.2	.25	—	.6
IV	1.2	1.4	1.0	1.7
III	12.0	3.6	1.0	6.3
II	89.0	9.5	17.0	9.8
I	100.0	100.0	100.0	100.0

[a] L. F. Schmeckebier, *The Public Health Service* (1923).
[b] Boston Police Commissioner, *Annual Report,* 1937, p. 86.
[c] Furnished by Griffenhagen and Associates.
[d] N. Y. City Fire Department, *Annual Report, Chief Engineer,* 1935, p. 8.

Hence arises the underlying and irreconcilable conflict in any promo- on system. Large numbers of employees, normally ambitious and intent n success in their vocation or profession and under heavy economic

[1] American literature on the subject of promotion is scarce. See William E. osher and J. D. Kingsley, *Public Personnel Administration* (1936), ch. 14; John . Pfiffner, *Public Administration* (1935), ch. 11; Walter D. Scott, R. C. Clothier d S. B. Mathewson, *Personnel Management* (2d ed. 1931), ch. 10; American Mu- cipal Association, *Salary and Promotion Policies in United States Cities* (mim. 33). The subject has been frequently discussed, on the contrary, in Great Britain. or illustrative literature see 5 *Pub. Adm.* 184-209 (1927); 7 *ibid.* 133-52 (1929); 8 *id.* 271-74 and 457-70 (1930); 12 *ibid.* 216-28 (1934); 15 *ibid.* 305-37 and 433-40 937).

pressure with the passing of the years, face a limited number of higher positions in which vacancies occur at relatively irregular and infrequent intervals. No form of promotion system can solve this dilemma; the best that can be done is to ensure that the most deserving have the first opportunity and that none are barred from consideration by artificial barriers.

Unfortunately many more or less artificial barriers exist in present promotion plans. The limitations on class or social lines which have been important in the public services of some countries have fortunately never been of consequence in the United States apart from the handicaps of the colored race. Political appointment to the higher administrative posts, on the other hand, has usually been present in greater or less degree. Another very common artificial barrier is the "Maginot line" between department and department, bureau and bureau, and even division and division. Promotion across these lines is not unknown but is relatively rare. Often this barrier is tacitly approved by the employees themselves who acquire a sense of vested interest and proprietary right in the particular position immediately above their own and a corresponding indifference to similar openings elsewhere. Pathetic illustrations of a really pathological sense of ownership are not unknown.

Quite a different handicap to absolutely free movement lies in the deepening specialization which comes with the years. In the professional and scientific pursuits, specialization sets in at once: a cytologist is not in line for a higher vacancy in agronomy; a civil engineer is not equipped for aeronautical engineering assignments; a lawyer and a public health expert climb wholly different ladders. In the clerical, administrative and fiscal service, specialization need not work its effects so soon; but the tendency is strong in the direction of particularism. A partial remedy lies in varied training and work assignments in the early years of official life.

In lesser jurisdictions, such as a city of ten or fifteen thousand population, the rural counties, and the smaller states, promotion is severely limited by the restricted size of the organization, and by disinclination to appoint an "outsider." A police force of seventy men will require not more than five sergeants, two or three lieutenants, a captain and the chief. This is the complete promotional structure. A city clerk's office is small in most instances, and the occurrence of a vacancy is infrequent even for political reasons. As Jefferson once wrote, "Few die and none resign."

Where extensive promotional opportunities do or might readily exist, as in the larger administrative units, the principal questions are, where should the final responsibility for selection for promotion rest, and on what principles and by what methods should the choice be made?

Selection for promotion is almost without exception made by the official head of the agency concerned. In some quarters the civil service commission holds examinations to secure an eligible list but the final selection of one from among three or more is left to the department.

It is proper for the final responsibility in promotions to rest with line officials. In his testimony before the Commission of Inquiry, President Hoover took this view, which would be widely supported. "Of course the promotions," said Mr. Hoover, "must be left to the departmental heads. The Civil Service Commission can't go around and determine that. If it did there would be no discipline at all." [1] The function of the commission is primarily to see that the procedure required by law or regulation is observed, to lend assistance, formal or informal, in the search for qualified applicants, and where the law so specifies to hold an examination to weed out the less well qualified.

In large jurisdictions the central personnel agency may substitute qualifying examinations at two or three points on the promotional ladder in lieu of an examination for each and every promotion or at the other extreme in lieu of an entirely unregulated system.

More difficult is the problem of the criteria upon which promotion should rest. In a small organization the answer is simple: a department head acts on the basis of his personal knowledge of the men under his control. But this rule breaks down in the huge administrative units of the larger governments; the Superintendent of Schools in New York City, the Public Welfare Director of Ohio, the Commissioner of the Immigration and Naturalization Service cannot possibly depend on their own acquaintance with their subordinates.

Several methods are available where personal knowledge fails; they are used either alone or in combination with each other. They include selection either on the basis of a promotional examination, or an efficiency rating or service record, or seniority, or finally on the basis of the unabridged discretion of a higher official informed by conference with his immediate advisers.

Preliminary to a discussion of these bases of selection, it may be said that the usual area of eligibility is the administrative unit recognized by the appropriation act. In some cases, as in a police or fire department, this corresponds to a definite vocational specialty; in other cases it does not. Here we find one of the chief reasons for "blind-alley" employ-

[1] Commission of Inquiry on Public Service Personnel, *Minutes of Evidence* (1935), p. 476.

ment; a small appropriation unit means a limited opportunity for promotion. Every effort is required to ensure that each position finds a place on a promotion ladder which leads to responsible work. This does not mean that every employee will reach the top of the ladder, but no one should be stopped by purely artificial limitations.

A promotional examination may be an open competition, a limited competition, or merely a pass examination. In the first case, persons not in government employ or employed in other departments or agencies are eligible to compete. This creates the so-called "open" system of promotion. It is defended on the ground that it brings in new blood and fresh ideas and that present employees suffer no loss of rights since they will benefit on the examination by their special knowledge of government work. It is criticized because it tends to destroy morale to bring in outsiders, even by examination, who take the higher jobs from those who "deserve" them. Where an outsider is appointed on a basis other than merit the harm is even greater.

Open competitive examinations for promotion are uncommon as such but in the guise of an original entrance examination for a high position they are frequent, especially in the national government. Thus in 1935 the United States Civil Service Commission held examinations for such positions as administrative assistant to the Director of the Census, senior soil technologist, principal architect, associate biologist and principal statistician. These are positions of responsibility which would normally be filled by the promotion of a person in the next lower grade in the same organization, or by the transfer or promotion of a person doing similar work in another organization. The announcement of an open competitive examination for such posts is an indication either that the recruiting process in previous years has been unsuccessful in producing good prospects or that too little effort has been made to develop available material. In the national service both situations prevail, especially the latter.

Examinations limited to those in specified lower positions are mor[e] common. In the uniformed forces they are almost invariable; forma[l] written examinations are often required as high as the rank of polic[e] captain. Persons outside the service are entirely excluded, thus followin[g] the "closed" promotional system. In general, the closed system is mor[e] common than its opposite and is usually preferred by students of pro[-]motion questions, except where a reasonably adequate supply of super[-]visory talent is not discovered in the normal processes of recruitmen[t].

A third type of promotional test is the pass examination, in which [a] specified individual is nominated by the department head subject t[o] proof of minimum attainments by examination, either written or no[n-] assembled. In this case discretion is lodged with the department, subject to this qualifying test. This is the customary procedure in the national administrative system, where the qualifying test is usually merely the submission of the individual's education and experience record.

Employees often prefer the rule of seniority, by which the eligible longest in service is automatically awarded the promotion. Within limits, seniority is entitled to consideration as a criterion of selection. It eliminates favoritism or the suspicion thereof; and experience is certainly a factor in the making of a successful employee. Seniority is given most weight in promotions from the lowest to other subordinate positions. As employees move up the ladder of responsibility, seniority is given less and less weight. When seniority is made the sole determining factor, it is a dangerous guide. It does not follow that the employee longest in service in a particular grade is best suited for promotion to a higher grade; the very opposite may be true. Consistent application of the rule of seniority up the scale to supervisory and administrative positions would in itself cause the resignation of the better men and thus invite progressive deterioration in the higher grades where special competence is particularly needed.

In many instances, some weight is given to the service records or efficiency ratings. This subject is discussed in the next section. It will suffice to state here that although they have value it is unsafe to make them the determining factor in selecting employees for promotion. The wiser rule is that they should be considered for as much guidance as may be proper in the light of the character and quality of the rating, but that the decision should not be automatically governed by a numerical or other symbol. It is especially undesirable to grant or withhold promotion on slight differences of a fraction of one per cent. The efficiency rating is or may be a useful guide but as a mechanical determinant it is too arbitrary to be useful.

If the good judgment, freedom of action, and good intent of higher officials could be taken for granted at all points the best basis for making promotions would be found in the free discretion of the responsible officials, informed by reference to service records and other relevant data. Unfortunately, good intent may be and sometimes is obscured by political, factional or personal considerations.

Despite these objections, the final decision must be left to the judgment of the official responsible for the continuous operation of the organization. No mechanical substitute has been devised which can weigh and evaluate the many delicate factors which play a part in the final conclusion that A is more likely to succeed than B in a specific situation. An examination may test what applicants know about the job ahead and may throw some light on their personalities. At best it is a rough and approximate measure, failing to take into account many elements of first-rate importance, such as adaptability, industry, cooperativeness, loyalty and courage. The presence or absence of such qualities may be partly revealed by a service record, but the ratings cannot safely be summarized in a mathematical figure which precludes the exercise of judgment. In the nature of things, seniority will play a conspicuous part in the final decision, whether given a definite weight or not. The discretion of the responsible officer will be checked by these considerations as well as by the criticism of organized employees, but it should be preserved.

Probably the best provision for handling promotions under normal circumstances in a large organization consists in a procedure by which all eligibles (broadly construed) are considered on the basis of experience and capacity to perform new duties. These qualifications are determined in part by previous record, in part by personal characteristics, and in part by examinations of one type or another, especially for the lower grades. The final selection is then made on the recommendation of the personnel officer by the official head of the organization on the basis of all the evidence at hand. In a small organization less extensive procedures are adequate, but some formality based on a record is always desirable if for no other reason than to discourage outside pressure.[1]

Whatever the instrument of selection one underlying consideration must always be held in mind. Success in a given position is not an infallible symbol of success in a higher position. In positions involving technical operations alone, such as laboratory work, a good junior will presumably develop into a good senior technician. But higher positions are usually supervisory in nature, and require ability to work with others, to coordinate, and to lead, as well as possession of special knowledge.[2]

Consider for example the research scientist who is promoted to become the head of a scientific bureau, a position whose duties require him to maintain sound public relations, and to plan and supervise the work of others. In his testimony before the Commission of Inquiry on Public Service Personnel, Dr. W. W. Stockberger, then Director of Personnel in the Department of Agriculture, testified, ". . . in our department we have spoiled many excellent research men by making them into rotten administrators." [3] A man of high scientific attainments may also be a fine administrator, but the two types of ability are different. The domi-

[1] For discussion of transfer, lay-off and reinstatement, see Mosher and Kingsley *op. cit.*, pp. 277-81, 304-5, and Pfiffner, *op. cit.*, pp. 229-33. These important but secondary topics are not discussed in this volume.

[2] Henri Fayol, *Industrial and General Administration* (1930), p. 14.

[3] Commission of Inquiry, *op. cit.*, p. 52.

nant interest of the scientist is discovery, not management. The scientist is interested in laboratory techniques rather than in the manipulation of administrative situations. The training of scientists is not particularly conducive to the development of managerial skill. On the other hand scientists who have administrative talent are ideally fitted for promotion to the highest supervisory posts in the professional bureaus.

2. Service Records (Efficiency Ratings)

Among the common operations in personnel administration the rating of employee efficiency is perhaps the least standardized and the most subject to criticism. Despite a long history no rating form has earned widespread adoption or maintained an undisputed record of successful achievement.[1] Despite dissatisfaction with present forms, some type of written record of performance is indispensable in any large organization; the larger, the more indispensable. It need not be a numerical rating scheme, but it must be periodic, written, and indicative of actual performance, so far as possible on a uniform and comparable basis.[2]

Inspection of the forms now in use in various American jurisdictions reveals three major types of efficiency ratings. They are production records, the graphic rating scale, and the personality inventory. Many forms combine one or more of these basic types.

A production record is particularly applicable in types of work which are repetitive and which involve relatively little judgment, although often a high degree of attention and technical skill. An illustration is the work of a card-punch operator. The production record, combined with a factor to give weight to accuracy, can probably be applied much more widely than is now the case. The work of typists on plain copy, stenographers operating in a large pool without differentiation of work, file clerks on large files, and machine operators of various types affords illustrations.

The production record may be combined with other factors, such as punctuality, industry, and attendance. The hazards of such combinations and permutations are illustrated by the system worked out as early as 1892 by the National Bank Redemption Agency. Production was combined with other elements and so weighed that the net result was to make it possible for an employee who did no work whatever to secure a passing efficiency rating, provided he came regularly and seemed to be occupied.

[1] English experience is recorded in a valuable study published by the Institute of Public Administration, *Staff Reports in the Public Service* (1936).

[2] There is a brief summary of the history of rating in F. F. Bradshaw, "Revising Rating Techniques," 10 *Personnel J.* 232-45 (1931-32).

Although a carefully organized production record is the best single index of efficiency, it is not always adequate standing by itself. An employee with a high production index may be blessed with a personality which irritates colleagues to the point where their own efficiency is adversely affected. And conversely an employee with an average production record may have that rare type of personality which makes for harmony, good will, and esprit de corps in his group; such an employee may be worth infinitely more than a mere production record would indicate.

The production index alone is also inadequate when selection for a supervisory position is required. Manual or mechanical aptitude or capacity for repetitive work (which are important aspects of a production index) may be relatively irrelevant for supervisory work, where a different set of qualities is needed. When it can be fairly used, the production record is, however, one of the safest guides to many personnel decisions.

Obviously the production record cannot be used in a large part of the public service and some indirect approach involving subjective judgments by supervisors becomes necessary. The major part of the experimental work in service ratings during the last fifteen years has been devoted to the task of restricting or guiding these subjective opinions, with the hope that the subjective element could eventually be controlled or eliminated. The mere fact that a rating system is subjective is not necessarily a condemnation. If the subjective judgment of the supervisor is honest (as it usually is) and conforms to generally accepted standards (which may be progressively realized), it may be quite good enough for the limited use to which a formal rating should be put. None of the forms yet devised, apart from production records, have eliminated subjective judgments, although much has been done to make these judgments more thoughtful and complete.

The two major forms which have resulted from this experimental work are the graphic rating scale and the personality inventory. For purposes of illustration the United States rating form in use from 1923 to 1934 and the Probst system will be used in the following discussion.

The rating form employed in the national civil service for about a decade and until it was substantially revised in 1935 was one of the earlier and one of the most highly developed graphic scales.[1] As used in Washington, the form included fifteen traits or qualities, against each

[1] The army rating scale is shown in *The Personnel System of the United States Army* (1919), vol. 2, p. 260; cf. H. P. Rugg, "Is the Rating of Human Character Practicable?" 12 *J. of Educ. Psychology* 425-38; 485-501 (1921); 13 *ibid.* 30-42; 81-93 (1922). For the early graphic rating scale, see D. G. Paterson, "The Scott Company Graphic Rating Scale," 1 *J. of Personnel Research* 361-76 (1922–23).

of which was placed a horizontal line along which were found five subdivisions with appropriate adjectives under each indicating the degree in which the characteristic to be checked was possessed. A check on each line "rated" the employee on the corresponding trait. For different types of work, different combinations of four or five traits were specified for use by the rating officer, the single sheet thus serving for a wide variety of occupations. The rating scale is reproduced on pages 378-79.

The resulting score, expressed in a numerical figure carried out to two decimal places, was worked out by clerks and was subject to review by one or more higher officials. They sought to equalize the grades of the "hard-boiled" supervisor with those of the "soft-hearted" (a considerable majority) by adding to or taking from whole blocks of ratings, or even by modifying individual grades. The end result was consequently not that prescribed by the original rater and he naturally declined to take responsibility for it. Just how these alterations were made on review was seldom clear to the employee, and the consequent confusion was a constant source of irritation.[1]

The use of the graphic rating scale was also affected by certain legislation and regulations known as the "average" provision. The average numerical rating was understood to be 82.5; and the regulations required that as many ratings below average be assigned as those above average. While the end in view was a proper one—to prevent the ratings from rising steadily with universal perfection as the ultimate goal—it was never achieved. The "average" in many cases showed constant improvement to an amazing proficiency. Thus the average of nearly a thousand employees of the U. S. Civil Service Commission for 1934 was 92.5, a gradual ten-year progression from the "normal" 82.5.

But if this objective was not attained, other deplorable results were achieved. The regulations (drafted originally by the Bureau of Efficiency) required that increments within the salary scale be allotted in strict accord with the efficiency ratings, and further legislation prohibited the rate of pay in any category in an office to exceed the average of the scale. To ensure an increment to an employee already over the average, it was therefore necessary to give him a high efficiency rating; but it was necessary also to avoid exceeding the average efficiency rating of 82.5 as well as the average pay. The newcomers at the bottom of the salary range were depended upon generally to balance the older employees in maintaining these averages; but among the efficiency ratings of the latter, weird manipulations were the order of the day. If A

[1] Herman Feldman, *A Personnel Program for the Federal Civil Service*, H. Doc. 773, 71st Cong., 3d sess. (1931), ch. 9.

Efficiency Rating Form No. 8

CLASSIFICATION SYMBOLS		
SERVICE	GRADE	CLASS

GRAPHIC RATING SCALE

NON-SUPERVISORY .... ☐ (CHECK ONE)

SUPERVISORY .... ☐

Name .... Department ....
(Surname) (Given name) (Initial)

....
(Bureau) (Division) (Section) (Subsection)

ELEMENT NUMBER	SERVICE ELEMENTS	NOTE: MARK ONLY ON ELEMENTS CHECKED IN LEFT-HAND MARGIN					Do not use Space Below
☐ 1	Consider accuracy; ability to produce work free from error; ability to detect errors.	Highest possible accuracy.	Very careful.	Careful. No more than reasonable time required for revision.	Careless. Time required for revision greatly excessive.	Practically worthless work.	
☐ 2	Consider reliability in the execution of assigned tasks; dependability in following instructions; accuracy of any parts of product appraisable in terms of accuracy.	Greatest possible reliability.	Very reliable.	Reliable.	Doubtful reliability.	Unreliable.	
☐ 3	Consider neatness and orderliness of work.	Greatest possible neatness and orderliness.	Very neat and orderly.	Neat and orderly.	Disorderly.	Slovenly.	
☐ 4	Consider the speed or rapidity with which work is accomplished; the quantity of work produced in a given time; the dispatch with which a task of known difficulty is completed.	Greatest possible rapidity.	Very rapid.	Good speed.	Slow.	Hopelessly slow.	
☐ 5	Consider industry; diligence; attentiveness; energy and application to duties; the degree to which the employee really concentrates on the work at hand.	Greatest possible diligence.	Very diligent.	Industrious.	Inattentive to work.	Lazy.	
☐ 6	Consider knowledge of work; present knowledge of job and of work related to it; specialized knowledge in his particular field.	Completely informed.	Unusually well informed.	Well informed.	Poorly informed.	Lacking.	
☐ 7	Consider judgment; ability to grasp a situation and draw correct conclusions; ability to profit by experience; sense of proportion or relative values; common sense.	Perfect judgment.	Excellent judgment.	Good judgment.	Poor judgment.	Neglects and misinterprets the facts.	

No.	Factor						Rating
8	Consider success in winning confidence and respect through his personality; courtesy and tact; control of emotions; poise.	Inspiring.	Unusually pleasing.	Pleasing.	Weak.	Repellent.	
9	Consider cooperativeness; ability to work for and with others; readiness to give new ideas and methods a fair trial; desire to observe and conform with the policies of the management.	Greatest possible co-operativeness.	Very cooperative.	Cooperative.	Difficult to handle.	Obstructive.	
10	Consider initiative; resourcefulness; success in doing things in new and better ways and in adapting improved methods to his own work; constructive thinking.	Greatest possible originality.	Very resourceful.	Progressive.	Rarely suggests.	Needs detailed instruction.	
11	Consider execution; ability to pursue to the end difficult investigations or assignments.	Completes assignments in shortest possible time.	Completes assignments in unusually short time.	Completes assignments in a reasonable time.	Slow in completing assignments; or does not complete assignments.	Takes inordinately long and accomplishes little.	
12	Consider organizing ability; success in organizing the work of his section, division, or department, both by delegating authority wisely and by making certain that results are achieved; ability to plan so as to complete tasks on schedule.	Highest possible effectiveness.	Effective under difficult circumstances.	Effective under normal circumstances.	Lacks planning ability.	Inefficient.	
13	Consider leadership; success in winning the cooperation of his subordinates and in welding them into a loyal and effective working unit; decisiveness; energy; self control; tact; courage; fairness in dealing with others.	Most capable and forceful leader possible.	Very capable and forceful leader.	Capable leader.	Fails to command confidence.	Antagonizes subordinates.	
14	Consider success in improving and developing employees by imparting information, developing talent, and arousing ambition; ability to teach; ability to explain matters clearly and comprehensively.	Develops employees of highest possible caliber.	Develops very efficient employees.	Develops competent employees.	Fails to develop employees.	Discourages and misinforms employees.	
15	QUANTITY OF WORK (To be used only where accurate and comprehensive OUTPUT RECORDS are kept.)	Highest possible output.	High output.	Good output.	Low output.	Practically no output.	

On the whole, do you consider the deportment and attitude of this employee toward his work to be satisfactory?....................
Answer "Yes," "No," or "Fairly so"

Total....................

Rated by:.. **Reviewed by:**..
(Rating officer) (Date) (Reviewing officer) (Date)

Final rating....................

secured a rating of 90 in 1930 to ensure his increment, he might be reduced to 80 in 1931 to make possible a rating of 90 to B without disturbing too seriously the sacred average of 82.5. Naturally A became disturbed at these gyrations, especially when in 1933 and 1934 many lay-offs occurred which were based in part upon the efficiency rating.

The basic difficulty was not the graphic form as such. The highly fictitious numerical rating, derived from the graphic rating scale and refined to a hundredth part of one per cent, was made an important and at times a determining factor in controlling salary increments, promotion, lay-off during reduction of forces, and demotion or dismissal for inefficiency. Fraught with such consequences, the integrity of the rating scale simply broke down; some supervisors would not give low ratings, others in all good conscience declined to force their subordinates to walk the gangplank in competition with other employees whose supervisor was known or thought to be trying to protect his staff by favorable ratings. An unhealthy competition thus developed which could not be restrained by the revising power of the reviewing boards. Their efforts often caused new complications.

The close correlation of efficiency ratings and rates of pay with eligibility for promotion and liability for demotion was logical enough but introduced the fatal error of putting too much responsibility on the rating. If anything is clear from this decade of experience at Washington, it is that the efficiency rating should not become the determining element in handling personnel decisions, but merely a factor to be weighed with others; for if it is to control, it will be manipulated out of any semblance to reality.

A second major fault of the former national system was the refinement of numerical ratings to the second decimal point. Judgment of human efficiency is not accurate enough to warrant any such refinement. The difference between a rating of 84.91 and 85.00 is purely fictitious, but it was accepted as a good and sufficient reason for withholding salary increments to real persons. This multiplicity of minute differences also served to increase the occasions for heartburning and jealousy among employees and to antagonize subordinates and supervisors.

These two underlying weaknesses, added to an undesirable secrecy, variations in standards, faults in judgment, and occasional prejudice, progressively undermined the whole system, until by 1934 it had no friends in any quarter. The U. S. Civil Service Commission, after a year's close study in cooperation with representative committees, promulgated a much simpler scheme in 1935. This plan eliminates numerical ratings, substituting five broad categories (excellent to unsatisfactory) which in turn are derived from three relatively simple judgments on

Form 3200—(April 1935)
U. S. Civil Service Commission

Classification Symbols		
Service	Grade	Class

SERVICE RATING FORM

(Read instructions on back of this form)

Check one:

Supervisory .... ☐

Nonsupervisory....... ☐

Name .... Department ....

....
(Bureau) (Division) (Section) (Subsection)

On lines below mark employee:
✓ if neither strong nor weak point.
− if weak point.
+ if strong point.

1. Underline the elements which are especially important in the position.
2. Mark nonsupervisory employees on all elements except those in *italics*.
3. Mark supervisory employees on all elements.

In boxes below rate employee:
1 or 2 if Excellent.
3 or 4 if Very Good.
5 or 6 if Good.
7 or 8 if Fair.
9 or 10 if Unsatisfactory.

Rating Officer | Reviewing Officer

I. QUALITY OF PERFORMANCE

...... (a) Acceptability of work; thoroughness
...... (b) General dependability; accuracy.
...... (c) Neatness and orderliness of work.
...... (d) Skill with which the important procedures, instruments, or machines are employed in performing his duties.
...... (e) *Effectiveness in getting good work done by his unit.*

☐

II. PRODUCTIVENESS

Base rating primarily on element (a), if known; otherwise on (b) and (c).

...... (a) Amount of work accomplished.
...... (b) Application of time, interest, and energy to duties; industry.
...... (c) Promptness in completing assignments; speed.
...... (d) ....
(State any other elements of this class considered)
...... (e) *Effectiveness in securing adequate output from his unit.*

☐

III. QUALIFICATIONS SHOWN ON JOB

...... (a) Knowledge of duties and related information.
...... (b) Ability to learn and to profit from experience.
...... (c) Judgment, sense of proportion, common sense.
...... (d) Initiative and resourcefulness.
...... (e) Cooperativeness; ability to work with and for others.
...... (f) ....
(State any other elements of this class considered)
...... (g) *Effectiveness in developing and training employees.*
...... (Custodial only) Ability to perform such physical work as the job requires.

☐

Sum of ratings . . . .

Rated by .... (Rating officer) .... (Date)

Reviewed by .... (Reviewing officer) .... (Date)

Report to employee ....

On the whole, do you consider the deportment and attitude of this employee toward his work to be satisfactory? . . ..
(Answer "Yes", "No", or "Fairly so")

Sum of Ratings	Report to Employee	Significance
3 – 7	Excellent.	Promotable within grade if below top salary.
8 – 13	Very Good.	Promotable within grade if below top salary.
14 – 19	Good.	No salary change if receiving middle salary or above; if below middle, promotable not beyond middle salary.*
20 – 24	Fair.	Reduce one step if above middle salary.*
25 – 30	Unsatisfactory.	Dismiss from present position.

* For Cu-2 and Cu-3, the fourth salary rate will be considered the middle salary

quality of performance, productiveness, and qualifications shown on the job. The law with reference to "averages" still exists but its force has been softened; and the former regulations correlating increments with ratings have been greatly eased by the new form. The form is shown on page 381.

The many difficulties which surrounded the use of the graphic rating scale in the Washington service were partly adventitious. As a device for securing a formal record the graphic form has considerable merit, and deserves to rank today as one of the useful rating instruments. Like all other records, it cannot rise above the level of intelligence and honesty with which it is used nor can it obviate differences of standards among supervisors. These are inherent defects in any written record. The form is sound as far as it goes and may be recommended for use.[1]

The personality inventory seeks a comparative record of service by different means, or at least with a markedly different emphasis on some common means. The best known illustration is the Probst Rating scale, invented and developed by Mr. J. B. Probst, Chief Examiner of the St. Paul Civil Service Bureau, and shown in reduced form on page 383.[2]

The essential feature of the Probst system is a comprehensive, descriptive list of traits or characteristics which, taken as a whole, are intended to include almost any possible combination of human qualities relevant to employment. From among these qualities of personality the rating officers (two or three for each employee) select the particular items descriptive of the employee in question. From ten to twenty-five such items are usually picked out without difficulty. A number of special forms have been devised for different types of employees, such as policemen, firemen, librarians, and teachers, in addition to the basic form which is adaptable to a wide variety of employment.

The rating officers do not arrive at a rating themselves and are not given the weights which, on the basis of extensive trial and error experiments, have been attached to each item. The rating, which is expressed by a letter indicating one of eleven groups (A to E–), is derived by adding the proper weights to the selected factors, plus or minus, and by reading the appropriate letter from a numerical scale.

The Probst system, like the graphic rating scale, is subjective and cannot avoid the hazards of lack of intelligence or good will on the part of rating officers. It does have the great merit, however, of putting supervisors on record in so detailed a manner as to make downright

[1] Some of the difficulties are discussed by Forrest A. Kingsbury, "Analyzing Ratings and Training Raters," 1 *J. of Personnel Research* 377-83 (1922–23), and "Making Rating Scales Work," 4 *ibid.* 1-6 (1925–26).

[2] J. B. Probst, *Service Ratings* (1931).

Probst Service Report (General Form)

DIRECTIONS: Place an X mark next to each of the items on this page which you know from your own knowledge will describe or fit this employe. Do not guess; check only if you are reasonably certain.

Check Columns 1	2	3	
☐	☐	☐	Lazy
☐	☐	☐	Slow moving
☐	☐	☐	Quick and active
☐	☐	☐	Too old for the work
☐	☐	☐	Minor physical defects
☐	☐	☐	Serious physical defects
☐	☐	☐	Indifferent; not interested
☐	☐	☐	Talks too much
☐	☐	☐	Too blunt or outspoken
☐	☐	☐	Too much self-importance
☐	☐	☐	Good team worker
☐	☐	☐	Not a good team worker
☐	☐	☐	Resents criticism or suggestions
☐	☐	☐	Antagonizes when dealing with others
☐	☐	☐	Might often be more considerate
☐	☐	☐	Usually pleasant and cheerful
☐	☐	☐	Unusually courteous
☐	☐	☐	Cranky disposition
☐	☐	☐	Often seems dissatisfied
☐	☐	☐	Often grumbling or complaining
☐	☐	☐	Uses poor judgment
☐	☐	☐	Might often use better judgment
☐	☐	☐	Generally uses good judgment
☐	☐	☐	Always uses good judgment
☐	☐	☐	Does not do his (her) share of work
☐	☐	☐	Generally looks for the easy work
☐	☐	☐	Must generally be told what to do
☐	☐	☐	Work often slightly behind
☐	☐	☐	Often needs prodding
☐	☐	☐	Work always up to date
☐	☐	☐	Turns out unusually large amount of work
☐	☐	☐	Steady worker most of the time
☐	☐	☐	Always busy at work
☐	☐	☐	Does not accept responsibility
☐	☐	☐	Accepts responsibility
☐	☐	☐	Does not always obey orders willingly
☐	☐	☐	Visits too much with others
☐	☐	☐	Needs considerable supervision
☐	☐	☐	Works well without supervision
☐	☐	☐	Fine self-control; seldom or never loses temper
☐	☐	☐	Loses temper easily
☐	☐	☐	Easily rattled
☐	☐	☐	Lacks self-confidence
☐	☐	☐	Too easy-going
☐	☐	☐	Learns new work slowly
☐	☐	☐	Learns new work easily
☐	☐	☐	Understands instructions readily
☐	☐	☐	A willing worker at all times
☐	☐	☐	Takes unusual interest in the work
☐	☐	☐	Might be more orderly
☐	☐	☐	Very orderly and systematic
☐	☐	☐	Often forgetful
☐	☐	☐	Often does careless work
☐	☐	☐	Makes many mistakes
☐	☐	☐	Usually accurate
☐	☐	☐	Hardly ever makes a mistake
☐	☐	☐	Accurate but very deliberate
☐	☐	☐	Is highly expert in own work
☐	☐	☐	Not generally reliable or dependable
☐	☐	☐	Usually reliable and dependable
☐	☐	☐	Always reliable and dependable

Check Columns 1	2	3	
☐	☐	☐	Active and strong
☐	☐	☐	Active but not strong
☐	☐	☐	Usually careless of personal appearance
☐	☐	☐	Usually neat personal appearance
☐	☐	☐	Has a pleasing voice and manner
☐	☐	☐	Very tactful in dealing with the public
☐	☐	☐	Poor technical training for the work
☐	☐	☐	Good technical training for the work
☐	☐	☐	Poor head work in sudden emergencies
☐	☐	☐	Good head work in sudden emergencies
☐	☐	☐	Often assigned to other important positions*
☐	☐	☐	Often assigned to fill a higher position*
☐	☐	☐	Sometimes goes on a "tear"
☐	☐	☐	Drink is one of principal failings

These items are for supervisory or administrative positions only:

Check Columns 1	2	3	
☐	☐	☐	Willing worker, but is not a leader
☐	☐	☐	Does not plan or lay out work effectively
☐	☐	☐	Plans work well but lacks snap in getting it done
☐	☐	☐	Unusual ability in planning and laying out work; good organizer
☐	☐	☐	Makes quick and accurate decisions
☐	☐	☐	Too lenient in maintaining discipline
☐	☐	☐	Maintains good discipline
☐	☐	☐	Discipline too harsh
☐	☐	☐	Exceptionally skillful in handling difficult situations

In the following spaces you may add such other items of your own as you believe will further describe this employe.

Check Columns 1	2	3	
☐	☐	☐	
☐	☐	☐	
☐	☐	☐	
☐	☐	☐	
☐	☐	☐	

REMARKS

* Temporary assignments

dishonesty vastly more difficult. High graders and low graders still upset the best results, but the second or third rating by higher officials does something to iron out these discrepancies. The third rating (by an official two degrees removed from the subordinate) is frequently difficult to secure and when secured is not always based on adequate knowledge.

The personality inventory is much more flexible than the graphic rating scales, and as developed by Probst offers a very wide range of choice. This very range, however, tends to discourage rating officers at first. Unless carefully watched, they work out certain patterns which they are inclined to repeat in case after case, thus destroying the real value of the plan.

No other single rating scale has been so widely experimented with or so widely used. The evidence indicates that satisfactory results can be secured with it. The best results here as in other systems require close supervision and eternal vigilance on the part of some higher authority, either from within the department or from the personnel agency. The same deteriorating factors already noted above may weaken the usefulness of the Probst system as well as any other scheme.[1]

In the light of the foregoing analysis, what can be said of American experience and point of view with reference to formal records of efficiency? Influenced no doubt by the underlying philosophy of scientific management, American experts have pushed their experiments toward an "objective" and automatic system boldly and hopefully, but not always with adequate insight into the hazards of their venture. Production records are reasonably objective criteria of efficiency, but all judgment ratings are subjective and are not cured of the inevitable variability of human opinion by being spread out on a graphic rating scale or in an elaborate personality inventory.

Inspired by an extraordinary faith in the validity of various schemes, they have been put to work in some jurisdictions with a thoroughness which cast caution to the winds. Men and women have been singled out to lose their jobs, to sacrifice a part of their income, and to abandon prospect of promotion because a mathematical conversion of a series of check marks by supervisors totaled less than an arbitrary sum. The effort to control the judgment of supervisors to this degree and to govern the fate of individuals in this way is not sound personnel policy.

The defense made for it is that unless a formal record is established and made conclusive, the bias, prejudice, or ill will of supervisory offi-

[1] An interesting form of rating was introduced in New York City in 1935 which seeks to secure objective evidence to support exceptional ratings. See Samuel C. Ordway, Jr., and J. C. Laffan, *Approaches to the Measurement and Reward of Effective Work of Individual Government Employees* (1935), and the annual reports of the New York City Civil Service Commission.

cials will produce even worse results. There are doubtless illustrations of personal malice or poor judgment among a small minority of officials; but no one should suppose that they will be more reliable in making out an efficiency record than in taking any other action. The only cure is more intelligent and trustworthy supervisors. In other words a formal rating by a supervisor cannot be expected to achieve indirectly what the supervisor does not intend or is not able to do directly.

Experience with formal rating systems indicates definitely that careful supervision of the rating officers is essential even to moderate success. Such supervision may come from high officials in the department if the promotion and lay-off system is departmental in scope. But if promotions and lay-offs are service-wide and the efficiency rating is one of the factors of decision, the supervision must come from a central agency such as the civil service commission. This supervision should be primarily educational and advisory, continuous in nature, and directed toward securing uniformity and accuracy. After the records are deposited, they require careful analysis to reveal variations in standards or other errors, which guide subsequent supervision.

Another type of supervision may be secured by allowing individual appeals to the civil service commission. In the interest of maintaining the authority of the departmental officials such appeals are not recommended. On the other hand an opportunity for departmental appeal and review should certainly exist.

Most of the difficulties encountered with efficiency ratings in the United States may be alleviated by (a) broad simple categories of performance; (b) caution in the use of the results, and (c) greater skill and care among the supervisors who make the ratings.

What are the real uses of a formal efficiency rating? Partly, without doubt, to furnish one basis of judgment in handling personnel; partly to protect employees against the snap judgments, prejudice, and ill will of some supervisors; and partly, in a well-managed organization, to point out to employees their strong and weak characteristics.[1] The finest type of personnel work consists in aiding employees to make the most of themselves and their opportunities. A flexible system of efficiency ratings which commands respect and which will bring out points of personality, character, and skills is a helpful device. The emphasis of the last two decades upon the efficiency record as the automatic and unerring hand of fate—"the moving finger writes and having writ, moves on"—is

[1] An undeveloped but important use of service ratings is as an aid in the day-by-day supervision of employees. The technique of supervision is a sadly uncultivated art which is gradually being organized by Dr. L. J. O'Rourke of the U. S. Civil Service Commission. Consult Ordway Tead, *The Art of Leadership* (1935); U. S. Department of Agriculture, *Elements of Personnel Administration* (1935).

unwholesome and unnecessary. A new emphasis in which the objective is to aid the employee by calling attention to his weak points, if any, and to facilitate vocational counseling and career possibilities rather than to concentrate on the negative and policing elements of earlier practice might go far to make efficiency ratings a greater asset to the public service.

Chapter Twenty-five

FORMS AND METHODS OF DISCIPLINE

DISCIPLINARY methods in public office have gradually evolved from a rough and ready policy of "hire and fire" without restriction or supervision, for any or no reason, into more formal procedures. The enactment of civil service legislation marked the chief transition point, since the merit system conferred relatively permanent status protected by certain formalities intended to prevent separation for other than just cause.[1] A similar trend is to be observed in large industrial organizations in many of which the power of the foreman to discharge has been vested in or made subject to review by the plant superintendent or the personnel officer. In public office the trend has gone farther in some instances both in establishing the specific causes for removal and in creating formal methods of appeal and review. No standard practice has been developed nor is there yet any widespread agreement in principle, especially concerning the right of review.[2]

The infrequency with which formal cases of discipline arise is no index to the importance of discipline in systems of public administration, or indeed in any social organization. Subtle forms of discipline are constantly making their influence felt although no overt action is taken or is required; and it is perhaps these more than the formally recognized methods with which a wise administrator will concern himself. In any event discipline is not a conscious concern of the great majority of employees whose personal standards make formal external direction unnecessary; it is a specific and more or less regular necessity for a few and a marginal concern of others.

A number of terms are loosely used in reference to certain classes of disciplinary action. To avoid misunderstanding, the particular meaning

[1] Early experience in removal procedure under civil service is noted in Clay Lawrence, "Police Removals and the Courts," 20 *Pol. Sci. Q.* 68-90 (1905); and in Charles Kettleborough, "Removal of Public Officers: A Ten-Year Review," 8 *Am. Pol. Sci. Rev.* 621-29 (1914).

[2] This chapter will not deal with the constitutional and legal aspects of the removal power, which may be studied in such references as W. W. Willoughby, *The Constitutional Law of the United States* (2d ed. 1929), vol. 3, ch. 84; James Hart, *Tenure of Office under the Constitution* (1930); *Myers vs. U.S.*, 272 U.S. 52 (1926), and *Humphrey's Executor vs. U.S.*, 295 U.S. 602 (1935).

which is attached to these terms in this book may be stated at this point. Separation is a general phrase applying to the termination of employment, with or without prejudice; thus it covers such different cases as lay-off, resignation, discharge, removal, and retirement. It is the usual unit employed in the calculation of rates of turnover. Furlough is a word used to describe an enforced vacation without pay for a determinate period, usually to reduce expenditures. A lay-off is an indeterminate separation under the same circumstances. Neither has any disciplinary connotation. Suspension is a term usually associated with discipline; it means the enforced relinquishment of duties for a determinate period without pay. Discharge and removal are two phrases implying permanent separation; both are used for separation for cause. Resignation indicates a permanent separation brought about by the initiative of the employee, normally without prejudice or the suggestion of offense. An employee in the merit system who resigns retains rights to reinstatement; but one who is separated as a penalty can be reinstated only upon proof of good character. The foregoing are the customary meanings attached to these terms, but they are often inaccurately employed; and in some cases different meanings are given by law or regulation.

In a healthy organization the staff possesses a high morale which relegates discipline of any type to a position of secondary importance. For most persons the attitudes and morale of the group are a sufficient guide to conduct; and where effective leadership and good supervision exist problems of discipline largely disappear. The basic attack on disciplinary problems is therefore an indirect one, rather than the search for new forms of action or the imposition of heavier penalties.

Discipline in the public service is especially important where the temptation is greatest and the pressure is most severe. It is therefore not surprising to learn that police departments offer the most difficult instances of discipline in municipal government, and that in the federal administration such groups as the customs service, the border patrol, the anti-narcotic force and the investigators of the Department of Justice present special aspects of the general problem. By contrast, discipline is less rigid in such agencies as the National Archives service, the clerical services of a state office, or a city library. The nature of the problem varies also with the character of the personnel; thus the situation is different in an organization manned by professional and scientific workers than in an agency chiefly composed of individuals without a professional outlook.

The need for disciplinary action arises under a great variety of circumstances. The ordinary causes which put in motion some form of discipline include (1) inattention to duty—tardiness, laziness, carelessness, breakage or loss of property, etc.; (2) inefficiency; (3) insubordination, violation of law or regulation, disloyalty; (4) intoxication; (5) immorality; (6) lack of integrity, including violation of a recognized code of ethics, failure to pay debts, soliciting or accepting a bribe or deliberately neglecting to enforce the law.[1] A common formula which is elastic enough to cover a multitude of sins is "conduct unbecoming an officer."

The broad distinction between indirect and informal types of discipline and the direct and recognized forms has already been suggested. The informal methods of discipline are legion in form and circumstance. They may involve only a chill in the atmosphere. They may mean reassignment to less desirable work, closer supervision, or the loss of privileges. They may involve failure to invite the "disciplinee" to confer or consult in relevant matters, or rejection of his proposals by a superior officer. They may include reduction in his estimates and curtailing of his authority, or a reorganization the effect of which is to diminish his responsibility. In fact disciplinary measures may take any one of a hundred forms without resort to any of the procedures established in law or regulations. The reason for this active and omnipresent system of control lies in the fact that many offenses are too slight, or too subtle, or too difficult to prove to warrant direct and formal action.[2]

Formal types of discipline vary from a timely notice to judicial prosecution. Some well-established types of penalty include: informal notice and warning; reprimand, with or without entry on the record; requirement of overtime (especially in police departments); loss of seniority rights or delay in salary increment; suspension; demotion; removal for cause; judicial prosecution.

These penalties fall into two general classes, varying according to their severity and often requiring different procedures. One group, which may be called penalties of the first degree, is minor in character, including warning, reprimand, delay in salary increment, and loss of seniority rights. These are usually imposed and enforced by the head of the office or division on his own responsibility and without review. A second group includes the more severe penalties—suspension, demotion, removal, and judicial prosecution. While practice varies greatly these sanctions usually require action by the head of the department, and in many jurisdictions the employee is allowed to appeal to an independent administrative agency or, more rarely, to the courts. In Euro-

[1] See Florence E. Allen, "Remedies Against Dishonest or Inefficient Public Servants," 169 *Annals* 172-83 (1933).

[2] William E. Mosher and J. D. Kingsley, *Public Personnel Administration* (1936), ch. 17; Lewis Meriam, *Public Personnel Problems* (1938), ch. 9.

pean administrative systems an appeal to an administrative tribunal is the established practice but not in Great Britain, where the position of the head of the organization is carefully protected.

Great diversity exists in American practice with reference to the more severe instances of discipline. Four cases may be distinguished: the first leaves all disciplinary authority in the department head, as for example in the state of Mississippi among many other jurisdictions; the second stipulates cause as the prerequisite for removal but gives substantially no review, as in the federal system; a third provides formal administrative review, as in Chicago; and the fourth, judicial review, as in Massachusetts.

The situation in Mississippi is typical (although in varying degree) of many state, most county, and some municipal governments. There is neither a merit system nor a civil service commission; there are few legal restrictions upon the unlimited right of the head of a department or office to discipline or discharge his subordinates for any reason or no reason. The position resembles that found in many industrial and nongovernmental agencies, in which the right to "hire and fire" is unlimited. It is the historic tradition in this country. It emphasizes the complete responsibility of the head of the office, institution or department. So long as no sharp factional disputes arise within the dominant party in those areas where one party is usually in control, serious damage may not occur; but the wholesale displacement of trained personnel in Pennsylvania and other states subsequent to change of party control in 1933 throws a lurid light upon the calamitous consequences to the public service which an unrestricted right of removal may entail.

Reasons of public policy therefore dictate some restriction upon the unlimited freedom of the head of the agency to remove, whether a formal merit system prevails or not. In the national government definite limitations are imposed by law and by the civil service rules, although final responsibility (with two exceptions) remains in the head of the department or establishment. An act of August 24, 1912, prescribes the fundamental requirements.[1]

Sec. 6. That no person in the classified civil service of the United States shall be removed therefrom except for such cause as will promote the efficiency of said service and for reasons given in writing, and the person whose removal is sought shall have notice of the same and of any charges preferred against him, and be furnished with a copy thereof, and also be allowed a reasonable time for personally answering the same in writing; and affidavits in support thereof; but no examination of witnesses nor any trial or hearing shall be required except in the discretion of the officer making the removal; and copies of charges, notice of hearing, answer, reasons for removal, and of the order of removal shall be made a part of the rec

[1] 37 Stat. 539.

> ords of the proper department or office, as shall also the reasons for reduction in rank or compensation; and copies of the same shall be furnished to the person affected upon request, and the Civil Service Commission also shall, upon request, be furnished copies of the same: *Provided, however*, That membership in any society, association, club, or other form of organization of postal employees not affiliated with any outside organization imposing an obligation or duty upon them to engage in any strike, or proposing to assist them in any strike, against the United States, having for its objects, among other things, improvements in the condition of labor of its members, including hours of labor and compensation therefor and leave of absence, by any person or groups of persons in said Postal Service, or the presenting by any such person or groups of persons of any grievance or grievances to the Congress or any Member thereof, shall not constitute or be cause for reduction in rank or compensation or removal of such person or groups of persons from said service. The right of persons employed in the civil service of the United States, either individually or collectively, to petition Congress, or any Member thereof, or to furnish information to either House of Congress, or to any committee or Member thereof, shall not be denied or interfered with.

The rules of the U. S. Civil Service Commission require like penalties for like offenses although the Commission has no legal power to enforce its findings. Suspension is allowed for a maximum of ninety days. The Commission is vested with authority to investigate only when it is alleged that the procedure required by law or rule has not been followed, that unequal penalties have been imposed for like offenses, or that political or religious discrimination has been exercised. The Commission has no jurisdiction to investigate the sufficiency of the reasons for a removal, which are finally determined by the appointing officer. Nor do the courts have jurisdiction to review the sufficiency of reasons for the action of an appointing officer in removing an employee.[1] In the national service an employee's fitness, capacity and attention to duty are questions of discretion and judgment to be determined by the head of his department.

The effect of these provisions is to leave the power to discipline and to remove in the departmental authority, subject to the requirement of notice, orderly procedure and publicity in case of removal. The power to discipline is not restricted by the civil service status of the employee, nor by the supervisory influence of the Civil Service Commission. The widespread impression that a merit system employee cannot be effectively disciplined or removed is without foundation in the national service as in most other merit jurisdictions. If discipline is lax and if incompetent employees are not removed, the fault lies with the responsible officials in the department, not with the protected status of the workers.

In fact discipline in the established national agencies under the merit system is generally well maintained. The number of discharges for cause

[1] *Taylor vs. Taft*, 24 App. D. C. 95 (1904).

is not large but other types of discipline are freely used. The same generalization holds for state and local civil service jurisdictions. Employees not under the merit system are likely to cause more trouble since the real center of authority and control may lie outside rather than within the official hierarchy.

For some years there has been agitation in Washington for an independent court of appeals to hear employee grievances. Pressure for such a body is gradually increasing and it is possible that some form of appeal will be authorized in the near future. The problem has been intensified by two significant cases. The first involved an employee of the National Recovery Administration, John Donovan, who was summarily discharged by General Hugh Johnson. Donovan's friends picketed the General's office, claiming that he had been discharged for union activity and that section 7(a) of the National Industrial Recovery Act should apply to require his reinstatement. An agreement was reached to lay the matter before the National Labor Relations Board, which found that Johnson's action "must be considered in its effects, whatever the subjective intent, as a blow to legitimate union activities." Donovan's reinstatement was ordered and effected.[1]

The second case involved an employee of the Federal Power Commission, Robert Y. Durand. It was alleged that his removal was ordered because of union activities. The case was heard in the autumn of 1936 by an *ad hoc* committee presided over by Edwin S. Smith of the National Labor Relations Board. After extensive hearings the committee reached the conclusion that the discharge was "to some extent animated by . . . adverse feelings on the organized activities undertaken by him and his associates for bettering the welfare of the employees prior to and during the period of promoting a union in the Commission." Durand's reinstatement was ordered and put into effect. In their decision the committee recorded their opinion that a standing tribunal should exist before which employees could bring individual grievances.[2]

The case for such a tribunal rests in part upon the protection of the right of employees to form unions, which was recognized in 1912, in part upon the desirability of protecting employees against the unjustified action of supervisors. In such a large organization as the federal civil service injustice is doubtless done in some cases, although probably the number of cases is not great.

The arguments against an independent tribunal have so far prevailed. Opponents of the proposal assert that it overemphasizes the rights of the employee and fails to give sufficient recognition to the interest of the

[1] The decision is printed in full in the *Washington Post,* August 22, 1934.

[2] This case was reported in the daily press of January 21, 1937.

responsible official in maintaining proper control of his office. Decisions of an independent board against a department or institution and in favor of an employee tend, it is said, to undermine the position of the principal, to create undesirable attitudes on the part of the subordinate and of his friends, and to nourish feuds and divisions within the organization. Nor is it certain that the decisions of an outside agency, which can never be as intimately informed as the department itself, are either wiser or fairer than properly safeguarded decisions of the latter. An independent agency to which appeal can be made, moreover, tends to make administrative discipline a matter of formal proof with increasing emphasis upon rules of evidence and technicalities of procedure rather than a matter of employment management.

The desire for an independent court of appeals to review disciplinary cases in such a large organization as the federal administration is understandable even though it is subject to some objections. However, the case for conciliation committees organized within the departments and commissions is impregnable. Their function is not to replace the authority of the responsible official but to supplement it, and by informal negotiation to seek the reconciliation of conflicts without incurring the necessity for formal action by any outside body. A representative conciliation committee in sympathetic hands can perform a major service and is a useful part of any large organization.[1]

Such conciliation agencies were recommended by the United States Civil Service Commission in 1934 and a conciliation committee was established within the Commission. Three of its members are elected by the employees, three appointed by the Commission. While it has found little business, it has successfully ironed out several difficulties which were potential sources of friction. Its existence alone is a symbol of the desire of the Commission to meet halfway all proper complaints. Conciliation committees look in another direction than arbitration boards. They recognize that many behavior disturbances call for treatment rather than discipline. The connection between carelessness and poor health, between lack of attention and financial worries, and between a short temper and eye strain are well established. They point to more adequate supervision rather than to the use of either formal or informal types of discipline.

In a relatively small number of instances, which we shall illustrate by the case of Chicago, removals can be effected only after hearing and order by the civil service commission. The power of the head of the department or institution is confined to the making of charges and the

[1] Cf. U. S. Department of Agriculture, *Personnel Relations Policy and Procedure*, Memorandum No. 753, May 4, 1938 (mim.).

offer of proof. The Illinois municipal civil service law of 1895 contained the following provisions which are still in force in Chicago:[1]

> No officer or employe in the classified civil service of any city, who shall have been appointed under said rules and after said examination, shall be removed or discharged except for cause, upon written charges and after an opportunity to be heard in his own defense. Such charges shall be investigated by or before said civil service commission, or by or before some officer or board appointed by said commission, to conduct such investigation. The finding and decision of such commission or investigating officer or board, when approved by said commission, shall be certified to the appointing officer, and shall be forthwith enforced by such officer.

This procedure does not apply to laborers or persons having the custody of public money for the safe-keeping of which another person has given bonds.

The character of the hearing in Chicago has had an interesting evolution. From 1895 to 1901 the employee against whom charges were filed was required to petition for a hearing. But in 1901 the Commission decided to investigate independently all charges filed with it and to hold hearings in each case. The amount of business naturally increased greatly and in 1904 an attorney and two investigators were added to represent the Commission in preparing cases. The hearings became more and more like a judicial trial, involving legal counsel, witnesses, and rules of evidence. Trials consumed days and even weeks of the commissioners' time. "The departmental trouble maker with a nice point of law had not only his day, but his weeks in court before the trial board. The commission went at a plain question of employment through pleas of 'guilty' and 'not guilty,' answers, demurrers, rulings, citations of authorities and appeals, and, in course of time, created a system of jurisprudence about the words 'removed or discharged except for cause on written charges and after an opportunity to be heard in his own defence.' "[2]

After two prolonged trials in 1906 important changes were made. The special police and fire trial boards were abandoned; the Commission heard all charges directly; the case was decided, usually without the presence of professional counsel, from the point of view of an ordinary employer. The Commission came to regard itself more as an administrative or disciplinary body than as a court and was able to reduce substantially the amount of time required for hearing cases. In 1915 the Commission reported that the trial work did not consume more than

[1] Illinois Laws 1895, p. 85, sec. 12.

[2] Robert Catherwood, "The Development of Efficiency in the Civil Service," in *Proceedings of the National Civil Service Reform League*, 1910, pp. 163-75.

our hours a week; now the Commission sits usually Wednesday morn-ng and afternoon, and sometimes on Thursday morning of each week.

That independent review by the Chicago Civil Service Commission as actually saved some accused employees from discharge is clear from he following table of cases:

TABLE IX

DISPOSITION OF CASES BEFORE THE CHICAGO CIVIL SERVICE COMMISSION

YEAR	CHARGES FILED	REMOVED FROM SERVICE	ACQUITTED
1915	514	86	132
1920	414	65	121
1925	667	101	269
1930	336	24	120
1935	174	26	97

Judicial review of decisions of the Civil Service Commission is pen on grounds of irregular procedure and bad faith on the part of the ommission, including absence of evidence on which the decision can e based. The sufficiency of the evidence is usually accepted by the ourts as prima facie; in rare cases it has been rejected as inadequate.

The chief value of an independent administrative review is to secure onsideration by an impartial and disinterested body. Public confidence the impartiality of the Chicago Civil Service Commission has been aken from time to time by some extraordinary decisions which it has eached. Thus the Commission sustained charges in 1918 against the econd deputy commissioner of police; but on certiorari, the Supreme ourt quashed the removal, saying, “. . . there is nothing in the return ade to this writ from which the court can see that there was any tempt to prove any of the facts or what was the particular state of cts upon which he was found guilty.”[1] Over ten years later a mem-er of the Commission was indicted for malfeasance, but died before e case came to trial. Unless a commission is absolutely impartial and is enerally recognized to be impartial, its review of charges leading to moval is of dubious value.

Chicago city employees, however, are practically unanimous in re-rding the review by the Civil Service Commission, such as it is, as a tal protection both to their own interests and to the merit system. his opinion is confirmed by the ruthless disregard by both political rties of the status of merit system employees in the Illinois state serv-

[1] *Funkhouser vs. Coffin*, 301 Illinois 257 (1922).

ice, where no such protection has been available since 1917. On the basis of two years' experience as a member of the Chicago Commission I reached the conclusion that in the circumstances prevailing in this city an independent review of removals by the Civil Service Commission is desirable; it would be more desirable if confidence in the Commission were enhanced.

The ultimate stage in the process of protecting employees against unfair action by superior officials is illustrated by the law of Massachusetts, which provides opportunity for state, county, city and town employees to appeal to the courts for final decision of important disciplinary issues. Present limitations on the right of removal began in 1894. In this year legislation provided that veterans could be removed from classified city positions only after a hearing by the mayor. In 190[illegible] the same protection was made to cover reduction in rank or compensation of veterans. In 1911 an entirely new system of protection was established by law. All civil employees, veteran or nonveteran, were granted the right of a public hearing of charges before the officials responsible for removal or reduction in rank and compensation; and the police, district or municipal courts were vested with authority to review the findings and order of the administrative official. ". . . a new function of district judges as arbitrators of administrative matters was established." [1]

The law governing removal from classified positions in the public service of the Commonwealth of Massachusetts in its present form contains these provisions:

> . . . every person holding office or employment in the classified public service of the commonwealth, or of any county, city or town thereof, shall hold such office or employment and shall not be removed therefrom, lowered in rank or compensation or suspended, or without his consent transferred from such office or employment to any other, except for just cause, and for reasons specifically given him in writing within twenty-four hours. . . .
>
> If within three days thereafter, the person sought to be removed, suspended, lowered or transferred shall so request in writing, he shall be given a public hearing in not less than three nor more than fourteen days after the filing of the request, by the officer or board whose action affected him as aforesaid, and he shall be allowed to answer the charges preferred against him, either personally or by counsel, and shall be notified, in writing within three days after the hearing, of the decision of such officer or board. In default of such hearing, said person shall forthwith be reinstated. A copy of said reasons, notice, answer and decision shall be made a matter of public record in the department. . . .
>
> Within thirty days after the hearing . . . the person so removed, transferred or lowered in rank or compensation, or suspended, or whose office or position is abo

[1] George C. S. Benson, *The Administration of the Civil Service in Massachusetts* (1935), ch. 5.

shed [except certain police] may bring a petition in the district court of the judi- ial district where such person resides, . . . praying that the action of the officer or oard may be reviewed by the court, and after . . . notice . . . it shall review such ction, hear the witnesses, and shall affirm the decision of the officer or board unless t shall appear that it was made without proper cause or in bad faith, in which case aid decision shall be reversed and the petitioner be reinstated in his office without oss of compensation. The decision of the court shall be final and conclusive upon he parties.[1]

Benson notes that two other channels of judicial appeal are open to a eparated employee. On points of law he may petition directly to a ingle justice of the supreme court for a writ of mandamus if he has xhausted the statutory remedies, with subsequent opportunity for re- iew by the full bench. The number of these cases has not been great ut they have been instrumental in settling disputed points of law. A less requently used method is action of contract on wages due an employee. The most common method is the statutory review described in the pre- eding excerpt from the law.

Under this procedure, district court judges have been compelled to ass on such questions as whether or not employees have come to work n time, the physical condition of a kitchen attendant, the level of sal- ries for hospital employees, the efficiency of a bookkeeper, the neces- ity for a hospital superintendent, the proper lubrication of a machine y a mechanic, and whether a water department foreman was discharged or reasons of economy. The courts generally limit themselves to a re- iew of the action taken, avoiding a retrial with resubmission of evi- ence and offer of new evidence. Apparently most of the cases go gainst the employee.

A similar procedure has been developed for the members of the New ork City police department. The New York City Administrative Code rovides that no member of the police force shall be fined, reprimanded, emoved, suspended or dismissed from the police force until written harges have been preferred and heard before the police commissioner r deputy. This procedure has been held judicial in character and re- iewable by the courts on writ of certiorari. Contrary to the original ractice, the courts now review the competency and weight of the evi- ence as well as the procedure before the commissioner. The court will ot, however, consider whether the extent of the punishment was too evere.[2]

In the fourteen years prior to 1912, 683 policemen sought reinstate- ent through the courts. Of these cases only forty-six were decided

[1] General Laws of Massachusetts, 1932, c. 31, secs. 43, 45.

[2] Elmer D. Graper, *American Police Administration* (1921), pp. 100-3.

against the department, twenty-six on account of evidence, and twent cases on grounds of irregular procedure. During the years 1914–191 there were one hundred and twenty-six dismissals after administrati trial and only three judicial reinstatements. In three years, 1935, 193 and 1937 there were 200 dismissals and four reinstatements by cou order.

What conclusions can be reached as to preferred disciplinary pr cedures and safeguards? Is the historical business pattern of "hire an fire" a better solution than the judicial protection against arbitrary di ciplinary action which has been espoused by Massachusetts? Or is ther a reasonably clear midway solution which avoids the dangers inhere in either extreme position?[1]

The answer has to be framed not entirely in the light of the prefe ences of responsible officials, whose term of office is usually brief, n entirely in the interest of the employees. Their legitimate interests a subordinate to the superior interest of the people for whom the who system of administration exists. The public interest itself requires som guarantee of fairness, justice and stability in the administrative corp otherwise its agents will work under conditions which induce bad fee ing, fear, intrigue and lowered morale. But the public interest als requires adequate disciplinary authority and its proper use. On th whole there has been too little rather than too liberal use of disciplinar power.

Generalizations are, however, almost certain to be misleading. In on jurisdiction may be found settled traditions of good government an fair play which maintain high standards without formal procedures an without inducing the necessity for protective devices; in another, tradi tions of political and factional reprisal destroy the very expectation o fair treatment and induce elaborate protective devices of one type o another.

Orderly procedure in cases of formal disciplinary action, includin full publicity, is a minimum requirement. Protection against removal o discrimination for reasons other than the good of the service—specifi cally for reasons of politics, favoritism, race and religion—is an essentia element in any jurisdiction. Opinions differ as to the proper procedur by which such fundamentals can best be safeguarded.

From one point of view elaborate safeguards against removal seem t be consonant with the purposes of the merit system; but they may i the end convince the public that the merit system is bought at too grea a price—the price of an uncontrolled bureaucracy. In the balance o

[1] Foreign experience is summarized by Herman Finer, "The Civil Service and th Modern State: Discipline and Rights," 7 *Pub. Adm.* 323-42 (1929).

interests, it is probable that we should avoid independent review of disciplinary action by courts; that review and decision by a civil service commission or a court of appeal should be exceptional and available only for unusual cases and serious penalties; and that much greater emphasis should be laid on better personnel work, buttressed by conciliation committees within the departments.

Chapter Twenty-six

RETIREMENT SYSTEMS

THE establishment of a satisfactory retirement system for govern ment employees has taken on new importance in recent years. Or the one hand, the number of public employees benefiting by a retirement allowance has greatly increased due to the expansion of old agencies and the appearance of new ones. The actual or apparent finan cial burdens placed upon the taxpayers have increased, partly on accoun of more favorable terms of retirement, partly by the mere growth in numbers, partly by a more complete realization of the amount of futur commitments made without actuarial advice. On the other hand, th Social Security Act extends the principle of old-age security to the grea mass of citizens, but excepts employees of public authorities. The de mand on the part of government employees for similar protection in cases where no retirement system is in force has logic on its side. W may therefore expect to see considerable expansion of retirement sys tems for public employees in the near future, and eventually discussion of the ways in which these systems may be coordinated each with th other.[1]

1. The Development of Retirement Systems

Civil pensions in the federal government became an object of interes

[1] For a broad discussion of pension policy, see Henry S. Pritchett, *The Soci Philosophy of Pensions* (1930). The principal work on public retirement systems Lewis Meriam, *Principles Governing the Retirement of Public Employees* (1918 Important official studies were made by Herbert D. Brown, *Civil Service Retire ment*, S. Doc. 290, 61st Cong., 2d sess. (1910), and S. Doc. 745, 61st Cong., 3d ses (1911); see also H. Doc. 732, 62d Cong., 2d sess. (1912). A brief treatment of hi torical interest is, Pension Committee of the National Municipal League, "Pensior in Public Employment," 11 *Nat. Mun. Rev.* 97-124 (1922). The sixth report of th New York State Commission on Pensions contains valuable data, Legislative Do 111, 1922. The federal system may be studied from the annual reports of the Boar of Actuaries and of the U. S. Civil Service Commission and from the quinquenni valuation of the Board of Actuaries. Local pension plans are described in Mass chusetts H. Doc. 1501, 1936. A recent proposal for a state pension plan is the *Repo of Commission Appointed to Study Pension Systems in the State of Connecticu* Conn. Public Doc. 88, 1937.

as early as 1845.[1] In that year a committee of the House of Representatives reported, "The list of officers becomes a pension roll; the public departments are sought to be converted into national poorhouses." The committee urged as the panacea for this "un-American" predicament that the term of office be limited to a period so short "that the incumbents will hardly be able to forget that they are once more to become private citizens."

In 1867 a writer in the *North American Review* stated: "If parts of the public offices are thus degenerated into dormitories, other parts of them are nothing but asylums, where the aged and infirm luxuriate, as far as their scanty salary permits, in a kind of official hospital of invalids, constituting a formidable though venerable reserve force of incapacities."[2]

From time to time comments were made in the course of debate in Congress which indicated a "rapidly growing civil pension list," and after 1904 there was a more or less continuous demand from department officials for some form of retirement legislation. Great impetus was given the movement by the carefully prepared report of the President's Commission on Economy and Efficiency in 1912, and by the leadership of President Taft in urging retirement legislation. Congress, however, was reluctant to act and it was not until 1920 that a retirement system was finally established.[3]

Meanwhile, however, retirement systems had been put into effect in many local jurisdictions, especially for policemen, firemen and teachers. The earliest of these is the New York City pension fund for policemen, established in 1857. The New York City Teachers' Mutual Life Assurance Fund, founded in 1869, was the first formal teachers' retirement plan.

Growth was slow until the advancing merit system established the rule of continuity of employment, but with the second generation of civil service employees the demand for a retirement system became widespread. A large majority of existing state and city pension plans were established subsequent to the World War.

By 1938 twelve states, including Massachusetts (1911), Maine and Connecticut (1919), New York (1920), New Jersey (1921), Pennsyl-

[1] John T. Doyle, "The Federal Civil Service Retirement Law," 113 *Annals* 330-38 (1924). Army and navy officers and men have long had the advantage of generous retirement allowances. An officer who has reached the age of 62 may be placed on the retired list; at the age of 64 retirement is compulsory. The retirement allowance for officers is 75 per cent of the pay of the rank held at the time of retirement.

[2] Unsigned, "Civil Service of the United States," 105 *No. Am. Rev.* 479 (1867).

[3] 41 Stat. 614 (1920).

vania (1923), Minnesota (1929), California (1931), Colorado (1931 Rhode Island (1936), Maryland (1937) and Ohio (1938), had state-wic retirement systems.[1] Others have partial systems, so that only ten stat (1936) had no retirement legislation. The *Municipal Year Book* f 1938 reports data on 559 retirement systems in cities over 10,000.[2] T National Education Association reported in 1937 thirty state-wide teach retirement systems and fifty-six local systems.[3] Retirement of civil ser ice employees has clearly become one of the settled conditions of publ employment and it is only a matter of time until all permanent emplo ees are covered in one form or another.

Retirement systems vary in form and structure.[4] They may be enact by state legislatures to cover all or part of the state employees, or addition all or part of the employees of local governments. They m be organized on the actuarial reserve or the cash disbursement pla They may be contributory or noncontributory. They may provide wide range of benefits, including superannuation, disability, death, eith ordinary or in performance of duty, and special benefits to widows a children. American retirement systems are usually contributory a compulsory for new entrants. They have been organized on both t cash disbursement and actuarial reserve plan, but with a tendency in t last fifteen years toward the latter form.

Many retirement systems are small and many rest on insecure fina cial foundations. The interests of the government and of the employ alike are best conserved by the establishment of retirement systems co ering a large number of individuals, with substantial funds, sound act arial advice and competent administration. These considerations sugg the creation of state-wide retirement systems which would include n only state employees, but the employees of county and municipal go ernments.[5] One management could thus perform the task of ma better qualified executives would be available for the single major u dertaking, sound actuarial advice could be secured, and the handling funds would command greater attention. The device of a single fu for all public employees within a state allows any desirable variation

[1] U. S. Bureau of Labor Statistics, *Public Service Retirement Systems*, Bull 477, 1929; and Kansas Legislative Council, *Retirement Systems for State Employ in Kansas* (1937).

[2] *Municipal Year Book,* 1938, pp. 310-38.

[3] National Education Association, "Teacher Retirement Systems and Social Se rity," 15 *Research Bulletin* 91-151 (1937).

[4] Able discussions of pension laws are found in the reports of two Illinois P sion Laws Commissions, 1916 and 1918–19.

[5] This situation prevails in New York and New Jersey. See A. L. Doris, " Operation of the New York State Retirement System in Municipal Governme 10 *Municipal Finance* 5-8 (1938).

benefit for particular classes and at the same time is more likely to possess the advantages of stability and sound management.

In some states lack of confidence in state authorities and strong organizations of local government may suggest another solution. In his study of retirement systems for Virginia, Egger suggested two methods of dealing with the small municipality. He proposed either group insurance or the establishment of an intermunicipal cooperative pension plan through the means of an incorporated Employees' Pension Association.[1]

Public attitudes toward civil pensions have gone through a process of basic reconstruction. In 1911 President Taft said in a message to Congress, "I am aware that there is a strong feeling in both Houses of Congress, and possibly in the country, against the establishment of civil pensions, and that this has naturally grown out of the heavy burden of military pensions." Within a quarter century, Congress had adopted a comprehensive civil retirement plan and twice liberalized its provisions; had imposed a retirement plan upon the railroads and had enacted an old-age pension plan for the mass of the civilian population. The country has become pension-minded, aided by the proposals of Dr. Townsend. The issue ahead is not shall there be retirement plans for public employees, but what form shall they take? In view of the immense sums of money involved, this question deserves the most careful study.

2. Objects Sought by Retirement Systems

At first pensions were provided by governments for their employees as a benevolence, but gradually the idea spread that the "old and faithful public servant" was entitled to an allowance as a reward of merit. This idea has in turn given way to the belief that retirement allowances are, in fact, deferred pay to which employees are entitled as of right.

Although the government as employer is the party primarily concerned in the retirement system, the interests of the employee and of the taxpayer are important. The general purposes sought by the government are enumerated by Lewis Meriam as follows: (1) to eliminate from active duty those who have lost their efficiency because of age or long service; (2) to eliminate those who have lost their usefulness by reason of accident or disease; (3) to improve the morale of the remainder; (4) to retain in the service the best of the present employees, many of whom in the absence of a retirement system resign to accept positions elsewhere; and (5) to attract to the service higher grade men

[1] Rowland A. Egger, *The Retirement of Public Employees in Virginia* (1934), pp. 149-50; see also Donald C. Stone, "How Can Cities Set Up Retirement Systems?" 19 *Pub. Man.* 357-61 (1937).

and women. While the precise effect of a retirement system cannot be measured except in numbers of employees actually retired for old age or disability, there can be no doubt that a retirement plan aids in some degree to improve the service along all the lines indicated in this analysis.

The main object of a retirement system is to terminate the employment of men and women who are no longer able to "pull their weight" by reason of age. These employees block the road to promotion of younger men in subordinate positions; to the extent that they occupy higher posts, they are likely to resist the introduction of new ideas or methods. Consequently there is sometimes a tendency toward a lack of energy and progressiveness. There are, of course, many brilliant exceptions, but they only emphasize the normal expectation.

If the primary object is to retire the aged, where shall the line be drawn? The taxpayers' interest tends superficially to an advanced retirement age; the interest of good administration tends toward a lower age, with exemptions in individual cases; and while employees as a group tend to favor a low retirement age, in individual cases they are almost invariably reluctant to terminate their life work. These somewhat conflicting interests lead to no obvious conclusion. In this country, 70 is a common age for termination of public work and receipt of a pension. The national system accepts 70 as the normal age, but fixes 65 for some groups, and 62 for others, with a minimum of 15 years' service. Police and firemen are often eligible for retirement at 60 or 65. Some provision for exceptions in special cases is desirable. In any event, a specific determination of retirement age must appear in the statute in order to enable the proper actuarial computations to be made and to protect the interests of government and employee alike. A weakness of some pension plans is the provision for retirement after a number of years' service rather than at a given age. Such provisions result in violation of the public interest by permitting retirement and payment of benefits to employees in middle age and in full possession of their faculties.

Should retirement be compulsory or optional with the employee, or the government, or both? Normally retirement is compulsory at a specified date. A retirement system leaving the date of retirement optional with the employee alone gives no protection to the public service. It is natural for men and women to postpone the moment when they terminate their life work and face an uncertain future of relatively empty days. Experience with retirement systems leaving an option to the employee and tying the hands of the administration has been exceedingly unsatisfactory. Retirement should be compulsory at a certain age, with a certain number of years' service. Optional retirement at 60 with a minimum of 30 years' service, the option to be exercised either by the government or the employee, was proposed in 1936 by the United States Civil Service Commission. The employees are unwilling to concede the government the option.

Employees occasionally assert that they should be free to make their own plans for old age by means of insurance, annuity or otherwise. There is only one method by which the government can make sure that its employees will have a degree of economic security which will facilitate the termination of their employment when superannuated. This method is compulsory membership in the official retirement plan. A system which employees may enter or not at their discretion fails to ensure the main object of a pension plan. Membership cannot therefore be optional, either at the discretion of employee or the government.

A second major objective of a retirement plan is to safeguard the service against the retention of employees incapacitated by reason of disability, whether from accident or sickness. The presence of men and women who are unable on account of disability to perform efficient work handicaps administration as certainly as do elderly incompetents.[1] This is equally true whether the disability was incurred in line of duty or otherwise; indeed, the cases of disability in performance of duty are small in number and in proportion. In the New York City police department the number exposed to risk from 1908 to 1914 was 63,330 of whom 1,295 were retired because of disability, and of these only 89 were disabled in actual performance of duty.[2]

The third principal objective of a retirement system is to provide benefits to dependents in case of death of an employee before retirement, whether in line of duty or in case of ordinary death. To take the latter case first, one may argue that the government is not interested as an employer in making contributions under this head, the obligations of which are a primary duty of the individual, readily met by ordinary life insurance; that it is inequitable to force employees who have no dependents to contribute toward a death benefit; and that the expense of the retirement system is largely increased.

The government has no immediate object in providing death benefits in the event of death from ordinary causes before retirement, but it has an interest in maintaining conditions of employment which will preserve the good will and loyalty of its employees. The chief hazard to which they feel themselves exposed is early death before they have been

[1] On this topic see Edwin O. Stene, *Provisions for American Public Officers and Employes Disabled in the Course of Duty* . . . (mim. 1936).

[2] *Report of the Pension Funds of the City of New York* (1916), Pt. 2, p. 43, quoted in Meriam, *op. cit.*, p. 208.

able to make adequate provision for their dependents. A retirement system which makes no provision for benefit in the event of death is therefore very unpopular.

The interest of the government is different in the case of death in the performance of duty, because in many branches of the public service, of which the police and fire departments are illustrative, the government demands action involving great personal risk. Death benefits are an essential guarantee to its employees in such cases, as the *quid pro quo* in return for unhesitating compliance with duty. High wages only partially meet the problem of dependents. The general principle that the economic losses arising from death in the actual performance of duty are part of the costs of the service, to be borne by those who derive benefit from the service, here finds a good illustration. The claims to compensation for death in the performance of duty are so strong that most cities have made special provision for policemen and firemen. This benefit is usually on a noncontributory basis.

Benefits in case of death after retirement are of interest to the government only remotely and are exceptional. But the residue of annuity payments made by an employee available at time of death clearly belongs to the estate of the deceased annuitant and is almost invariably paid over to the estate. A proposal enabling employees subject to the national retirement system to make additional payments in sums of $100 or multiples thereof to be held and administered for the purpose of an increased annuity has been endorsed by the United States Civil Service Commission. In this case the pension authority acts as an agent of the employee in the handling of the annuity funds and payments, in lieu of a private insurance company.

In short a retirement system for civil employees is primarily designed to facilitate the termination of employment of men and women whose powers have failed on account of age or disability by granting allowances for past service; to provide benefits to dependents in case of death; and to improve the morale of the service by creating a sense of economic security. From the point of view of the employee, the retirement system helps to compensate for modest scales of pay, relieves anxiety for the future, and furnishes a convenient means of regular saving.

3. Establishment and Maintenance of Funds

A number of important issues arise concerning different methods for the establishment and maintenance of the necessary funds which systems of retirement require. Brief notice will be given to four of these: the actuarial reserve or the cash disbursement plan, the contributory or noncontributory plan, the indirect contributions of the government, and the method of handling accrued liabilities.[1] The highly technical questions involved in these matters are omitted in order to concentrate attention on the major problems.

a. Cash disbursement vs. actuarial reserve. Many pension funds have been administered in the United States on the cash disbursement plan. By this method, current collections, whether from government or employees, are used to pay current obligations. The payments made into the fund are treated as flowing into a single great reservoir, from which obligations are met as demands are made. The duty of maintaining an adequate supply of funds in the reservoir soon falls on the government since the contributions from employees are rarely sufficient. Put in another way, the cash disbursement plan accepts contributions from John Smith, a present employee, to ensure funds to cover the cost of his ultimate retirement and then uses his contribution to pay the retirement allowance of John Brown, a presently retired employee whose own contributions commenced too late to meet the full cost of his allowance.

This plan was in operation in the federal system from 1921 to 1926. It was severely criticized by the Board of Actuaries, and in the 1926 revision of the pension law the actuarial reserve plan was adopted. The Comptroller General was required to establish accounts, and the government recognized its responsibility for annual appropriations to meet its share of the normal cost of the retirement system.[2] The actuarial reserve plan was effective in 183 of 545 city retirement systems reported in 1938.[3]

The cash disbursement plan is condemned by most students of retirement systems. Two arguments are advanced in its favor; it is simple, and safe. "No elaborate collecting and investing machinery is required and no nice actuarial computations and valuations are needed." [4] The money is left with the taxpayers until needed, thus obviating incidentally any loss through mismanagement or bad investment. The objections to the cash disbursement plan are summarized by Meriam under the following heads: (1) it is unbusinesslike and conducive to extravagance, (2) it requires constantly larger appropriations which are subject to attack in times of economic pressure, (3) it is inequitable because the generation which establishes the scheme escapes almost all financial responsibility while succeeding generations must bear a constantly in-

[1] I.e., those sums required to meet maturing pension obligations which have not been covered by previous contributions of either annuitant or government.

[2] See Board of Actuaries, *Annual Report*, 1927, pp. 8-10.

[3] *Municipal Year Book*, 1938, p. 310.

[4] Meriam, *op. cit.*, pp. 328-29.

creasing burden, and finally (4) it is not readily adaptable to give employees fair benefits in the event of death in active service, voluntary resignation, or dismissal. Of these defects, perhaps the most dangerous is the first, since the apparent absence of financial burden makes it relatively easy to obligate the government to costly benefits, the expense of which is obscured until later years. In a word the cash disbursement plan is conducive to blind assumption of unrecognized obligations.

The actuarial reserve plan commences with a calculation of the amount of contribution necessary at each present age to provide the legal benefits at the retiring age. A fund is then established into which is paid at regular intervals, usually on pay days, a sum which will be sufficient with compound interest to pay for all the benefits established by law for each employee.

Three distinct differences between the actuarial reserve and the cash disbursement plan make clear the advantages of the former system. First, under the actuarial reserve plan the taxpayers who receive the service pay all the obligations incurred by the government in respect to that service, whereas under the assessment or cash disbursement plan the taxpayers at the time the service is rendered pay the immediate wage only and leave for some future taxpayers the payment of the prospective benefits which have accrued in respect to that service. Future taxpayers under the assessment or cash disbursement plan pay the immediate wage for the services rendered them plus the retirement benefits which mature in their day in respect to services rendered to a prior generation. Under the cash disbursement system the generation establishing the system escapes with little or no payment and passes the burden to the future, whereas under the actuarial reserve system each generation pays its share.

In the second place, under the actuarial reserve system, the money available for payments comes in part from taxes and contributions and in part from the interest earned by this money in the time between its collection and its disbursement, whereas under the assessment or cash disbursement plan most of the money comes directly from taxes and relatively little interest is earned because little time elapses between the collection of money and its disbursement. On the other hand, it is true that the money otherwise earning interest in the pension fund is in the hands of the taxpayers, earning interest for them. The security of the fund, however, is not properly safeguarded in this case, especially against the hazard of altering the benefits in time of depression to save current tax payments.

Finally, under the actuarial reserve plan the amount required from the taxpayers annually for the retirement system bears practically a fixed proportional relationship to the sums raised for the immediate wages of those in the service, whereas under the assessment or cash disbursement plan the proportion between the amount required for retirement benefits and the amount required for wages constantly increases over a long period, although eventually reaching a stable point, for a stable force.

The objections to the actuarial reserve system are first, that it is complicated, requiring a complete system of records, periodical actuarial computations, and the maintenance of investment machinery; and second, that the existence of the large reserved sums is dangerous because the power which control of the fund gives may be used for political purposes, because the administrators may prove dishonest, and because the fund may be lost through unwise investment. Meriam concludes, however, in favor of the actuarial reserve plan, "The government could thus secure for its system honest and conservative control; it might not be brilliant control, but safety with a reasonable return is all that is expected." The same conclusion is reached in a recent study of the Municipal Finance Officers' Association,[1] and it is the consensus of the experts in this field.

Retirement funds for civil employees have often been poorly planned and inadequately financed. The result has too frequently been insolvency and either costly reorganization or loss of benefits. An Illinois official report stated, "These acts have been built up blindly. The liabilities under them have crept up almost imperceptibly, as the service given by the public as an employer has expanded. Through these laws the state and many of its municipalities today are in effect in the position of holding out dishonest promises to the men and women in the employ of the public . . . the deficit of the policemen's fund of Chicago is $21,000,000 and that of the firemen's fund $7,000,000, . . . the deficit of the Chicago Teachers' fund is about $6,000,000 and that of the Municipal employees about $5,000,000."[2] Despite some remedial legislation which has put some Illinois systems on a sound basis, other funds are still actuarially unsound.[3]

The introduction to Egger's study of pension legislation contains a colorful description of the financial difficulties of certain municipal retirement systems in Virginia. "A descriptive approach has not been utilized for the very obvious reason that there is little to describe, and that little were better left unportrayed. The statute establishing the

[1] Municipal Finance Officers' Association, *Retirement Systems for Public Employees* (1938), p. 2.

[2] Illinois Pension Laws Commission, *Report*, 1918–19, p. 13.

[3] Arthur S. Hansen, "The Social Security Status of Employees of Government in Illinois," 16 *Ill. Mun. Rev.* 111-14 (1937).

Teachers' Retirement System is one of the most quixotic bits of wishful thinking in the annals of legislative *imponderabilia;* its administration has been as fantastic as its original pattern, and its utter bankruptcy has been assured from the outset. The two municipal systems attempting to establish reserves have likewise been bankrupt since the day of their inauguration. Three other municipalities offer pensions under general ordinances without any contributions and without attempting to fund the liability; they likewise are headed toward annihilation when the true magnitude of the burden which they have assumed becomes apparent. . . . These pension 'systems' require interment, not analysis; it is no part of the purpose of this study to squander printer's ink on their obituary." [1]

A survey of seventy local pension funds in New York State in 1931 revealed that "None of the funds studied was found to be in a sound actuarial condition." [2] Retirement plans established since 1920, however, are more commonly put on a sound financial base, and old funds are being renewed.

Fortunately there is now a growing body of literature contained in careful investigations of the retirement problem and in the experience of a number of well-administered funds, which makes repetition of these faults as unnecessary as it may be hoped they will become uncommon. The whole problem of superannuation has, however, been obscured by the early mistakes committed in pension legislation.

b. Contributory vs. noncontributory funds. The necessary funds may be collected from the government alone, in which case the plan is called noncontributory, or from the government in part and the employees in part, in which case it is known as a contributory plan. Theoretically, all the contributions might come from the employees, the government acting merely as a depository and as disbursing agent, but in fact almost no such arrangement exists.[3] In America most retirement funds are contributory, each party usually sharing equally, although in Chicago the municipality pays nearly double the amounts collected from the employees.

Differences of opinion over making a retirement system contributory or noncontributory are not infrequently based on misapprehension concerning the real issues involved. There is, for instance, no necessary difference in the character of the benefits paid, nor is the cost of the benefits affected, nor does one method of deriving revenues rest upon

[1] Egger, *op. cit.*, p. ix.

[2] Albert H. Hall, *A Summary of Actuarial Surveys of Seventy Local Police and Fire Pension Funds in New York State*, New York State Conference of Mayors, Publication No. 34, 1935.

[3] This method was recommended by the Taft Commission on Economy and Efficiency, H. Doc. 732, 62d Cong., 2d sess. (1912).

the actuarial reserve while the other involves the cash disbursement plan.

So far as new employees are concerned the question has little economic importance, for if a noncontributory plan is established, wages and salaries tend to be depressed to the extent required to meet the government's contribution without an increase of total pay-roll costs. With regard to employees already in the service, the government almost always pays off the accrued liability without their contributions; by future accumulations employees can pay only a part of the ultimate benefits, so that either plan means for them a net increase in financial expectation. Their gains are somewhat greater if the retirement plan is noncontributory.

The real differences between the two plans are moral and psychological. A contributory plan escapes the flavor of charity or philanthropy and is less open to attack in periods when taxes are high. Employee representation on the managing board is more certain under the contributory plan, and the tendency toward "treasury exploitation," i.e., use of retirement funds for other than retirement purposes, is perhaps less.

c. Indirect contributions. Under either contributory or noncontributory systems the government makes certain special contributions. It usually bears all the expenses of management, although sometimes they are carried equally by the public authority and the employees.

The government has a moral obligation to sustain the solvency of the retirement system, the benefits of which are a part of the compensation. Legal limitations on the extent of governmental liability to pay the promised benefits are "highly improper." The government establishes the system and is under an obligation to know that it is sound. No individual about to become a public employee can ascertain for himself whether the system is actually sound. He must assume the solvency of the plan and the certainty of the expected benefits. The government, on its part, should have such competent actuarial advice that every actuarial reserve system will stand the test of experience.

The earning power of any fund is, of course, dependent largely upon the rate of interest. The benefits are calculated on a given expected rate, failure to earn which tends to create a deficit. To avoid these contingencies the government frequently guarantees that it will contribute any sums necessary to maintain the assumed rate.

d. Accrued liability. At the moment when a retirement plan is put into effect, every employee in the service becomes entitled to its benefits. No prior contributions have been made, of course, by any person or authority to meet these obligations when they fall due. The prospective normal contributions of employees and/or government for the years remaining before retirement are not sufficient to meet the cost of the benefits of those who retire after a few years. The amount necessary to make good these deficiencies is called the "accrued liability." The government assumes the burden of the accrued liability and usually discharges its responsibility by paying in an annual sum which will extinguish the obligation over a period of years.

The accrued liability can be closely estimated by actuarial computations, and often runs into very large figures, depending on the number of persons and the scale of benefits. The federal retirement system involved an initial accrued liability, on the basis of the 1920 benefits, of $248.8 millions, which was promptly increased by the failure of Congress to appropriate the 1.06 per cent of the pay roll representing its share of the current normal cost. Due to the increased benefits provided by subsequent legislation the accrued liability had mounted by 1934 to $730.1 millions, assuming that the government fully met its current normal costs of 2.45 per cent of the pay roll. Commencing in the fiscal year 1929 Congress appropriated $20,000,000 annually to the retirement fund, and in 1935 increased the amount to $40,000,000.

4. Administration of the Retirement Funds

The investment of the funds of the United States retirement system is in the hands of the Treasury Department. Individual accounts of employee and government contributions are maintained by the Comptroller General. Determination of eligibility for retirement allowance is made by the Civil Service Commission, on the basis of the Opinions of the Attorney General, the Opinions of the Comptroller General and the decisions of the courts. Actuarial supervision and guidance are supplied by the Board of Actuaries, which has been fortunate in securing the services of distinguished actuaries at nominal cost. The employee contributors to the fund and the annuitants are not represented on any of the governing bodies.

In states and municipalities various provisions for the administration of funds are encountered. The administration of funds and the determination of eligibility for allowances are frequently vested in a board of trustees, often comprising representatives of the members of the system as well as the employing authority. The degree of representation varies; in some cases an effort has been made by contributors and annuitants to secure majority control of the board. In view of the fact that the retirement system is established primarily for the advantage of the government, the public authority is entitled in all cases to maintain control of the funds and of the award of retirement allowances. In some instances the election of representatives by the members tends toward the choice of the candidate who promises most to his constituents, not always with proper regard to the interests of the retirement fund, the taxpayer or the employing authority. The substantial investment which employees have in a retirement fund, however, gives ground for some representation on the governing board of the system. At the very least, full publicity of all operations is essential.

The function of the board of trustees is policy determination; the actual administration of the retirement system is best placed in the hands of a competent executive director. Expert actuarial advice is essential, both in the original establishment of the system, in watching the mortality experience, and in considering the effect of proposed amendments. Without such advice, ill-considered commitments are almost certain to develop. Funds are usually retained in the custody of the treasurer of the jurisdiction concerned. In state and local governments their investment is ordinarily governed by the board of trustees.

5. Some General Observations

The rise of so many civil service retirement systems since 1900 is intimately connected with the expansion of the merit system. Retirement benefits at the close of a lifetime of service are a symbol of the human need for security, which on a larger scale and at a later date was provided for citizens generally by the Social Security Act. In another place, T. V. Smith and I have suggested that the way of life of a civil servant who enjoys the satisfaction of secure opportunities to practice his skill over a lifetime in return for a modest income and a protected old age may become a more common and a more enlightened pattern of American living.[1]

One effect of accruing retirement rights is to stabilize the service. While this is desirable from the point of view of moderating political rotation, it may be harmful in closing still tighter the doors to free movement from one jurisdiction to another. The desirability of freedom to transfer among the professional, scientific and technical employees is particularly great, and some means must be found to avoid the "rooting" effect of pension rights. Within the states, a single state-wide retirement system covering state, county, city and rural governments seems an adequate solution. Between states, and between the state and federal governments some arrangement to transfer retirement credits is essential.[2] The time is ripe to work out this unsolved problem.

An analogous result of a retirement system is to handicap severely the separation of unsatisfactory employees who have accumulated considerable pension accruals. Mere incompetence will not usually suffice to

[1] Leonard D. White and T. V. Smith, *Politics and Public Service* (1939).
[2] Lewis Meriam, *Public Personnel Problems* (1938), pp. 199-200.

bring about separation in view of the weight of the penalty, i.e., the loss of retirement rights. It is not likely that the reluctance of supervisors to be "hard-boiled" will be changed, which suggests that the introduction of retirement systems ought to be accompanied by increasingly careful initial selection, by higher standards both of mental and physical fitness, and by elimination of the less qualified either during the probationary period (which might well be extended to at least one year) or in the early years of employment.

The levels of retirement income vary widely but in almost every instance they are much higher than the level provided by the Social Security Act. It is unlikely that an effort will be made to grade down retirement benefits to the level now established for industrial employees. It will, however, probably be necessary to coordinate public retirement systems with the benefits of the Social Security Act in order to meet the situation of those who pass from private to public employment and back again.

The principal technical problems arise in the management of funds, the calculation of benefits, the periodic evaluation of systems, and the coordination of benefits promised with income provided. We have entered an era of old-age protection by civil pensions and we shall doubtless not withdraw. We shall, however, face many problems of coordination and adjustment.

Chapter Twenty-seven

PROFESSIONAL AND OFFICIAL ASSOCIATIONS IN THE PUBLIC SERVICE

THE quality of any public service is deeply affected by the training, experience and point of view of its members. At one time the quality of the American public service was fixed by the political interests and allegiance of its members; at another time (1916–20) it was surcharged by the dissatisfaction caused by inequities in pay and opportunity. In increasing measure the quality and the performance of the civil service reflect the influence of professional, scientific and technical personnel and of their associations.

When the government was founded there were no organizations of public officials or employees and none were imagined. Now there are thousands of such organizations, unofficial in nature although composed of officials or public employees. At one level men and women formed professional, technical and specialist organizations for the exchange of information and experience and for the advancement of their profession or calling. At another the crafts and the clerical rank and file came together in unions primarily for their economic advancement and self-protection. Substantial numbers still remain untouched by either movement, especially in the rural and small-town regions, but the character of our administrative system has been and will continue to be greatly affected by these developments. The present chapter is devoted to the consideration of the professional and official associations; the following will deal with the public service unions. The dividing line is sometimes obscure, for these two groups overlap to some extent and gradual changes in point of view and purpose may cause an organization to drift in one or the other direction.

1. Scientific and Professional Techniques in the Public Service

The origin of the professions is found in the middle ages, during which law, medicine, and theology emerged in connection with the guilds and the universities.[1] Of these the first was always closely related

[1] A. M. Carr-Saunders and P. A. Wilson, *The Professions* (1933).

to the public service and the connection has never grown less intimate; medicine was to become a branch of the public service only in the nineteenth century and has really come into its own within less than the last fifty years; the influence of theology has steadily decreased in administrative and governmental circles.

It was during the eighteenth-century growth of Brandenburg and Prussia that a definite flavor of professionalism began to attach itself to the civil service of Frederick the Great and his successors, a service marked by continuity, high and exacting standards, specific responsibility, definite training, and career opportunities.[1] The modern German public service has been deeply affected by this distant origin of its well-known esprit de corps.

Naturally this point of view did not emerge among the forests and prairies of a new continent. The American public service has traditions of an entirely different order. But the demands of national housekeeping in the United States of the twentieth century are as exigent as were those of Prussia in the eighteenth; and under an entirely different political structure we have been putting the professions and the sciences to work in our system of administration. It is not uncommon, indeed, to speak of the public service as a profession, although this is an exaggeration.

The conduct of government in 1850, whether federal, state or municipal, made slight demands upon the professional and technical corps other than in the field of education: a few lawyers, a few physicians, a somewhat larger number of engineers and surveyors, a very few scientists. The rest of the public service comprised law enforcement officials, tax collectors, bookkeepers, postal employees, clerks, messengers and custodians, amateur fire fighters, craftsmen, and unskilled laborers; in short, persons who needed common sense, good judgment, diligence, manipulative skill and often knowledge of special routine, but not technical or professional training.

The remarkable change which has transpired chiefly since 1900 is well illustrated in police administration. A well-organized police department in 1890 might have employed as technicians a photographer and a Bertillon measurement expert. In 1938 a highly developed police department will outfit patrolmen with vest-pocket cameras and at headquarters will have elaborate photographic apparatus and equipment for making blueprints, photostats and enlargements; the Bertillon expert has been

[1] Walter L. Dorn, "The Prussian Bureaucracy in the Eighteenth Century," 46 *Pol. Sci. Q.* 403-23 (1931), 47 *ibid.* 75-94, 259-73 (1932); F. M. Marx, "Civil Service in Germany," in L. D. White and others, *Civil Service Abroad* (1935).

replaced by fingerprint experts and the rogues gallery supplemented by enormous collections of fingerprints; the department has become motorized and keeps in touch with its squad cars by two-way radio; in the laboratory are experts in the identification of handwriting, hair, and dust; with the aid of the science of ballistics an expert identifies bullets and weapons; statisticians survey the crime front through the lenses of elaborate tables and spot maps showing the occurrence of crime; and the expert in *modus operandi* ("m.o.") focuses suspicion on a limited number of known criminals for certain types of offense. Thus side by side with the essential but relatively simple duty of foot patrol still performed much as it was fifty years ago, there exist many very highly specialized operations derived from the application of science to police problems.

Determination of the coefficient of expansion of a concrete slab on a modern highway, measurement of the stresses and strains in an airplane wing, preparation and administration of standardized preventive serums, discovery of sources of contamination in an oyster bed, breeding rust-resistant wheat are merely samples of the type of problems which have caused the increase in the number and variety of the professional and scientific bureaus and personnel. New types of problems in recent years have been making demands upon other groups of experts. The management of agricultural production and the search for ways and means of securing a national balance between agricultural and industrial production are opening new duties to the agricultural economists and statisticians; the overhead coordination of ever larger organizations is developing a new race of administrators; the desperate needs of persons in economic distress and requiring relief and rehabilitation have led to an unprecedented increase of technically qualified social workers in the public service.

In many directions, therefore, one observes the emergence of professional, scientific and technical operations and personnel in the functions of government, operations based on scientific achievement and invention, and reflecting both the enlarged scope of public activities and a public expectation that these activities shall be well performed for the general welfare.

2. Technical and Official Organizations

As late as 1900 most administrative officials and professional, scientific and technical employees lacked regular contacts with other public service employees in the same calling; they worked alone, too often in ignorance of the procedures, problems and solutions of their fellow workers in other jurisdictions; each struggled with common problems without the aid of mutual counsel and advice. But by 1938 a complicated network of official and semiofficial organizations brought most professional, scientific, and technical employees into regular contact with others.[1]

a. Professional organization of public officials. The teachers were the first public service group to form a professional association (1830).[2] In 1857 the National Teachers' Association was organized and eventually grew into the present National Education Association. The police chiefs met in council for the first time in St. Louis in 1871 and in 1893 assumed the title, "International Association of Chiefs of Police." [3] The fire chiefs commenced their corporate activities in 1873. In 1878 the National Association of Insurance Commissioners was organized, and six years later appeared the Conference of State and Provincial Health Authorities of North America. These illustrations indicate that even before 1900 the trend toward professional and technical organization was well established. These groups came into their own, however, in the twentieth century. A few illustrations will indicate the trend.

The engineering field, for example, is now highly organized. Engineers employed by government naturally belong to one or more of the national engineering groups; in addition there are a considerable number of organizations catering primarily to engineers in public employment. Among these may be noted the American Water Works Association (1881); the American Society of Municipal Engineers (1894); the American Road Builders' Association (1902); the American Association of State Highway Officials, the members of which are not always engineers (1914); the American City Planning Institute (1919); the International Association of Public Works Officials (1920);[4] and the Institute of Traffic Engineers (1930).

In public health administration there are many active official associations, some of which are concerned chiefly with scientific problems, others with operating problems. The following list presents a few of the large number of national, state and local organizations.

[1] The rise of professional influence in the public service is discussed in a series of papers in 189 *Annals* 58-96 (1937); see also David H. Kurtzman, "Influence of Organizations of Local Government Officials," 195 *Annals* 103-9 (1938).

[2] C. S. Foos, *State Educational Associations*, U. S. Bureau of Education Reports, 1909, vol. 1, pp. 251-74.

[3] Lent D. Upson, "The International Association of Chiefs of Police and Other American Police Organizations," 146 *Annals* 121-27 (1929).

[4] Now the American Public Works Association, by merger in 1937 with the American Society of Municipal Engineers.

American Public Health Association	1872
Conference of State and Provincial Health Authorities of North America	1884
Association of Dairy, Food and Drug Officials of the United States	1897
Conference of State and Territorial Health Officers	1902
International Association of Dairy and Milk Inspectors[a]	1911
American Association of Medical Social Workers	1918
Conference of State Sanitary Engineers	1920
National Conference of Tuberculosis Secretaries	1921
National Committee of Health Council Executives	1926
American Association of School Physicians[b]	1927

[a] Now the International Association of Milk Sanitarians.
[b] Now the American School Health Association.

A number of semiprofessional groups, such as chief executives, civil service commissioners and the like, are concerned with general aspects of administration. The Civil Service Assembly of the United States and Canada, established in 1906 as the National Assembly of Civil Service Commissioners, was a forerunner of this group. The history of this association has been an interesting one. Commencing with a membership whose technical interests were slight, for nearly twenty years the Assembly was chiefly a forum for the exchange of experience. About 1924 a new interest in classification, testing, statistical procedures and other technical phases of personnel work and research became evident, and in recent years the annual and regional conferences have been notable for the close attention given to strictly technical matters and to reports of research studies.

In 1906 the International Association of Comptrollers and Accounting Officers (since 1932 the Municipal Finance Officers' Association) was established, open to all state, county, and city accounting officers as well as to private accountants who are regularly engaged on government work. In 1915 the National Association of State Auditors, Comptrollers and Treasurers was formed to bring together the responsible state accounting officers.

The National Association of Secretaries of State was established in 1904 and the National Association of Attorney Generals in 1906. The National Association of Purchasing Agents, Inc., formed in 1915, has a section comprising official purchasing agents.

The International City Managers' Association, founded in 1914 with a membership of eight, has grown steadily to a 1938 manager membership of 329. This Association has an unmistakable professional flavor. In addition to the annual meeting devoted to discussion of municipal problems, it maintains a secretariat in Chicago, publishes a valuable magazine, *Public Management*, and *The Municipal Year Book*, prepares correspondence training courses and engages in research.[1]

Significant signs of present trends are the American Public Welfar Association (1930), the National Association of Housing Officials (1933) and the American Society of Planning Officials (1935). These sample are illustrative only and in no way exhaustive; they may perhaps serv to indicate the rich variety of organizations of officials which now contribute to the better conduct of public affairs. Total membership canno even be conjectured; eighteen associations reported a membership i 1937 of approximately 45,000.[2]

b. Organization among governments. Organization of governmenta authorities, as distinguished from public officials, commenced among th cities. The municipalities of Indiana joined hands as early as 1891; i 1898 state leagues of municipalities were organized in California an Iowa, followed the next year by formal organization in Indiana. By 193 there were leagues of municipalities in forty-two states and since 192 these leagues have acted together for informational and other purpose through the American Municipal Association.[3] Under the pressure o depression emergencies, the larger cities organized the United State Conference of Mayors. From the outset (1932) the Conference exerte an active influence upon national agencies touching municipal conditions, especially public works, municipal loans, and relief.

The subject matter dealt with by the municipal leagues is much th same from Virginia to California, but the emphasis varies. All are inter ested in maintaining and developing the legal powers and the fiscal right of the municipal corporation and for this purpose look primarily to th state legislature. All are concerned with the improvement of adminis trative methods, for which they depend upon exchange of informatio at the annual conventions, the monthly magazines whose combined ci culation approximates 100,000, and frequent special studies of selecte topics. Of recent years they have been in closer contact with the nation government. Each league, within its own state, is both a pressure grou and a service agency; the American Municipal Association is, howeve almost exclusively a service agency. All are nonpartisan in character.

The "sovereign" states were slower than the cities in making commo cause, but they too have been driven into associated action, partly t

[1] Leonard D. White, *The City Manager* (1927); Lyman S. Moore, "Twenty-fi Years of a Profession," 20 *Pub. Man.* 259-64 (1938); and a forthcoming work l Don C. Price, Harold Stone and Kathryn Stone on council manager government.

[2] "Professionalization of the Municipal Service," in *Municipal Year Book*, 193 p. 365.

[3] Clifford W. Ham, "State Leagues of Municipalities and the American Municip Association," 31 *Am. Pol. Sci. Rev.* 1132-37 (1937).

consider genuine administrative problems, partly to exert influence on broad questions of constitutional reconstruction. The beginning was made in 1908 with the Governors' Conference, initiated, incidentally, by the President of the United States. The Governors' Conference has never developed sufficient cohesion to make it an effective instrument of state action for common purposes. Such an instrument is being gradually forged through the Council of State Governments. In succession Senator Henry W. Toll and his associates developed the American Legislators' Association for the individual members of state legislatures (1925), then the Interstate Assembly, a semiofficial conference of delegates from the upper and lower houses (1932), and finally the Council of State Governments (1933), an organization of state authorities including governors, legislators, and the principal state officials. Under the pressure of depression conditions, the states are rapidly moving toward associated activities in place of their historic "rugged individualism."

With less certain steps the courts of the various states seem to be moving in the same direction through the establishment of judicial councils. In 1938 twenty-nine such councils had been authorized and most were in actual operation.[1] No coordinating agency has yet been created for them.

Not until the publication of the first edition of the *Directory of Organizations in the Field of Public Administration* in 1932 was there any conception of the extraordinary number of official and technical organizations which have been illustrated in the preceding paragraphs. The first edition of this inventory (1932) showed 1,744 organizations; the fourth edition (1938) described 2,067, of which 558 were national in scope, 1,342 were state organizations, 80 were regional and 87 were Canadian.[2] No attempt has yet been made to list local organizations of officials, whose number is legion.

Since 1929 some of these associations of officials and of governmental authorities have tested the possibilities of mutual assistance by establishing their headquarters offices in cooperation with each other in Chicago, in the neighborhood of the University of Chicago but with no formal connection with this institution.[3] In 1934 they established relations with the International Union of Local Authorities and the International Institute of the Administrative Sciences, whose headquarters are in Brussels. These associations are service agencies for their respective constit-

[1] 22 *J. of Am. Judicature Society* 72-80 (1938).

[2] Public Administration Clearing House, *Public Administration Organizations: A Directory 1938–1939* (4th ed. 1938); see also a companion volume, published by the Joint Committee on Planning and Cooperation (Brussels), entitled, *A Directory of International Organisations in the Field of Public Administration* (1936).

[3] Hal Hazelrigg, "The '1313' Group in Chicago," 199 *Annals* 183-89 (1938).

uencies, possessing only the capacity to give advice and, upon reques to conduct inquiries. Their activity becomes daily more extensive an more intensive. A national capital of state and local government is i process of taking shape in Chicago under the skillful hands of Loui Brownlow and his colleagues—a capital without a shred of power, bu with the substantial influence which comes from good intent, unselfis purpose, and special knowledge. These organizations and their wor represent one of the most significant and most promising development in the contemporary administrative scene.

3. Programs and Policies

The enumeration of these associations gives an idea of their variet and chronology, but it tells little about their programs and policie While these naturally vary from case to case, it is feasible to describe i general terms both what they seek and what they avoid. The nature o their contribution to good administration will become more clear as w examine their objectives.

Associations of individuals with similar skills and training are natura especially when they serve the same or a corresponding employe Doubtless early organizations were intended chiefly to promote persona acquaintance among individuals with common interests and problem The impressive value of such acquaintance is apparent on every hand Each individual becomes a member of "his" group; he derives satisfac tion from this identification of self with something larger and mor powerful than self; he is anchored in society and is no longer an isolate unit. He discovers someone who knows his problems by having experi enced them, to whom he can tell his successes and confide his failures from whom he can learn and profit. His personality expands, his moral is heightened, and as he becomes a leader in his group his prestige grow with his morale. All this is true of membership in any group, especiall a skill group; the particular point is that these values develop withi associations of public officials.

This, however, is but the beginning. As men meet and talk they de velop standards in the process of exchanging experience. The associa tions, through their annual conventions, their committee meetings, thei publications, the correspondence among their members, broadcast meth ods to colleagues and to the world. The speed of diffusion of good prac tice is vastly accelerated as the "mastery of the mystery" is thus directl or indirectly cultivated. Over and over again are repeated the words "I always learn something from our annual convention."

The headquarters offices of the associations carry on other useful en terprises. They prepare and circulate technical information to member and citizens on all sorts of public questions; they answer endless inquiries on administrative problems and with the aid of their members formulate procedures in the interest of good administration. In this way they exert a steady influence upon the improvement of administrative standards.

In many instances no answer is known to the questions which are hrust upon them, and consequently they are driven to set in motion tudies, great and small. The amount of research which they undertake aries from time to time, but in the aggregate it is impressive. Through heir professional and technical magazines they spread the results of heir inquiries and cement their members into an organic whole.

Upon request of the official bodies the headquarters staffs of these ssociations undertake special studies or investigations in a particular ommunity. The associations, however, refrain from entering a comnunity on their own initiative. When invited, they investigate, report nd advise; they act in accordance with the governing body but never n hostility to it. The amount of this kind of advisory, consulting work onstantly grows greater, already exceeding the capacity of most associations to meet the demand.

Some groups, such as the leagues of municipalities, are active in seekng the enactment of legislation within their respective states. National rganizations often advise, but seldom advocate publicly, although the ne may grow indistinct.

Many of these groups set up standards of conduct for themselves in e form of codes of ethics which express their responsibilities to each ther, to their employer, and to the public. A well-known example is e code of ethics of the International City Managers' Association; there e many others.[1]

It is also possible to indicate in general terms what these associations f officials avoid. Above all, as associations, they avoid participation in olitics, national, state or local. They take no part in campaigns; they ve no candidates for public office, and they refrain from attempting to ntrol public policies apart from the provision of technical advice. hey will not seek to influence the making of budgets or the issuance bonds, although they may advise on the form of the budget or the ethods of floating a loan.

They refrain from seeking any monopoly of public employment for eir members or special privileges for their constituents. Their task is aid all officials, not to cultivate the personal interests of some. For is reason they usually avoid maintaining placement services for their embers, although it is inevitable that they should often be called upon

[1] See ch. 29, *infra*.

for advice. They do not seek to improve the economic status of their members, nor do they intervene in particular instances where their members may be in difficulty with their superiors or with the governing bodies. These are their principal taboos.

4. Professionalism and the Public Service

The firm establishment of the professions in the public service and the rise of strong associations of professional, scientific and technical employees of government have already had a substantial effect upon the tone of the service itself. The army and navy are well recognized as professions; so are many sections of the civil service, although as a whole it is hardly entitled to such recognition at the moment. Clearly the trend is in this direction. The extension of techniques based on the professions, on science and invention will undoubtedly strengthen and extend a professional point of view into branches of the public service which are now recognized only as vocations. There is no insuperable barrier to the recognition of police work, or food and drug inspection as professions; and street cleaners may develop an esprit de corps under good leadership which approaches the professional spirit.

A professional or technical point of view, supported by an appropriate organization, is an asset to the public service. Professional and scientific workers are nonpartisan and progressive in their outlook; moreover, a position which is recognized as scientific in nature is usually left alone by the patronage brokers, partly because they recognize its special character, partly because they are less likely to have clients anxious to try their hand at it. Science and patronage do not mix, and while there are cases where harassed or hungry politicians have interfered with scientific and professional workers, they are exceptional.

Professional and scientific employees raise the intellectual standard of the public service. They usually possess a college or university training and come to the government service with a relatively broad outlook. They maintain contact with their professional colleagues in the world outside. They are inclined toward long-range views and policies as well as concerned with the exigencies of immediate programs. They have within themselves the spring of continuing achievement—the desire for recognition among their fellow scientists. Hours mean nothing when the pursuit of a scientific problem grows hot. The prestige of the public service is consequently raised.

England can point to distinguished administrators whose achievements shed luster on the whole service; the United States displays a splendid group of scientists and professional men and women in government service whose achievements are as brilliant—Elwood Mead, former head f the Bureau of Reclamation; Dr. L. O. Howard, one-time chief of the Bureau of Entomology and Plant Quarantine; Stephen K. Mather, first director of the National Park Service; Dr. Lyman J. Briggs, director of the National Bureau of Standards; George R. Putnam, for a generation head of the Bureau of Lighthouses; Grace Abbott, the former head of the Children's Bureau; Sanford Bates, the former director of the Bureau of Prisons, a penologist with a national reputation, and many others. It is not without significance that the federal service, which has the largest and perhaps the ablest body of scientists in its employ, has the highest prestige of any of the American jurisdictions.

In brief, as long-range implications of the trends of the last quarter century are examined, the importance of the growth in numbers and influence of the professional, scientific and technical groups in the public service assumes large proportions. The competence of the public service is favorably affected; its impartiality and objectivity are more nearly assured; its capacity to serve long-time programs intelligently is increased; its prestige is elevated. Without any conscious effort on the part of government, professional and scientific ideals have taken possession of substantial parts of the civil service. This is clear gain.

Chapter Twenty-eight

PUBLIC SERVICE EMPLOYEE UNIONS

WHILE one section of the public service has been developin the professional and technical point of view described in th previous chapter, another section has been exploring the ad vantages of unionism. The origins of the union movement in the publi service are not as remote as those of the professional and technic groups, but the unions may look back upon a good half century of slo but steady growth, marked by conflict and secession as well as by sul stantial achievement. In the official as in the industrial world unionis has progressed at varying rates of speed, with the result that toda some branches of the public service are almost wholly unionized, whi others are still completely untouched by union influence. Public att tudes vary as greatly; in some jurisdictions the public service unions a freely accepted, in some they are tolerated, and in others they are tabo It is important to know how and why they have come into existenc what is the legal structure within which they operate and what are th practical means by which they seek their ends, for they are sure to exe a substantial influence upon the conditions of public employment of th future.

1. Origin, Growth and Present Extent of Public Service Unior

It was natural that the Post Office Department should be the scene early efforts at organization on account of the large numbers of en ployees engaged in similar work, but in addition many post office grie ances, especially the matter of hours, hastened organization at a rel tively early date.[1]

The National Association of Letter Carriers was organized in Bostc in 1889 and survived an early but acute controversy over the issue affiliation with the Knights of Labor, who conveniently solved the prol

[1] The principal reference is Sterling D. Spero, *The Labor Movement in a Go ernment Industry* (1924). Through Mr. Scott Hart, Mr. John P. Simpson call my attention to the Provident Association of Clerks organized (and apparently d banded) in Washington in 1817. That present problems are not new is evidenc by the quotation from a notice in the *Daily National Intelligencer* of May 1817: "It is earnestly requested of those members who have not paid their su scription money, that they come prepared to do so, as punctuality in this respe is indispensable."

lem for the carriers by disappearing from the scene. This group has become the largest and most prosperous of all the postal organizations. Its attitude has always been conciliatory, and is well expressed by a declaration of a former president: "I shall continue to adhere to the same safe and sane and conservative policy of conciliation and persuasion in advancing the cause of the men and promoting the growth of the National Association of Letter Carriers." Not until 1917 did the Association affiliate with the American Federation of Labor.

The postal clerks have had a more stormy and spectacular history han the carriers. A local association was formed in New York City in 888, but its officials were dismissed from the service and it suffered rom the unbounded hostility of the local postmaster. In 1890 the Naional Association of Post Office Clerks was organized in Washington vith the tacit consent of the Post Office Department. By 1895, however, he attitude of the Department had changed, and postal employees were orbidden to visit Washington for the purpose of influencing legislation efore Congress. Two years later a secession was brought on by facional troubles, leading to the formation of a rival organization, the Jnited Association of Post Office Clerks. The breach was healed in 899 by the formation of an entirely new association, still in existence, alled the United National Association of Post Office Clerks, and someimes referred to as the "Unapocs."

In 1897 the American Federation of Labor began to interest itself in ost office employees, but the United National Association early came o a settled conviction that it had nothing to gain by affiliation. This ecision, coupled with factional disputes, led to a new secession movement, and the formation in 1906 of the National Federation of Post Office Clerks, which promptly affiliated with the American Federation f Labor. It has remained to this day the rival of the United National ssociation. From the beginning the methods of the Federation have een more aggressive; on several occasions some of its officers or emloyees have been removed from the post office on account of their ctivities. The audacity of its comments may be inferred from a quotaon from the *Union Postal Clerk*, referring to the retiring Postmaster General in 1921: "Mr. Burleson of Austin, Texas, who almost succeeded finishing what Ben Franklin started, our postal service; if his involunry retirement brings him the joy it brings us, he is a happy mortal."

Other branches of the postal service have likewise been organized. he Railway Mail Association, formed in 1898, comprises the "aristoats" of the postal service. Its chief objectives are to furnish low cost surance and to lobby for legislation. It has a membership of about ,000 and publishes *The Railway Post Office*. It does not have a substantial interest in the labor movement, although affiliated with the American Federation of Labor.

The National Rural Letter Carriers' Association was organized in Chicago in 1903. It is not affiliated with the American Federation of Labor since labor union psychology has little influence with the rural carriers. A small organization catering to the same group, the National Federation of Rural Letter Carriers, is affiliated. The depression brought special problems to the substitute post office employees, who in 1933 formed the National Association of Substitute Post Office Employees an organization cutting across the recognized craft lines.

Over a period of a half century, the post office employees have thus succeeded in establishing strong and active unions in the various branche of the service, each major group organizing independently as a craf union, and nearly all cooperating on common legislative programs in Washington. Certain information concerning the principal unions, as o 1936, is summarized in the following tabular presentation.[1]

TABLE X

POST OFFICE UNIONS

NAME OF ORGANIZATION	YEAR ORGANIZED	PUBLICATION	AFFILIATED WITH A. F. OF L.	1936 MEMBE SHIP
National Association of Letter Carriers..................	1889	Postal Record	1917	54,0
United National Association of Post Office Clerks of the United States............	1890; 1899	Post Office Clerk	No	45,0
Railway Mail Association....	1898	Railway Post Office	1917	20,0
National Rural Letter Carriers' Association..............	1903	National Rural Letter Carrier	No	35,0
National Federation of Post Office Clerks............	1906	Union Postal Clerk	1906	40,0
National Alliance of Postal Employees..............	1913	Postal Alliance	No	4,8
National Federation of Rural Letter Carriers..........	1920	Rural Delivery Journal	1920	1,0
National Association of Substitute Post Office Employees	1933	Postal Sub	No	3,0

[1] Estelle M. Stewart, *Handbook of American Trade-Unions* (1936), U. S. Bure of Labor Statistics, Bulletin 618, 1936.

Clerical employees have been slow to turn to unionism in other coun-ries as well as in the United States; but within the last twenty years hey have organized in this country rapidly and on the whole effec-ively, although the degree of organization ranges all the way from the npressive clerical unions in Washington, New York State, San Fran-isco, or Chicago to the complete absence of any clerical organization n many parts of the country.

The earliest, and still by far the largest clerical organization in the ederal service, is the National Federation of Federal Employees, launched n 1917 under the aegis of the American Federation of Labor. The con-litions out of which it developed—the high cost of living, inadequate alaries, and an attack in Congress on the seven-hour day—are typical of he circumstances responsible for protective organization among public mployees.

The National Federation of Federal Employees (N.F.F.E.) is not rganized on craft lines, but is open to a wide variety of occupational roups in the federal service, excluding, however, the postal employees nd the recognized crafts. The Federation has thus a variety and breadth f membership quite unlike that of the typical craft organization, but it as never sought to become "the" industrial union for the federal serv-ce. The Federation also draws no line between the higher supervisory fficials and the rank and file, and many of the former are included in s membership.

Despite some fluctuations the membership of the Federation has rown steadily from about 12,000 at the close of 1917 to about 70,000 n 1938. There are over 650 locals scattered throughout the United tates and its possessions.

Favored by exceptional leadership the Federation has achieved many f its basic objectives. It successfully defended the seven-hour day, was nstrumental in winning the war-time bonus, and was chiefly responsible or the enactment of the classification legislation of 1923. It has fol-owed the administration of this act closely and helpfully. The Federa-ion was also deeply interested in the enactment of the original pension w of 1920 and its subsequent liberalization and administrative improve-nent. From the outset, in common with other employee organizations, he Federation has been a staunch defender of the merit system and has vorked for its extension. In 1935 it authorized the collection of a fund f $100,000 from its members for the defense of the merit principle, a ractical demonstration of support which is without precedent. Exten-ion of the merit system, extension of classification to the field service, doption of a $1,500 minimum salary for all full-time adult workers, establishment of a civil service court of appeals, and improvements in the retirement act are its principal objectives.

The methods of the National Federation are conservative but strenuous. The officers maintain a lobby in Washington, prepare legislation and seek its passage, consult with administrative officials, and through the monthly publication, *The Federal Employee*, and otherwise, "make medicine" in favor of their program. Extreme forms of pressure such as the strike are not countenanced under any circumstances, nor does the Federation openly enter political campaigns.

Affiliation with the American Federation of Labor, which was a cardinal principal with N.F.F.E. for many years, was terminated in 1932. The skilled crafts of the American Federation of Labor had been alert over a period of years lest the breadth of jurisdiction of the National Federation of Federal Employees lead to poaching on their recognized membership; this was one of the sources of difficulty. The other concerned the classification under the act of 1923 of employees engaged in the crafts, whose wages were usually fixed by wage board negotiations. During the campaign for the Classification Act of 1923, the National Federation had made it clear that it did not desire to force the crafts into classification if they preferred existing pay scales at the "prevailing rate" as fixed by a wage board.

The issue arose again in 1931 with reference to the proposed extension of duties classification to the field service. In the 1931 convention of the American Federation of Labor certain craft leaders, concerned over jurisdictional issues and alarmed over classification and wage problems, succeeded in defeating a resolution sponsored by the N.F.F.E. endorsing the proposed classification act. The National Federation, failing an amicable settlement, thereupon voted (16,649 to 11,537) to sever its connection with the American Federation of Labor and has remained aloof despite the belief of its leaders that under favorable conditions affiliation is desirable.

The American Federation of Labor proceeded in 1932 to charter a second union of government employees with competing membership known as the American Federation of Government Employees. In authorizing this rival organization the American Federation of Labor laid the foundations for a situation similar to that which raised havoc among the postal clerks for a generation.[1] The American Federation has had a stormy and somewhat spectacular history, with a leadership at times hardly distinguished by balance and foresight. Its objectives are much

[1] Sterling D. Spero, "Employer and Employee in the Public Service," in Carl Friedrich and others, *Problems of the American Public Service* (1935), p. 217.

he same as those of the National Federation, but its aims have been :onfused by internal friction. Its membership was 18,000 in 1936.

The split in the American Federation of Labor which led to the for-nation of the Committee for Industrial Organization produced new livisions in the ranks of federal employees. In 1937 a C.I.O. affiliate was organized to compete with the American Federation of Government Employees and the older National Federation of Federal Employees, with the title, United Federal Workers of America. The U.F.W.A. in-herited some seceding lodges of the A.F.G.E. and started a campaign for membership on a program which on its face was not distinguishable from the platforms of existing groups.

Conditions in the state governments have not been favorable to the development of employee unions. In only fifteen states do public em-ployees have established tenure; in most states party control is still so strong that the workers seek political influence rather than the strength of independent employee organizations. Employees are widely scattered and in a majority of states the predominating culture is rural-agricultural rather than urban-industrial. In 1937, state-wide associations of employ-ees existed in nine states, all but one of which have merit systems. They are shown in the following table.[1]

TABLE XI

ORGANIZATIONS OF STATE EMPLOYEES

NAME	DATE OF ORGANIZATION
ssociation of State Civil Service Employees of New York	1910
irginia State Employees (Union No. 17659)	1923
Iassachusetts Commonwealth Service Association	1925
Iassachusetts State Engineers Association	1925
:ate Employees Beneficial Association of Ohio	1925
hio State Public Service Employees Association (Union No. 17931)	1927
olorado State Public Service Employees Association (Union No. 18025)	1928
alifornia State Employees Association	1931
'isconsin State Administrative Employees Association	1932
:aryland Classified Employees Association	1935
:nnsylvania State Employees Association	1937

To this list of state-wide organizations must be added the state locals stablished by the American Federation of State, County, and Municipal mployees since 1936, including in November 1938 the Wisconsin State mployees Local Union, and locals in Ohio, Minnesota, California, Con-ecticut, Illinois, Iowa, and Michigan, together with locals in other ates with membership of less than 1,000.

[1] The situation is changing rapidly in the states and this table is consequently :ely to be soon out of date.

In the cities, employee unions are well established in New York Cleveland, Detroit, Chicago, Milwaukee, Seattle, San Francisco, an Los Angeles. In others they lead either a diffident or a rather precariou existence. In many cities they are nonexistent, excepting "benefit" or ganizations and the widespread International Association of Fire Fight ers, which is affiliated with the American Federation of Labor. Teachers unions are found in a number of the larger cities but are often oppose by superintendents of schools; the national union is the American Fed eration of Teachers, also affiliated with the A. F. of L.

New impetus was given to the organization of state and local em ployees in 1936. The drive started with the American Federation o State, County, and Municipal Employees, formed under the leadershi of Dr. Arnold Zander of Wisconsin. It affiliated with the A. F. of L and started a vigorous campaign among state and local employees. I was destined soon to have a C.I.O. rival in the State, County and Munic ipal Workers of America, organized in 1937. Meanwhile a third grou rejecting any affiliation with organized labor, came into existence (1936) the National Civil Service Association. This Association is based on group of urban counties in New Jersey and the cities of Cleveland an Chicago. Membership figures as of November 1, 1938, gave the Amer can Federation about 42,000, the National Civil Service Associatio about 20,000, and the State, County and Municipal Workers of Americ about 52,000.[1] The International Association of Fire Fighters also showe renewed activity, pushing the number of its locals to 313 and its mem bership to nearly 40,000. Until 1938 the A. F. of L. affiliates includin the organized crafts outnumbered their rivals on the state and loc scene, but the situation was not a stable one.[2]

The aims of the municipal groups are much the same as those of th state and national organizations: security against arbitrary action, sough in part by permanent tenure, in part by means of formal procedures i disciplinary cases, in part by the protective intervention of the organ zation; improvement in scales of pay, hours, working conditions, leav retirement benefits, and the like. None of these organizations aspire t share the responsibilities of authority; they are essentially conservativ

[1] Lyman S. Moore, "Organizations of Local Government Employees," in *Munic pal Year Book*, 1938, pp. 339-53. An extensive list of local unions is found at th citation. See also James W. Errant, "City-Wide Organizations of Municipal Em ployees," *ibid.*, 1937, pp. 232-40.

[2] Arnold S. Zander, "The American Federation of State, County and Municip Employees," 19 *Pub. Man.* 259-61 (1937); Abram Flaxer, "State, County and M nicipal Workers of America," *ibid.* 262-64; Gordon R. Clapp, "A New Empha in Personnel Administration," 189 *Annals* 111-18 (1937).

n point of view, except for a bold willingness in a few cities to defy he governing powers by short-time strikes.

Broadly speaking, municipal unions tend to use political as well as ther resources in seeking their ends. They often bargain with local olitical leaders; the New York (City) Forum, a group of city, county nd state employees, is political in its outlook and behavior. Individual nembers may use their political influence to secure promotions, transers, and other advantages, supplementing the established civil service rocedures. They cannot be wholly blamed for this, since the "civil ervice" is in some cases controlled by the politicians and is diverted to ecome a part of the political mechanism of rewards and punishments.

In municipal government, employee unions have had to struggle against nany adverse circumstances.[1] The municipal service is heterogeneous in he extreme; the police and fire personnel have little contact with other roups; the teachers are usually independent of the city hall; the engieers find little in common with the clerical force; the laborers fall into heir customary craft unions between which and the white-collar roups there is little common feeling. In the smaller cities, public opinon is likely to be hostile to any form of organization beyond the recretional or beneficial; in the larger cities the unions are in constant danger ither of losing their independence to strongly entrenched political nachines, or of saving their independence at the cost of futility in pracical achievement.

This quick review of the evolution of a half century indicates that ublic employee unions have become well established in the post office nd in the clerical force of the national government, that they have reently secured a foothold in states which have a permanent staff, and hat they are well entrenched in the larger cities but practically nonxistent in the smaller towns and in all but a few of the highly urbanized ounties. Conditions favorable to the growth of public service unionism nclude the present (1938) friendly attitude of the national government oward labor unions, offset somewhat by public concern over union nethods and practices; the gradual establishment of a large block of egularly employed public servants in the lower and middle brackets; nd the gradual but accelerating transition of the United States into a ype of society where most individuals seek protection of their interests hrough associative action. The immediate circumstances which precipiate organization vary; they have usually been related to acute dissatis-

[1] An illuminating study of Chicago civil service unions has been written by one f the principal participants: James D. Errant, "Trade Unionism in the Civil Serve of Chicago" (ms. 1938), University of Chicago Library.

faction with scales of pay, hours, and conditions of service. In many instances lack of foresight and good judgment on the part of the constituted authorities has been a major consideration. In any event, public service unions must now be counted among the elements which are entitled to consideration in determining future conditions of public employment. Their influence will increase, rather than diminish, unles irresponsible leadership destroys their usefulness.

2. Law and Practice of Public Service Unions

In the search for their objectives, the officers of public service employee unions have to deal constantly with the constituted authoritie —legislative bodies, chief executives and administrative officials, and in some cases with the courts. They also are mindful of the value of citizen support and of strong cohesive organization of their own number, whic leads them into the realm of public relations on the one hand and o organization technique on the other.

In most jurisdictions there is practically no law governing their activities apart from the general law of trade unions and of public officers In the national government there are fragmentary provisions of law enacted in the light of specific conditions, which grant certain immunities and impose certain obligations, but even here there is no systemati treatment of the subject.

In general it may be stated that the existing law of public servic unions is chiefly ameliorative in nature, confirming rights and privilege claimed by employees but not always freely conceded by administrativ heads. Several cases may be passed in review.

a. The right to organize. There was no Congressional legislation o the right to form civil service unions until 1912, although several impor tant organizations had been in existence for many years. In 1912 Con gress formally recognized the right of members of the classified civ service to form organizations.[1] For another ten years, however, the atti tude of the Post Office Department was hostile and not until 1921 wer working relations firmly established between the postal unions and th government. So far as is known, there is no state legislation on thi point. In some cities ordinances restrict or prohibit unions, especially i the police department. In general there are few legal barriers to th formation of public service unions; but public opinion is hostile to ther in many communities.

b. The right to lobby. In 1895 the Postmaster General issued a regu lation forbidding postal employees to "visit Washington, whether o leave with or without pay, for the purpose of influencing legislatio

[1] The Lloyd-La Follette Act, 37 Stat. 539, 555 (1912); see *supra*, pp. 390-91.

before Congress." This policy was amplified by President Theodore Roosevelt. In its final form the so-called "gag-rule" read:

All officers and employees of the United States of every description, serving in or under any of the Executive Departments or independent Government establishments, and whether so serving in or out of Washington, are hereby forbidden, either directly or indirectly, individually or through associations, to solicit an increase of pay or to influence or attempt to influence in their own interest any other legislation whatever, either before Congress or its committees, or in any way save through the heads of the departments or independent Government establishments in or under which they serve, on penalty of dismissal from the Government service.[1]

This executive order was legislated out of existence in 1912 by the Lloyd-La Follette Act, one section of which provided:

The right of persons employed in the civil service of the United States, either individually or collectively, to petition Congress, or any Member thereof, or to furnish information to either House of Congress, or to any committee or Member thereof, shall not be denied or interfered with.

Since 1912 the right of federal employees to lobby has not been questioned, and in fact each of the major organizations maintains its headquarters and agents in Washington. For some years the National Legislative Council of Federal Employee Organizations has served to coordinate most of these several lobbies.[2]

As a matter of fact, the public service unions have been and still are chiefly concerned with legislation, since the basic improvements which they desire are usually attainable only by action of Congress. The unions have found, moreover, that Congress is more responsive to their representations than some departmental officials; and mandatory requirements of law cannot be easily disregarded administratively. It is generally recognized in Washington that the public service lobby is a powerful one, especially when supported by the American Federation of Labor.

c. Right of collective bargaining. On this point President Franklin D. Roosevelt stated the official position in the following excerpt from a letter to the National Federation of Federal Employees. After pointing out that it is both natural and logical for organizations of government employees to present their views on employment matters, President

[1] *Civil Service Act, Rules and Executive Orders*, 1906, p. 65.

[2] The program of the Council for 1936 included six points: Preservation and extension of the merit system, optional retirement at 60 after 30 years' service, government payment of official bonds required by law, maintenance of present rates on first-class mail, extension of classification, and liberalization of sick and annual leave. Of these, the merit system was singled out as the paramount issue.

Roosevelt continued: "All Government employes should realize that the process of collective bargaining, as usually understood, cannot be transplanted into the public service. It has its distinct and insurmountable limitations when applied to public personnel management. The very nature and purposes of Government make it impossible for administrative officials to represent fully or to bind the employer in mutual discussions with Government employe organizations. The employer is the whole people, who speak by means of laws enacted by their representatives in Congress. Accordingly, administrative officials and employes alike are governed and guided, and in many instances restricted, by laws which establish policies, procedures or rules in personnel matters." [1]

On issues of pay, hours and working conditions, public employee groups often "bargain" with members of legislative bodies, but these negotiations are different in principle from those which prevail in industry. In the latter case the workers may abstain from work and do; in the former case they usually renounce voluntarily such means of bargaining and confine themselves to representations and negotiations.[2]

d. Maintenance of a closed shop. The recruitment of public service employees by open competitive examination prevents the maintenance of the closed shop principle in government offices, although different situations may prevail in governmentally operated industrial undertakings. The normal rule is disclosed by the policy of the Tennessee Valley Authority: "No employee of the Authority and no one seeking employment shall be required as a condition of employment, transfer, promotion or retention in service to join or to refrain from joining any organization or association of employees"; and further, "there shall be no discrimination against representatives of employees of the Authority nor shall employees suffer discrimination because of membership or nonmembership in any organization or association of employees." [3]

e. The right to engage in political activity. Individual political activity of federal employees is curtailed by Rule I of the Civil Service Commission, which reads: [4]

> No person in the executive civil service shall use his official authority or influence for the purpose of interfering with an election or affecting the results thereof. Persons who by the provisions of these rules are in the competitive classified service while retaining the right to vote as they please and to express privately their opinions on all political subjects, shall take no active part in political management or in political campaigns.

[1] *Washington Evening Star*, Sept. 26, 1937.

[2] Tennessee Valley Authority, *Employee Relationship Policy* (1935), however uses the term, collective bargaining.

[3] *Ibid.*, secs. 4 and 5.

[4] *Civil Service Act and Rules, Statutes, Executive Orders and Regulations*, 1937 pp. 12-13.

This rule is fundamental in the effort to diminish the influence of politics in the classified civil service, and is supplemented by the limitations of the Pendleton Act on political contributions by merit employees.

Although the rule is construed to apply also to *organizations* of federal employees, it is difficult to find any effective means of enforcement against a union whose officers are usually not in the public service. The issue arose in 1932 over a letter sent by the president of the Railway Mail Association to members of the Association which indicated how certain candidates for office voted on measures of interest to the clerks, and advised that it was entirely proper that "you should remember your friends on election day." [1] The Civil Service Commission ruled that this was political activity. "To make public attack on a candidate for public office is to take active part in a political campaign. . . . If the attack is made by the joint action of several employees the guilt is still personal and attaches to each employee separately and severally for the purpose of administration of the Civil Service Law."

As a matter of fact, organizations of federal employees have entered Congressional campaigns in cases of unusual aggravation. Sound tactics, however, suggest caution; and it is this consideration rather than the penalties of the law and rules which, with rare exceptions, has kept federal public service unions out of political campaigns.

f. The right to affiliate. Affiliation between public service unions and the American Federation of Labor occurred well before any legislation permitting or denying it was on the books.[2] This situation was clarified in 1912 by the Lloyd-La Follette Act in the form of a limitation upon the right of removal. The statute provides:

> membership in any society, association, club or other form of organization of postal employees not affiliated with any outside organization imposing an obligation or duty upon them to engage in any strike, or proposing to assist them in any strike, against the United States, having for its objects, among other things, improvements in the condition of labor of its members, including hours of labor and compensation therefor and leave of absence, by any person or persons in said postal service, or the presenting by any such person or group of persons of any grievance or grievances to Congress or any Member thereof shall not constitute or be cause for reduction in rank or compensation or removal of such person or groups of persons from said service.

[1] Quoted in Spero, "Employer and Employee in the Public Service," *loc. cit.*, p. 195.

[2] See *Carter and Others vs. Thompson*, 164 Va. 312 (1935), sustaining an order by a city manager forbidding membership of the fire division of Portsmouth in any firemen's organization affiliated with any outside organization, specifically the International Association of Fire Fighters.

This act is construed to apply to other than postal employees and settled any doubt as to the legal propriety of affiliation under the prescribed circumstances. Three large national groups remain outside the American Federation of Labor—the United National Association of Post Office Clerks, the National Rural Letter Carriers' Association, and the National Federation of Federal Employees, the two former on principle, the latter through bad management in the Vancouver convention of the American Federation of Labor.[1]

Opinions as conservative as those of former Postmaster General Burleson, who believed that "the interests of employees will always be protected by public sentiment," and that consequently organization is unnecessary, are rapidly disappearing as this country moves along paths already well worn by others.

No disposition on the part of the public authorities to dispute the privilege of affiliation between public service unions and labor organizations can now be discovered, except in the case of the police and the teachers. In 1919 Congress forbade affiliation of the District of Columbia police and firemen with any organization which claims or uses the right to strike;[2] similar prohibitions are common in municipal ordinances for policemen, but firemen are usually freely allowed to join the International Association of Fire Fighters, which has long been affiliated with the American Federation of Labor.

The question may be asked, what is involved in affiliation? Affiliation establishes an organic connection between the government employee and organized labor. This connection may indicate much or little; it may mean merely an occasional contact between the officers of organized social groups, with little real sympathy or understanding among the rank and file. By the rules of the American Federation of Labor affiliation involves the payment of monthly and special assessments to the

[1] The United National Association has taken an emphatic stand against affiliation, stating its attitude in the following quotation from the *Post Office Clerk.*

> As civil service employees, post office clerks have certain obligations, certain restrictions, not common to the civilian world. They take an oath to their country similar to that taken by soldiers and sailors. They are forbidden to participate in politics for their own good. Participation in politics means promotion for reasons other than merit; it means political assessments by various political parties; it means the debauchery and spoliation of the civil service. Civil service employees are forbidden to threaten the government either openly or by implication. They are forbidden to strike against the government. . . . Affiliation [with the American Federation of Labor] can have but one object and that is to threaten the government. Outside labor organizations insist on the right to strike against the government, and also participate in politics. . . . No greater danger faces the country than the possibility of domination of the government service by labor organizations. It means a politico-labor bureaucracy. . . .

[2] 41 Stat. 363 (1919).

common treasury, but not to the strike fund. Affiliation involves the obligation to send delegates to the annual meeting of the national organization and provides opportunity to participate in the discussion and settlement of problems of interest to organized labor.

Affiliation also means that the national organization, the American Federation of Labor or Committee on Industrial Organization, will be ready to assist government employees in securing approval of their requests by Congress or by the departments. Such assistance has taken the form of appearance before legislative committees, appeals to the President, general publicity, and aid at the time of elections for the support or defeat of candidates. Assistance may be expected in furthering the growth of the organization and in mediating between rival organizations. In the cities affiliation normally means representation for the government employee on the central labor union council although this privilege is not always used. Affiliation with the American Federation of Labor does not mean that government employees assert a right to strike, nor are they encouraged to strike by the Federation, nor can the Federation require them to participate in a sympathetic strike. A similar situation prevails with respect to the C.I.O. Affiliation may be supposed to result in a sympathetic attitude on the part of the government employee toward organized labor, although it does not appear (with some exceptions) that this attitude is now widely extended.

The fact is that, apart from the craftsmen and unskilled workers, the great bulk of public employees in the United States are not "class conscious." No class lines are drawn in recruitment and no artificial barriers block the way to advancement. The public service is a branch of employment where men and women of diverse educational background, coming out of widely variant economic circumstances, and of different race, religion and politics, work together in an official organization where each has his part to play. The heterogeneity of social environment and the prospect of advancement on personal merit combine to strengthen a common "white-collar" variation from the point of view and methods of labor unionism. A substantial change in attitude must intervene before public service affiliation with the organized labor movement becomes a connection of spirit rather than one of form.

g. The right to strike. The law of public employment with reference to the act of a strike by public employees is incomplete and in many jurisdictions nonexistent. This reflects the fact that in most jurisdictions the issue of a public service strike has never arisen, and has consequently never been considered.

The Lloyd-La Follette Act, which has already been quoted, by indirection frowns upon a strike of federal employees. In the postal service there have been one or two instances of a concerted cessation of work, or a threat thereof. In the Fairmont, West Virginia, case (1915) the entire staff of twenty-five postal employees handed in their resignations; they were placed under arrest and eventually pleaded guilty to a charge of "conspiracy to obstruct the mails." [1] The District of Columbia police and firemen are forbidden by law to strike as well as to affiliate with an organization which uses the strike.

Municipal ordinances frequently contain a direct or implied prohibition against strikes by the police and fire departments. Other classes of employees, however, are not subject to this prohibition, and in highly organized cities like Chicago, brief strikes of street cleaners, city truck drivers, electrical workers, and other groups are not uncommon. A strike of sewage disposal employees occurred in Philadelphia in 1938.

Apart from the spectacular Boston police strike of 1919, there have been no important strikes of public employees in this country, nor have they become entangled in any great industrial strikes as some of the civil service unions in England became involved in the general strike of 1926. The influence of the Boston police strike upon the temper of the country has remained decisive.

In short, while the law on strikes by public service groups is very sketchy, the issue has not become a vital one because the problem has never assumed any importance except for a brief time in the troubled years following the war. Although the conditions of public employment were seriously affected by the depression, there was no recourse to extreme measures by organized employees. Reasonable adjustment of working conditions from time to time by the appropriate authorities will easily maintain this satisfactory situation.[2]

3. Summary

This survey of the law with respect to public service unions indicates that the state assumes a different position in handling its employment problems from that which it imposes upon private employers. The terms and conditions of private employment may be fixed by collective bargaining; in public employment they are fixed by law and by official determination. The influence of organized employees in the industrial world is buttressed ultimately by the power to withhold labor, but in the official world this measure of constraint is forbidden by law or by

[1] See Spero, "Employer and Employee in the Public Service," *loc. cit.*, p. 184; 35 Stat. 1127 (1909), sec. 201.

[2] A systematic defense of the right of public employees to strike is found in Sterling D. Spero, *The Labor Movement in a Government Industry* (1924). Spero takes the view that even the so-called primary functions of the state have no inherent qualities which entitle them to special consideration with reference to strikes.

custom. In the industrial world there is full freedom of organization and affiliation, but in government employment these rights are recognized only in certain jurisdictions and even there are forbidden to certain classes. The political rights of industrial workers are not curtailed by law, but the public service employees in the merit system are forbidden to participate actively in politics. The "closed shop" ceases to have meaning when employees are selected on the basis of competitive examinations.

The constitutional right of the state to impose these restrictions is undoubted. They are defensible from the point of view of maintaining an impartial public service, undisturbed by industrial conflicts and not subject to the temptation of divided loyalties. At the same time, public service employees who are subject to these limitations are clearly entitled to freedom of collective action in making their claims known and in seeking legislative or administrative acceptance of them. Employees are also entitled to the protection of their individual interests which may arise from union support in case of need.

Review of the influence of the postal and clerical groups in Washington over the last twenty years leads to the conclusion that it has been constructive and beneficial. Support of the merit system, retirement legislation, and duties classification are as much in the public interest as in the interest of the employees immediately affected. The record is not so clear in local government where less effective leadership is common. But the Municipal Employees' Society of Chicago and the Cleveland Municipal Employees' Association furnish striking illustrations of sound leadership and helpful influence. Traditions of honest and intelligent government make it easier for employee unions to march forward along routes mutually advantageous to workers and government alike.

Chapter Twenty-nine

PRESTIGE AND MORALE

A VENERABLE text recites, "Ye shall not live by bread alone." The life of any established organization, public or private, constantly illustrates this ancient wisdom. In diverse ways a government department or bureau or commission is affected by many circumstances, the combined effect of which is to produce in its members an attitude or point of view which may deeply affect their behavior as individuals and as an organization. In the army this truth has gradually become well recognized, leading to conscious efforts to sustain the morale of the armed forces and to destroy the morale of the enemy.[1] Many civil administrators also recognize the value of esprit de corps and do what they can to cultivate it.

The "state of mind" of an organization is a real element in its capacity for performance. An administrative machine is an instrument of action. It cannot act effectively if it is hamstrung by vacillation, indifference, internal dissension, or disloyalty. Other things being equal, its capacity for action varies directly with its esprit de corps or morale.

The inner life of any group, especially as stable an association of men and women as a public service organization under the merit system, becomes more and more specific with the passing of the years. Departments acquire a history and a tradition, symbolized perhaps by great figures such as Pepys, or John Stuart Mill, or Robert Morant; in this country by Alexander Hamilton in the Treasury, or the two Adams in the State Department. The United States Civil Service Commission has had a continuous existence of over fifty years, accumulating traditions and understandings, memories of controversy and adjustment, of success and failure. Into its ranks have come and gone many who have labored in its service, the best known of whom was Theodore Roosevelt; each one has left an impress upon it, and without his conscious will has contributed to its standing in the community and to the "state of mind" which as a body it now possesses. So also every continuing association of human beings.

Two aspects of the many phases of the "group mind" of the public

[1] Sir Ian Hamilton, *The Soul and Body of an Army* (1921).

service are suggested in the preceding paragraphs: the esteem which an organization commands, i.e., its prestige; and the morale which an organization possesses, its esprit de corps.

These terms are related but not identical. For the purposes of this discussion they are understood in the following sense. Prestige means the attribute of social appreciation which may attach to a person, a group, or an institution. It is external to the person or group concerned. Thus we may speak of the prestige of the Forest Service, or of the scientific services of the Department of Agriculture, or of Mr. J. Edgar Hoover. Morale is the state of mind of an individual or a group with respect to work and work environment. High morale is a state of mind in which men and women voluntarily seek to develop and apply their full powers to the task on which they are engaged by reason of the intellectual or moral satisfaction which they derive from their own self-realization, their achievements in their chosen field, and their pride in the service; it is also a social situation in which men and women are aware of the degree to which they are mutually affected by these motives and respond to this knowledge. Low morale is defined in opposite terms. Morale is implicit in the group, not external to it. A high prestige aids to support a high morale, although good morale may exist in a group with a neutral prestige. A low prestige undoubtedly lowers morale.

A healthy public service is characterized by a high prestige and a high morale. It is an important duty of the responsible officers of any organization, and especially of the personnel officer, to build up prestige and morale so far as possible. They have a responsibility to hand on their department, office, or institution to their successors in the best possible condition for continued service to the public, a responsibility which ought not to be submerged by the desire for temporary personal or political advantage. The complex responses which form both prestige and morale are subject to observation and analysis and to certain types of measurement. They are also subject within limits to management. In the following pages the prestige of the public service and the bases of a high morale are summarized in the light of some of my earlier studies.

1. The Prestige Value of Public Employment

Prestige is a relative quality. One individual or group may have greater or less prestige than another, but there is no obvious fixed point from which prestige may be measured. The prestige of the civil service may be compared with the prestige of the army or the church, or the educational corps of the country, or any other definable group. In two research studies an effort was made to compare the prestige value of the public service with that of corresponding private commercial and industrial employment.

The prestige of the public service as thus ascertained may vary with the individual or group whose opinion is registered. For instance, the attitude of a recent immigrant from a foreign country where the public service has had a high standing for generations may differ from that of persons born in this country; and among the latter, opinions may vary in accordance with the particular traditions of government in different parts of the country.

Setting aside for the moment the question, what creates prestige, we may turn to a short summary of the results of this inquiry.[1] Two parallel studies were devoted respectively to the prestige of public employment in Chicago and in the country at large. In each case the sample (4,680 and 7,168 persons respectively) was inadequate to warrant more than the most tentative conclusions, but the two studies revealed the same general pattern. The evidence in each case was based chiefly on individual choices within twenty paired occupations (public and private); on completion tests designed to reveal opinion on the relative efficiency, honesty and courtesy of public and private employees; and on the answers to fifteen questions designed to compare public and private service on as many different qualities, each of which was thought to have relevance to prestige.

The broad result of the studies indicated that the standing of the public service among the persons interviewed was less favorable than that of private employment. But in each case it was curious to observe that the personal contact with the public service by those interviewed had been satisfactory, by a majority of better than two to one. The low-prestige stereotype was clearly fixed by other factors than personal experience.

Three questions were given special treatment in a completion test in which the subjects could select any one of nine possible answers, ranging from complete endorsement of the public service as against private, through a neutral position to the opposite pole. These dealt with efficiency, honesty, and courtesy and gave results hardly flattering to the public service. The broad result of the two studies indicated that approximately one-third of the persons interviewed (30%) could see no distinction between the efficiency, honesty and courtesy of public and private employees; over one-half (57%) believed with various degrees of emphasis that preference should be given to private employees; and only about one-tenth (11%) thought that the efficiency, honesty and

[1] For details, see the author's *The Prestige Value of Public Employment* (1929) and *Further Contributions to the Prestige Value of Public Employment* (1932).

courtesy of government employees exceeded that of industrial employees. A few failed to answer the question.

These are the generalized views of the mass of persons taken as a whole. The views of different groups varied greatly, and gave us considerable insight into the prestige indexes of public employment among important sections of the population. The opinions of the persons interviewed were analyzed by sex, age, education, occupation, and race or nationality. Some extraordinary differentials appeared which ran consistently through each study.

The sex differential. On the basis of these experiments men have a less favorable view of public employment than women. In the Chicago study the index of the men was eleven points lower than that of the women; in the nation-wide study it was sixteen points lower.

The age differential. The prestige index of public employment varies inversely with age. The combined results of the two studies appear in the following table.

TABLE XII

PRESTIGE INDEXES BY AGE GROUPS

AGE GROUP	PRESTIGE INDEX
15–19	+17.01
20–24	+ 4.22
25–29	− 1.33
30–34	−13.52
35–39	− 8.82
40–44	−14.26
45–49	−16.62
50 and over	−21.03

The age group 35–39 behaved atypically in each experiment, the reasons for which are not clear. With this exception it appears that each succeeding five-year group possessed less confidence in the public service than its predecessor.

The education differential. The prestige index of public employment varies inversely with education, so far as this sample of the population is concerned. The public service enjoys the greatest esteem among persons with a common school education, less among those who have passed through the secondary schools, and least among the college graduates.

Occupational differentials. Although the evidence is not adequate, it appears broadly that labor, skilled and unskilled, tends to show greater esteem for government employment; that the professional and executive-proprietor groups have a very poor opinion of government service; and that the "white-collar" clerical workers and housewives occupy a position midway between these two extremes.

The nationality differential. The evidence of both prestige studies indicated that the prestige index was affected by the fact of native or foreign origin. Persons of foreign birth showed a characteristically higher prestige index than that of the native born; and native-born persons with foreign or mixed parentage fell midway between. So far as these small groups are concerned, we find verification of the hypothesis that foreign-born persons are more friendly to government than the native born. The index of the colored group was higher than that of the white.

Federal-state-municipal differential. Which of our three systems of administration possesses the greater prestige, and to what degree? The experiment confirmed a preliminary guess by demonstrating that the national system stands highest, the states next, and the cities at the bottom. On a numerical scale of 100, the cities rated 58, the states 69, and the national government 81.

It is obvious, therefore, that we cannot speak of the prestige of the public service as an indivisible entity, for it varies widely among different sections of the population. The studies which have just been summarized are studies of opinion; they are not necessarily rational or informed or unprejudiced opinions. They may in fact stray far from an accurate understanding of the facts about the public service. They are stereotypes, mental pictures of a vague composite of a city hall: elective officials, politicians, postal carriers and other public employees, perhaps a state house and the public buildings in Washington, gossip about public affairs and public men, newspaper comments and cartoons, personal experience, direct or indirect, with government. They are effective to a degree wholly unrelated to their correspondence with reality.

A study of the relative prestige of business and government employment is the most severe test to which the public service could be put, because the dominant prestige elements in the United States presumably cluster around business, or did at the time the studies were made. Foreign visitors often observe that we lack a sense of the state. Since the advent of the depression the population has acquired a sense of the state more acute than ever before in our national history, except in war. It is probable that the prestige of business has fallen absolutely since 1929, and likely that that of government has risen absolutely as well as relatively. The attitudes of young men and women in institutions of higher learning reflect this change in point of view; and the unhappy experience of 20,000,000 persons on relief has undoubtedly left a marked impress upon their attitude toward government—precisely what no one knows.

These prestige studies have sometimes been quoted as proving a low public esteem for the public service. To the contrary, we may note the evidence that large sections of the population in fact entertain a high respect for the public service. Labor, skilled and unskilled, persons under twenty-five years of age, women as a group and persons born abroad characteristically acknowledge a favorable standing to the public service. These are numerically very large sections of the population. Furthermore, these studies were conducted in the cities, chiefly in the larger metropolitan areas. We have no evidence concerning the attitudes of the rural population. The sample, moreover, is too small to warrant anything more than preliminary tentative hypotheses. Any conclusions as to the public mind of America about the public service must therefore be drawn from this evidence with the greatest of caution and with important reservations.

The prestige standing of the public service has a definite relation to a number of important operating problems. Its effect is most noticeable in recruitment, a fact eloquently stated in the Brookings Institution report on the organization and administration of Oklahoma.[1] "All those questioned on the subject in Oklahoma, both in state employment and out of it, advise against the state service, unless the young man wants a fling at politics. As the state administrative departments are now run, they are not attractive except as short-time jobs; and short-time jobs in normal times do not attract the best candidates. In fact, one new executive in an important agency at the Capitol said that he would not object so much to the horde of job hunters he had to interview if among them he could find the kind of employees needed; but, he complained, 'The kind of people we really need are not applying for state jobs.' The public educational system of Oklahoma has trained plenty of them; and there is an adequate supply. The trouble is that, very properly, the well equipped ambitious youth does not want to work under conditions that at present prevail in the administrative service of Oklahoma. The wise youth is looking, not for a temporary political job that may last four years, but for an opportunity for a career. If the good private corporation offers him that opportunity, while the state sticks to patronage and rotation in office, he will naturally prefer private business or else he will leave his own state to work for some other government."

In general terms the pulling power of any public service varies directly with its prestige. An organization with a high prestige will attract first-rate men and women to its ranks; but one whose prestige is low will

[1] Brookings Institution, *Organization and Administration of Oklahoma* (1935), p. 357.

have to be content with much less than the best. Over a period of years the effect in either case is cumulative.

A high prestige operates favorably to keep competent men in the service. Professional and scientific workers in the National Bureau of Standards, the Geological Survey, the Department of Agriculture and other public agencies not infrequently decline lucrative opportunities elsewhere. Among the considerations which keep them in the service is the quality of prestige.

Prestige is also related to morale. It may or may not be one of the major factors which make a high morale, but lack of public esteem may become an important factor in lowering morale. The obviously increasing public impatience with the effort to enforce the eighteenth amendment and the indifferent public esteem which the prohibition unit commanded had a definite influence in reducing its morale. *Per contra,* the popularity of the Federal Bureau of Investigation undoubtedly enhances the morale of its members.

It remains to inquire what are the elements or determinants of prestige. We have no direct experimental evidence on this point, but it is probable that they vary widely with circumstances. Presumably each type of occupation has a cluster of prestige determinants more or less specific to it. Thus the prestige of a man of letters rests upon insight, imagination, and skill in the use of words; it is effective in relatively small groups of the population. The prestige of an all-American football player rests upon athletic skill, dramatic success on the field, and a good press; it is probably effective among large numbers.

In public office, the significant cluster of prestige determinants might include such specific elements as the wearing of a uniform, association with well-known persons, security, or capacity to exercise power. Generally the prestige of the public service has not been enhanced by a good press. Nor has it been elevated by the published opinions of many leaders of business. The scandalous dictum of a former president of the United States Chamber of Commerce to the effect that the best public servant is the worst one has often been quoted. More recently a representative of a great motor car company stated, "Government, as such, creates nothing. . . . The more government takes, the less each one has." Such inaccurate and misleading observations by men who command public attention are unnecessary handicaps to raising the prestige of the public service. They press heavily upon the steadily rising standards of government operations and hinder the progressive improvement of administrative operations, irrespective of what the state undertakes.

Apart from the special determinants of the prestige of the public service, certain general considerations probably count for as much here as in other groups. The prestige of any group is raised by public recognition of a high standard of integrity maintained by it. In the public service, standards vary from place to place but in general a cross section of the standards of the civil service is probably somewhat higher than those of the community as a whole, especially where the merit system is carefully enforced. The case of the prohibition unit is instructive. The ill-repute into which this organization fell was certainly due in part to the extraordinarily low character of many prohibition agents selected under the patronage system. When this unit was placed under the merit system, sixty-five per cent of the staff were found ineligible, hundreds by reason of failure to pass the character investigation.

Capacity to achieve results is also a general element in prestige, perhaps peculiarly so in this country where action rather than reflection is widely admired. "Those who can, do; those who can't, teach." This gem of wisdom from a "doer" illustrates the pattern of ideas. The success of the Federal Bureau of Investigation in tracking down a considerable number of "public enemies" is a spectacular instance where prestige is made by success. In informed circles the scientific work of the Department of Agriculture benefits by the same recognition of achievement. So also the income tax unit of the Treasury, the New York State Department of Farms and Markets, and the state agricultural research stations.

This is in part a result of maintaining high standards of individual competence. The excellent reputation of the governments of Milwaukee, Cincinnati, Berkeley (especially the police department), Richmond and other cities rests upon the reputation of the managers and mayors and the department heads in these communities, and upon the tradition of continuing service which develops sometimes with, sometimes without, the support of the merit system. The excellent standards maintained, for example, by the United States Public Health Service, the Bureau of Public Roads, the Patent Office, and the Bureau of Home Economics in Washington confer prestige upon these agencies in the scientific and professional groups concerned and among the public. The indifferent standards of personal ability tolerated in many police departments, in some assessors' offices, and in clerical forces outside the merit system destroy whatever prestige may arise from competence.

There is also a glamor about the public service which attracts many persons. Most young people dream of representing their country abroad in a diplomatic or consular post; and to a lesser degree other branches of the public service carry a halo, somewhat sentimental perhaps, but different from the emotions which attach to the United States Steel Corporation or the Ford Motor Company.

Other factors of prestige undoubtedly play their part. They are among the intangible elements which a wise administrator recognizes and turns to such account as he may from time to time. The course of government in recent years strongly suggests that as an agency of social protection and improvement its prestige is destined to rise; and as it mounts, the general standards of administration will be advantageously affected.

2. Morale

Morale is an inner possession of an individual or a group. Although the term had been used earlier, it became general during the World War, in military circles. Since 1920 there has been much discussion of the nature and value of industrial morale. Leaders in any activity—sports, education, business, religion, politics, advertising, transportation—deal with morale more or less consciously and specifically. A football team is "keyed" for the crucial game; the campaign manager stirs his precinct workers to the final drive for victory at the polls; a sales manager puts on a "pep" campaign among his salesmen—these are familiar illustrations of morale techniques.

A wholesome morale is an invaluable adjunct to effective administration. It adds the force and energy which make for achievement. More than this, morale fights indifference and even without conscious vigilance maintains safeguards against the endless variety of small incidents which *en masse* may scuttle good administration. A wholesome morale stimulates loyalty, cooperation and teamwork, all of which are so essential for the smooth coordination of many individuals in a single organization.[1]

Morale is both an individual and a group possession, each interacting upon the other. It would be difficult, for example, to maintain a high group morale among individuals who were harassed by personal worries. Studies in the field of industrial personnel show that failure during work hours may be due to conditions wholly unrelated to occupation, personal in nature.[2] On the other hand, a high group morale may help tide over an individual who is perplexed and distressed by personal matters.

These considerations indicate how wide are the potential interests of

[1] The World War induced considerable writing on morale, but there has been little in recent years. Among the World War books are the following: William E. Hocking, *Morale and its Enemies* (1918); G. Stanley Hall, *Morale, the Supreme Standard of Life and Conduct* (1920); Edward L. Munson, *The Management of Men* (1921); and Sumner H. Schlichter, "Industrial Morale," 35 *Quarterly Journal of Economics* 36-60 (1921).

[2] Elton Mayo, *The Human Problems of an Industrial Civilization* (1933).

personnel officers. It is their duty to maintain the morale of their organization at the highest possible pitch; and to do this, they cannot overlook any circumstances which may affect the attitudes of workers, individually or collectively. While their primary mission will remain with working conditions, in some instances they will be concerned with matters far removed from the immediate work environment.

What are the broad bases on which a wholesome morale can be maintained? Without seeking to explore the special circumstances of particular cases, we may describe a number of general considerations which underlie a wholesome morale in most, if not all, cases.[1]

Knowledge of the purposes and objectives which an organization seeks to achieve, buttressed by conviction of their social value, is a driving force of greatest importance. Such convictions underlie great historical movements, sending medieval knights to the Crusades, sustaining the strength of armies in every major modern conflict, and lending power to the great emancipation movements of the last century. These powerful drives are not ordinarily captured by the organs of civil administration and usually they are not needed. But cast in less heroic molds they are equally valuable.

In a number of contemporary fields, notably those which are highly controversial in nature, sympathy for the end in view is particularly important. It was not without reason that the Tennessee Valley Authority inquired into the attitude of its directing and research personnel toward the aims of the Authority, and that the Rural Electrification Administration selected its important staff members with an eye to their loyalty to the aims of the organization.

In lower and routine positions, a belief in the general objectives of a public agency is less essential; but if neutrality or indifference shade over into disbelief and opposition, the morale of the group is adversely affected. Experience indicates, moreover, that specific effort is needed to keep the members of an organization informed about policy, if knowledge is not to be displaced by rumor and hearsay. Taking steps to keep the members of a group informed makes a positive contribution to morale in and of itself, for it cultivates the feeling that everyone "belongs," and that all have a share in the enterprise.

From another point of view this suggestion is related to the sense of the "worth-whileness" of one's work. There are few more depressing circumstances than the haunting feeling that what one is doing is not worth doing. It is not enough that work provide a living; it should pro-

[1] R. O. Beckman, "How Cincinnati's New Government is Improving Civil Service Morale," 18 *Nat. Mun. Rev.* 232-36 (1929); C. R. Stampe, "The Provision and Equality of Opportunity in the Public Service," 8 *Pub. Adm.* 44-55 (1930).

vide a positive satisfaction in the performance. That so frequently this is not the case is one of the unsettling forces in modern life. A high morale is essentially joined with a belief in the importance and value of the work which each individual performs. The assurance of such a conviction so far as may be possible is one of the broad responsibilities of management and deserves not to be left to chance alone.

Dealing with the same problem in industry, Oliver Sheldon wrote, "Without some general motive, the appeal for cooperation in industry is a voice in the wilderness. The motive for cooperation must be accepted before cooperation can become effective. A society cannot be formed without an object to which all the members can subscribe." [1] In the public service, a sustaining motive for good work lies in an understanding and acceptance of the great ends for which the state exists, and a realization that the daily efforts of each contribute in some measure to these ends. The device of the English Society of Civil Servants, bearing the words, "We serve the State," symbolizes the devotion of the service to these essential human purposes.

Another important element in making morale is confidence of the rank and file in the integrity and good intent of associates and superiors. The splendid example of the city managers affords an illustration of what can be done to sustain morale by high standards of integrity in public office. It is difficult, on the other hand, to maintain esprit de corps in an organization whose leaders are suspected of unfairness, favoritism, sharp practices or corruption. The morale of some civil service commissions has been shattered at different times because the commissioners conspired to violate the spirit if not the letter of the law to secure jobs for political friends. The low morale of some police forces has been due in part to lack of confidence in the commanding officers who were suspected of "collecting" from organized vice. Rumors spread through the force like an insidious poison, and the weaker members of the lower ranks decide to "get theirs." Fortunately such extreme cases are rare, but they attract public notice. The grosser forms of corruption are uncommon, but a single-minded devotion to the public interest, as against party interest or business favor, has not been reached on all fronts.

Morale is related to loyalty. Exceptional administrators will inspire an unlimited devotion among their subordinates. There is no formula for such a result; one man will win loyalty in one way, another quite differently, but in any case the quality of fairness to the staff on the part of the leader is of cardinal importance. It is fatal to morale to play favor-

[1] Oliver Sheldon, *The Philosophy of Management* (1923); see also Ordway Tead "Purpose as a Psychological Factor in Management," 10 *Bulletin of the Taylor Society* 254-67 (1925).

ites for political, religious or personal reasons; or to be suspected thereof. This breaks down the essential confidence in superior officers on the part of their subordinates.

Morale is a matter of attitude, opinion and belief. High morale depends upon the belief among the rank and file that personnel operations are fairly handled. There are never enough opportunities for promotion to satisfy all employees and some are consequently bound to be disappointed. Those passed over will not always concede the justice of the selection of another; but the fairness of the personnel officer and chief administrator in making assignments, allowing increments, granting leave, securing transfer, making promotions and maintaining discipline should be so apparent that individual disappointment in particular cases may be overborne by recognition of good intent and impartial (if mistaken) judgment.

This result, so helpful to maintaining morale, can hardly be attained if in fact employment conditions are unsatisfactory. These conditions often depend on elements beyond the immediate control of the official in charge of a bureau or institution. Scales of pay and often individual salaries are fixed by the appropriating body; lines of promotion are often limited by the structure of the organization; bad housing conditions may be the fault of the central agency which controls office space, or due to overcrowded conditions for which no one is directly responsible. Public employees, like other Americans, enjoy their constitutional privilege to grumble, and employee organizations have no difficulty in finding points at which employment conditions can be improved. They will never be perfect; but they can readily become so imperfect as to cause havoc in the morale of the service. Failure to handle the compensation problem effectively during and after the World War had a disastrous effect upon the morale of the federal employees. The inevitable reaction in extreme cases is sabotage by employees, more or less disguised.[1] A campaign of passive resistance or noncooperation is quite enough to hamper any program and to ruin some. There is considerable evidence that unsatisfactory working conditions were responsible for the impaired morale of the Boston police force at the time of the police strike in 1919. Sound and wholesome conditions of employment are certainly among the important bases of a wholesome morale.[2]

Stimulating leadership is also important. This phase of group esprit de corps has been explored at length in a recent treatise.[3] The qualities of

[1] For the analogous case in industry, see Stanley B. Mathewson, *Restriction of Output among Unorganized Workers* (1931).

[2] Will H. Hays, "Value of Good Will in Government Employment," 9 *Proceedings of the Academy of Political Science* 668-78 (1922).

[3] Ordway Tead, *The Art of Leadership* (1935).

leaders in the political world have been analyzed in some detail, but less is known of the qualities of administrative leadership.[1] They are very likely much the same. Effective leadership will use many morale-making devices, but in and of itself it makes morale; for a great leader will by his personality and influence bring to bear on his associates and subordinates forces of incalculable value. This is elementary in military circles. In this country leadership in civil administration is somewhat fortuitous, whether political or career, because capacity for leadership is not given as great consideration in selecting directing staffs as is political availability or technical competence. Nevertheless administrative leadership often rises to stimulating levels and sometimes to genuine heights.

From the standpoint of the individual employee what circumstances tend to improve morale?[2] Among the more ambitious, opportunity takes high rank. It is possible in the public service as elsewhere to miss the chance to grow to one's full capacity, merely by reason of the accidents of placement, assignment, supervision, or contacts. The ablest persons usually drive through these hazards to success. But morale can be sapped if others fail to achieve their more modest success and gradually realize with increasing bitterness that they are doomed to a lifetime of work exacting less than their best, rewarded by less than enough to meet their needs. There is a sense of frustration among some persons in the public service, much of which could be avoided by more intelligent handling of personnel problems. The gradual achievement of a career service will tend to provide opportunity for all grades and classes, so far as the major structure of the service will permit. Certainly a steadily expanding opportunity is one of the conditions of man's growth, and success in meeting new responsibilities one of the enduring satisfactions which make morale.[3]

Inevitably many employees will remain in the rank and file. For all, satisfactory personal adjustments to work and leisure are essential. Perfect adjustment is reserved for other worlds than this, but a working accommodation to the conditions of life is open to achievement. This is highly individual. Within the framework of generally sound employment conditions, most employees make suitable adjustments to their fellow workers, supervisors, subordinates and to the work itself. In many cases an unobtrusive and wise personnel officer can expedite this

[1] Charles E. Merriam, *Four American Party Leaders* (1926); Harold D. Lasswell, *Psychopathology and Politics* (1930), ch. 8.

[2] For brief analyses of public service incentives, see Marshall E. Dimock, "The Potential Incentives of Public Employment," 27 *Am. Pol. Sci. Rev.* 628-36 (1933); and three articles in 12 *Pub. Adm.* 250-81 (1934).

[3] Thomas Naughten, *Scope for Initiative in the Junior Grades of the Civil Service* (1935).

process. In some his aid becomes essential. In a few he will have to go beyond ordinary means to seek help from physicians or social workers, psychiatrists or friends. Here he will need the wisdom of Solomon, the patience of Job, and the insight and understanding of a Jane Addams. But the building of morale is his task, and he cannot avoid this aspect of his job.

Opinions differ concerning the extent to which supervisors should go in seeking to aid their subordinates. Some believe that the life of the worker outside the office is irrelevant to performance at his desk. This is an untenable position. Others believe that official efforts to make an effective adjustment should be limited to office hours and office matters, leaving outside problems to be handled by friends or by community agencies. In many cases this course will be adequate. Where, however, failure in work springs from disturbances outside the office which cannot be dealt with otherwise, a personnel officer must follow the cause of failure to its source.

Finally, morale rests upon recognition. It is human to crave notice of one's achievements and to respond to public attention given to the success of one's efforts. In professional and scientific circles, the recognition of one's peers is one of the greatest, perhaps the greatest incentive. The competitive industrial world grants recognition in terms of wealth secured in the market place, a type of social distinction of great weight in America but perforce closed to those in the public service. Hence it is the more important both for the prestige of the service and for the morale of civil servants that other forms of recognition be substituted so far as may be feasible. These will probably be found in terms of public and professional notice for work of exceptional merit.[1] It is strange that a type of human response which is so well understood and implemented in the military and naval service should have been so generally disregarded in the civil service. This is not a suggestion in favor of a civil uniform, or the civil equivalent of an Iron Cross. Within proper limits of the psychology of the civil service, appropriate forms of recognition could be found. They might become a distinctive element in making morale.

Reflection upon the conditions which have depressed the morale of the public service in this country leads to the opinion that its greatest handicap has been political interference in administrative circles. Politics has time and again disrupted an effective organization by replacing its members with party henchmen who clamored for their reward. Politics has often broken the morale of public office or institution by prostitut-

[1] Myra Curtis, "Treatment of Suggestions from Staff," 12 *Pub. Adm.* 168-77 (1934).

ing it to partisan ends. At times politics has played havoc with the very purpose for which an administrative agency exists, not on the ground of public policy but for immediate party advantage. Politics has driven fear into the hearts of the permanent employees under the merit system as well as the members of the precarious branch of the public service; and fear destroys morale. These conclusions do not refer to the consequences of changes in public policy, which may and often must bring in their train changes in administration and administrators; they are concerned only with the consequences of narrow party intrigue, with a mean type of temporary personal dictatorship for purely partisan or personal gain, with the effort to ensure continued dominance of a party machine irrespective of the effect upon the public service.

The morale of the public service has suffered also from a bad press. Every breakdown in the integrity or efficiency of the public service is news; the steady performance of good work week after week is not news. This is inevitable, but as a result the social values created by the steady performance of government routines are seldom appreciated. It is doubtful, too, whether the civic education of boys and girls in the secondary schools gives a proper foundation for understanding how essential are the contributions of government to society.[1] These young people are the more easily impressed by newspaper criticism. Many newspapers, moreover, reflect the attitude of certain sections of American business which are hostile to government regulation of the economic order; it is to their interest to decry government activity and to raise the alarm against the "bureaucrats." We cannot expect the ablest men to aspire to a service subject to the irresponsible criticism which frequently is hurled against public officials and employees.[2]

The morale and prestige of the public service have been deflated somewhat by the widely accepted opinion that "business" commands the finest talents. This conclusion may be easily exaggerated, for the public service has had and now has in its ranks many exceptionally able men. But the prevailing belief runs to the conviction that the public service is the haven of the second best despite definite evidence that in some types of employment the contrary is true. The great financial prizes have, of course, been available only in business, and in a country where wealth spells prestige, this element has undoubtedly played a substantial role.

[1] Charles E. Merriam, *Civic Education in the United States* (1934).

[2] For an attractive account of the real achievements of one section of the public service see T. Swann Harding, *T. N. T., These National Taxeaters* (1934).

3. Codes of Ethics

One of the signs of a group which has attained a wholesome morale is the formulation of a code of ethics. Such codes in turn attract favorable public attention and help to raise prestige. Many public service agencies and organizations of officials have developed such codes of ethics, following the example of the established professions. The canons of legal ethics were first formulated in 1908; the canons of judicial ethics in 1924; but some state bar association codes had been formulated earlier. The principles of medical ethics were adopted in 1912. Engineering codes were drawn up by various groups from 1911 to 1927. The National Education Association Code was drafted in 1929 from earlier state teachers' codes.[1]

A code of ethics supplements legal provisions governing the conduct of a professional or technical group. It is normally self-imposed, although in the public service many ethical standards are stated in office rules officially promulgated and a few may find their way into the statutes. A code is concerned in general with the relations of members of the group to each other and to the public; in public service codes, with relations to superiors and to subordinates.

Membership in a profession imposes definite ethical standards, apart from the existence of formal codes of behavior. A profession is defined by the *Oxford English Dictionary* as a "vocation in which a professed knowledge of some department of learning or science is used in its application to the affairs of others or in the practice of an art founded upon it." A professional man is expected to give his services whenever called upon without exercising capricious discrimination. An obligation to give only the best service and to subordinate personal considerations to the interests of the client is widely recognized. The mental attitude associated with profit seeking is incompatible with devotion to a professional calling. The attitude of a professional man is one of pride in service given rather than of interest in opportunity for personal profit.[2] These broad considerations are progressively affecting the point of view and the actions of important classes of public service employees who as yet are not generally recognized as comprising a profession.

In the municipal field a well-known code of ethics is that adopted by the International City Managers' Association in 1924. Its provisions, as revised in 1938, follow.

[1] See C. F. Taeusch, "Professional Ethics," 12 *Encyclopaedia of the Social Sciences* 472-75 (1934), and A. M. Carr-Saunders and P. A. Wilson, "Professions," *ibid.* 476-80.

[2] A. M. Carr-Saunders, and P. A. Wilson, *The Professions* (1933), pp. 421 ff.; see also Benson Y. Landis, *Professional Codes: a Sociological Analysis* (1927).

In order to achieve effective, democratic government, the council-manager plan provides that municipal policy shall be determined exclusively by a legislative body elected by the people and that the administration of policy shall be vested in the city manager who, as administrative head of the city, shall be appointed by and responsible to the council. The International City Managers' Association is a professional organization of city managers; its purpose is to increase the proficiency of city managers and to aid in the general improvement of municipal administration. To further these objectives, the Association believes that these ethical principles should govern the conduct of every professional city manager:

1. No member of the profession seeks or accepts a position as city manager unless he is fully in accord with the principles of council-manager government and unless he is confident that he is qualified to serve under these principles as city manager to the advantage of the community.

2. The city manager has a firm belief in the dignity and worth of the services rendered by government and a deep sense of his own social responsibility as a trusted public servant.

3. The city manager is governed by the highest ideals of honor and integrity in all his public and personal relationships in order that he may merit the respect and inspire the confidence of the administrative organization which he directs and of the public which he serves.

4. The city manager believes that personal aggrandizement or personal profit secured by confidential information or by misuse of public time is dishonest.

5. The city manager is in no sense a political leader. In order that policy may be intelligent and effective, he provides the council with information and advice, but he encourages positive decisions on policy by the council instead of passive acceptance of his recommendations.

6. The city manager realizes that it is the council, the elected representatives of the people, which is entitled to the credit for the fulfillment of municipal policies and leaves to the council the defense of policies which may be criticized.

7. The city manager keeps the community informed on municipal affairs but keeps himself in the background by emphasizing the importance of the facts.

8. The city manager, in order to preserve his integrity as a professional administrator, resists any encroachment on his control of personnel, insists on the exercise of his own judgment in accomplishing council policies, and deals frankly with the council as a unit rather than secretly with its individual members.

9. The city manager handles all matters of personnel on the basis of merit. Political, religious, and racial considerations carry no weight in appointments, salary increases, promotions, and discipline in the municipal service.

10. The city manager curries no personal favors. He is the administrator for all the people and handles each administrative problem without discrimination on the basis of principle and justice.

These declarations represent a high standard of official conduct.[1] The Association maintains no standing committee on ethical conduct, but the observance of these standards is customary, even to the point where a manager sacrifices his immediate economic advantage.

In the national government a number of codes have been developed

[1] Read also City Manager Edy's letter to persons about to enter the employ of the city of Berkeley, California, printed in L. D. White, *The City Manager* (1927), pp. 331-34.

each for a particular office. They are often confused with office rules and regulations and seldom make an effort to state all the norms of conduct which in fact are expected. They are usually of official origin; indeed, so far as is known, no organized group of federal employees or officials has developed a code of ethics on its own initiative.

These official codes usually refer to the duty of diligent and courteous service, care in the use of government property, abstention from political or factional intrigue, loyalty to the responsible authorities, and care to prevent the disclosure of public business. They enjoin impartiality and fairness in dealing with the public, promptness in paying personal debts, forbearance in borrowing money from fellow employees, and forbid the sale of goods in office hours or the solicitation of contributions.

Special problems arise at a number of points where right and wrong are not as readily discernible as in these instances. Indulgence in speculation is one case. Obviously it is improper for an official or employee to take advantage of special information acquired in the course of official work and not otherwise available for the purpose of speculation for private gain. Certain employees in such federal agencies as the income tax unit of the Treasury, the Interstate Commerce Commission, the Federal Trade Commission, the Securities and Exchange Commission, the Federal Communications Commission, and certain bureaus of the Department of Agriculture are regularly in possession of confidential information on the basis of which they could easily speculate to their private advantage.

While sound service ethics bars such speculation, what can be said of a purchase on the stock market for investment? And should public employees be forbidden all speculation, or merely that which uses official information not in general circulation? The difficulties of distinguishing between investment and speculation are so great that no definition has been reached for the federal service at large; but prohibition against speculation in commodities or securities affected by an official agency on the part of the employees of the agency is common. The same problem arises in state administration in the case of utility commissions, tax commissions and the like; and in city government in real estate speculation. Neither laws, regulations, nor codes of ethics have been wholly successful in preventing official speculation. But standards are doubtless rising.

Complicated issues arise with regard to public criticism of the official acts of superiors or of the policy of the government or the chief executive. In the national government political activity is forbidden classified employees; but a wide margin still exists for criticism. Mere irresponsible grumbling, display of bad temper, and the like may call for minor discipline. A different case arises when the criticism is a reasoned and thoughtful disagreement on matter of policy. We may start from the constitutional guarantees of freedom of speech and of publication and reach one conclusion, or we may start from the doctrine of loyalty and reach a contrary view. Should a classified employee publish in professional journals or elsewhere arguments and views which are contrary to those supported by his responsible superiors? Should they be published anonymously? Should disclosure of official acts which might bring criticism of the government be tolerated in the interest of more complete information to the voting public?

No clear answer to these issues emerges and in any specific case the decision is governed by a host of attendant circumstances. In general subordinates in fact refrain from public criticism of their superiors. In cases of serious disagreement, however, subordinates will at times disclose their views publicly. In some instances, where the public interest is being betrayed, it is their duty to do so, even at heavy cost to themselves. In others, ethical considerations will lead an employee to resign and then to make a public statement of his reasons for doing so.

An ethical problem which admits a reasonably precise conclusion arises when scientific findings are rejected because they are politically unsatisfactory, followed by either a refusal to publish or by a request for their modification. To the credit of scientific and professional workers, such circumstances are customarily followed by absolute refusal backed up if necessary by resignation. A scientist will not and ought not to allow trifling with his findings.

Another instance which is clear in principle involves action in a case in which the official is directly or indirectly concerned. The judicial rule is that a judge never hears or decides such a case. A similar rule governs the decisions of administrative officials; the rule is often imposed in the statutes, and is always implicit in any code of public service ethics. Borderline cases may lead to a legitimate difference of opinion as to whether an official has an indirect interest which might be presumed to affect his impartiality, but the rule is a clear one. It is as important for administrative authorities to be free from bias, and to be known by the public to be impartial, as it is for the bench.

These are merely examples of the types of problems which arise in the public service and for which some guidance is often found in the codes of ethics of officials and employees. They do not exhaust the subject; indeed, they hardly illustrate it. We lack any general study of civil service ethics, but a subject which offers such interesting possibilities will doubtless soon be explored.

The qualities of prestige and morale are intangible, but they count heavily. They are inescapable, whether for good or for ill. They respond to changing circumstances, and themselves play a part in shaping events. They are compounded out of the complex of daily routines, built from the maze of personal contacts between public and officials and between the members of the public service. They are manageable within limits, and it is the thesis of this study that it is an obligation of responsible authorities to foster the prestige and morale of the public service. For the capacity of the service for action in the solution of the great human problems which vex the world is directly conditioned upon success in handling these intangible attributes of men at work.

PART V

FORMS OF ADMINISTRATIVE ACTION

Chapter Thirty

NONCOERCIVE FORMS OF ADMINISTRATIVE ACTION

THE analysis of the American system of public administration which has occupied the previous chapters deals with internal problems of departments, commissions and agencies: how government is or-anized for the daily performance of its varied functions; how officials et funds and account for their use; how the army of officials and em-loyees is selected and managed to secure effective operating results. But ublic administration is not a self-regarding enterprise. It does not exist or its own sake, but for the sake of social amelioration achieved in the xecution of public policy. It looks outward, not inward. Its task is not ompleted when it has created an effective instrument of action; it is nly then ready to face its real responsibilities, which lie outside its own orders among the mass of individuals and groups throughout the length id breadth and depth of society.

Through representative institutions, democratically responsible, citi-ens agree that certain services shall be carried on as public enterprises, id that conduct shall be influenced or controlled in certain particulars the interest of the general good. Public officials and employees exist provide these services and to ensure compliance with these standards conduct.

In either case officials and employees are concerned with the mass of tizens. In the provision of services, the relationship is beneficial and oblems of adverse interests arise infrequently; in the regulation of nduct, the relationship is restrictive and the limits of official authority e often challenged by those whose freedom of action is curbed—the ctory owner who furnishes a machine alleged to be dangerous to the erator; the broker who offers securities alleged to be fraudulent; e real estate owner who constructs a building alleged to violate the ovisions of the building code.

These outward-looking relationships are the essence of administration action. If they are effective, the great ends of state are achieved; if ey are inadequate or inefficient, public policy is blunted or diverted om its intended course.

The content of these external relationships varies with each field o administrative activity. In public health the subject matter includes principally the mass phenomena of disease; in crop production control th subject matter is the mass phenomena of price, production and consumption; in traffic regulation the subject matter is the mass movemen of persons and vehicles. Every field of administration thus has its ow special and peculiar content.

The methods employed by officials in every field, however, hav much in common. The task of securing compliance on a large scale in evitably leads administrators to similar, if not identical means of action varying in their intensity with the social urgency of compliance, bu nevertheless following certain common patterns. They are the subjec matter of this and the following chapters.

We therefore now leave the study of the administrative system as a instrumentality and turn to ask the question, by what means does th system operate in its contacts with citizens? How do administrative officials educate, inspire, cajole, restrain, or coerce 130,000,000 persons t behave as the law expects them to behave in the manifold relations o person to person in the endless complexity of modern society?

Fortunately it will not be necessary to examine all contacts betwee officials and public. The whole vast range of governmental service, i which there is no attempt to regulate or influence individual conduc unless in a way purely incidental to the provision of the service, fal outside this field of our study. Thus all activities such as the maintenanc of lighthouses and air beacons, the delivery of mails, the loan of book from a public library, the analysis of specimens in a public health laboratory, the making of a geological survey, the building of roads, park and public improvements, are set aside; they do not involve problem of law enforcement or compliance except in the incidental rules whic may be established for the use and enjoyment of the facilities or service provided.

Likewise excluded from the purview of the present inquiry are th research and publication activities of government, although they ma have important secondary and ultimate effects upon problems of la enforcement. The great research laboratories maintained by the National Bureau of Standards, the National Advisory Committee for Aeronautics, the state agricultural experiment stations, the Forest Produc Laboratory at Madison, Wisconsin, and by many other publicly supported institutions are designed not to enforce law but to extend th boundaries of useful human knowledge.

We are concerned with those administrative methods which are designed to establish a pattern of behavior among citizens in conformit with public policy as declared by law or by official regulation in conformity with law. Thus the maintenance of air beacons does not involve enforcement problems, but the licensing of air pilots does. A geological survey to plot oil resources falls outside this part of our study, but governmental regulation of oil production by private producers falls within. The maintenance of a health laboratory is a public service; but the requirement to render certain medical reports to the laboratory imposes an obligation upon private physicians, the enforcement of which involves, or may involve, administrative pressures upon this group of citizens.

Amidst the multitude of specific cases of law enforcement which occur every day, indeed every hour, all sorts of methods are used by public officials. There is no one, indeed, there are no few methods of reaching the ends fixed by law. Some administrative methods are prescribed in the statutes; some (notice and hearing, for example) derive from the common law; many are inventions of the public official who has a job to do and who proceeds as best he may with one eye cocked on the law of official liability, and with one ear close to the ground to catch rumbles of public reaction.

The methods prescribed by law or adopted by officials swing all the way from the relatively mild to the relatively severe. Some are noncoercive, more are coercive in greater or lesser degree. The choice of method will be dictated by a number of circumstances which can be identified in general terms. Thus the force of the means employed will vary directly with the urgency of securing compliance. Administrative action to prevent the spread of hoof-and-mouth disease is summary and requires the killing of diseased cattle. By contrast administrative pressure brought to bear on a householder in Chicago to reduce the amount of smoke from his soft-coal furnace is almost innocuous.

Without multiplying illustrations we may note that administrative methods of law enforcement are also likely to vary with the number of persons affected and with the concentration or dispersion of the population; with the degree of popular consent to or dissent from the law to be enforced; with the extent of departure from established habits which is required; and with the kind of compliance involved, whether merely abstention or positive action.

Our treatment of this general problem will proceed from a survey of those administrative methods which have the least degree of coercion to those which involve a greater degree of force, although it is not always possible to establish a certain order in view of the variable penalties and sanctions attached to noncompliance. We propose, as a matter of convenience rather than of logic, to consider in turn the noncoercive types of law enforcement (if this be not a contradiction in terms), including public relations as an aid to law enforcement; inspection; licensing; orders of individual application and rules; and administrative adjudication. Then follows a discussion of the various types of administrative sanctions, including the withholding or withdrawal of benefits and the summary destruction of property and detention of the person. These are by no means all the methods of law enforcement which officials use. They are illustrative only, although they are among the most common.

In an ideal society the noncoercive action of public officials would be the normal type: hortatory, declaratory, persuasive, perhaps at times minatory. Even in the imperfect world in which we live there is an enormous amount of official action not involving coercion, although at times influenced without doubt by the realization of ultimate weapons of coercion to which recourse might be had.

From one point of view, indeed, it might appear that there are two types of noncoercive action. In one, the true type, there is not even a reserved power of compulsion; what compliance is achieved must be achieved by agreement and free consent. In the other, compliance is in fact achieved without overt compulsion, but coercion stands in the background. If we should include in the class of noncoercive administrative action the latter type of response, we would be forced to conclude that the bulk of the day-by-day work of government is noncoercive. The flow of traffic responds to the traffic lights or the policeman's whistle, not by virtue of compulsion but by common recognition of general convenience—but the policeman has the power to arrest for violation of the traffic rules. Quarantine of a child afflicted with scarlet fever is usually "enforced" by the good sense of the family and the self-interest of the neighbors rather than by the official order and the forbidding notice of the health department—but in the last analysis the health department may remove the sufferer to a contagious-diseases hospital. Voluntary submission to smallpox vaccination is widespread, but by no means universal; in cases of urgency it can be required in most states.

Since, however, ultimate coercive power even though seldom invoked lies behind these examples of administrative action, they will not be accepted as conforming to the purely noncoercive type which is under discussion in this chapter. There are other forms of official action which definitely lack any aspect of legal compulsion but which nevertheless are effective within limits in guiding the action of individuals; a number of these are described in the following paragraphs. Lines of demarcation are not easy to establish and in some of the cases which we have chosen there may seem to be a degree of coercion. Anyone may make his own selection of cases and assignment to categories.

1. Declaration of Public Policy

From time to time the executive branch of the government may declare the policy of the "government of the day" as a guide to private action, hoping that a substantial proportion of the citizens will act accordingly. These declarations have no force of law and may be disregarded with impunity. Thus in the early years of the depression of 1929 President Hoover made a number of statements of public policy designed to encourage business men to increase industrial employment. In 1937 President Franklin D. Roosevelt stated in a press conference that he hoped reductions in wages and salaries would be withheld by private employers. In such instances there are no administrative or other methods of compliance; these declarations are merely appeals to the conscience and good judgment of citizens. They represent administration at its vanishing point, since no official has any authority to take any action.

In the early days of the crisis in Ethiopia in 1937, the Department of State indicated its desire that shipments of certain war materials be withheld. From time to time the attitude of the department on foreign investments has had a definite effect upon banking operations.[1] Thus President Wilson in 1913 disapproved American participation in a loan to China on the ground that it was "obnoxious to the principles upon which the government of our people rests." In 1928 the sale of Russian bonds and the payment of interest thereon through certain United States banks were opposed by the Department of State. In such instances no direct enforcement problem arises. Compliance may follow in part, however, from secondary or collateral consequences where government assistance would be needed or from fear of possible prosecution on some technicality which might be overlooked in case of an approved loan. Despite uncertainty concerning the constitutional authority of the government, the expression of opinion on foreign loans is not uncommon and is often effective, despite lack of legal means of enforcement.[2]

2. Declaration of a Legal Obligation, with no Sanction for Nonobservance

Whenever a rule of action is prescribed by any public authority for the violation of which no penalty is provided, subsequent official action

[1] Benjamin H. Williams, "Capital Embargoes," 43 *Pol. Sci. Q.* 229-48 (1928).

[2] The purchase or sale of bonds of governments in default to the United States was forbidden by act of April 13, 1934, 48 Stat. 574.

to secure compliance is noncoercive in nature. Such cases are not common, and usually reflect wide differences of opinion in the community concerning the wisdom or justice of the policy involved.

During the nineteenth century there was considerable declaratory legislation with respect to hours of labor, beginning in New Hampshire in 1847. By 1896 seventeen states had legislation of this kind, the majority making eight hours the legal working day. In each case, however, contracts for longer hours were permissible, and the courts usually assumed the existence of such where longer hours were the custom. This legislation was ineffective.[1]

3. Establishment of Voluntary Commercial Standards

In the course of administration the fixing of standards is one of the most common procedures. Often such standards are intended to have binding effect and in case of infraction some penalty is provided. In some cases, however, the standards are worked out merely as guides, without any binding effect. The purpose in mind may be merely public convenience, in which case the administrative function is purely a service one; or the government may seek some degree of voluntary compliance for the effectuation of a desired public policy.

The establishment of commercial standards by the federal government is principally limited to interstate commerce, but such standards may in fact have a persuasive influence throughout the trade. The Cotton Futures Act of 1914 and the Grain Standards Act of 1916 put two large staple crops on an official grading system for interstate shipments; these standards have been voluntarily adopted for most transactions, because no one could foretell which cotton or grain would be sold in interstate or intrastate commerce.[2]

Most departmental grades are optional and permissive, except for government purchasing and for official inspection, if any. Thus the food standards of the Food and Drug Administration are wholly advisory and compliance is a voluntary matter on the part of the manufacturer. They do, however, represent a standard of purity and quality which the government believes desirable and which would be enforced if authority permitted.

The National Bureau of Standards has devoted much effort to the

[1] John R. Commons and associates, *History of Labor in the United States, 1896–1932* (1935), vol. 3, pp. 540-41.

[2] The Tea Importation Act of 1897 (29 Stat. 604) set standards which automatically became universal since there is no domestic production. See also the Butter Act of 1923 (42 Stat. 1500) and the canned food products legislation of 1930 (46 Stat. 1019). Requirement of safety devices on freight cars moving in interstate commerce was automatically effective for most intrastate commerce as well, since no railroad company could readily restrict certain cars for exclusively intrastate use.

development of national commercial standards.[1] While the Bureau has no means of enforcing such standards it has invented an ingenious plan of certification to facilitate their use. The Bureau compiles lists of manufacturers who are prepared to certify to purchasers that their material is guaranteed to meet the requirements of federal specifications. In 1932 about 8,000 firms were thus listed; in 1936 more than 21,000.[2] These lists are distributed to the purchasing agents of all federal departments and establishments, to the public purchasers of all the states and of the more important cities and counties, and to tax-supported colleges and hospitals.

4. Provision of Standard by Example: the Government as a Model Employer

Somewhat analogous to the previous case is action taken by the government with reference to its own affairs with the intention in part of stimulating voluntary action by private parties along lines thought socially desirable. Conditions of employment in the public service with respect to hours, leave, compensation for injuries, and salaries and wages in the lower brackets are affected somewhat by this consideration.

The government may use its purchasing power as a very strong inducement to conformity to standards which Congress, at least, has no constitutional authority to impose directly. Thus the Walsh-Healey Act of 1936 imposed a number of labor standards upon contractors supplying materials of value in excess of $10,000 to the United States Government.[3] They must pay not less than a minimum wage as determined by the Secretary of Labor; maximum hours are fixed at forty per week; child labor is forbidden; the products of convict labor are not accepted; and the plants must be free from unsanitary, hazardous, or dangerous conditions. These regulations are not and could not be imposed upon manufacturers generally; they are standards which the federal government sets up for its own guidance in selecting its contractors.

5. Educational Campaigns

The coercive forms of securing compliance themselves break down at times or give evidence of inadequacy as, for example, in traffic regulation. Despite all the laws and penalties the toll of highway accidents and

[1] See U. S. National Bureau of Standards, *Standards Yearbook;* National Industrial Conference Board, *Industrial Standardization* (1929); *Industrial Standardization and Commercial Standards Monthly;* Gilbert Sussman and S. R. Gamer, "Standards and Grades of Quality for Foods and Drugs," 2 *Univ. of Chicago Law Rev.* 578-99 (1934–35); *The Protection of the Consumer of Food and Drugs: A Symposium,* 1 *Law and Contemporary Problems* 1-133 (1933–34).

[2] U. S. Secretary of Commerce, *Annual Report,* 1936, p. 79.

[3] 49 Stat. 2036 (1936).

fatalities is beyond all reason. Supplementing the efforts of highway patrols, a number of states and cities have undertaken educational campaigns to induce more careful driving. These include traffic schools for citizens, the circulation of literature, radio talks, and billboard advertising. It is possible that for many drivers these methods of securing conformity are more effective than the remote anticipation of arrest and a small fine.

The campaign for the use of the "Blue Eagle" in 1933 and 1934 illustrates a nation-wide effort to produce a given result in the shortest period of time by voluntary cooperation. It rested principally on a public appeal heavily tinged with an exhortation to patriotism. On a much less dramatic scale, the inspectional services of federal, state and municipal governments depend very heavily upon educational rather than coercive means of securing compliance.[1] Crime *prevention* is essentially educational in nature; but the *apprehension* of criminals proceeds on other grounds.

In many fields, therefore, we find examples in which the administration tries to spread mass habits and responses by means which are essentially educational and persuasive in nature, rather than by invoking the coercive penalties of the law.

6. Demonstration

By demonstration is meant explanation by example or exhibition of a preferred method or device, in the expectation that its superiority will lead to its voluntary acceptance. Government has supported demonstrations for many years, especially in the field of agriculture.

The most extensive example of demonstration is the work of the county agent, initiated in 1906 and placed on a cooperative federal-state relationship by the Smith-Lever Act of 1914.[2] The county agents, home demonstration agents, and county boys' and girls' club agents numbered over 6,000 in 1930. They have no power to compel any farmer to do, or to refrain from doing anything. Their work is educational and promotional. The emphasis of county agents' work until 1933 was on the improvement of crop and livestock production. Since 1933 they have also been engaged in planning crop quotas and in many ways assisting the program of the Agricultural Adjustment Administration and other federal "action" agencies. They remain, however, demonstration agents,

[1] See ch. 31.

[2] See A. C. True, *A History of Agricultural Extension Work in the United States, 1785–1923* (1929); C. B. Smith and M. C. Wilson, *The Agricultural Extension System of the United States* (1930); William A. Lloyd, "Extension Work, Agricultural," 6 *Encyclopaedia of the Social Sciences* 31-36 (1931); Gladys Baker, *The County Agent* (1939).

destitute of coercive power but exercising much influence in farm management and agricultural methods.

The maintenance of safety museums for the display of approved machinery and safety methods is another form of demonstration. These museums are also used for training safety inspectors.[1]

In the modern field of housing, the activities of the federal government have been based chiefly on the idea of demonstration in the hope that local government and private capital would assume the major responsibility. Thus the rural and suburban housing enterprises of Resettlement Administration were intended to demonstrate types of economically sound projects. The urban housing projects of Public Works Administration were also in part demonstrations, combined with a program of slum clearance. In each case it was regarded as unwise for the federal government to build and manage local housing from Washington. The Wagner-Steagall Housing Act of 1937 represented an experimental balance between federal and local authorities in low-cost housing, with the initiative now transferred to the local authorities.

The federal government's experiment in water transportation, the Inland Waterways Corporation, was hailed at its inception as a mere demonstration which would soon be turned over to private capital. The shift has not yet occurred (1938). Other examples indicate that government not infrequently resorts to the process of demonstration to achieve its policy when it lacks legal authority or does not wish to use coercive means to accomplish the end in view. A substantial part of the vast publication output of the federal government in fact is a form of demonstration, through which new methods and new ideas are brought to the attention of the people.

7. Conferences

A common device to aid in law enforcement is the holding of conferences of private parties whose interests are affected. This type of conference may be distinguished from those which are held for the purpose of formulating policy, either in legislation or in rules having the force of law.

A well-established form of the conference which is directly related to law enforcement is the trade practice submittal of the Federal Trade Commission. These conferences bring together representatives of a certain trade or industry for the purpose of discussing trade practices and of reaching an understanding on the part of the trade concerning acceptable practices. No official action is taken by the conference or by the Federal Trade Commission; no prosecutions are initiated; but the

[1] For example, New Jersey Museum of Safety.

common understanding of "unfair practices" developed through such conferences has been very advantageous. Henderson reports "that the educational influence of a single trade practice submittal is as valuable as the coercion of a host of formal complaints and orders."[1]

Under the National Industrial Recovery Act an extraordinary number of trade conferences were held, chiefly for the drafting of the various codes, but partly for consideration of problems of compliance. The administration of the crop production control programs of the Agricultural Adjustment Administration and of the subsequent soil conservation programs involved a huge number of conferences with farmers and farmer organizations. The operation of the Securities and Exchange Act has required frequent conferences between federal officials and brokers. Some of these conferences relate to conditions for the enforcement of which ultimate coercive methods are available; but the noncoercive methods, especially in the early stages of administrative enforcement, are constantly becoming more significant.

In state governments the enforcement of much labor and industrial safety legislation is facilitated by conference between officials and manufacturers. In all large jurisdictions there is a constant give-and-take between administrators and private parties with reference to the forms and methods of enforcement proceedings which in substantial measure eliminates the necessity for the use of coercive methods of securing compliance. The great majority of citizens desire to fulfill the obligations which the law lays upon them and conference is a powerful means of facilitating their cooperation.

8. Mediation and Conciliation

These forms of official action are common in handling labor disputes. Hypothetically the state might adopt a policy of complete hands off with respect to labor troubles. In fact the inconvenience and, in some cases, the danger to the public arising from labor conflicts, strikes, and lockouts are so great that most modern states intervene in one form or another to bring them to a peaceful and early termination. By constitutional amendment strikes and lockouts might be prohibited, or arbitration of disputes might be made compulsory with enforced acceptance of the awards, but with rare exceptions the state has chosen noncoercive rather than coercive methods in this field of its activity.

Mediation and conciliation machinery is maintained by the national and most of the state governments. It is the duty of a government conciliator to discover the facts of an industrial dispute, to make suggestions and to offer advice to the parties at issue in order to find a means of

[1] Gerard C. Henderson, *The Federal Trade Commission* (1924).

bringing them into agreement. In most cases the acceptance of an offer of conciliation is optional with the parties; in some cases the law requires that conciliation must be accepted before a strike or lockout may occur. In the latter case, the methods of securing consent to the intervention of official conciliators are undeveloped; and after conciliation has been undertaken, there is no compulsion upon the parties to agree upon a settlement. In the last analysis, therefore, conciliation is a noncoercive undertaking on the part of government.[1]

Despite the lack of sanctions, the usefulness of mediation and conciliation agencies is not open to doubt. A substantial proportion of all labor disputes is successfully terminated by this form of government intervention, and in a number of industries permanent unofficial conciliation boards have made unnecessary any official action to maintain industrial peace. The labor conciliator performs a most difficult and delicate task, and one which illustrates the important role which administrators play even where they lack coercive power.[2]

9. Purchase of Capacity to Act; Purchase of Consent

In some instances government finds it convenient to purchase the consent of a section of the population, rather than to coerce it; and in some instances in which the federal government has no specific constitutional authority to act, it may purchase consent to a policy through its power to raise and disburse funds "for the general welfare." In other cases it may purchase a resource, such as land or a power site.

The latter case is illustrated by the purchase of submarginal land by the federal government in recent years, through Resettlement Administration and other agencies, for the purpose of withdrawing it from cultivation. The prevention of erosion in certain arid sections is also sought by the purchase of land in order to put it into erosion-resistant types of plant life. Both constitutionally and politically it would have been impossible for the federal government to have removed the population by coercive methods; it was, however, quite feasible to purchase their holdings. The government then has all the rights of any landowner and can manage its property as it deems wisest in the national interest.

The purchase of riparian rights to construct public improvements is exemplified in the construction of the lake-front park and boulevard in Chicago, an improvement extending nearly twenty miles along Lake Michigan and involving a large number of riparian rights including

[1] For example note the functions of the National Mediation Board with respect to railway labor disputes, 48 Stat. 1185, 1193 (1934).

[2] For a brief survey, see B. M. Squires, "Conciliation, Industrial," 4 *Encyclopaedia of the Social Sciences* 165-69 (1931).

those of the Illinois Central Railroad. Purchase was certainly a more convenient, if not practically the only feasible method of procedure.

The principal example of purchase of consent to a national policy is the production control program of the Agricultural Adjustment Administration. Payments to farmers for reduced production were undertaken on a huge scale, the funds being provided at the outset through the processing tax.

10. Compliance through Publicity

The purpose of this method of law enforcement is to induce compliance by the economic and social effects of adverse publicity, but without resort to legal means of compulsion.

The case is well illustrated by the procedures of the Massachusetts Minimum Wage Commission in extending the observance of a noncompulsory minimum wage. The Commission is authorized after investigation to announce a minimum wage for women in a specific trade or industry. After a hearing, it is authorized to publish the names of employers who fail to observe the recommended wage.[1] The manufacturer may be required also to post notices of wage hearings and of decrees which apply to the employees. The force of public opinion is thus sought in support of a minimum wage which has no legally binding effect. Similar legislation is found in other states induced by adverse decisions of the Supreme Court on compulsory minimum wages.[2]

11. "Yardstick" Regulation

The history of public regulation of utilities is principally the story of evolving coercive measures ranging from early legislative enactments through franchise limitations and advisory administrative commissions to regulatory commissions vested with power but subject to judicial review. None of these methods have proved wholly satisfactory. Within recent years the "yardstick" theory of utility regulation has been invented and is now being applied in some instances.

In essence, this type of public activity consists in government competition with privately owned utilities in order to develop tested data concerning profitable rates, and to induce proper commercial rates and services by holding out to consumers an alternative source of supply. The government, by entering a given field as producer, thus supplies a yardstick by which it and the consuming public may measure the services and rates of private producers.

The view may be taken that in such a case the government is in fact

[1] General Laws of Massachusetts, 1932, c. 151.

[2] For examining powers, see Ernst Freund, *Administrative Powers over Persons and Property* (1928), ch. 9.

applying coercion, and that consequently this form of securing compliance falls in another category than the noncoercive. From one point of view this argument is well-founded; economic pressure may be brought to bear to force better services or lower rates. From another point of view the government is applying no legal forms of compulsion. The private utility is subject to no new obligations, requirements or penalties; it is merely faced with a new competitor.[1] It may continue to do business, making whatever adjustments may be necessary to retain its position in the field.

This type of noncoercive administration, if such it deserves to be called, is illustrated by the Seattle municipal power system, which has developed important power facilities on the Skagit River, and which competes in Seattle with the Puget Sound Power and Light Company. The most spectacular instance is furnished by the Tennessee Valley Authority, which is competing with the Commonwealth and Southern Corporation and other utilities in furnishing electric light and power.

These examples of noncoercive forms of administrative action indicate how varied are the means open to officials short of compulsion. Their usefulness naturally differs from one situation to another, and in general they cannot be relied upon where the need for compliance is pressing. In a democracy, however, there will be preference, just so far as may be possible, for the milder forms of establishing the mass habits which the law prescribes.

12. Public Relations and Administrative Publicity

The extent to which noncoercive methods are adequate will vary with many circumstances, among them the quality of the relationship between governors and governed. If there is a mutual confidence and respect, the necessity for resorting to compulsion will be relatively slight; if the contrary, relatively great. It consequently behooves a thoughtful government to maintain good relations between itself and the public.

"Public relations in government is the composite of all the primary and secondary contacts between the bureaucracy and citizens and all the interaction of influences and attitudes established in these contacts." [2]

[1] For the purposes of this presentation it is unnecessary to enter into a discussion of the all-important question of the financial and economic character of the competition, and of the propriety of governmental activity of this sort, all highly controversial questions.

[2] This definition and much of the following analysis are taken from a forthcoming work by James L. McCamy, *Federal Administrative Publicity*. See also three papers by S. H. Wood, C. Kent Wright, and A. P. Ryan, "Intelligence and Public Relations," 14 *Pub. Adm.* 41-65 (1936); T. S. Simey, "A Public Relations Policy for Local Authorities," 13 *Pub. Adm.* 242-50 (1935); and a forthcoming study by Maure L. Goldschmidt, *Public Relations Techniques in Municipal Administration.*

It is in large part the stuff out of which prestige is won or lost for the public service. The quality of the relations existing between any administrative agency and the people may vary with a thousand subtle distinctions from a public attitude represented overtly by outright hostility, sabotage and resistance to one in which quick acquiescence and affirmative support are regularly forthcoming. Quite clearly the problem of effective administration is vitally concerned with maintaining public support through good public relations.

Practically any phase of administrative activity may have an influence upon public relations. It is an error to assume that the formation of good public attitudes is the sole responsibility of a public relations expert. All officials and government employees, especially those who deal directly with citizens, are public relations agents whether they realize it or not. They may please by an attitude of courtesy and helpfulness, or they may irritate by an attitude of superiority and a show of authority. The United States Civil Service Commission, to take one example among federal agencies, is especially careful to select as information clerks employees who have a pleasing personality and a steady disposition. They are a real asset to the Commission.

The correspondence of a public authority is another foundation on which good or poor public relations may rest. Dispatch in answering letters is a first necessity if public attitudes are to remain friendly; silence over a period of weeks or months (as is sometimes forced for mere lack of adequate appropriations) is certain to create bad feeling on the part of the correspondent. Letters themselves may be courteous or abrupt, responsive to the question or evasive, clear or ambiguous, couched in the active or the passive voice. They are endless emissaries from the official to his public, and a wise official sees to it that they go bearing peace, not war.

Many of the qualities which confer prestige, discussed in chapter twenty-nine, are also determinants of good public relations. It is unnecessary to repeat them here. It is essential, however, to point out that every government agency has its own special public with which its relations are peculiarly important. Thus the Department of Commerce looks especially to good contacts with business men; the Department of Labor with organized and unorganized workers; the Civil Aeronautics Authority with the expanding airship industry; the milk inspection service of a city health department with dairymen, and so on through the whole list of public agencies. It is more immediately important to each agency to have healthy public relations with its own public than with the public at large, but in the long run the latter cannot be overlooked.

A specialized "public relations service" has made less headway in government than in business. Until recently government has not been concerned with selling either itself or its products to the public. More and more definitely it is realizing that its major tasks can be facilitated by conscious cultivation of good will; and in gradually increasing measure government is selling specific products under circumstances where consumer good will is important—for instance, the sale of power and light by municipally owned utilities, or the sale of electrical appliances by the Electric Home and Farm Authority.

In the last analysis, the making and conservation of wholesome public relations are the end result of the functioning of the total mechanism. A specialized public relations office may actively pursue the end sought, but it can be won only as the outcome of the work and attitude of the whole organization from top to bottom. The object in view, to keep public attitudes sweet, or to sweeten them if they have gone sour, is of primary importance.

The public official whose duty it is to manage a public relations program has, however, a delicate task. The proper limits of his activity are not certain, and he is likely to encounter hostile forces on many sides. Opponents of the policy which is to be carried out are certain to look with disfavor upon a public relations campaign to facilitate its public acceptance. Members of legislative bodies are often critical of the sums spent for "informational" and related purposes by public officials, and hard-pressed taxpayers usually center their criticisms on official "publicity." The line between "propaganda" and information is not easy to draw, nor is it easy to differentiate in practice between facilitating compliance with an accepted policy and inducing agreement with a proposed policy.

A conservative view limits public relations activity to the dissemination of facts about the work of an organization in an atmosphere of complete neutrality. A less conservative attitude accepts the duty of placing such work in a favorable light with the definite intent of securing a friendly response. A more radical view accepts the responsibility of "selling" the program of an organization to the public by much the same methods used by a commercial producer to sell his product.

In any event, here is one of the noncoercive methods of facilitating compliance, modern in its conception and expanding in its scope and energy. While it is related closely to the newer commercial operations of government, it is not limited to them; and in its application to other types of administrative activity it raises important problems for future consideration. In the words of an English student of American facilities for public information, "their constant daily operation and development will, in the long run, have a significant influence on public opinion: an influence which will be found not only to have been informative, but fruitful in the more practical virtues of toleration, goodwill, and co-operation by which the task of government can be so greatly eased." [1]

A special aspect of public relations is administrative publicity, "the conscious effort to tell a public what public officials are doing, why they are doing it, and what subject matter is involved." [2] It is a phase of public relations which has been assiduously cultivated in recent years; indeed it is probably the first aspect of public relations to crystallize into specific forms.

The most spectacular example of administrative publicity is the weekly press conference of President Franklin D. Roosevelt. This bold and unprecedented experiment was extraordinarily popular in its early years, but more recently the nonquotable "off-the-record" comments and occasional evasions or refusals to speak have cooled the ardor of some newspapermen. In general the daily press is the principal medium used for administrative publicity, and city managers, governors, department heads and presidents all guard their press contacts carefully.[3] A hostile press in a city manager town is almost certain to break the manager sooner or later; a friendly press is one of his chief assets.

The effort of administrative agencies to inform the public is enormous. The various research and informational services of the national government, such as the National Bureau of Standards, the Bureau of the Census, the Bureau of Foreign and Domestic Commerce, the crop reporting services, the Weather Bureau and many others send out a never ending stream of scientific and statistical material. Similar agencies in the states (geological and biological surveys, agricultural experiment stations, health laboratories) add to the volume of printed matter designed to inform, to educate, and to assist the citizen in any one of his manifold activities. Apart from the scientific and statistical output, there is a huge quantity of reports, summaries, presentations of factual material, annual operating reports, financial statements and similar material, designed to inform citizens rather than to direct their conduct.

McCamy's study of administrative publicity in Washington confirmed the position of the newspaper as the principal medium of official publicity, and ranked in order the following additional outlets: maga-

[1] F. R. Cowell, "Government Departments and the Press in the U. S. A.," 9 *Pub. Adm.* 214-27 (1931). For a more extensive discussion of this topic, see John M. Pfiffner, *Public Administration* (1935), chs. 22-23.

[2] McCamy, *op. cit.*; George Michael, *Handout* (1935); Arthur Krock, "Press vs. Government—a Warning," 1 *Public Opinion Q.* 45-49 (April, 1937); Arch A. Mercey, "Modernizing Federal Publicity," *ibid.* 87-94 (July, 1937); Cedric Larson, "How Much Federal Publicity is There?" 2 *ibid.* 636-44 (1938).

[3] The principal study on this general point is by Leo C. Rosten, *The Washington Correspondents* (1937).

zines, radio, pamphlets, "own movies," posters and film-strips.[1] The three principal categories from the point of view of content were (1) releases announcing the achievements, progress and policy of the agency; (2) releases describing the methods of work, the nature of the function performed, or the equipment of the agency; (3) releases presenting facts from the records or from research studies. Several municipalities have developed their own movies and it is likely that motion picture and radio publicity will grow more rapidly than other forms in the future. The extraordinary films of the Agricultural Adjustment Administration, "The Plow that Broke the Plains" and "The River," suggest a new world in official publicity.[2]

"Press agents" in government departments have been and to a certain degree still are objects of suspicion on the part of legislators. Representatives of the people fear that press agents may become propaganda agents who will suppress the unfavorable and "ballyhoo" the favorable aspects of governmental work, eventually influencing public opinion and thus expanding the power of the bureaucracy.

So considerable was this alarm in Washington in 1913 that Congress forbade spending appropriated funds for "publicity experts" unless specifically authorized.[3] This prohibition still prevails, but is largely avoided by spending funds for directors of information, directors of publication, editors and the like instead of for publicity experts. A further prohibition, the nature of which will be obvious, prevents the use of public funds for services, messages, or publications designed to influence any member of Congress in his attitude toward legislation or appropriation.[4]

The body of experts who deal with administrative publicity is small. In Washington, McCamy was able to secure data on 212 such specialists.

[1] Cf. Victor Rosewater, "Municipal Government and the Newspaper," 18 *Nat. Mun. Rev.* 158-63 (1929); F. R. Cowell, *op. cit.;* T. Swann Harding, "Informational Techniques of the Department of Agriculture," 1 *Public Opinion Q.* 83-96 (Jan. 1937); Hal Hazelrigg, "A Newspaper Man looks at City Hall," 20 *Pub. Man.* 67-70 (1938).

[2] During the last ten years much attention has been given to public reporting, especially annual reports. This topic is not dealt with in this volume, but the following references will direct the interested reader to the principal recent sources of information. Considerable beneficial influence was exerted by the National Committee on Municipal Reporting in its work, *Public Reporting*, published in 1931 by Municipal Administration Service. See also Wylie Kilpatrick, *Reporting Municipal Government* (1928); Herman C. Beyle, *Governmental Reporting in Chicago* (1928); Phillips Bradley, *Making Municipal Reports Readable* (1935); Clarence E. Ridley's annual appraisals in the *National Municipal Review* and more recently in *Public Management;* J. T. Barton, *Municipal Public Reporting in Texas* (1936). One of the best pieces of municipal reporting in recent years is *New York Advancing: 1934–1935* (1936), edited by Rebecca B. Rankin.

[3] 38 Stat. 208, 212 (1913).

[4] 41 Stat. 35, 68 (1919).

This figure may be compared with the 208 Washington correspondents discovered in 1936 by Rosten, i.e., active political correspondents for American newspapers and press associations of a general circulation of 75,000 or over. The number of government publicity men increased sharply with the Roosevelt administration and intense publicity work took place in many of the New Deal agencies. Some publicity officials and employees have been patronage appointees, others have been selected by the usual methods of civil service examinations. Neither process has given uniformly good results.[1]

In state and municipal governments no such body of experts exists. In city halls, the mayors or managers and their private secretaries deal directly with the press, as do department heads in their fields of interest. In state capitals hardly greater attention is given to administrative publicity.[2] Busy reporters maintain their official and subterranean contacts, but the administration as such does not usually formalize its publicity efforts.

Does the array of federal publicity experts, along with the mounting tide of official releases, films, pamphlets and speeches constitute a threat to freedom of opinion? Are we again faced, as the civil service reformers declared the country was faced in 1880, with an overpowering force which may undermine democracy at its very source—this time not patronage but publicity?

There is no present evidence to this effect. Government publicity competes with nonofficial publicity in the open market and on a relatively minor scale. As a tool of administration, publicity creates no policy and makes or enforces no rules; it reflects only the policy and the rules of the official agencies by which it is used. If these agencies are responsible, their publicity is not likely to become a danger.

13. Summary

A survey of administrators at work reveals, in summary, that at various points their efforts lack means of compulsion. On one front or another, they must proceed by persuasion rather than by command. Here especially the maintenance of friendly public relations is important; but even where the power to command exists, progress in achieving ends is

[1] Top publicity specialists rank high in the official hierarchy. In 1936 the Director of Information in the Agricultural Adjustment Administration was paid $9,800; in Farm Credit Administration $8,500; and in Public Works Administration, the Social Security Board, and a few other agencies $8,000. The average salary of the whole group was about $4,000. They are predominantly former newspaper men. The rise of this new body of specialists is reflected in an article by Don J. Kinsey, "Training Employees in Public Relations," 20 *Pub. Man.* 171-74 (1938).

[2] See, however, Fred E. Merwin, "Public Relations and the State Government," 14 *Journalism Q.* 342-52 (1937-38).

facilitated by wholesome public attitudes. By example, by persuasion, by education, by demonstration, by conference, by the purchase of consent, by publicity, by "yardstick" competition and by building up an attitude of cooperation, public officials march forward as far as they can on the platform of administration by consent.

Under what circumstances is the use of noncoercive methods by public officials indicated? First and necessarily, noncoercive methods must be used where there is no constitutional authority to use coercive methods. The federal structure of the American administrative system multiplies instances where national action is desirable but where national power is either wanting or doubtful. The purchase of consent or other noncoercive means of action is a convenient substitute for constitutional power.

In the second place, noncoercive forms of administrative action will be preferred where they are adequate to the end in view. This is a relatively narrow area, but it exists; and as the influence of government is sought for the amenities of life as well as for its sterner necessities, noncoercive methods may expand within modest limits. The city beautiful, or the city clean, may perhaps be achieved by leadership better than by fines.

Where mass resistance to coercion or mass sabotage is probable and the end is not urgent, noncoercive forms of action may be the only ones which will produce any results, for in a democracy it is costly from every point of view to enforce law which encounters mass resistance, passive or otherwise.

In new fields of government activity, the milder measures of conference and education may be deliberately chosen as the prelude to coercive forms of administration at a later stage. The law is gradually fitted to those who are affected by it; and an interval of adjustment creates both a better disposition to acceptance and a corresponding lessening of the number of cases where coercion becomes necessary.

Finally, noncoercive methods may be adopted merely because funds are lacking to ensure adequate enforcement by compulsory process. Results may be disappointing, but they may be better than complete official neglect.

Apart from the provision of services, some degree of coercion, however modest, is associated with most administrative action involving citizens. Noncoercive forms are exceptional, although in such fields as the adjustment of labor disputes they are well established and give no present indication of yielding to more drastic types of state intervention.

Chapter Thirty-one

INSPECTION

THE sequence of noncoercive methods for securing complianc with public policy described in the preceding chapter led peril ously close to forms of coercion, economic and social rather tha legal in nature. Inspection, while buttressed by legal forms of compu sion, proceeds in most instances not by coercion but by educatio persuasion, exhortation and cajolery. Narrow is the borderland betwee the coercive and the noncoercive forms of state action!

Inspection is the examination and evaluation of some matter with re spect to standards of public policy. These standards may be expressed i laws or in rules made in pursuance of law. Inspection is essentially th viewing of a condition and the making of a judgment as to whether th condition is in compliance with public policy.[1]

The typical form of inspection is that in which the state examines condition and stands ready to use sanctions unless minimum standard are observed. A variant is the inspection of school pupils in which sub standard health conditions are noted and called to the attention of th students or their parents. In this case there is generally no element c compulsion unless the health of one is endangering the health of other

Inspection may be distinguished from traditional police enforcemen on several grounds. It is specialized, relating to one subject matter, fc example, food laws. It may be a continuing surveillance, as in the cas of federal meat inspection where every carcass is examined to determin its wholesomeness, or it may be periodic, as in the case of an annu inspection of steam boilers. Whether periodic or continuing, inspectio agencies attempt to determine compliance or noncompliance of all pos sible violators within a selected field, a task which the police cannot at tempt in the broad field of criminal law.

Another distinction is one of emphasis. Although police administratio is giving more consideration to crime prevention, most of its efforts ar still devoted to the investigation of law violations and the apprehensio of violators. On the other hand, inspection is concerned as much wi the prevention of violations as with the punishment of offenders.

[1] See Edith Ayres, "Inspection," 8 *Encyclopaedia of the Social Sciences* 71- (1932).

Inspection is one of the most common of administrative operations. ts development is related to several factors. Progress in the development)f the sciences of medicine and hygiene has made possible much modern nspection by providing a body of knowledge regarding the causes of lisease and means of control. For instance, no attempt to control the vholesomeness of milk was possible prior to the findings of Pasteur. Of :qual importance is the development of mechanization and the use of)ower in industry. These changes in the technique of production)rought hazards to life and limb with which workers could not cope, acking both knowledge of methods and the necessary power to enforce hanges. Related to the technological revolution, another condition unlerlying inspection is urbanization. The compact life of the city brings nany hazards to health and safety which are so great that the enforcenent of legislative correctives cannot be left to the regular law enforcenent officers. Social reform movements and labor unions, which with arying success have influenced public policy, expedited the introducion of the use of inspection. Leaders of these movements were not satsfied merely with reform legislation, but demanded its enforcement by pecial officers who would insist upon compliance.

. History of Inspection

One of the earliest forms of inspection is found in the public market. ledieval town authorities used this means for supervising standards of uality, price and weight in their markets and imposed stiff penalties n violators. It seems likely that these authorities were primarily intersted in preserving the good name of their markets so that the town ight become known as a fair place in which to trade. Early nineteenthentury American records show the same use of the inspectional device.

Influenced by the doctrines of mercantilism, Massachusetts and other tates maintained an extensive system of inspection of products, chiefly vith reference to the export trade, during the eighteenth and early part f the nineteenth century. Beef, butter, bread, chocolate, hops, smoked lewives and herring, gunpowder, firewood bark, salt, and paper were mong the commodities for which grades were fixed and inspection rovided.

The inspection of beef illustrates the practice. Legislation enacted in 800 in the Bay State prohibited the export of beef except such as conormed to the standards specified in the act. Provision was made for randing every barrel, the making of which was also prescribed in deil. The governor and council appointed an inspector general of beef, vho appointed numerous deputies to examine all export beef. Various nes were set for fraud in inspection and for attempting to evade inspection. The master of every ship was furthermore required to tak oath that all beef in his cargo was properly branded.[1]

Among the more modern uses of inspection as a means of law en forcement, one of the earliest is the inspection of places of employmen to ensure observance of the child labor laws. Massachusetts led the way by authorizing such inspection in 1867, Connecticut in 1869. In 187 Massachusetts created the first state factory inspection service with thre inspectors to enforce safety legislation and hours of labor for women as well as the child labor regulations.[2]

State factory inspection was not adopted rapidly. "As late as 1896 substantial proportion of American labor legislation was still in what w have called the pre-enforcement stage." [3] During the next eighteen year there was a considerable acceleration in the movement. The number o inspectors increased, their powers were enlarged, and additional state adopted inspection for the first time. Conflagrations, such as the Tri angle Shirt Waist fire in New York in which 145 were killed, gave im petus to the movement. The analysis of accident statistics stimulated th reform groups. During this period the improvements were largely thos of extending the powers of specialized policemen. It is since 1911 tha the factory inspector has been "transformed from a specialized police man into an expert acting as an instructor and advisor."

While the states developed inspection for the enforcement of thei labor laws, the expanding cities were also developing the same devic for the enforcement of social legislation. Although inspection has long been used in the municipal field, "The bulk of inspectional activity ha been undertaken in comparatively recent years, as technological devel opments and scientific investigations have furnished the tools for pro tection against various long-existent or newly created hazards. . . . Thi is a tendency which seems to be increasing rather than decreasing an the future is likely to find it of even greater significance both as t personnel and expenditure than it is now." [4]

The extent to which a modern municipality inspects and the period o introduction of each type of inspection appear in a study of Detroit.[5] The city was organized in 1824 and started out inspecting weights an measures and fire hazards. No further inspection was introduced unti

[1] Acts and Laws of Massachusetts, 1800, vol. 2, c. 69.

[2] Elizabeth Brandeis, "Labor Legislation," in John R. Commons and associates *History of Labor in the United States, 1896–1932* (1935), vol. 3, p. 629.

[3] *Ibid.*, p. 630. See also W. F. Willoughby, *Inspection of Factories and Work shops* (1900).

[4] Edna Trull, *The Administration of Regulatory Inspectional Services in Ameri can Cities* (1932), p. 176.

[5] Lent D. Upson, *The Growth of a City Government* (1931).

1867 when the sanitary patrol was established. Prior to 1900 we find nspection of food and meat (1879), construction of buildings (1885), nilk (1887), plumbing (1894), boilers (1896) and electric wiring (1896).

The field of inspection steadily enlarged, as Detroit became a greater netropolis and as new problems arose. In 1902 smoke inspection sought o abate the evil of pollution of the air. Safety considerations governed he inspection of elevators and signs (1911), and all inflammables (1915). Other forms of inspection include maternity hospitals (1913); refriger-tion (1916); foodhandlers (1918); day nurseries (1922). In 1926 was dded inspection of explosives, negro housing, hairdressers, and cosmeti-ians. No new subjects of inspection were established during the de-ression.

Since 1875 the federal government has adopted the inspection tech-ique for several purposes. Steam vessels, locomotives, and railway afety appliances, drugs and biological preparations, meat, airplanes, anding fields and aeronautics schools have all come under federal in-pectional supervision. Most inspection, however, falls to the state and ity governments.

. The Uses of the Inspectional Method

At present the inspectional procedure is applied to attain numerous bjectives. Safety in transportation is sought through the inspection of eam vessels, railway equipment, motor vehicles, airplanes and their cilities, and elevators. The protection of the public health is sought rough the inspection of food, its manufacture and distribution, drugs d biological preparations, housing, the adequacy of sanitary facilities, ospitals, nurseries, barber shops, beauty parlors, conditions causing ccupational diseases, the sources and character of water, sewage dis-osal, and the direct physical examination of school children and others. Safe conditions of work are sought through the inspection of mines, arries, boilers, factories, workshops, and construction. The prevention f fire and its attendant tragedies is attempted by the inspection of mate-ils, plans and modes of construction, the adequacy of fire-extinguishing cilities, the freedom of egress from buildings in which numbers of rsons assemble, the conditions of "housekeeping" likely to cause fires, d by surveillance over highly inflammable or explosive materials.

Commercial honesty and the informing of consumers and buyers of mmercial products are secured by inspectional enforcement of stand-ds of weight, price and quality, and by the grading of food, seed and merous other products. The preservation of the quality of the human ock is attempted by the enforcement, through inspection, of child labor laws and of hours of labor legislation. There is no presumptio that this list is complete.[1]

The matters which have been selected by government for inspectiona surveillance suggest that the device is used largely to foster publi health and welfare and to meet and control the hazards of a cultur that has become increasingly industrial and urban. In order to give clearer picture of the procedures and techniques included in the inspec tional methods, more detailed consideration of two cases, factory in spection and food and milk inspection, will be helpful.

3. Factory Inspection

The laws under which factory inspectors operate tend to be one o two types.[2] In one jurisdiction the law will specify the duties of factor inspectors in considerable detail, describing the factory condition which are approved and disapproved. In another, the legislative grant o power will be quite general in terms and the discretion of the inspecto is consequently enhanced. In the latter case the law is supplemented b administrative rules and regulations.

The standards of public policy regarding factories, whether embodie in law or administrative rules, deal with a wide variety of matters: th types of building in which manufacturing may be housed, their lightin and ventilation; the placing of machinery and the guarding of machin ery likely to cause injury; the wearing or use of safety appliances; th care of dangerous materials, and the housing of processes detrimental t health; the adequacy of sanitary facilities, the general orderliness c "housekeeping," exit facilities, child labor, hours of labor of womer "day of rest," provision of first-aid and medical facilities, and recor of workers and accidents.

A factory inspector is generally assigned to a district for which he responsible. In the ordinary course of events, he will go from factory t factory making his inspections until he has seen each factory in his di trict. This regular schedule may be altered, however. Accidents, de pending upon their severity and the probability of a violation of safet regulations, may cause a prompt inspection. Some inspectors make a attempt to investigate every serious accident, whereas others investigat only those thought to have resulted from violations. Complaints of vi

[1] Ernst Freund, *Administrative Powers over Persons and Property* (1928), ch. unsigned, "Investigatory Powers of the Securities and Exchange Commission," *Yale Law J.* 819-41 (1934-35); see also three articles on the place of the inspect in central and local government, 11 *Pub. Adm.* 236-58 (1933).

[2] See International Labor Office, *Factory Inspection* (1923); John B. Andrew *British Factory Inspection*, U. S. Department of Labor, Division of Labor Stan ards, Bulletin 11, 1937; William A. Robson, "The Factory Acts, 1833-1933," 5 *P Q.* 55-73 (1934).

ation received by the inspection agency may also alter the normal order f inspections. The agencies tend to encourage this sort of aid and some f them announce that all such information will be considered confiden-al. In the three years ending in 1936 the New York State factory in-pection agency received 2,763 complaints of the violation of factory ws, three-fourths of which were anonymous. About half of the infor-nation secured in this manner was found to be correct.[1] The regular ourse of inspection may also be altered by reinspections to determine hether defects noted have been corrected.

Before starting to inspect a plant, an inspector will make use of the ccident records and records of previous inspections of the plant in rder to familiarize himself with the conditions which he is to observe. Ie may thus be forewarned as to the degree of care he must take and s to the kinds of violations for which he should look.

The inspector starts his work by making his presence known to the nanagement. He then proceeds to view the factory, usually in the com-any of some member of the management, possibly a safety executive. Ie may check a printed form listing all the conditions to be observed r he may merely take notes of matters which should be corrected. He nust be an astute observer, for known violations overlooked by the in-pector will not enhance the management's respect for his ability or his anding with the chief inspector.

If the inspector regards himself merely as a law enforcement officer, e will complete his record of violations, if any, give directions, and ave for his next inspection. Factory inspection has, however, generally ecome much more than mere viewing and the issuance of orders. The nspector often develops all possible means of personal influence for curing compliance with good standards of safety and health.

On his visits to factories, he may become an appreciated source of formation on the duties of the factory operator under existing laws nd rules. He can recommend methods for removing hazards. His head-uarters office may have provided him with the results of research in fety techniques which he can pass along to factory managers. His own bservations of factories may have given him information as to inex-ensive correctives which will not interfere with efficient production. t one time Wisconsin inspectors would not ask factories to guard articular machinery unless a method of protection could be suggested. he inspector by his technical knowledge may be able to give plant nanagers economically valuable advice.

Partly because factory inspection is only periodic and partly because the roportion of accidents due to mere lack of care and unsafe practices

[1] Industrial Commissioner of New York, *Annual Report*, 1936, p. 13.

is increasing, it has become apparent that factory inspectors need to inculcate safety attitudes in the minds of factory operators. Speaking of this problem, one factory inspection official says, "In the course of his work the inspector meets many men of many minds and moods. Some welcome him, others do not conceal their intense willingness to say good-bye to him at the earliest possible moment. Some are agreeable, some are grouchy, and still others are just busy."[1]

In order to secure the desired attitude toward industrial safety and health hazards, inspectors use a variety of appeals that would do justice to a high-pressure salesman. From experience in investigating accidents they may relate how a worker was injured in circumstances similar to those found in the plant, thus appealing to the sense of humanity. They may appeal to the manager's interest in increased production by telling him how his plant conditions produce fatigue, or how guarded machinery permits a worker to keep up his speed without fear of injury, or how more orderly, cleanly housekeeping contributes to efficiency as well as to safety and health. Use of economic pressure is to be found in the compensation laws of some states which allow additional awards in cases where injury resulted from a violation of the factory laws. Cajolery may even have its place. One factory inspector reports, "I have often found that by kidding them about such conditions as not being able to see out the windows, or keeping the scrap on the benches and the tools on the floor, one can get further than by talking to them about accidents."

The inculcation of safety-mindedness in factory operators by inspectors takes other forms than preaching. Conferences of factory managers for discussion of safety matters are aided or promoted. Regular forums on safety may be held for plant foremen and superintendents. Aid is given factories in setting up workers' safety groups within the factory. In every New Jersey factory having more than fifty workers the state labor department appoints an employee, nominated by the management, as "factory chief" for safety purposes. This individual organizes workers' safety activities in the plant, does some regular inspection, receives safety literature published by the state department and acts as the inspector's contact with the plant. This same state also conducts contests between factories for safety records. In these promotional activities factory inspectors will be found cooperating with the National Safety Council and its local units.

The device of inspection thus displays considerable flexibility. But if information, advice, and encouragement are inadequate to secure com

[1] United States Department of Labor, Division of Labor Standards, *Report o Proceedings of a Training Course for State Factory Inspectors,* Bulletin 6, 1936, p.

liance with the state's standards there remains the possibility of sanc-ions. Behind the factory inspector's informal discussion with plant nanagers there is the veiled warning that if necessary the state will use s powers. Yet inspectors are not eager to use coercion. So long as they an secure cooperation they stand on a better basis for continuing their vork. Prosecutions, furthermore, are costly, requiring much time for ne preparation of legal proof and appearance in court.

In cases where changes are difficult or extensive, inspectors are willing o allow time for compliance to be forthcoming. Prosecution will follow reinspection on an agreed date shows that required changes have not een made. In practice extensions of time are frequently granted where n attempt to comply is being made.

In cases where violators are slow to comply, the inspectional agencies ave developed several methods of warning offenders. Firm letters urg-ng compliance and threatening prosecution are sent to offenders from eadquarters. Formal notice that a hearing at which the offender may now cause why he should not be prosecuted may bring compliance efore the time set for the hearing. With regard to some matters there an be no excuse for delayed compliance. Laws regulating child labor, ne hours of work of women, the wholesomeness of meat and milk, do ot need or permit delay in compliance. Building and manufacturing onditions which create a grave hazard deserve no forbearance in the rompt use of sanctions.

Because the laws and rules providing for factory safety may be diffi-ult to interpret in specific cases and because factory inspectors may be ger to secure high standards of safety regardless of the specific terms the law, it is important to secure some uniformity in interpretation d application. There are various ways in which wide discretion in terpretation may be stabilized. Ordinarily an inspector gives only erbal warnings or orders while he is in the plant. The formal order is sually sent from the state office, where some uniformity in standards ay be applied. Another means of stabilizing the interpretation of the w is by frequent conferences of inspectors at which problems of fety standards and the interpretation of the law may be discussed. ome states call persistent offenders to the state office to show cause hy they should not be prosecuted. This hearing gives an opportunity r a central leveling of interpretation, as well as being a useful device r frightening violators into compliance.

The activities of the United States Department of Labor through the ivision of Labor Standards may tend to give some interstate uniformity labor standards. Detailed standard codes of safety and health which e prepared by the Department of Labor, usually in cooperation with state departments or private associations, tend toward national uniform ity. The state inspectors' schools held about the country by the Divisio of Labor Standards are a means to the same end.

Factory inspection is in short a blend of coercive and noncoerciv forms of securing compliance. In the last analysis a recalcitrant employe may be prosecuted for noncompliance, and in the background of mos inspectional activity stands the ultimate authority of the court. Over period of many years, great progress has been made in securing highe standards of health, safety, comfort and convenience through inspec tion by agents of the state. This progress is due without doubt in sub stantial measure to the tact, diplomacy and salesmanship of the inspecto perhaps in lesser measure to his authority to issue an order and to en force compliance through a court.

4. Food and Milk Inspection

Factory inspection seeks to ensure the safety of urban working popu lations. Food and milk inspection involves a large section of the rur farming population whose food products move into the city for con sumption. The scattered, numerous and isolated units and the rugge individualism of the American farmer present special inspectional prob lems, aggravated by the universal inadequacy of inspectional forces.[1]

Most food and milk inspection is done by city and county healt departments, with some guidance and coordination from the state healt department. Food products moving in interstate commerce may be in spected by federal officials, and the largest single food inspection un in the country is the meat inspection service of the United States Burea of Animal Industry. Slaughter houses handling only intrastate shipmen of meats are inspected by state or local officials.

While the locality in which inspection occurs is thus usually the cit or county, the hand of the inspector may reach far afield. Thus the in spection of oysters by the health department of Chicago not long ag disclosed sources of infection which led to an embargo upon the sale oysters. To lift the embargo, city inspectors eventually went to the eas

[1] From Pennsylvania the following: ". . . physically it is impossible for the St Department of Health with 28 men to supervise adequately 80,000 farms, 7,000 de ers, 5,000 raw milk producers, and about 3,000 to 3,500 ice cream manufacturer See *Annual Report*, 1936, of the International Association of Milk Sanitarians, 166. It is not unusual for the state to delegate part of its inspectional duties to surance company inspectors; for example, the *New York State Industrial Code I lating to Factories*, 1919, pp. 94-95. In 1930 insurance companies made 21,784 bo inspections in Wisconsin while the state made 1,831 (A. J. Altmeyer, *The Ind trial Commission of Wisconsin* [1932], pp. 149, 160). Pennsylvania depends up unofficial milk inspectors to a large degree. Kansas has delegated much of its f tory inspection to insurance companies, lacking an adequate official staff.

oast oyster beds, and after inspection certified beds from which oysters ould be sold in Chicago. Eventually the certification was taken over y the United States Public Health Service.

Milk inspection is regularly carried on throughout the milkshed hich supplies any city. Milk inspectors go from dairy to dairy, in-pecting cattle for tuberculosis and other infections, supervising the leanliness of barns and of milking utensils, checking pasteurization and ansportation and suggesting improvements in the interests of health-al conditions. Like inspection in other fields, coercion is a last resort; ersuasion, education, appeal to self-interest are more usual methods. "I ecided after much thought," writes an inspector, "that in order to be f real service to all concerned, I would have to add to my duties as an ispector, those of a salesman and an educator." [1]

The necessity for tact and for a nice adjustment of means to ends is xaggerated by the more personal character of rural relationships. Peo-le know each other; and it is not difficult to develop a country reaction gainst the city, which does not help the inspector. One of them, in ommenting on the value of voluntary rather than compulsory inspec-on, asked his fellow milk sanitarians, "Have you ever been responsible or the grading of milk supplies, or have you had to institute legal action gainst a violator of some provision of the milk ordinance, in a com-unity in which the mayor, or several councilmen, or the probate idge, or a member of the board of county commissioners owned a mily cow, and sold milk to neighbors? . . . It is obvious that Mayor nith will be reluctant to convict and fine Councilman Jones or Judge rown for violating the milk ordinance." [2]

The model milk ordinance recommended by the United States Public ealth Service includes two enforcement devices: revocation of a ermit to sell, and lowering of the grade of the milk, or degrading.[3] It more difficult to revoke a permit than to degrade the product, and or even serious violations degrading nearly always secures the desired sult without the trouble and expense of court cases." A seasoned milk

[1] R. J. Powell, "Practical Aspects of Dairy Farm Regulation," in International As-ciation of Milk Sanitarians, *Annual Report*, 1936, p. 278; see also American Mu-cipal Association, *Milk Control: Governmental Regulation of the Dairy Industry the United States* (1937).

[2] C. A. Abele, "Milk Control in Small Communities on a Mandatory versus a oluntary Basis," in International Association of Milk Sanitarians, *Annual Report*, 36, p. 384.

[3] This ordinance was drafted in 1923; see Public Health Bulletin 220, 1936. By 35 there had been about 600 adoptions by cities and other local jurisdictions. The blic Health Service publishes annually a list of cities reported by the state health partments which reach a level of 90 per cent enforcement. Only about 13 per nt of the 600 communities reached that level in 1935.

inspector testifies to this, saying: "Several years of enforcement wor indicate definitely to me that the permit revocation principle shoul and can be used satisfactorily only in *extreme* cases. In all routine in spection work the 'degrading' principle should most definitely b used." [1]

The control of milk subsequent to its delivery by the farmer to th wholesaler is less difficult. The number of wholesalers is limited, opera tions are on a fairly large scale at a few central points, the possible los of investment and business by a revocation of permit is too serious t make effort at evasion easy or profitable. The purpose of inspection a this point is principally to ensure cleanliness of premises, utensils an operations, and proper pasteurization.[2]

In taking leave of these two examples of inspection, factory and foo we may generalize the inspection process. Inspection involves: (1) standard, fixed by law or by administrative rule or order; (2) an obliga tion on the part of individuals to observe the standards, with prescribe penalties for nonobservance; (3) an obligation to submit to inspectio (4) the actual viewing of the premises to determine compliance or nor compliance; (5) an order to make such alterations as may be require to secure compliance; (6) usually an opportunity for an administrativ appeal; (7) an eventual opportunity for court review to determir whether the penalty for noncompliance should be exacted, which in volves all aspects of the legality of the inspection and order.

What are the conditions under which inspection is most effective Continuous inspection, as in the inspection of meat, produces the be record. Where periodic inspection is more suitable, or an econom necessity, adequate, usable records of previous inspections may give semblance of continuity. Ideally the frequency of inspection should b governed by the need, rather than by the number of inspectors, b budget limitations are rigid.

One of the principal conditions of successful inspection is the adequac of the standards which the inspectors use in making their judgment The vocational training of inspectors may provide standards which a

[1] J. R. Jennings in International Association of Dairy and Milk Inspectors, *Ann Report*, 1935, p. 21.

[2] A more complex and far-flung example of inspection may be studied in t work of the United States Food and Drug Administration. For a glimpse of t variety and interest of the scientific problems, see C. W. Crawford, "Techni Problems in Food and Drug Law Enforcement," 1 *Law and Contemporary Pro lems* 36-43 (1933–34). This whole issue is devoted to food and drug legislation a administration.

[3] On this topic see John B. Andrews, *Administrative Labor Legislation* (193 ch. 4. The Wisconsin procedure is described in Arthur J. Altmeyer, *The Industr Commission of Wisconsin* (1932).

lequate. Persons trained in public health or sanitary engineering, or as umbers or electricians, know what are and what are not good praces in their fields. Inspection in fields of the established vocations involves relatively little difficulty with administrative standards; where a ody of accepted practice is wanting, standards are more difficult to evelop.

An example of good practice for securing suitable administrative andards in regulatory inspection is found in the procedures of the Visconsin Industrial Commission. The statutes authorizing inspection e general in nature and permit the Commission to set up rules for lministering them. The Commission with the collaboration of interted parties draws up codes in which the standards are incorporated. he inspectors contribute information from their experience. Experts in e field may be called upon for advice. Advisory committees of reprentatives of employers and workers in the enterprises governed by the de have an opportunity to discuss the rules that are to affect them, d to question their necessity or adequacy. As a result, the codes emdy the best practices tempered by practical necessities.

Analysis of the history and character of the inspectional method of w enforcement gives some basis for suggesting the fields of law enrcement for which the method is most appropriate. Inspection is an propriate means of enforcing laws when individuals directly conrned are not in a position to have recourse to the ordinary methods of w enforcement. Thus, employed persons cannot generally afford the k of making open complaint about illegal conditions of their labor. ne enforcement of laws requiring special knowledge of the matter gulated or specialized technical proficiency is facilitated by inspecon. Likewise, the inspectional method fits the type of law enforcement which it is necessary to give personal instruction of a technical charter as to the method of compliance with the law. Finally, inspection an appropriate means of enforcing those laws which touch hazards life and property too great for reliance upon private initiative or the ditional judicial methods of law enforcement.

The Inspector

The first glimpse of law enforcement through inspection demonstrates at the inspector is a technician. The meat inspector requires special owledge of animal diseases and their identification; the building inctor, a knowledge of building materials and of structural weaknesses; elevator inspector, a knowledge of machinery and skill in observing wear and tear; the factory inspector, a knowledge of hazards to peral safety from complex machines and equipment.

In addition, the inspector is a technician in the sense that he mu know intimately and accurately the law and the rules which he is t enforce, the judicial decisions which interpret the law, and the powe and the limits of power which he possesses. Furthermore, it is clear th for real success he must be a rare combination of a salesman, an edu cator, and an artist in human relations.[1]

It follows that inspection as a method of law enforcement is as goo or as mediocre as the inspector, given a reasonably satisfactory law. follows also that care and judgment should govern the selection of a inspector, his training, his supervision and direction. Unfortunately in spectors too often have been mere political creatures, uninformed the outset and quite likely to be ousted by the time they have learne their job.

Inspection by the federal government is on a relatively high level competence and integrity. Inspectors are selected by open competiti examination, enjoy the permanence of the civil service system, and a protected from political or other influence. Standards are illustrated the examination for poultry inspector announced by the United Stat Civil Service Commission in 1938. The duties of an assistant poultry i spector, at $2,600 a year, are, "under immediate supervision, to be e gaged in inspection or grading of live or dressed poultry for hum consumption." The educational requirements are successful completi of a full four-year course leading to the degree of Doctor of Veterina Medicine in a college of veterinary medicine of recognized standin with the possibility of substitution of additional experience for ea required year of education. The assistant inspector must have had, addition, at least two years of experience of a responsible nature, i volving inspection of animals in wholesale commercial plants operati under federal, state, or municipal supervision. Applicants must be sound physical health and have a high degree of physical stamina a endurance. These are the minimum requirements; the inspection servi secures those who pass highest on a competitive examination.

Among the states the methods of selecting inspectors vary widel In the states with civil service laws, relatively good standards are usual maintained. In other states the situation varies from good to indefensib In 1916 a survey conducted by the International Association of Dai and Milk Inspectors showed almost a complete absence of techni preparation for inspectional work in state and city offices. The edu tional standards of New Jersey (a civil service state) in 1925 requir a college agricultural course for dairy inspector, high school or equi

[1] Mary Anderson, "Personnel Equipment in Factory Inspection," 113 *Am* 321-28 (1924).

ent for food and drug inspector, common school for meat inspector. rom this level, standards run off to the case reported by the National ivil Service Reform League, "our food inspectors must be under sixty ears of age" and in another case "have common sense." [1]

Inspection forces have been favorite hunting grounds of patronage oliticians.[2] Gradually they are being given the protection of the merit ystem. The tragic results of stupid inspection are so irreparable that very inspector should be a permanent, tested, trained and impartial ublic servant. A fearful example of the hazards of unskillful inspection ccurred in 1934 in Chicago, when a water tower crashed through the oof of a factory, killing and injuring a number of workers. The build- g inspector who had examined the water tower was put on the stand the coroner's inquest. He admitted that he knew nothing about the uilding trades or the materials used. An excerpt from his testimony ollows.

Q. How long have you been a building inspector?
A. Nine months.
Q. What were you before that?
A. I was a malt salesman.
Q. When you were made a building inspector did you know anything about the ork?
A. No, I didn't know anything about it.
Q. When did you inspect the building and the tank?
A. It was in January.
Q. Did you find anything wrong with the tank?
A. No, it looked all right to me.
Q. Are you in a position to know whether it was all right or not?
A. No. I'm just the same as you or anybody else who might inspect it.
Q. Did you inspect the anchor plates?
A. Well, I looked at them.[3]

The attitude of the technical inspectors toward their personnel prob- n is ably stated by the director of the city health department of ouisville, Kentucky:

. . there is one factor abating progress that this Association should deal with finitely and firmly. I refer to the custom of paying political debts with public alth positions. The lack of confidence in the health department causes numerous ficulties in the adoption and enforcement of an ordinance. In many cases the

National Civil Service Reform League, *Study of Personnel in Food Inspection* im. 1925), pp. 15, 27.

A report from Pennsylvania stated, "We still have the situation in the state ere some dealers keep rushing to their local politicians to see if there is not some y by which they can circumvent a health regulation." International Association Milk Sanitarians, *Annual Report*, 1936, p. 165.

Chicago Tribune, June 2, 1934, p. 5.

> milk industry would welcome and support such a program as the public healt service milk ordinance were it not for the fear, and justly so, that the positions creates would be filled with incompetent "ward heelers." Legitimate industry h opposed milk control programs because it is unwilling to place its investment the mercy of politicians and the spoils system.[1]

A symbol of the direction in which the technical inspectional service are moving is found in the formation of associations of inspectional per sonnel. The Association of Dairy, Food and Drug Officials of the Unite States was established in 1897. It represents the official bodies concerne with inspection of foodstuffs. The International Association of Dair and Milk Inspectors was organized in 1911, and in 1936 adopted th name, International Association of Milk Sanitarians. The Association o Chiefs and Officials of Bureaus of Labor (1883) and the Internation Association of Factory Inspectors (1887) amalgamated in 1914 to forr the organization now known as the International Association of Gov ernmental Labor Officials. The meetings of these bodies are devoted t technical problems. Another sign of the times is the training course fc state factory inspectors instituted in 1936 at Johns Hopkins Universit under the auspices of the United States Department of Labor.

6. Summary Observations

Factory inspection celebrated its one hundredth birthday in Gre Britain in 1933; in the United States inspection of one type or anothe also reaches back over a century. Viewing the results in the large the remains no doubt that this form of securing compliance with the law of primary importance. Reliance upon the historic means of judici enforcement by persons whose rights have been infringed is to le upon a weak reed in controversies involving workers and employe under modern conditions of mass production. Social interests in mai taining standards of health, safety and convenience require preventi rather than punitive action on behalf of the state. This is provided b inspection and by the process of education and suggestion which go with inspection.

Resistance to inspection steadily diminishes but never disappears, new entrepreneurs enter the field and as competition grows tight among producers. The fixing and maintenance of certain standards b a force of inspectors establish a common foundation below which pr ducers cannot be driven by competition. The manufacturer sensitive standards of working decency thus finds protection against irresponsib competitors who cannot "chisel" so long as inspection is adequate.

[1] J. R. Jennings in International Association of Dairy and Milk Inspectors, *A nual Report*, 1935, p. 22.

The legal form in which inspection eventuates is an order of individual application requiring a specified individual or corporation to do, or to refrain from doing, a specific stated act.[1] The requirement ordered by an inspector may be relatively simple and inexpensive, or it may involve large expenditures. In the latter case, the economic effect upon the enterprise may be of first magnitude, threatening profits or even the existence of the undertaking.[2] Here arise the principal resistances to compliance, and many realistic adjustments are doubtless made between the ideal and the feasible. Here, too, come the most severe pressures from outside—political and otherwise.

Recognizing the gaps which may be discovered between complete success in ensuring compliance through inspection and actual results, we may nevertheless conclude that inspection provides one of the leading administrative means of law enforcement. The principal lines of advance are clearer and more precise standards, better trained and more adequately protected inspectors.

[1] See ch. 35 for further discussion of the various forms of legal action.

[2] The economic aspects of governmental intervention are not dealt with in this volume. See E. Pendleton Herring, *Public Administration and the Public Interest* (1936), *passim;* Carl L. Alsberg, "Some Economic Consequences of Commodity Control," 1 *Law and Contemporary Problems* 44-49 (1933-34).

Chapter Thirty-two

LICENSING

THE procedures of inspection which were described in the previous chapter may have much or little coercive power. The process of licensing involves formal and explicit power of compulsion through denial and through suspension or revocation, an authority sometimes vested with administrative officials, sometimes with the courts.

In simplest terms, a license is an official permit to carry on a particular business or profession, or to do a particular thing otherwise forbidden. In terms of Freund's definition, "licensing . . . is the administrative lifting of a legislative prohibition. The primary legislative thought in licensing is not prohibition but regulation, to be made effective by the formal general denial of a right which is then made individually available by an administrative act of approval, certification, consent or permit." [1] A license is not a grant of freedom, but an instrument of restraint.

In human terms we may conceive of licensing in such fashion as this. Citizens stand before their government, one saying, "I desire to sell alcoholic beverages," another, "I wish to treat the sick," another, "I want to design buildings," still another, "I intend to teach the young in the public schools." To each of them and to others the government says, "Your proposed life work is so important to your fellow citizens that they require you to demonstrate fitness and capacity before you may undertake it and to maintain such ability while you serve the people. If you can meet the established standards, you will be licensed to practice your calling or profession, but not otherwise."

This form of administrative action is accurately illustrated in federal legislation requiring registration (i.e., licensing) of aircraft and airmen. It is made unlawful to navigate any aircraft in interstate commerce unless such aircraft is registered, and to act as airman without an airman certificate; the Secretary of Commerce (now the Civil Aeronautics Authority) is authorized to register aircraft under specified conditions and to issue and revoke airman certificates.[2] Various penalties are provided for failure to observe these requirements.

[1] Ernst Freund, "Licensing," 9 *Encyclopaedia of the Social Sciences* 447-51 (1933); see also Freund's *Administrative Powers over Persons and Property* (1928), ch. 7.

[2] 44 Stat. 569 as amended.

Control through licensing involves an administrative advance judgment regarding the presence of legal requirements or the absence of legal objections. The broad end in view is to secure law observance "by eliminating at the outset the most obvious or serious sources of future trouble," thus avoiding slower remedial processes either administrative or judicial in nature. One of the most typical examples is the grant of a license to sell intoxicating liquor. The value of the licensing power from the point of view of effective law enforcement turns in part on the fact that it throws the burden of proof on the individual applicant, not on the official. To inspect, the official must take the initiative; to secure a license, the individual must take the first step by demonstrating affirmatively his right to favorable action. The precise degree of official power inherent in the granting of a license varies considerably from case to case, depending upon a number of elements in the licensing process. These are passed in quick review in the following paragraphs.[1]

The requirements prerequisite to the issue of a license may be perfunctory, as in the grant of a dog license or a hunting license, or they may be extremely formidable, as in the case of the professional examinations preceding the issuance of a license to practice medicine, law or engineering. The weight of administrative power varies principally with the amount of discretion which attends the grant or refusal. The law may specify in considerable detail the conditions under which a license shall be granted, leaving little to the discretion of the official. On the other hand and more commonly, such terms as reasonable, adequate, reputable, suitable or safe are used, which imply official judgments on values or future probabilities. Wide discretion is vested in such cases.

The weight of official power is also affected by the duration of the license. In some cases, such as the issuance of a building permit, official authority is exhausted in the original decision; in other cases, such as the issuance of a professional license, the grant runs for the lifetime of the holder, unless it is suspended or revoked for cause; in still other instances, the license must be renewed annually, as most trade licenses and automobile licenses. In the latter case, the administrative body makes a periodic review of the desirability of continuing or discontinuing the licensed privilege.

Another criterion of the importance of the licensing power as a means of administrative law enforcement is whether administrative discretion in granting or refusing a license may weigh community needs

[1] Hugo Wall, *A Study of the License Laws in Eighteen Selected States* (mim. 1929), Ph.D. thesis, Stanford Univ.; C. C. Ludwig, "Administration of Regulatory Licenses," 20 *Pub. Man.* 227-31 (1938).

and the adequacy of existing supply: in the last analysis, a subjective judgment of the licensing authority. These are legitimate considerations in some instances, but not in others. Apart from the liquor trade, for example, where the limitation of the number of saloons is usually an important consideration, notice may be taken of the "certificate of convenience and necessity," authorizing new public utility undertakings. Such a certificate always involves a judgment of community need. Some of the codes drawn under the National Industrial Recovery Act utilized an analogous authority in other than the public utility field.

The importance of the licensing power is also extended if the grant of the license may be burdened with conditions. Although the weight of judicial opinion indicates that conditions may not be attached without express legislative authority, the tendency is in the direction of granting such power. In the field of railroad legislation, for example, the power to impose conditions was a "conspicuous feature" of some of the most important licensing requirements of the Transportation Act of 1920. Here the conditional permit was authorized in connection with pooling, leases, consolidations, new construction, extension, abandonment, and the issue of securities.

Official authority in the field of licensing is also emphasized in cases in which a power of modification subsequent to the initial grant is vested. Such power is rather unusual, although apparently when discretion to grant the license exists, it is lawful to issue a license with such stipulations as may be accepted by the licensee.[1] To the extent that the power to alter a license may be reserved, or accepted by stipulation as a condition of grant, the latitude of official control is expanded. Finally, the degree of official influence is substantially affected by the power or lack of power to suspend or to revoke a license, a topic discussed below. To the extent that the administrative body has this right, it is in an extremely powerful position.

There are some fields of activity where no power to license exists. Exactly where the line is drawn between those activities which are constitutionally subject to the licensing power and those which are beyond is not established. Nevertheless there are certain limits, as evidenced by the decision of the Supreme Court denying state power to require a certificate of convenience and necessity in the business of manufacturing ice.[2]

We may conclude, therefore, that the power to license, where it exists, is normally one of great weight, but that its actual importance

[1] Ernst Freund, *Administrative Powers over Persons and Property* (1928), p. 117.
[2] *New State Ice Company vs. Liebmann,* 285 U. S. 262 (1932).

varies from one case to another according to the specific terms in which it is vested in administrative officials.

1. Growth and Extent of the Licensing Power

Administrative power to issue licenses is an ancient one. It was well established in the common law, and was well understood by the English colonists in America. The extent to which recourse is had to this, as well as to other forms of state action, depends upon public attitudes favoring laissez faire or intervention as the case may be. Thus Freund notes that toward the middle of the nineteenth century it was possible to discern a tendency hostile to the multiplication of license requirements. Early attempts to license medical practitioners broke down by the Civil War.[1] Early control over admission to the bar also was relaxed in many jurisdictions during the middle of the nineteenth century. In the absence of a general history of licensing, it is not feasible to venture beyond the general statement that while the principle of licensing reaches far back in Anglo-Saxon history and beyond, its effective use as an administrative device for law enforcement in the United States is very largely a development of the period subsequent to 1870.

Since the licensing power is usually associated with some phase of the police power, it follows that its native habitat is the state rather than the federal government. Federal licensing is principally associated with the power to regulate foreign and interstate commerce, and as such has been exercised since 1789. The licensing of ships and seamen was one of the early concerns of the first Congress.[2]

Federal licenses were rare, however, prior to 1900. An early example of the modern use of this procedure is found in the requirement of a license for the preparation of viruses and toxins for human use when moving in interstate commerce,[3] which in 1913 was extended to the preparation of animal viruses. Another early instance is the requirement of a license for the importation of nursery stock in 1912.[4]

The United States Warehouses Act of 1916 is described as "the first of the great licensing acts."[5] It was followed in rapid succession by others—power licensing under the Federal Water Power Act of 1920, the licensing of commission men by the Packers and Stockyards Act of 1921 and of grain exchanges by the Grain Futures Act of1922; radio licensing in 1927; potential (but not actual) licensing of business under

[1] Henry E. Sigerist, *American Medicine* (1934), pp. 135-37.
[2] 1 Stat. 55 (1789).
[3] 32 Stat. 728 (1902).
[4] 37 Stat. 315 (1912).
[5] Charles V. Koons, "Growth of Federal Licensing," 24 *Georgetown Law J.* 293-344 (1935-36).

the N.R.A. and the A.A.A. in 1933; and the licensing of the sale of securities in 1934. This enumeration of the principal federal licensing laws indicates how modern is the use of license as a means of federal control.

In the states the curtain rises earlier. Lacking any history of licensing on general lines, we may note its use in a few selected fields. Before we turn to these examples, however, an idea of the frequency and variety of licensing powers may be gained by noting the new licensing powers vested in the authorities of one state in one session of the legislature. In 1937, North Carolina placed power to license in the hands of the State Board of Alcoholic Control, the North Carolina Board for Licensing Tile Contractors, the Board of Examiners of Electrical Contractors, the Dry Cleaners Commission, the North Carolina Real Estate Licensing Commission, the Board of Health (for making mattresses and for operating sterilizers for old mattresses), and the county or city superintendents of public welfare (for child labor permits). This is a goodly crop for one year!

Professional licensing: medicine. Most professions are now subject to a state license system: medicine, law, engineering, architecture, accountancy, teaching in the public schools, and others. The purpose of the license in most cases is to protect the public against danger to safety or health incident to unqualified practitioners; in some instances, to guard against incompetence in fields having special public importance, as in teaching. The development of medical licensure, while not in all respects similar to other professional license systems, is illustrative.[1]

The issuance of medical licenses by state medical societies and by authorized medical schools, instituted as early as 1781 in Massachusetts and New Hampshire, eventually fell into disrepute. In 1873 Texas initiated the state board of medical examiners, a device permitting a combination of control by the state and by the medical profession. The plan spread throughout the states and has now become the standard method of issuing a medical license. The state board is usually appointed by the governor, sometimes with the consent of the senate; the members are exclusively or predominantly medical practitioners of one school or another. Legislation prohibits practice without a license; the state board holds periodic examinations to test the qualifications of applicants and on the basis of demonstrated fitness grants the professional license.

Over a long period of years the required standards of competence

[1] Cf. two unpublished theses, Univ. of Chicago: Fay E. Bates, "The Development of State Control of Medical Practice in Massachusetts" (1933); Helen E. Cobb, "Development of State Control of the Right to Practice Medicine in California" (1935).

have been raised. The examination now consists of, first, a difficult, comprehensive written examination which may be taken upon graduation from medical school; second, in most jurisdictions, a practical oral test, given in the hospital at the close of the interneship. In practice there is considerable variation from state to state in the severity of the test, and some states offend by allowing failures to make repeated efforts to pass.

Commencing with Connecticut and Wisconsin in 1925, nine states and the District of Columbia have also imposed additional examinations in the basic sciences, usually including anatomy, physiology, chemistry, bacteriology and pathology. These additional requirements for a medical license are designed to exclude poorly prepared practitioners who specialize in some particular form of healing.

The National Board of Medical Examiners is an unofficial body organized in 1915 for the purpose of conducting medical examinations which would admit to practice in any state. The prestige of this Board and the excellence of its examinations are such that all but seven states (in 1938) accepted its credentials. There are also reciprocity arrangements between the state medical examining boards which remain the official agencies for the grant of medical licenses.[1]

In taking leave of the subject of professional licensing with this brief example, we may note that licensing is sometimes sought as a privilege tending to establish professional status, rather than endured as an official restriction or interference. The social workers, for example, have inaugurated an unofficial system of certification in California which may be destined, if the social workers prevail, to become an official system of certification or license designed to establish standards of competence and to exclude the incompetent. The nurses have already preceded the social workers in this undertaking.

In some instances, licensing is also apparently sought in part as a means of establishing a trade or occupational monopoly. In such cases, the licensing board will be found in the hands of the organized trade or labor group. Licenses are required, for example, in Connecticut (and other states) for "hairdressers." They are granted by a board of three appointed by the governor from a list nominated by the Connecticut Hairdressers' Association. Two must be experienced hairdressers, one a cosmetician. Registration is annual, and licenses are granted on condition that the place of business "is, with respect to its location and ap-

[1] Analogous arrangements exist for other professions, of which law and engineering provide two of the leading examples. Studies of the administration of licensing and its growth in special fields are needed.

pointments, suitable and sanitary, and will be conducted in compliance with the law and with the rules and regulations of said board. . . ."[1] There is inadequate evidence to suggest how widely licensing becomes a means of controlling access to a trade or occupation.

Health, safety and morals. Licensing, as well as inspection and the issuance of orders of individual application (see next chapter), plays an important part in the protection of public health, safety and morals. An example may be taken from the regulation and control of the liquor traffic.

The hazards arising from the excessive use of alcoholic liquor have induced a great variety of official restraints in most parts of the world. Two principal methods have been employed in the United States: prohibition, both state and national, and local option with license. The latter is the only one which requires notice here, although passing reference may be made to the significant fact that a third method, state monopoly of distribution and sale, is now being tried in the United States.[2]

Over a large area of the United States for a long period of time, licensing has been the principal means of administrative action to control the liquor trade. Before the prohibition amendment, every state except Kansas and North Dakota had tried the licensing system at one time or another. Usually the licensing authorities were municipal officials or local judges. Among the restrictions of the licensing system were a limitation on the number of saloons, prohibition of saloons near schools, posting of a heavy bond conditioned upon the observance of the law, closing on certain days and hours, and prohibiting sales to minors or to intoxicated persons. The fee for the license varied widely and was fixed in part in the light of potential revenue; the amount of surveillance also varied widely. Failure of the licensing system to reduce the number of saloons and the consumption of alcohol eventually led to the experiment of national prohibition. The difficulties encountered in this change of policy again turned the tide toward either a licensing system or state monopoly.

The large number of liquor licenses now issued is indicated in the following table.[3] While it is impossible to construct a table showing the

[1] General Statutes of Connecticut, 1930, sec. 2896. See also "Recent Regulation of Useful Occupations by License Requirements," 26 *Columbia Law Rev.* 472-76 (1926).

[2] George E. B. Catlin, *Liquor Control* (1931); Leonard V. Harrison and Elizabeth Laine, *After Repeal: a Study of Liquor Control Administration* (1936); Frederick A. Johnson and R. R. Kessler, "The Liquor License System—its Origin and Constitutional Development," 15 *New York Univ. Law Q. Rev.* 210-51, 380-424 (1937–38).

[3] From Harrison and Laine, *op. cit.*, p. 58.

total number of licenses issued for all purposes by all governments, these figures suggest how important this method of administrative action is.

Licenses in the regulation of business. The enormous field of business regulation through licensing can only be suggested by two recent examples, broadcasting and the sale of securities. Early regulations over export trade imposed by the state involved both inspection and license, but with the decline of American mercantilism these licenses largely disappeared. Modern control of business through license is principally a development of the post Civil War period, and, aside from the regulations designed to protect safety, health and morals, is in part a reflection of the anti-monopoly, anti-business drives of the last half century.

TABLE XIII

NUMBER OF LIQUOR LICENSES ISSUED IN CERTAIN STATES IN 1935, AND NUMBER OF EMPLOYEES IN STATE LICENSING AGENCY

STATE	NUMBER OF LICENSES	NUMBER OF STATE EMPLOYEES IN LICENSING AGENCY
Arizona	2,532	15
Arkansas	3,371	6
California	73,189	475
Connecticut	6,280	53
Delaware	457	29
Maryland	108[a]	14
Massachusetts	6,609	42
Nevada	100[a]	2
New Jersey	20,231	256
New Mexico	857	6
New York	59,296	229
North Dakota	1,959	30
Rhode Island	2,309	40
South Carolina	3,858	8
Wisconsin	3,676[a]	93

[a] Exclusive of retail licenses.

A crisis in broadcasting had emerged by 1927 due to the "mad scramble" to take possession of the ether. Congress, faced with a rapidly developing and novel technical problem, decided to seek its solution by administrative action. Broadcasting was forthwith prohibited except under a license granted by the Radio Commission. The Commission received little guidance from "the Hill"; it was directed to grant a license to any applicant "if public convenience, interest or necessity will be served thereby." It was also directed to make such a distribution of licenses and power among the different states and communities as to give "fair, efficient and equitable radio service to each of the same." [1] Broadcasting policy and the regulation of radio were, in fact, laid in the lap of the Radio Commission to be developed through the administrative means of licensing broadcasting stations.[2]

The pressure of conflicting interests in the broadcasting field, aided and abetted by some members of Congress, filled the years of the Radio Commission with controversy. It is clear from this experience that success in the granting of licenses under such circumstances requires as definite a statement of legislative policy as may be possible.

Another recent application of licensing in the business world is found in the Securities Act of 1933.[3] The essential phase of law enforcement underlying this legislation is the prohibition of interstate movement of securities for sale, and the denial of all interstate facilities of transportation or communication for the purpose of selling securities for which no registration statement is in effect. The granting of a registration statement by the Securities and Exchange Commission, subject to extensive conditions and qualifications, is a license reopening interstate channels for the sale of registered securities.

The control of the sale of securities was pushed forward another step in 1934 by extending the licensing power to exchanges on which sales of securities take place. The requirement of a license is made to support broad inquisitorial powers. In case of failure to list securities, the Securities and Exchange Commission may suspend trading privileges for any or all classes of traders.[4]

These examples must suffice to illustrate a very wide range of licensing powers. Since 1900 the federal government has made wide use of this power in agricultural marketing and other aspects of interstate commerce. The states have taken principal responsibility for licensing the professions. Cities have developed licensing in a wide variety of businesses and occupations, partly for revenue purposes; a recent survey identified no fewer than 131 city business and occupation licenses.[5] The range of licenses in a great metropolis is suggested in this excerpt: [6]

When you walk into a theatre, when you buy a newspaper, when you have your laundry washed, when you have a key made, when you play billiards, or visit an employment agency, when you buy ice, when you use a public porter, when you

[1] 44 Stat. 1162 (1927).

[2] See E. Pendleton Herring, *Public Administration and the Public Interest* (1936), ch. 10.

[3] 48 Stat. 74 (1933).

[4] 48 Stat. 881 (1934).

[5] American Municipal Association, *License Taxes as a Source of Municipal Revenue* (mim. 1933), p. 10.

[6] Rebecca B. Rankin, ed., *New York Advancing, 1934–1935* (1936), p. 265.

have a massage, when you do business with a second hand dealer, when you have your furniture moved or your piano hoisted, when you dive into a swimming pool or visit Coney Island or check your hat, when you go to the movie or play a "pin game" machine,–the *License Department* stands vigilantly by to see that you get fair play and fair treatment.

2. Operations in the Grant or Refusal of a License

Recalling that a license is the lifting of a legislative prohibition by administrative action under conditions specifically or broadly stated in the statute, we may now turn to observe the usual operations involved in this method of official action.

Since one of the requirements of administrative work is that it must be consistent and not capricious, a licensing agency is at once faced with the necessity of finding and stating the standards on which its discretionary action will be based. The degree of freedom allowed officials at this point will vary with the text of the legislation. Specific, objective criteria may be found in the law; the standard is then a legislative, not an administrative one. Or the legislation may merely require that a license shall issue if public convenience will be served. Here wide discretion as to standards and bases of decision is left to administrative officials.

Common standards are (1) skills and knowledge established by formal written examinations, as in the professional licenses; (2) character and moral or financial reliability, as in pawnshop licenses; (3) consent and approval of locality, as in liquor licenses; (4) public safety, as in licenses to operate a barber shop or a stationary engine; (5) public convenience and advantage, as in the certificate of public convenience and necessity required for utility extensions.

Administrative operations involved in the actual issue of the license are three: receiving applications; conducting hearings, examinations or investigations; and granting or denying the license. The application may be merely an oral one; more usually it involves at least a written form. The application for a license in cases involving large property interests, as in broadcasting, utility extensions, security registration, and power development, is usually a formidable presentation of legal, economic, and financial data, requiring expert analysis on the part of the official agency. Where adverse private interests are involved in the grant of a license, notice to all parties is common, but, in general, notice and hearing are not prerequisites to the grant. They are more commonly required for denial, and most frequently in case of revocation.

The licensing authority must inform itself whether the requested license should be granted or denied. To this end all sorts of means are available. Apart from formal examination, investigation by field examiners is a common method. Thus the inspection staff of a state liquor commission may investigate persons desiring a liquor license. Practical tests are usual in granting motor drivers' licenses, and doubtless constitute one of the greatest mass testing procedures in the history of man.

The conclusion of the investigation is either the grant or refusal of the license. In rare cases some substitute or equivalent privilege may be offered, as in radio facilities. In many cases, the granting of licenses creates collateral administrative duties. There is the ever present task of discovering and prosecuting persons operating illegally without a license, a duty divided between the city and state police and specialized inspectional forces. Then, too, licensees frequently enjoy their status subject to conditions, the observance of which must be checked and enforced. A substantial degree of surveillance thus often accompanies licensing.

The significance of these collateral tasks is greatest in licenses involving public safety and morals, especially the sale of liquor. "The key to successful liquor control," write Harrison and Laine, "is the investiture of adequate discretionary powers in the regulatory body. The exercise of wide discretion can be wisely entrusted only to an administrative personnel of the highest quality. If mediocre administrators are brought to the exacting task of liquor control, they will of course fall down, regardless of whether or not they are given an ample range of discretion; but even able administrators will fail to achieve significant results without it. . . . If liquor-control administration is to work positively toward a progressive elevation of standards, and not negatively, merely guarding against infraction of the laws and regulations, full discretion to grant and revoke licenses and to promulgate rules must not only be given in the first place, but must also be preserved against attrition of any kind." [1]

The revocation of a license, the principal sanction attached to licenses, is discussed below in chapter thirty-five. At this point we may note that there is no general power to revoke implied in the power to grant a license, and that in fact revocation is often vested in the courts, especially where important interests are in jeopardy. As a means of law enforcement, the revocation of a license by administrative action is swift and effective: "a revocation is worth fifty routine inspections."

Conclusion. No better conclusion to the subject matter of licenses can be stated than that of one of the most profound students of administrative methods, Ernst Freund.[2] "Where safety, health and morals are involved, where private activities trench upon the conservation of public

[1] Harrison and Laine, *op. cit.*, p. 9.

[2] 9 *Encyclopaedia of the Social Sciences* 451 (1933).

resources or where nationalistic interests are to be safeguarded, the license always suggests itself as a ready means of making regulation more effective, if only as a temporary measure pending the discovery of substantial principles of regulation.

"As compared with the nineteenth century the present is an era of intensive governmental regulation. Even without a disposition to enhance official powers, perhaps notwithstanding a strong feeling against bureaucratic government, there are many fields in which administrative intervention and even administrative discretion are indispensable. The choice in these fields lies between administrative orders and administrative licenses. The former probably represent a more conservative exercise of public power; but with the burden of initiative thrown upon the government, the check is likely to be sporadic and confined to exceptional cases. A licensing system is the path of least resistance; it lends itself equally to wide discretion and to nondiscretion, and private interests are usually able to accommodate themselves to it without undue difficulty. It is so convenient a method of checking the observance of governmental regulations that its permanence in the economy of legislation and administration appears to be assured; but the elaboration of administrative detail with a view to the most effective reconciliation of public and private interest will necessarily be a matter of prolonged experimentation."

Chapter Thirty-three

ADMINISTRATIVE ORDERS AND RULES

AS THE difficulty and urgency of administrative tasks are intensified, the need for more powerful means of reaching the ends of public policy increases. The attainment of some objectives may be left to persuasion or to the beneficial effects of mere publicity; others require the constraining effects of inspection; still others are sought by licensing and the imposition of various conditions as prerequisites to the license. In this chapter we pass on to consider the authority of administrative officials or boards to issue orders of individual application and general rules having the force of law.

1. Orders of Individual Application

". . . the normal function of an administrative order," wrote Ernst Freund, "is to make a generic statutory prohibition or requirement definite. The directing power is given because the legislator finds himself incapable of foreseeing the precise duty of the individual . . ."[1] Usually there is no occasion for orders of individual application when the statute imposes a specific, unconditional obligation upon an individual, unless the order be merely a warning or notice of prosecution for noncompliance. In more and more cases, however, the statutes do not foresee the precise duty of the individual. Discretion is vested with officials to state in detail what the legislature meant in its enactments. Exact duties and obligations are contained in the orders of individual application.

The administrative order may be contrasted with other devices for law enforcement. In his analysis of administrative acts, Ernst Freund distinguished among others the enabling power, such as license and permit, and the directing power, the authority to issue orders of individual application. The former permits administrative influence to play a part at the moment when an individual must have official consent to proceed and, by revocation or threatened revocation, to exert some degree of continuous influence over the conduct of the licensee. The latter requires no initial authority to be obtained by private persons, but

[1] Ernst Freund, *Administrative Powers over Persons and Property* (1928), p. 148.

reserves the general right to intervene at any time to correct acts contrary to law or rule by specific requirements having only individual application.

Both licenses and permits on the one hand and directing orders on the other normally affect only individual persons or cases; they vary, however, in their nature, the one being intrinsically in the nature of an authorization, the other in the nature of a corrective intervention.

a. Development. In American law there is no general inherent administrative power to issue orders to individuals. Such a power belongs only to courts of equity, and also to common law courts for the purpose of compelling the attendance of witnesses and the giving of evidence.[1] Specific power in this field has been vested in administrative officials by legislation over a period of many years. In the early days of our administrative history, the making of orders of individual application by federal authorities was highly exceptional. Apart from the assessment of imports, Freund notes early grants of this authority only in the repair of vessels (1852), in safeguards against fire at sea (1871), and in the exclusion of aliens. In the states, the power was associated with early health legislation and with assessments for taxation, but here too it was exceptional.

It was the Interstate Commerce Act which opened the door to the modern use of the directing power. This legislation introduced the "cease and desist" technique. It authorized the Commission in case of a violation of law not only to notify the carrier, but also to serve "a notice to cease and desist from such violation." [2] The Hepburn Act of 1906 extended Commission authority over rates by vesting power to "determine and prescribe what will be the just and reasonable rate." Official action consequently could take the form of an order to *a* carrier with respect to *the* rate for *a* given class of commodities.

The directing power has since become the chief instrumentality of federal economic legislation. It was written into the Federal Trade Commission Act, the Shipping Act, the Packers' Act, and such "New Deal" legislation as the Securities Act, the Communications Act, and the Labor Relations Act. It has also been adopted by the public utility laws of most American states.[3]

The course of development of the power to issue orders of individual application in the states is suggested by the experience of New York. Apart from certain desultory instances affecting New York City, a general directing power was not vested in any official until 1867. Boards

[1] *Ibid.*, p. 140.
[2] 24 Stat. 379 (1887), sec. 15.
[3] Freund, *op. cit.*, pp. 145-46.

of health were then granted an extraordinary range of authority to issue orders, in these terms: "to make, without publication thereof, such orders and regulations in special and individual cases—not of general application—as they may see fit, concerning the suppression and removal of nuisances and concerning all other matters in their judgment detrimental to the public health. . . ." [1] Other grants of the directing power have been made in the labor law, the banking law, the insurance law, tenement house legislation, and similar enactments.

Apart from such relatively formal instances of the authority to issue orders of specific application, there are countless examples of the making of orders in the ordinary course of day-by-day operations of many departments. Quarantine orders imposed by health departments, notices left by restaurant inspectors, police orders controlling traffic, directions given to workmen picketing an industrial plant, such official orders flow in an endless stream. They have relatively little legal significance, since ordinarily they establish no new general rights or obligations, nor are they intended to clarify uncertain or vague rights or obligations. They are partly "beneficial," i.e., a warning against eventual penalties for noncompliance, partly merely a public convenience. They have, however, great practical importance.

b. Procedures. The procedures surrounding the device of administrative orders vary from the most elementary, summary forms to the most complex and highly developed. Matters of urgency involving public health and safety may frequently be treated by summary administrative action. On the other hand, matters involving valuable interests or conflicts between private persons or groups tend to be dealt with through formal, complex procedures designed to protect all the interests involved.

So informal as to be almost without procedure are the directions given by a traffic patrolman in regulating the movements of motor cars and pedestrians at a busy corner. Other police directions such as orders to stop, to remove obstructions from a sidewalk, or to submit to arrest may be summary.

Slightly more developed in procedure are the actions of inspectors. Orders resulting from inspection are generally based on findings of a systematic, periodical viewing of matters under surveillance. Evidence of more developed procedure is found in the customary practice of making and preserving a detailed record of inspectors' findings. In some cases, inspectors may not issue orders upon their own findings but must

[1] New York Laws, 1867, c. 790.

submit them to a superior who decides whether and in what form the order should issue.[1]

In contrast to orders issued upon such routine procedures are those issued after special investigation. Examples may be found in the procedures of the Securities and Exchange Commission and the Federal Trade Commission. These agencies, upon complaint or other information, undertake investigations of suspected violations of the laws they enforce. In the first phase these investigations are informal, investigators interviewing complainants, the accused, and others affected by the suspected wrong action. If such informal investigation confirms the agency's belief that there is a violation, an order for a formal investigation may be issued. This order empowers officials to require persons to appear and give testimony and to produce books, papers and any other material relevant to the inquiry.

The most highly developed procedures accompanying the issuance of administrative orders are to be found in agencies which adjudicate disputes.[2] The order in these cases is generally the last step in a long line of actions including complaint, investigation, negotiations to settle dispute, formal charge, hearing before an examiner, examiner's intermediate report of findings and a recommendation, review of the case by the adjudicating agency and the making of the final administrative decision. Such a procedure allows for persuasive as well as coercive techniques, adapts itself to the easy as well as the difficult cases, and provides methods for the conserving of all interests.

c. Types of orders. Orders of individual application may be directed to the remedying of conditions in any of the multitudinous subject matters of public administration. So far as their effect is concerned, they fall into a number of fairly well-defined classes. Thus one simple class is the *order of convenience* in which, for example, highway patrolmen impose one-way traffic over a stretch of new construction.

Another form is the order to produce books, papers and records and to give testimony, i.e., *ancillary orders* supporting other forms of administrative action. Though administrative agencies often have this authority, they do not possess the power to punish for contempt in case of refusal but must rely upon subsequent orders of a court.

In a third group there is the *corrective order* intended to control directly the action of individuals or groups. Thus a property owner may be directed to replace a fire escape; a common carrier may be told what rate to impose; a broadcasting station may be assigned a specific wave length. In this class also are to be found the administrative

[1] See ch. 31.
[2] See ch. 34.

orders revoking professional, vocational and business licenses; revocation of automobile licenses; orders which remove incompetent physicians from medical practice, and defective types of aircraft from air commerce, and which close improperly operated taverns.[1]

An example drawn from the practice of the Securities and Exchange Commission illustrates the use of this kind of admistrative order in a new field of economic regulation.

> In the matter of the Gold Hill Operating Company
> Stop Order
>
> . . . the Commission . . . finding that said registration statement contains untrue statements of material facts. . . .
>
> It is ordered . . . that the effectiveness of the registration statement filed by Gold Hill Operating Company, Tacoma, Washington, be and the same hereby is suspended.[2]

The class of corrective orders of individual application is most widely illustrated by those which attempt to correct a wrong by stating an individual's specific legal obligation in a particular situation. Such an order may be either a statement of his exact duty under the law, or it may be a statement of prohibition, notifying the individual that his actions are in violation of law. Orders of this kind flow from the whole law enforcement system: the police, inspectors of all kinds, bureaus, boards and commissions.

These orders are often made by inspectional agencies. The restaurant inspector may order chewing gum removed from the underside of counters, chairs and tables, or forbid the open display of pastries. The building and fire inspectors may order the removal or repair of signs or awnings, the repair of doors or the installation of fire extinguishers. The bank examiner may order the calling of loans from persons who have moved to another location. The factory inspector may order the guarding of a particular machine or forbid the use of certain chemicals. In short, many persons learn their specific obligations under the law and administrative rules are given explicit form in the directions given by inspectors.

Other corrective orders stating specific obligation arise from formal administrative adjudications, a subject treated in the next chapter. Thus compensation cases, if the claim is found just, end in an order to pay the injured person a specified amount. Orders of duty state specifically what the individual must do to avoid violation of law, whereas orders of prohibition, styled "stop orders" or "cease and desist" orders, define particular acts whose continuance would involve prosecution.

[1] See ch. 35, section on revocation of licenses.

[2] 1 *Federal Register*, 1376 (1936).

The orders of the Federal Trade Commission to cease and desist are perhaps the best known examples of this administrative device. A not untypical and somewhat amusing instance is given in abbreviated form.

> In the matter of the Lur-Eye Products, Inc. . . .
>
> It is further ordered that the respondents . . . cease and desist from
>
> 1. Advertising . . . that said cosmetic preparation (a) will grow, increase the length of, or change the texture of eyelashes; (b) that it is a competent treatment for . . . granulated eyelids; that it will penetrate to or reach the follicles . . . of eyelashes, . . . or that said preparation will relieve eyestrain.[1]

During the fiscal year 1937, the Federal Trade Commission issued 294 cease and desist orders, dealing with such varied violations of the law as false advertising, suppressing competition, misrepresenting the value of medicinal preparations, false allegations by correspondence schools claiming some connection with the United States Civil Service Commission, and false disparagement of products sold by competitors.

The administrative orders so far considered have all had the characteristic of being particularized directions for compliance with public policy. A partial exception to this characteristic is found in administrative orders which exempt an individual from the force of a general law or rule. *Orders of exemption*, authorized in law by a specific grant of administrative discretion, have the purpose of giving relief in exceptional cases in which the general rule is onerous.

The operation of orders of exemption can be seen in the administration of city zoning ordinances.[2] If an individual wishes to build a type of building at a location where such buildings are prohibited by the zoning ordinance, he may generally present a request for a "variance permit" to a board of appeals. By holding hearings, and in some cases viewing the proposed building site, the board determines whether the general rule for buildings in that area imposes practical difficulties or unnecessary hardships upon the applicant in such a degree that an exception should be made in his case. The situations in which variances are granted differ widely and the variance orders are not always clearly defensible. A typical case is the lot which is on a steep hillside, so that adherence to a set-back would make it impossible to build a house. Likewise, along the borders between building zones, practical difficulties and the shifting of trends in the use of land frequently bring this form of administrative discretion into use.

Orders of exemption from the strict rule of a law are not always grants of complete freedom from obligation, for the agency making the

[1] 1 *Federal Register* 117 (1936).

[2] Edward M. Bassett, *Zoning: The Laws, Administration, and Court Decisions During the First Twenty Years* (1936), pp. 117-69, esp. 120-31.

grant may be authorized to impose conditions upon the applicant.[1] Thus, continuing with the zoning illustration, the board of appeals may, when granting a variance, specify the style and materials of construction and the uses to which the proposed building may be put. Through imposition of such conditions in granting exemptions the administrative agency may not only provide relief in difficult cases but may protect others from suffering from such action.

d. General observations. From the foregoing analysis of types of orders of individual application—orders of convenience, ancillary orders, corrective orders and orders of exemption—it will be clear that the occasion for their issuance may and does occur in the flow of administrative operations which also involve other forms of administrative action. The order of individual application may be associated with inquisition, inspection or adjudication and may lead to the making of administrative rules. The web of administrative operations is complex, but within it the order finds its place as a characteristic form of official action.

Each order of individual application is effective only against the person or corporation named in the order. While this specific application is one of the limitations of the directing procedure, the actual effect of some orders may be in fact much more extensive. An order may set a precedent; it may be widely discussed in trade journals and a series of specific orders may substantially terminate undesirable forms of private activity. In due course of time, the trial-and-error method of dealing with the individual case may lead to the promulgation of a general rule, and eventually to legislation.

An order embodying a precedent is illustrated by a fragment of a decision taken from the records of the National Labor Relations Board.

In the matter of R.C.A. Manufacturing Company, Inc. and the United Electrical & Radio Workers of America

> . . . Following these cases [cases interpreting the word "majority"] the phrase, "majority of the employees," in the Act must be interpreted as meaning a majority of the employees who participated in the election, so that the organization receiving a majority of the votes cast is entitled to certification. Such an interpretation is both consistent with the broad declarations of the Act in favor of the procedure of collective bargaining, since it facilitates the choice of representatives to carry on that bargaining, and is in accord with the general concepts and court decisions concerning elections.[2]

The Board proceeded to certify the union as the representative of the employees, thus ordering the employer to recognize the union as the collective bargaining agent for all the employees in the defined unit.

[1] *Ibid.*, pp. 128-31.

[2] National Labor Relations Board, *Decisions and Orders*, vol. 2, 1936-37, pp. 159, 177-78.

Orders of individual application as a method of administration offer several advantages. The device is useful where the field of regulation is experimental and the matter regulated is complex. In such situations these orders allow an administrative finding of the precise standards by intensive study of particular cases and by trial and error. As has been noted above, such finding of standards over a period of years may result in establishing rules which complete the elaboration of the statute. In cases in which statutes do not authorize the administrative elaboration of general legislative standards into a body of specific rules, the device of the order of individual application is the only available coercive method short of prosecution.

The order of individual application also gives persons concerned specific notice of their legal obligations in the manner of a declaratory judgment. Thus, an individual receiving an order has an official interpretation of his obligations, generally without suffering penalty.

In view of the fact that the discretion of the directing or ordering power is to a considerable extent amenable to the control of the courts, Freund concludes that it may be the most desirable form of administra-ive discretion. It would thus become "the appropriate instrument of egislative policies that attempt to establish control by the trial-and-error nethod of corrective administrative intervention." [1]

2. The Rule-Making Power

By means of the power to issue orders of individual application, administrative agencies are able to specify corrective action in particular cases; these orders eventually may work into a pattern of conduct which becomes recognized and accepted as a general rule, although such ules may arise in other circumstances. By means of the power to issue ules and regulations, the administration is able to prescribe required conduct in a general fashion for all persons rather than through the ndividual instance. The authority to make rules having the force of aw is therefore one of the important administrative means of law nforcement.[2]

[1] Freund, *op. cit.*, p. 174.

[2] The principal general references on this topic are: Cecil T. Carr, *Delegated egislation* (1921); James Hart, *The Ordinance Making Powers of the President f the United States* (1925); John P. Comer, *Legislative Functions of National Administrative Authorities* (1927); Frederick F. Blachly and Miriam E. Oatman, *dministrative Legislation and Adjudication* (1934); John B. Andrews, *Adminis-ative Labor Legislation* (1936); James Hart, "The Exercise of Rule-Making ower," in President's Committee on Administrative Management, *Report with pecial Studies* (1937), pp. 310-55; Great Britain, Committee on Minister's Powers, *eport* (Cmd. 4060, 1932); Edwin E. Witte, "The Preparation of Proposed Legis-tive Measures by Administrative Departments," in President's Committee on Administrative Management, *op. cit.*, pp. 357-78 (1937).

A satisfactory formal definition of this power is that of James Hart: "The rule-making power may be defined as the legal authority of administrative officers or agencies of government to prescribe discretionary or interpretative rules and regulations of general applicability and legal effect, or to determine the existence of conditions under which contingent statutes are to become operative."[1] Such rules may be made by the chief executive, by heads of departments, by boards and commissions, by administrative tribunals, and by government corporations such as the Tennessee Valley Authority. With no known exception the power is vested only in determinative authorities, that is, those which by law have final administrative disposition of certain types of cases it is not vested in subordinate personnel.

Standard terminology has not yet been developed in this field. No accepted distinction is made between rules and regulations, although the latter term is sometimes used as subordinate to the former. Rules are also called administrative legislation, or sublegislation. Different types of rules are not distinguished by class names.[2] For the purpose of this book, the term rule will be understood to mean a prescription of genera import made by an administrative authority and affecting the rights and privileges of citizens; the term regulation will be understood to mean merely directions for office management, for internal operations or for public convenience in dealing with public offices. The latter wil be excluded from further consideration.[3] It is principally the forme which are concerned with law enforcement.

a. Development of rule-making power. Contrary to the history of th power to issue orders of individual application, the authority to issu rules reaches back to the beginning of our constitutional and adminis trative system. In the early days of an agricultural economy, howeve the use of the rule-making power was infrequent, and did not touc the daily interests of the individual citizen. Administrative legislatio on its present scale is the product of an urban, industrial civilization.

During the first decade of the federal government, there were onl nineteen instances of delegated rule-making power.[4] With apparentl only a few exceptions, administrative legislation was limited until 189 to cases involving revenue, the armed forces, Indians, and government privileges or bounties such as pensions, land grants, mail, supplies, an claims. Two examples, however, foreshadow the use of administrativ

[1] James Hart, "The Exercise of Rule-Making Power," *op. cit.*, p. 319.

[2] *Ibid.*, pp. 320-21.

[3] See ch. 6 for notice of internal regulations.

[4] Comer, *op. cit.*, p. 50.

rules to prescribe and direct the conduct of individuals in their daily occupations: the vesting of power to make rules to prevent disease in animals, and to prevent deception in the sale of oleomargarine.

Since 1890 the authority to issue rules has grown by leaps and bounds, especially during the World War period and the emergency legislation following 1933.[1] The most recent compilation indicates that the authority was vested in 1936 in 115 federal agencies, on the basis of 964 statutory provisions and 71 executive orders and proclamations.[2] This count does not include the multitudinous code authorities under the National Recovery Administration which fell with the Schechter decision, and whose rule making rose to an unparalleled volume.

There are no statistics to indicate the volume of sublegislative enactments which flows from these authorizations, but it is very great. Blachly and Oatman state that the published rules and regulations cover altogether about eight or ten times as many pages as the acts passed by Congress. During the N.R.A., thousands of rules, amendments and exceptions were hatched by the Blue Eagle.

Not only has the rule-making power thus become "a normal method of government" in Washington; it also has become well established in the states. Here it was early associated with health departments, as for example in quarantine; later it developed in the administration of labor laws, in the regulation of utilities, in the supervision of the professions, and in many phases of urban life.

For purposes of illustration, the growth of administrative legislation in the field of labor will serve.[3] By the end of the last century industry had created a need for a quantity, flexibility and type of labor legislation which legislative bodies could not produce. They not only lacked technical understanding of the problems and time for deliberation; their procedure, their very numbers, and the prevalence of political considerations joined to make effective legislation unlikely. To meet the need, various departments and boards began to receive authority to "fill in the details," or more broadly to develop and promulgate administrative codes.

The break away from detailed labor legislation with relatively little sublegislative delegation to general legislation with broad delegation came in Wisconsin in 1911 with the enactment of the Industrial Commission Act. Massachusetts, among other states, had already begun to move in the same direction; following two serious boiler explosions,

[1] Hart, "The Exercise of Rule-Making Power," *op. cit.*, pp. 310-55.
[2] *Ibid.*, p. 313; see also Blachly and Oatman, *op. cit.*, p. 10.
[3] See specially John B. Andrews, *Administrative Labor Legislation* (1936).

delegated rule power had been given to the State Board of Boiler Rules in 1907, and in 1910 the State Board of Health was authorized to exclude children from injurious occupations.

The nature of the Wisconsin Industrial Commission Act, which is described by Altmeyer as "nothing less than a work of genius," is illustrated in its central section.[1] "Every employer shall furnish employment which shall be safe for the employes therein and shall furnish a place of employment which shall be safe for the employes therein and for frequenters thereof." The generality of this obligation is clear enough. To reduce it to workable dimensions, the Industrial Commission was authorized to fix reasonable standards and to prescribe reasonable orders. A quarter century of successful experience has demonstrated that with a competent public service this method of government intervention is preferable to rigid, detailed statutory requirements in such fields as labor administration.

The Wisconsin experiment was quickly followed. In 1913 five states enacted similar legislation and by 1935 twenty states had delegated broad rule-making power in industrial safety. By 1935 there were also sixteen states with minimum wage laws and seven with laws dealing with hours of women and children, all of which included the rule-making power. "In all, a total of thirty states have explicitly delegated to their labor department officials some measure of power to issue legally enforceable administrative regulations."[2]

The extent to which codes and regulations have been issued by state and federal administrative agencies in the field of labor law is indicated by Table XIV, based on data gathered by Andrews.[3]

TABLE XIV

NUMBER OF LABOR CODES AND REGULATIONS ISSUED BY FEDERAL AND STATE AGENCIES

YEAR	NUMBER
1906–1910	3
1911–1915	27
1916–1920	92
1921–1925	91
1926–1930	97
1931–1935	25
TOTAL	335

[1] Arthur J. Altmeyer, *The Industrial Commission of Wisconsin* (1932), pp. 106-7. Compare similar Wisconsin legislation concerning hours of labor of women, and the broad recognition of rule-making power in *State vs. Lange Canning Co.*, 164 Wis. 228; 157 N. W. 777; 160 N. W. 57 (1916).

[2] Andrews, *op. cit.*, p. 21.

[3] *Ibid.*, pp. 122 ff.

In a few states the device of administrative rules and codes has now become the principal method of industrial regulation, while in others it is quite absent. The trend, however, is clearly toward a wider use of administrative legislation in this field and elsewhere.

b. Constitutional limitations on the grant of the rule-making power. The complex constitutional problem of justifying the grant of subleg-islative authority in the face of the doctrine of separation of powers has been threshed over by courts and students of public law *ad infinitum.* This note is intended chiefly to indicate the nature of the problem, the attitudes of the courts, and the limitations, if any, which arise to hamper administrative operations.

The doctrine of separation of powers is construed by the courts to prohibit the vesting of legislative power in either the executive or judicial branches of government. Chief Justice Marshall was early faced with the problem of constitutionality of the exercise of power by the executive branch which on its face looked like legislation: i.e., the prescription of a rule of future conduct. He succeeded in laying the basis for the guidance of courts by holding that it was permissible to authorize administrative officials to "fill in the details" of statutes.[1] The implied fiction, later developed as the performance of "quasi-legislative" acts, sufficed for over a century to sustain a steadily expanding delegation of administrative legislation. The state courts, with many exceptions, also took a liberal view concerning the possibility of delegating various types of subordinate authority resembling legislation, while at the same time consistently holding to the main doctrine that the separation of powers forbade vesting legislative power in the executive branch.

In 1933 the Supreme Court seemed to open even wider the door to administrative legislation. Justice Cardozo, speaking for the Court in *Norwegian Nitrogen Products Co. vs. United States*, said, "What is done by the Tariff Commission and the President in changing the tariff rates to conform to new conditions *is in substance a delegation, though a permissible one, of the legislative process.*"[2] It might have been supposed that the course of expansion of administrative power would henceforth turn on the Court's willingness to allow various examples of actual delegation of real legislative power.

The tide turned, however, in 1935 with the decisions in the "hot oil" case and the Schechter case.[3] In each case the Supreme Court held that delegations of rule-making power to the President under the Na-

[1] *Wayman vs. Southard*, 10 Wheat. 1 (1825).

[2] 288 U. S. 294, 305 (1933). Italics are author's.

[3] *Panama Refining Co. vs. Ryan*, 293 U. S. 388 (1935); *Schechter Poultry Corporation vs. United States*, 295 U. S. 495 (1935); see also to the same effect, *Carter vs. Carter Coal Co.*, 298 U. S. 238 (1936).

tional Industry Recovery Act were invalid as violating the doctrine of separation of powers. In his concurring opinion in the latter case Justice Cardozo wrote, "This is delegation run riot. No such plenitude of power is susceptible of transfer." For the first time in its history, the Supreme Court found some limits to the delegation of legislative power.

How serious are these limitations from the point of view of effective use of rule making as a part of administrative law enforcement? They are probably not important. The court will require the legislature to indicate in general terms the end to be sought, the standards to be followed, and the procedure to be observed, but these are requirements which can readily be met. The development of administrative legislation in the national government will not be delayed by the present restrictions of the Supreme Court. Without entering upon a review of cases in the state supreme courts, it may be added that the rule-making power is adequately recognized in most states.[1] Constitutional requirements as to rule making do not hamper administrative necessities.

c. Rule making as a method of securing compliance. In all cases where a statute can be drafted in terms which impose an unconditional obligation, there is no necessity for administrative legislation to aid compliance. The rules could do no more than restate the specific obligation. Most legislation once took this form.

In cases where the statute imposes only a conditional obligation, or an obligation which is general, vague, undefined, or ambiguous, supplementary steps must be taken to support action looking to compliance. In its original statutory form, such legislation may be substantially unenforceable simply because of the indefiniteness of the obligation. Theoretically, and historically, compliance might be sought by prosecution before the courts by the attorney general in any case which came to his attention. In fact, direct prosecution on the basis of the statute alone has been substantially abandoned in this type of case.

One alternative is that already discussed, the issuance of administrative orders of individual application based on the general terms of the statute and themselves enforceable eventually by judicial action. The Federal Trade Commission, for example, is permitted to proceed only in this way in seeking to prevent unfair practices in interstate commerce. Another alternative is the issuance of a rule having the force of law, based on the organic act. Such a rule may (1) state in detail the requirements or prohibitions implied in the act; (2) establish standards, norms, or principles; (3) interpret the meaning of the act; (4) authorize exemptions from the act; (5) in exceptional cases, add to the

[1] *State vs. Whitman*, 196 Wis. 472 (1928).

scope of the act; (6) determine when the act shall go into effect; (7) prescribe the procedure for taking advantage of the act. In any case we find an example of delegated administrative legislation.

Additions to and exemptions from or changes in the law are exceptional, but apparently well established. With specific authority of legislation, officials may add to the statutory list of dangerous employments from which children are excluded.[1] As early as 1916 the board of health in twenty-four states had been given power to add to the list of reportable diseases.[2] Since 1915 the New York State Industrial Commission has been authorized to amend the provisions of the Industrial Commission Act as well as its own rules. Its authority is vested in the following language.[3]

> If there shall be practical difficulties or unnecessary hardship in carrying out any provision of this chapter, or rule or regulation adopted by the industrial board thereunder, affecting the construction or alteration of buildings, exits therefrom, the installation of fixtures and apparatus, or the safeguarding of machinery and the prevention of accidents, the industrial board shall have power to make a variation from such requirements if the spirit of the provision or rule or regulation shall be observed and public safety secured. . . . If the board shall permit such variation it shall be in the form of a resolution and such variation shall apply to all buildings, installations or conditions where the facts are substantially the same as those stated in the petition. At least three affirmative votes shall be necessary for the adoption of any such resolution. Such resolution shall contain a description of the conditions under which such variation shall be permitted and shall be published in the manner provided for rules and regulations of the board. A record of all such variations shall be kept . . . and shall be open to public inspection during business hours.[4]

The immediate effect of the issuance of a rule is to make definite an obligation which was indefinite, to make certain what was uncertain, or to put into effect what was merely contingent. These results are essential to effective administrative action in securing compliance.

Where a rule can legally and practically be made, it has advantages over the order of individual application. The rule gives advance notice of the obligation; the order (other than beneficial) gives none, unless its application is suspended. The rule gives relatively complete information on the scope and nature of the obligation; the order covers only a single, perhaps unique case. The drafting of the rule may and often does permit conference between the government and the parties at interest, and consequently a broad agreement which tends toward vol-

[1] Andrews, *op. cit.*, pp. 19-20.

[2] U. G. Dubach, "Quasi-Legislative Powers of State Boards of Health," 10 *Am. Pol. Sci. Rev.* 80-95 (1916).

[3] Laws of 1915, c. 719, sec. 52a.

[4] The number of such variations is considerable; see N. Y. State Department of Labor, *Report of the Industrial Commissioner*, for any recent year.

untary compliance; the order does not always permit this procedure, although it may.

Nor is this all. The rule permits a definite statement of policy without litigation or compulsion; the order necessarily implies compulsion upon an individual or corporation and can be challenged only in an adverse proceeding. The avoidance of litigation as far as possible is a definite gain. Finally, amendments to a rule have the same general notice and publicity as attend its making, while a change of policy tucked away in an order may be lost to every interested party except one.

For these reasons the rule is a useful and convenient means of aiding in securing compliance. The rule itself will in its turn support orders of individual application as well as inspection and possibly license; and the mere existence of the rule does not destroy the necessity for the order. Both are advantageous, indeed often necessary means of administrative action.

d. Rule and law. Early fears that administrative rules would be so transitory and changeable as to throw industry into confusion have largely disappeared. The need for certainty in law is, however, so great that law should leave as little as possible to rule, and in fields of human activity where rights and obligations have become relatively stable and clearly understood, the need for administrative rules is small. In many directions, however, such certainty is impossible, and rule making becomes an adjunct to policy forming as well as to policy execution.

The advantages of administrative legislation in lieu of detailed statutory legislation are substantial.[1] The rule is more adaptable and more easily adjusted to changing circumstances than the statute. The rule is drafted by experts in the appropriate department who are familiar with actual conditions. The rule can more readily be prepared in consultation with interested parties than can the statute, although the difference is one of degree.

Equally important, the rule can be written in the light of what is administratively feasible. "If a legislative rule is both specific and unworkable, the administrator is in a dilemma. He must either try to work the unworkable, and thereby invite litigation and defeat of the real purpose of the statute, or he must evade or ignore the letter of the law." [2]

In entering new fields, the first administrative rules may be relatively innocuous, with gradual stiffening until the full intent of the statute is achieved. Meanwhile the interest to be regulated is adjusting itself

[1] Blachly and Oatman, *op. cit.*, pp. 43 ff., for discussion of advantage to legislatures. See also Harvey Walker, *Law Making in the United States* (1934), ch. 18.

[2] Hart, *op. cit.*, p. 324. Cf. the case of the potato control act of 1935, which was in effect ignored by the Department of Agriculture until its repeal.

and the mixture of "suasion with command" may produce better results than immediate insistence on all requirements. This policy was followed in part by the Securities and Exchange Commission.

Against such advantages must be balanced potential and at times real perils. Flexibility may resemble instability and approach chaos. The multiplicity of rules and amendments may exhaust the patience and defy the endurance of those who would understand them. In many cases, the means of publishing rules are wholly inadequate or even nonexistent. Rule makers as well as legislators may be subject to political pressure, and turn the rules to special or private instead of public purposes. The experts may lack a sense of what is politically feasible, although wise enough about what is administratively possible.

The balance between rules and law was admirably stated by Ernst Freund in 1915.

> Weighing relative advantages, it may be expected that administrative action can be set more easily in motion than legislation, and that it can better plan a program of gradual development; that while administrative authorities have a better sense of what is practically enforceable, legislatures have a keener sense of what is politically expedient, that while the former can mix suasion with command, the latter can invest their commands with greater publicity and a higher moral authority. . . . Administrative action has, however, the indisputable, though incidental advantage, that it permits the process of establishing rules to be surrounded by procedural guarantees and other inherent checks which will tend to produce a more impartial consideration than the legislature is apt to give, and which should in the course of time, if not immediately, substitute principle for mere discretion.[1]

In fact there has been a steady undercurrent of concern and occasionally protest against the extension of sublegislation.[2] This is not confined merely to those who want to be let alone. The complaints are sufficiently justified to cause general acceptance of a number of reasonable safeguards against potential dangers.

e. Safeguards. These precautions were first stated in a little English classic on administrative rules[3] in the form of five propositions: (1) that the delegation of legislative power should be to a trustworthy authority which commands general confidence; (2) that the limits within which the delegated power is to be exercised ought to be definitely laid down; (3) that if any particular interests are to be specially affected, the legislating authority should consult them before making its laws; (4) that adequate measures should be taken to ensure publicity; and (5) that there should be means of amending or revoking delegated legislation.

[1] Ernst Freund, "The Substitution of Rule for Discretion in Public Law," 9 *Am. Pol. Sci. Rev.* 666-76 (1915).

[2] James M. Beck, *Our Wonderland of Bureaucracy* (1932); Leverett S. Lyon and others, *The National Recovery Administration* (1935), esp. pp. 79-82, and ch. 10.

[3] Cecil T. Carr, *Delegated Legislation* (1921).

Experience in the United States confirms the importance of each of these suggestions. Recent studies of the rule-making power, and some legislation, find us in about the following position.

Delegation to a trustworthy authority. Too many agencies have been vested with uncoordinated power to make rules. Blachly and Oatman suggest for the national government that the power be vested exclusively in the President, and that a special reviewing agency act on his behalf in controlling the form and content of rules in addition to the scrutiny now given them by the Bureau of the Budget and the Attorney General. Assuming an effective staff agency for this purpose, the recommendation is sound; in any event, the grant of the rule-making power should be consolidated, not further dispersed. The President, of course, will not study every proposal for a rule; the advantage of requiring his approval is that it permits an agency advisory to the President to review the whole output of administrative legislation from the over-all point of view. Greater uniformity and consistency would naturally be expected. In the states, the preference has been in favor of conferring the rule-making power upon the appropriate departmen or commission, rather than upon the governor. Hence there is much dispersion of authority.

In any event, the rule will be drafted in the first instance by the agency concerned with its enforcement. In this connection we may take notice of the opinion expressed by a leader in labor legislation and regulation, John B. Andrews. "From the practical experience of more than twenty years, there is ample support for the conclusion that rule-making is most properly and effectively used when vested in boards or commissions rather than in individual officers."[1] This is common, bu not universal practice.

Definite limits. The United States Supreme Court has already spoken decisively on this point; better legislative draftsmanship and clearer understanding and statement of policy will be required from legislativ bodies.

Consultation. In such states as Wisconsin, consultation is standar practice. In general it is usual, although often not required. It is one c the chief advantages of sublegislation and ought consequently to b exploited.

Publication. The Federal Register Act of 1935 substantially mee publication needs for the national government.[2] The Panama Refinin Company case indicates how intolerable the situation had become. Th case was heard in the lower federal courts in part on a supposed ac

[1] Andrews, *op. cit.*, p. 26. For a contrary view, see Walker, *op. cit.*, pp. 457-58.
[2] 49 Stat. 500 (1935).

ninistrative rule which in fact did not exist, a situation unknown alike o the persons affected, the prosecuting authorities and the courts.[1] n the states the facilities for publication are still often deplorably inade- quate. Since 1917 Massachusetts has required every rule and regulation of a general character to be filed with the secretary of the common- vealth.

Amendments and repeal. The authority which can make a rule nor- nally is empowered to modify or repeal it. The same safeguards of notice and consultation are desirable. In some cases the terms of the rant of rule-making power seek to prevent hasty and frequent altera- ions. Thus the Cotton Futures Act directed the Secretary of Agricul- ure not to change or replace cotton standards within a period of less han one year after promulgation, and only after one year's notice. uch restrictions are uncommon; the customary grant is "to adopt easonable and proper rules and regulations and to alter the same."

In the Securities and Exchange Act of 1934 there was introduced new provision designed to protect individuals against prosecution for cts done under the protection of a rule later modified. After granting e power to make rules, the law continues, "No provision of this title nposing any liability shall apply to any act done or omitted in good ith in conformity with any rule or regulation of the Commission . . . otwithstanding that such rule or regulation may, after such act or nission, be amended or rescinded or be determined by judicial or her authority to be invalid for any reason." This protection is en- rely reasonable.

f. Summary. Powers to make orders of individual application and to omulgate general rules having the force of law greatly expand the fectiveness of administrative officials. These, together with the power inspect and to license, are the characteristic elements of modern ministration in action, especially in new fields of state intervention. hile their origins reach far back in our administrative history, their oad application is found principally in the last half century, and in e states chiefly in the last three decades.

The orders and rules of administrative bodies are subject to judicial lidation; but when a precedent has once been accepted by the courts, bsequent applications of precedent naturally pass unchallenged. It llows that the great mass of orders and rules are conclusive so far the individual is concerned. Protection against "an offensive bu- ucracy" at work with these powerful tools consequently becomes part a responsibility of elected representatives, in part a duty of the

[1] See remarks of Chief Justice Hughes in this case, 293 U. S. 388 (1935).

higher supervisory officials.[1] In fact the chief protection is already found in some cases in the superior quality of the personnel, in their recognition of the delicacy of their tasks, and in their frequent consultation with the groups whose interests they regulate.

The powers to issue orders of individual application and rules having the force of law are not likely to diminish in the foreseeable future. They will probably increase, since advancing legislation finds constantly greater difficulty in specifying precisely either the ends in view or the means necessary to achieve these ends. A civilization which is changing so rapidly and in which the currents of collective action for social and economic security are running so strongly will continue to depend in considerable measure upon administrative legislation and upon orders of individual application issued by public officials in particular cases.

[1] E. Pendelton Herring, *Public Administration and the Public Interest* (1936) shows that the "public interest" is also jealously watched by private groups.

Chapter Thirty-four

ADMINISTRATIVE ADJUDICATION

THE most formal type of administrative action is adjudication. Superficially the work of administrative tribunals seems almost to become that of a court, separated by a broad gulf from the noncoercive and the relatively informal types of administrative action which were described in earlier chapters. The importance of the property or personal interests in question is sometimes of first rank; the moral authority of administrative determinations and the prestige of the administrative body rise to higher levels; and the impressiveness of official action is greatly enhanced.[1]

An administrative tribunal is not, however, a judicial court. Most such tribunals operate with a degree of informality which is suited to the nature of the issues involved. Formal rules of evidence, as developed in common law courts, need not be observed; legal counsel is not necessary in many of the humbler matters which require adjustment; the facts are quickly developed by question and answer and a conclusion reached without delay. The decisions are reached, moreover, by persons expert in the subject matter rather than by persons expert in the law. Thousands of disputed cases involving claims for workmen's compensation, for example, are settled every year, finally and speedily, by these informal hearings. The elaborate requirements of judicial proof, with appeal to higher courts and expenses out of all proportion to benefits finally decreed, are thus avoided.

Administrative adjudication has aroused widespread interest and attention for thirty years among lawyers and publicists. They have been concerned with the nature of "quasi judicial" power, with the application of the doctrine of separation of powers, with due process of law, and especially with the extent of judicial review of administrative adjudication. These important matters are adequately discussed elsewhere; those interested primarily in administration are more concerned to learn what part this procedure plays in the general area of law enforcement as one of the many means by which officials cultivate patterns of behavior which correspond to law.

[1] See James M. Landis, *The Administrative Process* (1938).

1. Growth of Administrative Adjudication

Dickinson notes some early instances of administrative adjudication at the beginning of the nineteenth century.[1] Although the courts were not unfriendly at the outset, hostility began to appear after the middle of the century. It was not, however, until the rise of state intervention in such fields as public health, industrial safety, and utility regulation that administrative adjudication really came into its own.

Most federal administrative adjudication was authorized subsequent to 1900, and the bulk of it is the product of the last quarter century. An early example is the authority lodged in the General Land Office in 1875 to adjudicate claims to public lands.[2] The Interstate Commerce Act of 1887 vested powers of adjudication in the Commission, which were extended in 1889 to cover reparations cases.[3] A new application of the adjudicating power was made the next year in the Meat Inspection Act, vesting authority in the Secretary of Agriculture.[4] In 1891 the Secretary of Commerce and Labor was authorized to take aliens into custody and to direct their deportation in certain cases.[5] These are the principal instances before 1900.

An important new field of adjudication was opened in 1906 with the enactment of the first food and drug law, enforced by the Department of Agriculture.[6] The Plant Quarantine Act of 1912 further extended the adjudicating work of this department.

The investigational work of the former Bureau of Corporations was expanded in 1914 into the Federal Trade Commission, the essential aspect of whose activity is adjudication in the determination of unfair practices in restraint of trade.[7] Similar jurisdiction was vested in 1916 in the Shipping Board, now the United States Maritime Commission. The Air Commerce Act of 1926 vested incidental adjudicatory power in the Department of Commerce (since 1938 the Civil Aeronautics Authority) with respect to aircraft, airmen and air transportation. In 1927 the Radio Act, now administered by the Federal Communications Commission, vested adjudicating authority in another new field.

The principal novel examples of federal administrative adjudication since 1933 are found in the Securities and Exchange Act (1934), the

1 John Dickinson, *Administrative Justice and the Supremacy of Law in the United States* (1927).

2 Charles R. Pierce, "The Land Department as an Administrative Tribunal," 10 *Am. Pol. Sci. Rev.* 271-89 (1916).

3 I. L. Sharfman, *The Interstate Commerce Commission* (1931), vol. 2, ch. 10.

4 26 Stat. 414 (1890).

5 William C. Van Vleck, *The Administrative Control of Aliens* (1932).

6 1 *Law and Contemporary Problems* 1-133 (1933-34).

7 Gerard C. Henderson, *The Federal Trade Commission* (1924).

National Labor Relations Act (1935), the Petroleum Conservation Act (1935), the Railroad Retirement Act (1937), and the Bituminous Coal Conservation Act (1937).

This brief sketch of the emergence and expansion of adjudicating powers in the United States government excludes those instances in which a privilege, grant or bounty is chiefly concerned, as in the hearing of claims of applicants for civil service employment and claims for payments to veterans, and also omits cases involving liability to taxation (Customs Court, Court of Customs and Patent Appeals, Board of Tax Appeals). The instances cited represent the application of administrative power to the activities of private parties in what were once considered private domains. The impact of the federal government on the economic life of the country through administrative adjudication commenced, in short, with the Interstate Commerce Act of 1887; adjudicating authority has accompanied most extensions of federal power in this all-important field.[1]

Data are lacking to present a comprehensive account of the growth of administrative adjudication in the states. In general it is true that the great bulk of present-day adjudication of this type originated subsequent to 1900, although in some fields it reaches back into the nineteenth century. The development of administrative adjudication in the field of workmen's compensation is a useful illustration of the trend. Until 1910 recovery for injuries incurred in course of employment could be had only through suit against the employer in the proper court, before which the employer could assert the traditional common law defenses of assumption of risk, fellow servant, and contributory negligence. There was no administrative agency of any kind (apart from the newly established United States Employees' Compensation Commission, 1908) to assist in recovery or to assess damages.

The results were so deplorable that strong agitation developed to follow the example of several European countries by providing an administrative remedy. The first effort was to force the old law of liability into workable shape; this failed. Doubts concerning the constitutionality of compulsory workmen's compensation laws led to the enactment of several optional statutes; these also failed. In 1917 the Supreme Court validated a compulsory compensation act,[2] and within a few years, as indicated in the table below,[3] the new administrative procedure for determining damages had swept the country.

[1] A thorough study of the history of the administrative adjudicating power is greatly needed.

[2] *N. Y. Central Railroad Co. vs. White*, 243 U. S. 188 (1917).

[3] Taken from U. S. Bureau of Labor Statistics, *Workmen's Compensation Legislation of the United States and Canada as of January 1, 1929*, Bulletin 496, 1929, p. 8.

TABLE XV

ENACTMENT OF WORKMEN'S COMPENSATION ACTS BY THE UNITED STATES, THE STATES AND TERRITORIES

YEAR	NUMBER
1906–1910	1[a]
1911–1915	33
1916–1920	13
1921–1925	1
1926–1929	3

[a] United States public employees.

By 1934 only four states (Florida, South Carolina, Mississippi and Arkansas) continued to depend on the old liability principles.[1]

The advances of the last half century in the field of administrative adjudication are not likely to be curtailed; it is more probable that they will be expanded. Liability for automobile accidents might well be handled by the same method now almost universal for handling claims for industrial accidents.[2] A new field of administrative jurisprudence will develop around contemporary social security legislation. Wages and hours legislation and price fixing will open up new necessities for administrative adjudication.

2. Nature of Administrative Adjudication

For the purpose of this book administrative adjudication means the investigation and settling of a dispute on the basis of law and fact by an administrative agency.[3] This agency may or may not be organized to act solely as an administrative court, and may act with varying degrees of formality and finality.

Two principal types of dispute arise. The most common is in substance an attack upon some official decision instituted by an individual or corporation whose interests are affected; the individual and the administration are opposing parties; and the decision of the administrative tribunal will be enforced like a judicial decision unless appeal is allowed to some higher authority, either administrative or judicial.[4]

A less frequent case involves only the rights of private parties in the investigation and settlement of which the administration acts as an impartial umpire, applying the law to the facts in much the same way

[1] Walter F. Dodd, *Administration of Workmen's Compensation* (1936).

[2] Patterson H. French, *The Automobile Compensation Plan* (1933).

[3] Frederick F. Blachly and Miriam E. Oatman, *Administrative Legislation and Adjudication* (1934), p. 91.

[4] *Ibid.*

as might a court. The most common example is the making of awards in workmen's compensation cases by industrial commissions.[1]

Administrative adjudication may be broadly distinguished from "mere" administration on the one hand and from judicial adjudication on the other. In their regular work of handling cases, administrative officers may and often do hold hearings, listen to experts, interpret laws and decisions, draw inferences from facts and make decisions. So long as those affected do not dispute the decisions, such operations may be considered as simple administration. "When, however, an interested person objects that some administrative act, finding, or decision invades his legal rights in any way, it becomes necessary for an investigation to be made and a decision rendered on the points of controversy. If the investigation and decision are made by an administrative agency or tribunal of any kind, . . . this function is administrative adjudication." [2]

The border line on the side of the courts is drawn by Blachly and Oatman in these terms. "The only distinctions of primary importance and fundamental validity between administrative adjudication and ordinary adjudication . . . depend upon the nature of the acts adjudicated and the nature of the authority that is adjudicating. . . . If acts are administrative in nature, and if they are adjudicated either by agencies which carry on administrative duties or by administrative tribunals, the function thus performed is administrative adjudication." [3] Pragmatically the distinction is one between an adjudication by a court and by a body not a court, which, as a corollary, is not bound by the rules of procedure that hedge the court.

In the last analysis these are subtle distinctions. For our purpose it is enough to observe that alongside the field of established judicial determination there now lies a large and growing field of administrative adjudication which is not merely supplementary but is replacing in part the work of the courts. This new field of administrative adjudication has been deliberately created by statute; it is not the invention of administrators. The expansion of this form of administrative action

[1] An analogous case involves the determination of rights and obligations of officials with respect to each other by a higher administrative body. See Charles S. Hyneman, "Administrative Adjudication: An Analysis," 51 *Pol. Sci. Q.* 383-417, 516-37 (1936).

[2] Blachly and Oatman, *op. cit.*, p. 100.

[3] *Ibid.*, p. 104. The distinction is pushed further by John Dickinson. "The *purpose* of administrative adjudication," writes Dickinson, "is to inform administrative officers what to do, rather than to determine the individual rights which will be affected by their resulting action or failure to act. The two things are in the nature of the case inseparable, but there is a difference of emphasis which is precisely the distinguishing factor between administrative adjudication and adjudication by a court. . . . An administrative tribunal . . . adjudicates for the direct purpose of informing itself how best to perform its functions of enforcement." *Op. cit.*, pp. 23-24.

is facilitated, not so much because an eventual appeal to the courts is denied, but rather because the results of administrative adjudication are accepted by the parties. The scope and range of administration have been greatly expanded by the growth of the power to make determinations affecting private rights, and by the wide acceptance of these decisions on the part of the individuals concerned.

3. Types of Federal Administrative Tribunals

A previous section suggests that administrative adjudication has deep historical roots. It has in fact become one of the normal methods of administrative action. There were in 1936 approximately fifty administrative tribunals in the federal government.[1]

The most important categories into which these federal tribunals fall include *first*, the independent administrative courts: the United States Customs Court, the United States Court of Customs and Patent Appeals, the Board of Tax Appeals and the Court of Claims. With some exceptions, the members of these bodies are called judges; the appointment of members is during good behavior; the independence of the courts is protected by their separation from other agencies of government, and by the exclusion of political influences; their procedures resemble the procedures of judicial courts.

Second, special administrative tribunals within government departments. Here we find the Board of Appeals in the Patent Office, the Board of Veterans' Appeals and Insurance Claims Council in the Veterans' Administration; the deputy commissioners of the Employees' Compensation Commission; and the Board of Labor Review, Public Works Administration. The common characteristics of this group are these: they are integral parts of some government unit; the members of the tribunal are also members of the larger body; they are not called judges but board members or commissioners; they need not be lawyers, although they do work which is essentially judicial in nature; they neither exercise the rule-making power nor perform administrative work in the narrow sense.

Third, the regulatory authorities, including the Interstate Commerce Commission, the Federal Trade Commission, the Federal Communications Commission, the Federal Power Commission, the Securities and Exchange Commission, the United States Maritime Commission and the National Labor Relations Board. These bodies exercise all classes of powers: sublegislative, quasi judicial, and administrative. Their members are not called judges; they are appointed for fixed terms; but

[1] Blachly and Oatman, *op. cit.*, p. 121. The following analysis is borrowed from this work.

since the decision of the Supreme Court in the Humphrey case, they apparently are, or may be, protected against the unrestricted right of the President to remove them.[1]

Fourth, licensing authorities; for example, the Bureau of Marine Inspection and Navigation which reviews appeals regarding the suspension and revocation of licenses and refusal to grant licenses in shipping; and the Civil Aeronautics Authority (formerly the Secretary of Commerce) which licenses aircraft and airmen.[2]

The number and variety of administrative adjudicating authorities, each with its special procedures, have naturally suggested the desirability of a more carefully organized system, possibly even the institution of a structure of administrative courts resembling that which has long been a part of French governmental institutions. This topic is discussed in chapter thirty-seven. Here it may be said that the historical development of the last half century and the present uncoordinated structure both give reason for belief that in due course of time an administrative court system will take its place in the institutions of this country.[3]

4. Practice and Procedure of Administrative Adjudication

a. Workmen's compensation. In order to present a clear impression of the form and procedures of administrative adjudication, two cases will be described in the following sections, dealing with the award of claims in workmen's compensation by industrial commissions and with the award of reparations to shippers by the Interstate Commerce Commission.

The functions of industrial commissions enforcing workmen's compensation acts are threefold: administrative, "quasi legislative" and "quasi judicial," the two latter categories being functions "in fact judicial or legislative in character, but which the courts hold may be exercised by administrative or executive officers without violating the principle of separation of powers." The administrative function includes such activities as the enforcement of requirements that accidents be reported; the investigation and approval of agreements to settle uncontested claims; supervision of payments; and supervision of insurance companies and self-insurers to assure financial capacity. The legislative function is concerned with rule making.[4]

The quasi judicial function includes the action of administrative bod-

[1] For the Humphrey case, see ch. 4, *supra*.

[2] Blachly and Oatman list other categories of somewhat lesser general importance.

[3] The topic of procedure before administrative tribunals is not discussed in this book. Consult Harold M. Stephens, *Administrative Tribunals and the Rules of Evidence* (1933).

[4] Dodd, *Administration of Workmen's Compensation* (1936).

ies in passing upon contested claims; the approval or disapproval of compromise or lump sum settlements; and the review of compensation awards for the purpose of increasing, diminishing or terminating them. It is this phase of the work of industrial accident commissions with which we are here concerned.

The necessity for close supervision and adjudication of claims and awards became evident at an early date. An investigation of results in New York under a system which favored unsupervised agreements and handicapped administrative review revealed an estimated underpayment to injured employees during 1918 alone of a half million dollars. Agreements showed gross underpayments for injuries sustained, incorrect reporting of wages, termination of payments too soon, and disregard of some types of accidents. Legislation consequently put an end to direct settlements in favor of official review of all claims.

Under the legislation of 1921 and subsequent amendments, an industrial board of five members formulates and enforces an industrial code and reviews decisions in contested cases. If the parties fail to reach an agreement on the amount of the claim, the dispute is heard in the first instance by a referee who makes an award. If the parties are satisfied, the decision of the referee becomes the decision of the board.

If disagreement still prevails, an appeal is open to the industrial board at which new evidence may be introduced. The hearings are conducted by one member of the board who, after taking evidence, makes his award, which is regarded as the award of the industrial board. A further appeal is allowed to the Appellate Division of the Supreme Court of New York. In other states, Massachusetts for example, the administrative adjudication is by three or five members of the industrial accident board, a body comprising seven members.

Although there is wide diversity among the adjudicating procedures in the various states, Dodd summarizes the usual form of action in four stages:

(1) A hearing by a referee, examiner, arbitrator, or by a member of the administering body;

(2) A review, with the possibility of introducing new testimony, before a board of several persons or before an officer superior to the one who held the original hearing;

(3) An appeal to a trial court or to an intermediate court of review, with the issues in most cases heard by the court on the basis of the record made in the administrative review;

(4) A further judicial review by the highest state court, also based on the record made in the hearing before the administrative body, and usually limited to points of law.

The extent to which administrative adjudication is in fact final and conclusive is indicated by the analysis of Illinois industrial claim cases during the year 1926–1927.[1]

TABLE XVI

DISPOSITION OF INDUSTRIAL ACCIDENT CLAIMS IN ILLINOIS, 1926–27

Compensable accidents reported	57,535
Claims for arbitration	12,209
Decisions by arbitrators (first administrative hearing)	2,828
Review petitions (second administrative hearing)	1,512
Writs of certiorari to circuit court	237
Applications for writ of error to Supreme Court	104
Applications for writ of error to Supreme Court allowed	50

Of 57,000 reported compensable accidents, over 45,000 involved no contest. Of 2,800 cases settled by an arbitrator, all but 237 were finally adjudicated and settled by the Illinois industrial commission.

Analogous results are reported from Wisconsin. In twenty years of experience (1911–1931) appeals were taken to the court in only 988 out of 36,256 compensation decisions, and in these the commission was upheld in 741 cases.[2]

b. Reparations cases before the Interstate Commerce Commission. The Interstate Commerce Act imposed a liability of carrier to shipper for violation of the law, and authorized the shipper to present his claim either before the Commission or a court.[3] Hence arise the so-called reparations cases, involving questions "peculiarly fitted for jury trial."

In requiring the Commission to assume this judicial function, Congress was trying to render somewhat less formidable the task of obtaining compensation for losses sustained as a result of violations by carriers, especially since the individual claims were usually small. The specific judicial nature of the procedure is indicated in that a shipper can proceed, by the terms of the law, either before the court or before the Commission.

Reparations cases, although still numerous, do not now form an essential part of the regulatory process. The Commission relied in large measure, although without much success, upon reparations proceedings as a method of controlling rates prior to the passage of the Hepburn Act in 1906. Until then the Commission had no power to fix the

[1] Dodd, *op. cit.*, p. 115.

[2] Arthur J. Altmeyer, *The Industrial Commisssion of Wisconsin* (1932), pp. 84-95.

[3] This section is based on the invaluable study by I. L. Sharfman, *The Interstate Commerce Commission* (1931–1937), especially vol. 3-B, pp. 329 ff.

maximum rate, but it could order repayment of the surplus of an excessive rate. Subsequent to 1906, however, reparations cases have had no public interest; they involve only the settlement of private claims.

Awards are made chiefly in connection with rates found excessive or discriminatory and with departures from published tariffs. The procedure of the Commission has been governed by the judicial character of the reparations function. Investigation and hearing are indispensable prerequisites to the issuance of an order; the findings of fact are required by law to be included in the report and the findings must be supported by substantial evidence. The findings and order are not conclusive or self-enforcing; the successful complainant must appeal to the courts for an enforcement order if the carrier declines to make payment. Such instances are rare. If the plaintiff elects to present his claim to the Commission in the first instance rather than to the court, he has no redress in court if the Commission denies him relief.

Following the Hepburn Act giving the Commission power to fix a maximum rate, the number of reparations cases increased, although their public significance diminished. Still "in a vast number of cases" they were the occasion for the initiation of rate proceedings. As the burden of these cases steadily increased, the Commission sought to return them to the exclusive jurisdiction of the courts. In 1916 the Commission observed, "If we had no power to award reparation, a mass of cases which now require consideration and decision, with all their attendant detail work and expense, would be kept off the Commission's dockets." [1]

In the annual report for 1930, the Commission complained more vigorously. Reviewing the work of the preceding decade, the Commission found that it had issued reports in 9,231 rate cases; reparation was sought in 6,367 of these, or sixty-nine per cent. "The amounts of reparation sought and awarded have increased year by year during that period. In a large proportion of the cases the amounts involved are small, and no question of particular public interest is involved. Our awards have amounted to approximately $4,000,000 per year. . . . The increased number and complexity of these so-called reparations cases have so encroached upon our time and energies as to deprive us of adequate time for the thorough consideration of the many larger and more important problems continually coming before us." [2]

Congress, however, has turned a deaf ear to these recommendations, suggesting that it still sets store by the administrative determination of claims for money damages in rate cases. On the other hand, the New

[1] Interstate Commerce Commission, *Annual Report*, 1916, p. 76.
[2] *Ibid.*, 1930, p. 92.

York Public Service Commission has expressly requested that it be allowed to adjudicate claims of overcharge.[1]

5. Organization and Personnel Aspects of Administrative Tribunals

The usual assumption that administrative tribunals are independent agencies outside the major frame of government is erroneous. Blachly and Oatman describe many federal adjudicating agencies which are within the departments, as well as some very important ones outside the departments. For example, the Department of Agriculture handles adjudications in connection with the Warehouse Act (1916); the Packers and Stockyards Act (1921); and other acts.

The recommendations of the President's Committee on Administrative Management in favor of the gradual integration of the nonjudicial functions of these adjudicating bodies with the departments has already been discussed.[2] The course of debate in Congress in 1938 revealed how strong is the independent position of such agencies as the Interstate Commerce Commission. At the same time, evidence is accumulating to show that Congress is reluctant to create new independent adjudicating bodies.

Within the states the independent position of administrative adjudicating bodies has not been substantially affected by the course of state reorganization during the last twenty years. Even where they have been placed "in a department," as in Illinois, their independence in making determinations has been carefully protected.

The question arises, to what authority are such independent bodies responsible? They clearly are not responsible to the chief executive, nor in any realistic sense are they responsible to the legislative body. Their work is subject to review by the courts, and in this sense they may be said to be responsible to or at least controlled by the judiciary. It is more accurate to say that they are primarily responsible to the law under which they operate, although this is often defined by their own decisions. To this extent they appear responsible to themselves.

[1] Case studies in administrative adjudication in a number of fields would be of great value. Patent decisions may affect only private parties, or may involve the government and a claimant; the exclusion or deportation of aliens involves the alien and the government, represented by the Department of Labor (see W. C. Van Vleck, *The Administrative Control of Aliens* [1932]); the administration of the Longshoremen's and Harbor Workers' Compensation Act of 1927, 44 Stat. 1424, provides an interesting case; the adjudication of complaints concerning the issue and revocation of aircraft and airman certificates deserves study, among many other examples.

[2] See ch. 8.

The origin and quality of federal commissioners were studied by E. P. Herring in 1936.[1] Standards of competence for appointment as a commissioner are rarely found in the statutes, but in general Congress apparently desires to maintain commissions not identified with any one class, party or section. A review of the educational background of commissioners showed that a majority had some college education; a few were "real scholars"; more were trained in law than in any other discipline. Their education was representative of various school facilities, and as a group their academic work was a prelude to the practice of law or the holding of public office. Herring found that prior public service in Congress has not been a useful qualification for work on administrative boards—a judgment confirming the general opinion of most "lame-duck" appointments.

Motives of presidents in selecting commissioners vary. Wilson endorsed the ideal of independent commissions and sought able men holding the broad views of public policy which he himself entertained. Harding depended heavily upon personal friendship with much less concern about technical competence. Coolidge was greatly influenced by political considerations and sought to keep commission policy in line with his own views. Hoover tended to allow the commissions a free rein. Franklin D. Roosevelt sought commission adjudications in harmony with his policy, but was balked in his effort to assert unlimited presidential power of removal. In general, political reliability and "soundness" of views on public policy are important considerations in the selection of commissioners. Herring rightly concludes, "Presidential policy is bound to be reflected in the type of men placed upon these commissions and boards." The actual level of statesmanship achieved on federal adjudicating bodies varies widely. In general, an excellent level of ability is attained, and in individual instances extraordinarily able men serve the government in this capacity.[2]

The level of competence reached in state regulatory and adjudicating agencies varies very widely. In some states, Wisconsin, New York, Massachusetts, and Virginia, for example, the level is almost uniformly high; in other states it is almost uniformly mediocre; in still others one administrative tribunal will command respect while another will not. In his study of administrative adjudication, Hyneman concludes, "it is imperative that the personnel, organization and procedures of American administrative tribunals be improved."[3]

[1] E. Pendleton Herring, *Federal Commissioners, a Study of their Careers and Qualifications* (1936).

[2] Biographies would be very useful to students of administration.

[3] Hyneman, *op. cit.*

So far as the technical staff is concerned, it may be said that the federal government is well equipped. The engineers, accountants, examiners and other experts are usually selected by competitive civil service examinations and by long service become highly qualified. In the states various conditions obtain, but it is not unusual to find a technical staff which is better equipped for its task than are the commissioners for theirs—including states bereft of any merit system. It is no exaggeration to say that the competence of the technical staff in an adjudicating body is of primary importance, nor to take the view that it is at this point among others that administrative tribunals usually surpass courts. The protection of the merit system is a primary need for these technical experts.

6. Reasons for Expansion of Administrative Adjudication

The search for the conditions which favored the rapid expansion of administrative adjudication in preference to action by courts leads into some underlying aspects of our system of government and public law. They may best be suggested against the background of the historical relation of courts to law enforcement and in the light of the changing character of legislative enactments.

With rare exceptions, the early pattern of law enforcement was based on a specific, definite, and readily understood obligation or right expressed in statute or recognized at common law; in case of violation of right or obligation, recourse was had to the ordinary courts for relief, usually in the form of civil damages, the initiative being taken by the injured party. It was assumed that public interests (apart from criminal actions) would be adequately conserved by private action in the judicial courts on the basis of the rights and obligations defined in the law.

This simple, direct method of law enforcement made almost no demands upon administration, apart from the realm of the criminal law. Enforcement through administrative action of any kind was in fact exceedingly rare, and the simple administrative system of a hundred years ago was chiefly concerned with the collection of taxes, the keeping of records, the elementary protection of person and property and the construction of a limited number of types of public works, such as canals and highways, rather than with law enforcement.

The economic and social evolution which changed so fundamentally the role of administration has been sketched elsewhere.[1] By 1900 public evidence of dissatisfaction with the achievement of either personal or community protection through a system of law enforcement de-

[1] See ch. 2.

pending on specific legislation and court adjudication on petition of private parties was everywhere apparent. Administrative action of various sorts, including administrative adjudication in some cases, was invented and extended in the interest of more effective state action for broad social objectives.

Incident to this development was a profound change in the character of legislation. Faced with complex and shifting economic and social situations and perplexed by many competing proposals for their management, the legislature gradually ceased the effort to prescribe in exact detail the pattern of conduct which it believed desirable. Specific legislation prescribing exact rights and obligations yielded in some degree to general legislation laying down broad objectives and establishing administrative agencies to work out in detail the precise pattern of behavior. This change in the form of legislation underlies the expansion of administrative rule-making and ordering powers, as well as administrative adjudication.

Special reasons, however, account for the swing away from the courts. For a half century there has been growing dissatisfaction with court procedure. Litigants are faced with exasperating delay due in part to crowded dockets, in part to an excessive right of appeal to higher courts; they find the technical rules of evidence sometimes inappropriate and conducive to dispute among lawyers rather than to a just and early settlement; they are dubious about the value of the jury in many kinds of cases; and the cost of judicial action, including attorney's fees, sometimes reduces victory to a hollow success. Evidence of this dissatisfaction is spread throughout the legal literature; the growth of commercial arbitration, implying the partial abandonment of the court as an adjudicating authority in certain types of cases, is symptomatic.[1]

One set of reasons for preferring administrative adjudication is then to be found in the desire to avoid the delay, uncertainty, and cost of judicial trial. The task of reconstructing the judicial system to meet new demands for rapid decision in large-scale adjudication (as in workmen's compensation cases) was abandoned in favor of building up a secondary system of administrative adjudication.

Another important consideration was the desire to secure adjudication by a body of experts in the subject matter of litigation rather than by a body expert in the law. The character of the issues which began to appear before courts as the state extended its regulatory and controlling activities was novel, and in the traditional sense often not wholly legal in nature. What is the proper basis of valuation of a far-flung rail-

[1] Wesley A. Sturges, "Arbitration, Commercial," 2 *Encyclopaedia of the Social Sciences* 151-53 (1930).

road property? What is a fair return on investment? What is a reasonably safe factory? What is a proper minimum wage? When does public convenience and necessity require a permit for utility construction?

These and many other problems rose to perplex courts and administrators alike, but it seemed apparent that a better answer might be forthcoming if the problem were turned over to a body of men who were, or who might become experts in the field. This consideration weighed heavily in the movement to establish utility commissions in the states, and in the creation of such federal agencies as the Court of Customs and Patent Appeals, the Board of Tax Appeals, the Federal Trade Commission and the Securities and Exchange Commission.

Underlying these considerations was the desire to place authority for interpretation of general statements of law with a body able and willing to give weight to considerations of public policy. Early experience, and some recent experience as well, demonstrated that when courts were faced with the necessity of giving meaning to the broad generalizations common in much vital current legislation, they found that meaning in the maxims of the common law or in the precedents. The whole significance of the legislation, however, was to strike away from the conceptions of earlier generations and to make new law through which would breathe the spirit of new social aspirations. The courts faltered in this enterprise, and administrative adjudication arose to modify the attitudes of the courts.

Here is the deepest significance of the expansion of administrative adjudication in the last half century. It is recognized in these words of John Dickinson. "Under the old system of adjudication by courts of law alone, the process of adjudication went on within a separate cell or compartment, as it were, tightly closed off from the sphere of governmental action. There was thus made possible a single-minded attention to the individual rights of the parties immediately before the court, with only an accidental regard for the interests of the public at large, and with a disregard for the exigencies of social policy which has been congenial to the naive individualism embedded in the philosophy of our law. The introduction of administrative justice, on the other hand, with the resulting opportunity for policy and discretion to affect the determination of individual rights, is one of the ways in which the newer philosophy of social solidarity has been making its influence felt. It marks a recognition of the fact that in the determination of the rights of individuals, as well as in the conduct of governmental enterprises, the interests of the community as a whole ought to be consulted." [1]

Society has not changed, nevertheless, to the extent that old rights and

[1] *Op. cit.*, pp. 29-30.

liberties must yield completely to new forms of social intervention. These rights and liberties, too, represent an essential aspect of living together, and are not to be abandoned but only adjusted to new conditions. How much the forces making for change may be given precedence over the ancient rules is the never ending problem with which all institutions of government are concerned and to which all make their contribution.

The balance at any point of time is deeply affected by the extent to which administrative adjudication is subject to review by courts from which original jurisdiction has been removed. If the courts may try the case *de novo* on questions of fact as well as of law, older concepts of social adjustment may prevail. If judicial review is curtailed, or in exceptional cases eliminated, the door is open to the play of policy entertained by the administrative body, but with potential risk to old established private rights. Legislative bodies have sought in many ways to curtail judicial review; the courts have yielded reluctantly and in some cases have denied any restriction upon their authority to re-examine the work of administrative adjudicating agencies.[1]

[1] For further comments see ch. 37, "Judicial Control of Administrative Action."

Chapter Thirty-five

SANCTIONS

IN THE preceding discussion of methods of administrative action, occasional reference has been made to the penalties which non-compliance with law or official action entailed. It remains now to onsider more systematically the subject matter of sanctions, both ad-ninistrative and judicial.

In any settled community there exists a predisposition to obey the w, which in itself is one of the principal foundations of all administra-ive activity. This normal expectation of compliance and conformity reaks down only when the law pushes out far beyond the settled con-ictions of the people (as in the prohibition amendment), or when narked differences exist between opposing groups (as in employer-mployee labor relations), or when some irreconcilable or revolutionary novement appears. In the ordinary situations of life, obedience to law is ne normal reaction of the vast majority of the individuals in the com-nunity.

This pattern of behavior is supported by the moral authority of the tate and of its representatives: legislators, judges, and administrative of-cials. A decision by a recognized administrative authority carries veight in and of itself, whether it be a decision of an industrial com-nission awarding damages for a factory accident or the order of a po-ceman to "move on." Back of compliance may be a fear of the conse-uences of refusal to comply but not always or exclusively. Individuals re motivated by considerations of public convenience and usefulness in large area of conduct where guidance is enough to secure results.

. Nature of Sanctions

In other, less accepted areas of official action, mere guidance is inade-uate. Some means of compulsion, great or small, is required, either enerally or for the small minority of persistent law-breakers. To secure theoretically uniform compliance a complex network of sanctions xists, the great bulk of which involve judicial action in some form. In ome cases, however, the official may select and impose certain kinds of enalties, and very slowly the tendency is toward expanding this means of administrative pressure. It is the principal task of this chapter to inquire how far, by what methods and under what circumstances officials may impose sanctions without recourse to the courts.

A sanction is a means of enforcement; in formal terms "a conditional evil annexed to a law to produce obedience to that law." [1] The most common forms of sanction are fine and imprisonment; less common are forfeiture of goods or property, loss of citizenship, voting rights and the right to hold public office; and of growing frequency are the withdrawal of benefits generally provided by government, but subject to loss as a means of inducing compliance.

Historically sanctions were imposed by courts, and even today it is exceptional for administrative officials to be given power to enforce a sanction other than the withdrawal or refusal of a privilege or benefit conferred by government. In a few cases the penalty fixed by an official is final and beyond review by the courts; more frequently such action, while complete in itself, is followed by opportunity to secure judicial review and relief; and in some cases the action of the official has no binding effect until it has been embodied in a court order upon request of the official body. In the latter case judicial enforcement of sanctions alone is involved; in the others the administration imposes the penalties or determines the liability to penalty, at least in the first instance.

The sanctions or penalties themselves may be set specifically by law, permitting no discretion as to their weight. Or the penalty may be, and frequently is, set in terms of a minimum and a maximum. In this case it is usually the court which exercises discretion as to the exact punishment, but if the sanction involves the withholding of a benefit some administrative official may determine the exact weight of the penalty.

That there is a type of sanction extra-legal in nature is well recognized; some examples of legally noncoercive but persuasive administrative methods were suggested in an earlier chapter. Adverse publicity, handled by public officials for purposes laid down in law and public policy, is a type of sanction. Direct economic competition is another highly effective means of securing certain results; the objection of private producers to government competition is very strong and the threat of such competition may bring about substantial compliance with policy

2. Refusal or Withdrawal of Benefits

The principal means by which administrative pressure produces results, especially on a large scale, lies in the capacity of officials to refuse or to withdraw benefits. Exclusion from valuable benefits which others enjoy is a weapon the effectiveness of which in securing conformity

[1] 56 *Corpus Juris* 125.

varies with the benefit in question. It has become, and doubtless will continue to be, one of the major administrative sanctions. Some examples follow.

Exclusion from the use of the mails in certain cases is a long-standing instance of the withdrawal of a privilege or service. The power to bar in cases of fraud and to prevent the circulation of obscene and objectionable matter is vested in the Postmaster General. The long battle over birth control centered on the right to send birth-control literature through the post office.

Exclusion from public employment through open competitive examinations for certain offenses, by order of a civil service commission, is designed both to protect the public service against an undesirable type of employee and also to protect the integrity of the examinations.

A new phase of this sanction is found in the Walsh-Healey Act excluding certain concerns from bidding on public contracts. These manufacturers may continue employment practices which are thought undesirable but which are beyond the direct authority of the federal government; but if they do so, the privilege of bidding for lucrative government contracts is withdrawn.

In administering workmen's compensation acts the power to withdraw benefits is used as a subsidiary means of enforcement. Thus in New York, failure of a workman to submit to a physical examination may result in reduction or suspension of payments, the purpose being to ensure such examinations. In the state of Washington, the industrial commission may suspend compensation if a worker indulges in unhealthful habits retarding recovery.

The prevention of fraud or deception in quite a different field but by the same method is illustrated in the Frazier-Lemke Farm-Mortgage Act. A farmer guilty of fraud in applying for the time extension benefits of the act was penalized by losing this benefit and thus becoming immediately liable to suit for his debts.

The most extensive and by all means the most spectacular application of this administrative sanction was developed in connection with the program of the Agricultural Adjustment Administration. In bare essence, a nation-wide program of crop control was made to pivot on contracts entered into between individual farmers and the Secretary of Agriculture, governing the number of acres of certain crops to be grown by the farmer. Millions of such contracts were executed. In return for agreement to reduce acreage, the Secretary of Agriculture undertook to make certain payments, conditioned on the fulfillment of the contract. Withdrawal of these benefits was the principal sanction for noncompliance; judicial intervention either to compel performance, or to award damages, or to impose a fine would have been obviously im possible on the huge scale of A.A.A. operations.

The National Industrial Recovery Act envisaged both administrativ and legal sanctions. The principal pressure to secure compliance, whicl for a year was disastrously neglected, came through administrativ means, the withdrawal of the use of the Blue Eagle. By this procedure popular boycott of "chiselers" was sought. Throughout the short his tory of N.R.A., the inadequacy of the legal staff was so great that a sys tem of "selective justice" was developed by means of which a few vio lators were selected for prosecution as examples, with no pretense o prosecuting other cases of similar nature but in the hope of creating psychological state of fear conducive to compliance.[1] In fact chroni violators operated with impunity, and the prestige of the N.R.A., th code authorities, and even the government suffered in consequence.

The possibilities of finding sanctions in administrative power to with hold or to withdraw benefits are still relatively unexplored. In all case where large numbers of individuals are involved, as for example in labo controversies with employers, this technique may be found the onl useful one. Old forms of coercion such as fine and imprisonment fai when five thousand or fifty thousand employees are involved. The ex treme difficulty of law enforcement in case of wrongful seizure of prop erty in a sit-down strike illustrates the perplexing problems which en forcement agencies, whether judicial or administrative, may encounter Tear-gas bombs and revolvers, called into play by the police at th Republic Steel Strike in Chicago, are not a method of mass law enforce ment which the people will tolerate.

3. Denial or Revocation of License

In some ways the refusal to grant a license or the suspension or revo cation of a license is equivalent to the withdrawal of a benefit. In ever instance where administrative action hinges on a license or permit, th normal sanction is refusal to grant or to renew, or suspension or revoca tion of the license.

In most cases some form of judicial review of these penalties is pro vided, in view of their severity. In the case of the licensed profession the revocation of a license bars one from his means of livelihood and i surrounded by guarantees more rigid than in the revocation of a permi to hang an awning over a sidewalk.

Where large property values have become vested as a result of licens the power to revoke may be denied to the administrative body whic

[1] Leverett S. Lyon and others, *The National Recovery Administration* (1935 pp. 267-68.

ranted the license and vested exclusively in the courts. This is the case or instance in the revocation of water power licenses issued by the 'ederal Power Commission. Frequently, however, the authority to susend or revoke a license is an administrative power, complete in itself ut subject to review by a court.

Broad licensing powers over interstate industries were vested in the 'resident by the National Industrial Recovery Act but were not actully invoked. Commenting on the lack of safeguards in this instance, the pecial Committee on Administrative Law of the American Bar Assoiation observed, "This, in essence, is tantamount to delegating power ɔ determine what kind of punishment shall be inflicted for violation of ıe law or regulations, in addition to the penalties provided by Congress. 'o subject a business to a license system is to subject each individual ngaged in that business to the temporary or permanent loss of the right ɔ continue in that business as a punishment for violation of the law or a egulation. There is no more drastic kind of punishment. . . ." Federal ıcorporation of interstate businesses would open up opportunities for dministrative regulation analogous to those inherent in license.

Summary Action by Administrative Officials

In a number of exceptional cases, officials are authorized to employ ımmary powers, i.e., "administrative power to apply compulsion or ɔrce against person or property to effectuate a legal purpose, without a ıdicial warrant to authorize such action."[1] Freund points out that in nglo-American jurisdiction such a power constitutes an anomaly, ince normally the way to compulsion leads through the courts." A ımmary power leaves no room for disobedience, but at most for resistıce. In these cases, the administrative officer applies immediately and irectly the sanctions which normally come into play only subsequent a court order. His action may be and usually is subiect to later judial control.

The state reserves summary powers to enforce the collection of reveıe. The general rule laid upon the taxpayer is, pay first and contest ter. The usual provision is for the sale of the delinquent's property by lministrative process; this is especially effective in the collection of unıid customs dues since imported merchandise automatically passes into ıe hands of the customs officers.

Quarantine of persons or property as a protection against the spread disease prevents another analogous case. Here the individual is put ıder restraint for a period of time, and in case of necessity may be re-

[1] Ernst Freund, *Administrative Powers over Persons and Property* (1928), p. 196. ıis section is based on chapter ten of Freund's work.

moved against his will to a hospital for contagious diseases. The federal government may impose a quarantine on the movement of animals or plants in interstate or foreign commerce; the states have corresponding power within their borders. As an incident to the power to quarantine there develops a power to inspect.

The protection of the public health is so important a subject of state intervention that it supports summary powers in a number of instances. Thus under the Federal Meat Inspection Act carcasses or meat preparations which the inspectors condemn are required to be destroyed in the presence of the inspector. On the other hand, unwholesome canned goods can be destroyed only on the basis of a court order.

The New York Farms and Markets Law illustrates summary action by state officials in this field. The commissioner may destroy animals or carcasses affected with communicable disease; he may seize and destroy any article of food in cold storage found to be unfit for human consumption; and he may deal as he deems necessary with diseased nursery stock.[1] Unlicensed dogs may be killed and false weights and measures may be destroyed. Summary powers are also granted in the enforcement of the New York Conservation Law.

Power to take over property provisionally is found in some instances illustrated by the law governing banks and insurance companies. Under the banking laws of New York, the superintendent of banking may take possession of the business or property of a bank or banker where a bank is unsafely conducted, and also where there is mere noncompliance with the orders of the superintendent. This, comments Freund, is "certainly a large power" in view of the probably disastrous effect upon the credit of the bank.[2]

On the other hand, the New York superintendent of insurance must go to the courts for an order to take over an insurance company. Patterson found that court intervention, at least in some instances, was a mere formality—"it seems tolerably clear that the court used a rubber stamp in approving the superintendent's findings."[3] The possibility of more effective judicial supervision at this point nevertheless exists.

Summary powers exist in connection with the movements of ships. A ship cannot move in international commerce without the papers re

[1] Freund, *op. cit.*, pp. 205-6.

[2] Cf. the authority vested in a police officer of New Orleans to impound an automobile parked in violation of the traffic ordinance and to hold for payment of three dollars, sustained in 173 La. 275 (1931). In the words of a commentator "Here the decision of an inferior administrative officer, a policeman, is final and binding." The Louisiana Supreme Court, however, recognized the owner's right to sue to recover the three dollars.

[3] Edwin W. Patterson, *The Insurance Commissioner in the United States* (1927), p. 440.

quired by general usage. When a ship enters a port these papers are delivered to the port officer and returned upon departure, which constitutes the clearance of the ship. Under an act of 1891 meat destined for export must have its condition certified before the vessel can get its clearance; and in 1908 this provision was extended to butter. The Immigration Law authorizes the withholding of clearance papers as a means of compelling the payment of a fine by a steamship company which brings an alien afflicted with a disease which could have been detected at the port of embarkation. This procedure was sustained by the Supreme Court.[1] Early Massachusetts legislation setting standards for exports occasionally provided fines upon masters of vessels for accepting unbranded or noninspected goods, but did not go so far as to prevent the sailing of the ship.

In rare instances forfeiture of property may be imposed by administrative action. The leading case involved the forfeiture and destruction of certain nets illegally used for fishing in New York. The Supreme Court of the United States sustained this administrative action.[2] Similar authority is sometimes vested to warrant the seizure and destruction of gambling devices, such as slot machines.

Recent examples of administrative power to seize property illegally held or used include contraband drugs (Narcotic Drugs Act, 1926);[3] hoarded gold and silver (Gold Reserve Act, 1934; Silver Purchase Act, 1934); contraband oil shipped in interstate commerce (Petroleum Act, 1935); and liquor illegally possessed (Liquor Law Repeal and Enforcement Act, 1935). In some of these cases, the power to seize is applied to property not harmful in itself, an extension of a drastic power into a somewhat novel area.

Administrative power over aliens is greater than that over citizens in view of the plenary power of the federal government to grant or refuse admittance. It has been held that the exclusion of an alien seeking admission may be determined by administrative order. Likewise the deportation of an alien who illegally entered or who under the law becomes subject to deportation may be ordered by the Department of Labor. In the decision of a well-known case which has since been somewhat modified, the Supreme Court even held that the issue of citizenship claimed by one seeking entrance to the country could be finally determined by

[1] *Oceanic Steam Navigation Company vs. Stranahan*, 214 U. S. 320 (1909).

[2] *Lawton vs. Steele*, 152 U. S. 133 (1894).

[3] 44 Stat. 635, 636 (1926). "Any narcotic drug . . . imported into the United States . . . contrary to law shall . . . be seized and summarily forfeited to the U. S. Government without necessity of instituting forfeiture proceedings of any character or without regard to its value."

administrative decision.[1] An alien who is denied a visa by a consul ha: no legal redress; only diplomatic channels are open to him.

In general, administrative officials are denied authority to impose fines This penalty is normally reserved exclusively to the courts.[2] An excep- tion may be noted in the alien immigrant case cited above. Here th liability to the fine, the amount of which was fixed by statute, wa finally determined by the Secretary of Labor.

Another more important exception is found in a number of adminis trative tribunals created by state constitutions and empowered thereb to fix penalties and commit to prison.[3] Thus, for example, the Californi Railroad Commission (Constitution, Art. XII, sec. 22) "shall have th power to administer oaths, take testimony, and punish for contempt i the same manner and to the same extent as courts of record." Hynema cites other examples, and gives a substantial list of administrative fine actually imposed.

Apart from such exceptional constitutional bodies, administrativ agents do not possess and cannot exercise the power to punish for con tempt. At this point they must go to a court and request judicial aid.

In some cases, therefore, officials have power to impose sanctions o varying degrees of severity. Characteristically they take the form o granting or withholding a benefit or privilege as provided by law. In ex ceptional cases, a penalty may be imposed summarily, with or withou eventual judicial review. As a rule, however, the administrator occupie a secondary place in imposing sanctions. Contrary to the opinion hel by some alarmists, he is no Jove choosing one thunderbolt or another t hurl into a contumacious people. In case of resistance to his authorit he often finds himself helpless until a court has come to his assistanc validated his action, and supplied the missing power of compulsion. Th "new despotism" is much less despotic than some would have us believ Moreover, if the official takes summary action and a jury later conclud that he made a mistake, he is usually personally liable in damages. Her is one reason why, for example, more substandard houses are not de molished under order of a housing inspector.

5. Judicial Enforcement

We are consequently led to inquire what ultimate means of compu sion the official may secure with the aid of the courts, and what role th courts play as law enforcers.

[1] *U. S. vs. Ju Toy*, 198 U. S. 253 (1905).

[2] See *Interstate Commerce Commission vs. Brimson*, 154 U. S. 447, 485 (1894 and discussion and citations in Charles S. Hyneman, "Administrative Adjudicatio An Analysis," 51 *Pol. Sci. Q.* 383-417, 516-37 (1936).

[3] Hyneman, *ibid.*, pp. 391-93.

All legislation, with rare exceptions, carries a sanction expressed usually in the form of a fine or a term of imprisonment for violation. It is the special duty of the court to sentence offenders in accordance with the scale of penalties. Where adverse private rights are involved, the court may be brought into action as a result of a civil suit with no administrative action in the premises. Where public considerations are involved, administrative officials may initiate action which requires the court to consider what penalty, if any, is appropriate. Where resistance to official orders occurs, the eventual sanction to compel obedience is usually found in the subsequent action of a court.

The scale of operations in imposing fines or imprisonment is very large. Thus the enforcement of the New York anti-noise ordinance in 1937 alone involved 15,411 arrests, 14,647 fines or forfeitures of bonds, and 81 imprisonments or committals to a hospital for the insane.

In addition to the statutory penalties of fine and imprisonment, the court may through its equity powers or by statutory authority issue its order for specific fulfillment. In such a case, an administrative order is often repeated or modified as a court order. Resistance then becomes contempt of court, which may be punished summarily by fine or by imprisonment as directed by the judge.

In the vast majority of cases where resistance to administrative orders or requirements develops, compliance can be secured only by means of these judicial sanctions. The mere order of the court confirming administrative action is usually sufficient; in only a small proportion of the cases is it necessary to force an unwilling individual to obey by taking his property in the shape of a fine, or by depriving him of his liberty of movement.

The order of the court imposing sentence is executed by another set of administrative officials, the United States marshal, the sheriff, the superintendent of prisons, and their subordinates. They, however, are executing judicial, not administrative orders. Normally, an official charged with the enforcement of the law cannot issue a writ to the sheriff to arrest and detain a person, or to seize and sell property. This type of sanction is reserved to the courts.

One further case requires mention. Mass resistance to a court order may require a heavy demonstration of force by the police (Fansteel Company strike in Chicago, 1937), by deputy sheriffs, or in the last instance by the armed forces of the state or the United States. Since the Whiskey Rebellion of 1793 there has been no doubt concerning the capacity of the federal government to enforce the orders of its officials and courts, and rare reminders such as the use of armed forces in the Pullman strike of 1894 are nevertheless frequent enough to demonstrate the ultimate sanctions which lie behind the acts of the governing power.

6. Administrative Discretion in Application of Sanctions

The formal distribution of power to impose sanctions between the administration and the courts thus ascribes by far the greater share to the latter. In all cases, however, where the courts are called into action as a result of preliminary administrative decision, a wide range of discretion remains with the official group. Such cases are numerous and significant; they include all criminal prosecutions, and practically all instances of state regulatory activity. The decision to prosecute, the form of the action, the time, the parties, the presentation of the evidence, and sometimes the choice of the court are in the discretion of the administrative official or authority.

These are powers of great dimensions which in fact go far to make the acts and decisions of officials as important as the work of the courts in law enforcement. It is well known that some officials use their powers with energy and skill, while others are mere shadows.

That indifference on the part of prosecuting officials may amount to nullification is suggested by a recent inquiry.[1] Wallace discovered that "the practice of nullification by administrative officers acting either on their own volition or under the pressure of local public opinion is a widespread and seemingly accepted process of government. . . ." Illustrative instances are cases of juvenile delinquency, in which the prosecuting attorney endeavors to salvage the delinquent rather than to punish him; cases in which juries will not convict; cases involving speed laws, blue laws and other obsolete measures; laws dealing with sex offenses; and antigambling laws.

Unwillingness to demand the application of sanctions proceeds from several impulses: the desire to conform to local public opinion; the desire to avoid waste of time where jury acquittal is believed certain; the belief that a conviction would produce injustice rather than justice; and the intent to secure better social results through administrative discretion than through the strict enforcement of the law.

In such cases and to a lesser degree in many other cases, it is the decision of administrative officials in the preliminary stages of enforcement which is in fact determinative of whether any sanctions shall be imposed

7. Conclusion

By a long sequence we are thus led from the relatively mild noncoercive forms of administrative action in law enforcement to the ulti-

[1] Schuyler C. Wallace, "Nullification, a Process of Government," 45 *Pol. Sci. Q* 347-58 (1930).

mate use of unadulterated force. A healthy social and governmental order depends almost entirely upon the moderate and restrained employment of the orderly processes of administrative and judicial action resting upon sanctions other than actual force, although they may perhaps be coercive in effect.

The number of daily instances in which more than three million public officials and employees come into contact with over 130,000,000 citizens passes all calculation. In the vast proportion of cases the moral authority of officials and the habit of obedience of citizens avoid the necessity for any formal sanction for administrative action. In a very real sense, the American people are operating a system of self-government.

Where, however, large property interests are involved, where the requirements of law are not widely accepted, where social tension is at a high level, and where individuals of a lawless nature are concerned, the sanctions of law assume a greater role. It remains primarily the function of the courts to impose penalties, the function of the administration to request the aid of the courts where necessary and to carry out the order of the court when the judge has spoken. In exceptional cases, the administrator may apply the sanction by his own authority; the modern form of granting or withholding a benefit constitutes the bulk of these.

The discovery of effective sanctions and their use is a far more perplexing problem now than in the days when this country was concerned chiefly with agriculture, fishing, and village store trading. Fines and imprisonment were enough then; they are far from adequate today in securing compliance from great corporations and from organized workers. We may face greater difficulties in the whole realm of law enforcement than are now apparent; it may well be that administrative action in granting or withholding benefits will become a more widely used method of securing compliance than it has been in the past. To the extent that this happens, the center of gravity of the compliance system will tend toward the executive branch.

PART VI

THE SYSTEM OF RESPONSIBILITY

Chapter Thirty-six

ADMINISTRATIVE RESPONSIBILITY

1. Forms of Responsibility and Trends

Government officials have always been subject to some form of responsibility. When Frederick the Great threatened a provincial tax collector with imprisonment if he collected one *thaler* more than was authorized, he spoke with an authority which left no doubt where the responsibility of the subordinate was due. With the gradual evolution of government the simple, direct and uncontestable system of responsibility which Frederick the Great enforced has become much more complex, but modern systems still reach back into the era of absolute kings and the formative period of the common law.[1]

Historically the direct responsibility of officials to a ruling king, who could and sometimes did lay heavy hands on his court assistants, was the most conspicuous form. Its modern counterpart is the disciplinary and directing authority vested in the chief executive and department heads. Nearly as ancient is the responsibility of officials to courts for action violating the rights of individuals. Courts still use the ancient writs, as well as more modern means of control. A new type of responsibility to a representative, legislative body was implicit in the English Revolution of 1688 and was formulated by Walpole in the institution of cabinet government. Under the American plan of an independent executive, the responsibility of officials to legislative bodies took a different form. In the United States of the last century, direct official responsibility to the electorate was pushed to an unusual degree, and still is widespread. Finally in the twentieth century we may observe a form of professional responsibility which, although outside the law, is probably destined to play an important part in the future.[2]

We have already used the term, system of responsibility. What does it mean? A system of responsibility is the sum total of the constitutional, statutory, administrative and juridical rules and precedents and the established practices by means of which public officials may be held ac-

[1] See John M. Gaus, "The Responsibility of Public Administration," in J. M. Gaus, L. D. White, and M. E. Dimock, *The Frontiers of Public Administration* (1936).

[2] See ch. 27, *supra*.

countable for their official actions. While the object in view is broadly the same in all jurisdictions, the means employed may vary considerably especially in the emphasis given to the different parts.

The administrative means by which internal responsibility is secured have been described in earlier pages.[1] We have now to consider the means of control external to the whole administrative and executive organization. In the United States, these are principally three: control by the electorate, by the legislature, and by the courts. The extent to which responsibility is enforced and the methods which are selected for this purpose reflect a shifting balance between the claims of officials for discretion, initiative, and authority on the one hand, and on the other the claims of citizens to be protected in their rights.

Quite obviously the trend of the last half century has inclined toward greater official discretion and authority. As a people we have assented to more official action and to less external control of such action, in the belief that the public interest would be thus advantaged. At the same time there has never been a cessation of the demand for responsibility which would be coextensive with the authority vested in the executive branch. The attitudes of legislative bodies and courts have swayed now this way now that, under the pressure of opposing forces.

The consolidation of administrative power in the hands of the chief executive, the ever widening range of governmental action, the broad delegation of discretionary power to commissions, the increasing impact of government upon personal and business relations, and the concern widely felt for democratic institutions in the light of contemporary events, all suggest the need for a truly effective scheme of responsibility. To maintain such a system, which at the same time will permit energetic fulfillment of public policy, is one of the major long-range problems of the future.

2. Administrative Responsibility to Citizens

"The contribution of the United States to the idea of responsibility in administration was made by requiring the chief executive—and later many minor executives—to submit directly or indirectly to popular vote."[2] Traditionally the American system of self-government united people and officials in an intimate union. The voters elected officials, high and low, far and wide, and elected them for the space of a year, two years at the most. Bureaucracy was submerged beneath a flood of ballots. The people were set on guard to protect their firesides from the real and imagined dangers of an office-holding class. As late as 1918 a well-known Democrat

[1] See chs. 4-7.

[2] Gaus, *op. cit.*, p. 30.

newspaper of Boston, opposing a constitutional amendment to extend the governor's term to two years, took up the famous dictum of Samuel Adams, "where annual elections end, tyranny begins."

Present-day administrative necessities may cause us to disagree with Adams' slogan, but the spirit it reflects has had a profound influence on our administrative system. Professor Charles E. Merriam calculates that about three-quarters of a million public officials still hold their mandate directly from the people. And although the theory of popular control by elections has suffered in the twentieth century, it still counts heavily in state and local governments.

The administrative consequences of direct election of nonpolicy-forming officials were to secure hardly more than an intermittent responsibility which was offset by a fatal dispersion of authority. On the other hand, the abandonment of popular election of officials leads directly to an integrated administration since the power of appointment (and thereby the rule of subordination) replaces popular election and official independence. But integration implies concentration of power, which in turn necessitates the amplification of control. Can this dilemma be solved and the public still retain any part in the relationship of the public powers?

Reliance upon annual or biennial elections to eliminate executives who prove incompetent or untrustworthy has been only partially successful. The trouble lies in the patent fact that the American voter seldom selects his mayor, governor, or president because he has administrative skill, but rather because he has an attractive program. The administrative issue can seldom be so focused that the voters have a clear-cut opportunity to declare for or against efficiency and honesty; where the issue is clear there is no reason to doubt their customary preference for good government. Elections alone, however, are not an adequate means of administrative control, either in finding or in dismissing our governors, high and low.

Some advocates of the traditional American democracy find a solution by shifting the emphasis from elections to recall. But the recall has been used and is likely to be used primarily to control policy rather than to dictate efficiency.[1] It hardly appears feasible to expect it to operate effectively as a means for settling administrative problems. Such issues are highly complicated, technical, usually without general or dramatic interest and ordinarily wholly unsuited for popular decision. Then too the issue can hardly be kept out of politics, the influence of which is

[1] Frederick L. Bird and Frances M. Ryan, *The Recall of Public Officers* (1930). Note the recall of the mayor of Los Angeles in 1938 as a result of the exposure of corruption in the city government.

already too great in administration. In Dayton and in some other manager cities, the city manager may be recalled by popular vote. In view of the position assigned to this official, his part in formulating policy does not seem extensive enough to necessitate such a degree of control, which is proper enough for the commission.

The initiative and referendum are other means of expressing public opinion on occasional issues of administration.[1] For the most part voters are not so well qualified to make a decision on purely administrative problems as is the legislature and in many cases both should yield to the judgment of the executive.

From one point of view the grand jury and trial jury are a means through which the public may make its influence felt in law enforcement. In the last analysis officials have to ask for convictions before the courts, and juries often determine guilt or innocence. The enforcement of unpopular laws is sometimes made impossible because of the unwillingness of juries to convict even in the face of unimpeachable evidence. An extreme example is found in the jury record in some states on liquor law violations during the prohibition era.[2]

"The most doubtful and difficult question connected with the administrative organization of a progressive democracy concerns its ability to obtain and to keep popular confidence. Democracies have almost uniformly distrusted administrative officials who tend to escape direct popular control." [3] The difficulty of maintaining wholesome contacts increases with the expansion of administrative work, the growth in the size of the organization, and the undertaking of activities in controversial fields. Croly advocated better education of the American democracy in order to help close the gap between the expert and the people. The experts, too, have a real obligation to familiarize the people with their work. Democratic administration must rest on a substantial degree of consent among the public. Officials are entitled to assume a certain degree of consent from the mere fact of the enactment of the statute which they are called upon to enforce; but it is also a part of their daily task to consolidate public support.

[1] Coker refers to Ohio initiated bills dealing with the regulation of the placing, use, etc., of electric poles, wires, etc.; creating a state board of drugless practice; regulating the practice of dentistry; creating a tax code commission; consolidating certain departments. See Francis W. Coker, "Interworkings of State Administration and Direct Legislation," 64 *Annals* 122-33 (1916).

[2] On Oct. 31, 1938, a Chicago jury acquitted a defendant accused of operating a handbook despite unimpeachable evidence of violation of the law. The defendant's attorney argued that the people did not want the law enforced and asserted, "It was never intended that the gambling law be enforced." The case was reported in the *Chicago Daily News*, Nov. 1, 1938.

[3] Herbert D. Croly, *Progressive Democracy* (1914), p. 371.

While these forms of direct control by voters and citizens are an essential part of our system of government, they are not the means by which an extensive and in some respects powerful bureaucracy can be adequately restrained. We must agree with John Gaus that "this form of responsibility is, nevertheless, very general and, on the whole, clumsy unless other forms of responsibility are developed whereby the ultimate responsibility of the great mass of public servants to the state as a whole can be made vivid and effective." [1]

This conclusion rests on a view of citizen control in which the citizen acts as a voting unit rather than in organized groups. His influence may be quite as great, in particular cases, when he acts through some organized interest group, not as a voter but as a pressure agency. Such groups are beyond counting; they are becoming the normal means by which citizens bring their influence to bear upon the special parts of administration which concern them.

Usually these groups represent an economic interest. The United States Chamber of Commerce is one of the means by which citizens engaged in business bring influence to bear upon public policy and its administration in the field of production, transportation, banking, foreign trade and the like.[2] The American Federation of Labor and the Committee for Industrial Organization represent citizens who work in the skilled and unskilled occupations in bringing pressure to bear on public policy and its administration where wage-earners are concerned: minimum wages and maximum hours, inspection of factories, prevention of occupational diseases, protection against employer interference in labor councils. The American Farm Bureau Federation links up the scattered farmers of the country to secure government aid in improving agriculture and in adjusting production to consumption. The influence which such national associations of economic groups bring to bear upon officials is as great, and more realistic than the influence of citizens as voters.[3]

There are other organizations which play a part, also, both in policy making and in administration. In recent years the National League of Women Voters has exerted a great influence toward the improvement of the public service, both by urging the extension of the merit system and by insisting upon its proper administration. The National Consumers' League has done much to support good administration of labor laws. Organizations of technicians themselves bring influence upon

[1] Gaus, *op. cit.*, p. 33.

[2] Harwood L. Childs, *Labor and Capital in National Politics* (1930).

[3] E. Pendleton Herring, *Public Administration and the Public Interest* (1936), *passim.*

department heads and chief executives to stand by good administration. On the other hand, local political organizations in town and country sometimes work in the opposite direction.

Citizens also are effective, in widely varying degrees to be sure, as members of advisory committees. We lack a systematic survey of contemporary experience with these committees, but there is some indication that they are becoming more significant as government takes a more prominent place in social administration.[1]

Officials thus stand in the midst of scores of conflicting, competing, cooperating, overlapping, commandeering groups whose efforts to "guide" administrators are never ending. They are perhaps more significant as means of citizen control than the formal means of citizen action through the ballot box. For as Gaus points out, "In a state in which the powers of government intermesh widely with those of industry, commerce, and finance the traditional restraints upon the discretion of the administrator through making him responsible to the electorate, the courts, and the legislators are inadequate. The injurious policy or action is taken long before review can attempt to undo the damage. It is only by having the interest which might be injured present and on the spot when the policy is determined and the action taken that substantial justice can be secured." [2]

3. Administrative Responsibility to Legislative Bodies

While the doctrine of separation of powers is accepted in the state and national governments, it is inevitable that each of the three branches of government should have contacts with the other.[3] Robert Luce, the

[1] John A. Fairlie, "Advisory Committees in British Administration," 20 *Am. Pol. Sci. Rev.* 812-22 (1926); W. Brooke Graves, "Citizen Participation in the Governments of Reorganized States," 16 *Social Forces* 492-502 (1937-38).

[2] Gaus, *op. cit.*, pp. 37-38.

[3] W. F. Willoughby describes the legislature in terms of a board of directors of a private corporation (*Principles of Public Administration* [1927], ch. 3). While the analogy has considerable validity, it is subject to important qualifications. The principal difference lies in the fact that while all the powers of the corporation are vested in its board of directors, the whole executive power in the national, state and many city governments is constitutionally vested in the chief executive. The practical operating differences between a board of directors of restricted numbers and a legislative body of two branches with two, three or four hundred members are also significant. The position of the board of directors toward the management and staff of a corporation and that of a legislative body vis-à-vis an independent chief executive and the departments are also different in quality, if not in kind. Legislators are subject to a degree of pressure from their constituents for jobs which is far greater than that experienced by business directors, and they have fewer means of resistance. While, therefore, the analogy is an interesting one, it is not exact.

In his *Principles of Legislative Organization and Administration* (1934), chs. 10-13, and elsewhere, Willoughby emphasizes the distinction between the executive distinguished Congressman from Massachusetts, is within the pure tradition of the theory of separation of powers when he takes the view that "the sole and legitimate function of Congress is to legislate–to make genuine laws." But Lindsay Rogers and other commentators are closer to the facts when they assert that legislatures in modern constitutional governments possess three purposes–to legislate, to control expenditures, and to supervise the administration.[1]

A legislature has legitimate functions to perform with regard to administration; these involve the power to legislate, to appropriate and to supervise. It may properly undertake to fix the main lines of policy and to see that administrative policy is in harmony with legislative policy; to ensure the legality and propriety of expenditures; to be satisfied that internal administrative controls are operating to secure economy and efficiency; and to inform itself of the conditions of administration in view of remedial legislation. Farther than this it does not need, and is not qualified, to go.

Such supervision does not mean that the legislative body itself should administer, or lay down specific methods of doing business (apart from procedural rules designed to safeguard private rights), or prescribe the exact use of funds, or deal with specific cases. This kind of legislative control leads to interference in matters which are more competently handled elsewhere.[2]

The following paragraphs concern the legislative body as a controlling authority to which the chief executive and the administrative agencies owe responsibility. To keep the balance clear, we must remember

---

function and the administrative function. The former he finds constitutionally vested in the chief executive, the latter in the legislative branch. The legal status of the administrative services is therefore one of subordination to the legislature; and the chief executive, in matters of administration, is said to act merely as an agent of the legislative branch. I am not able to accept this position as a realistic account of the administrative position of the chief executive either in the national or state governments. It overlooks the constitutional power vested in the chief executive to see that the laws are enforced, to appoint, to remove, and the derived power to direct and to supervise. It exaggerates the role of the legislature as the central office of the administrative hierarchy. Goodnow writes on this point, "The effect of recognizing that the President possesses these powers of removal and direction has been . . . to give him the administrative power and to make him . . . the head of its administrative system." (*The Principles of the Administrative Law of the United States* [1905], pp. 81-82.) Willoughby's analogies have closest application in the council manager cities.

[1] Lindsay Rogers, *The American Senate* (1926), p. 192; Marshall E. Dimock, *Congressional Investigating Committees* (1929).

[2] On this whole topic, see John A. Fairlie, "The Legislature and the Administration," 30 *Am. Pol. Sci. Rev.* 241-56, 494-506 (1936). Underlying all aspects of administrative control are the financial records and reports emanating from official bodies. Some aspects of the reporting problem are dealt with in ch. 30.

that the chief executive has considerable constitutional authority over the legislature, especially through the veto power, and much actual influence arising from his control of patronage and his prominent political situation. We must recall also that while the legislature has a wide range of control, it is becoming more and more dependent on administrative officials for assistance in the business of legislation itself.[1] While, therefore, in the intent of the constitution the legislative branch is primary, in the actual operation of our governing institutions leadership has often been, and now is usually found in the chief executive and his official subordinates.

a. Control of administrative policy. The major lines of policy are in the statutes, but the general and occasionally vague terms in which legislation is drafted leave constantly more room for substantive administrative policy.[2] Such lines of action are always subject to the overriding authority of the legislative body which by further legislation may amend, repeal, or confirm the rules and regulations of the administration. The legislature may order the administration to perform certain tasks, may impose certain methods, may overrule administrative programs, or even compel it to abandon established procedures. Control through legislation has been considerably relaxed in the last two decades by the "notable development" of permissive laws. Much "New Deal" legislation illustrates this trend.

At the same time much legislation is so specific and limited that it amounts to orders of individual application, with none of the guarantees of uniformity and technical competence which are usually characteristic of administrative action. A few examples from the laws of Massachusetts of 1937 will make the point clear.[3] Thus the office of the chief of police of Tewksbury was placed under the civil service laws (c. 2). The school committee of Dalton was authorized (c. 6) to retire a physically incapacitated janitor. The salary of the justice of the district court of Dukes County was fixed by law (c. 294). The city of Boston was authorized to refund to Dooley Bros., Inc., its deposit for a certain garbage removal contract (c. 222). The city of Lynn was authorized to pay an annuity to the widow of Roger Dwyer (c. 193).

The relative extent of legislation which is concerned with administrative matters is revealed by Dodd's analysis of the output of the Illinois

[1] Edwin E. Witte, "The Preparation of Proposed Legislative Measures by Administrative Departments," in President's Committee on Administrative Management, *Report with Special Studies* (1937), pp. 361-78.

[2] See ch. 33, *supra.*

[3] See the first edition of this book, pp. 427-28, for similar Massachusetts cases in 1924.

General Assembly for 1917 and 1927. His results appear in the following table.[1]

TABLE XVII

CLASSIFICATION OF LAWS ENACTED BY THE ILLINOIS GENERAL ASSEMBLY, 1917 AND 1927

CLASS OF LEGISLATION	NUMBER	
	1917	1927
State appropriations	63	69
State administrative matters	150	125
Local administrative matters	108	209
Laws relating to private rights	17	43
TOTALS	338	446

b. Control of appropriations. Every authorization to spend must come from the legislative body. The form of appropriation determines the degree of control, both directly and later through the audit. A lump sum appropriation confers wide discretion in the use of funds, a segregated or itemized budget may reduce discretion to the vanishing point. The gross amount of the appropriation governs the extent of activity in each field. A common means of controlling policy is through drastic reductions or expansions of appropriated funds. Thus civil service commissions generally have been allowed quite inadequate funds, the effect being a feeble enforcement of the merit system. For many years Kansas has omitted any appropriation for the state civil service commission. In the Independent Office Appropriation Act for 1937–38, the allowance to the Central Statistical Board was cut in half, the Senate having voted to eliminate all funds whatever.

The appropriations committees of the House and the Senate play an extraordinarily important part in the actual contacts of administrative bodies and the Congress. Officials appear year after year before the subcommittees or the full committees to defend their estimates. Minority as well as majority members play an important and useful part in the discussion of the work, programs, methods, and personnel of each administrative unit. Many questions are put, criticisms are voiced, new and less expensive methods are suggested, and general policy is reviewed at this time. Some organizations meet a hostile committee, others a noncommittal one, still others a friendly group of Congressmen. In any case the contact is an important one, and deserves study and analysis. A parallel situation is found in the states and the large cities.

c. Audit. The audit is a legislative enterprise, an examination of the

[1] Walter F. Dodd, *State Government* (2d ed. 1928), p. 175.

use of appropriated funds to ascertain whether they have been used for the purposes approved by the legislature in the appropriation act. It is one of the principal historic means of holding public officials to account.[1]

Legislative bodies have not organized themselves effectively to consider and act upon the findings of an audit. In most state legislatures the auditor's report is filed, accepted and printed but little attention is given to it. The reports of the Comptroller General of the United States have been completed so tardily that effective action by Congress is difficult, if not impossible. Congressional committees on expenditures, which originated as early as 1814, are designed to follow up the course of expenditures but they have rarely operated effectively. By contrast the Committee on Expenditures of the British House of Commons does excellent work.

The development of a "hot-audit," i.e., an audit which is continuously in operation on current claims, and the preaudit has greatly increased the influence and power of the auditor. In the minds of some observers, the preaudit tends to replace the judgment and authority of the administrative officials in the use of funds by the decision of the legislative auditor, while others maintain that only by a preaudit can legislative control be effective. The weight of evidence suggests that the Comptroller General of the United States, at least, has extended his authority to such a point as to weaken administrative efficiency. On all sides, however, there is agreement that an audit by an official responsible to the legislature or independently elected by the voters is desirable, indeed essential.

d. Personnel. Policy-determining officials (heads of departments, members of commissions, and a few others) are usually appointed by the chief executive with the advice and consent of the Senate. Heavy pressure was exerted in 1936 and 1937 by patronage-minded Senators and Congressmen to increase the number of such officials, and a few raids on the permanent service were successful. In general it may be said that there is no clear consensus as to where the line should be drawn. The interests of good administration suggest senatorial consent only for officials who have determinative authority with respect to public policy.

Legislatures possess some authority to remove officials, either by impeachment or in rare cases by other means. As a method of control either of the chief executive or lesser officials, impeachment is not especially useful. It has been abused by excessive use in a few states like Oklahoma; in general its use is infrequent. It is much too elaborate and

[1] See *supra*, ch. 17, for an analysis of auditing.

complicated an instrument to have significance in other than highly exceptional cases.[1]

Under the doctrine of the Humphrey case, Congress may impose limitations upon presidential removal of a certain type of quasi judicial federal official.[2] The effect of this case in extending Congressional power over removals is still uncertain. The case of Dr. A. E. Morgan, one-time chairman of the Tennessee Valley Authority, is likely to become a *cause célèbre* on this point. In general the power of removal is one which cannot be properly exercised by legislative bodies, and correctly belongs to the chief executive.

To this rule an exception may be recognized in the council manager form of government. Here the city council has full authority to "hire and fire" the city manager, the operating executive. But even in these cities the general power of removal of subordinates is vested in the manager, not in the council.

The legislative body usually retains the authority to fix the scales of salaries and wages, to lay down the general conditions of employment, to set up standards of competence and an examination system for some or most of the staff. Here the organized civil service employees exert their influence upon legislative bodies. Here also are made the general decisions on salary levels and conditions of employment which go far to determine what kind of a public service is possible. This form of control is real and ubiquitous.

e. Legislative investigations. The legislature has an undoubted authority to investigate in view of future legislation.[3] A legislative investigation, or the mere threat of an investigation, has a far-reaching effect, and investigations are sufficiently numerous so that no sensible official fails to reckon with their possibility and to safeguard his official acts accordingly. The result is perhaps to secure regularity and caution rather than boldness and energy, but there can be no doubt that the possibility of an investigation is an element in controlling official action.

[1] For data on impeachment, see C. A. M. Ewing, "Impeachment of Oklahoma Governors," 24 *Am. Pol. Sci. Rev.* 648-52 (1930); Frank M. Stewart, "Impeachment in Texas," *ibid.*, 652-58; Lewis Mayers, "Impeachment," 7 *Encyclopaedia of the Social Sciences* 600-1 (1932).

[2] See *supra*, ch. 4.

[3] On this subject, consult Marshall E. Dimock, *Congressional Investigating Committees* (1929); Ernest J. Eberling, *Congressional Investigations* (1928); M. Nelson McGeary, "Congressional Investigations during Franklin D. Roosevelt's First Term," 31 *Am. Pol. Sci. Rev.* 680-94 (1937); James M. Landis, "Constitutional Limitations on the Congressional Power of Investigation," 40 *Harvard Law Rev.* 153-221 (1926–27); George B. Galloway, "The Investigative Function of Congress," 21 *Am. Pol. Sci. Rev.* 47-70 (1927); Samuel Seabury, O. C. Herwitz and W. G. Mulligan, Jr., "The Legislative Investigating Committee," 33 *Columbia Law Rev.* 1-27 (1933).

The frequency of legislative investigations suggests their importance as a means of control, although many inquiries are concerned wholly with future legislation. In 1929 Dimock pointed out that both the Treasury and Interior Departments had been investigated about 50 times. The Seventy-third and Seventy-fourth Congresses authorized or conducted 165 investigations, of which 104 were initiated by the Senate.[1] Fairlie reports that from 60 to 80 state legislative investigations have occurred during each biennial period since 1909.[2] In the single year 1931, no less than 237 state committees and commissions were authorized to sit and investigate.[3]

The usefulness of legislative inquiries has been challenged by some. They are sometimes inspired by political motives and are usually subject to attack for this reason, rightly or wrongly. Although committees of inquiry have power to subpoena witnesses and compel the production of papers, they are not always able to get at the facts for lack of competent counsel. They often waste time and get sidetracked on irrelevant or unimportant details. They are not bound by the technical rules of evidence, a fact which has both its advantages and its disadvantages.

Despite these limitations, the usefulness of legislative investigations is very substantial. They often uncover situations of great public importance and help to focus attention on the need for reform. They are useful in educating the members of the legislature. They are certainly a deterrent upon officials, restraining them from conduct to which they are pressed but which would not stand the light of day.[4]

New techniques of inquiry have emerged in recent years, which raise the question whether legislative inquiries with their more or less inevitable political connotations may not be less useful in the future. There are on the one hand investigations and studies by special commissions of inquiry appointed by the President, as for example the committees which completed the studies preparatory to the Social Security Act and the Reorganization Bill of 1938. On the other hand are such unofficial, or quasi official, inquiries as the President's Research Committee on Social Trends and the Commission of Inquiry on Public Service Personnel. While these are useful bodies, they can hardly replace the legislative in-

[1] McGeary, *op. cit.*, p. 680.

[2] John A. Fairlie, "The Legislature and the Administration," *loc. cit.*, p. 502.

[3] 5 *State Government* 12 (Feb. 1932).

[4] Among recent examples, we may note the Seabury investigations in New York, the La Follette investigations on civil liberties, the investigation of the Bureau of Air Commerce, and the investigation of the Tennessee Valley Authority; somewhat earlier the Teapot Dome investigation.

vestigating committees with their power of compulsion and their appropriateness for study of situations involving high social tension.[1]

f. The Wisconsin "interpellation." In 1915 Wisconsin established means of bringing appointive state officers before either the Senate or Assembly on petition of six members of the former and seventeen members of the latter body. Here they were made subject to oral or written questions on any aspect of their work, or the manner of their appointment, or any appointment made by them. This law has been put to use several times; within a decade the Tax Commission was required to furnish information regarding income taxes; the Industrial Commission was questioned concerning its budget, and the Railroad Commission was brought before the Assembly. In 1935 the State Board of Control was questioned on its appointments, on purchases and on paroles from the state penal institutions.

g. Direct administration by local legislative bodies. The theory of separation of powers as well as practical operating difficulties have been substantial barriers in the federal and state governments against the development of administration directly by the representative body. In the city and county governments, however, this constitutional difficulty has never existed and in the commission governed cities there has been a widespread trial of management by elected commissioners.[2]

The commission plan broke through the crust of the cumbersome and antiquated municipal government of the nineteenth century. It sought to secure political responsibility as well as administrative efficiency by placing the city's business in the hands of five or seven men. In some ways this form of organization was a distinct improvement over the traditional municipal government, but from the point of view of sound administration it raised serious difficulties. It forced the business of the city into five or seven departments which often resulted in an artificial allocation of functions. It placed the business operations of the city in the hands of men who were elected by popular vote, and who were frequently not skilled administrators. Provided such successful political leaders allowed their professional subordinates to administer the city departments no harm was done; but the temptation to "run" the city was often too strong to withstand. In small cities this lay administration may

[1] The U. S. Budget and Accounting Act of 1921 authorized the Comptroller General to make such investigations as directed by either House or by any committee having jurisdiction over revenue, appropriations, or expenditures. He was also authorized to make recommendations looking to greater economy or efficiency in public expenditures. This investigatory power has been employed only infrequently.

[2] Ernest S. Bradford, *Commission Government in American Cities* (1911).

operate with reasonable success, but in the larger cities it involves serious risks.

Commission governed cities have been badly handicapped by the lack of administrative unity. Each department became something like a sovereign state, all held together for conference by a council of ambassadors. The council not infrequently became a hotbed for intrigue and "secret diplomacy," with the minority well placed to defy any decisions which displeased them. So far as the decisions involving policy are concerned, a majority may prevail by mere force of numbers; but in effectuating policies, the minority of a city commission may block an approved program by refusing to administer it, or by endless delay and evasion. The means of compulsion available against a recalcitrant political group within a commission are limited in number and dangerous to use.

h. Informal controls and contacts. The foregoing are the principal formal controls of administration by legislative bodies as established by constitution and law. As in the case of other political institutions, mere knowledge of the control pattern which crystallized into legal form at some time more or less remote is not enough. The real life of administrative and political institutions is imperfectly revealed in their legal description; and in the subtle give and take of representatives and officials in their mutual dealings with each other, different patterns may emerge. Study of the newspaper columns, the stenographic reports of committee hearings, the debates on the floor of the House and Senate, the memoirs and autobiographies of statesmen, yields much significant material from which to construct a nicer analysis than can be made from the bare terms of constitutions and statutes. When we learn that Mr. Taft, then Secretary of War, was ordered from the floor of the House of Representatives by an angry Congressman and retorted that he would leave as soon as the Congressman ceased to wait on the War Office for appointments, we catch an exciting glimpse of things as they are. More recently the reduction of a high official's salary by $500 by the Senate Appropriations Committee on account of a disagreement over patronage reveals a form of legislative pressure which was not debated by the "founding fathers."

The experience of the last three decades indicates that the traditional roles of chief executive and legislature are being recast. President Wilson pointed out in one of his trenchant speeches that the American people were no longer content with an executive who was not ready to take an aggressive lead in public affairs. By a variety of means he and other executives have abundantly verified this prediction. The relative position of legislative and executive authorities is also being profoundly affected by the radio. The possibility of direct appeal to the country, which Wilson tried with tragic results in 1919, is now a reality of the first order. Franklin D. Roosevelt's "fireside chats" have exerted an unparalleled effect upon public opinion, an effect which neither house of Congress as a body nor any individual member can duplicate. The ultimate results of this new type of executive leadership on administrative "independence" are still to be felt.

From time to time in state and municipal governments the traditional control situation has been reversed, the chief executive dominating the legislative bodies by personal vigor, political prestige, and the command of patronage. Illinois suffered from such a combination from 1921 to 1929; New York benefited by an analogous situation under Governor Alfred E. Smith. Too often legislative bodies lack the men to give effective leadership which in many states seems to be passing to executive mansions.

A different situation develops when there arises a private political boss powerful enough to control both executive and legislature. The constitutional hypothesis then vanishes into thin air, while the wires are pulled from behind the scene. One need only recall Mr. Elihu Root's dramatic exclamation before the New York Convention of 1915. "Then Mr. Platt ruled the state; for nigh upon twenty years he ruled it. It was not the governor; it was not the legislature; it was not any elected officers; it was Mr. Platt. And the capitol was not here; it was at 49 Broadway; with Mr. Platt and his lieutenants." [1] Cases like this are now rare. The real leadership of the state lies in its organs of government, although in a few cities the actual system of responsibility leads back to an old-time boss.

A special problem of legislative control arises with respect to government corporations.[2] One of the principal reasons for their formation is to free them from the controls which have been built up around the departments, other than judicial. The purpose is to give greater scope for initiative, corporate control of capital and earnings, and freedom from the meticulous audit of funds which tends to make officials cautious and safe rather than enterprising. This is an understandable purpose and, so far as operating problems are concerned, one commanding sympathy. The difficulty has been that the relaxation of control in some cases has gone beyond the field of operations into the field of policy, so that we discover multipurpose government corporations with broad powers moving into fields of public activity which were never specifically or consciously approved by the major policy-forming organs of government. Neither Congress nor the President has been able to exert an effective check on such developments of public policy.

[1] Harold F. Gosnell, *Boss Platt and His New York Machine* (1924), p. 71; see also pp. 209-10.

[2] See *supra*, ch. 9.

The powers and functions of a government corporation can be specifically defined to the end that the limits of its power and authority are clearly set forth and hence not likely to be expanded or exceeded except by formal amendment. Incidentally the single-purpose corporation is clearly a safer instrument than the multiple-purpose corporation. Within such explicit definition of purpose and function, wide freedom may be given the corporate body in its operating methods subject to the general review which arises from the annual operating estimates, the annual report, the annual audit, and legislative consideration of the success or failure of the corporation in achieving the ends for which it was constituted.

To summarize this analysis, we may say that our constitutional structure presupposes a wide range of control of chief executives and of administrative subordinates by legislative bodies in the interest of official responsibility to popular representatives. Representative bodies are entitled to guide and control administration by legislation, appropriation, audit, impeachment, and investigation. These are wide powers, and in the history of legislative-executive relationships they have often been used for the particular case rather than for the general rule. Despite this and other faults, legislative influence upon administration remains one of the essential features of the democratic balance of power, through which Americans conduct their public business. It should be conserved, and adapted to new and changing exigencies.

4. Adaptation of Administrative Responsibility to Legislative Bodies

Like all human relationships the legislative-administrative connection changes from time to time as new needs or new emphases appear. The basic idea of administrative responsibility to representative assemblies is an essential part of the American democratic regime. It will be retained so long as our existing institutions endure, but it may be better adjusted to its broad ends while at the same time better fitted to the needs of effective administration. Some possible lines of development are suggested.

(1) Legislative bodies should draft statutes as specifically and definitely as possible, so that officials will know what they are expected to do and their performance or nonfeasance will be more readily apparent. Vague and ambiguous legislation hampers effective responsibility as well as effective administration.

(2) Better provision for audit and for legislative consideration of audit reports will go far to increase the effectiveness of legislative supervision of official work. Present practice in this respect is markedly weak.

(3) The establishment of joint committees, including members of appropriations committees, to keep in continuing contact with each of the major public activities may be a useful arrangement in some jurisdictions.[1] To secure the best results, either the rule of seniority in selecting committee chairmen must go or the position of secretary or clerk to the committee must be built up. Through such committees or otherwise a more wholesome understanding might be developed. At present the atmosphere is too often one of distrust and suspicion on both sides.

(4) There may well be a relaxation of certain existing forms of legislative control, especially in the determination of detailed internal organization of departments, in the itemization of appropriations, in the enactment of "individual-order" legislation, and in requiring favored treatment of individual citizens or employees. Certainly the legislative body and individual representatives should refrain from influencing official decisions on individual cases of personal right or obligation under the law, except by presenting facts which are not otherwise available.

(5) Professor William Y. Elliott suggests the necessity of fundamental reconstruction of our legislative-executive relationships by abandoning the doctrine of separation of powers and adopting the cabinet form of government.[2] Such a change would doubtless clear up many present difficulties, but the secondary repercussions on the position of the Senate, and consequently on the federal system, are such that it is unlikely so drastic a change will take place in the foreseeable future.

"The responsibility of administration to the legislature," writes Gaus, "is best confined to general policy. . . ." He notes the general agreement among students of administration that legislatures have done far more harm than good by too detailed control of the organization of the administration.[3] With this statement we may concur, while recognizing the need and value of intelligent and sympathetic legislative guidance and oversight.

5. Lay Control of the Specialists

These various forms and methods of popular and legislative control of the administrative machine are the means by which the experts are subordinated to the major preferences of the population.[4] In a

[1] City managers generally deprecate such committees of council, and in small jurisdictions the case is different from that prevailing in the states and in the national government.

[2] W. Y. Elliott, *The Need for Constitutional Reform* (1935).

[3] Gaus, *op. cit.*, p. 34; see also Frederick A. Cleveland, "Responsible Leadership and Responsible Criticism," 8 *Proceedings of the Academy of Political Science* 29-41 (1918).

[4] See especially Herbert D. Croly, *Progressive Democracy* (1914), ch. 18.

democracy this subordination is accepted as a necessary condition of government; in a government operating on other than a representative popular basis these controls are unknown and will be irrelevant. In such governments individuals are subjects, not objects of administration; they accept the forms and purposes of administration which are imposed upon them, within the limits of public law but not within the restraints of public opinion.

A democracy may sacrifice some measure of administrative energy and perhaps (although less certainly) some degree of efficiency. The loss, if any, is compensated by the assets which a people accustomed to a degree of self-government cherish, and by the nearer approximation of government to the preferences and even the prejudices of the governed.

From another point of view, these popular controls are laymen's restraints upon technological and specialist administrators. It might be thought that social progress would be accelerated if the experts were free to apply their techniques. In some cases it is doubtless true that immediate social gains might be achieved through the unhesitating application of scientific knowledge by an unrestrained bureaucracy. Short of powers of compulsion far beyond those to which Americans are accustomed, and of a habit of obedience unknown to a population which still retains more than a trace of frontier independence, it is unlikely that the experts could impose such a regime of science.

It is more realistic to think of the legislative bodies as intermediaries between technicians armed with the weapons of science and citizens ready to accept the teaching of science and its application by administration as soon as they are satisfied with the objectives and the means proposed, but not sooner. From this point of view legislative restraints and controls are the regulators which adjust the speed of administrative application of technical progress, permitting new adaptations of government activity as rapidly as the time is ripe.

One further word. Legislators are politicians, and they deal with administration perhaps more frequently in the latter than in the former capacity. They often do harm to administrative integrity and competence under the compulsion of political necessities. Enlightened politicians will recognize a duty not only to supervise administration in their legislative capacity as the grand inquest of the nation, but also to protect and defend administration as a priceless asset of an organized people. A responsible administration, cherished and strengthened by those to whom it is responsible, is one of the principal foundations of the modern democratic state.

Chapter Thirty-seven

JUDICIAL CONTROL OF ADMINISTRATIVE ACTION

THE system of formal external control over officials and their acts falls into two main divisions, that exercised by legislative bodies and that imposed by courts. The purpose of legislative supervision is principally to control the policy and the expenditures of the executive branch; the end sought by judicial control of administrative acts is to ensure their legality and thus to protect citizens against unlawful trespass on their constitutional or other rights.[1]

The foundation of judicial control over administrative acts rests in the Anglo-American doctrine of the rule of law. The classic statement of the concept is that of Dicey.

> . . . no man is punishable or can be lawfully made to suffer in body or goods except for a distinct breach of law established in the ordinary legal manner before the ordinary Courts of the land . . . no man is above the law, but . . . every man, whatever be his rank or condition, is subject to the ordinary law of the realm and amenable to the jurisdiction of the ordinary tribunals . . . every official, from the Prime Minister down to a constable or a collector of taxes, is under the same re-

[1] The principal general works to be consulted on the subject matter of this chapter, which touches a very wide area, include the following: John Dickinson, *Administrative Justice and the Supremacy of Law* (1927); William A. Robson, *Justice and Administrative Law* (1928); Carl McFarland, *Judicial Control of the Federal Trade Commission and the Interstate Commerce Commission, 1920–1930* (1933); Gerard C. Henderson, *The Federal Trade Commission* (1924); Ernst Freund, *Administrative Powers over Persons and Property* (1928); Freund and others, *The Growth of American Administrative Law* (1923); Harold M. Stephens, *Administrative Tribunals and the Rules of Evidence* (1933); Frederick F. Blachly and Miriam E. Oatman, *Administrative Legislation and Adjudication* (1934); William C. Van Vleck, *The Administrative Control of Aliens* (1932); Patrick H. Loughran, *Judicial Review of Federal Executive Action* (1930); Walter F. Dodd, *Administration of Workmen's Compensation* (1936); I. L. Sharfman, *The Interstate Commerce Commission* (1931–37); *A Symposium on Administrative Law*, 18 *Iowa Law Rev.* 129-248 (1932–33); Frederick J. Port, *Administrative Law* (1929); Committee on Ministers' Powers, *Report* (Cmd. 4060, 1932).

The principal collections of cases dealing with the technical legal points involved in this chapter are Ernst Freund, *Cases on Administrative Law* (1911); Felix Frankfurter and J. F. Davison, eds., *Cases and Other Materials on Administrative Law* (1932); E. Blythe Stason, *The Law of Administrative Tribunals* (1937); Robert A. Maurer, *Cases and Other Materials on Administrative Law* (1937); Kenneth C. Sears, *Cases and Materials on Administrative Law* (1938).

sponsibility for every act done without legal justification as any other citizen . . . the general principles of the constitution . . . are with us the result of judicial decisions determining the rights of private persons in particular cases brought before the Courts. . . .[1]

This rule was brought to the United States as a part of the common law heritage and has been universally accepted.

The earliest application of this doctrine consisted in the right of the individual to sue an official in the ordinary courts for civil damages, or to enforce the official's criminal liability. Until after the Civil War, however, judicial control of administration by means of damage suits seems to have been, on the whole, relatively slight.[2] But subsequent to the Civil War arose a widespread tendency on the part of the courts to emphasize private rights against governmental encroachment, which was expressed in part in a willingness to hold officials liable to damages. "The judicial immunity of administrative officers was accordingly cut down at important points."

In due course of time a new type of administrative agency appeared: the independent regulatory commission vested with varying degrees of authority over businesses and occupations which had traditionally been subject only to the prevailing law of liability as enforced in ordinary courts. New obligations, often of a debatable nature, were laid upon persons through the rules and orders of these commissions. In order to balance these obligations with a more effective means of judicial intervention, a direct judicial review, either in the form of an appeal by the defendant or in the form of enforcement proceedings by the administrative body, was provided by law.[3] In addition, in many of the states the use of the ancient writ of certiorari as a means of reviewing quasi judicial acts of administrative agencies was enlarged. Judicial methods of control of administrative acts have, therefore, shown a tendency to expand with the growth of administrative power and activity.[4]

[1] A. V. Dicey, *Introduction to the Study of the Law of the Constitution* (8th ed. 1915), pp. 183-84, 189, 191. Dean Pound restates the rule in the following terms: "that the judiciary . . . may pronounce upon the legal validity of the acts of the king's ministers and servants and hence, in the United States, upon the validity of administrative, executive and legislative action with reference to the constitution and, in the case of administrative and executive action, the statutes governing such action." "Rule of Law," 13 *Encyclopaedia of the Social Sciences* 463-66 (1934).

[2] John Dickinson, "Judicial Control of Administration Discretion," 22 *Am. Pol. Sci. Rev.* 275-300 (1928).

[3] Cf. the Constitution of Oklahoma (1907). "The original jurisdiction of the Supreme Court shall extend to a general superintending control over all inferior courts and all commissions and boards created by law." Art. VII, sec. 2.

[4] Marshall E. Dimock, "The Development of American Administrative Law," 15 *J. of Comparative Legislation* 35-46, 3d series (1933).

1. The Issue

While the authority of courts to review the action of administrators is thus an ancient one and universally accepted in Anglo-Saxon countries, there is a growing difference of opinion as to whether there are not some limits to the usefulness of judicial intervention, and, if so, what those limits are. The old traditional view in Anglo-Saxon countries is that any aspect of administrative action which is alleged to violate a constitutional, statutory, or common law right or privilege of a citizen can and should be brought before a court for reconsideration *de novo* and for final decision. Another opinion holds that while a court review is and should be available, the court may be satisfied upon finding merely that the action is correct as to form and procedure and that there were reasonable grounds for the administrative action, although this action might not be the one which the court itself would have taken.

The consequences of judicial attitudes on the requirements to sustain administrative action are important, because if the court declines to validate what an official has done, the official may become personally liable in damages. If a court is strict in its requirements, officials are not likely to act unless they have an "open-and-shut" case; if a court is less strict, officials are more inclined to proceed in cases which in their judgment require correction. At one extreme, the rigor of judicial control may paralyze effective administration; at the other, the result may be an offensive bureaucratic tyranny. Exactly where the balance may best be struck is a major problem of judicial-administrative relationships.

In fact, the utmost variation exists. The amount of judicial intervention varies from subject matter to subject matter; it tends to be least in cases involving public health and safety, and greatest in cases concerned with public convenience or public amenities. It varies from state to state; there are forty-eight different schemes of court review of official action, plus the federal system. It varies from time to time; the pendulum swings this way and that in accordance with general trends and the attitudes of particular judges. As a result, it is practically impossible to state any general conclusions as to the actual extent or limits of court review of official decisions.

The orthodox opinion is that judicial review of administrative action is an essential feature of our constitutional and administrative system; that the courts should always be open to citizens to challenge the legality of the decisions of their officials; and that, if otherwise acceptable, the courts should be satisfied upon finding that there is reasonable evidence to sustain the administrative order or action. In actual practice all sorts of views representing greater or less departures from orthodoxy prevail.

2. The Occasions for Judicial Intervention

The courts are invited to validate, invalidate or correct administrative action for many reasons. The principal classes of cases are five: abuse of discretion; lack of jurisdiction; error of law; error in the finding of fact, and error of procedure. These categories are not clear cut; in their application to actual cases they become very indistinct at the margins; but they do point to five central points at which court review is common.

Abuse of power is illustrated in the rare instance when an official uses his authority vindictively to harm another for private reasons. Such cases are usually difficult to prove but certainly call for judicial correction. For example, the use of the power to inspect and to order changes in buildings or structures may become an instrument of punishment at the hands of an unscrupulous political machine.

Allegations of lack of jurisdiction provide a frequent cause of appeal to the courts. Every official has certain specified powers within a certain area; if he acts beyond these powers or outside the geographical limits of his government he has no jurisdiction and his acts have no force or effect. The interpretation of official jurisdiction leads directly into and overlaps questions of law and questions of fact, other categories on which many appeals rest.

If an official misconstrues the law which he is entitled to enforce and thus imposes upon citizens an obligation or responsibility which is absent from the law, he has committed an error which the courts do not hesitate to correct. Thus an overzealous inspector may order a fire escape on a two-story brick building when the law requires such exits only for frame buildings or for brick buildings having three stories or more.

Disputed questions of fact are always arising to bring administrative orders into the courts. A common case involves the condemnation of cattle afflicted with disease. The health inspector may order diseased cattle to be killed; the disputed question of fact is whether a specific animal was in fact diseased. If not, the inspector may be liable for damages for killing a healthy animal. And if the animal was not diseased, the inspector had no jurisdiction!

Finally, the courts will insist that administrative officials follow the procedure which is laid down in law as a prerequisite to action. Procedural requirements are often very detailed and specific, usually turning on the provision of adequate notice and hearing. If the record shows any gap or error in the procedure, the court will usually find the administrative action null and void.

These are the principal classes of instances which bring officials to courts on complaint of private parties. But conversely officials may and often do go to the courts for judicial writs to compel observance of the law. From the humblest police officer to the highest administrative tribunals, officials seek judicial orders to buttress their own decisions. Here, too, the court may issue the desired writ or not, depending upon its view of the legality and reasonableness of official action.

The judges and the administration are consequently colliding with each other at frequent intervals. Officials always act with the recollection that their action may be challenged in the courts and that under some circumstances they may be liable for damages if they make a mistake. The customary forms of judicial action against officials appear in the next section.

3. Forms and Methods of Judicial Control

a. Suit for damages, civil or criminal. This traditional form of judicial control is still very widely effective, although it has become progressively less important. It is the customary remedy for damage to property caused by unauthorized official action, for false arrest, or for deliberate abuse of power by an official and in cases where there is no other recourse. The development of the practice of bonding officials has made the suit against the bondsman a supplementary action, widely used by the government to protect itself against defaulting officials or employees. The impecunious condition of the official and employee class as a whole renders unlikely the collection of damages on any substantial scale. Furthermore, it is of doubtful public advantage to hold officials liable for damages for other than purely personal faults; the American law has gone too far in imposing liability on officials for "faults of the service." A suit to collect for damages already incurred, furthermore, does not prevent harmful action, and prevention is often the only useful remedy. Despite these qualifications, however, the suit to enforce civil and criminal liability remains one of the established forms of judicial control.[1]

b. Mandamus. This writ is issued by the court normally on petition of a private individual to compel the performance of a ministerial duty, i.e., one in the performance of which the official has no discretion.

[1] Study of these methods of judicial control of administrative acts can be pursued further in the standard casebooks on administrative law.

The principal use of mandamus is now in connection with the acts or omissions of public officers. It will lie also to compel the performance of a discretionary duty but without specifying the particular method of performance; that is, the court will compel the official to act one way or the other.

"An unqualified discretion is rarely vested in officials exercising authority over private rights. Although the official may be free to decide one way or another, it is his clear duty to consider the case and to proceed to some decision, to decide fairly and without favor and to confine his discretion to legitimate considerations but to take into account all those that are legitimate. Without his discretion being touched he may be judicially controlled in all these respects."[1] Mandamus can thus be used to correct an abuse of discretion.

In the federal service it is most widely used in cases brought against the Land Office, the Postmaster General, and the Comptroller General; but Blachly and Oatman declare that it is "practically useless as a remedy against erroneous decisions which may be made by most of the types of administrative tribunals. . . ."[2] In many other types of cases, however, it is more effective.

c. Injunction. The purpose of this writ in equity is to prohibit action, the result of which would be to cause irreparable damage to vested rights. It is used to protect rights at issue in private suits, and upon request of officials to restrain illegal action by citizens or upon request of private parties to halt official action. Prosecutors have secured injunctions, for example, against gambling dens and saloons; hence the phrase, "padlock injunction." The request for an injunction against pending official action is usually designed to initiate judicial review of the order, and is frequently used in the course of the regulation of business and the fixing of rates. The grant of a permanent injunction brings official action to an end so far as specified in the order. The frequency of injunctions issued by federal judges against the Interstate Commerce Commission induced Congress in 1913 to require the petition for such an injunction to be heard by three judges rather than by one.[3]

The mandatory injunction reverses the normal prohibitory effect of an injunction by using a double negative to produce a positive result. Thus a building inspector may be ordered to refrain from refusing to

[1] Ernst Freund, "Mandamus," 10 *Encyclopaedia of the Social Sciences* 84-87 (1933).

[2] Frederick F. Blachly and Miriam E. Oatman, *Administrative Legislation and Adjudication* (1934), p. 187.

[3] 38 Stat. 220 (1913); see further Blachly and Oatman, *op. cit.*, p. 191; Zechariah Chafee, Jr., "Injunction," 8 *Encyclopaedia of the Social Sciences* 53-57 (1932).

grant a building permit.[1] The effect is substantially equivalent to a mandamus.

d. Certiorari. In state jurisdictions the use of this writ has become the most usual method of reviewing the orders of public utility commissions, civil service commissions, industrial accident boards and similar agencies.[2] The writ has the effect of transferring a cause from an inferior tribunal to a court of higher jurisdiction for the purpose of review of the record and determination. The court takes jurisdiction in place of the administrative authority (or lower court) which has the case before it. The writ is not widely used in the federal government as a means of direct review by the Supreme Court of decisions of administrative agencies, although it is available in a growing number of cases. Each year the Supreme Court receives about 250 petitions for writs of certiorari involving some administrative questions, of which about 50 are granted.[3]

e. Habeas corpus. This ancient common law writ is designed to bring about the liberation of an illegally imprisoned individual. It requires the immediate production of the person in custody before the court to determine the legality of his detention.[4] Habeas corpus is widely used in determining the legality of detention of individuals by police departments. Counsel for suspected criminals held *incommunicado* by the police can usually "spring" their clients after a short interval unless the department is large enough to conceal the whereabouts of the suspect from his counsel by moving him rapidly from station to station. This game soon comes to an end, however. There has been abuse of the habeas corpus writ by some municipal judges. In state governments the writ has been used to determine legality of detention under quarantine or health regulations. In the federal service the writ is chiefly used in Chinese exclusion and deportation cases. The effect of the writ in any case is to cause the person under detention to be brought before the court for determination of the legality of his detention.

f. Quo warranto. This ancient writ, which first appeared in statutory

[1] *City of Dallas vs. McElroy*, 254 S.W. 599 (1923), cited in Kenneth C. Sears, *Cases and Materials on Administrative Law* (1938), pp. 137-40. For cases illustrating the writ of prohibition, which is not commonly used as a means of administrative control, see *ibid.*, pp. 26-39.

[2] John Dickinson, "Judicial Control of Administrative Discretion," *loc. cit.*, and by the same author, "Certiorari," 3 *Encyclopaedia of the Social Sciences* 317-19 (1930).

[3] Blachly and Oatman, *op. cit.*, pp. 194-95; Felix Frankfurter and Adrian S. Fisher, "The Business of the Supreme Court at the October Terms, 1935 and 1936," 51 *Harvard Law Rev.* 577-637 (1937-38).

[4] Pendleton Howard, "Habeas Corpus," 7 *Encyclopaedia of the Social Sciences* 233-36 (1932).

form in the Statute of Gloucester, 6 Edw. I (1278), has been replaced in many jurisdictions by a statutory substitute, the "information in the nature of quo warranto." The purpose remains the same, to try the right to a franchise or office. It may be used by the state, at the instance of the attorney general, or, with the leave of the court, by individuals who claim the right to office. The writ of quo warranto is the principal direct remedy for trying title to public office. It is used in cases of disputed elections (except for legislative positions) unless other special procedures have been provided. It is also regularly used to test charges of lack of qualification, and acts involving forfeiture. Title to office is also often adjudicated on a suit for payment of salary claimed by the appellant; both the Myers case and the Humphrey case were decided on this point.

g. Appeal; enforcement proceedings. The evolution of legislation and adjudication during the last half century has added to the time-honored writs just noted the device of a direct appeal from many administrative decisions or orders to the court, or its substantial equivalent, the requirement that the administrative body must itself turn to the court for the enforcement of its orders. Two questions of importance are, who may appeal (or who must appeal), and what weight is given by the appellate court to the findings and decisions of the administrative body.[1]

The original Interstate Commerce Act of 1887 prescribed that if any carrier failed or neglected to obey a lawful order of the Commis-

[1] There is voluminous literature on the general problem of finality of administrative decisons, from which the following items have been selected: Thomas Reed Powell, "Conclusiveness of Administrative Determinations in the Federal Government," 1 *Am. Pol. Sci. Rev.* 583-607 (1906–7); Thomas Reed Powell, "Judicial Review of Administrative Action in Immigrant Proceedings," 22 *Harvard Law Rev.* 360-66 (1908–9); Warren H. Pillsbury, "Administrative Tribunals," 36 *Harvard Law Rev.* 405-25, 583-92 (1922–23); Frank J. Goodnow, "The Growth of Executive Discretion," 2 *Proceedings of the American Political Science Association* 29-44 (1905); Nathan Isaacs, "Judicial Review of Administrative Findings," 30 *Yale Law J.* 781-97 (1920–21); E. F. Albertsworth, "Judicial Review of Administrative Action by the Federal Supreme Court," 35 *Harvard Law Rev.* 127-53 (1921–22); Ernst Freund, "The Substitution of Rule for Discretion in Public Law," 9 *Am. Pol. Sci. Rev.* 666-76 (1915); E. G. Baird, "Judicial Review of Decisions of the Workmen's Compensation Bureau of North Dakota," 3 *Dakota Law Rev.* 16-24 (1930–31); A. Martin Tollefson, "Administrative Finality," 29 *Mich. Law Rev.* 839-49 (1930–31); Joseph Kutten, "Judicial Review of Findings and Awards of the Missouri Workmen's Compensation Commission," 23 *Washington Univ. Law Q.* 99-116 (1937–38); Lewis F. Powell, Jr., "The Relation between the Virginia Court of Appeals and the State Corporation Commission," 19 *Virginia Law Rev.* 433-58, 571-93 (1932–33); Irwin S. Rosenbaum and David E. Lilienthal, "Court Review of Orders of the Ohio Public Utilities Commission," 2 *Cincinnati Law Rev.* 225-54 (1928); Elmer A. Smith, "Judicial Review of Decisions of the Illinois Commerce Commission," 24 *Ill. Law Rev.* 423-53 (1929–30); Forrest R. Black, "The 'Jurisdictional Fact' Theory and Administrative Finality," 22 *Cornell Law Q.* 349-78, 515-42 (1936–37).

sion, the Commission could apply to the appropriate circuit court for the enforcement of the order. If, after hearing, the court determined that the order was regularly made and duly served, and that the carrier failed to obey, the court enforced obedience by a writ of injunction or other proper process. In such cases, the carrier against whom the order was directed had to refuse or neglect to comply before proceedings could begin; refusal to comply did not itself involve liability to penalty; and the administrative body was the plaintiff.[1]

In the case of an order of the Federal Trade Commission, the matter may be taken to a federal circuit court of appeals either by the Commission to enforce its order, or by the party against whom the order is directed.[2] The appeal provisions of the Communications Act of 1934 are unusually broad.[3] Appeal lies to the Circuit Court of Appeals of the District of Columbia by any unsuccessful applicant for a radio station license, renewal, or modification; and also by any other person whose interests are adversely affected. After the filing of an appeal any interested person may intervene and participate in the proceedings.

The public utilities law of Illinois authorizes any person or corporation affected by an order or decision of the Illinois Commerce Commission to appeal to the circuit or superior court "for the purpose of having the reasonableness or lawfulness" of the order determined by the court.[4] Similar provisions are common in other states.

With respect to appeals initiated either by the government or by private parties, the most important question is, how far does the court find it necessary to go in reviewing the case? It may try the case *de novo*, accepting nothing from the administrative hearing and order; it may give "deference" to the earlier proceeding; or it may accord prima facie status to the finding of facts. The court may accept the administrative finding of fact as conclusive, if there is reasonable evidence in the record to support it, or it may decline to enter into any reconsideration of the finding; it may merely "try the trial," that is to say, inquire whether the prescribed procedure was observed.

The difference in the treatment of administrative findings depends partly upon the attitudes of judges and partly upon legislative directions to the courts concerning the intended status of official fact findings. Often the legislation will be silent on the weight to be given to such findings, but in the legislation of the last quarter century the effort has been made by legislatures to protect administrative findings to some

[1] 24 Stat. 379, 384; I. L. Sharfman, *The Interstate Commerce Commission* (1931), vol. 1, p. 22.

[2] 38 Stat. 717, 720 (1914).

[3] 48 Stat. 1064, 1093.

[4] Illinois Revised Statutes. 1937 (Smith-Hurd), c. 111 2/3, sec. 72.

extent. The trend is indicated by comparing the Interstate Commerce Act of 1887 with the Federal Trade Act of 1914 or the Communications Act of 1934.

In the former case, no preferential status was originally given to the findings of the Interstate Commerce Commission in its own application for court order to enforce its decisions. However, in cases where an injured shipper relied upon the findings of the Commission in a suit against a carrier for money damages, the court was required to accept them as "prima facie evidence of the matters therein stated." [1]

On the other hand, the findings of the Federal Communciations Commission when certified for judicial review are given special status. The law provides "that findings of fact by the Commission, if supported by substantial evidence, shall be conclusive unless it shall clearly appear that the findings of the Commission are arbitrary or capricious." [2] This language does not exempt the findings from judicial scrutiny, and the Supreme Court has been unfriendly to such exemption, but it does represent a shift from an earlier position.

To the general problem of the desirable extent of judicial review we turn in the next section.

4. Judicial Review of Administrative Acts

"Manifestly," writes Justice Rosenberry, "the determination of the extent to which a review should be had involves questions of public policy of the greatest importance. . . . One of the most persuasive arguments against a too generous employment of the right to a judicial review is the fact that courts are not equipped to review findings of fact in many technical fields. A judge, in order to be properly equipped to make an intelligent review of findings of valuation of a public utility, in addition to being a lawyer, should be an expert accountant, an engineer, an experienced operator, and a financier. An admission that he is not thus equipped may be made by any judge without a blush of shame. On the other hand, an unintelligent, improperly equipped administrative body, ignorant of fundamental legal principles, may by its findings and orders do such great injustice that one who suffers therefrom ought, according to the conceptions of justice which obtain among Anglo-American peoples, to be entitled to have them reviewed. Here we come to an impasse. . . ." [3]

The distinguished Wisconsin jurist continues, "The point where the

[1] 24 Stat. 379 (1887), sec. 16.
[2] 48 Stat. 1064, 1094 (1934).
[3] Marvin B. Rosenberry, "Administrative Law and the Constitution," 23 *Am. Pol. Sci. Rev.* 32-46 (1929).

irresistible force of growing administrative law most directly collides with the immovable body of law is as to the right of a party to have a review of a determination made by an administrative tribunal." Such a review normally exists; the issue concerns principally what the courts may properly accept as conclusive, if anything, from the preliminary work of an administrative agency.[1]

The case for giving the courts complete power of review, thus leaving no finality to any findings or acts of an administrative authority, rests upon the importance of preserving intact judicial determination of rights and obligations under the law in conformity with the procedures which courts have evolved to safeguard such rights and enforce such obligations. Administrative tribunals are not always required to follow judicial forms of procedure and may depart to some degree from the judicial rules of evidence, although where large interests are involved the tendency is to follow the rules of a court. Members of tribunals are not always learned in the law, although lawyers are frequently appointed. The tenure of members is not protected in many jurisdictions, and in some cases members have been appointed for obviously political reasons.

The possibility of misinterpretation of law, of overemphasis upon specialist considerations, of excess of zeal, and of partisanship cannot be overlooked.[2] "The courts, as the agency charged with the application and development of the whole law having a sweep perforce as broad as the needs of society, seem well fitted to adjust the narrower judgment of specialists to the larger considerations...."

The broad goal to be sought is some reconciliation of the claims of technical expertness, which on the whole administration provides, and the claims of adequate judicial protection of private rights, for which the courts exist. The terms of adjustment slowly change from generation to generation and, as in the case of all human institutions, there is a definite lag between a given system of official-judicial relationships and the public acceptance of necessary methods of reaching and attaining "the public good." On the whole the lag at this point now tends to carry over an emphasis on judicial protection of private right.

We are therefore led to inquire what are the social consequences of a legal situation in which administrative findings of fact are reviewed without restriction by the courts, as compared with the social con-

[1] See an especially valuable study by Charles G. Haines, "Judicial Review of the Findings and Awards of Industrial Accident Commissions," in C. G. Haines and M. E. Dimock, eds., *Essays on the Law and Practice of Governmental Administration* (1935).

[2] See Carroll H. Wooddy, *The Case of Frank L. Smith* (1931) (one-time chairman of the Illinois Commerce Commission).

sequences arising from a legal situation in which the courts accept the findings of fact of the administrative agency as prima facie or conclusive, thus reserving their control to questions of jurisdiction, procedure and abuse of power? Although data are not available to answer this question directly or conclusively, certain considerations suggest the direction of a solution.

(1) Many of the issues which may be brought before a court for review involve facts of a scientific or technical nature: engineering, chemical, biological, medical, geological and others. Administrative bodies, with appropriate technical staffs, seem better adapted to reaching findings of fact and of stating scientific conclusions from such facts than are courts.

An administrative commission may itself be an expert body when appointed, and usually becomes expertly informed in the natural course of its work. An administrative agency is appointed for the specific purpose of dealing with a given set of facts and handles only one kind of business.

A court, on the other hand, while expert in the law, is not and cannot be expert in the varied fields in which administrative action arises. The court deals with many types of judicial work, of which the review of administrative decisions is only one. The mind of the judge naturally turns to precedent for a solution rather than to relatively vague assertions about social consequences. Indeed the training of the lawyer-judge has not usually been conducive to an appreciation of the social consequences of public action.

In the technique of collecting evidence an administrative agency is undoubtedly superior to a court. A court acts only on complaint and considers only the evidence brought to it by the parties. An administrative body can act on its own motion and often has an extensive and well-trained staff to collect evidence. The trade submittal practice of the Federal Trade Commission illustrates the point.

(2) Some issues which come to courts for judgment involve the consideration of evidence and the forming of opinions in areas where standards of judgment are not fixed and where the opinions of "reasonable men" are helpful guides. Here the conclusions reached by administrative bodies would seem to warrant great respect by the courts. The determination of what is a "living wage" furnishes a good illustration. Is it appropriate to include an item for recreation, and if so, how much; does a child need two pairs of shoes or three a year at the bare edge of existence; what is a fair amount of insurance for a working man with a family of three children? These are questions involving

both a study of what is, the consequences thereof, and a decision as to what ought to be. No system of judicial logic is entirely adequate to their answer.

(3) The nature of the evidence submitted to define standards in these new fields of social regulation is also of a character the consideration of which is not especially facilitated by legal training. Deciding whether a compulsory minimum wage deprives an employer of due process of law or whether, conversely, it is a proper application of the police power raises intricate questions of the effects of low wage standards: the breakdown of family life, personal maladjustments, social irregularity, the warping of child life, and the tendency toward criminality. These are matters which cannot be disposed of by precedent. To validate a limitation of the hours of labor of women, complicated problems of fatigue and the physical structure and reactions of women must be weighed by the court, informed (or perplexed) by the testimony of physicians, neurologists, psychologists, and social workers.

(4) The points of contact at which has developed the chief criticism of judicial review of the work of administrative bodies usually involve new aspects of social policy, such as workmen's compensation, minimum wage, limitation of hours of labor, and safety devices. Legislation is often vague in defining the standards which are believed essential, and the burden of making a decision is passed on to an administrative body. It may be contended that such a body is better fitted than are the courts to perform this difficult and controversial duty, subject to protection against clearly arbitrary and unreasonable conclusions.

For such reasons as these, the social consequences of a legal system in which administrative findings of fact are given great weight by courts are likely to be superior to the consequences of complete judicial reconsideration. This conclusion does not foreclose judicial review, but suggests that the courts, in the exercise of their power, use "extraordinary tact and self-restraint."

It will obviously be easier for the courts to forego a meticulous review of each and every administrative act if fully adequate provisions exist within the executive branch to ensure a fair hearing and opportunity for an appeal within the administration itself. This brings us to a brief consideration of the gradual and partial development of a hierarchy of administrative tribunals and to proposals for a system of administrative courts.

5. Administrative Courts

The recognition of administrative law and administrative courts has been resisted in the United States, as in Great Britain, as a result of the predominant common law tradition. A considerable number of administrative tribunals now exist, both in the state and the national governments. For the most part, they form no hierarchy, and no general system of administrative appeals prevails. In some instances, however, such appeals have been provided, and the tendency is in the direction of extending them.

By way of example, a controversy may be taken from the chief examiners in the Patent Office to the Board of Appeals in the Patent Office and then to the Court of Customs and Patent Appeals, before it is possible to transfer the cause by certiorari to the Supreme Court. Decisions of the Insurance Claims Council of the Veterans' Administration may be brought to the Board of Appeals of this organization; here there is no appeal to or review by the judicial courts.

The Tariff Act of 1930 prescribed an elaborate set of administrative appeals. The initial appeal from an appraisal of imported goods is to a single judge of the Customs Court; a further appeal is allowed to a panel of three judges of the same court; and a third hearing may be prosecuted upon appeal to the Court of Customs and Patent Appeals. The Customs Court, of nine members, sits in New York. In general, however, administrative tribunal hierarchies of this type are exceptional.

At the same time another tendency is noted by Marshall E. Dimock which tends toward an administrative-judicial hierarchy, resulting from legislation giving to the District Court and/or the Circuit Court of Appeals of the District of Columbia the power to review decisions of administrative courts and officials. "If Congress continues to withdraw the appeal of technical administrative cases from the district courts and vests them in the courts of the District of Columbia, we shall have the substance if not the formal recognition of a hierarchical administrative court system." [1]

These tendencies, coupled with the increasing number of administrative tribunals, have naturally suggested the desirability of a system of administrative courts analogous to the well-known French courts of this type. The issue was presented for discussion to the American Bar Association by its Special Committee on Administrative Law in 1935. The proposal would have merged the Court of Claims, the Board of Tax Appeals, the Customs Court, and the Court of Customs and Patent Appeals. The new court would in addition assume jurisdiction now exercised by the District Court of the District of Columbia over mandamus

[1] Marshall E. Dimock, "The Development of American Administrative Law," 15 *J. of Comparative Legislation* 35-46, 3d series (1933).

and injunction proceedings against federal officials, as well as certain other causes.[1]

This proposal, however, did not in itself carry any specific recommendation with respect to the scope and limitation of judicial review of administrative acts. The establishment of a central administrative court with a body of judges holding permanent tenure, with both original and appellate branches, and with recognized expertness both in the law and in the substance of administration would, however, tend to build up respect for administrative tribunals in the judicial courts of a nature to diminish the scope of their review and control.

At the present time the absence of such a central administrative tribunal forces an excessive number of cases into the higher federal courts merely in [illegible]niformity of treatment. "...these regular cons[illegible]es a close observer, "are generally unfamiliar [illegible] governmental problems, and it is no easy task to [illegible]icate ninety-odd district courts, no matter how able the [illegible]be, in government cases which must, after all, form but a fraction of the regular work of such courts. Also, the diversities in conclusion reached by such courts in similar cases are simply staggering. ..."[2] An appellate administrative court could readily serve as a unifying agency and thus relieve the judicial courts from a mass of work, without derogation to an eventual judicial determination of issues involved.

Opposition to proposals of this sort arises from two sources. Members of the bar who have become familiar with the rules of the administrative court before which they practice show reluctance to the absorption of this tribunal into a larger body, with the probability of different rules and the possibility of a less favorable situation. More fundamental is the less vocal opposition which grows out of the belief that administrative justice is *per se* dangerous, and that its position should consequently not be strengthened by establishing a powerful central administrative court.

Concerning the details of any proposal it is not feasible to express an opinion. It seems certain, however, that the field of administrative justice, already large, is destined to expand, rather than to contract. In the light of this trend, it is desirable to work toward the most effective organization of administrative tribunals. Here, as elsewhere, the advantages of simplicity, orderliness, coordination, and responsibility

[1] *Reports of the 60th Annual Meeting of the American Bar Association* (1935), pp. 136-43; Louis G. Caldwell, "A Federal Administrative Court," 84 *Univ. of Penn. Law Rev.* 966-90 (1935–36).

[2] O. R. McGuire, "The Need for a Federal Administrative Court," 5 *George Washington Law Rev.* 43-64 (1936–37).

suggest an articulated system, rather than a scattered and formless aggregate of unrelated tribunals. Just as the judicial courts require an organization within themselves (with final jurisdiction vested at different points), so the administrative tribunals would appear likely to profit by an orderly relationship among themselves. A central administrative court, with both original and appellate jurisdiction, is, therefore, a desirable goal toward which to work, although the proposal of the American Bar Association Committee was not endorsed by the Association.

6. Summary

"The need of a formula to define the a[illegible] administrative immunity and judicial superiority is one of the mos[illegible] which the government is faced today." [1] The diffi[illegible] formula is enormous, not merely on account of the [illegible] questions involved. The weight of influence of those [illegible] ernmental interference with private initiative is natura[illegible] of judicial review of administrative action in its amplest extent. Conversely the friends of social progress through governmental intervention would like to see wide latitude for official discretion. The age-long conflict between authority and liberty thus reappears at this point of institutional adjustment.

The claims of authority were ably stated by one whose view was not less than world-wide in scope, Ernst Freund, who wrote, "Increased administrative powers call for increased safeguards against their abuses, and as long as there is the possibility of official error, partiality or excess of zeal, the protection of private right is as important an object as the effectuation of some governmental policy."

The claims of official discretion are reflected in the work of another author of international standing, Frank J. Goodnow, "What needs emphasis is no longer the inherent natural rights of the individual, but the importance, indeed the necessity, of administrative efficiency. For upon administrative efficiency depends the effectiveness of that social control without which healthy development in existing conditions is impossible."

The passing of the years seems to emphasize the soundness of Goodnow's view. But if officials are to play a greater role in social salvation, they must be themselves carefully selected, amply trained, adequately protected against political or other extraneous pressures, scrupulously

[1] Robert M. Cooper, "The Proposed United States Administrative Court," 35 *Mich. Law Rev.* 193-252, 565-96 (1936–37).

impregnated with the sense of justice and fairness, and supported by public recognition of their personal integrity and official competence. With such a public service, the need for judicial supervision and control, while never absent, should become progressively less.

EPILOGUE

THE preceding chapters may appear to leave the unfortunate official bound hand and foot by a myriad of restrictions and limitations upon his freedom of action: judicial, legislative, financial, auditing, and electoral, to say nothing of the weight of overhead management, of the auxiliary agencies and of the ever present pressure groups, one or more of which are almost certain to attach themselves to every major administrative enterprise. Amidst this tangle of apparent negation, how can positive achievement emerge?

In fact these controls and external requirements are not, or need not be hindrances to progress. They are rather the necessary channels which guide and direct the energy of the administrative organism. Between the banks and levees which are thus erected the stream of administrative power takes its way with only an occasional obstruction in the central flow of energy. But when the stream overflows its banks, or undercuts a levee, or threatens to strike out over the neighboring country in a new channel, the firm banks of the established order hold it to its accustomed course. The force and energy of administration in the performance of the work it is designed to achieve are not substantially impaired by the factors of control, despite some obstructions which impede navigation.

In its course the flow of administrative energy turns many wheels. It is a constructive, beneficial power. To think of governmental administration as negative in character or achievement, as an untamed and destructive torrent pouring down upon a defenseless plain after a mountain cloudburst, is to miss its most obvious quality.

Leaving the figure of speech, it is apparent in 1938 as it was not in 1925 that the American people are rapidly accepting government as a necessary and even as a welcome means of mass cooperation and protection. In my judgment they will continue to accept it on an even more ample scale as a useful means of achieving common tasks.

The outer limits of useful administrative enterprises are primarily two: first, effective agreement on the inevitable major compromises in the formulation of the public policy which administration must implement (for if irreconcilable groups emerge, administrators cannot be expected to bring them to terms—this is the task of statesmen); second, efficient operation of large-scale management under the conditions of public responsibility. This latter consideration is one of the principal concerns of public administration.

What, then, are the major tasks of the future in this field? Among others, these may perhaps deserve special mention: first, the clearer recognition of the many scattered parts of the existing system, federal, regional, state, rural and municipal; departments, bureaus, commissions, authorities, government corporations and mixed enterprises, as parts of a single whole, all engaged in the single task of caring for the collective needs of the American people. The strengthening of such a sense of unity will lead into gradual but vital changes in the structure of the existing organization: readjustment of functions among levels of administration, reallocation of revenues, reconsideration of areas, better coordination between Washington and state capitals, closer cooperation among state capitals, and broader services provided by the stronger for the benefit of the smaller jurisdictions.

Second, we note the further development of the technique of large-scale management, especially overhead direction, long-range planning, and the effective coordination of the parts of a constantly expanding machine. Here government may learn from the methods of great industrial organizations, where similar problems exist.

We may, furthermore, expect the steady application of technological improvements in administrative operations of all kinds. Already we make wider use of modern scientific and technical equipment than probably any other country of the world; and as new inventions appear and are tested, public officials will continue to accept them.

Finally, we must imperatively work out a better coordination and adjustment of the political party and active politicians, national, state and local, on the one hand with the administrative system and public officials on the other. This has been and still is one of the most perplexing practical problems, although well over a century ago William Coleman wrote (in 1801), "if every change of chief magistrate is to produce a similar change of subordinate officers . . . the management of public business will forever be kept in infancy and weakness." Weakness in administration has now become a handicap too great to be tolerated. We cannot "ignore the imminent perils in further advance of our heavy technical machinery over crumbling roads and shaking bridges."

In the closing pages of the first edition of this book, I wrote in 1926, "These, then, are the main lines of development: the steady growth of the merit system with its implications of permanent employment and the provision of a career; the constant limitation of the unregulated authority of the local area; the rise of the principle of administrative supervision and unified leadership; the emergence of the specialist and the expert; the origin of significant economic and professional organizations of public employees; and the rise of scientific inquiry into problems of government and administration."

The events of the last twelve years have reasonably confirmed these expectations. These trends are still in full swing and will probably dominate the developments of the next decade. The world framework of American public administration has, however, become vastly more significant, for it is now perhaps the principal example which will test whether a democracy can maintain a large-scale system of administration adequate to meet the needs of contemporary life. The cause of good administration thus becomes intimately identified with the progress of democracy itself in a world a large part of which has abandoned the art of self-government.

The following supplement, "Defense and War Administration, 1939-1942," is designed to record some of the vast changes which are taking place in American public administration under the impact of crisis conditions. Written in the middle of the crisis, these notes on current changes are necessarily fragmentary. They do, however, call to mind some of the major developments of the time.

In view of the fact that the crisis situation changes so rapidly, it has been thought wise not to index this supplementary material as a part of the index to the volume.

Supplement

DEFENSE AND WAR ADMINISTRATION, 1939–1942

SINCE 1939 the whole American system of public administration has operated within the framework of a crisis growing steadily more acute and in June, 1942, still unresolved. Unparalleled demands have been made, extraordinary achievements have been won, inadequacies and failures have developed, and at most points change has occurred with a rapidity characteristic of crisis periods. The fundamental forms of organization, relationship, and methods remained much what they were in 1939, but new agencies, new types of personnel, speedier methods, more drastic procedures, and ever closer interrelation of federal, state, and local authorities were the order of the day. As the reconstruction years after the war were projected in 1942, it seemed likely that new tasks of world-wide magnitude would have to be undertaken by the government through its administrative organization.[1]

Certain it is that the United States entered the crisis years beginning in 1939 far better equipped administratively than in the war years 1917–1918. The improvements in these two decades were great and many times over have proved their worth in the present struggle. In the federal government of 1917 there was no Bureau of the Budget, no central coordination and balance of the programs of a host of government agencies, no control of departmental competition or sabotage, and above all no central agency devoted to "administrative management," in the words of the President's Committee on Administrative Management to which so many of the most recent gains are due. In 1917 there was no effective executive office of the President, who traditionally had been assisted only by two or three skillful political advisers or journalists; the very concept of the presidency as the responsible center of federal administration was hardly recognized, and in no way was the President afforded the necessary technical assistance to permit him to be the administrative head of the government.

In 1917 the number of departments and agencies was already excessive and by 1936 had become so great as to paralyze effective coordination. During the intervening years the number of independent units—commis-

[1] This chapter was completed in July, 1942.

sions, corporations, authorities—had multiplied and the relative position of the presidency, while gaining in some respects, had clearly lost in this direction.

In 1917 the state systems of administration were weak, straggling, uncoordinated, ridden with patronage, and in many instances incapable of any impressive effort. The few exceptions only cast into darker relief the feebleness of the majority, faithfully reflecting an earlier era when government was not expected to do much beyond keeping the peace, building roads, and attending in some measure to the unfortunate. The administrative interrelationships of the federal and the state governments were numerous, but at relatively inferior levels of importance, and were marked by jealousy and distrust on one side and by a degree of competitive oversight on the other. To say that the whole administrative structure of the country was well integrated either for peace or war would have been a gross exaggeration.

It is easy to overemphasize the gap between 1917 and 1939 to the advantage of the present; the gap between 1939 and 1960 will doubtless make our present institutions of government administration appear inexcusably inadequate. Still the unmistakable ferment for betterment of the machinery of government had already begun to make itself felt by 1917 and by 1939 had made substantial strides. In 1917 the city manager plan of government was in the first flush of success; Governor Lowden was leading the way to reform of the states; budgeting was on its way; modern personnel techniques were just emerging from the chrysalis of civil service reform; administrative reconstruction was in the air.

By 1939 many impressive achievements had been recorded which were to count heavily in the war years. The President had powerful agencies for central direction of the whole administrative machine: his own executive assistants; the Bureau of the Budget, which had become a genuine central office for handling overhead management problems; the Liaison Office for Personnel Management, the Council of Personnel Administration, and a newly energized Civil Service Commission; the National Resources Planning Board for long-range thinking on policy; and the Office for Emergency Management (1940) from which was to stem the vast civilian war machine. The greater part of the poorly coordinated mass of administrative agencies had been pulled together into the ten departments and three agencies, although much consolidation still remained possible. Standards of management and operation were steadily rising, deeply influenced both by such older agencies as the Department of Agriculture and by newer agencies such as the Federal Home Loan Bank Board, the Farm Credit Administration, and the Tennessee Valley Authority.

The era of administrative competition between the state and the federal governments had substantially ceased with the recognized dominance of national institutions, and a healthier conception of coordination and mutual assistance was in the course of acceptance. The necessity for such cooperation was revealed again and again in the hard years of the depression and was symbolized by the dual structure of most aspects of the federal security program. The states themselves were somewhat slowly putting their administrative houses in order and thus becoming more effective partners in a steadily expanding area of joint enterprise. New connections had also been established between the nation and cities, whose administrative competence, especially in the city manager towns, was often of a very superior quality.

In short, the United States entered the years of defense and war with an administrative machine which was notably stronger in most respects than its counterpart of 1917. Crisis, however, speeds change; and in the years from 1939 to 1942 great changes occurred in the governmental structure—in part due to the crisis itself and in part to the momentum of earlier trends. It is the difficult task of this chapter to describe in proper balance and proportion the changes of general significance which the crisis has induced. The material falls into the following major divisions: (1) the agencies most immediately concerned with war—the armed forces, the Selective Service System, the War Manpower Commission, the Board of Economic Warfare, the Office of Civilian Defense, and others; (2) the War Production Board and its affiliates; (3) price control and rationing; (4) censorship and propaganda; (5) international aspects; and (6) finally, the principal administrative consequences of the war effort so far as they can now be seen.

1. War and Defense Agencies

The President is commander in chief of the Army and Navy as well as the sole depository of the executive authority of the government of the United States. For the discharge of his military duties he was advised by the Secretaries of the War and Navy Departments, traditionally nonprofessional men of standing, each of whom was advised by a professional general staff. Joint Army and Navy boards assisted in the coordination of their activities. In July, 1942, the President assigned Admiral William D. Leahy, formerly ambassador to the French government at Vichy, to be his personal adviser on military and naval affairs.

With respect to civilian aspects of the war effort, the Office for Emergency Management was the principal means of advising and assisting the President and of coordinating a considerable number of organizations. Most of the newly organized civilian agencies were established in or coordinated through this Office, itself a part of the Executive Office of the President. The Liaison Officer at the head of O.E.M. acted to protect the time of the President so far as possible in reaching decisions involving these numerous and often jangling agencies.

It must be recognized, however, that war requirements hit practically every federal department and agency, and consequently a complete account of administration in wartime would of necessity have to deal with the length and breadth of the national, state, and local governments. Through the Selective Service System, Office of Price Administration, and Office of Civilian Defense, especially, the state and local governments became integral parts of the war machine. Coordination at the top remained in July, 1942, less elaborate and apparently less effective than that which had developed in Great Britain. The O.E.M. was a major coordinator of newly established agencies, but there was need for an additional level of coordination beneath the President—one or more coordinators of the coordinators. This seeming complexity but actual simplification had been achieved in top organization for war in London.

a. The Army and Navy. At the outbreak of the Second World War the War Department and the Navy Department were organized substantially as they emerged from the experiences of World War I. A separate air corps was resisted by both departments; and in the early twenties both objected to a single department of national defense. The unsatisfactory coordination of each service to the other was dramatically revealed in the official investigation following the attack on Pearl Harbor.

Both armed forces expanded after September, 1939, but the demands of the Allied Powers for war equipment handicapped the Army, especially in 1941. In 1939 the National Guard was called to the colors for training; on September 16, 1940, the Selective Training and Service Act was signed; in midyear 1942, over 4,000,000 were in the Army and about 500,000 in the Navy, with substantial contingents already on service overseas.

The administrative structure of the Navy Department had not been substantially affected by war. The War Department had undergone a drastic reorganization to correct a lack of internal coordination and to reduce an unwieldy number of bureaus reporting directly to the Secretary of War. The organization of the War Department for military purposes in June, 1942, fell into three major divisions: the Army ground forces, the Army air forces, and the services of supply. The General Staff, reduced in numbers, continued as the central directing and coordinating authority, responsible to the Secretary of War.

b. Selective Service System. Following the precedent established in World War I, Congress enacted the Selective Training and Service Act in September, 1940, to provide for a democratically selected mass army. A nation-wide, highly decentralized structure based on many thousands of local selective service boards worked smoothly to provide the required number of recruits at the appointed time. The Selective Service System was a civilian organization, not connected with the War Department, responsible directly to the President. Originally directed by a distinguished civilian, Clarence A. Dykstra, its central organization in 1942 was manned almost entirely by army officers. The directors of the state headquarters, appointed in each case by the governor, were also military officers, with four or five exceptions. On the other hand the local selective service boards were composed of civilians.

In these local boards was vested responsibility for the classification of men and the determination of deferment. Their decisions were final, subject to an appeal to a civilian appeal board. From the earliest days of the Selective Service System a wide degree of discretion was left with the local boards, unimpaired by specific instructions from Washington. This policy was doubtless intended in part to permit decisions concerning liability to military duty to take into account the point of view of different communities, within the terms of the Selective Service Act. An inevitable consequence was considerable variation in the standards of classification; some boards were "hard-boiled," others were relatively "reasonable" in their decisions. These boards were citizen boards in every sense of the term—neighborhood residents, unpaid, serving often at considerable sacrifice as a contribution to the war effort. They have been an administrative success.

c. War Manpower Commission. The rapidly developing shortage in manpower occasioned by the induction of millions of men in the armed services and by the enormous expansion of war industry early gave rise to serious problems. One method of meeting the shortage was to train young people or retrain older workers for production; this program was directed by the Office of Education using funds specially appropriated for engineering, science, and management defense training (the E. S. M. D. T. program). To a certain extent military deferment was granted in a few crucial occupations, but in volume the exemptions were negligible.

On April 18, 1942, the President established the War Manpower Commission in the Office for Emergency Management and vested powers in it designed to coordinate and control the manpower needs of the armed forces, the civil service, industry, and the civil population.[1] The powers of the Commission were vested in its chairman, the Federal Security Agency Administrator, Paul V. McNutt. He was required to act only

[1] Executive Order 9139, in 7 *Federal Register* 2919–21.

after consultation with the Commission, which comprised representatives of the Departments of War, Navy, Agriculture, and Labor, the War Production Board, the Labor Production Division of W.P.B., the Selective Service System, and the U. S. Civil Service Commission. The powers vested in the Commission included the following: formulation of policies to assure the most effective integration of manpower; estimates of manpower requirements; coordination of all labor market data; control of all federal programs for labor placement in industry and agriculture; and control of policies governing the federal government's manpower requirements other than military and naval.

In order to ensure effective control of a highly competitive situation, the executive order creating the War Manpower Commission specifically directed a crucial list of federal agencies to conform to the directives of the chairman. They included the Selective Service System, the Federal Security Agency, the U. S. Civil Service Commission, the Bureau of Labor Statistics, the W.P.B. Labor Production Division, the Civilian Conservation Corps, the Work Projects Administration, and other agencies.

At the time of writing, the Commission had taken no drastic steps in allocating or controlling manpower. It had, however, intervened to prevent "pirating" of skilled labor by one war production plant from another. Before the formation of the Commission, furthermore, the President had approved a classification of all federal bureaus into five classes of priorities and authorized the Civil Service Commission to facilitate the transfer of employees from agencies with a low priority to those with a higher rating. While by June, 1942, the control of manpower (outside the armed forces) was therefore still relatively embryonic, it was clear that more forceful steps would be required in the early future, and that administrative machinery had been set up to take such steps.

d. The Board of Economic Warfare. Modern war is waged on many fronts—land, air, and sea; by armed force, by propaganda, by internal disruption, and by economic pressure. The Board of Economic Warfare, organized on July 30, 1941, as the Economic Defense Board, was designed to bring the weight of economic power to bear against the enemy.[1] The Board, for example, had to see to it that needed supplies did not leak through to the Axis powers by subterranean channels; it was empowered to buy materials for the United States in order to forestall purchase by hostile powers; it was concerned with exports and imports, transactions in foreign exchange, extension of credit, shipping, and the international aspects of patents.

The Board was principally a coordinating and planning agency, not

[1] Executive Order 8839, in 6 *Federal Register* 3823; Executive Order 8982, December 17, 1941, 6 *ibid.* 6530.

an operating body. It comprised the Vice President, as chairman, and representatives of the Departments of State, Treasury, War, Navy, Agriculture, and Commerce, the Attorney General and the Coordinator of Inter-American Affairs. The basic executive orders authorized the Board to develop measures of economic warfare and integrated plans for their pursuance, to recommend needed legislation, and to determine over-all estimates of materials required for economic warfare, other than lend-lease.

Administration of these policies remained with the appropriate departments, who "shall conform" to Board policies. In April, 1942, the Board received additional functions.[1] It received and executed directives from the W.P.B. concerning necessary war imports, other than munitions, and was authorized to create a corporation to obtain war materials and in general to strengthen the international economic relations of the United States. It was authorized to advise the State Department concerning terms to be included in the master lend-lease agreements and to represent the United States with other economic warfare agencies. The work of the Board occasioned some conflict with the State Department, which at the time of writing had maintained its dominance over foreign relations, even in this new field.

e. Office of Civilian Defense. Few war agencies have attracted more public attention than the Office of Civilian Defense, established May 20, 1941, by executive order,[2] and directed for a time by the colorful Mayor of New York City, Fiorello H. LaGuardia, with the assistance of Mrs. Franklin D. Roosevelt. Important steps had already been taken to encourage the formation of state and local defense councils and to coordinate local and national efforts through the Division of State and Local Cooperation of the Advisory Commission to the Council of National Defense.[3] This promising beginning was interrupted by the change of leadership in May, 1941; in February, 1942, a mounting tide of criticism led to the resignation of LaGuardia and the appointment of James M. Landis as director; Mr. Landis promptly emphasized the central duty of civilian defense against attack and discontinued a number of secondary activities which had attracted unfavorable comment.

Despite considerable opinion that civilian defense is inherently a military responsibility, the O.C.D. has remained a civilian agency for the sound reason that the task is essentially one which must be handled by

[1] Executive Order 9128, April 13, 1942, in 7 *Federal Register* 2809.

[2] Executive Order 8757, in 6 *Federal Register* 2517–18; amended by Executive Order 9134, April 15, 1942, in 7 *Federal Register* 2887–88.

[3] In 4 *Book of the States* 33–42 (1941–42) will be found the early record of civilian defense activities and an account of the basic ideas on which the system of state councils of defense rested; also a list of state defense councils as of February 15, 1941.

existing civilian agencies—police, fire, health, building, and welfare departments especially.

With one important exception the functions of the O.C.D. were to advise, suggest, stimulate, coordinate, and plan a program of civilian defense, the execution of which was a duty almost entirely of local governments. The organic executive order authorized the director to coordinate federal-state civilian defense activities, to keep informed of local problems, to assist states and localities to form defense councils, to study, plan, sponsor, and carry out civil defense programs, to assist in organizing volunteer service units, and to recommend further measures. An act of January 27, 1942, appropriated $100,000,000 to acquire necessary defense facilities to be assigned to local governments by the director. The control of these facilities gave the O.C.D. some leverage on local plans, but apart from this, the O.C.D. was not endowed with other than persuasive authority.

The central organization to perform these duties was subject to frequent reorganization. The most recent plan was announced April 27, 1942,[1] and included as the central divisions the following: civil air patrol, civilian protection division, medical division, mobilization division, and plant defense division.

The civil air patrol was designed to facilitate pilot training and under military direction to conduct missions of various sorts, including coast patrol. The civilian protection division engaged in the huge task of guiding the organization and training of local defense groups throughout the country, publishing a number of valuable handbooks on civilian defense against air raids. By 1942 most of the country was blanketed with air-raid warning devices and nearly every city block had its air-raid warden. The medical division was responsible for making provision for emergency medical services. The mobilization division was concerned with civilian morale and volunteer groups. The plant defense division was directed in May, 1942, to execute powers newly granted to assure the protection of essential facilities from sabotage.[2] The division acted to coordinate and stimulate action by other federal and state agencies.

At the suggestion of O.C.D.'s precursor, the Division of State and Local Cooperation, every state organized a state council of defense. The councils served as coordinating centers, receiving material and guidance from Washington, devising their own plans, and assisting in the formation and work of local defense councils. They were not always well constructed to serve as administrative bodies, but they were usually representative and by working through an executive committee they

[1] 3 *Victory* 32 (April 28, 1942).

[2] Executive Order 9165, May 19, 1942, in 7 *Federal Register* 3765–67.

served a necessary function. Later they were given important duties in the rationing and price control programs.

The actual achievement of the program of the O.C.D. was the responsibility of the local defense council, the head of which was usually the mayor of the city. Despite handicaps of funds and personnel, these councils worked often with feverish activity. The range of local duties and the way in which they were performed were well illustrated by the San Francisco Bay Region Metropolitan Defense Council.[1]

The offensive and protective power of the country at war is, of course, not fully described in the previous pages. The Coast Guard, the Foreign Broadcast Monitoring Service, the Air Ferry Command, the Defense Housing Division, the Health and Welfare Services, and the War Shipping Administration are examples of other governmental agencies directly concerned with the military effort.

The departments and agencies which are here described, briefly and inadequately, were, however, in the very center of the war effort. The Army, Navy, Marine Corps, and their respective air forces comprised the striking power of the United States. The Selective Service System and the War Manpower Commission furnished the men and women for fighting and for production. The Board of Economic Warfare sought to cripple the resources of the enemy and to strengthen the resources of the United Nations. The Office of Civilian Defense organized the home front for protection against hostile action of different types. These were the principal front-line agencies of war administration, themselves coordinated with each other and with related organizations in part through the Executive Office of the President, in part by the central direction of the President himself as chief executive and commander in chief of the armed forces.

Immediately behind these central offensive and defensive agencies was the vast machine for production of war supplies, directed by the War Production Board. To this complex organization we now turn.

2. The War Production Board

Modern war is an insatiable consumer of goods. Guns and ammunition, food and clothing, ships and airplanes, trucks and rails, coal and oil and steel, cotton and wool and fibers, delicate instruments of many kinds are needed in endless amounts. In the kind of war in which the world is now engaged there can hardly be too much of any type of war

[1] Samuel C. May and Robert E. Ward, "Coordinating Defense Activities in a Metropolitan Region," 2 *Public Administration Review* 104–12 (1942).

material. In spite of herculean efforts there was in June, 1942, far too little of some vital necessities, notably ships and rubber.

The normal production of the country is geared to a limited competitive market. War production is geared to an unlimited monopoly market. The producers of war materials were consequently faced with a unique problem—to produce in utter disregard of normal market limitations just as much as was humanly possible with available material and labor resources.

The keys to these enormous demands were industrial expansion and plant conversion. The task of the government was to facilitate and guide expansion and conversion to the utmost. The administrative responsibility for unlimited production through expansion and conversion rested in June, 1942, in the War Production Board, analogue to the War Industries Board of 1917–18. While there had been considerable confusion and some delay in the early stages of war production, the organization and direction of the W.P.B. seemed relatively stable in mid-1942 despite inescapable internal problems of adjustment and management consequent upon continuing rapid expansion of personnel.

The authority of the War Production Board, specifically vested in its chairman, Donald M. Nelson, was drawn from a variety of sources including powers taken from the Council of National Defense (the lawful parent of a varied and numerous progeny), the Office of Production Management, and the Supply Priorities and Allocations Board. Mr. Nelson's authority was great. He was authorized to "exercise general direction over the war procurement and production program. . . . Federal departments, establishments, and agencies shall comply with the policies . . . and procedures in respect to war procurement and production as determined by the Chairman." [1] He fixed total requirements of goods and materials needed for military, civilian, and other purposes; established policies for fulfillment of such needs; and formulated plans for equitable distribution, the basis for the rationing programs. He was authorized to requisition supplies and raw materials and to secure their proper distribution through a complex system of priorities. He planned and expedited the creation of new productive facilities, the financing of which was in large part a task of the Reconstruction Finance Corporation; and he was empowered to compel conversion to war production, if necessary to seize plants and direct their operation by the Army Ordnance Department.

The essential function of the War Production Board was to facilitate contracts between the government and private contractors for the production of war materials. Huge expenditures were funneled through

[1] Executive Order 9024, January 16, 1942.

prime contractors, at first on the basis of competitive bidding, later on the basis of negotiated contracts.[1]

One of the major production difficulties was to utilize the many thousands of small plants scattered about the country; the process of subcontracting and the development of "production clinics" went far toward solving this problem.[2]

The organization of the War Production Board in July, 1942, is shown in the diagram on page 12.[3]

By midsummer, 1942, Mr. Nelson announced that production was "over the hump"; Mr. Oliver Lyttelton, Minister of Production in Great Britain, admitted cheerfully that in the race for production the United States had outstripped his country; and guarded statements were made to the effect that American production of war supplies, including airplanes, exceeded that of Germany and her allies. Despite many internal difficulties and early hesitation, this record of conversion and production will doubtless be recognized as an administrative achievement of unparalleled magnitude.

Before leaving the War Production Board it is useful to recall its relation to the Office for Emergency Management and the latter's numerous affiliates. Formally the W.P.B. was one of the many defense and war agencies which were linked to the President through the O.E.M.; actually the W.P.B. operated with substantial independence. To the O.E.M. reported a galaxy of emergency agencies, including principally the National War Labor Board, the Office of Civilian Defense, the Office of Defense Health and Welfare Services, the Office of Price Administration, the Office of Defense Transportation, the Board of War Communications, the Office of the Coordinator of Inter-American Affairs, and the Office of Scientific Research and Development. The Office for Emergency Management was designed to relieve the President of immediate direction of such temporary agencies.[4]

3. Price Control and Rationing

After a futile effort to curb a rising price level without compulsory power, Congress finally enacted the Emergency Price Control Act in January, 1942.[5] This legislation recognized the Office of Price Administration, vested in it important powers of price control, but yielded

[1] 3 *Victory* 5 (March 10, 1942).
[2] Maurice F. Neufeld, "The New York State Defense Production Plan," 1 *Public Administration Review* 421–31 (1941).
[3] 3 *Victory* 5 (July 14, 1942).
[4] William H. McReynolds, "The Office for Emergency Management," 1 *Public Administration Review* 131–38 (1941).
[5] Public, No. 421, 77th Cong. (January 30, 1942).

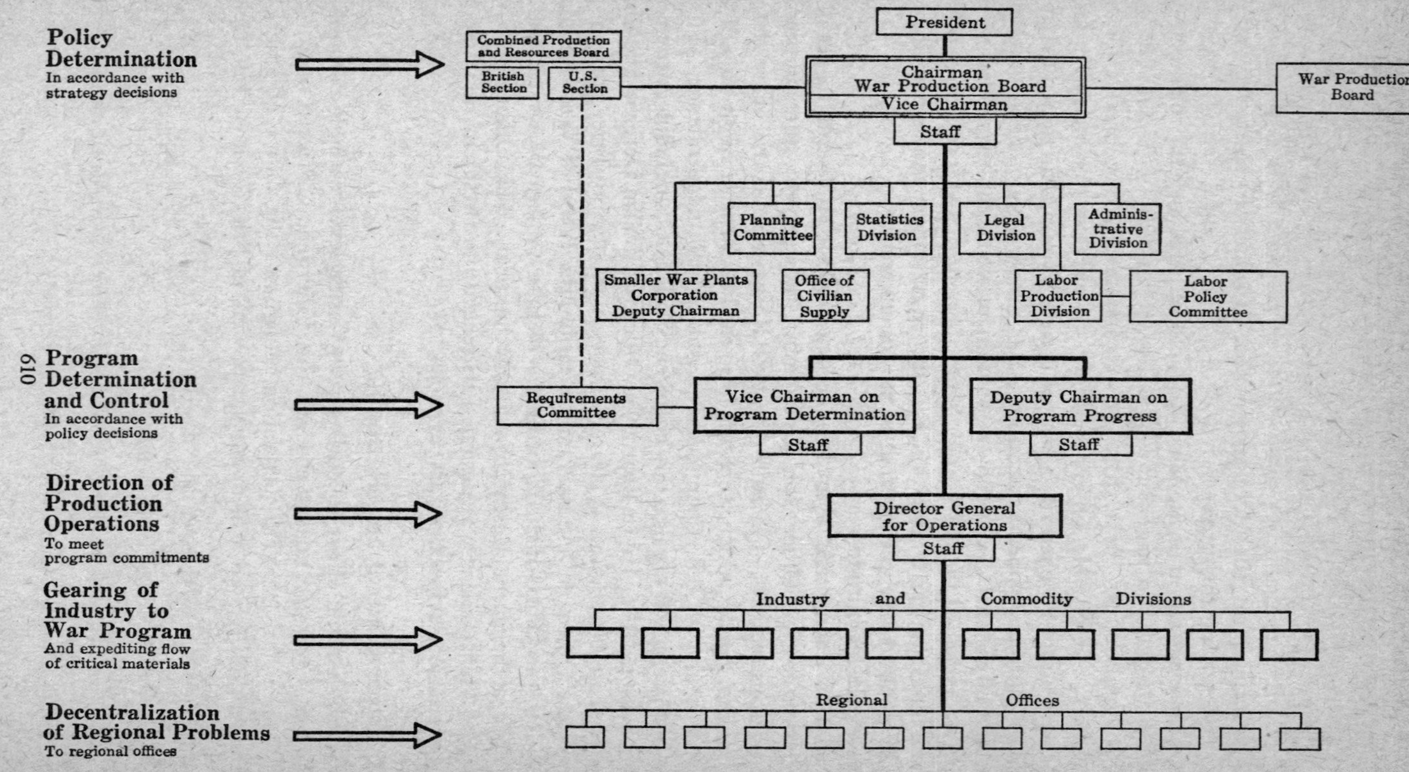
WAR PRODUCTION BOARD ORGANIZATION—JULY 8, 1942
Policy Determination
In accordance with strategy decisions
Program Determination and Control
In accordance with policy decisions
Direction of Production Operations
To meet program commitments
Gearing of Industry to War Program
And expediting flow of critical materials
Decentralization of Regional Problems
To regional offices
President
Combined Production and Resources Board
British Section
U.S. Section
Chairman War Production Board
Vice Chairman
Staff
War Production Board
Planning Committee
Statistics Division
Legal Division
Adminis-trative Division
Smaller War Plants Corporation Deputy Chairman
Office of Civilian Supply
Labor Production Division
Labor Policy Committee
Requirements Committee
Vice Chairman on Program Determination
Staff
Deputy Chairman on Program Progress
Staff
Director General for Operations
Staff
Industry and Commodity Divisions
Regional Offices

to a strong agricultural lobby by granting authority over farm prices to the Secretary of Agriculture.

The principal power vested in the O.P.A. was that of establishing maximum prices of commodities, after consultation with the affected industries. In defense areas rents were also subject to control. The administrator, furthermore, could regulate speculative practices and prevent hoarding. Enforcement lay ultimately in the power to prohibit sales except on the basis of a license, but at the time of writing publicity and complaints were relied upon to secure conformance.

Early price regulations affected automobiles, tires, and gasoline, later to be subject to the more stringent control of rationing. Effective March 30, 1942, maximum prices were set for seven important household appliances. On April 28, 1942, the O.P.A. froze the price of every major item affecting living costs by publication of the General Maximum Price Regulation. By May, 1942, rent orders had been issued in over three hundred defense communities.

The administrative organization for price control rested upon joint action with states and localities. Policies and decisions with respect to price ceilings were made in Washington and transmitted to the states and localities. The state defense councils appointed in each of the forty-eight states a price administrator who in turn set up in each county a price control office. Each of the largest metropolitan areas also had a price control office with numerous branches. The outlines of a huge administrative structure thus rapidly took form, with predictions that when fully in operation over 100,000 employees would be required.

The principal duties of the thousands of local price control boards were to make spot inspections of prices, to disseminate information, to receive and prepare reports, and to investigate complaints. The members of the boards, although selected under state authority, are sworn in as federal officials and their expenses are met from the federal Treasury. These boards are also the local authority for rationing.

Legal authority to ration was vested in the War Production Board but delegated by it to the Office of Price Administration.[1] Four days after Pearl Harbor the former Office of Production Management froze the supplies of rubber; on December 14, 1941, the O.P.A. was given the task of creating a rationing system; and on January 5, 1942, the system was in country-wide operation, an administrative feat due to the genius of Mr. Frank Bane, then director of field operations, O.P.A.

The state defense councils were requested to appoint a rationing ad-

[1] Frank Bane, "Cooperative Government in Wartime," 2 *Public Administration Review* 95–103 (1942); John E. Hamm, "Administrative Structure for Rationing," 15 *State Government* 119–20 (1942).

ministrator, who designated the municipal or county defense councils to be responsible for local operations; these in turn appointed local rationing boards usually of three persons. These boards, acting under the general policy fixed in Washington, then determined who were entitled to receive tires. Over 7,500 rationing boards were quickly set up and the tire rationing program operated with remarkable smoothness.

Sugar rationing was put into operation by means of the stamp book. The whole population was required to register, using the public schools as the registration agency. Every registrant received a ration book with detachable stamps, each of which was the necessary token for the sugar quota. Despite occasional misunderstandings, the registration took place in effective and orderly fashion, and the country settled down to a limited sugar consumption for the duration of the war. This organization proved effective from the outset and seemed likely to become the pattern for such extensions of rationing as might be necessary.

The administrative significance of these operations rested in the effective coordination of nation, states, and localities in a common enterprise. Policy was determined in Washington, but administration was local; rationing and price administration boards were locally selected from among local residents, state administrators were designated by the states, and both were given substantial responsibility for decisions. The same pattern was the foundation of the Selective Service System.

Gasoline rationing began on the east coast on May 15, 1942. The administrative pattern was similar to that developed for sugar, except that varying amounts of gasoline were allowed according to need. There was much criticism of the allocation of unlimited ration books, especially to congressmen.

4. Censorship, Propaganda, and Public Information

Warfare on the psychological front was widely exploited during World War I, but the truly devastating possibilities of an assault on the morale of the civilian population became apparent only as the consequences of German ideological penetration were laid bare in the early years of the present conflict. Every belligerent power took to the air in an effort to undermine the power of resistance of its enemies and to cultivate the good opinion of neutrals or allies. After December, 1941, the United States embarked on a program which in its early stages was confused, poorly organized, and ineffectively managed, but which after the formation of the Office of War Information in June, 1942, appeared likely to become a more effective instrument.

The three major aspects of wartime communications—censorship, propaganda, and information—were eventually organized in two principal agencies, the Office of Censorship and the Office of War Information, with a third agency in charge of propaganda, information, and commercial and cultural relations with South America—the Office of the Coordinator of Inter-American Affairs. The many interrelationships with other governmental agencies were facilitated by a representative Censorship Policy Board, a Committee on War Information Policy, and a Committee on Inter-American Affairs attached to the three principal agencies.

The Office of Censorship was established by executive order in December, 1941.[1] The director of censorship was empowered to censor "in his absolute discretion" communications by mail, cable, radio or other means between the United States and any foreign country. The Censorship Policy Board advised the director with respect to policy and coordination, but final authority rested with him. The Office has worked quietly but effectively. A competent critic made the following comment: "The Office of Censorship controls incoming and outgoing communications; helps to solve the perplexities imposed by 'voluntary censorship' to the extent it can; attempts to educate the military and coordinate the practices of the Army and the Navy, and to fit these into a pattern with the units of armament production. It is ably and intelligently administered."[2]

The Office of War Information was the outgrowth of a consolidation of the Office of Government Reports, the Coordinator of Information, the Office of Facts and Figures, and the Division of Information of the O.E.M., "in recognition of the right of the American people . . . to be truthfully informed about the common war effort."[3] The director of O.W.I. was the central directing and coordinating authority for the release of government information, in accordance with the war information policies of the President and the foreign policy of the United States.

The Office formulated and carried out information programs, at home and abroad, coordinated the war information activities of all federal agencies in the interest of consistency, acted as a clearinghouse, and issued binding directives. As a part of the information office reorganization, a new Office of Strategic Services was established under the direction of the U. S. Joint Chiefs of Staff to collect and analyze strategic information.

Here, too, we may notice the important function of the Federal Com-

[1] Executive Order 8985, December 19, 1941, in 6 *Federal Register* 6625.

[2] Arthur Krock, "The Limits of Censorship: a Symposium," 6 *Public Opinion Quarterly* 24–25 (1942).

[3] Executive Order 9182, June 13, 1942, in 7 *Federal Register* 4468–69.

munications Commission in operating the Foreign Broadcast Monitoring Service. This Service recorded, translated, analyzed, and circulated foreign broadcasts. It maintained four principal listening posts and picked up on a twenty-four hour basis the broadcasting of enemy and other countries. American broadcasts in June, 1942, were under the direction of the Office of War Information, except that a short wave broadcast designed for friendly listeners in enemy countries was maintained by a private chain in New York City.

The Office of the Coordinator of Inter-American Affairs was concerned with both commercial and cultural relations with South America. Established in 1941, it actively cultivated the countries south of the Rio Grande, at times raising problems of coordination with the State Department and other federal agencies.[1] The Office was directed by its organic order to "formulate, recommend, and execute" programs in the commercial and economic fields, to assist South American governments to increase their military and naval establishments, to cultivate hemispherical solidarity, and to serve as the center for the coordination of the cultural and commercial relations with Central and South America.

By June, 1942, then, the United States was active in the field of psychological warfare and public information. The central administrative organs were the Office of Censorship, the Office of War Information, and the Office of the Coordinator of Inter-American Affairs. Despite intelligent efforts in many directions—in too many uncoordinated directions, indeed—it was not clear that the net results had been wholly satisfactory. Our foreign broadcasting was criticized; and the confusion of voices on matters of war policy within the President's official family was disconcerting. A firmer hand at some points was indicated; but on the other hand a watchful and touchy press was on the alert to safeguard free access to its usual sources of information. The life of the censorship and war information authorities was not an easy one.

5. International Aspects

The earlier reference to the Board of Economic Warfare indicated one of the many international phases of administrative organization for war purposes. An elaborate structure had already been set up by midsummer, 1942, for the purpose of securing the most effective utilization of the combined resources of the United Nations. It was analogous to a corresponding series of over-all agencies which sprang into existence in 1917–18 principally as between the United States and Great Britain, agencies which were rapidly liquidated when hostilities ceased. There

[1] Executive Order 8840, July 30, 1941, in 6 *Federal Register* 3857–58.

appeared greater likelihood that the present structure might be more enduring.

In this sketch we note principally the Lend-Lease Act and its operation and the so-called combined boards. In the face of the Johnson Act prohibiting loans to countries in default on their debts to the United States, a critical problem developed in 1940 as the volume of British dollar balances in the United States available for the purchase of munitions and supplies approached liquidation. The problem of maintaining a flow of war supplies was solved without formally modifying the Johnson Act by the Lend-Lease Act of March 11, 1941.[1] This legislation authorized the President, in the interest of national defense, to sell, exchange, lease, lend, or otherwise dispose of defense articles—weapons, munitions, aircraft, vessels, machinery and parts, and "any agricultural, industrial, or other commodity or article for defense." An original maximum amount of $1,300,000,000 of lend-lease goods was later increased by Congress from time to time.

By the end of 1941, thirty-three countries had been declared by the President vital to the defense of the United States and lend-lease agreements had been concluded with ten of them. The nature of the lend-lease agreements was fixed by the master agreement with Great Britain, signed February 23, 1942. This document is a "preliminary agreement," setting out, however, some basic considerations. After confirming the intent of the United States to continue to supply the United Kingdom with defense articles, the agreement specified that the United Kingdom will not transfer title, and at the end of the emergency will return such defense articles, not destroyed, lost, or consumed, that the President determines are of use. Of greatest interest is the language of Article VII:

> In the final determination of the benefits to be provided to the United States of America by the Government of the United Kingdom in return for aid furnished under the Act of Congress of March 11, 1941, the terms and conditions thereof shall be such as not to burden commerce between the two countries, but to promote mutually advantageous economic relations between them and the betterment of world-wide economic relations. To that end, they shall include provision for agreed action by the United States of America and the United Kingdom, open to participation by all other countries of like mind, directed to the expansion, by appropriate international and domestic measures, of production, employment, and the exchange and consumption of goods, which are the material foundations of the liberty and welfare of all peoples; to the elimination of all forms of discriminatory treatment in international commerce, and to the reduction of tariffs and other trade barriers; and, in general, to the attainment of all the economic objectives set forth in the Joint Declaration [the Atlantic Charter].

[1] 55 Stat. 31.

The administration of lend-lease activities, while centered in the Office of Lend-Lease Administration in the O.E.M., involved a number of other agencies, principally the State Department, the Navy Department, the Board of Economic Warfare, and the U. S. Maritime Commission. Master agreements were negotiated by the State Department, with the advice of the Lend-Lease Administration and the Board of Economic Warfare. Negotiations for the manufacture and transfer of war materials were conducted by the Office of Lend-Lease Administration. By midsummer, 1942, lend-lease operations with Great Britain were diminishing in view of the policy of pooling resources.

To secure most complete utilization of resources and productive power a number of joint boards, or "combined boards," had been established during the early months of 1942. Six combined boards were in operation in June, 1942: the Combined Chiefs of Staff, the Munitions Assignments Board, the Combined Raw Materials Board, the Combined Shipping Adjustment Board, the Combined Production and Resources Board, and the Combined Food Board. These boards typically included one or more representatives of each of the two countries, especially informed on the subject matter in question and usually drawn from the administrative service. They were designed to secure direct and effective coordination by the experts.

These boards represented a departure from normal international relationships. They did not operate through the State Department although it had observers on the combined boards. In the interest of a consistent foreign policy the State Department has tended to view the activities of various administrative agencies in the foreign field with some concern—earlier, the overseas representatives of the Department of Agriculture; during the emergency, the Office of the Coordinator of Inter-American Affairs, the Board of Economic Warfare, the Lend-Lease Administration, and the combined boards. On May 20, 1942, word from the White House stated that the Board of Economic Warfare would continue to recognize that it is the function of the Department of State "to conduct or authorize the conduct" of negotiations with foreign governments. The phrase to "authorize the conduct" marks a departure from strict precedent.

By the end of the third year of the war, Washington was rapidly becoming the administrative center of the United Nations. Visits of royal heads in exile attracted the attention of newspapers, but far more important was the quiet but concentrated effort of officials and experts attached to the international administrative agencies typified by those outlined in this section. It already seemed certain that, upon the achievement of military success, the United Nations would face enormous tasks of restoring order, distributing food and supplies on a world-wide scale, allocating fiscal and other resources to invigorate a post-war economy, protecting the public health, and perhaps initiating a huge program of rebuilding devastated areas—all involving difficult problems of administration. The international administrative and fiscal center of the world might become Washington.

6. Administrative Trends

It remains to sketch rapidly the principal administrative changes that accompanied the operation of war policies, a few of which have been noted in previous pages. An immediate consequence was the urgent need for competent personnel of all kinds, especially directing and managerial. The basic administrative decision was taken at the outset in favor of utilizing the U. S. Civil Service Commission as the central personnel supply agency; this decision was confirmed on March 15, 1942, when new procedures, greatly simplified, were introduced for the duration of the war. These streamlined procedures were taken directly to the various operating agencies by "liaison officers" of the Commission who were authorized to make all possible decisions as to personnel on the spot and without delay. A special section of the examining division was established in the office of the Commission to expedite the discovery and appointment of top managerial personnel. Despite many obstacles, the record of central direction of employment during the crisis was an impressive one.

The magnitude of the war effort is illustrated by the expansion of the number of employees in the executive branch, as indicated in the following table.

TABLE I

CIVIL EMPLOYMENT IN THE EXECUTIVE BRANCH OF THE UNITED STATES GOVERNMENT AS OF SPECIFIED DATES [1]

DATE	TOTAL	WAR	NAVY
June 30, 1939	920,310	109,886	85,400
June 30, 1940	1,002,820	136,841	117,981
June 30, 1941	1,358,150	320,291	222,862
June 30, 1942	2,207,754	824,698	449,826

The rate of expansion in the spring of 1942 was such as to forecast a civil employment roll of perhaps 3,000,000 by July 1, 1943.

[1] Data from monthly and semi-annual reports of employment issued by the United States Civil Service Commission.

Coincident with this expansion occurred a heavy drain upon the states and cities whose officials and employees accepted civil and military positions in the federal government. While this movement benefited the war effort, it weakened the states relatively since no countermovement took place or was contemplated.

By the First War Powers Act Congress conferred upon the President wide authority to redistribute functions among executive agencies, reserving to Congress the abolition of any office found unnecessary.[1] This authority, which corresponds to the Overman Act of World War I, expires six months after the termination of the war. It was frequently used but not to initiate any spectacular interdepartmental changes.

The Bureau of the Budget greatly expanded its administrative influence after 1938 and became the recognized center for the consideration of administrative problems of many kinds. The somewhat negative point of view of the Bureau was erased by Director Harold D. Smith; a more constructive attitude toward administrative matters was encouraged, and the division of administrative management became an intensely active center of administrative studies and recommendations. Most of the major intradepartmental reorganizations of the early war years were developed by the experts in this division, a group notable for their skill in diagnosis of operating ills and for their accurate prescription of remedies. By 1942 the Bureau of the Budget was rapidly becoming the training center for the management experts of the future, fulfilling a function earlier discharged by the onetime Bureau of Efficiency.

The pressure of operations in Washington after 1939 induced two parallel but separate movements, geographical dispersion and decentralization (technically and more accurately deconcentration). A number of agencies were moved physically from Washington to other cities, New York, Philadelphia, Richmond, Chicago, and St. Louis, for example. This dispersion was forced by lack of office space in the District of Columbia and by mounting traffic difficulties in a city full of traffic problems.

Other departments and agencies, again under the pressure of an undue concentration of business at the center, took steps to decentralize their operations by transferring to regional offices the authority to make final decisions on specified matters. An early example was the decentralization of income tax decisions to regional offices, in lieu of the long-standing practice of concentrating all income tax returns and dispositions in the central offices of the Treasury. At the suggestion of the Reed

[1] 55 Stat. 838 (December 18, 1941).

Committee[1] and in the face of increasing business, the Civil Service Commission and the departments went some way in increasing the number of field service appointments handled in the field through regional offices.

The greatest changes in getting business out of Washington, however, occurred in the major operations of selective service, civil defense, price administration, and rationing. The decision in each instance was in favor of an administrative structure combining national policy decisions with state and local administration. With varying degrees of federal guidance and supervision, an immense fund of energy has been put to work in the communities of the United States to secure the realization of national objectives. There has been an impressive demonstration of the possibilities of coordinated administration.

An incidental consequence of the tendencies just described was to emphasize the magnitude and importance of the federal regional centers. No accepted pattern of federal regionalism has yet developed but the foundations were being laid on which a new structure may some day be built.

The War Production Board, the Office of Price Administration, the Board of Economic Warfare, and other war agencies drew in many top-flight business executives. Despite some criticism of the dollar-a-year men there can be no doubt that as a group the business executives made an important contribution. Their adjustment to the routines of government, and the adaptation of these to the habits of business moguls, are characteristically not easy and give rise to many problems. Two results may be anticipated: the improvement of government procedures and a better appreciation by businessmen of the integrity and competence of the public service.

[1] *Report of President's Committee on Civil Service Improvement*, H. Doc. 118, 77th Cong., 1st sess. (February, 1941).

INDEX

INDEX